Alfonso the Magnanimous: design for a medal by Pisanello, 1448

The Kingdom of Naples Under Alfonso the Magnanimous

The Making of a Modern State

BY

ALAN RYDER

OXFORD · AT THE CLARENDON PRESS

1976

Oxford University Press, Walton Street, Oxford OX2 6DP

OXFORD LONDON GLASGOW NEW YORK
TORONTO MELBOURNE WELLINGTON CAPE TOWN
IBADAN NAIROBI DAR ES SALAAM LUSAKA ADDIS ABABA
KUALA LUMPUR SINGAPORE JAKARTA HONG KONG TOKYO
DELHI BOMBAY CALCUTTA MADRAS KARACHI

ISBN 0 19 822535 0

© Oxford University Press 1976

Printed in Great Britain
at the University Press, Oxford
by Vivian Ridler
Printer to the University

To M, P, and J

PREFACE

MY attention was first drawn to Aragonese Naples by the late Miss C. M. Ady of St. Hugh's College, Oxford, who suggested that studies of fifteenth-century Italy had unduly neglected 'the kingdom'. Twenty years later that imbalance of interest persists. The artistic and literary flowering in Tuscany and the northern states understandably continues to fascinate scholars in many disciplines. Historians must none the less bear in mind that the future lay not with the republics, princedoms, and papal states of Italy, but with the larger monarchical states whose only Italian exemplar was the kingdom of Sicily *citra farum*. Any study of the influence of fifteenth-century Italy upon the political and adminis-trative institutions of Europe is therefore bound to pay some attention to developments in that kingdom where a conjunction of great significance was effected. By fusing together Spanish and Italian practice and experience, the kingdom for the last time fulfilled its historic role as the melting-pot of diverse traditions of government. As a result there came into being one of the first, perhaps *the* first, of European states to exhibit many of those characteristics that historians have labelled 'modern'—a bureau-cratic administration staffed by professional men, a crown domi-nant over nobility and clergy, a revenue derived mainly from universal, direct taxation, and armed forces recruited and paid directly by the crown.

The lack of interest shown by all but a handful of historians in the institutions of Aragonese Naples meant that this study had to rely almost entirely upon primary sources, which themselves appeared at first to be virtually non-existent. Destruction wrought in the Aragonese records in the Neapolitan state archives during the insurrections of 1647 and 1701 was completed by the Germans in 1943 when, as a reprisal measure, they burned the most valuable surviving records of the Angevin and Aragonese monarchies. A few scattered fragments, mostly belonging to the archives of the Sommaria, are all that survive of a once rich fund of documents. The staff of the Archivio di Stato of Naples have painstakingly assembled these fragments and over the past decade have made good progress with a project to publish the most important of them in the *Fonti aragonesi* series. By themselves, however, the remains of the Neapolitan archives would have been entirely inadequate as a basis for a detailed study of the institutions of government. In these circumstances I was fortunate to discover in the Archivo de la Corona de Aragón in Barcelona a large number of registers compiled in the chancery of Alfonso V during the years he reigned in Naples. Many of them, and in particular the series 'Privilegiorum' (Reg. 2902–19), were devoted exclusively to the business of the Neapolitan kingdom. These registers had been included, probably by mistake, along with others relating to the Corona de Aragón when the archives of Alfonso's chancery were transferred to Barcelona after the king's death. Thanks to these chance survivals the reign of Alfonso is today the best-documented period of fifteenth-century Neapolitan history.

Where so much has depended upon the use of archives I am greatly indebted to the staff of those in which I have worked, and in particular to those of the Archivo de la Corona de Aragón and the Archivio di Stato of Naples. To them all I give my thanks for their unfailing help and courtesy. To the University of Ibadan and my colleagues in the Department of History I owe a sabbatical year which has enabled me to finish this book.

A. R.

University of Ibadan
September 1973

CONTENTS

ABBREVIATIONS

ACA	Archivo de la Corona de Aragón
ACB	Archivo de la Ciudad de Barcelona
ASN	Archivio di Stato di Napoli
ASPN	*Archivio storico per le province napoletane*
BNN	Biblioteca Nazionale di Napoli
Cart.Com.	Cartas Comunas Originales Recibidas
Dip.Somm.	Dipendenze della Sommaria
Div.Somm.	Diversi della Sommaria
Fasc.Com.Somm.	Fascicoli Comune della Sommaria
Framm.Somm.	Frammento di Comune Summarie
Priv.	Privilegiorum
Reg.	Registros del Rey
Rel.Orig.	Relevi Originali
Signif.	Significatorie

I

THE ITALIAN AND
SPANISH ANTECEDENTS

FIFTEENTH-CENTURY Italy was a uniquely rich tapestry of constitutional patterns. Within the peninsula could be found exemplars of every form of state then known to Europe, but of the commonest form—monarchy—Italy possessed only one example, the kingdom of the south, which was often, for that reason, known simply as 'il Regno'. That other monarchies had not emerged may be explained partly by the vitality of the cities in central and northern Italy, and partly by the policies of the two suzerains of the peninsula—the Holy Roman Emperor whose sway extended nominally over most of the north, and the papacy which claimed overlordship of the centre and south. Neither had seen it expedient to bestow the coveted title of king on their Italian vassals, with this one southern exception which the papacy later had cause to regret. So it happened that much of the precocious political and administrative innovation which distinguished Italy during the Middle Ages took place in contexts outside the mainstream of European constitutional development. Only in 'the kingdom' can the institutions of monarchical government be observed evolving in an Italian setting.

If the achievements of the Italian city states in the arts of government and state building were remarkable, so too were those of 'the kingdom'. It stood at the cross-roads of Europe: the bridge between east and west, the highway which brought the peoples of northern Europe into the heart of the Mediterranean. People upon people in the first flush of their expansive energy fought to possess it and left upon its institutions the stamp of the originality and vigour that had carried them from their homelands in the Levant, Greece, Germany, Africa, France, or Spain. Successive stages in a cross-fertilization of cultures bred much that was new in many spheres of life: the south-Italian architecture of the twelfth century,[1]

[1] F. Heer, *The Medieval World* (London, 1962), p. 327.

the humanism that flourished in the court of Frederick II, Italian poetry which was born there. It produced too, according to Burckhardt, the first state as a work of art. Under four at least of its rulers—Roger II, Frederick II, Charles I, and Alfonso I— the kingdom stood in the van of governmental advance in western Europe.[2] That pre-eminence owed much to a series of able monarchs supported by capable advisers and the organizing genius of their native lands, much also to the unusually extensive foundations which each found already established within the kingdom. Relics of Byzantine provinces, Arab emirates, Lombard principalities and counties, and free city states, with all their diversity of laws, culture, customs, and language were the materials from which the Normans built their new state. The Hohenstaufen completed the edifice, and their arch enemies, the Angevins, did not seek to demolish it but only to furnish it in a French style.

An understanding of the state which Alfonso V of Aragon conquered requires some knowledge of these stages in its construction. The first two centuries of the kingdom's development demand particular attention because they saw the major organs of government established. The next century, which spans the death of Robert the Wise and the accession of Alfonso the Magnanimous, appears by contrast a barren period; a succession of weak rulers, assailed by their own baronage and foreign enemies, paid scant attention to administrative reform and were content to leave existing institutions to function as well as they could in the pre-vailing chaos. In relation to the Aragonese state the significance of this century lies in the decay of government and monarchical authority. Alfonso inherited a well-planned state but it came to him in a ruinous condition. Part of this introductory chapter will accordingly be devoted to outlining the origin and growth in the Norman, Hohenstaufen, and Angevin periods of those offices and institutions that were to play an important role in the Aragonese scheme of government. The remaining part will sketch the character of the Aragonese state and its relationship with the Italian kingdom culminating in the conquest of Naples by Alfonso V of Aragon.

[2] C. H. Haskins, 'England and Sicily in the twelfth century', *English Historical Review*, 26. viii (1911); E. Jamison, 'The Norman administration of Apulia and Capua, more especially under Roger II and William I', *Papers of the British School at Rome*, 6 (London, 1913), p. 265; T. C. van Cleve, *The Emperor Frederick II of Hohenstaufen* (Oxford, 1972); E. G. Léonard, *Les Angevins de Naples* (Paris, 1954), p. 33.

THE ITALIAN KINGDOM

The coronation of Roger II in Salerno on Christmas Day 1130 established the territorial framework of the Norman kingdom of Sicily by bringing together the kingdom of Sicily, the duchy of Apulia, the principality of Capua, and the honour of Naples, although it was not until after a struggle with Pope Innocent II that Roger succeeded in fixing his northern frontier in 1150 on the line of the rivers Garigliano and Tronto. Before the end of the century, when the brilliant direct line of the conquerors vanished, they had bestowed on their creation the character of a powerful, forward-looking state.

In fact the kingdom owed its existence to the military exploits of an alien people; in law it had come into being by acclamation of a general assembly in Palermo[3] and, more formally, by an act of the papacy which had invested Roger II with authority over these territories in return for an acknowledgement that the new state was a fief of the Church. There was thus created a relationship between neighbouring powers fraught with conflict and misunderstanding, for while the papacy claimed from it the full rights of temporal suzerainty, to the rulers of the kingdom it implied no more than a spiritual vassalage.[4] Against the quasi-feudal claims of papal overlordship the Normans set the pretensions of theocratic kingship.[5] Roger II proclaimed himself 'crowned by God' and extended to the whole of his new kingdom the 'Sicilian legation' by which Urban II had made his father perpetual legate and head of the church in the Sicilian lands. Not until 1192 was Celestine III able to wrest this overgrown privilege from the last of the Norman line, though in 1156 the Concordat of Benevento had once again restricted it to the island. The protection extended to clergy of the Greek church within the kingdom and the toleration accorded to Muslims[6] emphasized the independent stance of Roger and his successors in matters of religion. So too did the trappings of Byzantine and Islamic pomp and ceremonial with which they surrounded themselves.[7]

[3] D. Mack Smith, *Medieval Sicily, 800–1713* (London, 1968), p. 26.
[4] William I did, however, recognize the feudal overlordship of the papacy in the mainland territories.
[5] Cf. W. Ullmann, *Principles of government and politics in the Middle Ages* (London, 1966).
[6] Mack Smith, *Medieval Sicily*, pp. 17 and 29.
[7] Ibid., pp. 21 and 26, for the religious regalia of Roger I and Roger II.

Their wholehearted attachment to the principle of descending power was further manifested by the Norman kings' substitution of the hereditary mode of succession for the ancestral custom of choosing kings by election. For the pacts as between equals which had earlier regulated the dealings of rulers with provincial magnates and cities, the Normans substituted privileges granted from the plenitude of royal power.

At the centre of the state, which after the death of Roger I became fixed in Palermo, ruled the king, assisted by his six Great Officers. Among them a certain ceremonial pre-eminence attached to the office of admiral (derived from the Arabic title 'emir of emirs') whose holder controlled the armed forces of the crown, including the fleet. Two of the Great Offices—those of protonotary (head of the royal secretarial staff) and logothete (spokesman of the monarch)—which had a Byzantine origin, were often held by the same person. Normandy provided the model for the other three: the seneschal, the chancellor, and the chamberlain. The first of these supervised the royal household and forests; the second saw that effect was given to the royal will by dispatch of the requisite writs and letters;[8] the third controlled the chamber and hence the finances of the king.[9] Professional men of relatively humble birth, some of them Greeks and Saracens, commonly held these offices; only under the Angevins did they become the preserve of the feudal aristocracy. For most routine and confidential matters they were the ruler's chief advisers, the nucleus of his council; but for certain purposes, especially the discussion and promulgation of laws, a larger council, or Great Court, of barons and representatives of the cities would be summoned.

The idea of a *curia* as an assembly of nobles who gave the king advice and might claim some say in the administration of the kingdom was one aspect of the feudalism introduced into southern Italy by the Normans.[10] With it they planted in their new kingdom a fundamental contradiction between the feudal and autocratic

[8] The chancery employed Greek, Latin, and Arabic notaries. Cf. R. Weiss, 'The Greek Culture of South Italy', *Proceedings of the British Academy* (London, 1953), p. 27.

[9] The officials who, under the supervision of the chamberlain, looked after the finances were organized in two *duane* or *dohane* (from the Arabic 'diwan'). One, the *dohana de secretis*, managed the royal demesne and the direct and indirect taxes; the other, the *dohana questorum et baronum*, concerned itself with feudal business and revenues.

[10] Cf. Mack Smith, *Medieval Sicily*, p. 19.

modes of government.[11] Imperfectly restrained by the oath of fidelity to the crown, the feudal spirit was destined to struggle long and calamitously against the over-riding autocratic ethos of the state.

Throughout the island of Sicily and adjoining Calabria, controlled by the central administration at Palermo, the will of the ruler was paramount. In the more distant territories of the mainland, however, necessity imposed a substantial degree of devolution to the advantage of the feudal nobility. From the time of William I these mainland provinces were governed in the king's name by a *magister justiciarius* and a *magister comestabulus* who delegated their functions to subordinate justiciars and constables drawn from the tenants-in-chief.[12] Counts, the highest in rank of the feudatories, led their own men in the feudal host.[13] Lesser tenants-in-chief, owing one knight's service for every 20 *oncie*[14] of revenue, served under constables appointed by the crown from the feudal ranks. The authority of the Norman monarchy was none the less still great enough to impose on its vassals an extension of military service to ninety days instead of the forty days that were customary elsewhere in Europe.

In the administration of justice too counts enjoyed a great degree of independence, for they exercised all the functions of a royal justiciar within their own lands. Elsewhere local tenants-in-chief, usually acting in pairs, discharged the functions of the justiciar by perambulating their areas of jurisdiction in circuits which took in the most important towns once a year. Barons and judges from the neighbourhood of these towns formed their courts.[15]

The finances of the provinces were, by contrast, managed in a much more direct manner by servants of the crown: chamberlains

[11] Cf. Ullmann's discussion of the inherent opposition of feudal and 'descending' systems of government: *The Individual and Society in the Middle Ages* (London, 1967).

[12] Jamison, 'The Norman Administration of Apulia and Capua', pp. 282–3.

[13] The Norman kings created twenty-five counties in the mainland territories outside Calabria.

[14] The *oncia* was a money of account equivalent in value to 6 Venetian ducats.

[15] Justiciars administered the criminal law which embraced offences involving a breach of the king's peace. In civil matters their authority covered defect of justice in the courts of chamberlains and bailiffs, appeals from chamberlains, and feudal matters not reserved to the king's court; cf. Jamison, 'The Norman Administration of Apulia and Capua', p. 322.

in camerariates, which coincided in extent with the constabularies and justiciarates, and bailiffs in the towns. On these provincial chamberlains fell the duty of administering and safeguarding the crown's fiscal resources which were of three kinds: those that derived from the king's lordship in the royal demesne; those from feudal rights over tenants-in-chief; and those from his sovereign rights. Among the latter figured mints, saltworks, monopolies, wrecks, and—financially the most lucrative—customs dues. Hand in hand with their administrative functions chamberlains exercised extensive judicial authority, being empowered to use the procedure of the sworn inquest to establish royal rights and having jurisdiction in civil cases of a fiscal nature and an appellate jurisdiction over bailiffs. By means of this system the Norman rulers exploited the wealth of their kingdom with a thoroughness unexampled elsewhere in western Europe. With the richest treasury in the continent at their disposal they maintained a fleet and a mercenary army strong enough to countervail the feudal power of their subjects. Towards the end of the Norman period, however, the foundations of autocracy began to crack as feudal interests, already entrenched in other spheres of the administration, began to invade that of finance, to the detriment of revenues, discipline, and, ultimately, royal absolutism itself.

While the military and judicial system safeguarded the greater feudatories against direct royal interference in their possessions and gave them authority in their native provinces, the cities lost much of their former freedom as a result of the Norman conquest. Sporadic attempts to resist the suppression of civic liberties brought harsh reprisals. Venosa, Trani, Troia, Melfi, and Ascoli were burned and wasted in the wake of the Apulian revolt of 1133; William I razed Bari. Even loyal towns had to submit to the surveillance of resident royal officers. A winter of royal displeasure and suspicion blasted burgeoning city life in southern Italy and it never recovered to flourish as it did elsewhere in the peninsula. No substantial urban society was to stand as a moderating force between the crown and feudal aristocracy.

When he assumed effective power in the Sicilian kingdom in 1220, the Hohenstaufen Frederick II embarked on a programme of reforms designed in part to restore order and to recover those rights of the crown lost in the turmoil that had persisted since the death of William II; beyond that he strove to enhance the majesty of the crown to a degree surpassing that achieved by the great Norman rulers, and to depend no more upon mighty subjects as vital agents of his government.[16]

All corners of the state felt the autocratic wind. At the centre the Great Offices declined in importance as their functions passed piecemeal into the hands of lesser bureaucratic officials. The office of chancellor remained unfilled after 1221. As his chamberlain Frederick appointed first a man of obscure origin, who is thought to have been his chief eunuch,[17] and next one of mixed Saracen and Negro parentage who was moreover a Muslim. His admirals enjoyed no precedence outside the bounds of maritime affairs. By contrast to this drastic scaling down of the Great Offices, he strengthened the *magna curia* as a judicial organ by adding to it four judges, an advocate and a procurator fiscal, a *magister rationalis* or auditor general, and several notaries.[18] His most influential adviser, Pietro della Vigna, remained for much of his career no more than one of these judges of the *magna curia*.

Although they were symptomatic of the new spirit in the state, the changes which Frederick wrought at the centre of government did not overturn the Norman system. Far more drastic reforms were imposed on the provincial administration and in the relationship between the crown and the nobility. Frederick's strategy aimed at reasserting control over the crown lands in order that he might consolidate a demesne large and rich enough to raise him far above the nobles; at the same time he imposed on all his subjects a subordination to royal authority of unprecedented rigour. The edicts of Capua (1220) began the process of recovery by ordering the restitution of all demesne lands occupied by any title since 1189, the surrender, for confirmation subject to scrutiny, of all privileges issued in the same period, and the return of any villeins or burgesses who had decamped from crown lands. Castles built since the time of William II either passed to the crown or were dismantled; even those of older date were taken over

[16] The most recent study of Frederick is that by T. C. van Cleve, *The Emperor Frederick II of Hohenstaufen* (Clarendon Press, Oxford, 1972). An earlier work in English by G. Masson, *Frederick II of Hohenstaufen*, remains of value.

[17] The Hohenstaufen, like the Norman, royal household had a marked oriental character which lent colour to the despotic element in the government of those rulers.

[18] P. Giannone, *Istoria civile del regno di Napoli* (Palermo, 1762), III. xx, cap. 6, p. 48.

where they served to guard the northern approaches of the Terra di Lavoro and Molise, the most vulnerable of the land frontiers.[19] Other edicts promulgated at Capua brought the nobility sharply to heel. They forbade the alienation of fiefs, made their inheritance subject to the monarch's approval, and required his consent for the marriage of a tenant-in-chief and his children. The feudatory's relations with his tenants likewise came under royal scrutiny with the restrictions that Frederick placed on the services that might be demanded and his reaffirmation of the principle that all criminal justice belonged to the crown. In practice the Normans had been unable to enforce that canon of justice outside Sicily and Calabria; Frederick imposed it upon the whole kingdom.

In the royal towns a brief revival of municipal liberty or licence ended with the installation of crown bailiffs in place of the elected city fathers. The church too had to bow. Its lands were not exempted from the general recovery of the demesne. Restrictions were laid upon the gift of fiefs to religious bodies in order that service to the crown might not be jeopardized. Efforts to reassert the old Norman control over appeals to Rome and the nomination of bishops encountered determined opposition from the papacy, but were none the less relentlessly pursued. Jews and Muslims, valued financial and military auxiliaries of the crown, again enjoyed the protection to which they had been accustomed in the brighter days of Norman rule. 'Subversive' Christian sects, such as the Patarenes, on the other hand, often suffered savage persecution for their nonconformity. Thus did Frederick tighten his grip upon all his subjects, bruising the recalcitrant and encouraging those found serviceable.

Authoritarian as Frederick may have been, he did not demand mute obedience. Frequently he summoned parliaments or *curiae generales* which from 1232 included representatives of the cities as well as tenants-in-chief. In such gatherings he promulgated the remarkable series of judicial and administrative codes that constitute one of the chief glories of his reign. Parliaments of this kind, which had their antecedents in the Great Courts of the Norman kings, were supplemented by a new form of assembly— the *colloquia* or provincial gatherings—which were summoned for the first time in 1233. For eight days every May and November representatives of cities and towns, together with tenants-in-chief and bishops of the region, had an opportunity of laying their grievances before the king's representative before being informed of their tax obligations.[20] Thus did a watchful crown have the ear of its subjects.

All Frederick's legislation would have been of little effect had he not succeeded in creating a provincial administration staffed by royal servants in place of one run by local magnates in whom a combination of feudal and public authority menaced both crown and subjects. To that end he reorganized the mainland provinces into the shape they were to retain for centuries,[21] and put each under the control of a justiciar. Although these justiciars were still recruited mainly from the ranks of the feudal nobility, none could hold office in his native province nor in one where he possessed land; moreover the term of appointment was limited to one year, renewable *ad beneplacitum*.[22] Very extensive powers were conferred on this new breed of justiciar. Their jurisdiction covered all criminal cases of first instance and civil appeals. Assisted by paid professional judges, notaries, and clerks, they perambulated their provinces in frequent circuits. They seem also to have assumed the military functions previously performed by the constables, and to have supervised the administration of the direct taxes. To ensure an adequate supply of trained men for these and other administrative functions Frederick founded the University of Naples in 1224 as a state institution.

Even without the financial burden imposed on the kingdom by the imperial commitments of the Hohenstaufen, this elaborated hierarchy of salaried officials would have demanded a greater revenue than the one that had supported the Norman state; combined they called forth the most comprehensive exploitation of national wealth and resources known to medieval Europe. The Normans had gone some way towards introducing a general direct tax by transforming the feudal aid into a *subventio generalis* or *collecta*, but had levied this subsidy only on rare occasions.

[20] The assemblies met in four centres—Cosenza, Gravina, Salerno, and Sulmona. Cities sent four representatives, lesser towns and *castelli* sent two.

[21] Abruzzo, Capitanata, Terra di Bari, Terra d'Otranto, Terra di Lavoro, Molise, Principato, Basilicata, Val di Crati and Terra Giordana, Calabria. Later rulers subdivided the large provinces of Abruzzo and Principato.

[22] Vestiges of the Norman system remained in the division of the kingdom between two *magistri capitanei*—one for Sicily and Calabria, the other for Capua and Apulia. Using the same divisions, Frederick appointed regularly from 1239 two *magistri justiciarii* to supervise the provincial justiciars.

From 1229 onwards Frederick made it, despite protests, almost an annual imposition and the foundation of his revenues.[23] Ecclesiastical wealth did not escape the fiscal net, for while admitting the exemption of 'spiritualities' (i.e. tithes and offerings), Frederick insisted on taxing 'temporalities'.[24] Not surprisingly this novel taxation was viewed with vocal dismay by clergy and laity alike, and among the amendments promised them in Frederick's will was freedom 'ab omnibus generalibus collectis'. But such a device, having once revealed its potentialities to needy monarchs, could never again be restricted to its primitive uses. Sovereign rights, especially royal monopolies and customs dues, were systematically exploited. The crown stepped in to organize and tax the seasonal movement of sheep from their summer pastures in the Apennines to winter grazing in the plains of Apulia. State monopolies controlled the market in salt, silk, pitch, hemp, iron, steel, soap, wool, and dye-stuffs. Efforts to abolish internal customs dues were matched by increases in those levied at the frontiers. To the existing customs and tolls (the *jura vetera*) Frederick added no fewer than twenty-five *jura nova*, many of which fell on a variety of port services monopolized by the state, such as loading and weighing facilities.

In its brightest moments the Hohenstaufen fiscal system was creative as well as exactory because Frederick understood the importance of a prosperous economy. The institution of annual fairs at Sulmona, Capua, Lucera, Bari, Taranto, Cosenza, and Reggio, the construction of eleven new ports, the revival of Norman dues known as *marinaria* and *lignamia* which helped provide a fleet, may all be cited, along with the reorganization of the demesne, customs, and monopolies, as examples of a coherent policy of state-directed economic development. The hold of Pisans and Genoese on the external trade of the kingdom was broken, and the crown was not the sole beneficiary even if the royal demesne did prosper more than the rest of the kingdom. No small part of the Hohenstaufen tragedy lies in the distortion of these instruments of progress under external pressures into weapons of fiscal rapacity and destruction.

---

[23] When fully exploited, as in 1248, the *subventio generalis* is reckoned to have yielded 130,000 *oncie* (Masson, *Frederick II*, p. 170).

[24] H. J. Pybus, 'Frederick II and the Sicilian church', *Cambridge Historical Journal*, 3. 2 (1930).

Frederick dreamed of a new order in human affairs, a new order to be achieved through the agency of that imperial state of which he was the head and whose form he proclaimed in his kingdom of Sicily. The *Liber constitutionum* or *Liber augustalis* which he promulgated in the parliament of Melfi in 1231 was more than a constitution and code of law for the kingdom. It attempted to provide for the secular state of medieval Europe a common structure of law and order on the model of the imperial Roman codes. Sicily offered a pattern for the new Europe: 'Ut sit admirantibus omnibus similitudinis speculum, invidia principum et norma regnorum.'[25] Impressed by this vision, by the resuscitation of Roman law in Frederick's codes, by the emphasis on the secular and professional in his administration, many historians have stressed the modernity of his state.[26] Glaring anachronisms, though exciting to the distant observer, can nevertheless create breaking strains in a body politic. In the thirteenth century a ruler could not over-ride ecclesiastical and feudal powers with impunity, nor could the administrative and economic problems of southern Italy be solved when confounded with the fortunes of a ramshackle empire.

Although committed to uprooting from the Sicilian kingdom the works as well as the dynasty of the Hohenstaufen, Charles I of Anjou, once on the throne, strove to maintain the state as he had found it and to make as few concessions as possible to papal and feudal pressures.[27] Ignoring his earlier denunciations of Frederick's tyranny, Charles validated all the emperor's acts up to the time of his deposition. In their conception of monarchy too Charles and his successors endorsed the absolutist ideas of their dynastic foe. Their jurists, trained at the university of Naples where the Roman law continued to gain ground at the expense of the Lombard, championed the concept of sovereignty free of all trammels above and below. Only in a soft-pedalling of the divine nature of

---

[25] This phrase occurs in the *Novae constitutiones*: see van Cleve, *The Emperor Frederick II*, p. 147 n. 1.

[26] e.g. B. Croce, *Storia del regno di Napoli* (Bari, 1944), p. 6; van Cleve, *The Emperor Frederick II*, p. 533; E. G. Léonard, *Les Angevins de Naples*, p. 33.

[27] The most recent survey of the Angevin period is by E. G. Léonard (*Les Angevins de Naples*, Paris, 1954). Cf. P. Durrieu, *Les Archives angevines de Naples. Étude sur les registres du Roi Charles I (1265–1285)* (Paris, 1886–7); L. Cadier, *Essai sur l'administration du royaume de Sicile sous Charles I et Charles II d'Anjou* (Paris, 1891); R. Caggese, *Roberto d'Angiò e i suoi tempi* (Florence, 1921); R. Trifone, *La legislazione angioina* (Naples, 1921).

kingship is there any marked change from the earlier diapason in its praise, and that mutation owed more to a new relationship with Rome than to contrary convictions.

Charles I had none the less to pay a price for his throne. Though he confiscated the estates of those who rebelled against him after initial submission, he had to alienate large tracts of the royal demesne in order to enfeoff some 700 French followers whom he settled in the kingdom as a garrison of occupation. In the process many towns lost their demesne status and the crown dissipated that essential counterpoise to feudal power which Frederick II had striven so long to accumulate. So fundamental was the shift in the balance of forces that the state changed its very nature and became a feudal monarchy on the French pattern.[28]

The papacy too exacted substantial concessions from its champion and vassal. In the agreement made with the pope in February 1265 Charles promised to withdraw all the anti-clerical measures of Frederick II, to cede Benevento to Rome, and to bestow substantial privileges on the clergy of the kingdom. Chief among the latter were the freedom of clerical elections, exemption of the clergy from all lay jurisdiction save for feudal matters of a civil nature, exemption of churches and clergy from *collectae* and all other taxes upon their property, and renunciation of the crown's claim to the revenues of vacant benefices. Taken together these concessions amounted to a sizeable reduction in state revenue which the hard-pressed lay taxpayer had to make good.

While Charles I still reigned the Sicilian rebellion opened further breaches in royal authority because, to secure the support of his mainland subjects, he was driven to relax his grip upon them in a manner that benefited chiefly the church and baronage. The Ordinance of San Martino (1283) promised the latter payment for military service beyond the customary ninety days, removed many of the controls that Frederick had placed upon their marriages, authorized them to demand aids from their vassals without royal consent, and promised judgement by their peers in the *curia regis*. To the church he gave a state guarantee for the payment of tithes and tighter control over tenants on church lands. Furthermore the crown promised its support for the Inquisition—

---

[28] Cf. Léonard, *Les Angevins de Naples*, p. 81.

an action that symbolized the waning of the heterodoxy which had been one of the chief glories of the kingdom.

In subsequent reigns the process of baronial enfranchisement continued, matched by increasing subjugation of the peasantry to their feudal lords. Throughout the fourteenth century the nobles were rebuilding their castles and their military power. New titles enhanced their prestige: that of duke was first conferred outside the royal family by Giovanna I; Ladislas introduced that of marquis; orders of chivalry appeared to glamourize the warrior caste.[29] In numbers too the baronage waxed stronger; Ladislas was especially prodigal in his creation of counts and sales of demesne lands. Seigneurial control over the common people tightened with the gradual transfer of criminal justice from the crown to tenants-in-chief and with the introduction of a number of French feudal customs such as the *droit de moulin* and forced labour at harvest-time. According to Costanzo, Robert of Anjou was the first ruler to grant criminal jurisdiction to favoured nobles on a large scale.[30] After him the concession became more and more commonplace until by the reign of Giovanna II it was usual for fiefs to be bestowed with the full panoply of justice expressed in the formula *merum mixtumque imperium*. A century of development in that direction made the kingdom of Naples the most important centre of feudal jurisprudence in Europe.[31]

At the centre of the state also the nobility made inroads of some psychological significance. The Angevins modelled their household upon that of the French kings and it happened in Naples as in France that during the fourteenth century many of the higher domestic offices became a preserve of the nobility. Charles I left many of the Neapolitan Great Offices unfilled; they might have lapsed altogether had not the nobility put pressure upon his successors to bestow them upon great baronial families. As a result they became largely honorary dignities whose holders took little part in running the state. The functions of the *magister*

---

[29] The first non-royal duke was Francesco del Balzo, Duke of Andria; the second Tommaso di Marzano, Duke of Sessa. The later Angevins created two more dukedoms: that of Venosa in the Sanseverino family, and that of Atri for the Aquaviva. The first marquisate was that of Pescara conferred on Cecio del Borgo. The Order of the Knot (*Nodo*), founded in 1352, was the first order of chivalry in the kingdom.

[30] A. di Costanzo, *Historia del regno di Napoli* (Naples, 1710), vi. 161.

[31] Giannone, *Istoria civile*, ii. 306.

justiciarius in the *magna curia*, for example, were given to a professional lawyer who was nominally his regent, but in practice an appointee of the crown.

To the mass of the population the replacement of the Hohenstaufen by the Angevins brought little if any benefit. Despite promises to popes and people, Charles I maintained the established tax burdens which became only more inequitably shared because of concessions to the church and nobility. Before being invested with the kingdom he had undertaken to abolish *collectae*; instead he put them on a permanent, carefully regulated basis and made them the principal support of his finances. In 1282 the sum raised through this tax from the mainland provinces alone exceeded the one that Frederick II had taken from the whole kingdom. The fulfilment of a promise in the Ordinance of San Martino that taxes should be levied as in the time of 'good King William' was destined to become as remote as the good king himself. Charles II and Robert maintained the tax at a rate of between 40,000 and 45,000 *oncie* a year in the first half of the fourteenth century. We have little information about its fluctuations in the latter part of the century, but by the time of Giovanna II a figure of 40,000 *oncie* for the *collectae* had become accepted as customary and permanent.

Despite their financial problems, the earlier Angevins did, it is true, show some concern for the economic welfare of their kingdom. They encouraged mining and textile manufacture, improved roads, constructed ports, and enacted some laws favourable to agriculture and commerce.[32] Robert gave back to the towns of the royal demesne a measure of the self-government they had lost under Frederick II. Naples, Sessa, Barletta, and Salerno were allowed to elect municipal councils which exercised criminal and appeal jurisdiction. Small communities acquired the right to appoint minor tax officials (*sindaci, collettori, tassatori*) and those numbering more than 1,000 hearths were permitted in addition to name their own petty magistrates (*magistri jurati*). In demesne and baronial lands alike the period witnessed a movement to reduce communal customs to writing, especially those that regulated relations with an overlord. However, all this encouragement of municipal self-government did not lead to a significant development of town life and the growth of an active bourgeoisie.

---

[32] Cf. Léonard, *Les Angevins de Naples*, pp. 86–9.

Apart from Naples the towns declined; the urban middle class failed almost totally to expand its economic activity. Such evidence of urban liveliness as we have comes from the royal demesne whose constant diminution more than offset the effect of the freer conditions enjoyed by its inhabitants. The behaviour of most urban communities can best be interpreted as a defensive response to rampant feudalism; if any bourgeoisie was emerging, it was one of functionaries, not of entrepreneurs.

Within the restricted sphere of action left by their concessions to powerful subjects the first three Angevin rulers did much to improve the efficiency of their administration. Until their destruction in the Second World War the copious Angevin archives of Naples bore witness to their elaboration of bureaucratic routine. The castles and palaces of that rapidly growing city, where Charles I fixed his capital, afforded space for a convenient distribution of offices. Thus the physical transfer of the royal treasure to the stronghold of Castel dell'Ovo led in 1277 to the separation of the treasury from the chamber which remained in the king's residence at Castelnuovo.[33] The *magna curia* as a governing body disintegrated as the Great Offices lost their practical importance and the administrative offices of the state separated from the royal household. The name continued to be applied to those supreme tribunals that had once formed part of it, but these too lost ground to newer bodies. Under Robert the treasury acquired its own audit department, a tribunal known as the Sommaria presided over by deputy of the *magnus camerarius*. In theory the Sommaria made only a preliminary or summary inspection of treasury accounts— hence its name—the final audit being reserved to the older tribunal of the *magister rationalis* in the *magna curia* the members of which were nominated by the wards of the capital.[34] In practice the role of the latter body soon became a formality.

Another tribunal of the *magna curia* which suffered diminution was that of the *magister justiciarius*. In the reign of Charles I that official or his *locumtenens* continued to superintend royal justice, presiding over the supreme court and leading its judges on annual circuits. Finding that the volume of business was causing undue

---

[33] de Boüard, *Documents en français*, i. 11.
[34] Charles I bestowed this privilege on Naples, perhaps following the example of Philip Augustus who had appointed six burgesses of Paris to supervise the royal accounts.

delay in this single court, Charles II instituted another, known as
the Vicaria, to deal specifically with judicial irregularities and
appeals from the court of the justiciar.[35] Thanks to its more
flexible procedures and constitution, the Vicaria managed, at
least in the earlier years of its existence, to dispense justice more
swiftly than the *magna curia*, with the result that litigants sought
whenever possible to have their cases brought before it. This
pressure led to a steady extension in the scope of the Vicaria's
jurisdiction until it became virtually identical with that of the
magna curia. After a brief and unsuccessful attempt to unite the
two tribunals in 1324 they continued their separate but parallel
functions to the end of the Angevin era.

Until the death of Robert the Wise (1343) the feudal monarchy
of the Angevins functioned with reasonable efficiency, bestowing
on its subjects what seemed in retrospect a golden age of order and
prosperity. But even then the stresses that were to bring political
and social anarchy in the following hundred years lay close to the
surface. They can be seen bearing upon the justiciars whom the
Angevins retained as their chief agents of law enforcement. All-
powerful and alien under Charles I, they were highly successful,
if somewhat tyrannical. In the next reign they lost ground to lay
and ecclesiastical feudatories. Growing violence caused Robert to
confer extraordinary powers on them by means of the four 'arbitrary letters' which authorized them to act outside the procedures
laid down in constitutional codes when dealing with robbery,
arson, forcible abduction, illegal carrying of arms, clandestine
homicide, piracy, and other 'outrageous crimes'. Brigandage and
outlawry, like malaria, were old plagues of the Neapolitan countryside. Robert deserves some credit for tackling them energetically,
but the poverty and oppression that drove men outside the law
were not abated. Soon the 'arbitrary letters' lost their exceptional
character and became as permanent as the once temporary
collectae. Under Robert's successor Giovanna I (1343–82) and
again in the calamitous reign of Giovanna II (1414–35) the forces
of the state were corrupted and dissipated in endless civil wars and
struggles for power which drew in interested parties from outside
as well as those fomented within, until the kingdom became little
more than the helpless object of domestic and international

---

[35] C. Pecchia, *Storia civile e politica del regno di Napoli* (Naples, 1783), iii.
127 ff.

brigandage. Chaos paved the way for Alfonso and the Spaniards; it also ensured that restored royal authority would embark on a thorough reformation of the state.

THE CORONA DE ARAGÓN AND THE SPANISH INTERVENTION IN ITALY

The struggle that culminated in the Aragonese conquest of Naples had its roots in the thirteenth century, its motivation in the dynastic ambitions of the ruling house of Aragon and in the commercial aspiration of Catalonia. Before the union of the kingdom of Aragon and the county of Barcelona in 1137, the former had been a land-locked power absorbed in its rivalries with Castile and Navarre, and in expansion at the expense of its Moorish neighbours. Catalonia, on the other hand, dominated by the thriving port of Barcelona, had always looked to the Mediterranean as its natural sphere of territorial and commercial aggrandizement.[36] For almost a century after the union the seemingly ill-sorted state hung uncertainly between its continental and maritime destinies. Then, within the space of two years, came two battles which decided its future. Las Navas de Tolosa (1212), in which Peter II of Aragon fought alongside his fellow-Christian rulers of Castile and Navarre, broke the Almohad power in Spain and opened the way for the occupation of those Moorish lands assigned to Aragon in the treaty made with Castile at Cazorla in 1179; but it also assured Castile a dominant role in the future of the peninsula. In the following year Peter's defeat and death fighting in the Albigensian cause at the battle of Muret[37] marked the end of Aragonese domination in Languedoc and an important step towards the consolidation of a great French kingdom to the north. The long reign of James I (1213–76) saw the ambitions of Aragon adjusted to these new realities. With Louis IX he concluded the Treaty of Corbeil (1258) in which he renounced all claims to territory beyond the Pyrenees except for Cerdagne and the maritime regions of Roussillon and Montpellier.[38] By the Treaty of Almizra (1244) he renewed with Ferdinand III of

[36] Cf. F. Soldevila, *Història de Catalunya* (Barcelona, 1938), i, caps. xiv and xvii.
[37] R. B. Merriman, *The Rise of the Spanish Empire in the Old World and in the New* (New York, 1934–6), i. 284–6.
[38] Ibid. 392.

Castile the agreements of Cazorla that confined Aragonese expansion on the mainland of the peninsula to the coastal territory of Valencia.[39] Partly from choice, partly from necessity, James thus accepted the limitations imposed on his continental ambitions by his more powerful neighbours France and Castile. His fame as the Conqueror rests on his conquest of Majorca (1229–30), the kingdom of Valencia (1233 and 1236–45), and Murcia (1265–6) from the Moors[40]—achievements that pointed the way to a fruitful combination of commercial advantage and crusading zeal which might be carried to the farthest corners of the Mediterranean. Aragon now possessed the ports, the industries, the seamen, the merchants, and the shipbuilding timbers to compete with Italians and Provençals in Egypt, Tunis, Morocco, and Byzantium. It had also opened its eyes to a new sphere of political ambition and rivalry where the prize was no less than the mastery of the western Mediterranean.

In those states that comprised the Crown of Aragon political life was more constructive and sophisticated than in most parts of Europe. That liveliness derived largely from the dominant Catalan principality from which came also the ruling dynasty and the economic enterprise which established the Mediterranean empire. Catalan textiles and iron were the foundation of the trade which supported it. Catalan commercial prosperity helped in turn to entrench the power of an urban merchant class whose influence in public affairs outweighed that of the nobility. With few exceptions, the nobles of the Crown of Aragon lacked the great territorial estates which made their counterparts in Castile or southern Italy masters of the state. The victory of James II over the Union of Aragon in 1301 early averted any danger that the Aragonese state would become the tool of its barons. Instead a fruitful interaction between the crown and the merchant patriciates had evolved a constitutional system which enshrined the notion of contract between ruler and ruled, of a balance between effective government and the liberties of subjects. Where representative assemblies in the Italian kingdom remained the creatures of royal will, the Cortes of the Crown of Aragon steadily gained in authority and independence. Regular meetings, substantial representation of the towns, control over subsidies and legislation made

---

[39] Merriman, *The Rise of the Spanish Empire*, i. 289–91.
[40] Ibid. 294–6.

them indispensable partners of the crown in the business of government.[41]

From the Cortes evolved another powerful guardian of liberties in the institution known as the Diputació. Made up of representatives from each of the estates, its specific task was to administer the taxes and from the proceeds pay to the crown any subsidies voted by the Cortes; over and above that function it safeguarded the laws from violation by servants of the crown against whom it could organize effective sanctions. The Diputació appeared first in Catalonia; by the early fifteenth century Valencia and Aragon had established their own institutions on the Catalan model.

In the other scale of the balance weighed a royal administration which had been carefully adjusted to the needs of a scattered and heterogeneous empire. A Household Ordinance promulgated by Pedro the Ceremonious in 1344 and adhered to until the reign of Ferdinand the Catholic, detailed its structure with a precision unparalleled elsewhere in Europe.[42] Pedro reorganized the household in four main departments controlled respectively by the *mayordomens*, *camarlenchs*, *canceller*, and *maestre racional*, in that order of precedence. The *mayordomens*[43] were responsible for the feeding and provisioning of the household, and also for the royal stables, hunting dogs, and birds. Care of the king's person, his chamber and its contents, and supervision of the royal secretaries and *algutzirs*[44] belonged to two *camarlenchs*. The office of *canceller*, which carried responsibility for all judicial business brought before the king, was reserved to an archbishop or bishop holding the degree of doctor of laws; in the royal council he enjoyed pre-eminence by virtue of his duty to control its proceedings. A *vice canceller*, who had to be a doctor of laws not in holy orders,[45] a

---

[41] By the beginning of the fifteenth century Catalan jurists had elaborated a complete theory of a constitutional state and limited monarchy. Cf. J. M. Font y Rius, 'The institutions of the Crown of Aragon in the first half of the fifteenth century', in R. Highfield (ed.), *Spain in the 15th Century* (London, 1972), p. 173.

[42] The Household Ordinance of 1344 has been published by P. de Bofarull Mascaró, *Coleccion de documentos inéditos del Archivo General de la Corona de Aragón*, cuadernos 22, 23, 24 (Barcelona, 1850).

[43] They had to be *nobles cavallers* and were three in number: one from Aragon, one from Valencia or Mallorca, and one from Catalonia. Precedence among them was determined by the state in which the king was residing.

[44] Two knights who exercised jurisdiction, both civil and criminal, over the households of the king and queen.

[45] This provision ensured that he could act in criminal cases from which the *canceller* was debarred by reason of his orders.

prothonotari learned in Latin, who kept the seals and supervised the writing of legal documents, two *algutzirs*, twelve *scrivans de manament* for secretarial duties, five *oydors* who dwelt with petitions, together with numerous minor functionaries, completed the staff of the *canceller*. Although the royal chapel also came within his jurisdiction, it was immediately supervised by the abbots of Santa Creus. Last in the order of seniority came the office of the *maestre racional* whose task it was to receive and verify the accounts of all officials collecting or disbursing royal moneys. Under him functioned the treasurer and the *scriva de racio* who controlled allowances in money and kind given to members of the household.

The royal household of Aragon, like the households of other monarchs, was much more than a purely domestic apparatus. Together with officials such as the *mayordomens*, who served the personal needs of the king and his entourage, it numbered others, such as the chancellor, who exercised an authority which encompassed the whole state. Throughout Europe the fourteenth century witnessed an evolution of royal households leading to a sharper differentiation of these domestic and public functions, with a corresponding elaboration of offices which was especially marked in the public sphere. In Aragon the public role of the household became particularly important during the fourteenth century because it was the sole administrative bond holding together the diverse states that made up the Crown of Aragon. Each of these states had its own institutions functioning independently one of the other; only the person of the monarch and the public organs of his household served to unite them. An embryonic imperial government had thus developed in the Aragonese household possessing a supra-territorial character which made relatively easy the absorption of the Italian kingdom and the transfer of the seat of empire to Naples.

Even before the kings of Aragon turned their fleets and armies purposefully towards the Mediterranean there had been established a dynastic link of great significance for the future of that region. In 1209 Constance, the sister of King Peter of Aragon, married the youthful Frederick II of Hohenstaufen, and when in 1262 the time came for James I of Aragon to choose a wife for his heir he settled upon another Constance, the daughter of Manfred, Frederick's heir upon the throne of Sicily. For Manfred the marriage secured the friendship of a now formidable naval power. For James it meant influence in the central Mediterranean with a ruler enjoying close relations with those states of north Africa in which the Catalans had found profitable markets.[46] In the kingdom of Sicily too Catalan merchants had developed markets for their cereals and textiles. Neither party can have foreseen the revolution that was to be effected in Mediterranean affairs within three years of the marriage by the overthrow of Manfred and the installation of the Angevins on the Sicilian throne. James had good reason to oppose the domination of Italy by that branch of the French royal family which had already, in his view, filched Provence from him[47] and now threatened the long-term ambitions of Aragon in the central and eastern Mediterranean.[48] But James was unable to do anything about it and his subjects did not find their trade handicapped by the change of dynasty. The situation changed when the execution of Conradin (October 1268) left James's daughter-in-law Constance the best-placed champion of the Hohenstaufen cause. Already on the death of her father Constance had assumed the title of queen in her own right. After the departure of the old Aragonese warrior and the accession of her devoted husband Peter in July 1276, the recovery of the Hohenstaufen inheritance began to loom large in the calculations of the Aragonese court.[49]

Peter undoubtedly involved himself in plots against Charles I with the Greek emperor Michael Palaeologus, but the rising of the Vespers in March 1282 came spontaneously from the Sicilians themselves, and it was they who invited Peter to be their defender and king. Thus Aragon first set foot in Sicily as the champion of rebels against the rightful king and suzerain, Charles I and Pope Martin IV. Having ventured so far, political and military logic urged Peter to the conquest of the mainland territories, but mastery of the sea, which made him impregnable in the island, could not serve against Angevin and papal power on the mainland, nor secure his Spanish domains against the French invasion

---

[46] C.-E. Dufourcq, *L'Espagne catalane et le Maghrib aux xiiie et xive siècles* (Paris, 1966).

[47] Merriman, *The Rise of the Spanish Empire*, i. 288.

[48] S. Runciman, *The Sicilian Vespers* (Harmondsworth, 1960), p. 223; cf. Dufourcq, *L'Espagne catalane*, p. 250.

[49] One of Peter's first acts as king was to appoint John of Procida, once personal physician to Frederick II and chancellor to Manfred, as chancellor of Aragon. Cf. Runciman, *The Sicilian Vespers*, cap. 12.

launched in support of the Angevin cause. The outcome of this precarious balance between naval and military power was a century and a half of ruinous schism between Sicily and Naples.

Peter and his new subjects envisaged only a temporary union of Sicily and Aragon: on his death the island was to pass to his second son. Accordingly when Peter died in 1285, James became King of Sicily while his elder brother Alfonso inherited the Aragonese crown. Alfonso's early death in 1291 without an heir brought about a brief reunion of the crowns under James at a time when the papacy and Anjou had turned from war to diplomacy as a means of recovering the lost territory. James compromised profitably by agreeing to hand over to Rome the crown from which his father's and brother's wills already debarred him in exchange for rights of conquest in Sardinia and Corsica (Conference of Anagni, June 1295). Once again the Sicilians rebelled and chose their own king; this time it was James's brother Frederick whose coronation took place in Palermo in May 1296. Charles II struggled for a few more years to dislodge Frederick, then in the peace of Caltabellotta (1302) accepted the *fait accompli*.

The royal lines of Aragon and Sicily diverged from the time of James and Frederick until 1390 when the heiress to the Sicilian crown Maria married the only child of Martin I of Aragon.[50] Both husband and wife died before Martin I and left no issue, so in 1409, shortly before his own end, the last monarch of the Catalan line annexed Sicily to the Crown of Aragon and the whole inheritance passed to the new Trastamar dynasty established by the compromise of Caspe.

The Europe that witnessed the reunification of Sicily and Aragon at the beginning of the fifteenth century was very different from that which had brought about their separation one hundred years earlier. In the kingdom of Naples the direct line of Charles I had ended with the murder of Giovanna I in 1382; as a result the kingdom under the Durazzo branch of the dynasty had broken away from Provence under its Valois dukes.[51] The papacy, proud overlord of the kingdom, maker of kings, and scourge of emperors in the thirteenth century, now shook with the fevers of prolonged exile and schism; by endeavouring to become the master of princes it had become their plaything. The kingdom of France,

50 Merriman, *The Rise of the Spanish Empire*, i. 399–400.
51 Léonard, *Les Angevines de Naples*, pp. 471–2.

which had been first loyal servant then master of the papacy as
well as the most formidable supporter of the Angevin cause, came
to the end of the fourteenth century enfeebled by war on its own
soil, its government paralysed in the shadow of a mad king. Both
the Holy Roman and the Byzantine empires had failed to fulfil
hopes of their revival; by 1400 they had fallen into patent decay
and impotence. Castile had lived through a century of blood and
turmoil, its kings either weak or tyrannical, its nobility lawless and
grasping.

Such developments would have been sufficient in themselves to
call in question the settlement reached at Caltabellotta in 1302.
Still greater instability was threatened by the clearly impending
extinction of the Angevin–Durazzo line of Naples following
closely upon that of its Aragonese-Sicilian rival. Throughout the
reign of Giovanna II (1414–35) the all-powerful nobles of Naples
were looking to the future and inevitably some of them looked to
Aragon, now firmly entrenched on the threshold of the kingdom.
Giovanna, an impossible woman, devoid of political sense and
moral character, wallowed helplessly in the sea of intrigue that
surrounded her, grasping at one expedient after another and
casting each aside as it became irksome to her. In essence her
problem was to acquire, either through a husband or adopted heir,
the support of some power strong enough to repel rival claimants
to the succession and to master their factions within her kingdom.[52]
Her choice lay in effect between the royal houses of France and
Aragon, for only they could offer ready assistance and princes of
requisite rank; moreover both had a long-established interest in
the question which they were unlikely to waive at this critical
moment. But France was temporarily distracted by the madness
of its king, the recent struggle between Burgundians and Ar-
magnacs, and the impending attack from Henry V of England.
Giovanna's first instinct, therefore, was to turn to Aragon where
she found Ferdinand eager to offer his second son as a husband.
Perhaps it was the difference of age that made her draw back
(Giovanna was thirty years older than her proposed bridegroom),
perhaps a fear that Aragon might prove more of a master than an
ally, perhaps revulsion against surrendering her inheritance to the
hereditary enemies of her line. Whatever her motive, having

[52] Her first marriage to William, Duke of Austria, had shown that Giovanna
could not expect to bear children.

sharpened Ferdinand's appetite she abandoned the Aragonese marriage project and instead chose as her second husband Jacques de Bourbon, Comte de la Marche, a prince close enough to the royal house of France to secure its interest, but without the independent resources to overshadow the queen. The count spent four stormy years in Naples, three of them in prison, then fled gratefully to the shelter of a Franciscan monastery in France. Meanwhile another French prince, Louis III of Anjou, the representative of the Valois–Provence line, had begun to press through the papal suzerain those claims to Naples that his house had always maintained to the extent of using the royal title. Pope Martin V, anxious to reinforce the authority of the Neapolitan throne by the presence of a legitimate heir and also to re-establish the papacy in Rome, found it expedient to recognize Louis's right to the succession (November 1420). Having secured papal support and an understanding with the great *condottiere* Muzio Attendolo Sforza, that prince then prepared to install himself in Naples, by force if need be.[53] Again Giovanna felt her independence threatened and, realizing that a major ally would be needed to resist the combination of Anjou, the papacy, and Sforza, she appealed to Aragon to come to her aid.

Since 1416 Aragon and all its attendant territories had been ruled by Alfonso V, who, on becoming king, had shown himself impatient to win a heroic reputation befitting his own line and the inherited glories of Aragon. That ambition he allied to the aspirations of his Catalan subjects by fixing his eyes on Corsica, part of the price paid to James II for the renunciation of Sicily[54] but not yet collected, thanks to the manifest determination of the Genoese to defend with all their might an island that lay across the lifelines of their commercial empire. Supported by a powerful fleet and army, Alfonso began his expedition successfully in 1420 by settling the affairs of Sardinia and so securing his base of operations.[55] He then launched an attack on the port of Bonifacio in southern Corsica, but it soon became apparent that the Genoese had anticipated this move and that resistance would be tougher

---

[53] E. Pontieri, 'Muzio Attendolo e Francesco Sforza nei conflitti dinastico-civili nel regno di Napoli al tempo di Giovanna II d'Angiò-Durazzo', *Divagazioni storiche e storiografiche* (Naples, 1960).

[54] See above, p. 30.

[55] A. Boscolo, *I parlamenti di Alfonso il Magnanimo* (Milan, 1953), Introduction; Merriman, *The Rise of the Spanish Empire*, i. 412–13.

than he had expected. Fortunately for the king's military reputation, Giovanna's envoy, Malizia Carafa, arrived in Sardinia to request his intervention in Naples before the siege of Bonifacio had to be called off as a manifest failure. Checked by the Genoese, he accepted without much hesitation Giovanna's proposal that he should become her adopted heir and champion against Louis of Anjou. To his council's protest that it was a hazardous and unwise undertaking, he answered that 'no one has ever yet won glory without danger and difficulty'.[56]

The main objection that the counsellors had raised against the Neapolitan adventure—that it might ensnare Aragon in an endless, ruinous enterprise—proved to have some substance, for although Alfonso first entered the city of Naples triumphantly in July 1421 as the queen's heir,[57] twenty-one years passed before he was able to enter it again, this time by force of arms, and gain effective control of the kingdom. After quarrels with Giovanna had led in 1423 to his disinheritance, he played a waiting game, with the mastery that his father and brother, Juan of Navarre, displayed in other circumstances. Like a true Trastamar he knew how to overcome with time and gold as well as with steel. Events finally began to turn in his favour when in November 1434 Louis preceded Giovanna to the grave by three months, thus forcing on her a last-minute choice of a successor. She chose René of Anjou, brother of Louis III, and he was duly proclaimed king in Naples when Giovanna died on 2 February 1435. But René was far away, a prisoner of the Burgundians, while Alfonso, who proclaimed himself King of Naples from that same day, lay with a powerful fleet at Messina ready to support the faction he had fostered among the barons.[58] There ensued seven years of civil war in which Alfonso had to contend not only with the Angevin party in Naples, and after 1438 with René himself, but also with the Genoese and the papacy. Already suffering from Catalan commercial aggrandizement, Genoa threw its sea power into the struggle in a determined effort

[56] Beccadelli, *De dictis et factis*, i.

[57] The instrument of adoption dated 8 July 1421 is printed in C. Tutini, *Discorsi de sette officii overo de sette grandi del regno di Napoli* (Rome, 1666), pp. 137–42.

[58] On 25 Mar. 1435 Anthoni Vinyes, an envoy sent to the king by the city of Barcelona, wrote to the city council from Messina: 'E per aquest fet de Napols, es axi ansios e torbat que res al mon no li es plasent, sino parlarli del reyalme' (J. M. Madurell Marimón, *Mensajeros barceloneses en la corte de Nápoles de Alfonso V de Aragón, 1435–1458* (Barcelona, 1963), p. 86).

to prevent further Aragonese expansion. Pope Eugenius IV, after some hesitation, also decided that papal interests would be compromised by Aragonese domination of southern Italy; he therefore dispatched his warrior patriarch Vitelleschi to aid the Angevins. Feeling towards Aragon in the other Italian states ranged from unveiled hostility to unfriendly neutrality, for none believed that they stood to gain by an Aragonese victory.

The war began disastrously for Alfonso with the annihilation of his fleet and his own capture by the Genoese at the battle of Ponza (5 August 1535). Equally astounding to the whole of Europe was the counter-stroke by which the king turned naval defeat into diplomatic triumph. His Genoese captors had handed him over to their temporary suzerain Filippo Maria Visconti, Duke of Milan. Since he had first turned his attention to Naples in 1420 Alfonso had made many attempts to inveigle the duke into an alliance, but always without success, for Filippo Maria was not prepared to sacrifice his influence in Genoa to an understanding with Aragon. Now the king managed to turn his gaoler into a partner in a scheme for mutual aggrandizement by convincing him that a French prince in Naples would be a greater threat to Milan than a Spanish one. The humanists around Alfonso in later years chose to attribute this feat to his 'eloquence', but both parties had solid grounds for reaching a realistic understanding which was to remain a basic feature of Italian diplomacy until Ludovico il Moro overthrew it, with disastrous results for every state in Italy.[59]

His diplomatic triumph notwithstanding, Alfonso had failed in his plan to bring the war to an early end by a decisive blow at the city of Naples, and he had to meet the cost of that failure in a prolonged war of attrition in which gold, honours, lands, and promises counted for as much as fleets and armies.[60] Patiently and methodically he won over men and territory from the Angevin cause until at last, on 6 June 1442, his army stormed Naples. René of Anjou, recognizing defeat, abandoned the kingdom, and his last supporters began to make their peace with the victor.

[59] Pontieri, 'Alfonso V d'Aragona nel quadro della politica italiana', pp. 232–3.
[60] The best account of the war is by N. F. Faraglia, *Storia della lotta tra Alfonso V d'Aragona e Renato d'Angiò* (Lanciano, 1908).

II

THE KING AS LORD
AND VASSAL

ALFONSO V, the eldest son of Ferdinand of Antequera and Eleanor of Albuquerque, was born in Medina del Campo in 1396, spent his boyhood in Castile, and received his education there. Castilian was thus his mother tongue and remained throughout his life the language he habitually spoke and wrote,[1] though he later acquired an adequate command of Catalan and Italian.[2] In appearance Alfonso was short but well proportioned; his face was dominated by a strong, hooked nose and large, penetrating eyes; a broad, humorous mouth gave a pleasant touch to these otherwise severe features.[3] Most observers describe him as affable and even-tempered, calm in the face of both prosperity and adversity, and acutely conscious of the dignity of his office. In his habits he was restrained, preferring to dress in black or dark colours, drinking only diluted wine, and never using obscene language or losing his self-control. He had deep and conventional religious beliefs which he manifested in a strict observance of his personal obligations,[4] a veneration of the Virgin, saints, and relics,[5] a thorough reading of

---

[1] His autograph letters registered in ACA Reg. 2940 are all in Castilian except for one or two brief notes in Latin.

[2] Vespasiano da Bisticci recounts an incident when Alfonso spoke in Catalan to a deputation sent to him by the *remences* of Catalunya ('Vita del Re Alfonso d'Aragona', *Archivio storico italiano*, iv, pt. 1 (1843), 393).

[3] Cf. G. della Casa, 'Alfonsi regis vita', *Opere* (Venice, 1728), iv. 132. 'Statura fuit paullo minus quam mediocri, facie pleniore, et colore fusco: naso fuit oblongo, curvoque; oculis grandioribus, et vivacioribus; superciliis dignitatem promittentibus; ore latiore, et ad profusissimum risum exprimendum idoneo; brachiis, cruribusque graciolioribus; conspicuus erat in armis, et cujusvis, vel etiam indomiti equi sessor immobilis.' F. Martorell, *Alguns aspectes de la vida íntima d'Alfons el Magnànim* (Barcelona, 1938), pp. 4–5.

[4] For the character of Alfonso see A. Beccadelli, *De dictis et factis Alphonsi regis* (Basle, 1538); J. Vicens Vives, *Els Trastamares* (Barcelona, 1956), pp. 103 ff. According to Beccadelli (*De dictis et factis*, iv, proemium), Alfonso rose at daybreak to say the hours in his chamber and heard four masses every day; he strictly observed all fasts and performed the maundy ceremony.

[5] During the sack of Marseille in 1423 he organized a hunt for the body of

the Bible,[6] and a keenness for philosophical discussion of a religious hue.[7] Many of the *bons mots* recorded by Panormita (Beccadelli) show that he had none the less a dry sense of humour.[8] That same author undoubtedly exaggerates Alfonso's prowess as an original thinker in the realms of philosophy, but he had a shrewd mind, a facility for talking, and a passionate love of learning.[9] As a statesman his thoughts and actions revealed a realism which some among his opponents saw as cynicism and lack of scruple; few denied his political skill and invincible persistence.[10] Chroniclers seeking an appropriate cognomen for him after his death dubbed him 'the Magnanimous', and a modern historian, though critical of his activities in Italy, describes him as 'un gran signore nato'.[11] Only Francesco Sforza strikes a jarring note. Writing after the death of his old enemy, he said of Alfonso:

Egli era l'uomo più presuntuoso, non voleva ammetter nessuno al proprio livello come compagno. La sua arroganza, il suo orgoglio erano tali, che si teneva degno non solo di essere onorato tra gli uomini, ma

St. Louis of Toulouse and carried the relic away in his own ship. The royal chapel in Castelnuovo possessed relics of the Cross, the Crown of Thorns, and Christ's tunic which were displayed on Good Fridays. In 1453 Alfonso asked the pope to grant special indulgence to those who venerated these relics (ACA Reg. 2697. 154ʳ).

[6] He had read the Bible fourteen times and knew long passages by heart (Beccadelli, *De dictis et factis*, ii).

[7] Beccadelli describes his attendance at lectures given by theologians appointed to teach in the university of Naples (ibid. i); his participation in a discussion on the love of God which arose during a reading of Seneca's letters (ibid.); his exhortation to a dying courtier—a powerful exercise in the *ars moriendi* (ibid. iii).

[8] e.g. his remark, when being pestered by a garrulous old man while eating, that asses were more fortunate than kings because their masters allowed them to eat in peace (ibid. i); 'Married life can only be smooth if the wife is blind and the husband deaf' (ibid. iii). Of neutral Siena harassed by opposing parties in the Italian wars, he remarked that the Sienese were in the position of those who lived on the middle floor 'troubled by smoke from below and urine from above' (ibid. iv). Bisticci ('Vita del Re Alfonso') recounts the joke played by Alfonso on some foppishly dressed envoys from Siena.

[9] He listened to an address by some envoys from Barcelona for over two hours without saying a word. When they had finished he answered them point by point for more than one hour (ACB Cart. Com., vol. 23, fol. 45, Naples, 13 June 1453).

[10] Cf. E. Pontieri, 'Alfonso V d'Aragona nel quadro della politica italiana del suo tempo', *Divagazioni storiche e storiografiche*, cap. VI; E. Dupré Theseider, *La politica italiana di Alfonso d'Aragona* (Bologna, 1956.).

[11] Dupré Theseider, *La politica italiana*, p. 130.

anche adorato tra gli dei; pensava che persino gli alberi e le mura doves-
sero curvarsi innanzi a lui per fargli onore. Con lui non si poteva stabilire
nessuna comunanza di vita, nessuna amicizia.[12]

Sforza, who was not 'un signore naturale',[13] must have been
especially sensitive, for Alfonso seems not to have troubled others
in this manner.

His practical education as a ruler began at the age of sixteen
when he accompanied his father to Aragon and was soon taking
part in its government. In 1414 Ferdinand, wishing to support the
burgesses of Zaragoza against the excesses of the nobles and *ricos
omes*, entrusted control of the Aragonese capital to his son.[14] His
next assignment took him to the conference held at Perpignan
(1414–15) to prepare the way for a General Council which was to
heal the schism in the Church. There he met the Emperor Sigismund and many of the leading ecclesiastical and political figures of
Europe; it was an experience which probably helped to develop
in the young prince the cynicism with respect to ecclesiastical
politics that marked his later dealings with the Church.

Contact with the constitutional temper of his Spanish subjects,
and especially the Catalans among them, sharpened Alfonso's
autocratic predilections. In the Cortes of Barcelona (1412–13) his
father had encountered a well-organized offensive which sought
to restrict his legislative authority at the outset of his reign.
Alfonso in his turn often ran foul of that same spirit so that he
came to view with intense suspicion aristocratic and oligarchic
pretensions and seized every opportunity of weakening their
challenge to royal authority. In Catalonia, for example, the crown
became the champion of the restless peasantry: a constitution of
1448 freed the serfs and in 1455 Alfonso enforced a temporary but
complete suspension of the 'six evil customs' which gave the lord
certain rights over a serf's goods. Despite bitter recrimination
from the Catalan oligarchy the king confirmed the suspension in
1457. In the cities too he seized what opportunities offered to

---

[12] Quoted by E. Gothein, *Il Rinascimento nell'Italia meridionale* (Florence,
1915), pp. 118–19.

[13] Filippo Maria Visconti used this phrase to describe Alfonso when con-
trasting him with his Sforza son-in-law (Dupré Theseider, *La politica italiana*,
pp. 82–3).

[14] Macdonald, *Don Fernando*, p. 207. It was Alfonso who presented the new
municipal ordinance to the city. See A. Canellas, *El Reino de Aragón en los
años 1410–1458* (Palma, 1955), pp. 40, 161.

reduce the power of the ruling oligarchies. In Barcelona he took the part of the lesser merchants and artisans (the 'Busca' party) against the small ruling circle (the 'Biga') whose activities had long been a thorn in monarchical flesh. The system of filling municipal offices by balloting by lot, instead of by narrowly based election or co-optation, made its appearance in his reign; also he made the Catalan Cortes much more representative of popular feeling by increasing the number of cities represented in it from fifteen to forty. Such measures were not, of course, intended to encourage political aspirations in the sub-aristocratic classes—witness the fierce repression of the peasant revolt of 1450 in Majorca—but rather to turn to account the rising discontent of town and country-side by directing it against feudal and urban aristocracies and making concessions at their expense.[15] His Spanish experience had, in short, bred in Alfonso a hearty suspicion of the aristocracy, feudal and urban, and the institutions it controlled. Merriman has said of the nobility of Aragon that they were 'not only zealous for the welfare of their order as a whole, but also for that of the entire body politic',[16] but the king saw them, with some justice, as essentially the upholders of sectional privilege, local interest, and private passions. His dilemma, like that of all monarchs, was that his agents of government, his very household, were largely drawn from that same class and had to be weaned from opposition to support of royal interest by ties of honour, office, and profit; nor could he ever be certain that attachment to the crown would always prevail in any individual against the constant, general pull of family, region, and class.

In the kingdom of Naples Alfonso faced a situation different in many respects to that in Spain: a well-entrenched feudal aristo-cracy, barely leavened by a few town oligarchies, dominated the land and the people. It was, moreover, as the last century of Angevin rule had demonstrated, an aristocracy jealous of its independence and impatient of royal control. Frequent civil wars had brought the crown itself down into the arena of baronial politics and partisanship in a manner that had no parallel in Aragon. On the other hand, the Sicilian state in its formative

---

[15] Cf. the similar policy adopted in Sicily: in 1449 Alfonso approved a reform which gave the lesser citizens a share in the government of Messina (Mack Smith, *Medieval Sicily*, p. 102); he hung the ring-leaders in the Palermo riots of 1450 (T. Fazellus, *De rebus siculis decades* (Palermo, 1558), ix. 591).

[16] *Rise of the Spanish Empire*, i. 454.

years had been far more absolutist in spirit than Aragon, with the result that baronial interests had not become enshrined in those constitutional forms which in Aragon gave them a cloak of respectability and continuity and made them such a formidable rival to the authority of the monarch. Apart from the Great Councils or parliaments which met at the discretion of the king, the Neapolitan baronage as a class had no legal means of voicing its grievances or organizing opposition to royal policy. A strong ruler accordingly encountered little constitutional difficulty in imposing his will on the kingdom of Naples—administrative obstacles were another matter. Alfonso's liking for his new kingdom owed something to that circumstance; on several occasions he contrasted the authority he wielded there with that which was his in Spain, and always to the detriment of the latter. In 1450, for example, when the Cortes of Catalonia sent envoys to Naples to complain of the tardiness with which royal officials ministered justice in the principality, the king attacked the memorial they brought as 'indecent, impertinent and exceedingly dishonest; and moreover quite insufferable to his royal majesty and dignity'.[17] He went on to affirm that the real obstacles to justice in Catalonia were the 'usatges de Barcelona, constitucions e capitols de Cort de Cathalunya, privilegis e pretesos usos e libertats'. Against this image of trammelled justice he set that of 'lo present son Realme de Sicilia deça far per la sua Magestat adquisit e conquistat on ha la potestat absoluta, e no hi son fets tals opposits o allegacions pera empatxar la justicia'.

Having sworn no coronation oath and having promised to the papal suzerain only that the Neapolitans should enjoy the liberties of good King William, Alfonso could behave as 'princeps legibus solutus'[18] setting aside any law by the exercise of his sovereign power. Examples of such action and affirmations of the principle on which they were based occur frequently in the Aragonese registers. In a privilege issued for the Count of Brienza on 15 October 1456 is the clause 'Cassantes propterea et annullantes de plenitudine dominice et absolute potestatis omnia et quecumque

[17] ACB Cart. Com., vol. 20, fol. 48, 'indecents, impertinents e inhonestissimes mes encara son molt insoportables ala magestat e dignitat real' (Reply of king to the articles presented by the envoys of the Cortes).

[18] He pardoned Francesco Taurella of Naples for a wounding affray and quashed proceedings against him in the Vicaria by virtue of 'nostra dominica potestate legibus absoluta' (ACA Reg. 2915. 115ʳ; Torre d'Ottavo, 27 Oct. 1451).

privilegia quascumque provisiones cautelas cauciones constitu
ciones capitula concessiones ordinaciones consilia etiam generalia
edita ritus et observaciones editas . . .'.[19] This unfettered power he
believed was of divine origin; the theme appears again and again
in the documents of his chancery. 'Princeps prudens cui guber-
naculum suorum subiectorum dedit altissimus';[20] 'Rege qui
summi Regis ymaginem representat';[21] 'ut Omnipotente Deo,
cuius reges in terris in distribuenda iustitia imago sunt, quantum
possumus reddamur conformes, cui tot regnorum et vassallorum
sua clementia gubernacula commisit . . .';[22] 'calliditatibus et
erroribus aurificum pro interesse rei publice nobis ab alto comisse
sicut nostro incumbit regalis dignitatis officio providere volentes.'[23]
In the making of law, too, he was virtually a free agent, not being
bound to seek the advice and approval of his vassals save for
legislation which involved the imposition of new direct taxes. Not
since the heyday of Frederick II had a ruler of Naples enjoyed
such an unrestricted exercise of power.

Alfonso numbered his regnal years in the Neapolitan kingdom
from the death of Giovanna II on 2 February 1435 and styled
himself *Rex Sicilie citra et ultra farum*. The title had first been
coined by Boniface VIII in 1303 to signify the unity of the island
and mainland components of a kingdom that had by then ceased
to exist; Alfonso made use of it to mark the reunion of the two
under one monarch.[24] Politically and administratively, however,
the two remained apart, the kingdom of Sicilia *citra farum* (Naples)
having no link with Sicilia *ultra farum* other than a common
sovereign.

His ultimately unsuccessful rival, René of Anjou, he affected to
regard as a usurper, just as the first of the Hohenstaufen and
Angevins had treated their competitors in similar circumstances.

---

[19] E. Rogadeo, *Codice diplomatico barese*, ii (Bari, 1931), 367.
[20] ACA Reg. 2902. 232ʳ, Privilege for Maratea, Castelnuovo, 20 Sept. 1444.
[21] Ibid.
[22] Priv. anni 1449–51, fol. 111, cited by Toppi, *De origine tribunalium*, pt. II,
pp. 440–4.
[23] ACA Reg. 2902. 210ʳ, Naples, 20 May 1444.
[24] Cf. G. Romano, 'L'origine della denominazione "Due Sicilie" e un'orazione
inedita di L. Valla', *ASPN* anno xxii, fasc. III, 1897. The alternative formula
Rex utriusque Siciliae was also frequently employed; it appears at least as early
as 1443 in the record of the parliament. See N. de Bottis, *Privilegii et capitoli
con altre gratie concesse alla fidelissima città di Napoli, e regno per li Sereniss. Re di
Casa de Aragona* (Venice, 1588), fol. 2ᵛ.

The adoption by Giovanna in 1421 took precedence, he maintained, over any subsequent adoptions of other heirs and was, moreover, by its own terms, not subject to annulment; hence René's title was invalid. Although this argument was to assume some importance in the negotiations for papal recognition, it had not given Alfonso possession of the kingdom. That had come from conquest and it was in the stance of a victor that he sought recognition from his subjects, the papal overlord, and the states of Europe. Anjou refused that recognition. From Naples René had travelled to Florence where Eugenius IV had belatedly handed him the bull of investiture for the kingdom; nothing but that title remained to him when he returned to Provence at the end of 1442. But though thoroughly disillusioned with his Neapolitan supporters and Italian allies, René would not renounce his claims. In that direction Alfonso had to rest content with a truce signed in June 1443 and valid for only one year. Strenuous efforts by the Cardinal de Foix managed to bring about annual renewals until 1448, but a treaty of peace eluded all his endeavours. René resumed the struggle in 1458 when he sent his eldest son, who bore the title of Duke of Calabria,[25] to aid the Genoese against an all-out Aragonese attack.

Recognition by the other states of Italy, though not, except in the case of the papacy, juridically necessary to Alfonso's possession of the Neapolitan crown, was politically essential. In the summer of 1442 his only friend in the peninsula was Filippo Maria Visconti who, scenting fulfilment of the secret pact of 1435, demanded its renewal in the aftermath of Aragonese victory. Alfonso readily complied and sent a secretary to Milan in June 1443 to discuss how the treaty might be put into effect. Milanese influence soon secured him another ally in the person of Leonello d'Este, Marquis of Ferrara, whom Filippo Maria proposed as a husband for Alfonso's illegitimate elder daughter, Maria. The marriage took place in 1444. Relations between Ferrara and Naples were further strengthened by the visits which the marquis's brother Borso d'Este paid to Naples in 1444 and 1445, and the years which his youngest brothers, Ercole and Sigismondo, spent as pages in the

---

[25] This was the title customarily given to the heir apparent to the Neapolitan throne. Jean of Anjou reached Genoa in May 1458 as governor of the city in the name of Charles VII of France to whom the Genoese *in extremis* had offered the suzerainty of their republic.

king's court. But the rest of Italy showed little inclination to come to terms with the new regime in Naples. Florence and Venice, though reluctant to risk a direct confrontation, gave financial and diplomatic support to Francesco Sforza who at the end of 1442 still held a number of towns in the northern Abruzzi as well as the adjoining March of Ancona. Not until June 1450 and after a great deal of fighting did Alfonso make peace with Florence.[26] Venice followed suit a few days later.[27] Both powers then acknowledged his title to the kingdom. Genoa, a more determined opponent of Aragon than the other two republics, was nevertheless brought to a much earlier recognition of the king's success. From bases in Naples, Sicily, and Sardinia the Aragonese were able to threaten Genoese sea-routes to the east and west; their galleys harassed the Genoese coast itself through the winter of 1442–3; above all Alfonso was able to take advantage of the bitter rivalry between the Adorni and Campofregosi factions which kept Genoa in a state of almost perpetual civil war. In June 1443 the Doge Raffael Adorno asked for a truce which was with some difficulty converted into a peace treaty signed on 7 April 1444 on terms very favourable to Aragon.

Most important of all, Alfonso needed to force or cajole the pope into revoking the investiture belatedly granted to René of Anjou and transferring it to himself. Only then would his own position be constitutionally secure and a formidable pretext for rebellion disappear. In this delicate matter Alfonso gave one of his most adroit displays of diplomatic skill. He began to put pressure on Eugenius IV by adhering to the Council of Basle and opening negotiations with the conciliar pope Felix V who readily agreed to confirm Giovanna's act of adoption and invest him with the kingdom. But he knew that the anti-pope's crumbling authority could do nothing to secure his own position in Naples, so the matter was allowed to hang in suspense while a steady run of military and political success within the kingdom brought a reluctant Eugenius IV ever nearer to the moment when he would be forced to make a counter-offer. A further prod was administered through the 1443 parliament when the barons resolved to send a

---

[26] The text of the treaty signed on 21 June 1450 is printed in J. Du Mont, *Corps universel diplomatique du droit des gens* (Amsterdam, 1726), iii, pt. 1, p. 175. Mention is made of the investiture of the kingdom which Alfonso had earlier secured from the pope.

[27] Ibid., p. 178. The treaty with Venice is dated 2 July 1450.

delegation to the pope calling upon him to come to terms with their duly acknowledged sovereign or else face their repudiation of all obligations to Rome.[28] At the same time Alfonso let it be known that he would serve the church by driving Sforza from the March of Ancona which the *condottiere* was holding in defiance of papal authority—something he needed to do anyway in order to secure his northern frontier. Both sides moved cautiously. Beginning with a truce in the autumn of 1442, they proceeded to informal meetings of envoys first in Milan, then in Florence and Siena. In April 1443 Eugenius appointed Luigi Scarampo Paduano, Cardinal of S. Lorenzo in Damaso and Patriarch of Aquileia, a man with strong Aragonese sympathies, as his legate to conduct negotiations. They came to fruition in the agreement signed by the cardinal and the king on 14 June 1443 in the frontier town of Terracina.[29]

By the Treaty of Terracina Alfonso recognized Eugenius IV as the true pope. In return Eugenius undertook to confirm the king's adoption by Giovanna, to invest him with the kingdom of Naples, to legitimize his son Ferdinand and recognize him as heir to the kingdom.[30] Important as the substantive issue of the investiture might be, experience had shown that for practical purposes the crucial matter was the terms on which the papacy granted the investiture, and these had varied greatly through the Norman, Hohenstaufen, and Angevin phases of Neapolitan history. The statement in the treaty that these terms were to be 'those granted to earlier rulers of the kingdom' gave ample scope for Alfonso's resolve to obtain the most favourable interpretation. Eugenius, on the other hand, in a bull of investiture dated 15 July 1443,[31] took as his model the terms most favourable to the papacy, namely those granted to Charles I; they included an annual tribute of 8,000 *oncie* and an undertaking that the Neapolitans should enjoy the liberties bestowed by 'good King William'. Alfonso rejected this bull out of hand. Prolonged haggling ensued as he submitted objections and counter-proposals and instructed

[28] Cf. de Bottis, *Privilegii et capitoli*, fol. 9: '. . . possano recorrere ad debiti remedii de consilio o terzo loco . . .'.

[29] See Ametller y Vinyas, *Alfonso V de Aragón*, ii. 468; Giannone, *Istoria civile*, iii. 365.

[30] Alfonso formally recognized Eugenius IV as true pope in a letter dated 20 June 1443 and written in Gaeta (ACA Reg. 2652. 52ʳ). The papal bull legitimizing Ferdinand is dated 14 June 1444—text in Chioccarello, *Archivio*, p. 7.

[31] Text in Chioccarello, *Archivio*, p. 5.

his vice-chancellor to inspect the earlier bulls of investiture kept in
Rome in order to compare them with that offered to him.[32] The
outcome was another secret conference with the Cardinal of
Aquileia which took place at Teano in July 1444; there they
hammered out a detailed settlement of the terms of investiture
wholly favourable to the king. So much did the papacy concede
that it was agreed that a bull of investiture in the customary form
(that is, the form employed during the Angevin period) should be
published,[33] while the effective terms were to be embodied in a
number of post-dated secret bulls. The vice-chancellor Platamone
went to Rome to collect these in January 1445. Thus the bull of
15 July 1443 remained Alfonso's overt title to the kingdom. The
secret bulls, twelve in number, were dated September and December 1443, though they were not in fact issued until 1445.[34] They
freed the king of all financial obligations towards the papacy by
excusing him the payment of 50,000 marks for the investiture,
remitting all outstanding tribute and waiving all future claim to it
for Alfonso's lifetime.[35] The only token of suzerainty left to the
pope was a white palfrey which he was to receive from the king
every year on the feast of SS. Peter and Paul. The penalty of
deposition specified in the public bull for any contravention of the
terms of investiture was modified, again for the king's lifetime, to
a fine of 50,000 ducats. Equally significant were the papal concessions regarding the church and clergy of the kingdom. The open
bull forbade the imposition of any direct taxes upon churches and
monasteries, the clergy or their property other than in circumstances permitted *de jure* or by the constitutions of the kingdom.
Alfonso, relying upon the most favourable interpretation, argued
that the 'ancient constitutions' of the kingdom sanctioned the
imposition of tallage and *collectae* upon the clergy; presumably he
was referring to the constitutions of the Norman and Hohenstaufen period. The secret bulls conceded this point. Again basing his

---

[32] Berenguer de Erill, admiral of Aragon, and Batista Platamone were sent to
explain the king's objections to Eugenius. Their instructions, issued in Naples
on 26 Mar. 1444, are to be found in ACA Reg. 2698. 43ᵛ and 55ᵛ.

[33] Memorial for Platamone, Crotone, 23 Jan. 1445 (ACA Reg. 2698. 75ʳ). The
public bull is for the 'contentacio o satisfaccio al vulgar'.

[34] Texts in Chioccarello, *Archivio*, p. 6.

[35] At Teano it had been agreed that the amount of tribute should be negotiated
between Alfonso and the cardinal; they fixed a sum of 15,000 ducats which the
king was to keep as reimbursement of his expenses in aiding the pope against
Sforza (ACA Reg. 2698. 75ʳ).

case upon the 'ancient constitutions', he obtained recognition of his right to refuse to receive or admit any prelate elected or nominated to a benefice within the kingdom. Another of the bulls released him from his investiture oath to pardon Neapolitan rebels and restore their property. Another extended the right of succession from the direct male line to collateral branches, and another recognized Alfonso's *de facto* occupation of the papal territories of Benevento and Terracina by granting him the vicariates for life. One cannot wonder that Eugenius wished bulls so damaging to papal claims on the kingdom to be kept secret as long as he lived.[36]

Once the bargaining had been concluded, Eugenius sent Giovanni di Prima, the abbot of S. Paolo in Rome, to invest Alfonso with the kingdom. The ceremony must have taken place in Naples some time before 18 May 1445 when, in a letter to his wife, the king mentioned that he had received the investiture.[37] To the abbot Alfonso swore the oath of liege homage by which he acknowledged papal suzerainty.[38] There should have followed a coronation. In one of the secret bulls Eugenius had promised to send the Patriarch of Aquileia to perform the ceremony wherever the king wished,[39] and in the letter to Queen Maria mentioned above Alfonso wrote that he was shortly expecting a papal legate to arrive to crown him.[40] As early as July 1443 he had ordered jewels to be sent from Spain for his coronation[41] and in 1444 he had imposed a coronation aid.[42] In May 1444 the secretary Arnau

---

[36] Cf. G. A. Summonte, *Historia della città e regno di Napoli* (Naples, 1748–9), iv, bk. 6, p. 64.

[37] ACA Reg. 2690. 154ʳ, Castelnuovo, Naples, 18 May 1445: '. . . som en bona concordia ab nostre sant pare lo qual segons per altres letres scrit vos havem nos ha tramesa la bulla dela investitura daquest Reyalme en la forma que havem demanada, e la investitura nos es stada feta per lo Abat de Sant Pau de Roma en nom e vim de nostre sant pare.'

[38] This ceremony took place on 2 June 1445. The bull requiring the oath, supposedly dated 13 Dec. 1443, had to allow the king up to two years to swear it in order to get round the falsification of the dates. The full form of the oath is printed in Summonte, *Historia*, iii. 208.

[39] Bull dated 25 Sept. 1443 (Chioccarello, *Archivio*, p. 6).

[40] '. . . dins breus dies ab la aiuda de deu entenem ab les solemnitats degudes reebre de algun legat del dit nostre sant pare les insignits dela coronats de aquest Reyalme.'

[41] ACA Reg. 2939. 64ᵛ, 16 July 1443.

[42] Tutini (*Discorsi de sette officii*, pp. 80–101) prints the 'Cedula' of the 'Tassa collectarum felicis coronationis regis Alphonsi noviter imposita ad recolligendam a baronibus provinciarum Regni ultra terras demaniales.' He took it from the Sommaria register 'Commune 4 Anno 1445'.

Fonolleda was expecting the coronation to follow hard upon a conclusion of negotiations with the pope,[43] but none took place and Alfonso became the first King of Sicily and Naples not to receive the crown. The decision to dispense with the ceremony was presumably his own for he did not subsequently ask Eugenius IV or any of his successors to perform it. In the absence of any explanation for this change of mind we can only note that, having become an anointed king by virtue of his coronation in Aragon, Alfonso had not deemed it necessary to undergo that rite in his other kingdoms. A further coronation in Naples, he might have reasoned, could not enhance his status, might raise problems in other states (particularly in Sicily), and would certainly be a public manifestation of that papal suzerainty which he was otherwise striving to rob of all significance. Contemporaries within and without the kingdom presumably agreed that coronation added nothing essential to his authority in the kingdom for none ever brought forward its omission as an argument for challenging that authority.

As it happened, the king's relations with the next pope, Nicholas V (1447–55), proved reasonably harmonious, and conflict over the investiture only reappeared after his own protégé Alfonso Borja had ascended the papal throne as Calixtus III. Alfonso sent a magnificent array of Spanish and Neapolitan nobles and clergy to represent him at the papal coronation and perform homage to Calixtus in his name.[44] Negotiations for confirming the investiture, which Nicholas V had granted without demur, appear to have begun in earnest only in August 1456 when Eximen Roiz de Corella, Count of Cocentayna and formerly a close associate of the pope, was sent to Rome for that purpose.[45] Playing upon the pope's

[43] ACB Cart. Com., vol. 14. The ambassadors of Barcelona to the council of the city, Naples, 11 May 1444. 'Senyors asis diu per alguns que lo senyor Rey ha questa volta tot quant ha volgut del pare sant e entre les altres coses dien que la refermacio de aquest reyalme per a don fferrando. E per alguns e entre los altres lo secretari en fonolleda nos ho haurie dit que lo senyor Rey se coronaria fort prestament.'

[44] ACA Reg. 2660. 140ʳ, Instrument appointing the delegation to represent the king, Castelnuovo, 28 Apr. 1455; Reg. 2700. 90ᵛ, Memorial of the same date containing instructions for the delegation.

[45] ACA Reg. 2700. 113ʳ, Instructions for the Count of Cocentayna, Castel dell'Ovo, 16 Aug. 1456. There had probably been some preliminary bargaining. According to Aeneas Sylvius, the king had earlier asked Calixtus for the vicariates of the March of Ancona and other papal territories, but had been refused (Pii Secundi Pontificis Max. commentarii (Frankfurt, 1614), ii. 35). These other

well-known passion for the crusade, the count had instructions to begin his mission by revealing in strictest confidence that Alfonso intended to visit Spain where he would prepare an onslaught on the infidel. To facilitate his departure and the enterprise Calixtus was asked to confirm the bulls of investiture and the vicariates of Benevento and Terracina as granted by Eugenius IV and confirmed by Nicholas V. The pope's refusal to grant the requests of his erstwhile sovereign came as a rude shock to Naples even though relations with Rome had been distinctly lacking in cordiality ever since Calixtus's accession. His motives appear to have been a mixture of genuine concern for Christendom, political calculation, and blatant nepotism, all distorted by the mists of old age—Calixtus was seventy-seven years old when elected, and in poor health. Continuation of the Aragonese dynasty in Naples threatened, in his eyes, the newly recovered independence of the papacy. Alfonso's underhand support of the *condottiere* Piccinino against Siena and the papal states in the summer of 1455,[46] his marriage alliance with Milan in September of that year, and his constant hostilities against Genoa, taken together with his hectoring of the pope himself over matters such as clerical taxation and appointments, lend some colour to suspicions that he meant to dominate both Italy and the church.[47] He also fell into violent disagreement with the pope over crusading strategy. Self-interest and realism had led Alfonso to argue after the fall of Constantinople that the only sound policy for Christian Europe was to 'fight the Sultan where he now stands, rather than lose still more ground and be forced to fight for Italy itself'.[48] In practical terms this meant using all resources available in support of those Christian states of the Balkans that stood in the path of the Turks: warfare on the frontier of Islam in the crusading tradition of the Reconquista. Calixtus on the other hand dreamed of assembling the united

vicariates may have been those of Urbino and Pesaro which had allegedly been offered by Eugenius IV but refused by Nicholas V. Cf. ACA Reg. 2698. 180^r, Instructions for the secretary Andreu Gaçull, Tivoli, 19 Mar. 1447.

[46] Cf. L. Pastor, *The History of the Popes from the close of the Middle Ages* (Eng. trans.), ii (London, 1891), 360–4.

[47] Ibid. ii. 422–5.

[48] Contained in instructions given to the royal secretary de Reus, sent to Nicholas V (ACA Reg. 2700. 39^r, 8 Sept. 1453); 'Sera millor encara empachar lo e tenir li la guerra en aquelles parts on es que perdudes aquelles debatre ab ell deles senyories de Italia.'

forces of Christendom for a grand assault in thirteenth-century style upon the heartlands of the heathen. 'These exaggerated schemes'[49] had no prospect of being put into effect, much less of achieving success; yet there can be no doubt of the passionate sincerity with which Calixtus urged them, nor of the consequent bitterness of the recrimination that passed between him and the king on that account.[50] Further friction arose over ecclesiastical appointments which involved a head-on conflict between the unrestrained nepotism of pope and king.[51]

A seemingly unbridgeable gulf thus opened between the ruler of Naples and his suzerain at a time when Alfonso was growing old and could not afford to have papal hostility menacing the succession, as it clearly did following Calixtus's refusal to confirm the bulls of investiture, and in particular the one that enabled Ferdinand to succeed his father. Knowing the king's precarious state of health, Calixtus seems to have reckoned on procrastinating until death intervened to put the succession into his own hands, when a new ruler might be appointed on terms far more favourable to Rome than those extorted by Alfonso. During the king's last illness the Bishop of Modena, who had discussed the subject several times with Calixtus, wrote to the Duke of Milan:

Io credo firmiter che di nocte el papa stia suso questo pensar et desegno et expecta la morte del Re con summa leticia. . . . Dice ancora che dipoy che la M. del Re ha havuto questo reame may sancta chiesia ha havuto reposo et che sempre ha tribulato el papa Martino et Eugenoi et Calisto et che voria omnino morendo el Re liberare questo regno et

---

[49] Pastor, *History of the Popes*, ii. 406.

[50] Cf. the account of the dispute which Calixtus gave to the Milanese envoy in Rome. Jacopo Calcaterra to Francesco Sforza, Rome, 24 Aug. 1456 (Pastor, *History of the Popes*, ii. 548–9).

[51] See Pastor, *History of the Popes*, ii. 423 and 447; Ametller y Vinyas, *Alfonso V de Aragón*, ii. 828–33. Cf. the king's letter to Calixtus (ACA Reg. 2661. 148ᵛ, Casale Arnone, 25 Apr. 1457) refusing to accept certain papal provisions to Spanish sees unless Enrique, son of the Duke of Calabria, is made administrator of Zaragoza, and Juan, illegitimate son of the King of Navarre, Bishop of Valencia. Calixtus had already appointed his nephew Rodrigo Borja to his own former see of Valencia which had been a bone of contention ever since his elevation to the papacy. (See Pastor, *History of the Popes*, ii. 423; ACA Reg. 2700. 100ᵛ; Ametller y Vinyas, *Alfonso V de Aragón*, ii. 831–2.) When the pope refused to receive the king's ambassador in Rome to discuss the appointments, Alfonso instructed his envoy to draw up a public protest 'no podent ho pus ab paciencia suportar' (ACA Reg. 2661. 151ᵛ, Instructions for Antoni Torres, Castelnuovo, 10 May 1457).

li suoy successori de tanta servitute et conclude che totis viribus non supportaria che el duca de Calabria obtenghi el dicto reame.[52]

Whether Calixtus intended to bestow the kingdom upon a nephew or on René of Anjou need not concern us. He did carry out his threats against Ferdinand by publishing on 14 July 1458 a bull which claimed the kingdom for the papacy as a lapsed fief.[53] Ferdinand none the less proclaimed himself King of Naples immediately his father died and appealed to a new pope or council should his overtures to Calixtus prove of no effect. Shortly afterwards death again intervened to end the feud by claiming the aged pope on 6 August 1458; his successor Pius II, a man once charmed by Alfonso, found it politic to recognize Ferdinand as king.

Papal power in the kingdom of Naples had of course long since declined from its thirteenth-century zenith. Even among the loyal Angevins there had been rulers, such as Ladislas, who had not scrupled to reveal the reality. But it was Alfonso who took the kingdom in the teeth of papal opposition, compelled Eugenius IV to grant it to him on his own terms, and demonstrated beyond all mistaking that papal suzerainty over Naples had become a matter of empty form. It was a reverse of great significance for that restored papacy which had managed to re-establish its authority in Rome and over much of the papal states, but having failed to carry it further, and especially in its great southern fief lay in danger of being itself overawed by mighty secular neighbours. The convulsive effort of Calixtus III to undo the defeat of his predecessors served only to throw into higher relief the diminished capacity of the papacy to guide secular affairs. To the pope's threat, 'His Majesty should be aware that the Pope can depose kings', Alfonso could retort, 'Let his Holiness know that the king, if he wishes, can find a way to depose the Pope.'[54] He spoke from experience, for he had sent ambassadors to the Council of Constance to participate in the deposition of Benedict XIII, John XXIII, and Gregory XII, and in July 1429 he had forced the abdication of the anti-pope Clement VIII.[55]

[52] Rome, 11 June 1458 (Pastor, *History of the Popes*, ii. 557). The omission of Nicholas V from the popes whom Alfonso had troubled is significant.
[53] Ibid. ii. 469.
[54] Ibid., ii. 426.
[55] See Ametller y Vinyas, *Alfonso V de Aragón*, i. 235 and 288.

Holding that the kingdom was his by right of inheritance as the adopted son of Giovanna II, and faced from 1435 until 1442 by a hostile party which accorded that title to René of Anjou, Alfonso never sought formal recognition of his sovereignty from any parliament or baronial assembly. In the course of the civil war individuals and communities acknowledged him as king, as one after another they were attracted or forced into the Aragonese camp. By 1443 all but a small hard core of Angevin supporters had made their submission and sworn fealty and homage.

Establishing the succession to the throne—a matter of great political significance in the uncertainties of civil war—raised more complicated issues. Alfonso had no legitimate children and it seemed unlikely that he would ever have any for his wife, living apart from him in Spain, was by 1435 almost past child-bearing age.[56] Ferdinand I of Aragon had provided in his will that in default of a legitimate heir in Alfonso's line the succession in the Crown of Aragon should pass to the most senior of his brothers. From time to time Alfonso may have considered challenging that provision,[57] but he made no overt attempt to contest the claims of his brother Juan of Navarre to the Aragonese crown; on the contrary, in January 1436 he appointed him *locumtenens* in Aragon, Valencia, and Mallorca. In the Neapolitan kingdom, unaffected by his father's testamentary dispositions, Alfonso had a freer hand and he decided early in his reign there that it should pass to his illegitimate son Ferdinand; Aragonese history offered ample precedent for such a partition. A streak of contradiction had time and again manifested itself in rulers who struggled mightily to augment their state, only to divide it at their death for the benefit of their sons. Alfonso II (1162–96) detached Provence from Aragon for his second son. James the Conqueror did likewise with the Balearic islands and his remaining transpyrenean possessions.[58] No sooner had he acquired Sicily than Peter made testamentary dispositions to ensure that it should pass to a younger son. Perhaps the con-

---

[56] Alfonso married his cousin Maria of Castile in 1415. They did not see each other during the last twenty-five years of the king's life when Maria remained in Spain as regent of Catalonia.

[57] A bull (27 Apr. 1449) by which Nicholas V confirmed the egitimization of Alfonso's illegitimate son Ferdinand extended his right of succession to all states ruled by Alfonso (Chioccarello, *Archivio*, p. 8).

[58] Both these cadet branches were required to acknowledge the suzerainty of Aragon.

stantly changing, expanding frontiers encouraged the kings of Aragon to regard their territories as a family estate; geographical dispersion and ethnic diversity certainly made it difficult for either rulers or subjects to look upon them as a political entity. Many of the partitions have no apparent motive other than fatherly affection, and it may have been this feeling for his only son that prompted Alfonso. It is also likely that he and, more especially, the Neapolitan nobles were moved by considerations akin to those that had influenced Peter II in disposing of the Sicilian crown: namely a determination on the one part and an understanding on the other that an Aragonese victory should not mean a final end to local independence. The barons could ask no better gage than an heir presumptive effectively debarred from the succession in all other Aragonese territories.

In 1438 Alfonso had his illegitimate son brought from Spain to Italy. In February 1440 he legitimized Ferdinand and declared him eligible to inherit, making particular mention of the Italian kingdom.[59] A year later a parliament of Alfonso's adherents meeting in Benevento presented a petition asking that Ferdinand be proclaimed heir to the kingdom. The king preferred to wait until 1443 when he was able to muster a full parliament which dutifully repeated the request. On the evening of his triumphal entry into Naples (26 February 1443) the parliament waited on him:

There came to the king the aforementioned princes, dukes, counts, and barons and petitioned him that he might be graciously pleased to institute Don Fernando of Aragon his heir in the kingdom of Naples after his death, for they offered to perform homage to him immediately.[60]

Ferdinand was duly invested with the title of Duke of Calabria, customarily accorded to the heir apparent, and all the barons present in Naples performed homage.

Acceptance of Alfonso as king and of Ferdinand as heir to the throne sprang in part from the manifest military superiority of the

[59] The privilege of legitimization dated 17 Feb. 1440 is printed in Chioccarello, *Archivio*, p. 5.

[60] 'Aquella nit matexa vengueren al dit Senyor los dits princeps duchs comtes e barons, e suplicaren lo que fos de sa merce, que apres son obte volgues proveyir e heretar don fferrando de Arago del Reyalme de Napols; e aquell en lo dit cas los donas per Rey e senyor, car ells se offerien de continent fer li homenatge' (Anthoni Vinyes to the city of Barcelona, Naples, 28 Feb. 1443, ACB Cart. Com., vol. 13, fol. 18).

Aragonese over the Angevin party, and in part from Alfonso's skilful wooing of powerful individuals and families among the Neapolitan aristocracy. During the war influential nobles had been won over to the Aragonese cause by grants or confirmations of land, titles, and revenues. The means used to gain the support of Raimondo Orsini are a good illustration of the tactics employed. Raimondo, son of Giovanna II's justiciar, was one of the governors of the kingdom named in the queen's will and one of the first of the Neapolitan nobles to perform homage to the Duchess of Anjou.[61] Within a year Alfonso succeeded in weaning him from this decidedly pro-Angevin stance by an alluring combination of offices and estates. They included the principate of Salerno, the towns of Eboli and Nocera, and the office of justiciar. He also promised that Raimondo should marry Leonor, daughter of the Count of Urgel and hence a member of the royal house of Aragon, who would bring as dowry the duchy of Amalfi.[62] At whose expense were these benefits bestowed? Eboli and Nocera were fiefs of Francesco Zurlo, at that time a supporter of the Angevin cause; in 1438 he made his peace with Alfonso and was confirmed in possession of his lands, so that the grant to Raimondo Orsini did not take effect.[63] Salerno and Amalfi had formed part of the royal demesne until 1418 when Giovanna II gave them to Giordano Colonna[64] on whose death in 1422 they passed to his nephew Antonio Colonna. When the latter played a part in inviting Alfonso to invade the kingdom in 1432, Giovanna declared them forfeit to the crown.[65] Thus none of the grants which Alfonso made to Raimondo Orsini involved alienation of land then in possession of the crown; moreover at the time the grants were made all these lands were held by the king's enemies.

Carlo Ruffo, Count of Sinopoli, came to terms with the king in November 1432 with a confirmation of all his lands and privileges, including those recently granted by the Duke of Anjou; all alienations of his estates were annulled and vassals who had fled from him were to be compelled to return to their allegiance. His lands

---

[61] Ametller y Vinyas, *Alfonso V de Aragón*, i. 440, ii. 23.

[62] Ibid. ii. 110 and 276. Leonor strenuously opposed the marriage, but had to submit to the king's will. Her resentment flared out in 1461 when she joined the rebellion against Ferdinand. Raimondo Orsini received in addition a *condotta* of 400 lances.   [63] Ibid. ii. 187.

[64] Pontieri, 'Muzio Attendolo e Francesco Sforza', p. 103, n. 2.

[65] Ibid., p. 228.

were exempted from all taxes other than the general aids which they were to pay at the rate of no more than two a year, 'per la extrema povertate et necessitate che pati lu terreno de lo dicto signuri'.[66] Jews living on his estates were exempted from the *mortafa*, the special tax paid by Jews to the crown. The count was confirmed in his offices as captain and castellan of Bagnara *in perpetuum*, and he was promised the return of the dowry of his deceased daughter which had been carried off to Sicily by her husband. Alfonso confirmed these terms in April 1435, after he had assumed the title of king,[67] and added a further favour by appointing Ruffo justiciar of Calabria for life.[68] In December 1438 he gave Ruffo the county of Gerace,[69] but this grant was withdrawn when the pro-Angevin occupant of that fief, Battista Caracciolo, made his peace with the king.[70] Apart from this enlargement of his estates which did not take effect, the other favours bestowed on the Count of Sinopoli were confirmations of possessions and privileges he already enjoyed. The only substantial addition to them was the tax reduction which was primarily of benefit to his vassals. In return Ruffo gave the king military service and substantial loans in cash and jewels.[71]

The great majority of the agreements reached between Alfonso and individual barons up to the fall of Naples followed a similar pattern: they either confirmed existing titles and privileges, or else granted lands regarded as forfeit because their holders belonged to the opposing camp. Very early in the conflict barons began to insure themselves by seeking from Alfonso confirmation of their titles to lands, honours, and revenues. Antoni Vinyes described the scene in Messina in March 1435:[72]

Here in the court there are many men of the Duke of Anjou and from other parts of the kingdom who are asking for offices, counties, baronies and the revenues of certain places in that kingdom. The king quietly and calmly does nothing else but grant these favours; I believe he does it so that, once he has entered the kingdom, he will not be put to the trouble of attending to them.

---

[66] Mazzoleni, *Fonti aragonesi*, i. 7–10.   [67] Ibid. i. 11–14.
[68] Ibid. i. 14.   [69] Ibid. i. 19.
[70] ACA Reg. 2902. 174ᵛ, Confirmation of his lands and titles for Battista Caracciolo. The register is defective at this point and the last part of this privilege, with the date, is missing. However, it probably belongs to 1443.
[71] Mazzoleni, *Fonti aragonesi*, i. 14. These loans were made in 1435 and 1437.
[72] Madurell Marimón, *Mensajeros barceloneses*, p. 87.

While the business was undoubtedly brisk, Alfonso was not heedlessly disposing of what remained of the royal patrimony, nor was he auctioning the prerogatives of the crown.

As the outcome of the war became more certain, the movement of nobles from the losing to the winning side became a stampede; with it came a flood of privileges receiving these men into Alfonso's favour—privileges which mostly did no more than pardon them for their support of Anjou and confirm them in their lands and titles.[73] As latecomers into the Aragonese camp, they were not in a position to bargain for additional favours. Immediately after the fall of the captial the king proclaimed a general amnesty for all Angevin supporters.[74] There followed in 1443 an edict which confirmed all existing privileges and titles authenticated by documents issued by Alfonso himself or by any of his predecessors up to the death of Giovanna II,[75] and in 1446 another edict validated all titles derivable from periods before the death of Ladislas. Only titles derived directly from René of Anjou were wholly invalidated. By these measures Alfonso averted much litigation and disorder which might otherwise have frustrated his efforts to pacify the kingdom. Few Angevin supporters lost all, or even a large part of, their possessions. One of the most prominent of them, Antonio Caldora, who changed to the Aragonese side in 1439 only to desert it again in March 1442, lost his dukedom of Bari and some counties including Archi and Monteodorisio, but was permitted to retain his patrimony and the county of Trivento.[76] Alfonso gave the dukedom of Bari to the Prince of Taranto; Monteodorisio he restored to Perdicasso Barrile from whom Caldora's father had seized it;[77] Archi, Aversa, and some other towns in the Abruzzi were reintegrated in the royal desmesne. Michele d'Attendoli, Count of Cotignola, another last-ditch supporter of René, for-

---

[73] e.g. Giacomo Antonio de Marerio, Count of Marerio, was restored to his lands and titles after surrendering to Alfonso in 1440 (ACA Reg. 2902, 70^v, 7 Apr. 1440). He received a full pardon in March 1444 (ACA Reg. 2906, 97^v, 20 Mar. 1444). The Bishop of Potenza was restored to possession of the monastery of San Spirito after submitting in December 1442 (ACA Reg. 2904. 27^r). Marino Boffa surrendered in March 1439 and obtained a privilege confirming his feudal and other possessions (Faraglia, *Storia della lotta*, p. 146, n. 2).

[74] Ametller y Vinyas, *Alfonso V de Aragón*, ii. 412.

[75] Ibid. iii. 145.

[76] G. Zurita, *Anales de la Corona de Aragón* (Zaragoza, 1610), iii. 275; Ametller y Vinyas, *Alfonso V de Aragón*, ii. 419.

[77] ACA Reg. 2902, 57^r, 4 Aug. 1442, Sentence of the Sacrum Consilium in favour of Barrile.

feited his estates in Calabria some of which were given to the Duke of Andria and others to Iñigo de Guevara; Potenza was taken back into the desmesne. The most formidable of Alfonso's adversaries, Francesco Sforza, chose to lose all his estates within the kingdom rather than submit. From his great possessions Alfonso was able to create feudal endowments for the Castilian noble Iñigo de Guevara who became Count of Ariano and Apice, and for the Catalan Garcia Cabanyells whom he made Count of Troia. The estates of Sforza's wife, Polissena Ruffo, Countess of Montalto, the king sold to Covella Ruffo the mother of Marino de Marzano Ruffo as the principate of Rossano; on Covella's death in 1445 the principate passed, in accordance with the terms of the sale, to her son who had married Alfonso's daughter.[78] Andrea Matteo d'Aquaviva, an ardent supporter of Sforza, lost all his estates in Abruzzo ulteriore, but they did not pass out of his family, for the king gave them to his opportunistic uncle Josia d'Aquaviva, the Duke of Atri and Teramo.[79]

Once the confusion of war had settled men found that the feudal map of the kingdom had not drastically changed. Alfonso avoided large-scale confiscations and proscriptions. Despite the grievance felt by the native nobility at the appearance of Spaniards in their ranks,[80] the number so settled was small—insignificant indeed compared with the number of French nobles brought into the kingdom by Charles I. In order to win the war Alfonso had been obliged to shower favours on some nobles, but his victory had forced many others to submit to him on the terms he was prepared to offer even it those terms were usually not punitive. Furthermore he had, by the close of 1442, won a decisive victory and faced the disarmed barons in the 1443 parliament flushed with triumph and confidence. The barons, by contrast, were in a nervous state, fearing that the king meant to seize those he considered unreliable, and were only reassured by his amiable bearing during the parliament.[81] There followed the incident at the beginning of Alfonso's

---

[78] ACA Reg. 2908, 92ᵛ. [79] Ibid. 140ᵛ.

[80] Borso d'Este cited the bestowing of fiefs on Spaniards as one of the grievances held by the Neapolitans against Alfonso. In addition to those mentioned above the most notable fiefs bestowed on nobles of Spanish extraction were the county of Reggio (Alfonso de Cardona), the marquisate of Crotone (Antonio Centelles), the marquisate of Pescara and county of Monteodorisio (Iñigo de Avalos), and the county of Aiello (Francesch Siscar).

[81] Beccadelli, *De dictis et factis*, iii.

triumphal entry into Naples when the Prince of Taranto refused
the place in the procession allotted to him on the grounds that it
was inappropriate to his dignity as chief architect of the king's
victory. Although he was humoured, he obviously understood
that his days of influence were over, for he withdrew to his estates
and appeared at court only rarely.[82] Most of the other great nobles
were similarly excluded from playing any effective part in government. A few of the most exalted occupied the great titular offices
with their ceremonial duties; a rather larger number played a part
as courtiers and counsellors, enjoying the splendours of one of the
most magnificent courts of the age. All tenants-in-chief retained
their right to counsel the king in parliament—a right which became
more meaningful with the revival of that institution; a few were
active as military captains and diplomatic envoys. Those Neapolitans who held numerous important posts in the judicial and
financial offices came from the lesser and urban nobility. None the
less a majority of the barons, and especially the most powerful
among them, felt themselves alienated from the state. That alienation they expressed in attacks on the Catalans who, in their eyes,
had usurped the government. Borso d'Este, who wrote his memorial to Alfonso after a journey which had taken him through the
territory of the Orsini clan, was clearly echoing the sentiments of
the Neapolitan noble when he asserted that one of the reasons for
the king's unpopularity was his wholesale appointment of Catalans
to offices which ought to be held by Italians:[83]

. . . li quali, sequondo che a nui e monstrato chiaramente, plu tosto
desfano lo facto dela V. Maysta che lo fazano; e questo per le loro
superbie, mali modi et tiranie grandissime, che, evidenter, uxano verso
questi de lo Reame, et anche perche li voleno tenire sotto pedi et
segnorezarli con desonesti modi, e per ogni costa gli voleno dire vilania
e manazarli. Per la quale cossa pare che la V. Maysta non se fidi de
veruno Italiano, ne anche ne ami, ne voglia veruno.

The dangers of this gulf between the state and its most powerful
subjects was brought home more forcibly to Alfonso by his serious

   82 One of these rare occasions was the marriage of his niece to the king's son
in May 1444. According to the diary attributed to Tristano Caracciolo, 'ogni
volta che andava a vedere il Re se credeva remanesse carcerato' (BNN Bib.
Branc. MS. III E7, 102ʳ).
   83 Foucard, 'Proposta', p. 714.

illness in the spring of 1444. When it appeared that the king might die, the Prince of Taranto and Antonio Caldora began making warlike preparations while the Spaniards put themselves and their belongings behind fortified walls.[84] Instead of punishing those who had shown their hand against him, Alfonso determined on his recovery from the illness to try to bridge the gap by marrying his son and younger daughter into the Neapolitan nobility. The marriages took place in May 1444, Ferdinand marrying Isabella di Chiaramonte, a niece of the Prince of Taranto, and Eleonora the son of the Duke of Sessa. All the barons were summoned to Naples to attend the weddings.[85] When the testing time came, however, these ties proved no more effective than other dynastic alliances; both the Prince of Taranto and Eleonora's husband took up arms against Ferdinand. Nor was the general feeling of alienation overcome. The death-bed advice to rid himself of the Catalans which Alfonso is supposed to have given to his son, though probably apocryphal, none the less shows that opinion in 1458 had changed little from what it had been in 1444.

Contemporaries did not, in short, look upon the reign as a heyday of baronial freedom and influence. One might nevertheless argue that, much as the barons were obliged to disarm before the political will of the state and suffered for their more flagrant attacks on public order, they received in compensation greater control than hitherto over the lives and fortunes of their vassals. Such was the opinion of Giannone:

> Ma quello di che non s'ebbero molto da lodare i secoli seguenti, fù d'aver Alfonso conceduto a' Baroni il mero, e misto impero. Avendo questo Principe per la sua sterminata liberalità resi esausti tutti gli altri fonti, cominciò ad esser profuso anche delle più supreme regalie, che non doveano a verun patto divellersi dalla sua Corona, quando i Rè suoi predecessori erano stati di ciò cotanto gelosi.[86]

[84] 'Re Alfonso se ammalò et stette tanto grave che per tutto se disse ch'era morto, et li Catalani andavano salvando le cose loro per li castelli et molti Sri. havevano già pensato à fer novità et per uno Antonio Caldora se portò in Apruzzo Rostaino suo figlio, il Prencipe di Taranto vene de Puglia à speroni battuti' (BNN Bibl. Branc. MS. III E7, 101ᵛ).

[85] Cf. ACB *Cart. Com.*, vol. 14, fol. 71. During the wedding celebrations the Prince of Taranto received confirmation of the dukedom of Bari and of his right to the free export of foodstuffs from his estates (Summonte, *Historia*, iv. 74). Immediately before his illness Alfonso had been contemplating a marriage between Ferdinand and a daughter of the King of France (ACA Reg. 2698. 36ᵛ).

[86] Giannone, *Istoria civile*, iii. 400. For the *mero e misto impero* see below, p. 318.

Many more recent historians have been of the same view.[87] Whether or not the charge is accepted must depend upon one's assessment of baronial power in the period before Alfonso's accession. Bearing in mind that Ladislas and Giovanna II had already beat a general retreat, one may fairly say that Alfonso extended or made universal concessions which had already become commonplace, but did not open any important new vein of privilege to baronial exploitation. He yielded most in the line of jurisdiction. His grant of the *merum et mixtum imperium,* though not unconditional and general, did concede all that the tenants-in-chief had gained to date. In response to a petition of the 1456 parliament he further extended the scope of baronial justice by conceding to those exercising the *merum et mixtum imperium* authority to judge crimes hitherto reserved to the crown, including those that carried the death penalty. At the same time he allowed them to commute punishments involving mutilation or lesser corporal inflictions to fines which went into their own pockets.[88] These concessions subjected those living outside the royal demesne to baronial jurisdiction in the first instance for almost every crime except treason, and one must suppose that the abuses that attended the activities of royal officials in commuting criminal penalties to money payments were repeated by baronial agents of justice.

The eagerness with which barons sought these concessions was motivated by the prospect of financial advantage as well as by a desire to exclude royal officials from their lands. What amounted to state subsidies were essential to that class, and especially to the lesser barons, if they were to live peacefully and in the manner they expected on their estates. Some allowance for this factor must be made when appraising Alfonso's munificence towards individuals as well as to the whole group. The most common forms of income supplementation granted to the nobles were annual pensions charged on a tax (often one due to the crown from the noble's own vassals), exemptions from tax, fiscal concessions of a stated annual value,[89] and the outright grant of the proceeds from a

---

[87] e.g. N. F. Faraglia, *Il comune nell'Italia meridionale* (Naples, 1883), p. 119; V. Vitale, *Trani dagli angioini agli spagnuoli* (Bari, 1912), p. 160; P. Gentile, 'Lo stato napoletano sotto Alfonso I d'Aragona', *ASPN* (1938), p. 44; E. Pontieri, 'Alfonso V d'Aragona nel quadro della politica italiana del suo tempo', *Divagazioni storiche e storiografiche* (Naples, n.d.), p. 301.

[88] ASN Div. Somm. I. 52 (bis), 171[r].

[89] e.g. the numerous grants of duty-free export of grain to the nobles of Calabria and Terra di Bari (ASN Div. Somm. I. 10, 23[r]).

particular tax either over the whole kingdom or in certain places.[90] The fiscal privileges of Antonio di Sanseverino, Duke of San Marco and Count of Tricárico, will serve as an example of those enjoyed by a powerful baron who did not frequent the court. He received 600 ducats a year from the tax on the silk industry of Cosenza and other centres in Calabria;[91] another annual provision of 300 ducats came from the hearth tax on his lands,[92] and 360 ducats from the salt pans of Altomonte.[93] In addition he had a licence to export from Calabria every year 1,000 salme of grain free of duty, a concession worth 600 ducats a year.[94] This makes an annual total of 1,810 ducats of revenue diverted from the crown to the duke. In due proportion these 'baronial subsidies' extended down through the ranks of the nobility to the petty rural and urban knight. Most of the grants did not originate with Alfonso, but he readily confirmed those made by previous rulers and reassigned them on the death of the holders. While irregularities were pursued with some zeal by the Sommaria in a series of inquests,[95] no serious effort was made to recover these revenues for the crown. It may therefore be argued that the king had to increase other taxes in order to make good the revenue lost in this manner to the barons. On the other hand, it is by no means certain that the total by which Alfonso subsidized the baronage exceeded that lavished on them by earlier monarchs.

The extent to which Alfonso's ready creation of new titles increased the power of the nobility and the financial burden it imposed on the rest of the community are matters that admit of much dispute. Titles had been sparingly created up to the middle of the fourteenth century: that of duke was unknown outside the royal family until the reign of Giovanna I;[96] that of marquis first appeared with Ladislas.[97] Under Alfonso the ranks of the Neapolitan title-holders swelled dramatically. Between his accession and the close of the 1443 parliament he had, according to Summonte,[98] doubled their number. Borso d'Este in his Relazione listed two

[90] e.g. the grant of the mortafa (the special tax paid by Jews) in Calabria to Nicola de Leofante, a military captain (ACA Reg. 2909. 64ʳ, 6 Nov. 1443).
[91] ACA Reg. 2906. 168ʳ, 3 June 1445; ASN Div. Somm. I. 10, 16ʳ.
[92] ASN Div. Somm. I. 10, 6ᵛ and 21ʳ.   [93] Ibid. 16ʳ.
[94] Ibid. 16ʳ and 23ʳ.
[95] e.g. the inquest into titles to tolls, vacant benefices, offices, foundries, and mills instituted in 1456 (Gentile, 'Finanze e parlamenti', p. 218).
[96] Giannone, Istoria civile, iii. 228.   [97] Ibid. iii. 301.
[98] Summonte, Historia, iii. 21.

princes, ten dukes, two marquises, forty counts, and two countes-
ses.[99] Many of those who had served the Aragonese cause well
received their titles on the occasion of the king's triumphal entry
into Naples[100] and others were bestowed fairly regularly throughout the reign. The title of Duke of Scalea was created for Francesco
di Sanseverino in 1448;[101] a third princely title, that of Rossano,
was conferred on the king's son-in-law, Marino de Marzano Ruffo,
in November 1445;[102] another marquisate, that of Vasto, was
created for Iñigo de Guevara. Most of the new titles were attached
to lands confiscated from Angevin supporters or to new agglomera-
tions of extant feudal lands. None was created wholly at the expense of the royal demesne. Although such an arrangement was
contemplated in July 1449 when Alfonso reached an agreement
with Francesco Orsini to make him Duke of Manfredonia in
return for a loan of 30,000 ducats,[103] that transaction was never put
into effect. The growth in the number of title-holders did not,
therefore, seriously affect the balance, or rather imbalance, between the lands of the crown and those of the tenants-in-chief.[104]
Whether it strengthened the hand of the nobility in any other way
is rather open to doubt, for an over-generous creation of titles
tends only to devalue them.

Alfonso seems to have recognized, though perhaps not consciously, that the actions of the later Angevin rulers of Naples had
set in train certain irreversible developments in the structure of his
newly won kingdom. For at least a century the tenants-in-chief of

---

[99] Some individuals held more than one title.
[100] Before mounting the triumphal carriage Alfonso conferred these titles:
Gerardo Gasparo d'Aquino, son of the Count of Loreto, was made Marquis of
Pescara; Nicola Cantelmo, Duke of Sora; Alfonso de Cardona, Count of Reggio;
Francesco Pandone, Count of Venafro; Giovanni di Sanseverino, Count of
Tursi; Aimerico di Sanseverino, Count of Capaccio.
[101] ACA Reg. 2913, 20ᵛ. The Count of Buccino, Giorgio d'Alemagna, and two
other counts were charged with the investiture which consisted of placing a gold
coronet on the duke's head and handing him a standard.
[102] ACA Reg. 2908. 90ʳ.
[103] ACA Reg. 2697. 29ʳ, 6 July 1449. The king was to assign Orsini an annual
provision of 2,000 ducats on the revenues of Monte Sant'Angelo and San Giovanni Rotondo, the towns which were to constitute the dukedom. Orsini was to
name the king as his heir in the duchy and leave the appointment of castellans
in both towns in the hands of the crown.
[104] There was some movement in the other direction. The forfeiture of his
estates by Antonio Centelles, Marquis of Gerace, is the most notable instance.
In January 1458 the king gave orders for the reintegration of the counties of
Tagliacozzo and Albe in the royal demesne.

the crown had been shedding the military and financial obligations which bound them to the sovereign while they acquired ever greater control over their own tenants. Instead of fighting the tide, Alfonso went with it towards a destination of which both he and the nobility had little inkling. By generalizing what had hitherto been piecemeal though widespread concessions, he brought near completion the delegation to the barons of what one might call the primary level of administration, that is to say those judicial and fiscal functions that touched the everyday life of the ordinary citizen. Only within the restricted area of the royal demesne did such matters as the collection of taxes, the administration of justice in the first instance, and the appointment of municipal officials remain the direct concern of the crown. At the same time he endeavoured to ensure that the tenants-in-chief exercised these powers as agents of the crown, from which they held them *ad beneplacitum*, and not as petty sovereigns. If he was ready to allow the barons greater control of their vassals, he was equally concerned to emphasize his own power over them. To that end he reformed the institutions of government so as to create a machine largely independent of the nobility. Staffed by professional men, many of them not Italian, this revitalized bureaucracy strove with some success to foster a state interest distinct from, and in some respects antithetical to, that of the baronage.

III

THE KING'S HOUSEHOLD

ALFONSO'S conquest of the Italian kingdom enhanced still further the importance of his household as the sole institution common to all his states.[1] The last twenty years of his reign did, it is true, see very significant steps taken towards the establishment of specialized organs of government for the whole of the Aragonese empire; nevertheless the household, as an extension of the royal personality, remained the ultimate focus of political authority and action. Many of the most important officers of state still exercised their functions, in name at least, as servants of the household; many who performed domestic offices around the king were able to exert great influence upon the conduct of affairs. The Neapolitan kingdom, more than any other of Alfonso's territories, felt the impact of the household because there, and sometimes in other parts of Italy, he maintained it for twenty-three years.

While the struggle with the Angevins lasted, the court was an itinerant body accompanying its master and his army, taking up its quarters in a conveniently near-by town and often in tents. It acquired a more permanent abode only at the very end of the war when Naples fell and Alfonso made the capital his customary residence. Naples offered a number of ancient and uncomfortable fortresses for the accommodation of the king and his entourage; chief among them were Castelnuovo, Castel dell'Ovo, and Castel Capuano. Some work was immediately taken in hand to make them habitable, but it was only in 1449 when Alfonso, wearying at last of military life, settled permanently in Naples, that a wholesale reconstruction of royal residences in and around the capital began in earnest. Castel Capuano became the palace of the Duke of Calabria.[2] Castelnuovo, the great fortress of Charles I and the principal Neapolitan residences of the Angevin kings, was almost entirely rebuilt to make it both a fortress of advanced design and a

---

[1] Cf. above, p. 20.
[2] Cf. ACB Cart. Com., vol. 20, fol. 180, 4 Aug. 1450, Description of the baptism of Ferdinand's daughter Leonora in Castel Capuano.

palace embellished by some of the finest Italian and Spanish craftsmen of the age.[3] Whenever the king grew tired of Naples he could withdraw to one of several country palaces dotted around the shores of the Bay of Naples at Torre del Greco, Pozzuoli, and Baia. Alternatively he could indulge his passion for hunting at one of the hunting lodges in the hills and forests of the interior. Where the king went a nucleus at least of the court followed and the most important business of state was done, or left undone, amid idyllic surroundings. Aeneas Sylvius relates how a diplomatic mission undertaken on behalf of the Sienese was dragged out for several months as he followed Alfonso from one resort to another.[4] Some envoys from Barcelona found great difficulty in getting an audience with the king when he moved his court to Torre del Greco: 'In the morning after he has heard mass there is left only some two hours for those who need to do business with him; after dinner he shuts himself up in a garden so that no one can talk business with him.'[5] Such rustic seclusion enabled the king to avoid men and issues when it suited him.

As a connoisseur of courts, Aeneas Sylvius gave unstinted praise to that of Naples for its cultivated splendour. A host of other humanists eulogized a monarch who proved a generous patron and enthusiastic, if sometimes naïve, admirer of their works.[6] The impression they create of the court can however be misleading, for only in comparatively brief moments of leisure was the king surrounded by these men of letters. Without question they brought back to Naples an intellectual stimulation which had been missing for more than a century, but they had little direct influence upon policy and government. Where they did play their part in affairs of state was in supplying psychological and propaganda support for Alfonso's caesarian concept of his role in the world.

The true inner circle of the court were 'li governadori dela maiestá del Rè, i quali attende ala persona soa'.[7] In 1444 they were,

---

[3] The principal architect was the Mallorcan Guillem Sagrera. See R. Filangieri, *Castel Nuovo, reggia angioina ed aragonese di Napoli* (Naples, 1934).

[4] *Commentarii*, i.

[5] ACB Cart. Com., vol. 20, fol. 250, Naples, 18 Oct. 1450. The garden belonged to the king's mistress Lucrezia d'Alagno: '. . . en lo mati com ell ha hoida missa no ha de spay de fer affers ab les gents quil han mester sino entorn dues hores, e al depus dinar ell se tancha en un verger que nagu no pot comunicar de affers ab la sua senyoria.' [6] Cf. below, pp. 222–3.

[7] C. Foucard, 'Descrizione della città di Napoli e statistica del Regno nel

according to Borso d'Este, Iñigo de Guevara, Pedro de Cardona and his brother Alfonso de Cardona, Guillem Ramon de Moncada, Ferrer Ram, Eximen Perez de Corella, and Guillem de Vich. One is struck by the exclusively Spanish character of this group, and although most of them predeceased Alfonso, his intimates throughout the reign continued to be predominantly Spaniards. When he lay on his deathbed those summoned to witness his last will[8] were: the Bishops of Mallorca and Barcelona, Juan Ferrando, Arnau Roger de Pallars the Patriarch of Alexandria, the Archbishop of Siponto, Iñigo de Guevara, Sigismondo d'Este, Fernando de Guevara, Giovanni Antonio Caldora, and Martin de Lanuza—still only three Italians among ten, and only one of them belonging to the native Neapolitan nobility. Borso d'Este's warning that the king should show greater confidence in his Italian subjects by admitting more of them to this inner circle seems to have gone unheeded.[9] We should not seek an explanation solely in terms of mistrust between Alfonso and the Neapolitans. He was, after all, forty-six years old when he finally gained control of the kingdom and, despite his long absences from Spain, most of his life had been spent in the company of Spaniards and his deepest friendships had already been formed among them. Moreover, though he chose to remain in Naples, he remained the ruler of many states and his court served them all.

To dub the inner court 'Spanish' may be useful in so far as it highlights the absence of 'Italians'; it also serves to emphasize that it was drawn from most parts of the Spanish-speaking world— certainly not from Catalonia alone, as the Italian denunciations of 'Catalans' would lead one to imagine.[10] Some were Castilians, exiles from their native land because of their adherence to the Aragonese party in its civil wars. The brothers Iñigo and Fernando de Guevara belonged to this Castilian group; so too did Juan Ferrando of Cordoba who arrived in Naples in 1443 or 1444 on a mission from the King of Castile.[11] Ferrer Ram, Martin de

1444', *ASPN* (1877), 751. The description was compiled by Borso d'Este during his visit to Naples.

[8] ASN Priv. I. 186[r], Copy of Alfonso's will made in Barcelona, 19 Mar. 1667.

[9] C. Foucard, 'Proposta fatta dalla Corte Estense ad Alfonso I Re di Napoli, 1445'. *ASPN* (1879), 714. Borso wrote this memorial addressed to Alfonso after his return to Ferrara.

[10] e.g., Borso d'Este indiscriminately lumped all Spaniards together as 'Catalans'.   [11] Cf. below, pp. 83–4.

Lanuza, and Juan Garcia, Bishop of Mallorca, came from Aragonese families. Catalonia was represented in the groups mentioned above by Arnau Roger de Pallars and Joan Soler, Bishop of Barcelona; Valencia by Eximen Perez de Corella and Guillem de Vich. There was also an important element drawn from Spanish families which had settled in Sicily since the establishment of the Aragonese dynasty in the island; the Cardona brothers and Guillem Ramon de Moncada belonged to such families. These men and others like them drawn mainly from the higher ranks of the aristocracy had played a prominent part in the long struggle for Naples. Because they enjoyed Alfonso's confidence and had ready access to him they continued to exercise great influence in the government of Naples.

In structure Alfonso's household followed the Aragonese pattern. It had first been formed on that model when he ascended the throne of Aragon, and he felt no compulsion to abandon it for a household in the Angevin style when he assumed the title of the Neapolitan kingdom in 1435. At the same time he took care to fill those Great Offices of state which had under previous dynasties headed the Neapolitan household and whose nominal functions often duplicated or overlapped those of their counterparts in Aragon. The office of seneschal, for example, resembled that of the *mayordomons* in that it was mainly concerned with the business of feeding and exercising jurisdiction over the household.[12] The very extensive responsibilities laid on the Neapolitan chamberlain had much in common with those of the Aragonese *camarlenchs* where they concerned control of the personnel of the chamber and of the king's personal property, and of the Aragonese *maestre racional* where they concerned revenues of the crown.[13] Schedules of duties given to these Great Officers during Alfonso's reign continued to enumerate these functions,[14] so one might conclude, on such evidence alone, that considerable confusion must have reigned in the household offices. In practice the schedules bore no

[12] The office of seneschal had once existed in Aragon but had disappeared in the household reorganization of 1344.

[13] ASN Div. Somm. I. 52 (bis), 118^r, Appointment of Giovanni de Moncada count of Adernoni as chamberlain in succession to Lorenzo Colonna (d. 1423).

[14] See 'Commissionum diversorum regum et variorum annorum' (ASN Div. Somm. I. 52 (bis)). This volume is a formulary containing letters of appointment and schedules of duties for the Great Officers and their subordinates. Most are undated, but it is clear from internal evidence that many belong to the reigns of Alfonso and Ferdinand I.

relation to reality; the Great Offices had much earlier shed most of their household and administrative functions to become lucrative sinecures for great nobles.[15] Alfonso therefore did not find it difficult to establish his Aragonese household in Naples. But the presence of the alien court obviously rankled with many Italians: Borso gave the appointment of 'Catalans' to offices which used to be held by men of the kingdom as one of the reasons for the king's unpopularity. 'Per la quale cossa pare che la V. Maystà non si fidi de veruno Italiano, ne anche ne ami, ne voglia veruno.'[16] The household provided the most glaring example of the wholesale replacement of natives by foreigners.

Not all Spaniards who held household offices were eager to follow the king to Naples. Some had to be summoned in peremptory fashion to perform their duties.[17] Others, like the *mayordomen* Bernat d'Arinyo, took care to make excuses for their failure to leave Spain: '. . . vista encara la affectio bona e voluntat que haveu en venir nos servir açi sino per la indispositio de vestre sogre per la qual raho vos havem per ben scusat e us no agrahim tant com si ereu en lo dit servey açi.'[18] Many travelled backwards and forwards between Spain, Naples, and Sicily and, while retaining their household offices, were only intermittently at court. Identification of those active in the household must therefore rest on circumstantial evidence of their presence. Unfortunately most of the evidence that has survived is of an indirect nature—references in letters, signatures as witnesses to documents written in the chancery etc.—for the treasury accounts of household expenditure, which would have given a complete picture, have been destroyed.[19]

As a starting-point for a study of the royal household it will be convenient to look again at the office which by custom gave its holder pre-eminence in the Neapolitan court, namely that of seneschal. When Giovanna II died the office was held by Francesco

---

[15] Cf. above, p. 13. [16] Foucard, 'Proposta', p. 714.

[17] Cf. the letter to the *camarlench* Johan de Nava: '. . . decontinent vingau a nos si en disposicio sereu de poder venir e sino sereu en disposicio de venir nos servir scrivau la causa perque . . .' (ACA Reg. 2660. 132ᵛ, Castelnuovo, 19 Jan. 1455).

[18] ACA Reg. 2690. 11ʳ, nr. Pentonia, 28 Sept. 1442. D'Arinyo was still making excuses in 1446 (ibid. 211ʳ, 2 Mar. 1446).

[19] C. Minieri Riccio made use of these accounts in compiling his 'Alcuni fatti di Alfonso I di Aragona dal 15 apr. 1437–31 maggio 1458' (*ASPN* 1881) but his selection of data was very haphazard.

Zurlo, Count of Nocera and Montoro, who joined the Angevin party. Alfonso therefore appointed his own seneschal in the person of Francesco d'Aquino, Count of Loreto and Satriano,[20] until a timely change of allegiance by Zurlo in 1438 earned him confirmation of his lands and honours, including his court office. It is abundantly clear that Zurlo performed only duties of a public, ceremonial character, chief among them being attendance upon the king in parliament where the seneschal sat at the monarch's feet. The Count of Nocera duly occupied that position in the 1443 parliament, and this is the only known occasion upon which he carried out the functions of seneschal. A few weeks later, on 1 April 1443, he organized with the protonotary and the Duke of Melfi a spectacular tournament as part of the general round of festivities celebrating the king's victory,[21] and having thus graced Alfonso's triumph, the count seems to have withdrawn to his estates. That he enjoyed no special favour at court is suggested by the failure of his attempt in 1444 to extend his family possessions by purchasing from the crown the towns of Montella, Bagnoli, and Cassano, which border on the fief of Montoro. In July 1444 Alfonso reached agreement with the attorney of the seneschal and his brother Ruffo Zurlo to sell them the towns for 3,500 ducats,[22] but the transaction was never completed,[23] and in April 1445 the towns were sold instead to a trusted Spaniard, Garcia Cabanyells, for 5,000 ducats.[24] When Zurlo died late in 1447 his son Bernardo was confirmed only in his father's feudal possessions, not in his office of state.[25] Some time passed before a successor was appointed, for the lack of a non-functioning official was no handicap to the king, but rather a substantial saving on salary, and it was not until he found it necessary to summon another parliament in January 1449 that Alfonso faced the need for a new seneschal. On 26 December 1448 he gave the office to a Castilian, Iñigo de Guevara, Count of Ariano, Apice, and Potenza, who as *mayordomen* had for some years been effective master of the household.

[20] Faraglia, *Storia della lotta*, p. 77 n. 3.
[21] ACB Cart. Com., vol. 13, fol. 31, Anthoni Vinyes to Barcelona, Naples, 4 Apr. 1443.
[22] ACA Reg. 2903. 143ᵛ, 29 July 1444.
[23] ACA Reg. 2904. 163ʳ, ? July 1444. This privilege confirms the sale, but the incomplete dating seems to indicate that some hitch had occurred.
[24] ACA Reg. 2907. 94ʳ, 19 Apr. 1445.
[25] ACA Reg. 2912. 163ᵛ, 20 Jan. 1448.

Iñigo de Guevara stands first in the list of those whom Borso d'Este described in 1444 as 'li governadori dela maestá del Rè'.[26] Son of Ruy Lopez de Ávalos, he came of a family which had originated in Aragon, and later rose to a position of supreme power in Castile, only to fall and be forced to seek refuge in Aragon. With his brother Fernando, Iñigo joined the king in the expedition to Naples in 1435 and quickly gained great rewards and favour, among them the lands and titles forfeited by Francesco Sforza and Micheletto d'Attendoli in Calabria. Thus he acquired the counties of Ariano, Apice, and Potenza.[27] Later he received further dignity and properties with the marquisate of Vasto on the Abruzzi coast of the Adriatic. Two Neapolitan marriages helped to settle him permanently in Italy; first he married Lucrezia di Bisignano and then, after her death, Covella Sanseverino, sister of the Duke of San Marco. On many occasions he distinguished himself as a military commander: in the battle of Carpenone on 28 June 1442, in the campaign against Sforza in 1443, and in the final assault on Piombino (10 September 1448), when he led one of the columns which attempted to storm the town. His last military exploits were associated with the Tuscan campaign of 1453: in September of that year he joined the king's camp near Pontecorvo with several hundred horse and in October, when Alfonso fell ill, was given command of the cavalry sent to join Ferdinand in his attack on Florence.[28] Another bond between de Guevara and the king was their enthusiasm for the refinements of court life and amateur scholarship. According to Tristano Caracciolo, Iñigo was a skilled horseman, singer, and dancer, and a connoisseur of music;[29] he often participated in the king's philosophical soirées and is said to have collected a fine library. As *mayordomen* and then seneschal Iñigo de Guevara spent most of his time at court (his other offices as governor of Guglionesi[30] and governor general of

---

[26] Cf. above, p. 55.

[27] They were first conferred on him in June 1435, confirmed in December 1440 and again in October 1452 (ASN Priv. I. 40ᵛ, Castelnuovo, 23 Oct. 1452).

[28] ACA Reg. 2799. 42ᵛ, Camp near San Vittore, 12 Sept. 1453; Ametller y Vinyas, *Alfonso V de Aragón*, ii. 727 and 762.

[29] *De varietate fortunae* in Muratori, *R.I.S.* xxii (Bologna, 1934), 94: ' . . . quippe arma egregie tractabat, equorum studiosus, quos agree moderarique probe callebat; musicae non expers, cantare saltareque ad virilem dignitatem satis aptus.'

[30] ACA Reg. 2908, 59ʳ, 27 Aug. 1445, Privilege appointing him governor of Guglionesi for life.

Terra di Bari[31] he performed by deputy) and presumably played the leading part in the household assigned to those offices. His constant attendance at court is attested by the frequency of his signature as a witness on documents of state.[32]

Considering the Aragonese origin of the de Guevara family, it is probable that Iñigo held the office of *mayordomen* for the kingdom of Aragon.[33] It appears that he resigned it in favour of his brother Fernando when he became seneschal of Naples. Fernando witnessed a treaty between Castile and Aragon in his capacity as *mayordomen* on 16 March 1454[34] and is mentioned in the king's will as still holding that office. In other ways too he followed in the footsteps of his elder brother: he obtained an Italian patrimony in the county of Belcastro, distinguished himself as a soldier,[35] and won some renown as a scholar and poet.

Next to de Guevara among the leading figures of the household Borso d'Este placed Pedro de Cardona, whom he inaccurately described as a 'Catalan'; he came in fact from an Aragonese family settled in Sicily and held the county of Golisano and the office of *magister justiciarius* in that kingdom. Like Iñigo de Guevara he had been for many years the king's companion in arms.[36] At court he held an office usually designated that of *camarlengus*[37] with functions analogous to those of the *camarlenchs* in the

---

[31] The only reference I have been able to find to this office is a letter issued by de Guevara himself at Trani, 9 May 1453 (ASN Fasc. Com. Somm. 147ᵛ). In it he styles himself 'magnus senescallus ac provincie terre bari generalis gubernator'.

[32] e.g. to the appointment of Carlo de Urries as envoy to Eugenius IV (ACA Reg. 2690. 36ᵛ, 14 July 1443); to a commission for Pere de Besalu (ACA Reg. 2656. 82ʳ, Camp against Montecastello, 23 Nov. 1447); to a sentence of the Sacrum Consilium (ACA Reg. 2914, Torre del Greco, 22 Dec. 1449); to a provision for a visiting German prince, the Duke of Slesia (ibid. 150ᵛ, Torre del Greco, 16 June 1451); to a treaty with the Duke of Savoy (ACA Reg. 2697. 24ʳ, Castelnuovo, 27 June 1449).

[33] Cf. above, p. 19, n. 43.   [34] ACA Reg. 2700. 47ʳ.

[35] He and Luis dez Puig were given joint command of all royal troops in Lombardy for the defence of Milan in July 1449 (ACA Reg. 2697. 33ᵛ).

[36] He took part in the unsuccessful siege of Naples in September 1438 (Ametller y Vinyas, *Alfonso V de Aragón*, ii. 190), led the final assault on the city (ibid. ii. 410), commanded one of the five squadrons of the royal army in the battle of Carpenone (ibid. ii. 417), and led a column in the attack on Piombino (ibid. ii. 640).

[37] e.g. ACA Reg. 2656. 124ᵛ, Alberese, 7 May 1448. He witnesses a commission as 'Pedro de Cardona, camarlengus'; Reg. 2945. 70ʳ, Tivoli, 12 May 1447: Witnesses a grant as 'comes golisani, magister justiciarius Regni Sicilie ultra farum, camarlengus'.

Aragonese household ordinance. For example it was he who gave
the king's offering when the sovereign attended mass.[38] We also
find him acting in accordance with that part of the ordinance
which forbade the *camarlench* to divulge news of any illness of the
king without express permission.[39] Towards the end of March
1444, while hunting near Pozzuoli, Alfonso was seized with fever
and had to be carried back to Naples. His doctors put out reassuring reports which were generally believed until someone 'que es
del nombre stret de son servey' revealed to others of the court that
on 2 April the fever had worsened to such an extent that the king
had fallen into a coma. The alarm was great, and many, among
them the envoys from Barcelona, blamed Pedro de Cardona for
concealing this grave turn of events from them. He apparently
accepted the rebuke and excused himself by saying that he had
been too upset by the king's condition to think of keeping them
informed 'hour by hour' about it.[40] This incident serves to illustrate the much greater degree of intimacy with the king enjoyed
by his immediate entourage when compared even with such
weighty figures as the Bishop of Valencia.

Pedro de Cardona returned to Palermo in September 1450[41] and
died there a few months later. He was succeeded briefly as chamberlain and *magister justiciarius* of Sicily by his son Alfonso de
Cardona, Count of Reggio, who followed his father to the grave in

[38] e.g. at the Christmas mass in 1437 (Faraglia, *La lotta*, p. 109) and when the
king attended masses in the churches of Giovinazzo, Barletta, and Foggia in
January 1443 (ibid., p. 320, n. 2).

[39] Bofarull y Mascaró, *Coleccion de documentos*, p. 67.

[40] ACB Cart. Com., vol. 14, fol. 55, Naples, 9 Apr. 1444, Envoys of Barcelona
to the city: 'E de aço senyors merria mal lo camerlench don Pedro de Cardona
que ha special carrech del servey de sa persona al qual fou acordat per nosaltres
fos fet cert rahonament qui fou aquest en substancia, quens maravallavem molt
dell qui havia principal carrech dela persona de nostron senyor e Rey per son
offici de camerlench e que no divulgas a nosaltres missatgers de aquexa ciutat
e a uns semblants del bisbe durgell de valencia de mossen Johan ferrandis e del
comte Johan de Vintimilla de hora en hora lo mal del dit senyor, e lo punt en
que estava ... e quel pregavem que daquiavant ell servas e tingues altra pratica e
manera que no havie servada fins en aquella jornada ... e dehim vos senyors ab
tota veritat que lo dit don pedro no hac altre replicat en la resposta quens feu
sino quens dix que vertaderament ell devie haver fet aço que nosaltres li haviem
dit mas que ere stat ten torbat del mal e accident del dit senyor que noli anave
al cor en res, mas que dalliavant ell se ne seguiria ço que li haviem consellat
fahent nos gracies daço queli haviem dit.'

[41] Vilamari, captain of the king's fleet, was ordered to carry the chamberlain
from Naples to Palermo (ACA Reg. 2697. 69ᵛ, Torre del Greco, 20 Sept.
1450).

May 1452.[42] The career of the younger de Cardona had begun many years earlier with military services rendered to Alfonso in the war against Anjou[43] and in the Calabrian rebellion of Antonio Centelles.[44] His first reward was a substantial fief which included the city of Reggio given to him in November 1439.[45] On the occasion of the triumphal entry into Naples on 26 February 1443 the king bestowed on him the title of count in respect of that fief.[46] With his death the de Cardona family ceased to occupy an important role in the household because his son and heir Antonio was still a minor.

The man who effectively stepped into Pedro de Cardona's place as first chamberlain was another Spanish Sicilian, Guillem Ramon de Moncada, Count of Aderno. Among the oldest of the king's companions in arms, the count had served him throughout the Neapolitan adventure from the siege of Acerra in 1421[47] to the battle of Carpenone, in which he commanded one of the royal squadrons. For much of the war he had maintained a body of cavalry at his own expense, was twice taken prisoner,[48] and was left with Ramon Boyl to negotiate the surrender of Castel dell'Ovo to the Angevins in August 1439. He was rewarded with high office in the kingdom of Sicily: first that of seneschal,[49] then the chancellorship, and finally, after the death of Alfonso de Cardona, the office of justiciar. In the royal household he held the rank of a *camarlengus*. So long as Pedro de Cardona lived that office did not require de Moncada's assiduous attendance on the king, so he was often employed on diplomatic missions. The most spectacular of these was the one that took him with a train of a hundred attendants to the courts of France, Avignon, and Burgundy in the spring of 1444. The purpose was to explore the possibilities of a marriage between a daughter of the king of France and the Duke

[42] ASN Div. Somm. I. 149, 455ʳ.

[43] See Ametller y Vinyas, *Alfonso V de Aragón*, ii. 397 and 417.

[44] The king gave him authority to attack any rebel towns (ACA Reg. 2903. 177ʳ, Camp near Crotone, 8 Dec. 1444). Among those that fell to him were Montesoro on 27 Dec. (ibid. 189ᵛ), Polia, Menniti, and Monterosso on 29 Dec. (ibid. 194ᵛ), and Rosarno on 8 Jan. 1445 (Reg. 2907. 72ʳ).

[45] ASN Div. Somm. I. 149, 401ʳ.

[46] ACA Reg. 2904. 61ᵛ, Naples, 1 Mar. 1443.

[47] B. Facio, *De rebus gestis ab Alphonso primo, Neapolitanorum rege commentariorum libri x* (Leiden, 1723). ii.

[48] In 1423 by Sforza and at Ponza by the Genoese.

[49] His family had been hereditary seneschals of Catalonia until 1344. See above, p. 57, n. 12.

of Calabria,[50] and probably to arrange a prolongation of the truce with René of Anjou which de Moncada had negotiated the previous year. Having become principal chamberlain in 1452, he busied himself, like his predecessor, in the affairs of the royal chamber, though he did join the delegation sent to represent the king at the coronation of Calixtus III. His last public service to Alfonso was performed on 26 June 1458 in the Castel dell'Ovo when as chamberlain he sealed the king's will with the signet.[51] After the king's death he returned to Sicily where he did useful service to Juan II. His son Giovanni Tommaso de Moncada, whom Alfonso had made simultaneously a knight and a *camarlengus* on 25 January 1444,[52] had, so far as is known, little to do with the court.

Only one of Borso d'Este's 'governadori' could claim to have served in the royal entourage longer than Guillem Ramon de Moncada; this was Eximen Perez de Corella who had joined Alfonso in his Corsican expedition and remained a trusted confidant until his death in Naples on 17 October 1457.[53] In 1425 he held the office of *coperius* in the household;[54] in 1432 he and the Bishop of Valencia became joint governors and tutors to the king's son Ferdinand. De Corella remained with the boy in Valencia until 1438 then took him to join his father in Italy. There he continued to exercise his tutorship until in 1444 he led 'a great crowd of Catalans'[55] to bring his charge's bride, Isabella di Chiaramonte, from her home in Lecce to Naples. His performance as a tutor evidently satisfied both the king and his pupil for he was later given the same charge over the duke's sons and retained it to his death.[56] Alfonso also showed great confidence in his adminstrative abilities by appointing him viceroy in the province of Terra di

---

[50] ACA Reg. 2698. 36ᵛ, Instructions for the embassy given to de Moncada, Pozzuoli, 24 Jan. 1444.

[51] The Aragonese household ordinance required the senior chamberlain to keep the secret seal and not to affix it to any document which did not bear the signet or some other mark approved by the king.

[52] ACA Reg. 2914. 5ʳ.

[53] Madurell Marimón, *Mensajeros barceloneses*, p. 605.

[54] In that capacity he witnessed an instrument appointing plenipotentiaries to negotiate with Milan (ACA Reg. 2646. 2ᵛ, 10 Nov. 1425).

[55] 'una gran frotta de catalani' (BNN Biblioteca Brancacciana MS. III E7, *Diario di cose occorse in Neapoli dal 1266 al 1478*, 103ʳ).

[56] ACB Cart. Com., vol. 27, fol. 347, Naples, 16 Dec. 1457. In this letter his son Johan Roig de Corella informs the city of Barcelona that the king has confirmed him in all his father's offices including the tutorship of the Duke of Calabria's sons.

Lavoro and one of the governing council in Naples during the king's prolonged absences in the 1440s; indeed he appears to have been the senior member of that council.[57] Once the king had returned to take control in Naples, Eximen Perez de Corella's energies were diverted to diplomatic missions: in 1450 he was sent to Catalonia in connection with a meeting of the Cortes: in October 1451 Alfonso appointed him leader of an embassy to Castile.[58] His most dramatic assignment was his mission to Rome in 1456 when he confronted his former co-tutor, now Calixtus III. A phrase in his instructions, while reflecting the tension existing between Rome and Naples, harks back to the days when both men had shared the secrets of the king's council. 'On empero la sua Santidat en aquest negoci complaure noli vulla, covendra al dit Senyor recorrer e recordarse de usar dels remeys per sa Santidat en altre temps e consemblants materies recordats e aconsellats.'[59] The outcome was a blazing row and the two Valencians parted bitter enemies.[60]

For many years de Corella held the rank of a chamberlain in the household and towards the close of his life he acquired the higher dignity of *mayordomen*. He probably held that office in respect of the kingdom of Valencia of which he had for many years been governor, and where he had in August 1448 bought the fief of Cocentayna with the title of count from the crown for a sum of 80,000 florins.[61] How high he stood in Alfonso's esteem may be judged from the grant of the royal arms and insignia to him[62] and the direction that his annual provision of 3,000 ducats be the fourth charge upon the customs revenues of the city of Naples immediately after that of the king's daughters.[63] In the language of the chancery: 'in nostris dum vixit ingentibus serviciis strenue se gessit et in eisdem laudabiliter vitam finiit.'[64]

[57] Cf. below, pp. 100 ff.
[58] ACB Cart. Com., vol. 21, fol. 195, Anthoni Vinyes to Barcelona, Naples, 7 Oct. 1451.
[59] ACA Reg. 2662, 24ᵛ, Memorial for de Corella, Castelnuovo, 17 Aug. 1456. The matter in dispute was the translation of the Bishop of Urgell to the archbishopric of Monreal.
[60] Ametller y Vinyas, *Alfonso V de Aragón*, ii. 829–30.
[61] ACA Reg. 2943. 29ᵛ, Camp against Piombino, 28 Aug. 1448.
[62] Ametller y Vinyas, *Alfonso V de Aragón*, iii. 79.
[63] ACA Reg. 2902. 60ᵛ, Camp against L'Aquila, 10 Aug. 1442.
[64] ASN Div. Somm. I. 52 (bis), 48ʳ, Privilege recognizing Johan Roig de Corella as heir, 28 Oct. 1457.

Still following Borso d'Este's list of the king's personal attendants, there remain two to be considered: Guillem de Vich and Ferrer Ram. The household functions of de Vich were similar to those of his fellow-Valencian de Corella in that de Vich controlled the household of the king's daughters, Maria and Eleonora; for their expenses he drew 2,000 ducats a year from the Neapolitan customs revenues.[65] When Maria went to Ferrara to join her husband Leonello d'Este in April 1444, Guillem de Vich played the double role of escort and envoy to the king's new son-in-law.[66] Early in the following month his younger charge Eleonora was married to the son of the Duke of Sessa, thus bringing to an end his services in that direction. As early as 1425 he had been a *camerarius* in the household[67] and by 1440 had risen to the rank of *cambrero mayor*.[68] However, it would appear that, apart from occasional visits to Italy, he was until 1442 mainly occupied with his office of *magister rationalis* in the kingdom of Valencia, and with diplomatic missions to Castile. He was one of the Aragonese envoys who signed the five-year truce with Castile in July 1430[69] and went on other missions to that country in 1440 and 1444.[70] It is possible that he never returned to Naples from this last Castilian embassy, for he appears to have died late in 1445.

Like Guillem de Vich, Ferrer Ram had entered the inner circle of the household as an administrator and not as a noble companion in arms. A *doctor utriusque juris*, he succeeded his father in the office of protonotary in Aragon when Pere Ram died in 1443. Thereafter, though much in the king's confidence, his talents were employed more in diplomatic and financial missions than in the household, and from the beginning of 1444 until his death on 16 October 1448 he spent only a little over fifteen months at court.[71] Borso d'Este happened to be in Naples on one of those rare occasions—the summer of 1444—but it is clear that we cannot regard Ram as a regular member of the royal entourage.

[65] ACA Reg. 2903. 34ʳ, 3 Dec. 1442; Reg. 2901. 107ʳ, 29 Apr. 1443.

[66] ACA Reg. 2690. 57ʳ, Alfonso to Leonello d'Este, Castelnuovo, 6 Apr. 1444.

[67] ACA Reg. 2646. 2ᵛ, 10 Nov. 1425.

[68] ACA Reg. 2651. 170ᵛ, Alfonso to the King of Navarre, 25 Oct. 1440.

[69] Vicens Vives, *Els Trastamares*, p. 122.

[70] ACA Reg. 2696. 119ᵛ, Instructions for de Vich and Ram, Castelnuovo, 30 Aug. 1444; Ametller y Vinyas, *Alfonso V de Aragón*, ii. 345, n. 1.

[71] He was in Milan from March to June 1444, in Spain from November 1444 until August 1445, and his final mission, beginning in March 1446, took him to Rome and Spain from where he returned to Naples in August 1448.

Even if Borso's list is defective in a few particulars, it gives an invaluable contemporary impression of the king's closest attendants; they were still those noble knights prescribed by the Household Ordinance of 1344, and they still held the chief household offices of *mayordomen* and *camarlench*; moreover they were fighting men, leaders of the king's armies as well as attendants on his person. A full list of them would be difficult to compile and those to be added would be very similar in origin and background to those already described. Among the other *mayordomens* of whom we have some knowledge may be singled out Juan Ferrandez de Hijar, a descendant of the cadet branch of the dynasty of James I of Aragon. He had governed Calabria in Alfonso's name from 1421 to 1422, and again commanded the royal armies in that province at the time of Centelles's rebellion. He also played a prominent part in Alfonso's dealings with Castile.[72] Alfonso de Ávalos, another scion of the constable of Castile, became a *mayordomen* towards the end of the reign.[73] The ranks of the *camarlenchs* included Ramon de Perellos who had gone to Naples in 1420 to receive the adoption in the king's name;[74] Ramon Boyl, one of the most prominent of the military commanders;[75] Alfonso de Cardenas, viceroy of Terra di Lavoro beyond the Garigliano; Juan Ferrandez de Heredia;[76] Antonio Centelles, 'nostro amato camberlengo' before he became a rebel;[77] Lope Ximenez de Urrea who held the title of viceroy 'in utraque Sicilia';[78] and a scion of the Sicilian de Luna family, Lupo de Luna.[79] Many of these men

[72] E. Pontieri (ed.), *Fonti aragonesi*, vol. ii, p. vii; Ametller y Vinyas, *Alfonso V de Aragón*, ii. 109, 345, 495, iii. 644; ACA Reg. 2651. 170ᵛ, 25 Oct. 1440.

[73] ACA Reg. 2917. 161ᵛ, Castelnuovo, 3 June 1457, Privilege appointing Alfonso de Ávalos, *maiordomus*, castellan, captain, and governor of Melissa.

[74] Facio, *De rebus gestis*, i. He was given the title of *camarlench* in May 1421 (Faraglia, *La lotta*, p. 124, n. 4).

[75] He held the office at least as early as 1433. Cf. Ametller y Vinyas, *Alfonso V de Aragón*, i. 408.

[76] He appeared only briefly in Italy, joining the king in his camp at Tivoli in the summer of 1447 (ACA Reg. 2945. 81ʳ). As *camarlengus* he witnessed a letter *de gratia* dated 8 Aug. 1447.

[77] J. Mazzoleni (ed.), *Fonti aragonesi*, i. 19. The document in which this phrase occurs is dated 10 Dec. 1438.

[78] Beccadelli (*De dictis et factis* iii) cites this appointment as an example of the king's readiness to reward services; de Urrea had fought for him for twenty years. He was effectively viceroy of Sicily from 1441 to 1459. For the 'in utraque Sicilia' title see ACA Reg. 2660. 152ʳ, 13 June 1455.

[79] He received an annual provision of 500 ducats (ACA 'Real Patrimonio', 2951, March 1450).

spent only brief periods at court and their household duties, if
any, represented but an irregular and secondary aspect of the
services they rendered the crown. Only two Italians found a
prominent place in the chamber. One was Restaino Caldora, the
handsome son of Antonio Caldora, who grew up as the companion
of the Duke of Calabria and was at one time considered as a
husband for the king's daughter.[80] He gained a great reputation as
a polished courtier. The other was Ercole d'Este half-brother of
Borso and Leonello who, with his brother Sigismondo, had been
sent to the Neapolitan court as a page in 1445. In March 1454 he
was witnessing the ratification of a treaty with Castile as *camarlengus*,
and in the same capacity he witnessed the king's will, signing
after the seneschal Iñigo de Guevara and before the *mayordomen*
Fernando de Guevara.[81]

In the subordinate ranks of the household too men of Spanish
provenance held a majority of the important posts, though Italians
naturally appear more frequently than they do in the highest
offices. They were unusually well represented among the *copers*—
two esquires of noble or baronial lineage who served the king's wine
and ranked immediately after the *mayordomens* in the Aragonese
household. A Neapolitan, Rainaldo del Duce, became a *coperius*
after first serving as a page,[82] so too did Giovanni Antonio Caldora,
an illegitimate son of the *condottiere* Raimondo Caldora, who also
began his court career as a page.[83] Among the Spaniards who held
the office were Eximen Perez de Corella and Berenguer de Erill.[84]

[80] Ametller y Vinyas, *Alfonso V de Aragón*, ii. 369. He jousted in the celebrations for Ferdinand's marriage (ibid. ii. 519) and was among those who bore the
coffin of the king's brother Pedro in the reburial ceremonies in 1445 (ibid. 543).
A royal letter of 10 Aug. 1451 describes him as 'camarere nostro' (J. Mazzoleni
(ed.), '*Il 'Codice Chigi' un registro della cancelleria di Alfonso I d'Aragona re di
Napoli per gli anni 1451–1453* (Naples, 1965), p. 76). As a witness to the ceremony in which the tribute from Piombino was delivered to the king in May 1458
he figures as 'camerlengo' (ACA Reg. 2916. 97ᵛ).

[81] Cf. above, p. 61. For the treaty ceremony which took place in the king's
bedchamber at midnight 'segund la costumbre dela Ciudat de Napoles' see
ACA Reg. 2700. 47ʳ, 16 Mar. 1454.

[82] ACA Reg. 2908. 147ᵛ, Castelnuovo, 25 July 1446. As a *coperius* he is given
an annual provision of 200 ducats. By May 1451 it had risen to 300 ducats (Reg.
2914. 139ʳ, Castelnuovo, 20 May 1451). In May 1456 he was given command
of a body of troops sent to Albania (Reg. 2661. 118ᵛ).

[83] His signature as a witness to the king's will appears immediately after that
of Fernando de Guevara. For his feud with Iñigo de Guevara cf. Ametller y
Vinyas, *Alfonso V de Aragón*, ii. 816.

[84] Like the other *copers* de Erill entered the household as a young boy. A

After the *copers* in order of precedence came the *boteller* or *pinsernus* whose duty it was to keep the king's wine and water and deliver them to the *copers*. Martin de Santa Cruz, who had served in the household since boyhood, was *boteller mayor* in 1445 and still in 1452.[85] The carrying of cooked dishes to the royal table was entrusted to two 'squires of knightly lineage' known as *sobrecochs*. The name of one of these, Ferdinando de Argiona, appears frequently in the registers of privileges as the captain of various towns, and even as justiciar of Basilicata, but since these offices could be exercised by a deputy they did not interfere with the attendance on the king; indeed they illustrate the advantages enjoyed by such servants in acquiring lucrative offices.[86] Two *panicers majors*—Gonsalvo de Cordova was one of them[87]—served bread at the king's table, and two squires carved his meat.

In the Ordinance of 1344 the duties of the *comprador* or purveyor had been defined largely in terms of purchasing and accounting for the daily supply of victuals in the household.[88] In Alfonso's reign they extended to the general provisioning of the court, and the holder of the office needed to be a connoisseur of tapestries, jewels, and pictures, rather than of fish, meat, and vegetables, though the furnishing of the latter commodities still came within his province.[89] Four Catalans held the post in turn. The first of these, Jaume Amigo,[90] was succeeded by his son Luis Amigo.[91] Gabriel Davo was *comprador mayor* for only a few months in 1452

privilege for 'magnifico et dilecto consiliario et coperio nostro' mentions that he had served Alfonso 'ab eius ineunte etate' (ASN Priv. I. 16ᵛ, Castelnuovo, 29 May 1452).

[85] ACA Reg. 2909. 120ʳ, Bisignano, 12 Mar. 1445: appointing Martin, who had served the king from his youth, to be captain and castellan of Rocella, Reg. 2659. 56ᵛ.

[86] Cf. below, p. 337.

[87] He had an annual provision of 600 ducats on the salt tax of Naples (ASN Priv. I. 27ᵛ).

[88] Bofarull y Mascaró, *Coleccion de documentos*, p. 45.

[89] A number of specialist purveyors were appointed for particular commodities —e.g. Bernat Figueras was 'specier dela cambra' (Faraglia, *Storia della lotta*, p. 236, n. 1); Signorello di Fiore was court butcher (*macellarius noster*) (Mazzoleni, *Il Codice Chigi*, p. 274).

[90] ACA Reg. 2651. 98ʳ, Gaeta, 26 Sept. 1437. He also held the office of governor of Ibiza.

[91] The latest reference to Luis Amigo as *comprador mayor* is a letter the king addressed to him from Torre del Greco dated 13 June 1451 (Mazzoleni, *Il Codice Chigi*, p. 4). Shortly afterwards he went to the Abruzzi to carry out his duties as captain of Montagne di Abruzzi and Citta Ducale (ibid., pp. 90–2).

and then gave place to Andreu Pol.[92] This official had at his disposal an annual assignment first fixed at 12,000 ducats a year in June 1442[93] but shortly afterwards raised to 14,000 ducats.[94] That sum covered only the regular and basic provisioning of the household; special assignments were needed for the king's lavish entertaining and for the purchase of costly items such as jewels. Extraordinary expenditure of this kind was estimated by several contemporaries to have reached 100,000 ducats in the month of April 1452 when Alfonso played host to the Holy Roman Emperor Frederick III and his bride.[95] Every evening hundreds of the imperial retinue and the king's own subjects banqueted in the great hall of Castelnuovo; for two or three days red and white wine spouted from fountains of gilded and silvered wood set up by the lists in the Via Incoronata in front of the castle; and the king undertook to meet the cost of all purchases his guests made from merchants in the city. Pol made a number of journeys to Flanders in search of tapestries and other furnishings for the royal apartments,[96] and in Naples itself the purveyor was constantly purchasing luxuries for the chamber. A piece of gold brocade costing 745 ducats,[97] a piece of silk for 805 ducats,[98] furs to the value of 1,160 ducats,[99] and a collection of jewels bought from some Genoese merchants for 5,610 ducats[100] represent only a random selection from a multitude of similar purchases which made the office of *comprador* one of the great spending departments.[101]

'We can hardly tell you how much going about on foot is looked

[92] A letter dated 26 June 1451 refers to Davo as 'emptori maiori regie domus' (ibid., p. 37). An item in the treasury payments for 31 Aug. 1454 describes him as 'olim comprador' (Mazzoleni, *Fonti aragonesi*, i. 148). Pol had become *comprador mayor* by January 1452 (ACA Reg. 2659. 53).

[93] ACA Reg. 2902. 32ᵛ, Naples, 2 June 1442.

[94] ACA Reg. 2903. 34ʳ, Barletta, 3 Dec. 1442.

[95] Facio, *De rebus gestis*, ix; Beccadelli, *De dictis et factis*, iv; 'Come lo Imperatore Federico entrò in Napoli e poi lo 4 di entrò l'Imperatrice in Aversa', *ASPN* (1908), 481–500; N. F. Faraglia (ed.), *Diurnali detti del Duca di Monteleone* (Naples, 1895), p. 136; ACB Cart. Com., vol. 22, fols. 36, 38, 40, 57.

[96] Cf. C. Marinescu, 'Notes sur le faste à la cour d'Alfonso V d'Aragon, roi de Naples', *Mélanges d'histoire générale de l'Université de Cluj*, i (1927), 133–146; ACA Reg. 2661. 5ʳ, Letter to Pol about some tapestries to be bought in Bruges, Naples, 23 May 1453.

[97] ACA Reg. 2940. 32ʳ, 14 June 1447.   [98] Ibid. 35ʳ, 19 July 1447.

[99] Ibid. 118ʳ, 15 Feb. 1451. They were 580 marten furs.

[100] Ibid. 81ᵛ, 8 Mar. 1450.

[101] In November 1437 there was a *sots comprador*, Johan de Soria (Mazzoleni, *Fonti aragonesi*, i. 86). This office presumably continued to exist later in the reign.

down upon here for everyone rides a horse.'[102] So wrote the ambassadors of Barcelona seeking to convince their employers of the need to furnish themselves with horses while living in Naples. A king in this horse-conscious society needed a prestigious number of animals; he needed them for his favourite sport, hunting; he needed them still more against the eventualities of war. The stables were thus a vital component of the household and one on which the king lavished much care and money. In Aragon the Household Ordinance had deputed two *cavallerices* to supervise the stables. The same title appears in the Neapolitan court of Alfonso. One of the first to bear it was Paduano Pagano, a member of a prominent Neapolitan family.[103] It was also conferred on Gabriele Curiale,[104] Placido di Sangro,[105] and Giovanni Barrassa.[106] The only Spaniard among these masters of the horse was Pere Cases, the Hospitaller prior of Medina.[107]

Consideration of the stables leads us to the part of the court that ministered to the king's chief pleasure and relaxation—hunting. Many contemporaries wrote of his passion for the chase which burned undimmed by age.[108] In November 1456, when sixty years old, he left Naples for a prolonged hunting expedition in the cold, mud, rain, and mist of an Apulian winter, 'lunyes de affers e enten en sos plers'.[109] To be invited to join one of these taxing expeditions was the surest sign that Alfonso found a man congenial to his spirit.[110] Even war did not put a stop to the royal sport, for

---

[102] ACB Cart. Com., vol. 14, fol. 64, Naples, 29 Apr. 1444. The kingdom appears to have been an important centre of horse-breeding.

[103] He is mentioned as a 'cavallericie' in a letter ordering the treasury to buy fodder of the kind requested by him for the king's horses (ACA Reg. 2646. 85ᵛ, Capua, 28 Mar. 1440).

[104] Mazzoleni, *Fonti aragonesi*, i. 72. A document dated 31 Dec. 1448 names him as a 'cavallaricio'.

[105] Minieri Riccio, 'Alcuni fatti di Alfonso I', p. 457.

[106] Ibid., p. 357. He was sent to Burgundy in November 1450 to present four horses to the duke.

[107] On 25 July 1450 the king bought two horses from him as presents for the Florentine ambassador (ibid., p. 256). As 'cavallericio' he was to receive the pair of gilt spurs which Luis de Ispania owed the crown each year for a Valencian fief (ACA Reg. 2943. 40ᵛ, 9 Nov. 1452).

[108] Beccadelli, *De dictis et factis*, iv; Aeneas Sylvius, *Commentarius in libros Antonii Panormitae*, iv; Pere Boquet, an envoy sent to the king by the city of Barcelona, wrote in a letter dated 27 Jan. 1457, 'lo dia que no caça no s'i fa res ni ou negú' (Madurell Marimón, *Mensajeros barceloneses*, p. 552).

[109] ACB Cart. Com., vol. 26, fol. 174, Pere Boquet to Barcelona, Naples, 10 Nov. 1456.

[110] Antonio Beccadelli, *Epistolae campanae*, 47.

the king's falconers accompanied his army. In times of peace he organized ceremonial hunts, staged with a lavish pageantry to entertain the court and distinguished visitors. That organized for the Emperor on Sunday, 18 April 1452 probably surpassed them all in brilliance. It took place in the hunting grounds known as 'la caccia dell'Astroni' outside Pozzuoli and began with a feast that had taken eight days to prepare and required three hours to eat. Besides the official guests, large numbers who had flocked from Naples, Pozzuoli, Aversa, and Capua to see the sport were invited to eat and drink their fill. The noble ladies then took their seats on a covered platform erected on a small hill and the king's son Ferdinand, as master of the hunt, led a distinguished company of huntsmen against a motley collection of wild animals—stags, deer, bears, boar, even hares and porcupines—which had been herded into the area. With them went the pick of the royal hunting dogs, many of them presented to Alfonso from places as diverse as Turkey, Tunis, Brittany, England, and Corsica. One huge boar, 'big as an ox', was set upon by two English boar hounds and finished off by the Emperor and Ferdinand. When all was over part of the game was taken to Naples and the rest distributed among the spectators.[111]

To cater for this sport Alfonso maintained a body of huntsmen the senior of whom were known as *munterii majores*.[112] In the early years of the regin there were at least three men who held this title: Vasco de Gonea, Rodrigo de Lison, and Ferrando de Almaçan. Vasco de Gonea appears to have been the senior among them, and he was evidently a man of some importance. In 1440 Alfonso sent him to Portugal with letters for his sister, the queen of Portugal, and other members of the royal family.[113] He returned there in February 1451 to conclude negotiations for the marriage of the Princess Leonor to the King of the Romans,[114] and when that marriage was celebrated in Rome Alfonso sent Vasco to discuss with the new empress the visit which she and her husband were to

---

[111] 'Come lo Imperatore Federico entrò in Napoli', pp. 498–500. Cf. Faraglia, *Diurnali*, April 1445.

[112] This office did not appear in the Aragonese ordinance of 1344, but was known in Angevin Naples.

[113] ACA Reg. 2651. 157^r, Letter reporting his return to Italy with letters from the Portuguese royal family, Gaeta, 13 Sept. 1440.

[114] ACA Reg. 2697. 78^v, Torre del Greco, 3 Feb. 1451, Instructions for his embassy to Portugal.

pay to Naples.[115] The Castilian knight Rodrigo de Lison went to Castile in 1442 in order to buy horses and enlist men for service among the royal huntsmen. He managed to find altogether twenty-five men and eighteen thoroughbreds (*jinetes*), but had to send eleven men and eight horses back to Castile because he could not find a ship to carry them from Valencia to Naples.[116] When de Lison died a few years later, his place as *montero mayor* was filled by Vasco de Gonea's brother Fernando, who also held the office of herald of Catalonia. In 1450 Alfonso sent him to Portugal to negotiate a marriage between a Portuguese princess and the French dauphin,[117] a matter which his brother attempted to carry further the following year. The office of *submunterius major* was held, at least until 1447, by Garcia Ximenez de Aranjuez. He too was often employed on diplomatic missions. In 1446 he went to Burgundy and Brittany in search of horses and falcons,[118] but transacted at the same time some political business for which he returned to Burgundy in the following year.[119] In this manner members of the household served to carry on the business of the state as well as attending to the domestic affairs of the king.

The ordinary huntsmen were divided into four groups stationed in towns within easy reach of the capital. In 1445 there were sixteen at Pozzuoli,[120] thirty in Aversa,[121] thirty-five in Capua, and twenty-seven at Marcianise';[122] almost all of them were Italians. They enjoyed immunity from municipal taxation and jurisdiction, being subject directly to the *munterius major* and ultimately to the court of the *mayordomen*.

[115] Mazzoleni, *Il Codice Chigi*, pp. 268–9, 21 Mar. 1452. Vasco de Gonea's wife accompanied him to Rome.

[116] ACA Reg. 2901. 124^r, 8 May 1444. This letter to the *maestre racional* of Valencia deals with de Lison's expenses and cites the original instructions given on 29 Mar. 1442.

[117] ACA Reg. 2697. 68^v, 18 Sept. 1450, Memorial for Fernando's negotiations with the dauphin.

[118] ACA Reg. 2690. 213^v. 6 Mar. 1446, Letters from Alfonso to the Dukes of Burgundy and Brittany informing them of the purpose of the visit of his *submunterius major*. Further letters to the Dukes of Savoy and Milan ask for a safe passage.

[119] ACA Reg. 2699. 57^v, 4 Jan. 1447, Instructions for de Aranjuez and his fellow-envoy Francesch Davin. Among other things they were to receive the order of the Golden Fleece for Alfonso.

[120] ASN Fasc. Com. Somm. I. 81^v.   [121] Ibid. 98^v.

[122] Ibid. In 1455 this department of the household comprised 2 *munterii majores*, 2 *submunterii*, and 97 huntsmen (Minieri Riccio, 'Alcuni fatti di Alfonso I', p. 440).

An equally elaborate organization catered for the king's hunting of birds. At its head was the *falconer mayor*, a post held early in the reign by the Catalan poet Ausias March who, after relinquishing it, continued to breed birds for the king but did not accompany him to Italy.[123] There followed him Johan de Navarras,[124] Pere de Ladesma,[125] and Maso Barrese.[126] By 1455 the ordinary falconers numbered no fewer than ninety-eight.[127] For the benefit of the Emperor they put on a hunting expedition involving more than one hundred falconers and two thousand horses. The hunt took place in a plain surrounded by low hills two miles outside Nola and lasted for three days.[128] Hunting on this scale must have depleted the bird life around Naples, for in 1457 an attempt was made to stock the marshes near the capital with birds suitable for falconry.[129]

Responsibility for lodging and feeding the court when it was travelling and for arranging the transport of the royal baggage fell on an official known as the *sobreazembler*. And last of all in the hierarchy of the *mayordomens'* office as regulated by the 1344 ordinances came the royal musicians or *juglars* whose function it was to play at the beginning and end of all public feasts, except those that fell in Lent or on Fridays. The ordinance had provided for a quartet—two horns, a trumpet, and a kettle-drum—but musical tastes at the Neapolitan court were more sophisticated and the royal band had grown to include flutes, trombones, and harps.[130] It still continued to sound fanfares on ceremonial occasions and at feasts, but more important was the music played in the royal chapel, and for the dances and masked balls that became a regular feature of court life in the Aragonese era.[131] As with so many other features of his court, Alfonso held it a point of honour to ensure that his musicians were inferior to none in Europe, so his agents scoured the continent in search of *virtuosi*.

[123] A. Pagés (ed.), *Ausias March et ses prédécesseurs* (Paris, 1911).
[124] Mazzoleni, *Fonti aragonesi*, i. 121.
[125] ACA Reg. 2910. 41ᵛ, 28 Feb. 1446.
[126] ASN Priv. I. 85ʳ, 28 July 1453.
[127] Minieri Riccio, 'Alcuni fatti di Alfonso I', p. 440.
[128] 'Come lo Imperatore Federico entrò in Napoli', pp. 490–2.
[129] ACA Reg. 2917. 176ʳ, 4 Oct. 1457, Privilege authorizing Angelo de Rizardo, a skilled catcher and rearer of birds, to do this.
[130] M. Pietro of Caeta was the king's harpist in 1437 (Minieri Riccio, 'Alcuni fatti di Alfonso I', p. 8). In 1456 there were five flautists in the household (ibid., p. 444).
[131] Cf. B. Croce, *La Spagna nella vita italiana* (Bari, 1917), p. 43.

All those functionaries considered so far belonged to the general household staff controlled by the *mayordomens*. Turning to the chamber, which was supervised by the *camarlenchs*, we find that the Aragonese Household Ordinance makes provision for six *escuders* (squires) and six *ajudants* to take care of the king's clothes, jewels, arms, to make his bed and keep his chamber in order. The same designation appears in Alfonso's Neapolitan court applied to Giovanni Bassa,[132] Joan Prou, Tommaso Potenza, Guillen Pou, and Pere de Mondrago.[133] Very many others are described simply as *camerarius* or *cambrer*, a title which may sometimes disguise a specific function, but which seems to have been extensively employed by Alfonso either to attach a man to the chamber without assigning to him any of the functions specified in the ordinance of 1344, or else as a purely honorific title. Some of those so designated were military men. Galeotto de Bardaxi, a knight famed throughout western Europe for feats of arms, was summoned in 1448 to serve the king as a *cambrer* and given an annual provision of 120 *oncie* on the Calabrian revenues.[134] Another warrior *cambrer*, Francesch Marrades of Valencia, received a Calabrian fief as a reward for his services.[135] Luis Dez Puig, the Master of Montesa, also a Valencian, was a tall, strong man who played a leading part in the war against Anjou.[136] From 1442 he became one of the king's most trusted diplomatic agents and a master in the intricacies of Italian politics; in fact he came as close to being a professional diplomat as anyone of that age. Several other gentlemen of the chamber were employed in a diplomatic role: Felip Boyl went in June 1444 to sound the Emperor, the King of England, and the Duke of Burgundy, about an alliance with Aragon;[137] in September 1455 Gaspar Çapila delivered a gift of six horses to the king of Portugal.[138] The voyage to Flanders undertaken by Galceran Gener as captain of one of the king's ships was, by contrast, solely concerned with the business of the chamber—the transport of

---

[132] ASN Priv. I. 77^r, Castelnuovo, 7 June 1453.

[133] Faraglia, *Storia della lotta*, p. 251, n. 1; Mazzoleni, *Fonti aragonesi*, i. 87; Minieri Riccio, 'Alcuni fatti di Alfonso I', p. 457.

[134] ACA Reg. 2913. 1^r, Alberese, 12 Apr. 1448.

[135] ACA Reg. 2904. 228^r, Camp against Crotone, 18 Jan. 1445.

[136] Ametller y Vinyas, *Alfonso V de Aragón*, ii. 381. He led the king's troops in the storming of Biccari in July 1441.

[137] ACA Reg. 2939. 79^v, Castelnuovo, 18 June 1444, Instructions for Boyl, described as 'conseller camarlench e merechaunt'.

[138] ACA Reg. 2721 (2). 36^v, Castelnuovo, 28 Sept. 1455.

pictures, tapestries, and cloths purchased by royal agents in Flanders.[139] Several Italians too enjoyed at least honorary attachment to the chamber and they were well represented among the pages who served there. A list of the pages for December 1441 names four Italians against only two Spaniards.[140]

The department of the wardrobe was controlled by Pere de Mondrago, who ranked as a *sub camerarius*, and his deputy Antoni Cetina. Care of the king's clothing still figured prominently among their responsibilities. In his dress Alfonso affected sobriety and elegance. He preferred dark velvets, Florentine damask, oriental silks that came from Cyprus, Damascus, and Venice. Usually he wore a black doublet and hose enlivened with gold and pearls; fifteen embroiderers once spent a fortnight sewing pearls on one of his doublets. Catalan, Italian, Jewish, and Portuguese tailors made his clothes[141] which were sometimes ordered from Spain. His armour and weapons were cared for by the *armer maior*, Joan Lull,[142] and a *sotarmer*, Rodrigo de Medina.[143] For battle and the tournament he favoured armour of Milanese craftsmanship[144] and Catalan or French coats of mail.

Besides taking care of the king's apparel, the *sub camerarius* also saw to the safe-keeping of Alfonso's remarkable collection of tapestries, jewels, and pictures.[145] Until 1448 the jewels, objects of gold and silver, and a collection of antique coins were all housed in

[139] Mazzoleni, *Il Codice Chigi*, p. 56.

[140] Faraglia, *Storia della lotta*, p. 249, n. 1.

[141] Ayna Coeninch, one of the king's tailors who had followed him from Spain with his family, was granted Neapolitan citizenship when he settled in Naples (ACA Reg. 2908. 110ʳ, 17 Feb. 1446).

[142] He held this office by August 1437 (Minieri Riccio, 'Alcuni fatti di Alfonso I', p. 5). Martin de Lanuza, *baile general* of Aragon, also held the title (ibid., p. 8) but in an honorary capacity.

[143] Ibid., p. 5.

[144] Missalla of Milan made a suit of armour for the king in 1439 (ACA Reg. 2651. 94ʳ, Nocera, 29 Sept. 1439).

[145] Among other tapestries was a series by Roger van der Weyden depicting the Passion of Christ. Alfonso's agents in Flanders bought it for 5,000 ducats. Filangieri (*Castel Nuovo*) describes several other tapestries used to decorate the great hall. Of the king's jewels Tristano Caracciolo wrote (*De varietate fortunae*, p. 74): 'Gemmas, margaritas, carbunculos, ceteraque id genus pretiosa enumerare vanum esset, cum constet iis rebus reliquos suae tempestatis anteisse principes.' In his purchase of paintings Alfonso favoured Flemish artists. A Valencian, Jacme Baco, who probably introduced the technique of oil painting to Spain, was the resident court painter. See R. Filangieri, 'La Peinture flamande à Naples pendant le 15ᵉ siècle', *Revue belge d'archéologie et d'histoire de l'art*, 2 (1932), 128–44.

the wardrobe in Castelnuovo. At the end of that year many of them passed into the hands of merchants as security for loans; the remainder went to the chamberlain Eximen Perez de Corella for safe custody in the castle of Sant'Elmo.[146] They returned to Castelnuovo when the rebuilding of the Torre dell'Oro as a treasure house had been completed—probably by the end of 1453.[147] Alfonso took great delight in showing his collection of jewels, gold, and silver to visitors who went away duly impressed.

Because they were treated as the personal property of the king, a number of slaves, both black and white, came under the control of the wardrobe.[148]

Before he embarked on the conquest of Naples, Alfonso's passion for books had already led to the creation of a royal library which was looked after by Luis Cescases one of the king's clerks.[149] The collection followed the king to the mainland of Italy where it was housed until 1442 in Gaeta in the effective care of an official of the chamber, Joan Serra of Barcelona, though Cescases remained the nominal custodian.[150] After the court was established in Naples the library grew so much as to require the attention of a permanent staff, and in the course of the reign it became one of the most famous in Europe.[151] Alfonso first housed his books in Castel Capuano until the rebuilding of Castelnuovo had progressed far enough for them to be transferred to a permanent home in a room overlooking the Bay of Naples. With his library within easy reach, the king was then able to indulge what appears to have been a genuine delight in reading.

In Renaissance Naples it is a little surprising to find that all the

---

[146] ACA Reg. 2699. 141^v, 3 Oct. 1448.

[147] A contract for completing the Torre dell'Oro within thirty months was signed on 19 Apr. 1451 (Filangieri, *Castel Nuovo*, p. 53).

[148] Minieri Riccio, 'Alcuni fatti di Alfonso I', p. 456.

[149] 'Luis cestases qui ha carrech de tenir en custodia los libres del Senyor Rey' (Faraglia, *Storia della lotta*, p. 254, n. 5). G. Barzizza (*Orationes et epistolae* (Rome, 1723), p. 106) refers to 'Ludovico Cescases regio librario' in a letter of 1434 and relating to an incident that took place in Barcelona in 1432.

[150] G. Mazzatinti, *La biblioteca dei re di Aragona in Napoli* (Naples, 1897). p. xxii. On 14 July 1437 Serra was given some parchment for the use of the library (Minieri Riccio, 'Alcuni fatti di Alfonso I', p. 4). In December 1436 the books in Gaeta were handed over to some Florentine merchants as security for a debt (ACA Reg. 2651. 41^v, 3 Dec. 1436).

[151] See T. de Marinis, *La biblioteca napoletana dei re d'Aragona* (Milan, 1948).

royal librarians were Spaniards.[152] The office of *custos* passed sometime after November 1441 from Cescases to Tomas de Aulesa and
before January 1446 was duplicated in favour of Jacme de Casp.[153]
Another Catalan, Jaume Torres, a canon of Valencia attached to
the chamber, appears as *librer maior* in July 1451 and as *custos
bibliothece* in July 1452.[154] It would seem therefore that the Latin
and Catalan titles designated the same rank and that control of the
library was the joint responsibility of two or three *custodes*. Torres
made a number of journeys in search of books. In the autumn of
1455 he travelled to Spain armed with a list of works, mainly of a
scholastic nature, which he was commissioned to find and purchase. Another part of his duty was to run a school attached to the
library in which boys were taught grammar.[155]

Books which could not be bought were copied by a staff of
scribes assigned to the library. Highest paid of all was Jacopo
Curlo (or Curulo) of Spezia who drew an annual salary of 300
ducats.[156] Besides copying many books he acquired some reputation as an editor. It was during one of the reading sessions which
the king used to hold in his library after it had been installed in
Castelnuovo that Curlo was asked by Alfonso to edit the commentary on Terence by Donatus.[157] After the king's death he copied
and edited his friend Facio's translation of the life of Alexander by
Arrian at the request of the royal secretary Fonolleda.[158] Minia-
turists, among them an Alfonso de Cordoba[159] and Nicola Rabi-
cano,[160] decorated these manuscripts, and skilled leather-workers
brought from Granada and Cordoba bound them.[161] Many still

[152] A Baldassare detto Scarillo of Naples was 'adiutante nostre librarie' in
December 1451, but this was a junior post (ACA Reg. 2915. 137ᵛ).
[153] A privilege dated 25 Jan. 1446 refers to him as 'custos biblioteche nostre'
(ACA Reg. 2909. 187ᵛ).
[154] ACA Reg. 2939. 133ᵛ, Torre del Greco, 28 July 1451; Reg. 2550. 33ᵛ,
3 July 1452.
[155] ACA Reg. 2661, 100ᵛ, Alfonso to the Archbishop of Zaragoza asking him to
assist Torres in finding and buying the books, Castelnuovo, 22 Sept. 1455. The
payment of 50 ducats to Torres for the maintenance of the boys in the school on
16 Aug. 1453 is noted by Minieri Riccio, 'Alcuni fatti di Alfonso I', p. 423.
[156] This salary was first assigned him in May 1445 (ASN Priv. I. 7ʳ).
[157] Ametller y Vinyas, *Alfonso V de Aragón*, iii. 108.
[158] P. O. Kristeller in *From Renaissance to Counter-Reformation*, ed. C. H.
Carter (London, 1966), p. 66; Mazzatinti, *La biblioteca*, pp. vii–xii.
[159] Mazzatinti, *La biblioteca*, pp. xii–xiii.
[160] He is believed to have illuminated the copy of Strabo now in the Bibliothèque Nationale, Paris, MS. 4798.
[161] Moorish influence is perceptible in the arabesque decoration and maroon

survive, easily distinguished by the arms of Aragon and the devices of the open book, the castle, and the cross of Calabria emblazoned on the bindings.

Returning to the Aragonese order of precedence in the chamber —for the library was a post-1344 refinement—we come to those responsible for the king's health: a barber, two physicians, and two surgeons. Though he may still have been appointed, the barber does not figure as a person of any importance in the Neapolitan household. The number of physicians and surgeons, on the other hand, seems to have increased, and Alfonso adopted the Neapolitan practice of appointing a chief physician and a chief surgeon with the titles of *protomedicus* and *protocirugicus*.[162] As well as ministering to the king and his household, these two exercised authority over all others of their profession in the kingdom; they examined those who wished to practise either medicine or surgery, and on their report the necessary royal privilege was issued.[163] The first *protomedicus* appointed by Alfonso was Jacme Quintana of Barcelona, a master of arts and medicine who had served in the chamber from his youth. It is not known when he obtained the office, but it must have been before December 1442 when he examined Samuel of Barletta.[164] He died sometime before August 1457 and was succeeded by Gaspar Pelegri.[165] In May 1444 Quintana's authority was extended to all the king's dominions[166] and it was probably in consideration of these enlarged responsibilities that he received an annual provision of 300 florins on the revenues of Aragon.[167] We catch a glimpse of him tending the king

or reddish-brown sheep-leather bindings of many of the books (P. Lauer, 'Les Reliures des manuscrits des rois aragonais de Naples conservées à la Bibliothèque Nationale', *Bulletin philologique et historique*, 1928–9, pp. 121–30).

[162] See Summonte, *Historia*, ii. 459. A document of Giovanni I dated September 1380 mentions the *protomedicus*.

[163] e.g. a privilege issued for Marco Sibilia of Villafranca licensing him to practice surgery following an examination by the *protomedicus*. He was pardoned for having previously exercised his skill without licence or examination (ACA Reg. 2945. 13ʳ, 20 Dec. 1443). The majority of the recipients of these licences were Jews. But cf. below, p. 219.

[164] ACA Reg. 2904. 28ʳ, Barletta, 6 Dec. 1442.

[165] ACA Reg. 2662. 82ʳ, 26 Aug. 1457, mentions that Quintana has died; Minieri Riccio, 'Alcuni fatti di Alfonso I', p. 460, gives a reference to Pelegri as the *protomedicus*, March 1458.

[166] ACA Reg. 2904. 148ᵛ, 23 May 1444.

[167] ACA Reg. 2720. 130ᵛ, 15 Oct. 1449. Quintana had so far been unable to draw this salary because the revenues had been insufficient; he is therefore given first call upon them.

in that letter from the envoys of Barcelona in which they reported
their clash with Pedro de Cardona over his concealment of
Alfonso's grave illness:[168]

> We had the physicians—that is Master Quintana and Master Gaspar
> —come out and wished to know from them exactly how the king was;
> we also told them what we had said to Don Pedro de Cardona, which
> they greatly praised and said that they had already discussed between
> themselves that it was wrong not to have kept those who truly loved the
> king fully informed about the progress of his illness, but that they had
> to deal with young people. In the end the physicians and we agreed
> that each day they would give us a personal report of the course the
> king's illness was taking.

Salvador de Santa Fe, principal surgeon to the king, must have
been a much younger man than Quintana, for he died only in 1484
still holding the office of *protocirugicus* which he had occupied at
least as early as January 1442.[169]

The Gaspar Pelegri who succeeded Quintana as *protomedicus*,
and with him attended the king in his grave illness in 1444, is an
interesting figure because he had literary as well as medical
pretensions. These led him to write a laudatory history of Alfonso's
conquest of Naples entitled *Historia de actibus regis Alfonsi*, and
probably helped to obtain for him the post of prior of the university of Naples in July 1442.[170] Lorenzo Valla wrote scathingly to
Flavio Biondo about this would-be historian:

> Nam quod ad recentes pertinet Gaspar eius [sc. Alfonsi] medicus
> in commentarios retulit pene res ab illo gestas, sed ea adultatione, et de
> stilo ipso taceam, ne quis prudens scriptor aliquid ad fidem veritatis
> illinc mutuari possit. . . . Tu si voles huius medici scripta cognoscere,
> plusquam te medicum esse oportebit, ut de aegroto corpore historiarum
> tuas historias sanes efficias.[171]

---

[168] ACB Cart. Com., vol. 14, fol. 55, Naples, 9 Apr. 1444. Cf. above, p. 62.

[169] Minieri Riccio, 'Alcuni fatti di Alfonso I', p. 29. In August 1443 as *protocirugicus* he examined Cicco of Sulmona and found him 'licet ydiote et illiterate
tamen in pratica artis cirurgie provido discreto et suficienti' (ACA Reg. 2903.
92^r).

[170] Pelegri was physician to the king in October 1437 (Minieri Riccio, 'Alcuni
fatti di Alfonso I', p. 8). His appointment as prior of the university is in ACA
Reg. 2904. 55^v, 4 July 1442. The manuscript of his History remains unpub-
lished in the Biblioteca Nazionale di Napoli, MS. IX c. 22.

[171] L. Barozzi and R. Sabbadini, *Studi sul Panormita e sul Valla* (Florence,
1891), p. 106.

The other medical personnel of the chamber were Italians and men of some distinction. Alberto Strigio, 'a good doctor . . . and the king's astrologer'[172] who died of plague in 1458, received the exceptionally high salary of 600 ducats.[173] Silvestro Galeota, a man of sounder philosophical talents than Pelegri, began his career as a junior physician in the chamber at a salary of 300 ducats a year and in 1479 became *protomedicus* to Ferdinand.[174] Moyse de Bonavoglia was a 'mestre in medicina de casa del Senyor Rey' in October 1437[175] and still held the post in August 1443.[176]

Those secretarial duties ascribed by the Ordinance of 1344 to the two *escrivans secretaris* of the chamber will be examined elsewhere for their functions had by this time become identified with the administration of the state rather than with the domestic affairs of the household. Nor need attention be given here to such minor chamber offices as seamstress, apothecary, and porter. The office of *reboster major*, however, still had importance because the two holders of it were noblemen close to the king. Their function was to look after the gold and silver vessels used at table and various kinds of provisions—fruit, cheese, torches, candles, sugar, and salt. A master of lodgings (*aposentator mayor*) saw to the accommodation of the king and his household—finding suitable houses and allocating them according to rank—when the court was travelling.[177]

An interesting development had taken place in the status and possibly the functions of a group of chamber attendants known as the *uxers darmes*. According to the Ordinance of 1344 there were to be four of them, soldiers but not knights, to control access to the chamber. By the time of Alfonso the post had been upgraded in dignity so that those appointed to it were almost always knights and many were nobles. As with most of the household offices, Spaniards predominated in the ranks of the *uxers darmes*. Like the gentlemen of the stable and the hunt they were often employed as

---

[172] ACB Cart. Com., vol. 26, fol. 99, Pere Boquet to Barcelona, Naples, 7 June 1458.

[173] ASN Priv. I. 27ᵛ.

[174] C. de Frede, 'Un medico-filosofo del Rinascimento', *ASPN* (1958), 113. Galeota was born *c.* 1420 and died 8 Nov. 1488.

[175] Minieri Riccio, 'Alcuni fatti di Alfonso I', p. 8.

[176] Ibid., p. 242; Faraglia, *Storia della lotta*, p. 129, n. 4.

[177] The *aposentator mayor* in September 1455 was Garcia Betes. With another gentleman of the chamber, Diego de Lison, he delivered some hunting birds to the Kings of Castile and Navarre (ACA Reg. 2661. 102ʳ, 22 Sept. 1455).

envoys and diplomatic agents. Their watch over entrance to the royal presence made their favour worth seeking. Pere Boquet urged his masters in Barcelona to give them some present so that he might find it easier to have audience with the king.[178] The safety of the king's person was the responsibility of eight *porters de massa*, but he took no excessive precautions and would on occasion go about unaccompanied by armed guards.[179]

To complete this survey of the chamber it remains to consider the *algutzirs*, the constables who, with the assistance of a judge, exercised petty civil and criminal jurisdiction over all members of the household, kept the king's prison and sometimes made arrests on the order of the king or his council. Four of them are known by name: Jacme de Vilanova,[180] Johan de Perpenya,[181] Huguet de Maiorca,[182] and Pedro Gonula alias Amer.[183] All were knights as required by the Ordinance.

Most of those functions associated with the office of chancellor had shed their domestic character and cannot appropriately be considered in the context of the household. The important exceptions were the offices pertaining to the royal chapel and the king's spiritual advisers. Alfonso, who attached much weight to religious observances and ceremonial, paid correspondingly great attention to this department of his household, and those attached to it wielded much influence with him. At the same time he was in no sense priest-ridden; no prelate or churchman was ever permitted to forget his temporal subordination to royal majesty. He may never have said, 'Li preti sono homini da bastonate et non da preghiere', but these words attributed to him by contemporaries fairly represent his attitude.[184]

---

[178] Madurell Marimón, *Mensajeros barceloneses*, p. 535, 31 Oct. 1456: '... per haver millor e pus prompta entrada en la cambra'.

[179] Beccadelli, *De dictis et factis*, ii: 'Alphonsum nonnunquam solum absque comitantium pompa incedentem vidimus. Cum ob hoc a plerisque argueretur, suadereturque ut more aliorum principum et ipse armatorum manu stipatus graderetur, exhorruisse consilium visus est atque dixisse, se quidem minime solum, ut isti crederent, sed innocentia associatum vadere, neque esse quod benevolentia curium fretus, quippiam extimescat.'

[180] 'algutzir del Senyor Rey' in April 1439 (Faraglia, *Storia della lotta*, p. 164, n. 1).   [181] Ibid., p. 261, n. 1 (December 1441).

[182] ACA Reg. 2902, 22 Mar. 1443. Huguet is ordered to reinstate Giovanella di Gesualdo in possession of a fief.

[183] ASN Priv. I. 150ʳ, 15 May 1454, Privilege appointing Gonula governor of the prison of the Vicaria.

[184] Ametller y Vinyas, *Alfonso V de Aragón*, ii. 595.

His regular confessor throughout his reign in Naples was a Dominican named Juan Garcia. Though little is known about the relationship between the two, its long continuance suggests that Alfonso found Garcia a satisfactory confessor. Garcia received substantial rewards—the bishopric of Ales in 1439,[185] Syracuse in 1444, and that of Mallorca in 1446. We catch occasional glimpses of him going about his duties: an embassy to Eugenius IV in October 1436 when relations between the king and pontiff were extremely uneasy,[186] and a request that the pope should grant him authority to pronounce absolution on the king in case of illness.[187] Another confessor, Felip Faiadell O.P., once a monk in the monastery of S. Caterina in Barcelona, became Bishop of Gaeta in 1444.[188] Miguel de Epila enjoyed a considerable reputation as a theologian and preacher. He came to Naples from a Dominican convent in Zaragoza and won favour as a confessor to the king, but he refused the bishopric of Urgell when Alfonso had put pressure on Calixtus III to offer it to him.[189]

A good deal more is known about another confessor named Ferrando who, according to Vespasiano da Bisticci, had great influence with the king.[190] The cleric in question must have been Juan Ferrando of Cordoba who arrived in Naples in the summer

[185] C. Eubel, *Hierarchia Catholica medii aevi*, ii (Munster, 1913).

[186] Ametller y Vinyas, *Alfonso V de Aragón*, ii. 59; Faraglia, *Storia della lotta*, p. 80.

[187] ACA Reg. 2698. 43ᵛ, 26 Mar. 1444.

[188] ACA Reg. 2795. 3ʳ, Castelnuovo, 8 Oct. 1444, to the prior and brethren of the monastery asking them to let Faiadell have the property he had left there. He was 'confessor del Senyor Rey' in 1441 (Faraglia, *Storia della lotta*, p. 257, n. 1).

[189] He preached before the king at Torre del Greco in October 1451 (ACB Cart. Com., vol. 21, fol. 195, Anthoni Vinyes to Barcelona, Naples, 7 Oct. 1451). He was given an annual provision as a confessor in Aug. 1453 (Minieri Riccio, 'Alcuni fatti di Alfonso I', p. 423). For the bishopric of Urgell see ACA Reg. 2661. 148ᵛ, 25 Apr. 1457, Letter from Alfonso to Calixtus acknowledging receipt of the brief for Epila's appointment to the see. ACB Cart. Com., vol. 27, fol. 325, Pere Boquet to Barcelona, Naples, 22 Nov. 1457: '. . . es mort açi mestre epila qui avia esser bisbe de urgell'; Ametller y Vinyas, *Alfonso V de Aragón*, iii. 420–1.

[190] 'Vita del Re Alfonso', p. 398: '. . . uomo maraviglioso, e di santità di vita, e grandissimo teologo e filosofo. Questo fu di tanta santità di vita, che il Re, per la reverenza aveva in lui, non solo l'aveva in grandissima riputazione, ma egli lo temeva: perchè, quand'egli udiva cosa alcuna che Sua Maestà avessi fatto, che non fussi giusta e onesta, egli lo riprendeva . . .' Bisticci met Ferrando in Florence shortly after the king's death and describes him thus: 'Era uomo d'anni quaranta, grande di persona, magro, smunto, grave nel parlare, alieno a dissimulazioni e finzioni. Di sè stesso non diceva nulla, nè si laudava nè jattava, come fanno molti' (ibid., p. 414).

of 1444 on a mission from the King of Castile.[191] His extraordinary memory, wide learning, and knowledge of oriental languages roused the enthusiasm of Lorenzo Valla, though the humanist recommended that the newcomer be given a little polishing 'sub optime praeceptore'. Alfonso too was much impressed and took Ferrando into his household with the handsome salary of 600 ducats a year.[192] After broadening his experience with further travels in France and Germany, Ferrando found himself employed as an agent in the king's ecclesiastical diplomacy.[193] By July 1452 Alfonso was asking that he be given a cardinal's hat,

'no obstant que forse lo dit mestre ferrando no fos per natura o facultats de bens temporals de axi gran o egual conditio, car sens negun dubte sa santedat pot haver sperança que les obres de aquest seran axi nobles et virtuoses que no solament se egualaran mas forse sobraran les de alguns altres et suppliran encare les condicions de natura que en la origine sua fossen stades menys . . .'[194]

It was Ferrando, if Bisticci's account is correct, who broke the news to Alfonso that his doctors gave him no more than three or four weeks to live and who helped the king prepare for death.[195] Among the witnesses to the king's will he appears as the archbishop elect of Naples and *professor in sacra pagina* (a title probably conferred in respect of his teaching in the university of Naples), but neither here nor in the other documents that mention him does he figure as a confessor. Possibly Bisticci was misinformed in this respect.

The office of senior chaplain to the king (*cappellanus mayor*) belonged by tradition in Aragon to the abbot of Santa Creus. When Alfonso left Spain the abbot appointed Domenic Exarch, a monk of that Cistercian monastery, to accompany him as *locumtenens* of the chaplain.[196] By January 1441 Exarch had become *sots*

[191] A. Morel-Fatio, 'Fernand de Cordoue', in *Recueil de travaux à J. Havet* (Paris, 1895).

[192] Minieri Riccio, 'Alcuni fatti di Alfonso I', p. 245.

[193] ACA Reg. 2939. 130ᵛ, Torre del Greco, 25 July 1451, Instructions for the 'venerable mestre Joan Ferrando doctor en sacra theologia' as ambassador to Nicholas V; Reg. 2661. 35ᵛ, 12 Oct. 1453, refers to another mission to Rome undertaken by Ferrando.

[194] ACA Reg. 2939. 150ᵛ, Castelnuovo, 28 July 1452.

[195] 'Vita del Re Alfonso', p. 409.

[196] He appears in this capacity in May 1439 (Minieri Riccio, 'Alcuni fatti di Alfonso I', p. 21).

capella maior,[197] and by the end of the year *capella maior*.[198] Since it does not appear that he ever became abbot of Santa Creus, the king had by this appointment broken with the Aragonese custom. A few days after the fall of Naples he was given two of the four chaplaincies attached to the royal chapel of San Ludovico in the cathedral with the duty of arranging masses for past kings.[199] Three years later he became master of the royal chapel with responsibility for the discipline and education of the scholars attached to it.[200] Boys chosen for their voices came from all parts of the king's dominions to make the royal choir one of the finest of its day. Exarch lived in Santa Maria Incoronata, a church hard by Castelnuovo. When the monks of San Martino, to whom the church belonged, challenged his right to be there, Alfonso asked them not to disturb his chaplain because he found it very convenient to have him close at hand.[201] His preferment in the church entailed the usual tussle with the papacy,[202] but he finally achieved his bishopric, Agrigento, in 1451.[203]

When he separated the office of senior chaplain from the abbacy of Santa Creus, Alfonso appears to have treated it like the majority of household offices in that it was given to more than one person. Thus we find another Cistercian, Jaume Albarells, accompanying the king as *cappellanus mayor* on the Tuscan campaign of 1447-8, and conducting a visitation of royal churches and chapels in Calabria in 1451.[204] Exarch, however, remained the senior of the two,[205]

[197] Mazzoleni, *Fonti aragonesi*, i. 131.

[198] He is given this designation in a document dated November 1441, cited by Faraglia, *Storia della lotta*, p. 255, n. 1.

[199] He resigned these chaplaincies in 1447 in favour of a scholar of the chapel (ACA Reg. 2913. 62ᵛ, 6 Jan. 1447).

[200] Chioccarello, *Archivio*, p. 15, Privilege of appointment dated 19 June 1445. The name is wrongly transcribed as 'Fra Domenico de Tarquis'.

[201] Mazzoleni, *Il Codice Chigi*, pp. 331-2, Letter from the king to the prior of San Martino, Pozzuoli, 5 June 1452: 'nocte e iorno quando lo havimo mesteri subito lo havimo.'

[202] In 1444 Alfonso was asking that he be appointed almoner of the monastery of Ripoll *in commendam* (ACA Reg. 2698. 43ᵛ, 26 Mar. 1444). In the following year he had to exercise his *juspatronatum* to give Exarch an abbacy which Eugenius IV had refused (ACA Reg. 2690. 144ᵛ, 4 Apr. 1445).

[203] J. Vicens Vives, *Fernando el Catolico* (Madrid, 1952), p. 114, n. 121. Exarch remained Bishop of Agrigento until his death in 1471.

[204] He was with the king at Tivoli in June 1447 (ACA Reg. 2912. 81ᵛ, 7 June 1447). For his Calabrian visitation see P. Gentile, 'Lo stato napoletano sotto Alfonso I d'Aragona', *ASPN* (1937), 44, n. 3.

[205] In November 1455 and May 1457 Fr. Martin Cortes acted for him as *locumtenens* (Minieri Riccio, 'Alcuni fatti di Alfonso I', pp. 439 and 456).

and he it was who countersigned the great majority of privileges issued for the appointment of royal chaplains.[206]

Two of the royal chaplains performed the duties of almoners. The senior took charge of moneys destined for alms while the junior kept account of them. Both saw to the distribution among the poor of food left over from the tables of the dining hall and assisted the king in the ceremony of washing the feet of the poor on Maundy Thursday.[207] In the chapel they alternated in saying mass before the king and assisted with the other services. A Cistercian, Bernat Serra, was chief almoner in the earlier years of the reign. A friend of Valla, he had been sent by Alfonso to attend the Council of Basle in 1433 and died of plague in that city when he returned for another session in 1439.[208] He was succeeded by another Cistercian, the abbot of Poblet, who remained in his monastery and sent two of his monks to perform the duties of his office in the Neapolitan court.

Those who served in the household enjoyed the prized status of familiars which entitled them to food and lodging for themselves and any approved servants and animals, gave them the right to carry arms anywhere in the kingdom and exempted them from the jurisdiction of all tribunals save that of the court itself. Such privileges and the prestige of association with the household being highly valued, Alfonso was able to make lavish use of the *carta familiaritatis* to confer honorary membership of the household as a relatively inexpensive reward for services. The registers of privileges contain a multitude of these letters all couched in the following form:

Pateat quod illos in familiares nostros libenter accipimus et consortio nostrorum domesticorum familiarium agregamus quorum nobis fidei est note sinceritas quosque serviciorum grata prestacio virtus et probitas nostro conspectu representat. Sane ad quorundam familiarium et domesticorum nostrorum humiles intercessus necnon attendentes probitas et multipliciter virtutum dona Anthonii del oliver patris pauli del

---

[206] One of the earliest is dated Castel Capuano, 14 May 1443 (ACA Reg. 2903. 81ᵛ).

[207] Beccadelli, *De dictis et factis*, iv.

[208] Aeneas Sylvius gave this sketch of Serra: '. . . ut est consilio calidus, nequaquam directe ad conclusiones disputabat, sed furtim quaedam argumenta collegerat, quibus nunc hic, nunc illic praestaret impedimentum.' Cf. F. Marletta, 'Un uomo di stato', *Archivio storico per la Sicilia*, i (1937), 54. In 1436 Alfonso sent him to remonstrate with Eugenius IV (Faraglia, *Storia della lotta*, p. 62).

oliver filioli del oliver Nufrii del oliver et yiminii del oliver filiorum dicti Anthonii grataque accepta servicia per dictum Anthonium patrem nobis prestita et impensa queque prestare non cessat et infuturum tam patrem quam filios prestituros speramus dante domino meliora patrem et filios in familiares nostros domesticos et de nostra hospicio ex nunch in antea donech vixerint de certa nostra scientia tenore presentium recipimus. . . .[209]

Subjects of other princes sometimes received this honour. Honorary chaplaincies performed a similar function in attaching favoured clerics to the royal chapel. Unfortunately many of those thus distinguished did not display the *virtus* and *probitas* trumpeted in their diplomas, but used their privileges, especially the judicial ones, to evade civic obligations and oppress fellow-townsmen. Their excesses called forth protests from the afflicted communities, and remedies and rebukes from the king[210] as a result of which the immunities of familiars were in some places curtailed.[211]

Particulars of the resident members of the household, their salaries and allowances, were kept by a clerk 'skilled in accounts' known as the *escriva de racio* and his staff. It was also his business to see to the correct order of seating in the dining hall—apart from the king's table where the *mayordomen* regulated the seating—and keep out unauthorized persons. Three times a year he issued warrants for payment of salary to the domestics on his books, and once a year he gave them their clothing warrants. Another important function of his office related to the payment of troops in the king's service: the *escriva* received the muster rolls showing men, horses, and arms, and on that basis issued monthly payment warrants which the treasurer cashed.[212] By the fifteenth century

---

[209] ACA Reg. 2902. 69ʳ, near Tocco, 30 Aug. 1442.

[210] e.g. in a privilege directed against familiars who had been causing trouble in Amatrice: '. . . debeat omnes comprehendere divi non jure atque humano sit quodammodo in his familiaribus parcialis, quoniam si aliquem offendunt aut cuipiam debitores sunt non possunt coram his judicibus conveniri coram quibus ipsi alios conveniunt causa eadem concessimus namque ipsis familiaritatis indulta non ut aliis nocerent sed ut sibi ipsis aliter faverent absque aliorum jactura et dampno patrie sue . . .' (ACA Reg. 2912. 51ᵛ, 19 June 1447).

[211] e.g. the privilege for Atri (ACA Reg. 2912. 36ᵛ, 18 June 1447), subjecting familiars to the jurisdiction of the city courts, 'praeterque de familiaribus continue eius curiam serviciumque personale sequentibus'. Cf. order to Francesc Monlober, captain of Lucera, to give judgement in a dispute between Menelao de Mobilia and the *familiaris* Ventura de Raffino following a petition in which Menelao had pleaded the difficulty which he faced in taking the case before the seneschal (Mazzoleni, *Il Codice Chigi*, pp. 272–3, 21 Mar. 1452).

[212] e.g. Faraglia, *Storia della lotta*, p. 236, n. 2, cites an item from 'Cedole' 4,

this extra-curial activity of the *escriva de racio* had grown to a point where it overshadowed his household duties, thanks to the growth of armies and the control he exercised over related business of war, such as the provisioning of naval expeditions and building of fortifications. The personnel of the office appears to have been almost entirely Catalan and Valencian.[213] Antoni Olzina was the *escriva de racio* in the earlier part of the reign; Joan Dasin, at one time his deputy, followed him in the office.[214]

There exists no comprehensive description of the everyday working of this Aragonese court transplanted to Naples. Writing of that kind did not appeal to the taste of its many men of letters who preferred to depict their surroundings according to the current literary fashions. Beccadelli's *De dictis et factis Alphonsi regis* is full of anecdotes and observations which offer vivid glimpses of the king and his courtiers in their daily routine.[215] In his commentary on Beccadelli's work, Aeneas Sylvius drew on his experiences at the Neapolitan court to cap some of the stories: the king's pleasure when Joan Soler, a canon of Llerida, brought to him in Castelnuovo letters from two boys whom he had sent to study in Paris;[216] a conversation between Alfonso and an old, blind man during the Maundy ceremony;[217] Alfonso's delight when a coin of Nero was found at Pozzuoli.[218] This entertaining courtier's chatter is supplemented in the writings of the humanists by full-scale descriptions

fol. 188, for December 1441. 'Item doni an Jacopo Carbone senyor dela Padula hom darmes del Senyor Rey los quals li accorregui en la ciutat de gayeta ab albara de scriva de racio scrit en lo camp real dela Torre del grech a xxviii dies del present mes de dehembre en accorriment del sou e a compliment de la emprestancia de L lances etc. 440 ducats.'

[213] Up to sixteen clerks were employed in this office (Gentile, 'Lo stato napoletano', p. 26). Among them were Barthomeu Baruta, Nicolau Brusca, Innocente Cubells, Franci Desperers, Joan Quintana, Arnau Castell, Bernat Lopez, and a solitary Italian, Lorenzo Belluga, who was sent to pay the royal forces in the March of Ancona in November 1446 (Minieri Riccio, 'Alcuni fatti di Alfonso I', p. 251).

[214] 'Antonius Olzina miles scriba porcionis domus regie': thus Olzina styled himself in a receipt given on 17 Feb. 1449 (C. Salvati, *Fonti aragonesi*, iv (Naples, 1964), 107). Dasin was *locumtenens* of Olzina in October 1448 (ACA Reg. 2699. 141ᵛ) and had taken over the substantive office by January 1452 (ACA Reg. 2659. 56ʳ). An earlier deputy was Ramon Vidal who died in the summer of 1446 (ACA Reg. 2699. 44ʳ).

[215] G. Resta says of this work, '. . . è certo tuttavia che la figura di Alfonso, quale egli la presenta, spoglia di tutti i motivi cortigianeschi e laudatori, non è molto lontano dalla realtà, soprattutto in alcuni atteggiamenti che più colpirono i contemporanei' (*L'epistolario del Panormita* (Messina, 1954), p. 128).

[216] *Commentarius*, ii. 52.   [217] Ibid. iv. 1.   [218] Ibid. ii. 12.

of the most spectacular events of the reign, notably the triumphal entry of 1442 and the imperial visit a decade later. We have also the letters of visitors which occasionally let fall some light on the life of the court. Among the most useful of these is the correspondence of envoys sent at fairly regular intervals to the king by the city of Barcelona and the Cortes of Catalonia.[219] Frequent reference has already been made to their letters as a source of information about the household and its practices. Two further extracts from them will help to bring the picture to life.

In a letter written on 29 April 1444 two envoys of Barcelona describe an audience with the king:

That day we went quite early in the morning to Castelnuovo and when we arrived found that he was still at prayers. He heard mass—the first mass he had heard outside the chamber since his illness—and as soon as the mass was finished, he stood talking for a short time with two messengers who have come here from our Holy Father. Then, leading the way, he told us we should follow him and took us to a small room. He wished no one to remain there and made everyone go outside apart from Don Ferrando whom he had stay by a window quite far from us. The king sat in a chair which had been prepared for him and asked us to sit on a bench with a tapestry cover which stood in front of his chair. Then we began to explain our mission.[220]

A delegation from the estates of Catalonia sent home the following account of the reception accorded to Galceran de Requesens, governor of that principality:

The king gave him a great welcome and entertained him grandly. Indeed he did him a most singular honour such as we have not seen shown to any duke, count, baron or any other man since we have been here, for he has given a banquet solely for his sake in the Castel dell'Ovo. There he feasted and entertained him the whole day showing such

[219] See Madurell Marimòn, *Mensajeros barceloneses*.

[220] ACB Cart. Com., vol. 14, fol. 64. 'Nosaltres la dita jornada fom assats gran mati al castell nou e trobam lo que encare dehie ores com nosaltres hi fem, e hoyiu la sua missa lo qual era la primera missa que havie hoyda fore la cambra despuys que havie hagut lo mal, e de continent que fou dita lo dit senyor parla de peus e fort breu ab dos missatgers que hic son venguts de nostre sant pare. E apres metent se primer dix a nosaltres quel seguissem, e mes nos dins un petit retret en lo qual no volch negu hi aturas ans feu tot hom exir deffora sino don fferrando que feu star en una finestre assats luny de nosaltres. E lo dit senyor se segue en una cadera que li havien apparalleda, e volch que nosaltres nos assiguessem en un banch que stave al devant dela sua cadera cubert ab un bancal de ras. E llavors nosaltres . . . li començam explicar.'

pleasure that he might have been a kinsman. He had him sit at his table which up to now we have not seen done for anyone other than ambassadors of kings and the states of Italy; we have seen these invited to dinner occasionally (but never to supper) and sitting at his table, but other dukes, princes, counts and barons we have not seen sitting at the king's table. For love of him [i.e. Requesens] he invited the Master of Muntesa and Mossen Pere Vaca to keep them company. They were seated in this manner: the king at the head of the table, next to him Don Ferrando, next the Master of Muntesa, after him the governor Mossen Requesens and then Mossen P. Vaca. When they had dined the entertainment of the governor continued in a private room until supper, and so the festivities lasted until late at night.[221]

Accounts like this from the awestruck outsider often tell more than the consciously literary productions which are all that survive from within, but the former are unfortunately few in number.

[221] ACB Cart. Com., vol. 25, fol. 85, 25 Aug. 1455: 'Lo Senyor Rey la rebut molt be e ab gran cara e li fa gran festa, och li ha feta una singularissima honor tal que encara despuys que hich som no haviem vist lage feta a duch ni baro ni a home que hich sia stat, car hali fet un convit sol per amor de ell al castell del ou, e aqui la convidat a dinar e sopar e afastagar lo tot la jorn mostrant li tanta cara com a una persona conjuncta sen pot mostrar; och la fet seure en sa taula que fins açi no havem vist lo hage fet de negu si donchs embaxadors de Reys, o de aquestes comunitats de Italia no eran, aquells havem vist ha convidats alscunes vegades a dinar pero, mas no a sopar e seyen en sa taula mas altres duchs princeps comptes e barons nols havem vista seure en sa taula si bells ha convidats per amor de ell convida la mestre de muntesa e mossen. P. Vacha per fer li companyia; seyen axi lo Senyor Rey al cap dela taula, apres don fferrando apres lo mestre de muntesa, apres lo Governador mossen. Requesens e apres lo dit mossen. P. Vacha; e apres com foren dinats en lo retret tostemps festege lo dit Governador fins a sopar e axil tench festegant fins fou gran nit.'

IV

COUNCILS AND PARLIAMENTS

BOTH the Crown of Aragon and the kingdom of Naples had developed well-defined institutions through which the monarch could communicate with, and seek the advice of, his principal subjects. That they differed did not raise difficulties so far as the representative councils, Cortes, and parliaments were concerned, for these continued to function independently of each other and according to established practice. With the smaller, permanent council, however, whose function it was to be in attendance on the king, the acquisition of Naples aggravated a problem which had already caused some difficulty in the heterogeneous Aragonese state. In essence the difficulty was one of reconciling the king's free choice of his counsellors with the requirements of the laws and the interests of the different states over which he ruled. Various compromises had been tried; Peter IV of Aragon, for example, had promised in 1348 to maintain in his court four salaried counsellors learned in the laws and customs of Aragon, so that during his inevitable absences from the kingdom he should always have adequate counsel available when dealing with matters affecting it.[1] Alfonso found a partial answer by appointing members of his family to perform the functions of *locumtenens generalis* in the major states and attaching the appropriate council to them.[2] Later Spanish rulers overcame the difficulty by instituting a number of territorial councils at the centre of government.

The very fact that the problem had arisen in Aragon well before Alfonso transferred the seat of his government to Italy enabled him to meet it without any sudden and dramatic change in the structure and workings of his council. Instead he was able to get along for some years with a council of the customary kind and make his innovations at leisure. He was helped by the fact that in

[1] *Fueros y observancias del reyno de Aragon* (Zaragoza?, 1667), fol. 14.
[2] A. F. C. Ryder, 'The evolution of imperial government in Naples under Alfonso V of Aragon', *Europe in the Late Middle Ages*, ed. J. Highfield, J. Hale, B. Smalley (London, 1965).

his new kingdom the royal council had already become a flexible instrument in the ruler's hand. Its *ex officio* members, the seven Great Officers or collateral counsellors, had accepted an arrangement which gave them the dignity and salary of office while the king assigned all but the ceremonial duties to lesser functionaries.[3] Their attendance at councils became limited to the most formal occasions. Thus Alfonso inherited a situation in which he was able for most purposes to discount the collateral counsellors of Naples and choose his advisers at will without offending Neapolitan custom.

The body of titular counsellors was a large one. It included all those who held the title *ex officio* in the various states of the Crown of Aragon as well as numerous subjects and foreigners who received it as a mark of favour. For most of them it represented, like the title *familiaris*,[4] no more than a token of distinction. This must have been true, for example, of Martial Auribelli of Avignon, 'Ordinis Predicatorum, sacre pagine eximius professor, eiusdem Ordinis General', who became both *consiliarius* and *familiaris*,[5] and of the cardinal Lorenzo Colonna, a still more exalted *consiliarius*.[6] When, however, the title was bestowed on Tommaso Bibrio Cipriano, doctor of arts and medicine, in the same privilege that appointed him a personal physician to the king, it assumes significance as an adjunct to the new physician's professional standing in the household.[7] Yet it is most unlikely that Tommaso often, or indeed ever, attended a formal council. Moreover while many styled counsellors did not attend councils, some who had no such title did attend. For example, when Alfonso summoned a council on 25 August 1455 to decide whether he should undertake a crusade, the representative of Barcelona, who happened to be in Naples, was invited to be present though he was not a counsellor. Thus Alfonso had at his disposal a large body of potential advisers—nobles, soldiers, clerics, merchants, lawyers, administrators, men from all parts of the Aragonese empire and beyond, whom he could assemble in great and small councils as occasion demanded.

    [3] Cf. above, pp. 13 and 57.
    [4] Cf. above, p. 86.
    [5] ASN Priv. I. 157ʳ, 29 June 1454.
    [6] Mazzoleni, *Il Codice Chigi*, p. 209, 8 Jan. 1452. An order to the customs officials of the frontier refers to him as 'dilecto consiliario nostro'.
    [7] ACA Reg. 2908. 78ʳ, 20 Oct. 1445.

The greater council, opened to all counsellors who chanced to be at court and others specially invited, was a ceremonial body gathered for such occasions as the reception of ambassadors and major public acts when Alfonso liked to muster as large a number as possible. The envoys of Barcelona have left the following description of their audience before such an assembly:

After dinner on Saturday the 18th of the present month [sc. July 1450] we went to Castelnuovo to explain our embassy. The king gave us audience in his upper chamber, called the Glorietta, where was gathered his Council consisting of many counts, barons, knights and other important persons. We had received notice from the king that he would like us to explain our mission before his council. Therefore, before the king and in the presence of his council, we explained two matters only: first, that we had come to visit his high and royal majesty; secondly, that it might please his Highness to visit his kingdoms and lands in those parts from which his Majesty had been absent for more than eighteen years. And the king replied . . . We kissed his hand and wished to kiss his foot, but his Majesty would not permit it. Then we begged that his Majesty would grant us audience to explain the other matters for which we were sent before his Majesty alone.[8]

Another council of this magnitude met on 10 September 1450 to be told officially of the king's decision to visit Sicily, and to listen to 'certain considerations on which he asked for our advice' ('certs motius sobre los quals demana que lui consellavem'). Barons and knights from several kingdoms, as well as envoys from Catalonia and Barcelona, attended.[9] When he wished to sound opinion on the question of adhering to the Peace of Lodi, Alfonso summoned 'all members of the council and a great part of the

[8] ACB Cart. Com., vol. 20, fol. 168, Naples, 22 July 1450: 'Dissapte depus dinar que comptavem xviii del dit mes, nosaltres anam al dit Senyor al Castell nou per explicar la dita nostra ambaxada. E lo dit Senyor donans audiencia en la sua cambra dalt appellada Glorieta, a on era ajustat son consell de molts Comtes, Barons, Cavallers, e altre notable gent. E haviem hagut algun sentiment del dit Senyor Rey que trobaria pler nosaltres explicassem devant son Consell. E pertant nos devant lo dit Senyor e en presencia del dit consell explicam solament dues coses, la una com erem venguts per visitar la sua alta e reyal maiestat, la segona que fos plasent a sa excellent senyoria anar visitar sos Regnes, e terres de aquexes parts, dels quals la sua maiestat es absent mes ha de xviii anys. E lo dit Senyor respos . . . li besam la ma, e li volguem besar lo peu, sino que la sua maiestat non sofferi. Supplicam lo mesavant que deles altres coses per les quals erem tramesos a sa gran senyoria nos volgues donar audiencia en explicar aquelles devant la sua maiestat tant solament.'

[9] Ibid., fol. 213, Naples, 12 Sept. 1450.

barons of this kingdom to deliberate on this matter of the peace'
at Pozzuoli on 10 May 1454.[10] The advice the king received in
these grand councils was, it is clear, no more than general assent
to decisions reached previously by a small, inner council. Galceran
de Requesens, the *batle general* of Catalonia, gives a good example
of the relationship between the two categories of council in a letter
to the city of Barcelona in which he describes the deliberations on
the crusade.[11] Alfonso had first put his proposal to take the Cross
before a council held on 25 August 1455; on that occasion, wrote
Requesens, 'there were present no more than twelve barons and
counts', including the *batle general* himself. On the following day
there gathered in the king's chamber[12] an afforced council of 'all
the barons, knights and men of importance' ('tots los barons
cavallers e homens de stat') to hear an address in which Alfonso
told them he had decided to take the Cross and lead an expedition
against the Turks. Afterwards he asked for their advice and all
enthusiastically supported the proposal.[13]

Requesens did not reveal the identity of the dozen nobles who
comprised the smaller council on this occasion, but the fact that
they were all nobles highlights the largely political nature of the
issue brought before them. Alfonso's crusading proposals were in
truth a propaganda exercise designed to convince the new pope
Calixtus III that his erstwhile master was in earnest and to obtain
from Rome a crusading tithe.[14] For such a purpose a council composed of feudatories was entirely appropriate because, while striking the proper martial note, it could confine itself to generalities.

Other kinds of business required other forms of council. Fierce
dissension in Barcelona between the popular party, the 'Busca',
and the aristocratic party, the 'Biga',[15] led the former to send an
unofficial embassy to Naples in 1451 to present a petition for
a reform of the city government. To consider the petition the king
called a council composed of the Bishop of Urgell, chancellor of

10 ACB Cart. Com., vol. 24, fol. 64, Miquel de Manresa to Barcelona, Naples,
9 May 1454: 'tots los de son consell, e huna gran part dels barons de aquest
realme per fer desliberacio sobre lo fet dela pau.'
11 ACB Cart. Com., vol. 25, fol. 86, 26 Aug. 1455.
12 Alfonso was convalescing from a fever.
13 '. . . e daço volie lur consell; tots o an consellat ab una gran voluntat.'
14 Calixtus issued a bull granting the king a crusading tithe from all ecclesiastical revenues in his dominions on 11 Sept. 1455. Cf. above, p. 39.
15 Cf. above, p. 30.

Aragon and president of the council, Pere de Besalu the *conservator generalis*,[16] Galceran de Requesens, Rodrigo Falco a jurist, and Valenti Claver the vice-chancellor. Arnau Fonolleda, the protonotary of Aragon, and the secretary Joan Olzina were both excluded, presumably because they were known to be sympathetic to the 'Biga' party and friends of the envoy of that party who was then in Naples.[17] Fonolleda was however admitted to a council meeting held the following month to discuss a dispute between the crown and the city of Barcelona. The emissary of the 'Biga' sent the following report of the meeting for which the counsellors had been summoned to Capua where the king was hunting:

The Sunday before Christmas while Mossen. Requesens and I were in the king's chamber after dinner, the council assembled. After a time we were told on the part of the king that those who were not of the council should leave, and so Mossen. Requesens, myself and others left. Soon afterwards I learned that the king was closeted with the vice-chancellor, the protonotary, the *conservator*, master Rodrigo Falco and master Cola Anthoni.[18] In that Council was brought forward the business of Molindereig in the absence of Mossen. Requesens and myself. I have learned that the vice-chancellor began with a report hostile to the city; the king supported him, and so did master Falco who spoke in favour of Mossen. Galceran although the king allowed him to say only a few words. In spite of all this, master Cola Anthoni, the advocate of the patrimony, spoke with the king's permission and was of the contrary opinion to all the others. None the less the king stuck to his opinion.[19]

[16] Cf. below, pp. 205 ff.
[17] ACB Cart. Com., vol. 21, fol. 214, Anthoni Vinyes to Barcelona, Naples, 8 Nov. 1451.
[18] Nicola Antonio de' Monti.
[19] ACB Cart. Com., vol. 22, fol. 4, Naples, 12 Jan. 1452: 'Lo Diumenge ans de Nadal al depus dinar stant moss. Requesens e jo dins lo retret del Senyor Rey se ajusta lo Consell. E a cap de poch digueren de part del dit Senyor que qui no era de Consell hisques deffora. E axi lo dit moss. Requesens e jo ab daltres hisquem defora. Apres de continent sebi que lo dit Senyor stave apartat ab lo vicicanceller, prothonotari, Conservador, micer Rodrigo Falco e micer Cola Anthoni. En lo qual Consell fonch proposat, absents lo dit moss. Requesens e jo, lo fet de Molindereig. He sabut que lo vicicanceller comença a fer la relacio contra la ciutat, e lo dit Senyor de continent se adona a ell, e successive per semblant de micer falco, que lo dit Senyor apenes lo jaqui parlar sino molt poch, que de continent parlave en favor del dit moss. Galceran. Pero en tot axo ab bona licencia del dit Senyor micer Cola Anthoni advocat del Patrimoni del Senyor Rey perla, e fonch de contraria oppinio de tots los altres. Mes en tot axo lo dit Senyor stech en sa oppinio.'

On 19 December 1447 the council considered petitions from Majorca, Minorca, and Sardinia asking that the governors of those islands be suspended during an inquiry into their conduct in office.[20] The names of the counsellors present on this occasion are not recorded. When in 1451 Vinyes, the agent of the 'Biga' municipality of Barcelona, sought to have a commissioner appointed to inquire into the conduct of Galceran de Requesens as governor of Catalonia,[21] the king after much hesitation said he would refer the matter to Falco and Claver, and that it should then go to the council which he would personally attend 'both for the sake of justice and for his own interest' ('axi per la justicia com per son interes').[22] A great variety and volume of business was transacted in restricted *ad hoc* councils of this kind. The terms granted by the Prince of Taranto to the city of Barletta on its surrender were considered and confirmed 'dicti nostri consilii deliberacione matura' in September 1436;[23] an edict against the Florentines resulted 'ex deliberacione consilii' at the camp in Porto Barato on 17 December 1447;[24] in August 1454 it deliberated on the seizure of French ships around Minorca and subsequent French reprisals against the cattle and goods of the king's subjects.[25] Often proceedings were brief because most issues were initially referred for consideration to one or two or more counsellors, usually lawyers, who prepared a brief and sometimes a recommendation for the larger body. The dispute over Molindereig mentioned above, for example, was referred to Claver, Falco, de Besalu, and de' Monti.[26] The council could, if so instructed, meet and reach a decision without the king being present; the president would then take the decision to the king as a recommendation for his approval.

Subject to the principle that the king might summon whom he pleased to his council, official usage recognized the existence of a body of regular counsellors who were required to be constantly at hand and from among whom the council would normally be

---

[20] ACA Reg. 2656. 89ᵛ.
[21] Madurell Marimón, *Mensajeros barceloneses*, p. 382. There was much enmity between the 'Biga' of Barcelona and Requesens.
[22] Ibid.   [23] Rogadeo, *Codice diplomatico*, p. 19.
[24] ACA Reg. 2656. 87ʳ.
[25] ACA Reg. 2661. 72ʳ, Castelnuovo, 29 Aug. 1454, Instruction to the King of Navarre to give effect to the council's decision.
[26] Madurell Marimón, *Mensajeros barceloneses*, p. 399.

formed. The earliest indication we have of the composition of this body is the list noted down by Borso d'Este during his visit to Naples in April 1444.[27] He names seventeen 'permanent' members and seven others who might be summoned if the king wished.[28] This was not, as will be seen, a very meaningful distinction.

Alfonso Borja, Bishop of Valencia, was effective president of the council at the time of Borso's visit, though he was very soon to relinquish the post and move as cardinal to Rome.[29] Neapolitan practice gave precedence in the council to the protonotary, but the prerogatives of that Great Officer had fallen into such desuetude that Alfonso had no difficulty in overlooking them, except on certain public ceremonial occasions when it became politic to flatter Neapolitan feelings. Thus on 12 July 1450 the Count of Fondi as protonotary and head of the council led the procession which gave a triumphal welcome to the king's admiral Vilamari returning to Naples from a cruise in the eastern Mediterranean.[30] Three days later he received the king on his entry into the capital.[31] For other purposes Alfonso appears to have followed the custom of Aragon where proceedings in the council were directed by an archbishop or bishop who held the office of chancellor.[32] The presidents of his council, though not chancellors, were all distinguished clerics; the Archbishop of Naples followed the Bishop of Valencia, and on his death was succeeded by the Bishop of

[27] Foucard, 'Descrizione della citta di Napoli', pp. 756–7.

[28] Ibid.: 'La Maiestà del Rè congrega nel suo Conselyo queste infrascritte persone, quando che vuole far provixiione per suo stato e provixione da fare per lo suo Conselyo. Primo Monsegnor de Valenza, episcopo e capo del Conselyo. Item quelli sethe officialli delo Reame, che hanno quilli sethe officii predicti e sono prenominati ali soy officii. Item messer Anchorilya. Item lo Regente dela vicharia, che è messer Zuam de sam Soverim. Item messer Boffo. Item lo conte de monte de Risi. Item lo episcopo de Isernia de cha de monte Aquilla. Item messer Ponso de santa cruce, doctor decretorum, catelano. Item messer Guielmo de Vicho catelam. Item lo conte Zanni da vintimilya. Item lo conte de Purcino messer Zorzo de Alemania. Molti altri sono del Conselyo doctori e zentilhomini napolitani, che vanno quando volle e può andare, quando ie piace, zioè: Messer Michelle de Castelamare. Item Angelo da Napoli. Item Ziecho Antonio napolitano. Item messer Collella monopulo napolitano. Item messer Zuam Antonio Caraffa. Item messer lo iudice Matheo. Item messer Ponso, secretissimo de monsegnor de Valenza, il perchè scrive le secrette del ditto Conselyo.'

[29] He left Naples in June 1444.

[30] Madurell Marimón, *Mensajeros barceloneses*, p. 304. In the letter which the envoys of Barcelona wrote describing this event they called the count 'cap del Consell del Senyor Rey'. [31] Ibid., p. 305.

[32] Bofarull y Mascaró, *Coleccion de documentos*, pp. 109 ff.; cf. above, p. 19.

Urgell. In addition to the authority derived from their spiritual office, such men had a knowledge of law and experience of administration seldom found in laymen of comparable rank; these qualities, and not any desire to accord the church a pre-eminent place in the state, led Alfonso to make use of them.

All seven of the collateral officials of the kingdom appear in Borso's list of 'permanent' members, but their only regular activity as counsellors was to collect their salary of 1 *oncia* a day. Besides the president there were two other ecclesiastics—the Neapolitan Jacobo de Montáquila, Bishop of Isernia, and the Catalan Pons de Santa Creu, a *doctor decretorum* and familiar of the Bishop of Valencia, who acted as secretary.[33] The noble members included the powerful figures of the Count of Cocentayna and the premier magnate of Sicily, Giovanni di Vintimiglia, Marquis of Gerace. Like de Corella, the marquis had followed Alfonso loyally throughout the Italian wars and was still to command his armies in the March of Ancona and in the Balkans; in 1430 the king had appointed him viceroy of Sicily and in 1438 gave him the title of admiral in that kingdom. In addition to the collateral officials this council described by Borso d'Este included two other Neapolitan nobles—Perdicasso Barrile, Count of Monteodorisio, and Giorgio d'Alemagna, Count of Buccino. The choice of these two appears somewhat surprising, for neither wielded great influence as feudatories and the count of Buccino had adhered to René of Anjou to the end;[34] a pardon for his actions in support of the Angevin was issued only on 21 April 1444 when he had already entered the council.[35] A likely explanation for the favour shown them is that both had experience in the Neapolitan council, first under Giovanna II, who had named them among the governors of the kingdom in her will,[36] and later under René. Moreover Alfonso was a shrewd judge of human nature, well able to appreciate that a steadfast opponent might be turned into a staunch supporter.

The remaining 'permanent' members may be classed as financial and legal officials. One of them, Guillem de Vich, *magister rationalis*

---

[33] In October 1439 the bishop pressed Alfonso to write to the chapter of Valencia requesting the archdeaconry for Pons (ACA Reg. 2651. 130ʳ).

[34] Ametller y Vinyas, *Alfonso V de Aragón*, i. 276, 412, 414.

[35] ACA Reg. 2906. 73ᵛ. He had attended a meeting of the Sacrum Consilium on 27 Nov. 1443 (ACA Reg. 2913. 133ᵛ).

[36] Ametller y Vinyas, *Alfonso V de Aragón*, i. 440.

of the kingdom of Valencia, was a Spaniard. Two were Neapolitans: Marino Boffa, a president of the Sommaria, had played an important and generally pro-Angevin part in the affairs of Naples for twenty years until in 1438, to save the estates acquired through marriage to an heiress, he had thrown in his lot with Aragon and secured a leading position among the Neapolitan administrators around the king;[37] Giovanni di San Severino, regent of the court of the Vicaria, had gained favour through services rendered to Alfonso and his brother Pedro; his reward had been the life tenure of the regency.

Four of the counsellors classified by Borso as casual are readily identifiable as Neapolitan doctors of law in the service of the crown: Michele Riccio, Cicco Antonio Guindazzo, Angelo Tau, and Giovanni Antonio Carafa. The man he names simply as 'the judge Matteo' almost certainly belongs to the same group and may have been either Matteo di Girifalco or Matteo d'Afflitto. The absence from the list of any secretary other than the president's personal secretary is surprising, for other evidence suggests that meetings of the council were rarely held without one of the principal secretaries, either Fonolleda or Olzina, being present. In Aragon the king's secretaries were permanent members. Furthermore the list of casual members omits several other jurists serving in the courts of the Vicaria and Sommaria who occasionally attended the council about this time. Two general observations may be made about the council of 1444: the first is the preponderance there of lawyers who also served in the supreme tribunals, and the second, the predominance of Neapolitans and Sicilians among those lawyers. If Italians were largely excluded from the king's household, they still had a prominent voice in his council.

No important change took place in the state of affairs described by Borso d'Este until the winter of 1446 when Alfonso led his army into central Italy, thus beginning an absence that was to last two years. With him went many of his most intimate advisers as well as a fair number of administrators; from among these he formed his personal council wherever the fortunes of war took him. Behind him in Naples he left his sixteen-year-old son Ferdinand as *locumtenens generalis*[38] with an inner circle of three advisers: his

[37] Pontieri, 'Muzio Attendolo e Francisco Sforza'.
[38] The Duke of Calabria had been formally invested with this title in June 1442.

former tutor, the Count of Cocentayna, the secretary Olzina, and the treasurer general Matteu Pujades. It may be assumed that the full council of the *locumtenens* resembled that which had hitherto advised his father.

In the king's absence the administration ran down badly. Officials went unpaid for years—even the regent of the Vicaria had by 1448 received no salary for five years—and arrears of business in the courts and the Sommaria mounted alarmingly. Meanwhile from Tuscany came unceasing calls for money to prosecute the war.[39] Disgruntlement with this state of affairs grew clamorous, but it was only after defeat at Piombino had toppled his prestige and credit that Alfonso took measures to remedy it. The Count of Cocentayna and the Neapolitan banker Giovanni di Miroballo were summoned to the king's camp for consultations, then sent back to Ferdinand with detailed instructions for a major overhaul of the administration.[40] Since the first part of the instruction deals with the council, it may be presumed that it, like the other parts of the governmental machine, had not been functioning well. Although the nature of the fault is nowhere explicitly stated, the character of the remedy leads one to suspect that Ferdinand had relied too much on his three Spanish advisers, that the official members had neglected their duties, and that the non-officials had rarely been consulted. To improve matters Alfonso named a thirty-one-man council and gave certain instructions as to its functioning. In composition the new council closely resembled the old; indeed most of the counsellors of 1444 appear in it, which suggests that they had continued to serve in the intervening years. The Archbishop of Naples continues as president. There are still two other ecclesiastics, though not the same persons as in 1444; Alfonso's confessor, the Bishop of Mallorca,[41] and Pere Roig de Corella, a son of the Count of Cocentayna who held the office of papal protonotary and the archdeaconry of Jativa, replace the previous clerical members. The seven collateral officials are duly renominated with a significant proviso, 'mentre seran presents personalment en Napols'. The Count of Buccino is still there, but Perdicasso Barrile Count of Monteodorisio, who seems to have

[39] A. F. C. Ryder, 'La politica italiana di Alfonso d'Aragona, 1446–1448', *ASPN* (1960).

[40] ACA Reg. 2699. 141ᵛ, Instruction issued from the camp at Ansedonia, 3 Oct. 1448.

[41] Cf. above, p. 83.

fallen from grace, has gone.[42] Some of the official members of 1444 also have a place in the reformed council of 1448. Guillem de Vich had died in 1447, but Giovanni di San Severino retains his place *ex officio* as regent of the Vicaria, as does Marino Boffa as one of two presidents in a reformed Sommaria.[43] Michele Riccio, one of the casual members in 1444, acquires an *ex officio* place in his capacity as the second president in the Sommaria. The influential figure of the Count of Cocentayna looms as large in the new council as it did in the old.

Turning to the newcomers, one notes that a simultaneous shake-up in the Vicaria and Sommaria has resulted in the appearance of several *ex officio* counsellors. Both presidents of the Sommaria happen to have been in the earlier council, but the four new judges of the Vicaria whom Alfonso placed on the council are all fresh faces.[44] So too are Lupo de Speyo, the judge of appeals, Gabriel de Cardona, treasurer of the duchy of Calabria, Joan Dasin, *locumtenens* of the *escriva de racio*, and Joan Ferrer of the treasury. Olzina the secretary is formally nominated, though as one of the governing triumvirate during the king's absence he must already have been playing a prominent role in the council.

The inclusion of this solid block of officials recognized the leading role they had already assumed in the council; also it was hoped to improve administrative discipline and efficiency by subjecting them to a conciliar routine. The banker Giovanni di Miroballo was put in the council because, as part of the reorganization, Alfonso had ordered that all moneys received and paid by the crown should pass through his bank. Finally the reform brought into the council a representative of each of the five wards of the city of Naples, thus restoring the influence which the capital had enjoyed in the royal council in Angevin times. Because the city had resisted him so stubbornly, Alfonso had hitherto ignored the convention that gave places on the council to nobles from these wards, and the Neapolitans had been too chastened to raise the issue. His discomfiture in Tuscany now brought him to

---

[42] His county, which he had recovered from Giovanella de Burgo in 1442 (ACA Reg. 2902. 57ʳ, Judgement of the Sacrum Consilium, 4 Aug. 1442), he lost again to her by judicial process in 1452. In fulfilment of an earlier undertaking Giovanella subsequently gave the county to Iñigo de Avalos and his wife who was her niece (ASN Priv. I. 58ʳ, 28 Dec. 1452).   [43] Cf. below, p. 197.

[44] They were Clemente de Soncino, Antonio de Traetto, Francesco de Compli, and Geronimo de Miroballo.

make a conciliatory gesture to overburdened and maladministered subjects, though he took care that his nominees were all tried friends of the Aragonese cause.[45] It may also be that by appointing counsellors from the capital Alfonso hoped to convince the nobles of the kingdom that they had an effective voice in the council, for the collateral counsellors were seldom there to speak for them.

This council of 1448 differed from that of 1444 in that its function was to advise the *locumtenens generalis* in the kingdom of Naples on the affairs of that kingdom alone, and not the king on matters that might arise in any of his territories. Its terms of reference were to assist the Duke of Calabria 'in all things which shall arise and be needful, both in matters of justice and judicial appeal, in the business of the Sommaria, and in all other matters touching the state and service of the Lord King and the well-being of that kingdom, and also in business concerning monies of the said Lord King, so that all business may be duly despatched for the service of the said Lord King and the benefit of the said realm'.[46] Its Neapolitan character was further emphasized by the procedure laid down in the instruction, for it closely resembled that prescribed by Charles I in 1294 and revised in 1352 by Giovanna I. There were to be regular meetings every Monday, Wednesday, and Friday morning attended by the regent and four judges of the Vicaria, the two presidents of the Sommaria, and such other persons as the *locumtenens generalis* might direct for the purpose of considering petitions. The Duke of Calabria might, of course, summon other meetings of such persons and at such times as he thought fit. In effect, therefore, the former distinction between regular and casual members of the council persisted with the first group more narrowly confined to the senior judges of the crown; the non-official element still attended only at the will of the duke and not as of right.[47]

---

[45] The five nominated were Petriccone Caracciolo Count of Brienza, Carafello Carafa, Buffardo Cicinello, Matteo di Gennaro, and Dragonetto di Bonifaccio.

[46] '. . . deles coses que occoreran e seran necessaries tant en los fets dela justicia e recors de aquella quant en los dela summaria encara en tots altres fets tocant lestat e servey del dit Senyor Rey e benefici dela cosa publica de aquell Reyalme e encara per los negocis tocants pecunies del dit Senyor affi que tots los negocis vaien e sien tractats ab lorde ques pertany per servey del dit Senyor Rey e benefici dela dita cosa publica.'

[47] Ferdinand was told to take counsel 'with all these if they are present in Naples, or with those of them who happen to be present there'; but later 'or with such of them as the Lord Duke may think fit'.

Barely six weeks after ordering these reforms, Alfonso re-entered his torchlit capital still smarting from his reverses in the war with Florence. Effective authority in the kingdom now reverted to him and the council recently appointed to advise the *locumtenens generalis* gave place to the king's council. Whether he retained any of the new men and procedures ordered in October 1448 we do not know, but it would seem that for most purposes he continued his former practice of constituting his council on an *ad hoc* basis from a small group of legal experts and adminis-trators.[48] Where he did make a most significant innovation after 1448 was in developing the judicial functions of the council so as to differentiate clearly between its *ad hoc* administrative decisions and its judgements as the supreme tribunal for all his states. A degree of informality was appropriate in the procedures in-volved in making administrative decisions; judgement delivered as by the king himself called for a solemnity and formality at least as great as that found in lesser tribunals. The council had begun to emphasize this distinction as early as 1439 by constituting itself, for the purpose of hearing cases and delivering public judgement, into a more formal body which was to evolve into the Neapolitan Sacrum Regium Consilium. We shall look in vain for any act establishing it because such judicial power was inherent in the king sitting in council. Rather we must seek the evolution of the Sacrum Consilium in a series of administrative decisions taken within the council to determine the procedures it would follow when sitting as a tribunal.[49] One can only speculate on the pressures which may have led the council to take these measures at a time when most of its energy was devoted to winning the war with René of Anjou. There must have been an increasing flow of litigation over property within the kingdom as the Aragonese cause prospered; the prospect that Alfonso might triumph brought more and more tenants-in-chief before him with claims and counter-claims, many of them deeply entangled with the com-plicated twists and turns of events in the reign of Giovanna II. Only the final authority of the king supported by the judgement of lawyers and laymen fully versed in the highly developed feudal jurisprudence of the kingdom could effectively determine such

[48] Cf. above, p. 96.
[49] G. Cassandro, 'Sulle origini del Sacro Consiglio napoletano', *Studi in onore di Riccardo Filangieri*, ii (Naples, 1959).

issues. If in these circumstances Alfonso and his advisers needed some procedural precedent to guide them, they might have found it in the policy of the king's own forebears, the first Trastamar kings of Castile, who in reviving the royal council had developed the *audiencia* for the exercise of its judicial functions.[49a] This line of conciliar development must have been known to them and was directly relevant to their needs, which is more than can be said for other putative ancestors of the Sacrum Consilium such as the Roman Rota and the appeal tribunal of Valencia.[50]

In the reign of Alfonso the name Sacrum Consilium did not apply specifically to the council in its judicial capacity as it came to do in the kingdom of Naples in later years. One finds the epithet 'sacrum' used rather haphazardly. Sometimes it applies to the whole council without particular reference to its judicial function, as in a privilege which describes the Count of Fondi as 'nostri sacri consilii presidens'.[51] At other times it is applied to the council when clearly constituted as a body taking an administrative decision, as in the meeting held on 23 June 1445 when it was decided to extend the *nuova gabella* to the western coasts of the kingdom.[52] In fact the Aragonese chancery was very fond of the adjective 'sacrum'; 'sacra regia maiestas' occurs frequently in the documents that emanated from it; the Sommaria occasionally appears as 'sacra regia Sommaria';[53] while in Spain the council that assisted Queen Maria was sometimes dubbed a 'sacrum consilium'.[54] In other words, the occurrence of the name 'sacrum consilium' is not yet a ground for concluding that the council is in any particular instance acting as a supreme tribunal; that can

---

[49a] In Aragon too the *audiencia* developed during the fifteenth century, but almost nothing is known about it. Cf. Font y Rius, 'The institutions of the Crown of Aragon', p. 178: 'It would be interesting to discover just what the composition of this Royal Council was, and its integration into the heart of the Chancery, as well as its functions as a supreme tribunal and its conjoint or separate functioning in the different spheres of government.'

[50] Giannone (*Istoria civile*, iii. 373) suggests that either of these tribunals might have inspired the Bishop of Valencia with the idea of the Sacrum Consilium. Croce (*La Spagna nella vita italiana*, p. 43) follows him.

[51] ACA Reg. 2914. 60ʳ, 19 Apr. 1450. In this privilege it is acknowledged that the count succeeded his father as protonotary and president of the council.

[52] Salvati, *Fonti aragonesi*, iv. 21.

[53] Toppi, *De origine tribunalium*, iii. 241. In an entry in the accounts of the treasurer of Terra di Lavoro for 10 Sept. 1439. Cf. ibid., iii. 244, 'iura et consuetudines Sacrae Regiae Camerae', and a reference to the court of the Sommaria as the 'Sacro Auditorie' in a document which deals with the accounts of the treasurer Capdevila sometime after 1448.   [54] ACA Reg. 2659. 33ᵛ.

be determined only by a consideration of its procedure and the nature of the business before it.

When the council sat as a tribunal it was presided over by the normal president;[55] the king himself rarely intervened in its proceedings. Any counsellors might attend if they wished, and it was the custom to muster as many as possible for the sessions in which judgements were delivered in order to lend dignity to such occasions. The real business was, however, left to the legal members.

A suit was brought before the council by means of a petition addressed to the king. If on a preliminary examination the council decided to act on the petition, it deputed one of its jurists to take evidence from the two parties and prepare a report. Any lawyer member of the council might be charged with this task, though there is some evidence to suggest that in cases involving rights of the crown (as in a dispute over the possession of a fief) it would be entrusted to a chancery jurist, whereas a suit involving only private interests would be put in the hands of a judge of the Vicaria. The counsellor charged with examining the case then cited the plaintiff and defendant or their procurators to appear before him. Thus began a series of allegations, counter-allegations, and prorogations which continued until the commissioner was ready to present his report on the evidence and legal arguments adduced before him to a session of the council. In the presence of the parties and their counsel, or of the latter alone, he delivered his findings, the procurators addressed the tribunal and a day and time were appointed for delivering judgement. The council then reached its decision in a private session. Finally came the session in which the judgement was read and approved before a relatively full council.

Lata fuit hec sententia per nos seu in nostri personam per Reverendum in Christo patrem G. divina providencia Archiepiscopum Neapolitan. et vice prothonotarium ac presidentem in dicto regio consilio quod in quodam cancello hospitalis beate Marie Incoronate extra muros Neapolis more solito per ipsum Reverendum Archiepiscopum celebratur lecta et publicata de nostro seu ipsius mandato per fidelem scriptorem nostrum et notarium publicum infrascriptum Bernardum de Lobera die mercurii vii mensis octobris viii Ind.[56]

[55] Toppi (*De origine tribunalium*, ii. 3) cites a letter dated 20 Sept. 1440 which is addressed to the Bishop of Valencia as president of the Sacrum Consilium.

[56] ACA Reg. 2909. 48ʳ. Musello de Sacco had petitioned for the return of lands and goods which he alleged had been wrongfully seized by the sons of

The witnesses to this judgement were Giorgio d'Alemagna, Giovanni della Ratta, Giovanni di San Severino, Arone Cibo of Genoa, Giovanni di Forma, l.D., Antonio Musculo, a royal secretary and notary, Martino di Settembre, a clerk, 'et aliis pluribus in multitudine satis grande'.[57]

The length of time that elapsed between the presentation of a petition in the council and the delivery of a judgement varied with the complexity of the case, the pertinacity of the litigants, and the assiduity of the lawyer responsible for the report. A petition by the prior and convent of Santa Maria di Monteoliveto in Naples over a bequest in the will of the Duke of Sessa received a first hearing on 2 March 1447. Marino Boffa issued his first citations on 8 March 1447 but judgement was given only on 8 February 1449.[58] This was at a time when the machinery of the council had ground virtually to a halt in the king's absence. Much more typical was the course of a dowry dispute between Giovanni di San-severino and Emilia Capice, Countess of Marsico and San Severino. Proceedings had begun in the Vicaria on 26 April 1443, but the plaintiffs (the countess and her father) alleged partiality in the judge of that court because he was the brother of Emilia's deceased husband. On their petition that he evoke the case to the council, Alfonso directed it to his Spanish protonotary, Ferrer Ram, on 17 February 1444. On 27 March 1444 Ram, who had to travel to Milan on the king's business, passed the case to Antonio Becca-delli and the council gave judgement in favour of Emilia on 12 June that same year.[59] Not only did lawsuits tend to move more swiftly in the council than in other tribunals, there was also only one avenue of appeal from its judgements—directly to the king himself—and this factor helped to make recourse to it popular with those who wanted a quick, final decision. The Sommaria heard a case involving Carlo di Campobasso, Count of Trémoli, and the heirs of Giacomo de Zuzulo. Sentence was given against

Tommaso di Sanseverino. By describing the archbishop as acting in the capacity of vice protonotary care was taken to preserve the form, but not the substance, of Neapolitan usage which made the protonotary president of the council. Cf. ACA Reg. 2909. 74ᵛ, 12 June 1444: '. . . lata fuit hec sententia in dicto regio consilio quadam camera domus Archiepiscopatus Neapolis celebratur per dictum dominum Regem seu in eius personam per Reverendum in Christo patrem et dominum Alfonsum divina providencia Valentine episcopum con-siliarumque dicti domini Regis et vice prothonotarium . . .' Cf. above, p. 97.

[57] ACA Reg. 2909. 98ʳ, 7 Oct. 1444.   [58] ACA Reg. 2913. 108ᵛ.
[59] ACA Reg. 2909. 73ᵛ.

the latter who appealed, so the case came once again before the Sommaria. On their petition it was finally evoked to the council, 'ne causa fiat immortalis imo ut quam primum eadem dedicatur et fine debito terminetur', and the counsellors were exhorted 'in causa ipsa absque aliqua dilatione quam primum ferant sententiam'.[60]

Appeals against judgements of the council appear to have been uncommon, perhaps because Alfonso, to whom they were perforce addressed, was reluctant to permit any further extension of the judicial ladder. There is even some reason to think that a statute forbade them.[61] On the rare occasions when he did allow an appeal the king entrusted it to two or three legal officers of the crown. This happened when the council gave judgement in favour of Luigi di Gesualdo in a dispute between him and the Countess of San Severino over possession of a certain toll. The countess appealed and Alfonso sent the case to Valenti Claver, regent of the chancery, and two chancery lawyers, Rodrigo Falco and Nicola Fillach:

per vos omnes tres seu duos vestrum in absencia vel defectu alterius, videndam, decidendam et sine debito terminandam, mandantes expresse et de certa nostra scientia quatenus in causa ipsa procedatis iustitia mediante neutram partium iniuste gravando, eamque videatis decidatis et fine debito terminetis. Et quicquid decreveritis celeri executioni mandetis, procedendo in ea breviter, simpliciter summarie et de plano, sine strepitu, forma et figura iudicii, sola forma veritate attenta malitiis cavillationibus et diffugiis omnibus reiectis.[62]

The judgement of the council might be sought in any civil matter, both on appeal and in first instance. For a few favoured individuals it was even made the ordinary tribunal of first instance. Thus Petriccone Caracciolo, Count of Brienza, was promised that neither he nor his heirs should be cited before any other tribunal in respect of their feudal possessions. That it frequently heard cases in first instance is suggested by a petition from the city of Trani which complained that its privilege protecting citizens from being summoned outside the city in cases of first instance was being constantly infringed by summonses to appear before the

---

[60] Mazzoleni, *Il Codice Chigi*, pp. 39–40, 10 July 1451.

[61] A royal letter permitting an appeal begins 'Quacumque pragmatica sanctione seu constitutione non obstante . . .' (ibid., p. 75).

[62] Ibid., pp. 75–6, 28 July 1451.

council.[63] It could hear appeals from any other tribunal including the Sommaria and the Vicaria.[64]

Many, and perhaps most, of the petitions brought before the council related to disputes over feudal possessions. In the kingdom of Naples the chaos of prolonged civil war had raised a particularly flourishing crop of such questions. A typically involved example was the contest for the counties of San Severino and Marsico, one of the most substantial feudal holdings in the country. In the time of Giovanna II the counties had been held by Tommaso di Sanseverino who, dying without male heirs, had left his lands to his daughter Diana. Because Diana at the time had given her allegiance to Anjou, Alfonso declared the counties escheated to the crown and bestowed them upon Giovanni di Sanseverino, a brother of Tommaso. Diana first attempted to contest this action in 1442 after she had submitted to Alfonso. The council entrusted the matter to Battista Platamone and Alfonso himself delivered judgement in favour of Giovanni before a gathering of nobles in his camp on the outskirts of Lucera.[65] When Giovanni died in 1444 he directed in his will that Diana should receive 12,000 ducats if she would renounce her claims to the counties in favour of his son and heir Luigi who was still a minor.[66] That offer Diana rejected, and when in 1447 Luigi too died, leaving the title to the counties to his still younger brother Roberto,[67] she petitioned the council on two grounds: firstly she appealed against the judgement given in 1442; secondly she claimed the inheritance of her cousin Luigi on the grounds that he had died without heirs and that she, as granddaughter and heiress of the late Caterina di Sanseverino, Countess of San

---

[63] Rogadeo, *Codice diplomatico*, pp. 143–4, Petition of 5 Mar. 1444.

[64] Annechino Longobardo was appointed 'magister actorum in causis appellationum et nullitatum Magne Curie Vicarie, que coram Sacro Consilio et aliis iudicibus delegatis agitabuntur' (B. Mazzoleni, *Fonti aragonesi*, iii (Naples, 1963), 5, 6 July 1452).

[65] ACA Reg. 2902. 107ᵛ, 23 Oct. 1442: 'Lata fuit hec sentencia seu declaratio per nos dictum Regem sedentem pro tribunali intus tentorium nostrum in nostris felicibus castris fixis in silva civitatis nostre Lucerie.' Those present were the Prince of Taranto, the Duke of Andria, the Duke of Melfi, the Count of Capaccio, and the Count of Sant'Angelo. The secretary Fonolleda read the judgement.

[66] B. C. de Frede, 'Roberto Sanseverino Principe di Salerno', *Rassegna storica salernitana* (1951), p. 6.

[67] ACA Reg. 2912. 129ᵛ, Tivoli, 14 Aug. 1447, Privilege investing Roberto, aged seventeen, with the estates of his brother. The investiture is notified to, *inter alia*, 'presidenti insuper in nostro sacro consilio'.

Severino and Marsico, was next in line of succession.[68] Valenti Claver, regent of the chancery, investigated the case with the assistance of Marino Boffa and Geronimo di Miroballo. If the wording of the sentence can be taken at face value, the issue received exceptionally careful consideration:

Id circo Christi et gloriosissime matris eius virginis Marie nominibus invocatis habita prius matura diligenti et repetita discussione deliberacione nostri sacri consilii et concordi votorum prestacione famosissimorum utriusque juris doctorum nostrorum consiliariorum in unum votum eademque sentencia pariter concordancium . . .[69]

But once again the verdict went against Diana. The sentence of 1442 was upheld, and the issue of Luigi's inheritance was decided in favour of his brother Roberto partly upon the ground that a golden bull of King Robert directed that feudal possessions should pass to females only in default of male heirs. The council delivered its judgement on 22 December 1449 in an unusually solemn session presided over by the king in person at his country retreat in Torre del Greco. Arnau Fonolleda, the chief secretary, read the sentence in the presence of an exalted gathering which included the Duke of Calabria, Pedro de Cardona, Iñigo de Guevara, Eximen Perez de Corella, the governor of Valencia, Platamone the vice-chancellor, 'et pluribus aliis in multitudine copiosa'.[70] The reason for all this ceremonial and glittering assembly lay partly in the importance of the case, but more in Diana's marriage to Guillem Ramon de Moncada, the chancellor of Sicily. Thanks to his influence, she had been able to reach a favourable settlement with the guardians of her cousins before the court published its verdict. Once they knew the judgement would go in their favour—and this had been revealed to them by 5 December[71] —they had undertaken to pay her 30,000 ducats.[72]

Maria Capice brought a successful action against Petricone Caracciolo, Count of Brienza, for the return of her dowry. It had

---

[68] ACA Reg. 2914. 11ʳ, 22 Dec. 1449.   [69] Ibid.

[70] Ibid.: Lata fuit hec sententia pronunciacio sive declaracio per nos dictum Regem sedentem pro tribunali in solio maiestatis in quadam camera castelli ville Turris Octavi . . .'

[71] On that day the king had given an undertaking that the sentence would go in their favour and that he would permit no further litigation over the inheritance (ACA Reg. 2697. 43ᵛ).

[72] This settlement is mentioned in a privilege dated 10 Dec. 1449 (ACA Reg. 2914. 29ᵛ).

been lost to Caracciolo when the king confiscated and sold it along with the property of her husband, Pietro d'Alagnio, a supporter of the Angevin cause. The council ordered Caracciolo to repay Maria 200 *oncie* in view of the 'extreme poverty' to which she had been reduced.[73] In September 1446 judgement was given in a dispute over possession of the *baiulatio* of Lanciano.[74] In May 1443 the council found in favour of Marco di Cotignola who had complained that Antonio di Sangro and Antonio di Constanzo had seized thirteen horses, eleven oxen, and 300 sheep belonging to him, on the grounds that he was a rebel when he had already made his peace with the king and obtained a letter of pardon dated 5 February 1443.[75] Non-feudal property was the subject of another judgement which sentenced Nicolau Binot of Mallorca to pay 4,000 ducats to Mincio de Costanzio and Zullio di Viterbo of Messina as compensation for a ship which he had seized piratically off Calabria.[76] The crown itself could through the procurator fiscal bring an action before the council. This happened in 1452 when, after the outbreak of war with Florence, a ship suspected of belonging to the republic was seized off Gaeta even though it had hoisted the French flag after being challenged. Some Florentine goods had been found aboard, but the captain proved to be French and there were several French merchants among the passengers. The latter had appeared before the council to ask for restitution of their goods, which had been granted; the ship's master Nicolas Ferrat, on the other hand, had refused to appear and left Naples to lodge a complaint at the French court. After his departure the procurator fiscal began proceedings in the council to claim the ship for the crown on the grounds of a fictitious sale by its Florentine owners. Though representatives of the alleged French owners did eventually appear in Naples they refused to plead before the council which gave judgement for the crown.[77]

[73] ACA Reg. 2908. 149^r, 10 June 1446.

[74] Ibid. 182^r, Castelnuovo, 30 Sept. 1446.

[75] ACA Reg. 2906. 29^r, Castel Capuano, 20 May 1443.

[76] ACA Reg. 2918. 4^r. Judgement was delivered at Torre del Greco on 4 Nov. 1449. The king subsequently granted a stay of execution for eighteen months. On the expiration of that stay Mincio had petitioned in the king's Friday public audience for execution of the sentence; this was granted after further consideration by the council.

[77] ACA Reg. 2661. 1^r, 28 Jan. 1452, and 56^v, 13 Mar. 1454. Both these letters are addressed to the King of France in reply to others which he had sent to Alfonso protesting that the ship belonged to merchants of Montpellier.

The council also judged cases involving non-Neapolitan subjects of Alfonso. It decided in favour of Andrea Borromei, a Florentine merchant, in an action which he had brought against Rodrigo Dias of Valencia and entrusted execution of the sentence to Queen Maria.[78] It heard the case in which the city of Barcelona made claims on the estate of Arnau Porta, summoning Pere Boquet the city's representative to present the case before it.[79] On 8 June 1454 it gave a decision on a point of law which had arisen over the pardon granted to the Peralta family of Sicily after its rebellion against King Martin.[80]

In formal judgements such as these and in the procedures by which they were reached, the council acted in a manner later associated specifically with the tribunal of the Sacrum Consilium. Many of its decisions, however, though involving points of law, took the form of administrative directions, not judgements. Giacobella, described as 'pauperis et miserabilis persone',[81] presented a petition in which she complained that a certain Jacobo de Firmo, after wrongfully destroying documents relating to the dower of her late mother, had seized the dower. The result was an order ('de certa nostra scientia deliberate et consulto nostrique Sacri Consilii deliberatione pretereunte') to the notary concerned to provide Giacobella with new copies of the necessary documents so that she might take action for the recovery of her property. The intention here was to correct a denial of justice, not to give judgement. A petition 'ad nos et nostrum sacrum consilium' from the Duke of Scalea's town of Trécchina complaining that the governor of the town and the duke himself were ignoring privileges granted to it in 1426 and 1429 was referred to the counsellor Michele Riccio who found that the privileges had not been submitted for royal approval as required for concessions touching fiefs held *in capite*. Alfonso corrected this deficiency by giving his assent to, and confirming, the privileges.[82] Another matter

---

[78] ACA Reg. 2909. 79ᵛ, 28 Feb. 1444.

[79] Boquet had raised the question with Alfonso when the king was hunting at Foggia and had been referred to the council. Madurell Marimòn, *Mensajeros barceloneses*, p. 551, Letter from Boquet to Barcelona, 27 Jan. 1457; ibid., p. 571, Letter from Boquet to Barcelona, 18 Feb. 1457.

[80] ACA Reg. 2916. 1ʳ.

[81] Mazzoleni, *Il Codice Chigi*, pp. 106–7. This order to the notary of Manfredonia dated 28 Aug. 1451 is issued on the instruction of the Bishop of Urgell as president of the council.

[82] ASN Priv. I. 22ʳ, 15 Aug. 1452.

which the king decided 'cum matura deliberatione nostri Sacri Consilii' arose from a petition presented by the Count of Reggio asking that the governor of that county be permitted to proceed against a man accused of fomenting riot and sedition there notwithstanding claims by Messina that he could only be tried in the Sicilian city.[83] The demesne town of Francavilla, alarmed by a report that the king contemplated selling it to Francesco d'Aquino, dispatched two envoys to Naples to plead that its privileges expressly forbade such alienation. Battista Platamone and Ferrer Ram examined the case and reported favourably on the petition. 'De consilio ergo totius nostri sacri consilii matura deliberacione prehabita', Alfonso cancelled all documents of sale and confirmed the privileges of the town.[84] A licence to seize any goods belonging to Florentines up to a sum of 14,000 ducats resulted from a petition of the Count of Tagliacozzo examined by the council. He complained that the republic of Florence owed this money as stipend to his late brother Rainaldo Orsini, who had made him his heir, and that attempts to collect it had failed.[85] Often the procedure which the council followed in such matters differed in no important respect from that which resulted in a formal judgement and sentence—a petition, consideration of the petition by the council, assignment of the case to one or two of the legal counsellors, examination of witnesses and counsel if necessary, and a report upon which the council reached its decision—only the end product clearly distinguished a strictly judicial from an executive process.

Some months after his return from Tuscany Alfonso reformed his council in a manner intended to make it smaller, highly professional, and efficient in the dispatch of business. In particular the decree for its reform promulgated on 13 August 1449 carefully regulated the procedure by which it was to operate in its capacity as a supreme tribunal.[86] The scope of its jurisdiction did not alter; it continued to be a court of appeal and first instance for all states subject to the king; it also continued to take cognizance of cases

---

[83] Mazzoleni, *Il Codice Chigi*, pp. 342-3, Letter ordering the governor of the county to proceed against the accused, Castelnuovo, 6 July 1452.

[84] ACA Reg. 2690. 106ᵛ, 1 Sept. 1444.

[85] ACA Reg. 2915. 162ᵛ, Castelnuovo, 28 Dec. 1452.

[86] The text of the 'sacratissimi edicti' is published by Toppi, *De origine tribunalium*, ii. 440-4, and by A. Caruso, 'Circa l'origine del Sacro Regio Consiglio', *Il Rievocatore* (Naples, 1956).

from the Sommaria involving points of law.[87] Its membership on the other hand differed radically from those described by Borso d'Este in 1444 and those prescribed for the Neapolitan council as recently as October 1448. Apart from the Archbishop of Naples and the protonotary of Naples, who were to continue to enjoy their titular 'prerogatives and pre-eminence' whenever they were present at court, all the regular non-legal counsellors were excluded. Henceforth the permanent nucleus of the council was to consist of six jurists named in the decree: three were Neapolitans (Cicco Antonio Guindazzo,[88] Geronimo Miroballo,[89] Michele Riccio),[90] two Catalans (Valenti Claver and Nicolau Fillach), and one, the vice-chancellor Battista Platamone, was a Sicilian. Giovanni Antonio Carafa was added in December 1449,[91] Rodrigo Falco early in 1451[92] and Joan de Copons in July 1452.[93] These, 'our principal and privy counsellors', represented some of the foremost legal talent among Alfonso's subjects, and all had distinguished themselves in diplomatic missions and in administrative posts as well as in the law courts. They were paid a salary of 500 ducats a year and shared the customary *vicesima* paid by litigants in their tribunal,[94] but were forbidden to engage in private legal practice.

The key figure in the reconstituted council was the vice-chancellor, whom Aragonese usage recognized as effectively the principal legal officer of the crown.[95] It was evidently assumed that the Archbishop of Naples would, like the protonotary, rest content with a formal recognition of his status, and that the effective president would henceforth be the vice-chancellor, for it was the vice-chancellor who, in the absence of the archbishop, was to hold the council every day in Castelnuovo when the king was in Naples, and either in his own house, or in some other suitable place, when

---

[87] '... et etiam de omnes causas camere nostre Summariae in quibus de iure disceptabitur' (Toppi, p. 442).

[88] See Toppi, *De origine tribunalium*, i. 184–5. Guindazzo was a president of the Sommaria. He died on 15 Mar. 1488.

[89] Also a president of the Sommaria, and one of those appointed to the Neapolitan College of Doctors when Giovanni II founded it in 1428.

[90] See Toppi, ibid. Riccio, like the other two Neapolitan counsellors a president of the Sommaria, died before October 1457.

[91] Toppi, *De origine tribunalium*, ii. 445–6.

[92] Gentile, 'Lo stato napoletano' (1937), p. 2, n. 3.

[93] Mazzoleni, *Fonti aragonesi*, iii. 10. He was given a salary of 560 ducats.

[94] The proceeds of these payments were to be pooled and shared out every quarter.

[95] Cf. above, p. 19.

the king was absent. Meeting thus regularly, they were to receive
and dispose of petitions with all dispatch, assigning feudal cases to
at least three and other cases to at least two counsellors. In case of
disagreement the vice-chancellor was to add another counsellor.

Nothing prevented the king from summoning other counsellors
when he so desired and he continued to do so where matters of
state were concerned. Nevertheless the Neapolitan nobility found
the reform of August 1449 highly objectionable. They saw themselves excluded from the tribunal which had ultimate jurisdiction
in feudal affairs, and the notional pre-eminence of the protonotary
could hardly conceal the fact that the composition of the council
now paid little regard to Neapolitan custom. Ever mindful of their
independence, they regarded the reform as an increase of royal
power at their expense, so in the next parliament, which met in
March 1450, they launched a counter-attack. Among the petitions
presented to the king was the following:

Item supplicano li predicti che piatzia a la Maesta Vestra ordinare
et statuere che lo sacro vestro consiglio pro justicia ministranda stenga
firmo ne la cita de Napoli et che nelo dicto sacro consiglio habes ad
presidere lu prothonotario daquesto vestro Regno de Sicilia, secondo li
statuti de ipso Regno, et in sua absencia lo suo loctinente una con quelli
consiglieri ydoney et sufficienti et alcuni deli magnati de questo vestro
Reyame, li quali la Vestra Maesta deputara ad eleccione et taxacione
dela Maestra Vestra, et chel dicto locotenente sia regnicolo et de terra
demaniale del dito vestro Regno atzo che con bona maturita le tutte
cause se possano debitamente terminare.[96]

The barons do not contest the emergence of a supreme tribunal
within the council, nor do they dispute the king's right to nominate
the counsellors who shall constitute that tribunal, but they are
anxious to establish the principle that it is a Neapolitan institution
in direct line of descent from the Angevin Magna Curia and subject to the fundamental law of the kingdom. Hence they are concerned to safeguard the rights of the protonotary as president in
any form of the council 'secondo li statuti de ipso Regno'—something which the king had already conceded—and, more important,
to ensure that the effective president shall act as *locumtenens* of the
protonotary and be a native of the kingdom. Their other major
objective is to ensure the representation of the Neapolitan baron-

[96] Ametller y Vinyas, *Alfonso V de Aragón*, iii. 687–8.

age on the tribunal. It is rather curious that they did not urge the claims of the collateral officials, but they must have known that these, like the protonotary, were most unlikely to devote themselves to a routine office. No other magnates could claim admission to the council as of right, so the choice had to be left to the king. The request that the tribunal be located permanently in the capital is presumably intended to guard against the kind of breakdown that had followed upon the king's absence from 1446 to 1448.

Alfonso did not take kindly to attempts by subjects to invade what he considered the sphere of his prerogative. As the edict of August 1449 had stated clearly, the jurisdiction of the royal council applied to all his dominions; therefore there was no reason why it should be governed by the laws of Naples. His reply to the petition conceded nothing at all: 'placet Regie Magestati quod presideat prothonotarius vel eius locumtenens.' To drive home the point that rights already acknowledged would be respected, the protonotary Onorato Gaetano, Count of Fondi, was promptly given a privilege, 'quamquam necessarium non sit', confirming him 'unum ex ordinariis consiliariis nostris presidentemque dicti sacri nostri consilii in ipso nostro sacro reformato consilio residentibus atque deputatis'.[97] Designating the effective president *locumtenens* of the protonotary raised no problem when Alfonso ignored the part of the petition that asked that he be a native of the royal demesne in the kingdom of Naples.

To the request for baronial representation in the council he had returned no answer at all, but what he refused to grant in direct response to a parliamentary petition he conceded shortly afterwards by appointing six Neapolitan nobles as ordinary counsellors 'ad consulendum, dirigendum, regendum, opitulandum et faciendum occurencia nostra agenda et totius rei publice huius et aliorum regnorum nostrorum utique nostrum sacrum consilium confluentium'.[98] Those appointed were the trusted Count of Buccino, Giorgio d'Alemagna, Petricone Caracciolo Count of Brienza, Nicola Cantelmo Duke of Sora, Aimerico di Sanseverino Count of Capaccio, Francesco Pandone Count of Venafro, and Marino Caracciolo Count of Sant' Angelo. Their salary at 1,000

---

[97] ACA Reg. 2914. 60ʳ, 19 Apr. 1450.
[98] The letters of appointment, identical in wording, are dated 18 and 19 Apr. and 10 Aug. 1450—e.g. for the Count of Buccino, ACA Reg. 2914. 86ʳ, 19 Apr. 1450.

ducats a year was double that of the official counsellors. In return for it they were required to attend the council regularly. Francesco del Balzo Orsini, Duke of Andria, who was appointed to fill a vacancy on the council in August 1453,[99] found this requirement irksome and began to absent himself. Eventually he was asked to return the salary received during these periods of absence. After some negotiation that demand was dropped and he was permitted to continue as an ordinary counsellor with a reduced salary on condition that he attended the council whenever possible.[100] The Duke of Sora managed to retain his full salary when absent from Naples in 1452 but only because he was serving with the king's armies.[101]

A council that was to handle business from all the Aragonese states might be expected to include members from Spain and Sicily as well as Naples. There is indeed reason to believe that Alfonso intended to balance the six Neapolitan nobles with at least six drawn from other states. An appointment for the Catalan noble Gispert dez Far dated 16 November 1450 is couched in the same terms as those given to the Neapolitans; like them dez Far is to have a salary of 1,000 ducats a year while in attendance at the council.[102] But unlike them he is not required to reside permanently in Naples. Other appointments of non-Neapolitans almost certainly remain to be unearthed from the registers.[103] Visitors too were sometimes pressed into service as non-Neapolitan members of the council. This happened to Juan Ximenez Cerdan and Ramon de Palomar when the Cortes of Aragon sent them to Naples. Alfonso informed the Cortes that he had detained them in order that 'en algunas cosas graves que en nuestro sacro consello occorren nos podamos de su industria consillo e scientia servir'.[104]

Considerations of economy and efficiency probably dictated the concept of a council strictly limited in numbers, but before long supernumerary counsellors began to appear. Some of these were

[99] ASN Priv. I. 101^r, 4 Aug. 1453: '... assit et adesse debeat diebus horisque congruis debitis et consuetis . . .'

[100] Toppi, De origine tribunalium, ii. 462–3, 23 Jan. 1457.

[101] Mazzoleni, Il Codice Chigi, pp. 284–5, Order to the Sommaria to permit the duke to retain the full salary, 5 Apr. 1452.

[102] ACA Reg. 2914. 113^r, Castelnuovo, 16 Nov. 1450.

[103] Among the members of the council which considered the Peralta case (cf. above, p. 111) in June 1454 was Juan Ruiz Merino of Zaragoza (ACA Reg. 2916. 1^r).

[104] ACA Reg. 2660. 114^v, 15 Nov. 1453.

lawyers,[105] like the crown advocate Antonio Jacobo de Traetto who in March 1452 became 'unum ex eis ordinariis et in sacro nostro consilio penes ipsius consilii presidentem ad reddendam justiciam singulis eam querentibus deputatis quamquam de eis nostra pracmatiqua certus existat numerus prefinitus'.[106] By 8 June 1453 when Francisco de Pelatis of Padua became an ordinary counsellor the reference in the letter of appointment to a restricted number had disappeared.[107] Pressure of work on the lawyer members may have been responsible for this increase because the noble contingent was more rigorously restricted within the prescribed limits. Salaried ordinary counsellors had not been known in Naples—*ex officio* members had been paid in their other capacities and the rest had received gratuities in recognition of their services—but there were Spanish precedents. Peter IV of Aragon's salaried counsellors have already been mentioned;[108] the Castilian *alcaldes de corte* performed a similar function.

Why had Alfonso abandoned the concept of a small council composed exclusively of jurists assigned to that part of council business which concerned the administration of justice? The concept itself, one would imagine, originated with the legal officers of the crown who must have known that the lay counsellors had little or nothing to contribute in debates on legal technicalities. However the nobility—and the Neapolitans may not have been alone in this—saw matters differently; in their eyes the participation of tenants-in-chief was an essential element in all conciliar action, and to have acquiesced in its exclusion would have meant an immeasurable increase in royal authority. Alfonso may have been influenced too by the Aragonese practice which entrusted the examination of petitions to a body of *oydors* composed of equal numbers of knights and lawyers. In practice, the noble members of council probably did not take much part in the routine judicial business. The council which met in Castelnuovo on 8 June 1454 to give judgement on the Peralta pardon consisted of the Patriarch of Alexandria as president, seven lawyers (Claver, Palomar, Guindazzo, Carafa, di Miroballo, Riccio, de Pelatis) and Juan

---

[105] For some of these additional appointments see p. 113.

[106] ACA Reg. 2915. 182ᵛ, 1 Mar. 1452.

[107] Toppi, *De origine tribunalium*, ii. 466. De Pelatis was at the same time appointed a lecturer in canon and civil law in the university of Naples. His teaching duties were to take priority over his attendance in the council.

[108] Cf. above, p. 91.

Ruiz Merino.[109] Only two of the nobles—the Counts of Buccino and Brienza—attended a session which delivered a judgement on 12 May 1455.[110] The principle that some magnates had a right to attend the council had nevertheless managed to survive the ousting of the collateral officials.

The protonotary retained his right to attend and preside over the council, and very occasionally he did appear there.[111] The secretaries in drafting documents sometimes remembered to refer to his titular pre-eminence.[112] But, with these rare exceptions, the Archbishop of Naples continued to preside over the formal sessions in which judgements were delivered, while the vice-chancellor acted as president in the routine daily meetings. When the archbishop died on 29 April 1451, Alfonso gave the presidency to his Spanish chancellor Arnau Roger de Pallars, Bishop of Urgell and Patriarch of Alexandria, who is thereafter styled 'president of the council' without any reference to the Neapolitan protonotary.[113] In fact, by coupling de Pallars's presidency of the council with the chancellorship, Alfonso broke away completely from the Neapolitan tradition in favour of that of Aragon which accorded precedence in the council to the chancellor and relegated the protonotary to a place below that of the vice-chancellor.

In little more than ten years the judicial functions of the council had passed into the hands of a distinct tribunal whose regular meetings, carefully regulated membership, and procedure led contemporaries to attach to it in particular the name Sacrum Consilium which properly belonged to the more amorphous and general royal council. The underlying idea of entrusting certain categories of council business to specialized bodies, salaried and chosen by the ruler, had an important future before it, especially in the government of Spain and its empire.

Alfonso himself appreciated that the administrative device evolved for judicial business might usefully be employed for other purposes, and in 1455 he established another supreme tribunal on

---

[109] ACA Reg. 2916. 1ʳ.   [110] Summonte, *Historia*, iii. 101.

[111] e.g. on 29 Jan. 1452 (Toppi, *De origine tribunalium*, ii. 483).

[112] e.g. in an order for the observance of privileges granted to the Prince of Salerno (ACA Reg. 2914, 99ᵛ, 14 Sept. 1450) and the order transferring the case of the Count of Térmoli from the Sommaria to the council (Mazzoleni, *Il Codice Chigi*, p. 40, 10 July 1451).

[113] e.g. 'coram reverendissimo in Christo patre A. R. patriarca Alesandrino et archiepiscopo Montisregalis cancellario nostro et sacri nostri consilii presidente' (ASN Div. Somm. I. 52 (bis), 48ʳ, 28 Oct. 1457).

the conciliar pattern, the Consilium Pecuniae.[114] The moving spirit behind this body seems to have been Antonio Carusio, who had held a number of posts of a financial nature in Sicily and Naples,[115] and gained an oversight of financial administration in the whole of the Aragonese empire when he became auditor general (*magister rationalis generalis*) in June 1456.[116] What he had in mind was a tribunal which should uncover and punish financial mismanagement and peculation among officials, usurpation of crown rights and revenue offences among private citizens. This was work for lawyers and accountants, so the principal members of the council which met under Carusio's presidency in a building formerly occupied by the Neapolitan Magna Curia dei Maestri Razionali were the Spanish lawyer Jacme de Pelaya[117] and Goffredo di Gaeta, a president of the Sommaria.[118]

Unlike the tribunal of the Sacrum Consilium which was moved by petition, the Consilium Pecuniae normally initiated action by the procedure of inquest. In its first year it set in motion a general inquest into titles and privileges within the kingdom of Naples. This began with a decree dated 13 February 1456 annulling all titles to tolls and vacant benefices for which no privilege bearing the great seal could be produced. Exactly one month later it ordered the inspection of all grants of benefices, public offices, and licences to practise a profession. On 20 September 1456 it initiated an inquest into titles to mills and forges. Failure to produce a valid title of privilege resulted in forfeiture or a heavy fine; the city of Sulmona, for example, suffered a fine of 600 ducats for its deficiencies on that account.[119]

---

[114] On 5 Jan. 1456 a goldsmith was paid for a seal which he had made for the Consilium Pecuniae. It was a silver seal bearing the arms of Aragon and Naples (Minieri Riccio, 'Alcuni fatti di Alfonso I', p. 442).

[115] He had served as auditor of accounts in the Sommaria (ASN Fasc. Somm. 117ᵛ, December 1445) as *magister racionalis* in Sicily (ACA Reg. 2910. 69ᵛ, 23 Mar. 1446) and as president of the Sommaria (ACA Reg. 2914. 71ᵛ, 15 June 1450).

[116] In token of that office he was invested with a standard bearing the arms of Aragon, Sicily and Naples (Minieri Riccio, 'Alcuni fatti di Alfonso I', p. 451).

[117] He also served as a legal counsellor in the Sacrum Consilium and as crown advocate.

[118] A founder member of the Neapolitan College of Doctors (1428), Goffredo in 1460 wrote a commentary on the *Riti della Regia Camera* (Giannone, *Istoria civile*, iii. 193–4, 349).

[119] N. F. Faraglia, *Codice diplomatico sulmonese* (Lanciano, 1888), 21 May 1456. Sulmona was forgiven the fine.

Another council similar in composition and procedure to the Consilium Pecuniae was simultaneously probing corruption among officials within the kingdom of Naples and beyond. Known as the Consilium Subornacionum, it began its proceedings early in 1456 with a proclamation read in all the principal towns calling upon those who had part in or knowledge of any acts of corruption involving officials to denounce them in writing within twenty days. Those who lodged denunciations were guaranteed immunity from prosecution and the retention of any advantage they might have gained from the acts they reported. Towards the end of May the clerk Francesch Barbastre was sent to Sicily to publish the proclamation there and collect the resulting denunciations which he was instructed to deliver directly to the secretary Pere Salvator Valls.[120] It is probable that similar action was taken in the Spanish states.

Though notionally distinct, these two inquisitorial councils worked closely together, and in some documents are treated as virtually one body.[121] Consequently one cannot always be certain to which of them a particular action should be attributed, or whether they did not for certain purposes act jointly. Be that as it may, many communities and individuals came under their hammer and were severely punished for a variety of misdeeds. Several cities in Naples and Sicily, including Manfredonia and a group of Pisan merchants in Palermo were fined for trading with Florence in defiance of the ban imposed on the outbreak of war in 1451.[122] Giovanni di Miroballo, the royal banker and a president of the Sommaria, was condemned to pay 30,000 ducats for various offences. A fine of 40,000 ducats was inflicted on Trani for damage caused by a riot in that city. A large number of citizens of Barletta found themselves denounced for almost every crime in the calendar in the course of the inquests and proceedings started by the 'deputatos in consiliis subornacionum et pecunie'. By payment of a substantial sum all eventually escaped prosecution, save for Roberto della Marra who had to answer charges of treason and

---

[120] ACA Reg. 2916. 40ʳ, 23 May 1456, Text of the proclamation for Sicily; ibid., Castelnuovo, 25 May 1456, Instructions for Barbastre.

[121] e.g. the reference to 'magnificis consiliariis nostris deputatis in consiliis subornacionum et pecunie' in a pardon granted on 10 Oct. 1457 (Rogadeo, *Codice diplomatico*, pp. 419–24).

[122] For this and other actions of the council see P. Gentile, 'Finanze e parlamenti nel Regno di Napoli dal 1450 al 1467', *ASPN* (1913), 211–12.

coining.[123] Many prominent men in Molfetta, and especially Antonio Picarello the judge and assessor of the city, had to buy themselves out of trouble in similar fashion.[124]

Such a thoroughgoing scrutiny into the rights and actions of the most influential elements in the community produced a general consternation which was voiced in the parliament of October 1456. Many of the petitions of that gathering were clearly inspired by the recent activities of the councils; they asked for a general pardon for all crimes committed in the past, except for cases pending and high treason against the king's person; they wanted a general confirmation of titles to lands and rights; they requested that no strained interpretation be put upon their titles. Alfonso did not concede very much. His general pardon excluded treason against the state and officials of the king, as well as his person; it excluded also heresy and coining and offences committed by royal officials in their public capacity. Those guilty of suborning officials could obtain pardon on condition that they denounced the officials and offences concerned within forty days. He insisted that confirmation of feudal and allodial property extended only to that covered by valid title, but promised with respect to such titles 'quod non calumpniantur neque ad extraneum sensum trahantur per fiscales sue Maiestatis ad stimulandum et vexandum eos quibus concessi sunt'.[125] To a petition for a halt to all general and special inquests, except in matters of treason, coining, homicide, and heresy, he returned a flat 'non placet' on the grounds that it would be against the public interest to allow 'multa maleficia' to go unpunished. Although none of these first three petitions of the parliament mentions the Councils of Money and Subornation, their content and the nature of the king's replies leaves little doubt that they had those tribunals in mind. A later article expressed their apprehension of them directly: 'Item che da ciaschuno officiali ordinato da sua Maesta et specialiter dalo consilio dela pecunia se possa appellare ad sua Maesta et pendente appellatione

[123] Rogadeo, *Codice diplomatico*, pp. 413–17. The pardon is dated 8 Oct. 1457.

[124] Ibid., pp. 419–24, Pardon dated 10 Oct. 1457.

[125] ASN Div. Somm. I. 52 (bis), 171ʳ, Baronial petitions presented in the 1456 parliament. On 15 Nov. 1457 three members of the Orsini family—the Count of Gravina, his brother Jacobo, and Rainaldo Orsini—received a general pardon on condition that within four months they denounced any act of corruption involving royal officials that had come to their knowledge (ACA Reg. 2916. 80ʳ).

nichil debeat innovari'. This plea suggests that, as with the Sacrum Consilium, appeals against decisions of the Councils of Money and Subornation were rarely permitted. Alfonso in reply conceded the right of appeal to himself, but insisted that it should not delay the imposition of civil and financial penalties.[126] Neapolitan efforts to draw the teeth of these councils had thus met with little success and they pursued their course with vigour to the end of the reign.

In the course of 1457 they turned their attention on prominent officials and the usurpation of crown rights in the Spanish territories. A decree promulgated in April 1457 revoked all privileges, exemptions, graces, etc. granted *ad beneplacitum* in Valencia, Catalonia, Aragon, and Mallorca on the ground of fraud and loss suffered by the crown.[127] Jacme de Pelaya, who had been specially commissioned as a procurator fiscal for the purpose, was responsible for implementing this decree. To that end he sent his own agents to Spain to investigate the activities of several officials and institutions, among them the *generalidades* of Catalonia and Valencia. As a result of these inquiries some very highly placed persons found themselves under attack. Juan de Moncayo, regent in the office of governor of Aragon, was accused of various crimes and injustices which Queen Maria and the King of Navarre were ordered to investigate.[128] The secretary Francesc Martorell faced charges of corruption,[129] and towards the end of the year de Pelaya demanded the prosecution of the senior secretary Joan Olzina on a number of counts including bribery, malversation of funds during a mission to Spain, and mismanagement of the Aragonese barony of Huesca which he held on lease from the crown.[130] Accusations against men as powerful as these prompted vigorous counter-denunciations which the king is said to have encouraged. Jurists of the Sacrum Consilium[131] joined with

---

[126] 'Placet Regia Maiestati quod a consilio pecunie possit appellare ad sua Maiesta propterea tamen in civilibus vel pecuniariis non impedeatur exequcio . . .' (ASN Div. Somm. I. 52 (bis), 171^r).

[127] ACA Reg. 2662. 70^r, 25 Apr. 1457.

[128] ACA Reg. 2662. 81^v, 30 June 1457, Alfonso to Queen Maria and the King of Navarre. De Moncayo survived to become viceroy of Sicily under Juan II (Vicens Vives, *Fernando el Catolico*, p. 80).

[129] ACB Cart. Com., vol. 27, fol. 141, Pere Boquet to Barcelona, Naples, 23 June 1457.

[130] ACA Reg. 2662. 83^r, 29 Oct. 1457, Alfonso to the King of Navarre.

[131] Nicolau Fillach, Rodrigo Falco, and Cicco Antonio Guindazzo.

Martorell to incriminate the 'Sicilians' of the Consilium Pecuniae.[132] 'Thus', commented the envoy from Barcelona, 'the King listens to all, deals with all, and there is a great deal of heat on all sides.'[133] One is not surprised that bodies which aroused so much hostility among those with influence inside government as well as without should not, unlike the Sacrum Consilium, have survived Alfonso. But the idea of a supreme tribunal with council status acting as a watchdog over the fiscal interests of the crown was to recur often in the development of Spanish administration.

The same Pere Boquet who throws some light on the intrigues surrounding the Consilium Pecuniae refers, in other letters to Barcelona, to a body which appears to have been a council for naval affairs. He wrote in February 1456 that the king had appointed ten persons to organize a crusading fleet and that they were meeting for one hour every day at the arsenal of Naples.[134] Five were Italians (the protonotary of Naples, who presumably acted as president, the Count of Buccino, the Count of Sant' Angelo, the Count of Venafro, and another whose name he did not know) and five Spaniards (Juan Ferrandez de Hijar, Bernat de Requesens, Berenguer de Erill, Bernat Civiller, Pere Joan de Sant Climent) with Guillem Pujades acting as 'promovedor e solicitador'. The Italians, it will be noted, are among those appointed ordinary counsellors in 1450,[135] and it may be that the Spaniards had a similar status in the council. Over a year later Boquet referred to a 'Consell de mar' which had recommended Pere Joan de Sant Climent for the command of three of the king's ships then being armed in Naples.[136] On this occasion he mentioned by name only two of the members—Bernat de Requesens and the Count of Cocentayna. From these two references alone—and no others have yet come to light—it is impossible to judge whether this

[132] ACB Cart. Com., vol. 27, fol. 141, 23 June 1457, Boquet to Barcelona. The epithet 'Sicilian' suggests that Carusio had brought some of his fellow-countrymen into the Consilium Pecuniae. Martorell held the office of *magister portulanus* in Sicily, and it is likely that some of the charges against him related to that office on account of which he still owed the crown large sums when he died in 1466.

[133] Ibid.

[134] Madurell Marimòn, *Mensajeros barceloneses*, p. 511, 19 Feb. 1456.

[135] See above, p. 115.

[136] ACB Cart. Com., vol. 27, fol. 132, Boquet to Barcelona, Naples, 5 June 1457. Pere de Sant Climent was appointed to the command on 4 June 1457 (ACA Reg. 2800. 16ᵛ).

'Consell de mar' was merely an *ad hoc* committee of counsellors or a regular council responsible for naval matters. If the latter it would show how the king made use of his non-legal counsellors, and how rapidly the practice of government through a number of co-ordinate supreme councils was gaining ground in the final years of Alfonso's reign.[137]

What were undoubtedly *ad hoc* committees of the council came into existence during the king's last illness. Boquet is again the source of information.[138] Three 'consells' had, he wrote, been appointed, each consisting of twenty members. One was to investigate a rumour circulating in Naples to the effect that, should the king die, the 'Catalans' living there would all be 'put in their place'; the rumour had already caused many to flee the city. Another of the committees was to advise the Duke of Calabria on affairs of state; the third had the duty of attending with the doctors on the king so that they might have an exact idea of his state of health.[139] Boquet anticipated that once the king had recovered the last two committees would cease to function, but the first would remain in being until its inquiries had been completed.

PARLIAMENTS

Neapolitan parliaments had few powers and limited functions. They did not participate in the making of law, though they were sometimes the occasion for promulgating royal edicts.[140] Their advisory function was strictly limited by the ruler's power to summon and dismiss them at will and to determine what matters should be brought before them. They had no control over customs and excise duties which lay within the royal prerogative. But only a general parliament could grant extraordinary taxation, and therein lay their importance for sovereign and subject because no ruler could hope to manage without some supplementary income. Normally a parliament would make some fixed grant that

---

[137] Cf. the appointment of Cipriano de Meri as a counsellor 'in nostris conciliis tam iusticie et status quam aliis quibusvis in quibus nos aut Ill. Dux Calabrie . . . aut alii quivis nostri generales locumtenentes aderimus', Castel dell'Ovo, 2 Jan. 1458 (ACA Reg. 2916. 86ᵛ).

[138] ACB Cart. Com., vol. 28, fol. 80, Boquet to Barcelona, Naples, 30 May 1458.

[139] This arrangement may have been prompted by the experience of 1444. See above, p. 62.

[140] Frederick II in particular had made use of them for that purpose. See above, p. 8.

remained in force for the whole of a reign; crises that necessitated still greater expenditure, and hence heavier or new taxes, forced a ruler to resort to further parliaments.

General parliaments had taken shape in the time of Frederick II as gatherings of all tenants-in-chief, including prelates, and representatives of the demesne cities. The Angevin rulers did not cultivate them; demesne representation withered away and the clerical element, freed of taxation, did not attend; parliaments thus became the mouthpiece of a single order—the tenants-in-chief. During the last half-century of Angevin rule they lapsed almost completely.[141] When Alfonso proclaimed himself King of Naples the parliament of that realm was therefore an institution of inglorious past and uncertain future.

While civil war lasted neither side could summon a parliament whose authority would be beyond question, and, unless the destruction of records has entirely obliterated all reference to an earlier gathering, Alfonso did not attempt to hold a parliament until January 1441 when one met in Benevento.[142] Who attended, what was discussed, and what decided, we do not know, except for the petition that requested the king to proclaim Ferdinand as his heir.[143] Indeed it is possible that the Benevento assembly was in truth an afforced council.[144] But even if we leave it out of account, Alfonso's reign is still remarkable in that eight other parliaments were summoned in the space of fourteen years: one to consolidate his victory in 1443, four in the period from March 1448 to August 1450, and three between December 1453 and October 1456. Parliament had decidedly come back to life.

Alfonso not only revived the institution, he restored its representative character. That was not done immediately. For the parliament of 1443, following Angevin precedent, he summoned only tenants-in-chief numbering in all 127; the bishops were excluded and the only abbot present attended as a feudatory.[145] Little is known of the proceedings or composition of the next parliament which met in March 1448 to find money for the war

[141] A. Marongiu, *Il parlamento in Italia* (Milan, 1962), p. 232.

[142] Benevento was betrayed to the Aragonese on 19 Nov. 1440 (Ametller y Vinyas, *Alfonso V de Aragón*, ii. 343). [143] Cf. above, p. 43.

[144] For examples of such councils see above, pp. 93–4.

[145] The full record of the proceedings of this parliament, including the names of those summoned and present, is printed in de Bottis, *Privilegii et capitoli*, fols. 2ᵛ–10.

in which the king was then engaged in Tuscany.[146] Writs for the next meeting were issued soon after Alfonso returned from that campaign, and the parliament assembled in Naples towards the end of January 1449. For the first time in at least seventy years syndics from the demesne towns attended.[147] A document dated 20 February 1449 refers to 'parlamento generali Neapoli per nos celebrato de mense Januarii ac presente febroarii magnatibus baronibus et universitatibus eiusdem Regni';[148] another mentions the tax imposed in the parliament by the 'magnates comites barones ac universitates demaniales'.[149] Which of the demesne towns sent representatives we do not know, but it is likely that only a few did so; L'Aquila seems to have spoken for many of the demesne towns in the Abruzzi provinces.[150]

What inspired this restoration of demesne representation in parliament is nowhere explained, so we can only speculate about the king's motives. He may have decided to bring back the towns to offset in some measure the baronial grip on that institution; a few months later, it will be remembered, he attempted to unseat the barons from his council.[151] Experience of the various Spanish Cortes may have persuaded him that a parliament composed of more than one estate would be more manœuvrable than one constituted solely by the tenants-in-chief.[152] Some concession to popular feeling may have been needed to sweeten his demand for a further substantial grant of tax. Whatever the motive, it cannot have been one related merely to the circumstances of the moment, for the demesne towns continued to be represented in the other five parliaments of the reign. A letter addressed to the city of

---

[146] On 31 Mar. 1448 the king promised to repay Eximen Perez de Corella a loan of 5,000 ducats 'delas peccunias de los tres coltas que agora e havido del parlamento tenido en el mes de Março en Napoles' (ACA Reg. 2940. 50ᵛ).

[147] The notion that the royal demesne retained some tenuous footing in the late Angevin parliaments through the presence there of nobles representing the wards of Naples has been challenged by Marongiu. He argues (Il parlamento, p. 231) that these men probably sat in the 'general parliaments' of the city, not in those of the kingdom. They were certainly not present in 1443.

[148] ACA Reg. 2913. 95ʳ.   [149] Ibid. 159ʳ, 21 Mar. 1449.

[150] ACA Reg. 2913. 112ᵛ, Castelnuovo, 15 Apr. 1449. This document refers to a petition presented 'pro parte hominum baronie Carapelle et specialiter castri sancti stephani . . . vigore cuiusdam capituli presentati in parlamento generali per magnificos oratores civitatis nostre aquile'.

[151] Cf. above, pp. 112–13.

[152] Cf. the enlargement of city representation in the Catalan Cortes which he effected between 1449 and 1454. See above, p. 30.

Barcelona describes how, 'on the 11th day of the said month [sc. August 1450] were gathered here all the estates of this kingdom, including many barons and many of the communes'.[153] In Gaeta in December 1453 Alfonso held a parliament 'con li signori baroni regnicoli et universitate demaniale'.[154] For the last parliament (Naples, October 1456) we have a writ summoning the syndics of Bitonto:

Rex Aragonum utriusque Sicilie et cetera. Nobiles et egregii viri fideles nostri dilecti, nuy ad supplicacione de li baruni, che de presente so in la cita de Neapoli per cose concernente grandemente servicio nostro et beneficio de la republica de quisto reame, havimo deliberato tenere parlamento generale in la dicta cita a li x de lo mese de septembro proximo futuro, percio ve dicimo et commandamo che ordinate vostri sindaci cum ampla potesta, che per lo dicto di se trovano presenti allo dicto parlamento, et per niente manche. Data in Turri Octavi die x augusti MDLVI. Rex Alfonsus.[155]

Individual letters of summons were addressed to all tenants-in-chief, including women,[156] who were expected to attend parliament as a feudal obligation either in person or through a procurator. How many syndics a town sent depended upon its size: cities sent four and the smaller towns two as in the days of the Hohenstaufen. Letters of summons were dispatched between four and six weeks before the day fixed for the opening of the parliament.[157] Of the parliaments called by Alfonso, six met in the period between Christmas and the end of March. Financial necessities

---

[153] ACB Cart. Com., vol. 20, fol. 205, 4 Sept. 1450, '. . . a xi del dit mes foren açi ajustats tots los staments de quest Regne, en que foren molts barons, e moltes deles universitats'.

[154] ACA Reg. 2700. 45ᵛ, Gaeta, 23 Dec. 1453. A guarantee for the Prince of Taranto that the participation of the Duke of Andria as his procurator shall not prejudice any of his privileges.

[155] Rogadeo, *Codice diplomatico*, no. 225. The writ is addressed, 'Nobilibus et egregiis viris capitanio, universitati et hominibus terre Bitonti fidelibus nostris dilectis'.

[156] The writs for the 1443 parliament ran in part: '. . . vobis dicimus et districte precipiendo mandamus pro prima secunda et tertia iussionibus ac peremptorie, ut die xxxi et ultimo mensis Januarii de proximo secuturi apud dictam urbem (sc. Benevento) ubi duce altissimo erimus personaliter pro dicto celebrando parlamento compareatis inibique continuis diebus intersitis donec id per nos finitum licentiatumque fuerit, alioquin ad illius celebrationem et acta procedemus uti nobis visum fuerit vestri absentia non obstante et contumaciam exigente' (de Bottis, *Privilegii et capitoli*, fol. 2ᵛ).

[157] Letters dispatched from Barletta on 20 Dec. 1442 summoned tenants-in-chief to appear in Benevento on 31 Jan. 1443.

governed the timing to a certain extent, as it was necessary to make arrangements for the collection of any new tax well in advance of the beginning of the financial year in September. Account was also taken of the unhealthy atmosphere in the cities during the summer months when outbreaks of disease were liable to drive the wealthier citizens into the countryside. Meeting in the winter too presented its problems. The exceptionally severe weather of January 1443 made travelling so difficult that the opening of parliament was delayed for a whole month.[158] Again in 1450 the opening fixed for 20 February had to be postponed to 3 March, 'cum ad ipsum statutum diem ipsi magnates et barones non convenissent'.[159] But not all late arrival can be put down to bad weather. It arose too from a disinclination to attend gatherings likely to produce more burdens than benefits; and there were those who feared for their safety. Many barons, according to Beccadelli, went reluctantly to the 1443 parliament, afraid that the king would take the opportunity to lay hands on those who had opposed him.[160] On that occasion their misgivings proved unfounded and general confidence was established for the future. Even so, individuals with an uneasy conscience or with doubts as to the king's favour did not readily venture from the comparative security of their domains. Thus the Marquis of Gerace, whom Alfonso intended to arrest at the April parliament of 1455, ignored the summons.[161] Despite the delays and hesitations ninety-nine of the 127 tenants-in-chief summoned in 1443 made an appearance in the parliament either in person or through a procurator. No lists of attendance have survived for other parliaments.

Up to the time of Charles I the kings of Sicily had convoked their Neapolitan parliaments in various cities, but under the Angevins Naples as the capital became the regular meeting-place.[162] The

---

[158] The king arrived in Benevento on the stipulated day and had to wait: 'cum vellet ipsa regia maiestas praestolari alios ut supra vocatos qui hiemis asperitate nondum venerant' (de Bottis, *Privilegii et capitoli*, fol. 3ᵛ). Cf. Ametller y Vinyas, *Alfonso V de Aragón*, ii. 446.

[159] Ametller y Vinyas, *Alfonso V de Aragón*, iii. 684, Preamble to the *capitoli* of the parliament.

[160] *De dictis et factis*, iii.

[161] ACA Reg. 2700. 92ʳ, Castelnuovo, 2 Mar. 1455, King to viceroy of Calabria instructing him to allow the marquis to travel without hindrance to the parliament, 'car ve convocat e per nos demanat a parlament'. The marquis was wanted for a number of crimes against his vassals and royal authority for which he was arrested later in 1455 and condemned to death.

[162] Giannone, *Istoria civile*, iii. 38–9.

hostility of the capital to the Aragonese cause during the civil war upset this state of affairs. Alfonso held his first parliament or great council in Benevento when Naples was still held by René of Anjou, and in December 1442, as a mark of his displeasure towards that city, he summoned his first full parliament in Benevento. Naples, anxious to secure its privileges, protested against this departure from long-established custom, but only succeeded in having the parliament transferred within its walls by offering the king a victor's triumphal entry in classical Roman style.[163] All but one of the subsequent parliaments met in the capital, the exception being that held in Gaeta in December 1453. Naples thus managed, after an initial humiliation, to maintain its claim to be the meeting-place of parliaments. Besides being the administrative centre, one of its undoubted advantages was the number of large convents and churches within its walls, the chapter houses of which offered suitable meeting-places. The parliament of 1443 met in the convent of San Lorenzo,[164] in August 1450 it assembled in Santa Maria Incoronata and in 1456 in Santa Chiara. On the latter occasion the members heard the king's speech in the smaller hall of Castelnuovo.[165] Reconstruction work going on in the royal palace may have discouraged its use at other times; it is also possible that parliaments preferred to meet in a place less directly in the hand of the king.

Neapolitan custom prescribed that the king should attend parliaments in the company of the great officers of state: he entered the hall of assembly preceded by the constable bearing a naked sword and followed by the other six who took their seats on either side of the throne with the seneschal at his feet. Such, we may imagine, was the ceremonial observed in 1443 when these dignitaries were all present in Naples. In other parliaments many were not on hand,[166] so this procedure could not be followed. From 1448 Alfonso allowed his son the Duke of Calabria to play a prominent role. In that year Ferdinand opened the parliament as

---

[163] The triumphal entry is fully described in 'Racconti di storia napoletana', *ASPN* (1908), 474–544.

[164] The convent was paid 8 ducats compensation for damage done in the kitchen and refectory on the day the king gave a banquet for the barons attending this parliament (Minieri Riccio, 'Alcuni fatti di Alfonso I', p. 236).

[165] ACB Cart. Com., vol. 26, fol. 162, Boquet to Barcelona, 9 Oct. 1456.

[166] The Duke of Andria acted as procurator for his brother the constable on at least three occasions: March 1450, August 1450, and December 1453.

locumtenens generalis of the absent king; in March 1450 he presented the petitions of the barons to the king, and in 1456, as spokesman for the barons, he replied to the speech from the throne. These latter roles presumably fell to him as senior magnate of the kingdom.

Parliaments opened with an address in which the king set forth his reasons for summoning his subjects, and sometimes he made a specific statement of the assistance he expected from them. Pere Boquet has left an account of this opening ceremony in the parliament of 1456:

> Today [9 Oct. 1456] the king sat on his throne in the small hall of the castle [Castelnuovo] and all the dukes, counts, princes, and barons were present as a parliament. There he expressed his thanks for the services, aids, and true obedience that they had given him, and afterwards he told them that he was going to Spain and would leave them the duke his son who had been brought up among them, and that he would soon return for he held them in great favour. Then the Duke of Calabria spoke on behalf of them all, and so the parliament ended.[167]

In 1443 it was the logothete, the Count of Fondi, who rose after Alfonso had finished speaking and asked leave for the assembly to adjourn in order to discuss its reply. The evidence suggests that in those parliaments which included representatives of the demesne cities the latter held their consultations apart from the barons and returned separate petitions. Those *capitoli* (petitions followed by the king's reply) which have survived are all drawn up in the name of the tenants-in-chief alone, even for parliaments in which syndics of the demesne are known to have participated. Thus, the *capitoli* of the 1456 parliament bear this superscription: 'Li baroni de quisto Reame de Sicilia citra farum tanto in generale quanto in speciale per se ipsi et per nome et parte de loro vaxalli subditi incoli et habitatori de loro terre supplicano humilemente ala Maesta del Senyor che li conceda le infrascripte gratie.'[168]

---

[167] ACB Cart. Com., vol. 26, fol. 162, Boquet to Barcelona, 9 Oct. 1456: 'Huy lo Senyor Rey ha segut en son tribunal dins lo castel en la petita sala e tots los duchs comtes princeps e barons en forma de cort, e ali als fetes moltes gracies dels serveys fins açi fets donatives e bones obediencies, e apres los a notifficada sa anada aqui e quells laquia lo duc son fill criats entre ells e que prest tornaria deça per la bona voluntat quells te; e lo duc de calabria ha parlat per tots e axi an fet fi ala cort.'

[168] ASN Div. Somm. I. 52 (bis), 171ʳ. Gentile ('Finanze e parlamenti,' pp. 223–31) printed a version of these *capitoli* from the register Privilegiorum 2, fol. 263, of the Neapolitan chancery which has since been destroyed.

The inhabitants of the royal demesne are carefully excluded from the scope of these articles, but they did present petitions. Privileges granted to demesne subjects in Terra di Bari, Capitanata, and Barletta on 1 October 1457 arose 'ex capitulis parlamenti'.[169] Another privilege for Barletta dated 11 October 1457 is still more specific since it notes that it arises from *capitolo* number 47 of the petitions presented by the demesne representatives in parliament.[170] The syndics of L'Aquila introduced petitions in the parliament of 1449.[171] That no full *capitoli* for the royal demesne have survived from any parliament is probably due to the fact that, unlike those of the barons, they were not embodied in the form of a general privilege but dealt with in detail administratively.[172] Proffers of aid, on the other hand, seem to have come jointly from the barons and syndics of the demesne.

The record of the 1443 parliament shows that the barons, having deliberated, returned to the king with a reply consisting of a preamble and twelve articles which the royal secretary Joan Olzina read to the full assembly. It was then the turn of the king and his council to consider the requests and offer of aid contained in the articles. They quickly reached their decisions, and on the following day conveyed them to the parliament. Further discussion then ensued on a number of political issues such as recognition of Ferdinand as Duke of Calabria and heir to the throne, and on the problem of reconciling the king with the pope.[173] These matters the barons first discussed among themselves; they also pursued negotiations with the king for a modification of the answers he had returned to some of the earlier articles. In a final session on 9 March Alfonso announced further concessions and then gave those present leave to depart.[174] Though the disappearance of the record of proceedings for other parliaments makes generalization impossible, it is likely that later assemblies were conducted in a similar manner.

---

[169] Rogadeo, *Codice diplomatico*, pp. 409–12.

[170] Ibid., p. 424.

[171] See above, p. 126.

[172] The barons always took care to ask that their *capitoli* be drawn up in the form of a privilege and that each of them should have a copy—e.g. in 1456: 'Item supplicano li dicti baroni che delle dicte gracie et capituli se degne sua Maesta farene expedire uno privilegio con omne oportune sollempnita opur como vorranno dicti baroni et li possano tenere et usare a loro cauthela.'

[173] See above, p. 34.

[174] de Bottis, *Privilegii et capitoli*, fols. 8–10.

Since no accurate list of the parliaments which met in Alfonso's reign has yet been published,[175] a brief chronological survey is needed here. The uncertain status of the assembly held in Benevento in January 1441 has already been noted, [176] so the parliament held with the barons in Naples during March 1443 must still be counted the first undoubted parliament of the reign. Another did not meet until March 1448 when the king found himself obliged to ask, through his *locumtenens generalis*, for financial aid. We know nothing about it other than that it was held in Naples and granted the king three aids or *collectae*.[177] After his return from Tuscany Alfonso lost no time in calling another parliament for the end of January 1449 with the primary purpose of modifying the system of direct taxation. Its meeting in Naples lasted into February and led to the substitution of a general tax in place of the hearth tax that had been introduced in 1443 with disappointing results from the treasury point of view.[178] The baronial *capitoli* of the next parliament which assembled in Naples in March 1450 have been preserved in a register of the Archivo de la Corona de Aragón.[179] In that document we are able to observe the baronial reaction to the extensive administrative reforms which Alfonso had introduced in the previous year. But it seems not to have offered any financial aid to the crown, which was probably the reason why Alfonso called another parliament in August that same year. This assembly has entirely escaped notice. Ametller y Vinyas confuses it with the March parliament;[180] Gentile, while noting that writs of summons were sent out early in June 1450, believes that it never met.[181] Letters from some envoys of Barcelona newly arrived in Naples rescue us from this uncertainty. They wrote on 6 July 1450, 'It is certain that the king has summoned a parliament

---

[175] The best surveys of the Neapolitan parliament in this period are those of A. Marongiu, *Il parlamento in Italia* and 'Il parlamento baronale nel 1443', *Samnium*, 4 (1950), 1–16.

[176] See above, p. 125.

[177] Cf. above, p. 125. A letter addressed to Giovanni di Miroballo specifies certain crown revenues from which he may recover loans made to the king: among them are the proceeds 'collectarum trium novissime in parlamento celebrato Neapoli in toto dicto Regno generaliter impositarum' (ACA Reg. 2913. 39ᵛ, Piombino, 29 Aug. 1448).

[178] For the hearth tax and general tax see below, pp. 210 ff.

[179] ACA Reg. 2914. 52ʳ–55ᵛ. They have been published by Ametller y Vinyas, *Alfonso V de Aragón*, iii. 684–92.

[180] *Alfonso V de Aragón*, ii. 686–95.

[181] 'Finanze e parlamenti', p. 190.

of barons in this city on the 10th August next.'[182] On 22 July they had an audience with the king at Torre del Greco. To their renewed request that he would visit his Spanish possessions he replied 'that for the moment he could not speak to us with any certainty about these matters because he had summoned a general parliament of the kingdom in this city for the 10 August coming, and that the principal purpose of it would be to put this kingdom in order'.[183] When it met they were invited to attend the opening ceremony: 'The king addressed them at the Incoronata and wished that we should be present at the address. The said parliament came to an end after ten days and offered the king a subsidy of 70,000 ducats.'[184]

An interval of more than three years elapsed before another parliament met in December 1453, this time in Gaeta. Nothing is known of its proceedings beyond the fact that it gave the king a forced loan of 220,000 ducats payable by barons and demesne towns alike.[185] The next parliament, which met in Naples in April 1455, is also ill documented. From it Alfonso managed to cajole further extraordinary aid in the form of a levy of one-fifth on all provisions and salaries for an indefinite period, save for certain officials who were to pay one-sixth for one year only. The proceeds of the levy were supposed to build twelve galleys for the defence of the kingdom and for use in a crusade.[186] Alfonso's last parliament met in October 1456 and may have been called at the instance of the barons rather than because the king wanted still more money. In the writ for Bitonto the parliament is said to have been summoned 'ad supplicacione de li baruni',[187] and if we consider the concern over the activity of the Councils of Money and Subornation which is reflected in the *capitoli*, we may well believe that both barons and demesne towns might have wished to have

---

[182] ACB Cart. Com., vol. 20, fol. 154: 'Es cert que lo dit Senyor Rey ha convocat parlament de barons en aquesta ciutat daçi a x del mes de Agost prop vinent.'

[183] Ibid., fol. 168, 22 July 1450: '. . . que ell ara bonament nons pot parlar clar dels dits affers, e aço pertant com ell ha convocat parlament general de aquest Regne en aquesta ciutat a x del mes de Agost prop vinent, e aço per principi de metre en orde aquest Regne.'

[184] Ibid., fol. 205, 4 Sept. 1450: 'E lo senyor Rey proposa devant lo dit parlament ala Coronada, lo dit parlament pres conclusio, e proferi al dit Senyor de donatiu setanta milia ducats.'

[185] Barletta was assessed to pay 3,000 ducats towards the loan, 'prout in parlamento generali per nos pridem magnatibus baronibus et universitatibus dicti ipsius Regni fuit ordinatum' (Rogadeo, *Codice diplomatico*, p. 310, 17 Apr. 1454).

[186] Gentile, 'Finanze e parlamenti', p. 211.   [187] See above, p. 127.

recourse to the forum of a parliament to defend their interests.[188] On the other hand, this parliament once more reformed the system of direct tax in such a manner that the burden was considerably increased,[189] so perhaps the wording of the writ should not be taken too much at its face value.

Marongiu has remarked, apropos of the 1443 parliament, that 'il modo di procedere e di deliberare è estremamente simile a quello delle *cortes* dei paesi della corona d'Aragona.'[190] This may well be true of procedure, for the virtual demise of the Neapolitan parliament before Alfonso came to the throne had stifled the growth of native traditions. In the influence they were able to wield in the state, however, the general parliaments of Naples were almost powerless when compared to their counterparts elsewhere in the Aragonese dominions. In Aragon, Sicily, and Sardinia the agreements reached between the king and his parliaments were drawn up in the form of a contract (*in vim contractus*) legally binding on both parties.[191] In Naples, as we have seen, the two estates treated separately, and the concessions the king made in answer to their petitions were granted either generally or individually in the form of privileges *ad beneplacitum*. The manner in which Alfonso interpreted his undertaking to maintain the pre-eminence of the protonotary in the council is one example of the discretion he enjoyed with respect to parliamentary *capitoli*. Withdrawal of a privilege did not affect a financial aid granted by the same parliament. An effort had been made by the 1456 parliament to establish a link between privileges and aids, if only on a contracting-out basis:

... se alcuna cita o terra o alcune citate o terre dello dicto reame non vorra o vorranno concorrere et pagare lo dicto supplemento, quella tale o tali non debia nec debianno gaudere le gracie remissioni et indulti contenti in deli capituli delo dicto parlamento, ma de quello se intenda et intendano excluse et exempti non obstante qualcuna razone in contrario se potessero adure et allegare et cussi se intendano deli baroni.[192]

The king firmly squashed the idea:

... nulla civitas castrum vel terra aut aliquis princeps dux marchio comes baro miles aut alius cuiuscumque conditionis fuerit pretextu aut

---

[188] Cf. above, p. 121.   [189] Cf. below, p. 214.
[190] *Il parlamento*, p. 333.
[191] Marongiu, 'Il parlamento baronale', pp. 10–11.
[192] ASN Div. Somm. I. 52 (bis), 171.

colore alicuius gracie privilegii vel immunitatis aut exemptionis sit liber aut exemptus a solutione vel contributione collectarum et adjunctionis predictarum immo teneantur et sint astricte solvere et contribuere in predictis.[193]

There must be no suggestion that the payment of taxes was in any way dependent upon the granting or enjoyment of privileges lest the Neapolitan parliament take a step towards the contractual agreements which restricted royal authority in other states.

From the manner in which the 1456 parliament worded its proposal on privileges and taxes one might imagine that the initiative had come from the syndics of the royal demesne: the emphasis is placed upon towns and cities, while the barons are seemingly tacked on as a last-minute addition. Hints such as this should make us cautious in assuming that the representatives of the cities were as passive as the scattered fragments of the parliamentary record might have us believe. Alfonso had brought the institution of parliament back to life in Naples, given it an important voice in determining the nature of direct taxation, and made it a forum in which his subjects could present their grievances. If his ends were mainly financial and political, it is still remarkable that he chose parliament as a major instrument for attaining them.[194]

[193] Ibid.

[194] Cf. Marongiu, *Il parlamento*, p. 332: 'Con ciò non ci vuol dire che l'avvento aragonese porti senz'altro con sè a Napoli un vero istituto ed una vera attività parlamentare. Ma si deve pur sempre constatare che le assemblee assumono d'ora in poi carattere ed importanza abbastanza nuovi e una concreta influenza su tutta la vita del paese. Questa rinnovata attività suscitata e richiesta del sovrano, non ha nè continuità nè periodicità. E ancora frammentaria, episodica, incerta. Ma ogni episodio è legato al precedente da una, non stretta ma pur evidente, connessione e tutto l'insieme è abbastanza diverso e ben più consistente di quel che non fosse in passato.'

V

JUSTICE

ANY attempt to describe the dispensation of justice as a distinct function of government in the kingdom of Naples, or indeed in any other state of that period, runs into the difficulty that judicial and administrative functions were not attributed to distinct categories of officials. Almost every office of state from the kingship downwards conferred power of both kinds on the person who held it. We have seen how authority in the royal household implied jurisdiction over the appropriate category of domestics or courtiers. In the Sommaria and treasury administrative and judicial functions went hand in hand. The mint had its own court. The office of chancellor conferred on its holder jurisdiction over those whom he appointed as public notaries; the admiral had a court with competence in a variety of matters related to his nominal function as commander of the naval forces of the kingdom. In other words, executive and judicial authority were for many purposes combined in the individual office-holder as they were in the sovereign whom he represented. A useful distinction can, however, be made between the limited jurisdiction—in terms of persons, territory, or matter—that belonged to the majority of offices, and the general jurisdiction attributed to certain tribunals and officials of the crown. It is with the latter that this chapter will be mainly concerned.

The hierarchy of judicial authority, as it existed when Alfonso had firmly established his administration, is set forth in a decree issued in 1454 to curb the excesses of its lesser agents:

Alguatzirii vero et alii officiales superius nominati qui meri exequtores existunt nisi in criminis fragrantia vel persequtione vel ubi aliis parte de jure liceret aliquem absque mandato nostro aut nostri cancellarii presidentis nostri sacri consilii vel vicecancellarii aut regentis cancellariam vel regentis vicariam vel aliorum judicum aut delegatorum habentium jurisdictionem et potestatem capere non possint.[1]

[1] ASN Priv. I. 165ʳ, 1 Aug. 1454.

Thus we have a descending order of the king, the chancellor as president of the council,[2] the vice-chancellor or regent of the chancery, the regent of the Vicaria and, finally, the general body of judges. It is a ranking that differs markedly from the earlier pattern of judicial authority in the kingdom. At the end of the Angevin period there existed nominally two supreme tribunals with general jurisdiction: the *magna curia* of the *magister justiciarius* and the court of the Vicaria.[3] Though at one time distinct in their functions and personnel, they had become, by the time of Giovanna II, for all practical purposes identical courts. The *magister justiciarius* or his *locumtenens* presided over both, both had three judges, the same procedural code, a similar organization, and a very similar competence; as a result they were often looked upon as two sessions of the same tribunal. Alfonso and his closest associates were accustomed to the very different system of Aragon where the chancery was the office of state that managed judicial business.[4] There the chancellor, the vice-chancellor, the *promovedors*, and the *oydors* were the key figures. By 1454 they had taken over in the Italian kingdom too.

The supreme jurisdiction of the council, which Alfonso developed for all his territories and which had a particular impact in Naples, has been described in the previous chapter; so too has the manner in which a Spanish chancellor came to preside over the tribunal of the council, the Sacrum Consilium, delivering judgement 'per dictum dominum Regem seu in eius personam'. Alfonso himself would very rarely intervene in that body. Every Friday morning, however, he held public audiences to receive petitions touching matters of justice ('singulis conquerentibus iusticiam ministrando').[5] These petitions he would usually refer to the council for consideration and appropriate action. Contemporaries praised the king for thus making justice available to those who might otherwise find their way barred in the costly and

---

[2] By this date the Spanish chancellor de Pallars had established himself as president of the council. Cf. above, p. 118.

[3] Cf. above, p. 16.

[4] The Household Ordinance describes the chancellor's office as that in which 'tots los negocis justicie concernents los quals a la nostra cort devoluts son espeegadors' (Bofarull y Mascaró, *Documentos inéditos*, V. 115).

[5] ACA Reg. 2918. 4ʳ, 3 July 1451. This document refers to the petition presented by the ship's master Mincio de Costanzio asking for execution of judgement against Nicolau Binot. Cf. above, p. 110.

intricate avenues of the law.[6] Occasionally too the king intervened in a judicial process already initiated—either to delay it, speed it, annul it, or transfer it from one judge or tribunal to another. In September 1445, when hard pressed for troops, he instructed his council in Naples to delay, 'under the most honest pretexts possible', proceedings in a case between Masello Sacco on the one hand and the brothers Aimerico and Michele di Sanseverino on the other, because the latter had offered to join his army with one hundred horse.[7] Sometimes he put a temporary but open stop upon proceedings that involved those called away on his service. Sometimes the intercession of 'friends at court' led him to intervene with a pardon which rescued an accused person from the clutches of a tribunal. This happened in the case of Galeazzo di Tarsia, lord of Belmonte, who stood accused in the Vicaria of several grave crimes including false imprisonment, torture, receiving fugitives from justice, leading an armed mob against Cosenza, and refusing entry to royal officials. At the instance of courtiers he was pardoned and the investigating judge, Michele Riccio, ordered to drop the case.[8] Homicide under circumstances of intense provocation or passion was frequently pardoned. The case of Antonio Toscano of Capua is typical of many. His wife had left him and gone to live in a brothel. After a number of warnings and attempts to get her back had failed, the husband had strangled her in a violent quarrel. To avoid scandal the relatives of both parties had agreed to petition the king for a pardon for Antonio.[9] Another pardon suggests a killing, possibly as the result of a duel, among members of the royal household. Diego, a Portuguese *familiaris*, and Jacobo de Borbo, the *magister scolarium cappelle*, had fought with Augustino de Labocca, the adopted son of a constable. Both Diego and Augustino had been badly wounded and Diego had died. Jacobo subsequently forgave

---

[6] e.g. Beccadelli, *De dictis et factis*, i. He represents the Friday audiences as being intended only for the petitions of the poor.

[7] ACA Reg. 2698. 103ʳ, 5 Sept. 1445.

[8] ACA Reg. 2914. 178ʳ, 20 Nov. 1451. A charge of murder against Andreu de Vesach was dropped at the instance of Frederick III (Reg. 2915. 197ᵛ, 10 Apr. 1452).

[9] ACA Reg. 2909. 174ʳ, 7 Jan. 1446. Da Bisticci ('Vita del Re Alfonso', pp. 393–5) has a story of a young man, related to the king, who was killed by the husband of a woman with whom he was having an affair. The husband, a courtier, went to report the matter to the king who pardoned him and ordered the relatives of the dead man not to molest him.

his opponent and had a public instrument drawn up to that effect by a notary. Just over a year later the matter was finally closed by a royal pardon:

Quamvis iusticia in terris necessaria sit adeo ut undiquemque delinquentem pena merita sequi debeat, frequenter tamen melius est erga peccatoris pietate et clementia uti quam severitate et rigore ad exemplum salvatoris nostri Jhesu Christi qui errores humanos quamcumque ingentes atque inmanes ad misericordiam semper retulisse visus est.[10]

Pardons of a political nature were common in the years immediately following the defeat of René of Anjou when supporters of the vanquished party were making their peace with Alfonso.[11] Those who had fought for the king too were often safeguarded against possible legal action for violence done in the course of the war by comprehensive pardons which usually covered any wrong they might have committed up to the time that the city of Naples fell.[12] A particularly striking instance of the king's intervention to transfer a case from one tribunal to another occurred in a lawsuit between Carlo di Campobasso and the heirs of Jacobo de Zuzulo. On 3 September 1449 he ordered the Sommaria judge Antonio de Carusio to stop his proceedings in the case and transfer it to the ordinary judge of Barletta in conformity with a privilege of the city which protected citizens from being cited before an outside tribunal in the first instance.[13] On 4 May 1450 Carusio received a further order to proceed with the case, give judgement speedily, and inform the king immediately by letter of the sentence, which he was not however to execute without the king's express command.[14] Only a fortnight later that instruction was again countermanded and the case given to the captain of Barletta.[15] One week later it was handed back to Carusio.[16] A tug-of-war at court between the interests involved usually lay behind this kind of interference.

Alfonso took his Spanish vice-chancellor with him to Italy. Jacme Pelegri, a Valencian, who had held the office since at least

---

[10] ACA Reg. 2914. 184ʳ, 1 April 1452.

[11] e.g. pardon for Giorgio d'Alemagna, Count of Buccino (ACA Reg. 2906. 73ᵛ, 21 Apr. 1444) and for Ottino Caracciolo, Count of Nicastro (ACA Reg. 2904. 88ᵛ, 24 Sept. 1442).

[12] e.g. a pardon for Jacobo and Marino de Lagonissa and Matalda de Stilliatis, their retainers and vassals, issued 25 Feb. 1444 (ACA Reg. 2909. 184ʳ).

[13] Rogadeo, Codice diplomatico, p. 212.

[14] Ibid., p. 222.   [15] Ibid., p. 223.   [16] Ibid., p. 223.

1423,[17] continued to act in that capacity as chief legal officer of the crown until his death in 1440/1.[18] The vice-chancellor who took part in the 1443 parliament was Ferrer Ram and it is likely that he had succeeded Pelegri.[19] But he did not remain long in that office, for towards the end of 1443 he moved into the office of protonotary of Aragon, left vacant on the death of his father. That Ram should have given up a vice-chancellorship to become protonotary suggests that the former office cannot have been the vice-chancellorship of Aragon which ranked above that of the protonotary. One may therefore surmise that, following the death of Pelegri, Alfonso decided to appoint a vice-chancellor specifically for the kingdom of Naples, and that it was this post that Ram held. It is certain that in December 1443, about the time that Ram assumed the office of protonotary of Aragon, a Sicilian doctor of laws named Battista Platamone became vice-chancellor for the kingdom of Sicily *citra farum*.

Platamone began his legal career as an advocate fiscal in Sicily in 1420,[20] rose to the rank of royal secretary in 1426, and in 1431 became a judge of the *magna curia*. He twice served on the Sicilian viceregal council in the king's absence. Alfonso also began to use his talents in diplomatic affairs when in December 1432 he sent him with an Aragonese delegation to Naples.[21] He subsequently undertook other missions to Rome, Milan, and Venice,[22] and took part in abortive peace negotiations with Genoa in 1443.[23] As a lawyer he had played a prominent part in developing the tribunal of the Sacrum Consilium; several of the earlier council judgements make mention of him as the counsellor to whom a case had been referred.[24] By the time he became vice-chancellor of

[17] Toppi, *De origine tribunalium*, ii. 127. Barzizza (*Orationes et epistolae*, p. 107) mentions that he was vice-chancellor in 1432.

[18] ACA Reg. 2901. 52^v, 17 Mar. 1442. This letter orders the payment of salary owed to the late Jacme Pelegri to his son and heir Guillem Pelegri, advocate fiscal in the kingdom of Valencia.

[19] In one of his letters to Barcelona written in March 1443, Vinyes refers to Ferrer Ram as the vice-chancellor (Madurell Marimon, *Mensajeros barceloneses*, p. 224). On 4 July 1443, in his capacity as vice-chancellor, Ram authorized the appointment of a constable to serve the captain of Naples (ACA Reg. 2909. 9^v).

[20] Platamone's career is described in some detail in Marletta, 'Un uomo di stato del Quattrocento: Battista Platamone'.

[21] Ametller y Vinyas, *Alfonso V de Aragón*, i. 363.

[22] Ibid., pp. 398, 443, 460.   [23] Ibid. ii. 493.

[24] e.g. he examined the disputed possession of the county of Monteodorisio (ACA Reg. 2902. 57^r, 4 Aug. 1442), another case of disputed possession in

Naples, Platamone had thus acquired an impressive experience
of legal, administrative, and diplomatic affairs. Lorenzo Valla,
who dedicated *De professione religiosorum* to him, described
Platamone as 'virum hoc tempestate singularem et omnes doc-
trinae maximarumque rerum peritissimum'.[25] Beccadelli compared
him to Hercules taking the burden of state upon his shoulders.[26]

The earliest extant document in which Platamone is styled vice-
chancellor bears the date 30 December 1443 and is concerned with
an investigation which he and Antonio Beccadelli had conducted
by order of the council into the insanity of the Duke of Andria.[27]
Although the instrument appointing him vice-chancellor appears
not to have survived, his later activities suggest that it must have
laid upon him duties very similar to those of the Aragonese vice-
chancellors. He attended the council, occasionally undertaking the
examination of petitions,[28] and acting generally as senior legal
adviser to the king; in the latter capacity he accompanied Alfonso
throughout the Tuscan war. Negotiations over the terms of the
investiture took him to Rome from March till May in 1444[29] and
again in March and April of the following year.[30] The reform of
the Sacrum Consilium in 1449 enhanced his status still further
by providing that he should preside over the conciliar court in
the absence of the Archbishop of Naples, and that the court
should meet in his own house when the king was not resident in
Castelnuovo.[31] Like the vice-chancellor of Aragon, Platamone also
seems to have been invested with the authority to read, correct,
and countersign letters emanating from the secretarial offices.
His countersignature appears on a very large number of documents.
Many of them touch on the financial interests of the crown:

Calabria (ibid. 91ʳ, 4 Oct. 1442), and a petition for restitution of a fief (ibid.
167ᵛ, 22 Mar. 1443).

[25] Resta, *L'espistolario del Panormita*, p. 231.

[26] *Epistolae campanae*, No. 19. The letter addressed to Platamone continues:
'. . . sed et te hortor ut fortunam serves quaeris quomodo hisdem artibus quibus
illam adsecutus es, humanitate, mansuetudine, diligentia, et gratitudine sis
gratus Principi qui te erexit ad coelum: sis diligens negotiis, quibus ille te
proposuit, sis mansuetus ad omnia, benignus in omnes.'

[27] ACA Reg. 2904. 115ʳ.

[28] e.g. with Ferrer Ram he examined a petition from Francavilla seeking confirmation of its inalienability from the royal demesne (ACA Reg. 2690. 106ᵛ,
1 Sept. 1444).

[29] ACA Reg. 2653. 31; Reg. 2698. 43ᵛ; Reg. 2690. 57ᵛ.

[30] ACA Reg. 2939. 20ʳ; Reg. 2690. 144ᵛ; cf. above, p. 36.

[31] Cf. above, p. 113.

a privilege granting the *condottiere* Piccinino all royal revenues in the Abruzzi to meet his *condotta*;[32] an order to officials not to hinder the Bishop of Spoleto and others in the collection of certain *gabelle*;[33] a privilege affirming the rights of the Duke of San Marco in the silk *gabella* of Calabria.[34] Others have a legal character: the extension of a justiciar's term of office;[35] confirmation of a fief;[36] a pardon for an Angevin supporter.[37] The countersignatures become especially numerous during the period of the Tuscan war (1447–8) when many officials who would normally have shared the task with him were left behind in Naples.[38]

Alfonso had not intended, when he appointed Platamone vice-chancellor, that his authority should be restricted to the kingdom of Naples, for such a limitation would place a severe handicap on his role in the council. Acting presumably with the consent of his sovereign, Platamone wrote early in 1444 to Pere de Sent Climent, *magister rationalis* of Catalonia, to ask whether he might not, like his Spanish counterparts, exercise his office in all lands subject to the king. His letter was passed to the city council of Barcelona which replied that it knew of nothing in the laws of Aragon to debar him from acting within the territory of the Corona de Aragón.[39] Fortified by that assurance, Platamone asked for transcripts of all documents relating to the office, only to be informed that it had since come to light that a vice-chancellor of the Crown of Aragon had to be a doctor of laws or jurist born and effectively domiciled in either Valencia, Aragon, Catalonia, or Mallorca.[40] There ended his pretensions to a sphere of authority

[32] ACA Reg. 2903. 119ᵛ, 25 Feb. 1444.
[33] ACA Reg. 2904. 120ᵛ, 21 Mar. 1444.
[34] ACA Reg. 2906. 169ᵛ, 3 June 1445.
[35] ACA Reg. 2904. 145ʳ, 23 May 1444.
[36] ACA Reg. 2903. 158ʳ, 25 July 1444.
[37] ACA Reg. 2906. 98ʳ, 20 Mar. 1444.
[38] The registers ACA Reg. 2656 and 2657 belong to these years and contain a very large number of documents countersigned by the vice-chancellor.
[39] ACB Lletres closes, No. 323, vi. 10. 128ʳ, 15 Oct. 1444. After thanking Platamone for the help he had given to the city's envoys in Naples, the letter turns to his query: 'com vos sots constituit en dubte si us serie permes de usar de vostre offici de vice-chanceller axi en lo Regne de Sicilia com encare en aquestes regnes e terres del dit Senyor deça mar constituits o si per qualsevol raho serie prohibit.' It concludes, 'nosem som veridicament informats e havem trobat en cert que constitucions leys dela terra e altres qualsevol obstacles nous fan nosa ne us contrasten en res de usar de vostra presidencia e vicicancellaria axi en Sicilia com deça en aquestes parts dela Senyoria del dit Senyor.'
[40] Ibid. 193ᵛ, 6 Mar. 1445, Council of Barcelona to Platamone.

extending to all the states ruled by Alfonso. Reporting his death, the envoy of Barcelona referred to him as 'Micer Babtiste de platamone . . . quis deze açi vicicancellari'.[41] Part of his salary was none the less assigned on the revenues of the seal of the Batle General of Catalonia,[42] and he occasionally countersigned documents concerned with Spanish business in his capacity as vice-chancellor.[43]

Having failed to make Platamone vice-chancellor throughout his empire, Alfonso appointed Juan de Funes vice-chancellor for the Crown of Aragon. The death of both Platamone and de Funes in the summer of 1451 presented him with a new opportunity, which he took on Holy Cross Day (14 September) 1451 by appointing Valenti Claver as his new vice-chancellor for all his realms.[44] Earlier in the year, it will be remembered, the Bishop of Urgell as chancellor had assumed the presidency of the council.[45] Thus were the highest offices and functions of the Aragonese chancery transplanted to Naples.

Claver came from an Aragonese family and had been long in royal service.[46] He rose to prominence in the Neapolitan administration as a jurist and administrator, acting as *locumtenens* of the chamberlain Iñigo de Avalos towards the end of 1445,[47] and as regent of the chancery in the frequent absences of Platamone. The Aragonese practice of entrusting the duties of the vice-chancellor to a regent of the chancery in the absence of the former official had appeared in Naples when Jacme Pelegri was vice-chancellor. At that time a Valencian, Pere Feliu (died 1441), had acted as regent when need arose.[48] Because Alfonso so often employed Platamone

---

[41] ACB Cart. Com., vol. 21, fol. 182, 19 Sept. 1451, Vinyes to Barcelona.

[42] See ACA Reg. 2720. 112ʳ, 28 Mar. 1449, Instruction to Fonolleda to pay Platamone without delay the part of his salary assigned on the revenues of the seal.

[43] e.g. an order for the sequestration of property from the estate of a deceased merchant of Barcelona found to be in debt to the crown (ACA Reg. 2656. 83ᵛ, 23 Nov. 1447).

[44] ACB Cart. Com., vol. 21, fol. 182, Vinyes to Barcelona, Naples, 19 Sept. 1451: 'Lo dit die de Sancta Creu lo dit Senyor provehi lo dit don Valenti Claver de vicicanceller per mort de micer Johan de Funes que vol dir per aquexes parts e per açi.'   [45] Cf. above, p. 118.

[46] He was a deacon of Zaragoza. One of his earliest assignments in Italy had been a mission to Genoa in 1428 (Ametller y Vinyas, *Alfonso V de Aragón*, i. 283).

[47] Numerous countersignatures in this capacity are to be found in the register ACA Reg. 2907.

[48] Feliu was regent when the king was still in Messina in April 1435 (Madurell

on missions abroad, a great deal of the routine legal business of the vice-chancellor in the council fell to Claver. This involved conducting the examination of cases referred to him by council, and sometimes acting as sole judge. In August 1451, for example, Alfonso revoked from the Vicaria a suit between Jacme Perpenya a Catalan knight of the household, and Luca Galgano in order that Claver might deliver final and speedy judgement:

quatenus vocatis coram vobis qui vocandi fuerunt eisque plene auditis de dicta causa cognoscatis decidatis ac sententialiter fine debito termine-tis prout de iure, usu et constitutionibus Regni inveneritis faciendum esse, et quod decreveritis debite esecucioni mandetis procedendo circa premissis breviter sumarie simpliciter et de plano, sine strepitu, forma et figura indicii, sola facti veritate actenta, maliciis et diffugiis omnibus ultroiectis.[49]

Silvestro de Sulmona, a *consiliarius* charged with investigating a land dispute in the Abruzzi, had orders to submit his findings 'clausum et sigillatum Maiestati nostre seu magnifico et dilecto consiliario et cancellariam nostram regenti valentino claver militi et legum doctori cui decisionem cause predicte commissimus'.[50] Reports that a notary was ill-treating his wife reached the council, were investigated by Claver, and led to an order, issued on the regent's authority to the Duke of Scalea, for the wife to be given into the custody of her sister; if the notary felt aggrieved, he was to appear in person before Claver 'qui in premissis faciet quod iuris fiendum erit'.[51] In effect there had developed a chancery jurisdiction, exercised by the vice-chancellor and regent, and co-ordinate with that of the council. It functioned entirely at the discretion of the king and council. In one of the rare cases of appeal from a judgement of the council, the appeal tribunal ap-pointed by the king consisted of the regent and two other chancery judges, Rodrigo Falco and Nicolau Fillach.[52]

Marimon, *Mensajeros barceloneses*, p. 90), and was performing the duties of the vice-chancellor on the mainland in August of that same year (Faraglia, *Storia della lotta*, p. 52, n. 4). In February 1448 Rodrigo Falco was appointed regent of the chancery in the Crown of Aragon because of the absence of de Funes (ACA Reg. 2720. 72ᵛ, 12 Feb. 1448).

[49] Mazzoleni, *Il Codice Chigi*, pp. 80–1, King to Claver, Torre del Greco, 17 Aug. 1451.

[50] ACA Reg. 2913. 112ᵛ, Castelnuovo, 15 Apr. 1449.

[51] Mazzoleni, *Il Codice Chigi*, pp. 115–17, Torre del Greco, 10 Sept. 1451.

[52] See above, p. 107.

Claver was not, like Platamone, inhibited from acting in legal business brought to Naples from Spain. As regent of the chancery he was responsible for an instruction ordering the governor of Rosellon and Cerdaña to reimburse a merchant of Puigcerda who had paid for offices in those provinces already promised to someone else.[53] He participated in a council review of criminal proceedings forwarded to Naples by the governor of Mallorca,[54] and he instructed the governor of Sardinia to investigate suspected fraud in the mint at Cagliari.[55] Barcelona presented him with 25 ducats 'pro diversis laboribus' in a suit to recover Terrasa and Sabadell from the jurisdiction of the governor of Catalonia.[56] After he became vice-chancellor a case between a merchant of Barcelona and a Catalan merchant resident in Naples was revoked from the Consulat del Mar of Barcelona for judgement by him.[57]

An increasing volume of legal business in the council, and in particular the requirement that the vice-chancellor should preside over daily meetings of the Sacrum Consilium, led in the 1450s to an increase in the number of those jurists empowered to act for the vice-chancellor. Sometimes they were styled regents, and sometimes vice-chancellors.[58] One of these was Rodrigo Falco, a Valencian doctor of laws who had become regent for the Spanish territories in 1448.[59] He was summoned to Naples, apparently early in 1451, appointed an ordinary counsellor with the usual salary of 500 ducats,[60] and on 2 May 1452 given an additional 300 ducats in respect of his duties as vice-chancellor.[61] The other supernumerary was Nicolau Fillach, like Falco a native of Valencia and a doctor of laws, whom Alfonso had brought to Italy in the autumn of 1448.[62] His services thereafter—attendance in the

[53] ACA Reg. 2720. 88ᵛ, 20 Jan. 1449.

[54] ACA Reg. 2654. 39ʳ, 10 May 1446.

[55] ACA Reg. 2657. 56ʳ, 29 May 1448.

[56] Madurell Marimon, *Mensajeros barceloneses*, p. 360, 26 Nov. 1450.

[57] ACA Reg. 2550. 94ᵛ, 24 Oct. 1452.

[58] A document dated 15 Nov. 1453 styles Fillach and Falco 'regents' (Toppi, *De origine tribunalium*, iii. 246–50). Another, of 2 May 1452, describes Falco as a vice-chancellor (ibid. iii. 251–3). Fillach participated in a meeting of the council on 28 Oct. 1457 as 'vice-cancellario nunc autem cancellariam regente' (ASN Div. Somm. I. 52 (bis), 48ʳ).   [59] Cf. above, p. 143, n. 48.

[60] Cf. above, p. 113.   [61] Toppi, *De origine tribunalium*, iii. 251–3.

[62] ACA Reg. 2719. 24ᵛ, 21 Sept. 1448, Berenguer Mercader, *baile general* of Valencia, is ordered to pay the expenses incurred by Nicolau Fillach and another lawyer, Gabriel de Palomar, in their journey to Italy at the king's command.

council,[63] extraordinary judicial commissions,[64] and diplomatic missions[65]—appear to have established him very firmly in royal favour. He became one of the first ordinary counsellors and within a year was performing the duties of vice-chancellor.[66] Thereafter he appears fairly regularly in that capacity; for example, in an order addressed to all Spanish officials on the subject of Catalan privateers whose activities against French shipping had led to reprisals,[67] and as witness to the deed of sale that conveyed the town of Caivano from the king to the Count of Fondi in July 1456.[68] It is clear, however, that Falco and Fillach only assumed the title of vice-chancellor in the absence of Claver. When both Claver and Fillach witnessed an agreement between Alfonso and a party of Genoese exiles in February 1458, Claver signed second as vice-chancellor and Fillach fourth simply as doctor of laws.[69]

A privilege conferring the degree of doctor of civil law upon Giacomo Cicario of Naples states that he has been examined by Felice Caposcrofa, 'huius regni Sicilie vicecancellarium'.[70] Another Neapolitan, Cicco Antonio Guindazzo, appears as vice-chancellor in a privilege dated 3 February 1454 which confers a doctorate in medicine,[71] and in another appointing a notary to the College of Doctors of Naples in the absence of the chancellor.[72] It is significant that these three documents (the only ones I have discovered which bear witness to the activity of a Neapolitan *vicecancellarius*) all relate to the university, of which the chancellor of Naples was *ex officio* rector. In this very restricted sphere, the Neapolitan chancellor or his deputy continued to function; the Aragonese chancery had, in any case, never taken responsibility for university matters.

[63] e.g. with de Palomar in a matter concerning the see of Valencia (ACA Reg. 2656. 172^r, 20 Apr. 1449) and the judgement concerning the county of San Severino (ACA Reg. 2914. 11^r, 22 Dec. 1449).

[64] e.g. as a member of a tribunal to hear an appeal from the council.

[65] He accompanied the Archbishop of Monreal to a peace conference in Rome (ACA Reg. 2939. 128^v, Torre del Greco, 25 July 1451, Instructions for the Archbishop and Fillach). Early in 1452 he was sent as sole envoy to Siena (ACA Reg. 2697. 122^v, Pozzuoli, 28 Feb. 1452, Memorial for Fillach).

[66] A letter dated 19 Mar. 1452 addresses him by that title (ACA Reg. 2659. 76^r).

[67] ACA Reg. 2661. 72^r, 29 Aug. 1454.

[68] ASN Rel. Orig. (Terra di Lavoro), 33. 57^r, 26 July 1456.

[69] ACA Reg. 2800. 51^v, 9 Feb. 1458.

[70] ASN Priv. I. 20^r, 17 Oct. 1452.

[71] Ibid. 111^r.

[72] ASN Priv. I. 181^r, 26 Oct. 1454.

Alfonso's purposeful development of conciliar and chancery jurisdiction inevitably damaged the prestige of the established Neapolitan tribunals. Nevertheless these continued to operate in modified form as the regular supreme courts of the kingdom, the jurisdiction of council and chancery being both more general and extraordinary in its scope. A figure-head *magister justiciarius* still stood in the fore of the Neapolitan judicial hierarchy. Raimondo Orsini, Prince of Salerno, succeeded his father Pirro Orsini in that dignity in the time of Giovanna II. Confirmation in it had been one of the conditions on which he had submitted to Alfonso in November 1436, and he retained it throughout the reign. His diploma of appointment, like that of the other great officers of state, carefully enumerated duties that had long since passed into other hands,[73] and subsequent general orders to the judiciary always gave pride of place to the master justiciar.[74] The prince was in truth a man of power and importance in the kingdom, second only to his cousin the Prince of Taranto whom he followed in the king's triumphal entry into Naples. A week later he rode through the city wearing the golden coronet of his rank and bearing three standards.[75] In April 1444 he joined the retinue which accompanied the king's daughter Maria to Ferrara, and he played a prominent part in the parliament of 1456.[76] These were the usual occasions for a great nobleman's intervention in public life: his chief interest in a highly technical office was the dignity and salary it conferred. One of the very few documents which show him acting as *magister justiciarius* is a privilege appointing a *subactarius* in the Vicaria; it is dated 4 January 1443 from his palace in Naples.[77] Even that modest exercise of authority was soon afterwards nullified by a reform of the Vicaria which obliged the prince's appointee to seek confirmation from the king.[78]

Only after he had taken possession of Naples was Alfonso able to make effective use of those courts attached to the office of the

[73] ASN Div. Somm. I. 52 (bis), 139ʳ. This diploma is undated, but is stated to have been given to the prince on the death of his father.
[74] e.g. Mazzoleni, *Il Codice Chigi*, p. 136, 1 Oct. 1451, an order concerning lepers addressed to 'Magnificis viris Magistro huius Regni Iusticiario eiusque locumtenenti Regenti et iudicibus Magne Curie Vicarie . . .'.
[75] BNN MS. X b2, Ant. Afeltri, Excerpta, 15ᵛ.
[76] He was the leader of the baronial delegation which conveyed the parliament's financial proposals to the king.
[77] ACA Reg. 2909. 167ʳ.
[78] Ibid. The king's confirmation of the appointment, 11 Dec. 1445.

master justiciar. The manner in which their identity had become blurred has been discussed earlier.[79] As a result their names gave rise to some confusion. The documents of the reign of Giovanna II printed by Minieri Riccio (*Saggio diplomatico*)[80] all refer to the *magna curia* of the justiciar alone and make no mention of the Vicaria which must have been subsumed. In Aragonese documents of an early date both names sometimes appear, but in such a manner as to indicate that they designated a single tribunal. In September 1442, for example, Nicola Antonio of Gaeta was appointed keeper of the prison 'magne nostre curie Vicarie et Magistri Justiciari'.[81] Sometimes the term used was 'magna curia Magistri Justiciarii',[82] but far more often it was 'magna curia Vicarie'.

Uncertainty over nomenclature was heightened by a reform promulgated in the 1443 parliament[83] whereby the court was reorganized on lines similar to those which Alfonso had followed in his reform of the Sicilian *magna curia* in 1433.[84] With a regent representing the master justiciar as president, the court was to consist of four judges, the same number as in the Sicilian tribunal. Baronial interest concentrated on the status of the president, and with the intention, presumably, of upholding the Neapolitan constitution, they asked that in 'la corte del mastro iustitiero in vicarie' the master justiciar should always be represented by his *locumtenens*. Alfonso promised in reply that the *locumtenens* as regent should preside over the 'magna curia vicarie' and honour was satisfied, as it had been with the protonotary's position in the council. What mattered was control over the appointment of the regent, and this Alfonso had already asserted when, before the fall of Naples, he made Giovanni di San Severino, a knight and doctor of laws, regent of the Vicaria and *locumtenens* of the master justiciar for life. Only afterwards did the Prince of Salerno go

[79] Cf. above, p. 137.

[80] C. Minieri Riccio, *Saggio di codice diplomatico*, ii (Naples, 1880).

[81] ACA Reg. 2902. 85ʳ, 28 Sept. 1442.

[82] ACA Reg. 2904. 122ʳ, 20 Apr. 1444, Appointment of Galeazzo Origlia as clerk of interlocutory decrees in the court.

[83] de Bottis, *Privilegii et capitoli*, fol. 5. There is nothing in the record of the parliament to support the assertion of Gentile ('Lo stato napoletano' (1937), p. 18) that the statute organized the court in three sessions, nor that the parliament petitioned that it be divided into two.

[84] Mario Muta, *Capitulorum regni Siciliae. Constitutionum et pragmaticarum*, iv (Palermo, 1614). Cf. R. Gregorio, *Opere scelte* (Palermo, 1845), p. 476.

through the motions of making a formal nomination of his *locum-tenens*; in a show of independence he tried to restrict the period of the appointment, but Alfonso brushed the limitation aside and confirmed it for life;[85] even the death or removal of the master justiciar were not to disturb the regent. In January 1448 the king went still further to assert his authority over the appointment of the regent by renewing the tenure of Giovanni di San Severino *ad beneplacitum* on the grounds that it had always been the custom of the kings of Naples to attribute functions of the great officers of state *ad beneplacitum*, and that the power of appointing a *locumtenens* given to the master justiciar was likewise subject to withdrawal by a ruler who wished to appoint the *locumtenens* directly on his own terms.[86] In this manner the master justiciar lost the last vestige of his authority over the administration of justice.

Giovanni di San Severino's last recorded act was to attend a session of the council on 8 February 1449,[87] and it is to be presumed that he died later the same year. Thereafter Alfonso reversed his former policy of having a life regent of the Vicaria and began to make changes almost annually. Joan de Copons, previously *promotor negotiorum curie*, was probably the first regent appointed after the death of di San Severino.[88] After him came Jacobo de Constanzo of Messina who held the office from May 1451 until the end of January 1452 when he left for Rome and Siena on a mission connected with the visit of the Emperor to Naples.[89] Well before de Constanzo's term expired the regency had been promised to a Genoese president of the Sommaria, Antonio Arone Cibo, in words which suggest that it was now looked upon as a useful means of repaying favours done to the crown:

Ne servitia per vos magnificum et dilectum consiliarium et presidentem Camere nostre Summarie Aronem Cibonem nobis prestita

---

[85] ACA Reg. 2906. 18ᵛ, 22 Apr. 1443.

[86] ACA Reg. 2912. 161ʳ, 4 Jan. 1448. This privilege also gives the regent jurisdiction over all subjects of the kingdom and power to inflict all punishments. He is allowed a staff of ten mounted men and twenty *familiares*.

[87] ACA Reg. 2913. 108ᵛ.

[88] A letter of the viceroy of Calabria dated 19 Apr. 1452 refers to letters recently received from 'dominum Johannem de Caponibus regentem olim magnam curiam vicarie' ASN Fasc. Com. Somm. 6ᵛ. de Copons was again regent in September 1453 (ACA Reg. 2660. 121ʳ).

[89] Mazzoleni, *Il Codice Chigi*, p. 234, 30 Jan. 1452, Letter notifying that a case has been withdrawn from the Vicaria.

absque aliqua remuneratione transeant, tenore presentis nostri albarani
in nostra regia bona fide promittimus et firmiter pollicemur vobis
eidem Aroni quod quam primum expiraverit tempus in quo magnificus
et dilectus consiliarius noster Iacobus de Constancio miles et legum
doctor officium Magne nostre Curie Vicarie huius Regni Sicilie citra
farum ex concessione nostra exercere potest et debet, officium ipsum
immediate vobis eidem Aroni et nemini alii comendabimus regendum,
exercendum et administrandum per vos cum omnibus et singulis
iuribus lucris emolumentis ac cognicione causarum eidem officio
debitis et consuetis sicuti nunc pro tunc ipsum officium vobis comen-
damus.[90]

On 15 September 1451 Cibo, who held no doctorate in law, was
duly appointed to the post.[91] As successor to the Genoese, a Venetian regent was suggested by the Aragonese ambassador to the
Adriatic republic. It would, he wrote, be diplomatically expedient
to bestow the regency on Andrea Donato.[92] The only objection
raised to a proposal, which so well emphasizes the devaluation of
the regency, was that the position had already been given to Cibo.
After Cibo's term of office had expired the regency reverted to
Copons.[93] He was followed by Nicolo de Porcinariis;[94] then came
the Sulmonese noble Gregorio de Merlinis[95] and Francisco de
Antignano of Capua.[96] The petition of the March 1450 parliament
asking for annual changes in the regency may lie behind what looks
like a deliberate down-grading of the office. Having lost the battle
to make the regent effectively a *locumtenens* of the master justiciar,
the barons presumably did not wish to see it in the hands of
a permanent royal nominee; the king, on the other hand, having
developed the judicial authority of the council and chancery, was

---

[90] Mazzoleni, *Il Codice Chigi*, pp. 38–9, Pozzuoli, 13 May 1451.

[91] ACA Reg. 2915. 109ᵛ, Torre del Greco, 15 Sept. 1451. The appointment is
for one year beginning 10 Apr. 1452. According to Toppi (*De origine tribunalium*,
i. 94), Cibo had been regent of the Vicaria in 1430 and held the office again in
1459.

[92] Mazzoleni, *Il Codice Chigi*, p. 300, Castelnuovo, 24 Apr. 1452, Letter to
the ambassador, Luis Dez Puig, explaining why it is not possible to appoint
Donato regent.

[93] He was regent in September 1453 when arrangements were made for him
to recover arrears of salary as regent and as a counsellor from the revenues of
the Vicaria (ACA Reg. 2700. 40ᵛ, 19 Sept. 1453).

[94] Regent in January 1456 (Gentile, 'Lo stato napoletano' (1937), p. 18, n. 4).

[95] G. C. Rossi, 'Sulmona ai tempi di Alfonso il Magnanimo', *ASPN* (1964),
190.

[96] Toppi, *De origine tribunalium*, i. 94.

nothing loath to see the older, native institution diminished in status.

In accordance with his undertaking to the 1443 parliament, Alfonso appointed four judges for the Vicaria. The names of the first four were noted by Borso d'Este as Simone de Pesce (Sicilian), Gabriele de Mastrillis (a Neapolitan from Nola), Marino Ballotta (a Neapolitan from Santa Agata), and Joan de Ruys (Reus?) a Catalan.[97] In later years almost all the judges were natives of the kingdom.[98] They received a standard salary of 300 ducats.[99] Each judge was assisted by an assessor or *magister actorum*,[100] and the court had a staff of nine clerks, seven being assigned to general pleas, one to appeals, and one to crown pleas. These clerks, or *subactarii*, were paid 24 ducats a year.[101] An 'erarius, perceptor et distributor' controlled the moneys of the Vicaria; Bernat Lober held that office until February 1445 when it passed to Joan Gener.[102] The judge Gabriele de Mastrillis had charge of the seals of the court for some years,[103] and when he died (c. 1449) they were given *in perpetuum* into the custody of Michele Riccio.[104]

[97] Foucard, 'Descrizione della citta di Napoli', p. 750.

[98] Gentile ('Lo stato napoletano' (1937), p. 19, n. 2) gives the names of the judges in 1447 as de Mastrillis, Ballotta, and a Catalan, Simone Senex. His list for May 1450 is: Clemente Mundo di Sonnino, Antonio Giacomo di Traetto, Francisco de Compli, and Francesco de Poseti. To these Toppi (*De origine tribunalium*, i. 110–12) adds Pietro Marco Gipsiis, Cristoforo Ricca de Sessa (1452), Onofrio de Camplo (1453), Mariano de Adam of Teramo (1454), and Nicola Cardoino (1457).

[99] Salvati, *Fonti aragonesi*, iv. 34. In 1457, however, Cardoino had a salary of 350 ducats (ibid. iv. 62).

[100] In 1447 the *magistri actorum* were Valerio Paolillo, Bacico Cuda, and Anichino Longobardo (Gentile, 'Lo stato napoletano' (1937), p. 19, n. 2).

[101] Borso d'Este put the number of *subactarii* at twelve, but must have been referring to a period before the following regulation came into force: 'Item per sept scrivents o subactares ala gran corte et un scrivent ales appellacions et altre scrivent ales causes fiscales a cascun vint quatre ducats lanni son per totes nou, monten ducentes sexi ducates' (ASN *Fasc. Com. Somm.* 120ᵛ, 2 Dec. 1445). This instruction to the treasurer of the Vicaria, having quoted the regulation, names the nine clerks who are to be paid.

[102] ACA Reg. 2904. 224ʳ, 11 Feb. 1445. This privilege appointing Gener, an official of the treasury, allows him to perform the duties by deputy.

[103] Toppi, *De origine tribunalium*, ii. 382. On one occasion de Mastrillis ran into trouble for not obeying a summons to present his accounts for the seals in the Sommaria (ibid. i. 273).

[104] When Riccio died in 1457 the office passed to his son, Perluigi, who was permitted to keep all the income from the seals without rendering any account (ACA Reg. 2917. 177ᵛ, 12 Oct. 1457).

The reorganization of the Vicaria had fixed the number of constables serving the court at three. Nicola Antonio of Gaeta had been appointed 'comestabulum et militem sive cavallarium necnon custodem carcerum' in September 1442.[105] Another was a Sicilian, Stefano de Iamplano, who in July 1445 was accused and eventually acquitted on charges of accepting bribes to allow prisoners to escape or evade arrest.[106] In May 1447 Alfonso added a fourth constable, Pino Mignienio, with the usual salary of 24 ducats a year.[107] Subsequently the number of keepers of the prison may have been reduced to one, because in 1454 the king appointed Pere Gomela of Mallorca to the vacant office 'custodis carceris magne curie nostre vicarie' with a salary of 72 ducats.[108] Numerous petty agents served writs, made arrests, guarded prisoners, and executed judgements.[109]

More than twenty procurators and thirty advocates practised in the Vicaria at the time when Borso d'Este was writing his description of Naples. Among them was an advocate paid by the crown to take care of the cases of the poor; a Sicilian lawyer, Bernardo de Neapoli, was the first appointed to this post by Alfonso. Pleas of the crown were the responsibility of the crown advocates and procurators. Although their activities were not confined to the Vicaria—they might appear before any tribunal—this will be a convenient place to consider them. The office of advocate fiscal must have been given to Giovanni di San Severino well before 1440, because in that year his salary was already sadly in arrears; he was given instead a vineyard in Gaeta confiscated from a partisan of René of Anjou.[110] Soon afterwards he became regent of the Vicaria and relinquished the office of advocate fiscal. A clearer picture emerges in January 1448 when Alfonso approved the appointment of Nicola Villano of Cava as substitute for either of

---

[105] ACA Reg. 2902. 85ʳ, 28 Sept. 1442.

[106] ACA Reg. 2909. 200ᵛ, 9 Feb. 1446, Judgement given by Claver as regent of the chancery dismissing the charges.

[107] When the other constables raised objections that this appointment increased the number of constables above that permitted, the king had to issue another privilege confirming it (ACA Reg. 2912. 113ᵛ, 15 Sept. 1447).

[108] The office had become vacant because Pere de Capdevila the treasurer, who performed it by deputy, had sold it to a man whom the king considered unsuitable (ASN Priv. I. 150ʳ, 15 May 1454).

[109] There were, according to Borso d'Este ('Descrizione', p. 750), 30 or 40 tipstaffs (birri), 30 mounted men, 50 armed footmen, and 2 couriers.

[110] ACA Reg. 2646. 88ʳ, 1 Apr. 1440.

the two crown advocates then serving 'in ipso advocationis fiscalis'.[111]
Villano had been appointed in the first place by Nicolo Antonio
dei Monti, presumably the senior of the two, to deputize for
himself and Matteu Malferit, 'similiter fisci nostri advocato'. The
substitute was authorized to act in the absence of either of the two
advocates, and was to receive a salary fixed by dei Monti. Both
dei Monti and Malferit enjoyed a great reputation for their legal
skill and learning. The former, hailed by Pontano as 'vir juris
Romani consultissimus',[112] served Alfonso throughout his reign
in many capacities in addition to that of advocate fiscal: as a legal
counsellor,[113] as president of the Sommaria,[114] and as *locumtenens*
of the chamberlain.[115] He lived to serve Ferdinand for many more
years.[116] His partner Malferit received lavish praise from Vespasiano da Bisticci for his deep interest in all kinds of learning: 'fu
litteratissimo in iure civile e canonico, e cavaliere, e universale
negli istudi di umanità; in altre facultà era universalissimo e di
maravigliosi costumi.'[117] Alfonso very frequently made use of him
as an envoy in his negotiations with the states of Italy: he went in

[111] ACA Reg. 2912. 168ᵛ, Castiglione della Pescaia, 30 Jan. 1448.

[112] Giannone, *Istoria civile*, iii. 487, quoting Pontano, *De obedientia*, iv,
cap. 6.

[113] He was present in a session of the council held in Castel Capuano under the
presidency of the Bishop of Valencia on Monday, 20 May 1443 to deliver judgement (ACA Reg. 2906. 29ʳ).

[114] e.g. the privilege in which the king approved the gift of Casalanguida to
dei Monti by the Countess of Loreto bears the annotation 'quia presidens
camere Summarie nihil solvat pro jure sigilli' (ASN Priv. I. 64ᵛ, 7 Jan. 1453).
The countess gave him the town for many services rendered, 'et presertim circa
recuperationem comitatus predicte [sc. Monteodorisio] quem noviter ipsius
patrocinio tanquam ad ipsam dominam comitissam iuste et rationabiliter
spectantem et pertinentem recuperavit . . .' (ibid.).

[115] From 1452 onwards his signature appears very frequently as *locumtenens*
of the chamberlain. In that capacity he appears often to have supervised the
Sommaria.

[116] In 1467 he spent three months in Rome as Ferdinand's envoy (Giannone,
Istoria civile, iii. 487).

[117] da Bisticci, *Vite* (ed. A. Bartoli, Florence, 1859), pp. 400–1. In this brief life
of Malferit, evidently based upon conversations between the author and his
subject, da Bisticci recounts that after twenty-two years in royal service,
Malferit had asked permission to marry and retire to his native Mallorca. This
permission was eventually granted—probably by Ferdinand. In the course of
their conversation Malferit complained to da Bisticci of the trials undergone by
those who served a ruler: '. . . piu volte si dolse meco della servitù e miseria
ch'era a stare con uno principe; e ugguagliava le corti de' signori grandi alle
gabbie degli uccellini, che quegli che vi sono drento, desiderano uscirne e
andarne fuori; e quegli che sono fuori, vi vorrebbono tornare drento.'

1443 to Milan, in 1444 to Genoa, in 1445 to Rome, in 1446 to
Florence, and so on until the end of the reign—in October 1457 he
was dispatched on a round trip to Florence, Venice, and Milan to
justify the king's action against Genoa and Rimini.[118]

Despite all his other commitments, dei Monti appears to have
retained his office of crown advocate; at least he was still exercising it in May 1452.[119] Whether Malferit too remained an
advocate is uncertain. Nevertheless, these two can hardly have
performed the duties very adequately, even with the assistance
of their substitute. Either the resignation of Malferit or the need
to strengthen the advocate's office presumably led to the appointment of Pietro Marco de Gipsiis as advocate fiscal in February
1451,[120] and of Jacme de Pelaya not later than October of the
same year.[121] The other advocate fiscal of whom we have knowledge was Antonio Jacobo de Traetto whom the king appointed
simultaneously an ordinary counsellor and crown advocate. His
office is described in the following terms: 'fisci nostri patronum ac
generalem advocatum in omnibus et singulis regnis et terris nostri
imperii tam occiduis quam citramarinis maxime quidem hoc in
regno nostro Sicilie citra farum.'[122] The other crown advocates,
whose letters of appointment have not survived, are likely to have
been given similarly wide terms of reference.

Turning to the procurators fiscal, we find that the senior among
them had been appointed sometime in the 1420s. This was the
Catalan Joan de Boxia (sometimes rendered as Buesa) whom
Borso d'Este indentified as the crown procurator in 1444.[123]
A Neapolitan procurator, Pietro Calense, had appeared by 1442;[124]
possibly he is identical with the procurator Petrus Albertus who

[118] ACA Reg. 2800. 37ᵛ, 19 Oct. 1457, Memorial of instructions for Malferit.
[119] ACA Reg. 2660. 35ᵛ, 22 May 1452. As advocate fiscal he countersigned
these instructions for an investigation into violations of the edict against trade
with Florentines committed in Catalonia.
[120] Toppi, De origine tribunalium, i. 177 and 269.
[121] D. A. Varius, Pragmaticae edicta decreta interdicta regiaeque sanctiones regni
Neapolitani (Naples, 1772), i. 392. Pelaya was later active in the Consilium
Pecuniae (Cf. above, p. 119).
[122] ACA Reg. 2915. 182ᵛ, 1 Mar. 1452. His salary was fixed at 500 ducats.
[123] Foucard, 'Descrizione della città di Napoli', p. 750. For the appointment of
Boxia see ACA Reg. 2912. 96ᵛ.
[124] A carta publici notariatus was issued from Foggia on 22 Nov. 1442 by
'virum nobilem Petrum Calensem de castro novo de Neapoli procuratorem
nostri fisci'. Calense was also a familiaris of the Neapolitan protonotary and gave
the letter as his deputy (ACA Reg. 2903. 26ʳ).

brought charges against the constable of the Vicaria in 1445.[125] A Nicola Palumbo of Capua held the office for a few years, but fell into disfavour in 1451 and was replaced by Antonello d'Angelo of Naples.[126] By this time Petrus Albertus and Joan de Boxia had moved to other offices, leaving a Spaniard named Pedro Salduno as Antonello d'Angelo's colleague.[127] The salary assigned these procurators was the relatively modest one of 24 *oncie* (144 ducats). Salduno and d'Angelo in turn either resigned or were replaced, and during the last two or three years of the reign the persons holding the posts of crown procurators were Bartolomeo Caputo[128] and Domenico Rustico.[129] We may conclude that the duties of crown procurator, like those of advocate, were normally discharged by two persons,[130] and in any court of the kingdom.

Statim receptis presentibus [so ran the letter of appointment for Antonello d'Angelo] ad sacram nostram audienciam magnam curiam vicarie cameram nostram sumarie curiam capitanei civitatis nostre Neapolis ac ad commissarios et iudices delegatos et delegandos aliosque officiales et tribunalia huius Regni nostri predicti te personaliter conferas et coram eis et unoquoque ipsorum omnes causas fiscales et fiscum nostrum tangentes contra personas quascumque defendas protegas et procurare studeas.[131]

Another official known as 'negotiorum curie promotor' belongs to this same group of lawyers responsible for legal proceedings on behalf of the crown. In February 1446 Ioan de Copons, *utriusque*

[125] Cf. above, p. 152. Marino Boffa acted as procurator fiscal in 1444 (ACA Reg. 2909. 47ᵛ).

[126] ACA Reg. 2915. 94ᵛ, 1 July 1451: '... considerantes itaque quod notarius Nicolaus Palumbus de Capua procurator erat noster fiscalis per nostram Curiam ordinatus una cum Petro Salduno similiter procuratore nostro fiscale. Et postmodum tempore notarius Nicolaus ex certis causis fuit ammotus per nostram curiam a dicto procurationis officio ...'

[127] Salduno had been wounded in defending Castelnuovo during the war. As a reward he was given in March 1446 the office of *notarius credencerius* in the coral *gabella* for the whole kingdom with a salary of 200 ducats (ACA Reg. 2909. 206ᵛ, 11 Mar. 1446). He must have become crown procurator at a later date.

[128] Toppi, *De origine tribunalium*, i. 177, mentions Caputo as a procurator fiscal in 1456. In May 1458 he was sent to Sicily; a letter to the viceroy describes him as 'procuratore fiscale generali' (ACA Reg. 2916. 69ʳ, 17 May 1458).

[129] Toppi, *De origine tribunalium*, iii. 78, for reference to Rustico as a procurator in 1457.

[130] In the appointment of d'Angelo occurs the clause, '... ut sitis duo procuressuri fiscales sicut erant prius de nostra ordinacione'. Evidently the number had for a time been varied (ACA Reg. 2915. 94ᵛ).

[131] Ibid.

juris doctor,[132] possessed that title. In the following year Joan de
Boxia, until then a procurator fiscal, became 'negociorum nostre
curie apud nos et in nostris audiencia sacro consilio et magnis
vicarie et sicle curiis et camera Summarie promotorem ordinarium'.[133] A further reference to this office occurs in an edict which
requires notification to the appropriate officials to be effected by
'promotorem negociorum nostri Sacri Consilii vel procuratorem
nostri fisci'.[134] From the terms of reference given to de Boxia the
duties of the office would appear to be very similar to those of
a procurator fiscal:

... possitis tam in ipso nostro audiencia sacro consilio et curiis predictis
ubicunque congregari seu celebrari contingat et signanter infra totum
regnum predictum Sicilie citra farum occurencia curie nostre negocia
de quibus in ipsis audiencia consilio et curiis tractari habebunt dedu-
cere ... et in audiencia consiliis et curiis ipsis intervenire et interesse.[135]

The difference between the two offices lies then mainly in the title:
that of procurator has a Neapolitan ancestry; that of *promotor* is
related to the *promovedor* of the Aragonese chancery.[136] A clause
in de Boxia's letter of appointment waiving the requirement that
he be a knight or doctor of laws,[137] emphasizes this latter relationship, for these are precisely the qualifications demanded of
a *promovedor* by the Aragonese Household Ordinance. Yet another
feature of the Aragonese chancery was thus superimposed upon
the judicial structure of the Italian kingdom.

The Vicaria, which had in its beginnings enjoyed a reputation
for swift and impartial justice,[138] had, like all tribunals, soon lost
its initial flexibility in the face of a growing volume of business,
inadequate staff, and the multifarious means by which the processes of justice could be indefinitely delayed. Long before the
Aragonese took Naples the venality of its judges and the quality
of its justice had brought repeated complaints from Angevin
parliaments. Alfonso's first general parliament asked him to
appoint suitable officials in the Vicaria; for his part the king took
the occasion to admonish the judges of that court that they should

[132] As a witness (ACA Reg. 2656. 9ᵛ, 28 Feb. 1446).
[133] ACA Reg. 2912. 96ʳ, 18 Aug. 1447, Letter of appointment.
[134] ACA Reg. 2656. 110ᵛ, 5 Feb. 1448.
[135] ACA Reg. 2912. 96ʳ, 18 Aug. 1447.
[136] Bofarull y Mascaró, *Coleccion de documentos inéditos*, p. 124.
[137] '... non obstante quod non sitis miles aut legum doctor ...'
[138] Cf. above, p. 16.

take nothing from litigants on pain of death and forfeiture of all their property. Two decrees promulgated in January 1444 attempted to bring the financial affairs of the court under tighter control. One (17 January) subjected its accounts to audit by the Sommaria and forbade judges to exact any fees other than the customary thirtieth. The second (21 January) sought to check abuses which were rampant in the procedure for compounding for a wide variety of crimes by a monetary payment. This facility, available daily in the Vicaria and periodically in the provinces through special commissioners, required henceforth the authorization of the Sommaria.[139] Disorder of another kind came to light in the proceedings for corruption against the constable Stefano de Iamplano.[140] Despite the dismissal of those charges, there followed towards the end of 1445 a general overhaul of the subordinate staff regulating its numbers, salaries, and duties.

That none of these measures much improved the performance of the Vicaria is evident from the angry tone of the king's instruction for further reform which he sent to his council in Naples in October 1448.[141] He had learned, so ran the instruction, that justice in the Vicaria was being administered neither properly nor promptly, as befitted the honour of the crown, the convenience of litigants, and the punishment of wrongdoers. His remedy was to make a clean sweep of the bench of judges. Four new men were appointed, all of them Neapolitan citizens, and all but one of them promoted from judicial posts in the provinces.[142] Each was to receive a salary of 400 ducats in four-monthly instalments, with a warning that the taking of any bribe or gift would be punished 'without mercy'. Failure to pay the judges and other officials of the court their salaries had certainly encouraged some of the earlier inefficiency and corruption; even the salary of the regent was five years in arrears by 1448.[143] For the future it was hoped, though in vain, that the salaries of all royal officials, including those of the Vicaria, would be paid regularly through the bank

---

[139] The effect of this reform may be seen in the order which the Sommaria sent to Pere Robert, a Catalan merchant, on 19 Nov. 1445. He was required to present in the Sommaria within twenty days his accounts as commissioner of the Vicaria in the provinces of Principato and Basilicata (ASN Fasc. Com. Somm. 95ʳ).

[140] Cf. above, p. 152. [141] ACA Reg. 2699. 141ᵛ, 3 Oct. 1448.

[142] For their names see above, p. 101, n. 44. The exception was Geronimo di Miroballo who was already a president of the Sommaria.

[143] Gentile, 'Lo stato napoletano' (1937), p. 20, n. 2.

of Giovanni di Miroballo, thus eliminating a perennial source of
demoralization.[144] Another notable feature of the 1448 reform was
the inclusion of the regent and judges of the Vicaria in the royal
council,[145] though it can be doubted whether their attendance
upon that body three mornings every week could have led to
greater dispatch in the business of their own tribunal. Finally the
king made another attempt to check the vexatious behaviour of
commissioners sent into the provinces by the Vicaria, and in
particular of those who collected the fines offered as composition
for other penalties. Ignoring the decree of January 1444, these
men had continued to extort money, demand free board and
lodging, and prolong their commissions in order to increase their
salaries. In future, Alfonso ordered, no commissioner was to be
appointed except on the direct authority of the Duke of Calabria
(at that time *locumtenens generalis* in the kingdom), and none was
ever to be sent to a province which had a resident commissioner.

The four dismissed judges were subjected to a judicial inquiry[146]
which investigated 'multas indebitas composiciones, extorsiones,
exacciones et fraudes in eorum officio et ex sui officii racione tam
iniurie nostre quam nostrorum fidelium huius Regni damnum.'[147]
Marino Boffa and Lupo de Speyo, both members of the reformed
Neapolitan council of 1448,[148] conducted the inquiry through the
usual procedure of summoning by public proclamation all those
who wished to lodge complaints or give evidence against the
judges under investigation.[149] In the end they presented to the
king a report which absolved all the accused, and these were
accordingly restored to their honours and dignities, but not to
their positions in the Vicaria.

Complaints about the court continued to figure with some
regularity in parliamentary petitions even after this comprehensive
overhaul. In March 1450 parliament demanded that the judges
should be natives of the royal demesne and doctors of law, that
they should hold office for only one year and submit to a general
inquest into their conduct when their term of office expired, and

---

[144] Cf. below, p. 184.   [145] Cf. above, p. 101.
[146] 'processum sindicacionis et inquisicionis' ACA Reg. 2914. 88ᵛ, a privilege
absolving one of the four, Marino Ballotta, of all charges, Castelnuovo, 12 Aug.
1450.
[147] Ibid.   [148] Cf. above, p. 101.
[149] '. . . cum solemnitatibus debitis emissis bannis per loca publica huius
civitatis Neapolis preconizando sindicacionem . . . ' (ACA Reg. 2914. 88ᵛ).

that they should be sworn to administer justice at the proper times.[150] In 1456 the barons asked that the regent and judges on entering office should swear to respect 'li capituli et immunitate che have questo reame',[151] and once again that they should be subject to inquest every year. The first parliament of Ferdinand in 1459 produced very similar petitions.[152] Alfonso's general reaction to such requests is summed up in his reply to the petition for annual inquests: 'Placet Regia Maiestati quod constituciones et capitula regni serventur.' Since the constitutions provided for inquest or sindication only on the expiration of office, and not annually, he was in effect rejecting the petition. He did so wisely, for such constant subjection of the judges to popular pressure would hardly have improved the quality either of justice or its dispensers. However, the total disappearance of the records of the Vicaria makes an independent assessment of parliamentary grumbles impossible.[153]

This chapter has so far concentrated on the structure and personnel of the supreme institutions of justice—the council, its attendant chancery organization, and the Vicaria. In all three Alfonso made innovations or reforms of far-reaching importance which integrated the judicial process more closely with the administrative functions of the state. One must go on to ask whether the result was a better dispensation of justice, a greater security of life and property, the restoration of order in a land ravaged by civil war and the breakdown of government.

If the court writers are to be believed, Alfonso thought and talked a great deal about justice. The duty of a king towards his subjects lay, he held, in the dispensation of justice, liberality, and benevolence, and of these justice stood first.[154] Many documents of the Neapolitan chancery contain in the exordium treatments

---

[150] Ametller y Vinyas, *Alfonso V de Aragón*, iii. 688.

[151] ASN Div. Somm. I. 52 (bis), 171ᵛ.

[152] Gentile, 'Lo stato napoletano' (1937), p. 20.

[153] In October 1455 the king paid Alfonso de Avalos 1,500 ducats for a house in which the Vicaria was to be installed (Minieri Riccio, 'Alcuni fatti di Alfonso I', p. 438). Perhaps this was the Palazzo Cavense in the Piazza San Giorgio Maggiore mentioned by Gentile ('Lo stato napoletano' (1937), p. 18) as the building in which the tribunal held its sessions.

[154] Cf. Beccadelli, *De dictis et factis*, I: 'Principes qui iusticiam non colerent, iis persimiles sibi videri dicebat, qui morbo caderent comitiali. Nam cum animae materia sit sola iusticia, qua tenetur ad vitam teste Lactantio, quid restat principibus sublata iusticia, hoc est sublata nutricatione et cibo, nisi caducarios videri.'

of this theme which we must assume met with his approval. Among the most eloquent is one belonging to the year 1449— a time when Alfonso was particularly exercised by the problems of justice:

Cum post acquisitionem huius praetiosissimi viridarii nostri regni Siciliae citra farum tot laboribus periculis et expensis, Deo actore, ac Sanctissima Ecclesia Romana approbante, iustissimo titulo a manibus tyrannorum et plurium invasorum recuperavimus et omnes guerrarum calamitates pacis lenitate sopivimus incredibilem itineribus et portubus securitatem praestando, bonos meritis exaltando, facinorosque et execrabiles ultore gladio e vita exterminando, omnes cogitationes et studia quamplures noctes vigilia transeuntes interposuimus, Cum virtutum regina sit sacratissima iustitia sine qua regna sunt latrocinia, sine cuius parte etiam qui contra eam nituntur vivere nequeunt, Deliberavimus iustitiae nostrae sceptrum praeexcellentibus viris scientia sapientia et moribus coruscantibus concedere, ut tanquam peritissimi nautes secundum iuris tramites ad portum veritatis omnem litigiorum litigantium controversias et omnes anfractus reducant, et semotis litigiorum calumnis iurgia quamcitius poterint expedire conentur cum publico fine sit finem imponi litibus, ut sit pacis tranquillitas qua parvae res crescunt, et iustitia huius sacratissimi regni nostri trahant perpetuum incolatum et inviolate custodiantur et sistant. Quoniam vero firmius est consilium quod plurimorum sententiis confirmatur, et causarum cognitio tot perspecta oculis tot gustata senibus, et tot palpata manibus extra omnem suspicionis fomitem, tum erroris, tum ignaviae divino humanoque iudicio comprobatur quamobrem ut Omnipotente Deo, cuius reges in terris in distribuenda iustitia imago sunt, quantum possumus reddamur conformes, cui tot regnorum et vassallorum sua clementia gubernacula commisit, et valeamus, Christo Jesu influente, nostri regiminis debitum calculum reddere . . .[155]

So began the decree which reorganized the royal council in August 1449. Alfonso professed to believe that the ideals it set forth had been realised in his Italian kingdom. To the ambassadors of Catalonia who visited him in 1450 he painted a glowing picture of the justice and order that reigned there:

He does justice and administers it in his own person and through his officials with such assiduity that, although before the conquest there were many wars and quarrels here not only between foreigners and inhabitants of the kingdom, but also among the natives themselves, and murders, thefts and robberies were perpetrated and committed in

---

[155] Toppi, *De origine tribunalium*, ii. 440–4.

the towns and on the highways as well as many other crimes, and justice was not administered, yet after the conquest His Majesty has not only established peace and wholly eliminated war among the natives themselves, but also between them and foreign peoples, and has so rooted out all crime, evildoing and wrongdoing that natives and foreigners alike with their goods and money go openly through the kingdom, along the roads and through the forests by night and day so safely and peaceably that they have no dread or fear of any evil or mishap; no injury or harm is done them.[156]

Beccadelli gives an equally reassuring account of law and order in the kingdom:

The most notable evidence for Alfonso's love of justice is that he completely rid the kingdom of Naples of robbers—something never known before. Today a man may travel where he will, alone and unarmed, by day or by night, in complete safety and carry even his valuables in his open hand.[157]

However exaggerated such claims may have been, they could hardly have been made to contemporaries had they been blatantly at odds with the facts. The registers contain a good deal of evidence to show the king's concern with the suppression of banditry. Decrees issued by Charles I and II were frequently invoked to deal with this menace. In July 1443 the viceroy of Gaeta received permission to employ the emergency powers contained in the decrees of Charles I in dealing with bands of robbers who were infesting that district. Disregarding the strict letter of the law, he was to proceed against them 'deum et justiciam solum habens pre oculis'.[158] When Giovanni di San Severino, regent of the Vicaria, became justiciar of the province of Principato citra in

---

[156] ACB Cart. Com., vol. 20, fol. 48. The context makes it clear that the envoys of the Cortes were paraphrasing the king's own words. '. . . fa e ministre per si e sos officials e ministres axi continuament justicia que jatsia ans quel conquistas hi hagues moltes guerres e dissensions no solament dels stranys ab los regnicoles del dit Realme, mas encare entre los regnicoles dessus dits, e si perpetraven e cometien en los poblets e per camins homicidis furts roberies, e molts altres crims, e justicia noy era administrada, empero la sua Maesta apres la dita conquesta no solament ha donat pau e extirpacio de tota guerra entre los regnicoles mas encare entre los regnicoles e los stranys e axi extirpats tots crims maleficis e delictes que les gents axi del dit Realme com strangers ab lurs diners e robes van publicament per lo dit Realme e per los camins e boschs de aquell de nit e de dia segurament e quiete que no han redupte o temor de mal o sinistre algu, nols es feta injuria o molestia alguna.'
[157] De dictis et factis, iv.
[158] ACA Reg. 2903. 88ᵛ, 19 July 1443.

1446 he received special powers to deal with bandits there.[159] In
later years, however, these extraordinary measures seem not to have
been employed, presumably because they were no longer necessary.

Part of the success in re-establishing law and order can be
attributed to the introduction of that useful Spanish police constable—the *alguacil*.[160] The Aragonese ordinance of 1344 had made
provision for two of them, with eight assistants, to keep the king's
prison and make arrests on the order of the council. They had
duly appeared in Naples. In April 1439, Jacme de Vilanova
'algutzir del senyor Rey' and three of his men had escorted the
condottiere Menicuccio de Amicis under arrest from Gaeta to
Sicily.[161] To the Neapolitan baronage this was an unwelcome
innovation which they endeavoured to counter with a petition in
the 1443 parliament; it asked that 'la maiesta vestra conceda che
nullo alguzino, considerato non ce foro mai in quisto reame, non se
habia ad impacciare de nullo homo regnicolo'.[162] Despite the
'placet' which the king returned to this petition, he proceded to
multiply the number of *alguaciles*. In May 1448, for example, he
appointed Monserrat Poch and Johan Gilabert as *alguaciles* to the
viceroy of Calabria and gave them powers which clearly embraced
his Neapolitan subjects. On instruction from the viceroy they
could hold court in demesne or baronial lands to hear either civil
or criminal cases, seize any wrongdoer 'fragrante [sic] maleficio',
and execute any sentence including death or mutilation.[163] In the
capital itself there were numerous *alguaciles* attached to the household,[164] the Vicaria, the court of the admiral, the captain of the
city, the mint, and a number of other tribunals. Inevitably some
abused their powers of arrest 'ut magis ab eis ius capture, mora-
baturi et carcelagii habeant et exigant quam de eis iustitia minis-
tretur'.[165] Such excesses became more intolerable as the number
of these officers increased and the state of law and order improved,

[159] ACA Reg. 2908. 161ᵛ, 11 Aug. 1446.
[160] The *alguacil* had already made an appearance in Sicily.
[161] Faraglia, *Storia della lotta*, p. 164, n. 1. Johan de Perpenya was an *algutzir*
(Catalan for *alguacil*) in December 1441 (ibid., p. 261, n. 1).
[162] de Bottis, *Privilegii et capitoli*, fol. 6.
[163] ACA Reg. 2913. 8ᵛ, 18 May 1448.
[164] e.g. commission to the 'nobili viro Uguetto de Maiorica militi alguazerio',
Naples, 22 Mar. 1443 (ACA Reg. 2902. 167ᵛ). Pere Gomela 'fideli algutzerio et
militi magne curie vicarie' (ASN Priv. I. 150ʳ, 15 May 1454). The *alguaciles*
seem all to have been Spaniards and knights (as required by the Ordinance).
[165] ASN Priv. I. 165ʳ, 1 Aug. 1454.

so in 1454 the king issued an edict to control their activities. In future any person arrested at the instance of another party was not to pay anything to the officer making the arrest, the fees involved being the responsibility of the one who had instituted the action.[166] Only a person arrested 'in fragrante crimine' could be obliged to pay the fee of his captor, and only in such circumstances were *alguaciles* to make summary arrests which they had to report to a competent judge within ten hours. The edict aimed to stamp out malpractices, not to curb the legitimate activity of these agents of the law. Exactly how far that legitimate activity extended still remained a matter of controversy after the failure of the 1443 parliament to exclude from it all natives of the Kingdom. In the last parliament of the reign the barons petitioned, 'che li alguzini non possano exercitare alcune jurisdictione contra li prefati baroni et loro vaxalli'.[167] This time the king stood on firmer ground than in 1443 and was able to reply, 'Placet Regia Maiestati quod serventur capitula super hoc concessa.'[168] In other words, things were to remain as they were, with the barons and their vassals subject in some instances to the jurisdiction of the *alguaciles*. The *capitula* regulating these matters, to which the king referred, have not come to light, but they are likely to have embodied the practices that governed the activity of the *alguaciles* attached to the viceroy of Calabria.

While one can believe that, in the later years of Alfonso's reign, justice was administered more effectively than at any other time in the previous half century, it is none the less evident that order and tranquillity did not reign everywhere in the kingdom. The king's reassuring 'state of the kingdom' speech to the Catalonian ambassadors almost coincided with an instruction to Bernardo de Raimo, his commissioner general in the Abruzzi, to investigate a wave of lawlessness in that province affecting both demesne and baronial lands. Royal captains and barons were failing in their duty to act against the criminals.[169] In 1456 Amatrice had to be given permission to pay its taxes to a royal treasurer in the town itself, instead of taking the money to Sulmona as required by law,

---

[166] e.g. on 3 Feb. 1453 Joan Rubio of the treasury paid for a copy of an order of the council to two *alguaciles* of the Vicaria who arrested him while he was listening to the sermon one Sunday in San Lorenzo (ASN Dip. Somm. 178. 10ᵛ).

[167] ASN Div. Somm. I. 52 (bis), 171ᵛ.   [168] Ibid.

[169] ACA Reg. 2915. 19ᵛ, 24 May 1451: '. . . patrati sint nonnulli excessus violencie homicidia insultos puplici crimina et delicta alia falsa moneta cusa . . .'

because of the insecurity of the countryside.[170] In Calabria nobles continued to oppress their vassals and sometimes openly resisted the attempts of royal officials to bring them to justice.[171]

Nor did the machinery of justice always run smoothly. In January 1453 the *promotor negotiorum curie* Joan de Boxia was ordered to expedite business pending in the courts of the Sacrum Consilium, the Vicaria, the mint, and the Sommaria. Crown pleas were his chief concern, but he was also bidden to take action to clear the backlog of private and communal cases, and to see that they were in future decided 'omnibus dilatione, cavillatione et procrastinatione cessantibus et reiectis adeo quod subditi nostri et presertim forenses et alii litigantes temporum longitudine ultra debitum litibus et sumptibus non vexentur'.[172] Impatience with the trammels of legal procedure shines through in many a royal command of the 1450s. When the Count of Venafro complained of certain persons wrongfully occupying some of his feudal land, the king ordered two judges to conduct an on-the-spot investigation by calling on all those holding of the fief to present themselves within a certain time, 'non obstante quod causa pheudalis sit, cuius cognitio de sui natura ad alios judices dignoscitur pertinere'.[173] The customary procedure had been set aside, 'ut aperta claritas depellat queque latencia nublia et incertitudo nodosa dissolvatur et tediosa confusionis materia minoretur'. In September 1452 he commanded the judges of the Vicaria and other officials to give every assistance to a procurator sent to recover moneys owed to the *condottiere* Jacobo Piccinino, 'procedendo in iis summarie, simpliciter et de plano sine strepitu forma et figura iudicii sola facta veritate attenta malitiis diffugiis dilacionibus et cavillationibus omnibus proculpulsis, non obstantibus quibusvis frivolis exceptionibus et aliis quibusvis iustitiam impedientibus'.[174] Such phrases become almost common form in

---

[170] Gentile, 'Lo stato napoletano' (1937), p. 22, n. 1.

[171] Cf. below, p. 168.   [172] ASN Priv. I. 73ᵛ, 16 Jan. 1453.

[173] ACA Reg. 2915. 1ʳ, 13 Apr. 1451.

[174] Mazzoleni, *Il Codice Chigi*, pp. 354–5, 12 Sept. 1452. The phrasing recalls that used in a letter of Charles II empowering the regent of the *magna curia* to proceed 'summarie de plano sine strepitu et figura iudicii ordine iudiciario pretermisso' in cases of oppression affecting widows, orphans, etc., 10 Nov. 1306 (Minieri Riccio, *Saggio*, Suppl. pt. II (Naples, 1883), p. 47). One is reminded too of an anecdote of Beccadelli (*De dictis et factis*, iv) about a clever but avaricious lawyer whose sophistries were causing havoc in the law courts; to put a stop to his activities, Alfonso decreed that all his suits should be judged lost.

instructions to those charged with special judicial commissions about this time. They reflect, on the one hand, the ingrained shortcomings of a system which bred delay and hence, often, injustice; on the other, a meritorious determination that the system should, where necessary, give way to simpler procedures in the name of justice.[175]

One is, however, conscious that the processes of law were bent most often in the interest of the powerful. However much royal edicts might thunder against the taking of unlawful fees and bribes, those who dispensed justice expected some gratification for services rendered. Even the president of the council, the Bishop of Urgell, showed that he expected some reward for his support of the 'Busca' cause in the council by complaining to the envoy of Barcelona that he was out of pocket on their account. To drive the point home he quoted the Catalan proverb, 'Who serves a child and a commune serves no one' ('Qui servex a infant e a comu, no serveix a nengu').[176] In 1450 the chancery judges Claver, Falco, and Fillach each accepted 25 ducats from Barcelona 'for their labour' in obtaining the jurisdiction of certain towns for the city.[177] As for the king, he seems to have acted in the belief that when great prizes were at stake in a lawsuit, those who stood to benefit handsomely from the justice dispensed by the state should be prepared to offer the state something in addition to the normal fees of justice. Those engaged in such suits understood this principle well enough for it pervaded the whole judicial system from top to bottom—and they acted accordingly.

Many examples might be quoted of men with cases pending in the royal courts offering money to the king. Tommaso Caracciolo, son of the Count of Gerace, became involved in a dispute with his grandmother Raimondetta Centelles over lands that had belonged to Cola Ruffo, Raimondetta's deceased husband and the maternal grandfather of Tommaso. The latter being a minor, his father first instituted proceedings on his behalf in the Vicaria, and then

---

[175] Cf. Alfonso's rejection of the petition from the barons in the 1456 parliament that action for crimes, apart from the most serious, should lie only with the aggrieved party: 'Non placet Regie Maiestati quoniam contra bonum publicum quia multa nefaria remanerent impunita verum eadem Maiestas confirmat capitulum editum per clare memorie Regem Robertum quod incipit Ut delatas ad nostram audienciam' (ASN Div. Somm. I. 52 (bis), 171). Cf. above, p. 121.

[176] Madurell Marimon, *Mensajeros barceloneses*, p. 561.

[177] Ibid., p. 360.

in April 1444, while these were still taking their course, he came to an agreement with the king to speed up matters.[178] In the first place the king gave him permission to reach a settlement out of court with Raimondetta on the property in dispute; for that favour the count was to pay 1,500 ducats. There remained the matter of a judgement that would validate whatever agreement might be reached:

... ad zo che lo dicto accordo abia piu celeri effecto et che interea non se perda tempo nella administracione dela justicia, pete lo dicto conte la prefata Maiesta abia informacione de suo sacro consiglio, nel quale presente li procuratori de ambe li parte so stati loro advocati plene auditi si nella causa de zo mota nella curte dela Vicaria si divia procedere innante non obstante alcune cose allegate in una supplicacione date per parte madamma Raymundeta. Et habita ipsa informacione che per justicia se debea procedere reduca la causa nelli termini quali era quando fo presentata la dicta supplicacione, et mandi a la dicta curte che proceda innante non obstante omni relacione et mandato facto per parte la dicta Maiesta per Johanni de Bosa,[179] o per altra persona. Et providere ita et taliter che per tucto lo mese de Jugno o Julio ad altius huius anni la dicta causa sia furnita et determinata per diffinitiva sentencia mediante justicia. Et interea lo dicto acordo se pora contractare et veniendo ad effecto la sua Maiesta lo reputi per accepto et abia per lucrati li dicti ducati mill cinquecento et lo litigio se restara ad non prosequirese.

Should Tommaso obtain the lands by agreement and subsequent sentence of the court, the king would excuse him payment of relief on them and receive another 4,500 ducats. If, on the other hand, the case went against him, or was not decided by July (Alfonso changed this to Christmas) the count was to recover his 1,500 ducats. The Vicaria did in the event give judgement in favour of Tommaso, though it was not until July 1445 that Raimondetta received an order to surrender two of the baronies in dispute.[180] It is worthy of note that this agreement came at a time when the king found himself 'in a greater need of money than ever

---

[178] ACA Reg. 2903. 155ʳ. The agreement was drawn up in Naples on 22 Apr. and registered on the 24 Apr.

[179] i.e. Joan de Boxia, the procurator fiscal.

[180] ACA Reg. 2907. 128ʳ, 28 July 1445. A judge of the Vicaria, Gabriele de Mastrillis, and a royal clerk were appointed commissioners to execute the judgement.

he was'[181] to pay the army which he had promised the pope to lead against Sforza. Again in the summer of 1446 when he was busy raising a large army, proffers for judicial favours were sympathetically received. Antonio de Fusco gave him a 'loan' of 1,000 ducats to be returned only in the event of an unfavourable verdict in a lawsuit between Antonio and the Duke of Melfi.[182] Sometimes the other party to the suit would join in the bidding to secure the advantage of royal discretionary power. This happened in another case involving the same Antonio de Fusco and the Archbishop of Salerno. In May 1446 the archbishop gave the king a 'loan' of 1,000 ducats which, with an additional 1,000, was to be converted into 'expenses' if the suit in the Sacrum Consilium went in his favour.[183] In August de Fusco capped the archbishop's bid with a 'loan' of 3,500 ducats in return for the king's undertaking not to revoke a two-year moratorium on the suit and to extend it *ad beneplacitum* on expiry; if the moratorium were revoked, de Fusco was to recover his loan.[184] A 'loan' of 1,000 ducats from the Duke of San Marco made in December 1454 was to be repaid if a suit with the Count of Arena went against him; but in the event of the duke obtaining the verdict, he was to give the king another 3,000 ducats 'quos nobis obtulistis ut in dicta causa iusticia mediante procedi mandaremus'.[185] Judges aware of the king's interest in accelerating or retarding the processes of law can hardly have remained entirely indifferent to it in reaching their verdicts. The most that can be said in defence of such transactions is that those involved could afford, and indeed expected, to pay.

Where criminal cases were concerned, there existed a standard bargaining procedure which permitted the accused to compound for their offences with a monetary payment to the crown.[186] Most of these matters were handled by officials and commissioners of the Vicaria, but occasionally they went to a higher level. That same Tommaso Caracciolo who profited from his father's arrangement with the king in a land dispute made his own bargain a few years later when he paid 1,500 ducats to compound for charges brought

---

[181] The secretary Fonolleda told the envoys from Barcelona that Alfonso was 'posat en la maior necessitat de diners que james fos per raho dela emprestança que ha a fer per exir en camp' (ACB Cart. Com., vol. 14, fol. 91, Naples, 6 June 1444).

[182] ACA Reg. 2699. 52ᵛ, 29 July 1446. [183] Ibid. 37ʳ, 26 May 1446.

[184] ACA Reg. 2699. 46ᵛ, 9 Aug. 1446.

[185] ACA Reg. 2700. 76ᵛ, 26 Dec. 1454. [186] Cf. above, p. 157.

against him by the crown.[187] But when he persisted in his acts of
oppression against his vassals and in defiance of the viceroy of
Calabria, Alfonso ordered his arrest. He was seized in Naples in
April 1455. His trial before the chancery judge Nicolau Fillach
and the advocate fiscal Jacme de Pelaya was a lengthy one;
thirty-three witnesses came from Calabria, and the viceroy spent
six months in the capital in connection with it. It ended with
Caracciolo being sentenced to death and the forfeiture of all his
property, a sentence which Alfonso later commuted to one of life
imprisonment.[188]

Whether many paid the penalty of death or mutilation is difficult
to judge because of the disappearance of the relevant court
records, but one gets the impression that these punishments were
imposed relatively rarely, all parties being usually ready to reach
a settlement that involved composition or compensation. The
judicial process could none the less crush the innocent as it did
a woman arrested and tortured on suspicion of being involved in
the theft of 800 ducats. She died of the torture and the thief
obtained a pardon on the charge of being implicated in her death.[189]

[187] ACA Reg. 2917. 69^v, 8 Nov. 1452. This pardon for the marquis, his
officers, and his vassals covers all offences except treason.
[188] Gentile, 'Finanze e parlamenti', pp. 207–10.
[189] ACA Reg. 2915. 129^r, 17 Nov. 1451, Pardon for Benenato Starconi: 'Et
licet etiam quedam mulier cum pro inquisicione ipsius furti per suspicionem
capta tormentis afficeretur et excruciaretur ob eadem ipsa tormenta insons a
dicto crimine expiraverat . . .'

VI

FINANCE

UNDER the Aragonese, as under the Angevins, the master chamberlain remained the titular head of those who managed the finances of the kingdom. Giovanni de Moncada, Count of Aderno, whom Alfonso appointed to that office in 1423, received a schedule of duties which translated into practice would have given him full control of the receipt and expenditure of the crown's revenues.[1] In reality the first of the Angevins had separated the treasury from the chamber,[2] while the second had finally allocated control of finance to the treasurer and the other administrative functions of the office to a vice-chamberlain.[3] The master chamberlain was in this manner freed from all regular financial responsibilities at a very early date. His name and title continued none the less to figure at the head of all documents emanating from the Sommaria and treasury, and either his own, or more commonly his *locumtenens*'s, countersignature upon all privileges, letters, orders, etc. of the chancery that touched upon royal rights, revenues, and property. The office was, therefore, one of great prestige, some profit, and little substance. It passed from the Count of Aderno to Ruggiero Gaetano,[4] from him to Ramon de Perellos,[5] and next

---

[1] A copy of the *capitoli* given to the count appears in ASN Div. Somm. I. 52 (bis), 120^r. Typical of its anachronistic instructions are the following: 'Item ad officium tuum spectat recipere omnem pecuniam cuiuscumque generis sit que ad cameram regiam mictitur. Item habebis similiter notitiam et conscientiam conditionis et status iurium fisci ac redditionum et proventuum regalium sive in cabellam vendantur sive in credentiam procurentur et debes assistere secretis et magnis procuratoribus et magistris salis ceterisque officialibus et procuratoribus et tenentibus domanie et bona curie in custodiam et procurationem ipsorum. Item singulis sex mensibus habebis a iusticiariis secretis et officialibus aliis terras et bona curie procurantibus quaternios introytus et exitus peccunie et rerum omnium officiorum ipsorum quos quaternios hiidem officiales tibi mictere teneantur.'

[2] Cf. above, p. 15.

[3] Trifone, *La legislazione angioina*, p. 35. This reform took place in 1302.

[4] Gaetano had died by April 1436 and his property devolved to the crown (ACA Reg. 2900. 1^r, 27 Sept. 1436).

[5] Ibid. 2^r, 22 Apr. 1436. He is described as 'magno camerario nostro in regno Sicilie citra farum'. Perellos took some part in administration—e.g. from Gaeta

to Francesco d'Aquino, Count of Loreto and Satriano, lord of Aquino, the head of one of the oldest and most powerful baronial families. When that corpulent personnage died in September 1449, Alfonso gave the office to a favourite Castilian courtier, Iñigo de Avalos, who held it for the remainder of the reign.[6]

In Aragon responsibility for the finances of the crown fell on the *maestre racional*; both he and the treasurer, whom he supervised, had permanent seats on the royal council. In practice, the office of the *maestre racional* performed an accounting function similar to that of the Sommaria, while the treasurers of Aragon and Naples had almost identical duties, the main difference between the two being that the Aragonese treasurer enjoyed a higher administrative status than his Neapolitan counterpart. Since the king maintained a single treasury, one is not surprised to find that Aragonese practice and Spanish personnel dominated it.

Bernat Sirvent, who was treasurer while the king was still in Catalonia in 1432, did not accompany Alfonso to Italy and seems to have died in 1435 or 1436. The office remained vacant until 22 June 1439 when it was given to Matteu Pujades, a Valencian who had served many years in Spain as receiver general of revenues.[7] Occasionally he would be addressed as treasurer general[8] —presumably to distinguish him from the host of regional and local officials who bore the title of treasurer—but more often he was given simply the title of treasurer. At the time of his appointment he was busy in Spain organizing a flow of money and supplies for the Italian enterprise, and it was only in the spring of 1441 that he joined the king. In October 1442 he returned to Barcelona to

on 7 Feb. 1438 he ordered Beccadelli to give effect to the *capitoli* regulating the sale of pitch, salt, iron, etc. in Ischia (V. Laurenza, *Il Panormita a Napoli* (Naples, 1936), pp. 64–5). Perellos also held the rank of *camarlench* in the Aragonese household. Cf. above, p. 67.

[6] Iñigo de Avalos was the son of Ruy Lopez de Avalos, Constable of Castile, and half-brother of Iñigo de Guevara. In the *Diurnali detti del Duca di Monteleone* (p. 129) he is described as a great favourite of the king—'home multo amato et intrinsico suo'. On 29 July 1450 he ordered the treasurer to allow the expenses he had incurred when assuming office. These included the making of cloths bearing the royal arms and his own, 'ut moris est', and a piece of green cloth to cover the tables of the Sommaria (Toppi, *De origine tribunalium*, i. 274).

[7] Gentile, 'Lo stato napoletano' (1937), p. 27, n. 2. A letter dated 28 Mar. 1441 concerning his accounts refers to 'tempore sue procuracionis et generalis olim recepcionis' (ACA Reg. 2901 2ᵛ).

[8] e.g. ACA Reg. 2901. 5ᵛ, 10 Apr. 1441. The kingdom of Sicily had its own treasurer—Antoni Sin.

arrange a large purchase of cloth and the redemption of crown jewels from the king's creditors.[9] Once there he became bogged down in many other transactions—especially in coping with the flood of bills of exchange which the king directed to him from Naples—and did not manage to return to Naples until early in 1445. He died there in December 1447.

Thus it happened that, during the first thirteen years of Alfonso's reign in Naples, for most of the time either the post of treasurer remained vacant or else that official was busy in Spain. In his absence the business of the treasury in Naples was conducted by a *locumtenens* or a regent. While Alfonso remained in Sicily preparing his expedition to Naples, Joan Cafont was *locumtenens* for the treasurer Sirvent.[10] Cafont died early in 1435 and was replaced in March of that year by Johan de Gallach who went to the mainland ahead of the king to distribute money among the supporters of the Aragonese cause.[11] On the death of Sirvent, Gallach assumed the title of 'regens officium thesaurarie ad presens vacans', but he too died in the autumn of 1437[12] and the regency passed to Jacme Amigo.[13] Amigo controlled the king's treasury in Italy until Matteu Pujades arrived there in 1441, after which he left to take up his post as governor of Ibiza. When the treasurer again departed for Spain in 1442, the post of regent was given to his nephew Guillem Pujades. Guillem, a clerk in the treasury,[14] had been sent to Italy by his uncle early in 1437 to deliver 7,000 Aragonese florins to the king and had remained to make a career there. He acquired, in addition to the regency, an Aragonese office hitherto unknown in Naples—that of *receptor* or receiver of royal revenues. In the Crown of Aragon one such official was appointed in each of the component states, with a receiver general at the

---

[9] ACA Reg. 2696. 112ᵛ, 8 Oct. 1442, Instructions for Pujades.

[10] Madurell Marimon, *Mensajeros barceloneses*, p. 89.

[11] Ibid., p. 86.

[12] ACA Reg. 2900. 1ʳ; Faraglia, *Storia della lotta*, p. 96, n. 1. A Johan de Gallach was regent of the chancery in Catalonia in 1448 (ACA Reg. 2656. 91ʳ) and later became vice-chancellor of Juan II (Vicens Vives, *Fernando el Catolico*, pp. 48 and 59), but it is probable that this was a son of the treasury official.

[13] See the payments made on his instruction in November 1437 Mazzoleni, *Fonti aragonesi*, i. 83). Also ACA Reg. 2901. 6ʳ, 13 Feb. 1441; Reg. 2646. 88ʳ, 1 Apr. 1440.

[14] Faraglia (*Storia della lotta*, p. 231, n. 2) refers to a document of September 1441 in which Pujades appears as a clerk. A privilege dated 3 Dec. 1442 styles him 'de nostra thesauraria Guillermo Puiades propter absenciam thesaurarii nostras pecunias administranti' (ACA Reg. 2902. 139ᵛ).

centre. In rank this latter office stood below that of treasurer, but the duties of the two overlapped so that confusion and rivalry were usually avoided by giving both posts to the same person. Thus Matteu Pujades on becoming treasurer had retained his former office of receiver general. The appeal to the king of a familiar system and the contribution that the kingdom of Naples made to his finances may both help to explain the introduction of the receiver's office there. Guillem Pujades himself may also have played a part, for he had much influence with Alfonso. The extent of it was described by the envoys of Barcelona when they advised the city council to listen carefully to what Francesc Pujades, Guillem's father, might have to tell them about the state of affairs in Italy, 'for he has better means of knowing them than anyone else, because of the high position of his son, Master G. Puiades, and the great favour he enjoys with the lord king who wishes that he should be called treasurer; and we tell you, gentlemen, in all truth that the favour he has is quite unbelievable'.[15]

Either as an act of policy or to gratify Guillem Pujades, the king did in the course of 1444 upgrade the status of the controller of his Neapolitan treasury. As the envoys from Barcelona noted, Pujades was accorded the title of treasurer;[16] he acquired also that of receiver general—'receptor general deles peccunies de nostre cort'.[17] Together they placed him on an equal footing with his uncle. When Matteu returned to Naples, however, he resumed full control of the treasury in accordance with the usual Aragonese practice which accorded precedence to the senior when two persons held the same office. Guillem soon afterwards moved on to become conservator of the royal patrimony in Sicily, and the dualism in the treasurer's office came temporarily to an end.[18] It reappeared again after Matteu Pujades's death when Alfonso appointed two treasurers general; one for the treasury in Naples, and the other for the rest of his territories.

For a few months after Pujades died, Gabriel Puig administered

[15] ACB Cart. Com., vol. 14, fol. 65, 29 Apr. 1444. Francesc Pujades himself carried this letter to Barcelona.

[16] e.g. in a warrant dated 1 July 1444 (ACA Reg. 2690. 88^r).

[17] Ibid., an order to him to see to the provision of artillery and gunpowder, 1 July 1444.

[18] ACA Reg. 2654. 52^v, 28 June 1446, a letter from the king to Francesc Pujades informing him that his son had been appointed conservator the previous day.

the treasury.[19] In May or June 1448 Perot Mercader, who had earlier been appointed receiver general in Spain in the absence of Pujades,[20] became treasurer general,[21] and on 17 October 1448 while at Civitavecchia Alfonso made Pere de Capdevila treasurer general specifically for the kingdom of Naples.[22] His duties were to make payments as directed by the king, to inspect the accounts of revenue officers and receive moneys from them, to investigate and punish fraud, extortion, and tax evasion, and to keep proper records of all receipts and expenditure. Capdevila had begun his career as a clerk in the treasury[23] and then moved to the office of the *escriva de racio*.[24] In 1446 he had gone to Sardinia to inspect the accounts of the royal procurator, and sometime after the death of Pujades (probably in March 1448)[25] he became regent of the treasury. In that capacity he accompanied the king during the operations against Piombino and earned favour by his energy in organizing supplies for the army. Less than five years later he was dismissed from all his offices following the discovery of large discrepancies in his accounts, and the office of treasurer general in the kingdom was given to Perot Mercader.[26] For the remainder of the reign Mercader held both the treasurerships, so the distinction between them became purely nominal.[27]

---

[19] Salvati, *Fonti aragonese*, iv. 91. Puig was administrator of the treasury between January and August 1448. Johan Ferrer then took over until the new treasurer general returned to Naples.

[20] His appointment as receiver general is dated 24 Oct. 1446 (ACA Reg. 2656. 25ʳ).

[21] The appointment must have been made on some date between 14 Apr. when he was still only receiver general (ACA Reg. 2656. 120ʳ) and 3 July when he was treasurer general (ACA Reg. 2719. 72ʳ).

[22] ACA Reg. 2913. 68ᵛ.

[23] He was a treasury clerk in November 1441 (Faraglia, *Storia della lotta*, p. 263, n. 2).

[24] Minieri Riccio, 'Alcuni fatti di Alfonso I', p. 31. The reference is to March 1442.

[25] When he went to Sardinia he was once more serving in the treasury (ACA Reg. 2690. 204ʳ, 8 Feb. 1446). Toppi (*De origine tribunalium*, III. 243) quotes from 'Cedula Gen. Thes. Petri de Capdevila, incepta a mense Martii 1448'. In July 1447 Capdevila acquired the office of 'perceptor et distributor' of the moneys of the Vicaria, but that office he performed by deputy.

[26] The fall of Capdevila seems to have taken place in June 1453. On 8 June he was still treasurer general (Toppi, *De origine tribunalium*, ii. 467); on 27 July orders were given for the sequestration of all his property (ACA Reg. 2661. 26ᵛ).

[27] Andreu Catala became *locumtenens* in Spain for Mercader (ACA Reg. 2721. 47ᵛ, 20 Sept. 1456; Reg. 2662. 60ᵛ, 2 Feb. 1458), Mercader was in Naples at the time of the Emperor's visit (Summonte, *Historia*, pt. III, p. 132).

Upon the treasurer general, treasurer, or regent of the treasury fell the unenviable task of managing a financial system plagued by a chronic shortage of ready cash and daunting administrative complexities. Even after victory over Anjou had been assured, there were few years which did not see Alfonso engaged in some treasure-consuming enterprise. A six-months campaign in the March of Ancona in 1443 cost, so he claimed, 800,000 ducats.[28] From Tivoli on 10 January 1447 he sent a memorial to his counsellors in Naples explaining 'com lo dit Senyor te tals negocis entre les mans de present que creu fermament que podent ell haver prontament L m. ducats o al menys XXXX m. faria granment sos affers e daria ley a tota ytalia';[29] a postscript raised the price of glory to 100,000 ducats. Entertaining the Emperor Frederick III for ten days is said to have cost more than 100,000 ducats. A rough estimate of receipts and expenditure shows that in a state of war ordinary revenues fell short of needs by between 200,000 and 300,000 ducats a year which had to be raised in Italy and Spain by every means available—customary aids, parliamentary grants, clerical subsidies, indirect taxation, sale of offices and privileges, fines, loans, etc. Sometimes the treasury could not, as Borso d'Este noted in 1445, produce 1,000 ducats in ready cash.[30] A year later the king had to admit to the governor of Mallorca that he stood 'en gran e extrema necessitat'.[31] He returned to Naples in November 1448 to find all his treasure in pawn to merchants as security for their loans.[32] A good treasurer was expected to navigate these crises, to see that the king had money when he needed it, to put off old creditors and find new ones, to ginger up debtors and revenue collectors; in short, to see that the creaking machinery of royal finance was by some means or other kept in motion.

The registers of the Aragonese archives amply illustrate the demands made on the treasurer. If he was in Spain, bills of exchange, warrants for payment, and orders for purchase arrived in a steady stream from Italy. One warrant, typical of many, was the result of a contract Alfonso signed with a Florentine merchant in February 1442. The merchant, Falducco Massi, lent the king

[28] ACA Reg. 2940. 19ᵛ, Alfonso to the Bishop of Lerida, Castelnuovo, 13 Oct. 1446.   [29] ACA Reg. 2699, 61ʳ.

[30] Foucard, 'Proposta fatta dalla Corte Estense', p. 711.

[31] ACA Reg. 2699. 40ʳ, 30 Apr. 1446.

[32] ACA Reg. 2940. 59ʳ, 27 Nov. 1448, Alfonso to Mercader: '. . . en poder de los mercaderes por su seguretat joyas oro argento quanto tengo.'

3,150 ducats, partly in cash, partly in cloth, on the understanding
that he would be repaid two months later by the treasurer of
Terra di Lavoro. When the latter managed to pay only 1,000
ducats, Alfonso came to an arrangement with the Florentine that
he should receive the balance from an aid granted by the Cortes
of Aragon. The appropriate warrant was dispatched to Matteu
Pujades in December 1442.[33] Bills of exchange from Italy were
made the first charge upon a clerical subsidy and maritagium ex-
tracted from Catalonia; having discharged these, the treasurer
general Mercader was to send the estimated residue of 20,000
ducats to Naples in coin.[34] Numerous payments had to be made for
shipments of salt, iron, and cloth destined for Naples. For example,
Matteu Pujades was told in October 1442 to spend 15,000 florins
on the purchase of 1,000 pieces of cloth 'of the colours and quality
which he knows are needed and current in the kingdom'.[35] In
1457 Miquel Bru, the receiver general in Spain, was ordered to
provide 1,000 cuirasses, 3,000 helmets for oarsmen, and 500
martinets for the king's forces fighting against Genoa.[36] Above
all the financial officials had to contend with the bills of exchange
by means of which Alfonso was able to draw with comparative
ease on the Spanish treasury, and more often, to anticipate in Italy
the proceeds from taxation imposed in Spain, Sicily, or Sardinia.
He informed Matteu Pujades in April 1444 that he had borrowed
'magnas summas' against bills of exchange drawn on the treasurer
and payable from a clerical subsidy of 140,000 florins. Should the
money from the subsidy not come in on time, Pujades was
authorized to raise the necessary funds by the sale of annuities.[37]
A letter to Mercader dated 7 June 1449 advised that the king intended taking bills of exchange to a value of 20,000 ducats against
the maritagium levied in Spain; the treasurer general was being
notified in advance so that the bills might be taken for the shortest
possible period and the rate of interest thus reduced.[38]

It took much less time to draw a bill of exchange or issue a warrant for payment than to collect a clerical subsidy or aid, whether
in Spain or Naples, so treasurers constantly found themselves in

[33] ACA Reg. 2901. 90ᵛ, 21 Dec. 1442.
[34] ACA Reg. 2699. 164ʳ, 5 Feb. 1449. If 20,000 ducats were not immediately
available, the king's galleys were to sail with 2,000 or 3,000.
[35] ACA Reg. 2696. 112ᵛ, 8 Oct. 1442.
[36] ACA Reg. 2661. 171ʳ, 15 Sept. 1457.
[37] ACA Reg. 2720. 15ʳ, 21 Apr. 1444.   [38] Ibid. 117ʳ.

difficulties in meeting the deadlines imposed upon them. Failure or delay exposed them to a barrage of letters mingling exhortation, plea and threat.

If the treasurer came to Italy, his life was hardly more tranquil, especially in those years when he had to meet the imperative demands of war and conduct his business from an armed camp. Capdevila's accounts for his first year as treasurer general suffered from those handicaps as the Sommaria recognized when it came to audit them:

Errantibus in calculo cuncta iura subveniunt, dummodo absit ab ipso eodem calculo fraus; cum igitur coram Excellentia et magnificent. vestrorum dominorum magni camerarii, presidentium et magistrorum rationalium Camerae Sacrae Maiestatis Regiae Petrus de Capdevila Thesaurarius Maiestatis eiusdem duos libros hucusque sui calculi seu rationis de administratis per eum pro Curia dederit datque etiam de presenti hunc librum tertium administrationis eiusdem et in ipsis libris diversae et maxime datarum aut receptarum copiae ipsarum administrationum existant, ob quod faciliter tam propter fragilitatem humanam quam propter ignorantiam aliquorum administratorum seu substitutorum Thesaurarii eiusdem cum propter crebras et repentinas plerorumque castrorum mutationes apud partes Tusciae ubi prefatus Thes. dictas in maiori parte fecit administrationes, tum et propter plurimas ac inopinatas hostium in ipsis castris insultationes, quibus ne dum scribendi partitas computorum ipsorum administrationum, sed etiam ad tuendas res proprias sepius potestas auferebatur, tum et alias, aliquis error in datis aut receptis forte posset reperiri non tamen ob culpam dolum nec fraudem Thes. eiusdem rationem reddentis et sic eidem debere minime imputari, sed ex causis predictis et propter longi temporis tractum multorumque et magnorum in ipsis administrationibus negociorum cumulum.[39]

Capdevila was not the only one to fall into these difficulties. Matteu Pujades, whom Alfonso had repeatedly assured of his confidence,[40] was found after his death never to have rendered any proper accounts: 'in vita sua compota administracionis sui thesaurarii officii non dederit.'[41] His heirs were therefore commanded to present the deceased treasurer's accounts in person before the king within the space of two months. When, after some

---

[39] Toppi, *De origine tribunalium*, iii. 243–5.

[40] e.g. in a letter dated 6 Oct. 1440: 'E som nos mes volguts playr de vos lo qual tenim per intrinsech servidor que de negun altre' (ACA Reg. 2651. 165ʳ).

[41] ACA Reg. 2656. 109ʳ, 14 Feb. 1448.

years, the inspection of the books had been completed, it was established that he had died owing very large sums to the crown, and orders were given for the sequestration of his property in Valencia.[42] The property was still in the hands of the crown when the king died, but in his will he directed that it be returned to the heirs.[43] Pere de Capdevila fared no better, despite the indulgence of the Sommaria. Examination of his accounts in 1453 revealed that he owed the crown 'molt gran quantitat de pecunia';[44] as a result he was dismissed from office and the crown seized all his property, including that in Spain. Perot Mercader must have been either more honest, more efficient, or more astute; at least he avoided the pitfalls that had trapped his predecessors.

Officials who died in possession of their offices commonly left their accounts in disorder; so too did those who fell suddenly into disgrace. Sometimes peculation or sheer inefficiency was to blame, but much of the trouble arose from antiquated methods of keeping accounts and conducting the audit. Transfers of money, goods, and credit among Alfonso's different kingdoms put enormous strains upon a system which had been devised for a relatively small and compact state. Great efforts were therefore made to adapt the accounting system to the new reality of a scattered empire dependent upon lengthy sea communications.[45]

Our particular concern is with the Neapolitan treasury, which was also in effect the central treasury of the Aragonese empire. In the latter years of the reign it was housed in a building in the ward of Naples known as the Seggio di Nido.[46] Its senior officials—

---

[42] ACA Reg. 2721. 43ᵛ, 23 Aug. 1452, Letter from the king to the Abbot of Poblet in which he mentions that the receiver general Miquel Bru is being sent to Valencia 'per fer execucio en los bens de Matteu Pujades'. Matteu's son and heir, also named Matteu, issued a receipt to cover 10,813 ducats which his father had received from the treasury official Joan Andreu de Vesach (Salvati, *Fonti aragonesi*, iv. 108, 24 Feb. 1449).

[43] 'Item volumus et iubemus quod sequestrum ad nostri fisci instantiam positum in bonis uxoris Matthei Puiades quondam militis thesaurarii nostri generalis penitus tollatur et bone que eidem pertineant sibi restituantur absque curie nostre alio impedimento' (ASN Priv. I. 186ʳ; cf. Gentile, 'Lo stato napoletano' (1937), p. 27, n. 4.

[44] ACA Reg. 2661. 26ᵛ, 27 July 1453, Instructions sent to Queen Maria, the King of Navarre, and Martin de Lanuza for the sequestration of Capdevila's property in the Spanish states.   [45] Cf. below, pp. 191–2.

[46] The building was rented from the secretary Olzina for 80 ducats a year (Minieri Riccio, 'Alcuni fatti di Alfonso I', p. 446). On the ground floor was a store-room for the king's stock of cloth (Gentile, 'Lo stato napoletano' (1937), p. 26, n. 6).

whether treasurers, treasurers general, regents, or *locumtenentes*—
were all Spaniards throughout the reign, Italians being found only
among the clerks and commissioners. Its basic procedures were
relatively simple. A person who had obtained a royal letter patent,
duly signed and sealed, authorizing a payment, would present it in
the office of the *escriva de racio*; that office would issue a warrant
(*albarano*) against which the treasury would make payment. Discharged warrants were filed on a spike in order of payment for
one month; at the end of each month they were made up into
bundles for eventual presentation in the Sommaria. In addition
the treasurer kept registers (*cedole*) of all expenditures and receipts.[47] Files of receipts (*apodixe*) served a purpose similar to
that of the warrants for controlling moneys paid into the treasury.

Besides receiving money from those responsible for the collection of royal revenues, officials of the treasury frequently went on
tax-collecting missions themselves. In February 1449 Angelillo de
Martino received a commission to collect the salt tax and two aids
in the province of Terra di Lavoro beyond the Garigliano.[48] The
Sommaria furnished him with a schedule of towns and baronies
detailing the tax assessment of each. With two assistants it took
him three months to complete the collection, for which he was
allowed 36 ducats as expenses. He collected altogether 6,455
ducats 2 *tarini* 2 *grana*, so the cost of tax gathering by this method
was very moderate indeed. Some he paid directly to the treasurer,
some through intermediaries,[49] and some through banks.[50] Capdevila the treasurer occasionally intervened to instruct the commissioner by word of mouth or by writing. For example, 'de
mandato petri de Capdevila regii Thesaurarii oretenus' he did not
collect two aids from Capua,[51] and he refrained from pressing
Marino de l'Aquila when he received the following letter.

Vir nobilis et amice carissime salut. Advisove per la presente como
marino de laquila e stato da me et havime narrato como vuy li donate
impazo alo facto de le colte et delo mezo thomolo de sale. Per tanto non

[47] Faraglia, *Storia della lotta*, p. 126, n. 1. The procedure is illustrated by
fragments of the *cedole* published in Mazzoleni, *Fonti aragonesi*, i.

[48] ASN Div. Somm. I. 133, a copy of his commission and accounts as presented to the Sommaria.

[49] e.g. he delivered 3,125 ducats to Dalmau Fenoses, another treasury official.

[50] The banks he used were those of Giovanni di Miroballo, Martin de la
Cavalleria, Pietro di Gaeta, and Pere Simart.

[51] ASN Div. Somm. I. 133, 9ʳ. A marginal note indicates that he presented
in the Sommaria a copy of a royal mandate remitting the aids for Capua.

vogliate dare impazo alo dicto marino supra ale dicte doy colte non anche alo dicto pagamento delo sale, ne ancho de foculeri per quanto me portate amore per che so bene accordato con ipso. Neapoli, die xviiii mensis Aprilis xii Ind.

P. de Capdevila, Thes.[52]

Another major task entrusted to officials of the treasury was the supervision of expenditure in public works involving large sums of money such as castle and harbour building and the construction of ships. In 1451 Alfonso decided to rebuild the walls and castle of Castellammare di Stabia, a small town on the bay of Naples. With Joan Rubio of the treasury acting as financial supervisor, the work began in September 1451 and continued for fifteen months, during which time Rubio lived in a house he had rented in the town. The treasury paid 1,000 ducats towards the cost, while the bishop, clergy, and town contributed another 971 ducats specifically for labour and building materials. The highlights of the operations were the laying of the foundation stone of the Torre Alfonsina on 19 July 1452 in the presence of the bishop and governor,[53] and a visit by the king in November to inspect the new fortifications. Rubio had to spend a good deal of his time riding around after the king in order to obtain warrants for the release of funds from the treasury and approval of the levy imposed on the town for the building.[54] Accounts have also survived for some of the work on the castle of Gaeta. Orders for the building of a new castle in the city were given in February 1436, soon after Aragonese forces took possession of it.[55] Work began in 1437 under the supervision of Francesco della Cava[56] and continued intermittently for much of the reign. The accounts we have related to the period from the end of 1448 to 1454 when work on the fortress, known as the Castel Alfonsino, was being supervised by Jacme Marti of the treasury.[57] Expenditure ran at the rate of approximately 5,000 ducats a year,

[52] The original letter is enclosed with Angelillo's accounts.
[53] A gold coin known as an *alfonsino* was placed beneath the stone.
[54] ASN Dip. Somm. 178, the accounts that Rubio presented to the Sommaria. In them he details the expenses incurred 'andando et venendo co uno cavallo et famillyo ad napoli et altre parte donde era la maesta de Re travallyando cola dicta maesta et colo magnifico messer Johanne Callyardo per potere avere dinare perlla dicta fabrica et dare ordine alo catasto che se devea fare per lla conta dela terra'.
[55] Minieri Riccio, 'Alcuni fatti di Alfonso I', p. 3. The Bishop of Lerida as viceroy of Gaeta first took charge of the work.
[56] Faraglia, *Storia della lotta*, p. 78, n. 3.
[57] ASN Dip. Somm. 189 (1), 189 (2).

though work ceased during the winter months from October to the end of January.[58] In all operations of this kind the actions of the treasury officials were controlled by a representative of the office of the *escriva de racio* who was likewise attached to the project.[59]

The employment of treasury personnel in the detection and punishment of fiscal misdemeanours can be illustrated by the commission given to Joan Andreu de Vesach on 1 March 1447.[60] There were, states the preamble, those in the provinces of Capitanata and Terra di Bari guilty of a great variety of offences: usury, the illegal sale of salt, selling foodstuffs to the king's enemy Francesco Sforza through the port of Ancona, retaining dues and taxes improperly collected when Manfredonia and other towns were in Sforza's hands, and illegally occupying feudal estates. The commission charges de Vesach to go in person to these provinces, hold an inquiry, and take proceedings against all suspected of these crimes 'pro ut iura ritus et consuetudines curie nostre Regnique huius constitutiones volunt atque mandant'. Assisted by a judge and notary (*magister actorum*) of his own choosing, he had 'plenissimam facultatem et potestatem condepnandi sententiandi et terminandi' and of executing the sentences imposed. He received too authority to compound any sentence for a monetary payment. A subsequent instruction stopped him using inquest procedure against usurers; he was told instead only to act on denunciation, as provided by the constitutions of the kingdom.[61]

Yet another type of commission was given to Paolo Brosco of the treasury in June 1451 following the death of the Archbishop of Otranto.[62] It ordered him to take possession of the property of the deceased and sell it by auction. The sales began in Lecce on 21 July 1451 and continued in Otranto, Taranto, Altamura, Venosa,

[58] Special stone for the foundations, doors, and windows was brought from Ischia; the remainder of the structure was built of softer stone quarried at Pizzofalcone in Naples.

[59] Cf. above, p. 88. Johan Lenes represented the *escriva de racio* in Gaeta. Each page of Jacme Marti's accounts bears the subscription, 'Ego Johannes Lenes testor'. In Castellammare di Stabia the corresponding official was Innocente Cubells.

[60] ACA Reg. 2690. 216ʳ, de Vesach, a noble and *familiaris*, had served in the office of the *maestre racional* of Valencia before going to the treasury in Naples in 1444. In November 1448 he was appointed commissioner for collection of the hearth tax due at Christmas in the provinces of Terra d'Otranto, Capitanata, and Terra di Bari (ACA Reg. 2913. 75ʳ, 20 Nov. 1448).

[61] Rogadeo, *Codice diplomatico*, pp. 188–9, Instruction dated 8 June 1446.

[62] ASN Dip. Somm. 314 (1), Accounts presented in the Sommaria by Brosco.

and Atella. Then, at the beginning of October, Brosco took some of the more valuable items to Naples where he held further sales 'in le banche de Napoli'.[63] He realized altogether some 3,000 ducats which he paid into the treasury either directly or through the bank of Pere Cimart.

These and many similar documents show us the officials of the treasury as men of considerable authority and standing—most of them were *nobiles* and *familiares*—occupied for much of their time on lengthy missions in the provinces, emissaries of the central government armed with a formidable array of judicial and executive powers. They travelled too outside the kingdom on a variety of business. Andreu de Capdevila, a brother of Pere, received in January 1443 instructions for a journey that was to take him to Castile to seek from Alfonso's brothers a confirmation of the treaty they had made with the Duke of Milan,[64] to Queen Maria in Catalonia with orders for the disarming of privateers,[65] and to the Archbishop of Zaragoza for money to pay troops in Italy.[66] In August 1446 Andreu, now regent of the treasury, embarked on another mission to Spain. Part of his business was again with Queen Maria,[67] but his principal assignment was an inquiry into allegations of fraud and corruption among royal officials in Mallorca; the proceeds of that inquiry were to discharge bills of exchange sent from Naples.[68] Miquel Bru, a clerk of the treasury, went on a similar money-hunting expedition to Spain at the end of 1451; his quarry was those who had contravened the laws against trading with Florence.[69]

[63] Most of the buyers in the sales held in Naples were Spaniards.

[64] ACA Reg. 2939. 55^v, 20 Jan. 1443.

[65] Ibid. 59^r, 21 Jan. 1443.

[66] ACA Reg. 2690. 19^r, 23 Jan. 1443.

[67] ACA Reg. 2654. 80^r, 3 Aug. 1446, Instructions concerning the appointment of a deputy in the office of *locumtenens* to the batle general of Catalonia.

[68] ACA Reg. 2699. 44^r, 3 Aug. 1446. The mission had previously been entrusted to Ramon Vidal, *locumtenens* of the *escriva de racio* (ibid. 40^r and 42^v), but he had died before reaching Mallorca. Both had instructions to explain to the governor of the island, Berenguer Dolms, that the king, being in great need of money to pay his armies, 'e volent se ajudar delo que a ell e ala sua cort pertany e bonament pot, essent informat que en lo dit Regne de Mallorques se son comeses moltes e diverses penes e confiscacions de persona e bens applicadas e adquisides ala sua cort segons davall es contengut, ha deliberat pendre cambis com de fet a presos sobre lo que resultara o prochira deles dites penes e confiscacions.'

[69] Madurell Marimon, *Mensajeros barceloneses*. p. 401, Letter from Antoni Vinyes to Barcelona, 9 Nov. 1451.

We also find treasury officials accompanying the king's land and sea forces as paymasters and general watchdogs of the crown's financial interests. In August 1452, for example, Alfonso decided to commission three vessels to attack the shipping of his enemies in the western Mediterranean. Pere de Niubo of the treasury was accordingly dispatched from Naples to join the ships in Spain and take command of the expedition; with him he took money for pay and provisions.[70] When the king's admiral, Vilamari, led a fleet of ten galleys against Florentine shipping and possessions, a treasury official, Johan Mates, sailed with him to supervise the distribution and sale of prize.[71] And ten years later, in the course of the final naval campaign against Genoa, the treasury sent Pere Johan to Vilamari with 500 ducats for each of the eleven galleys under his command.[72]

Not all the cash received or disbursed for the crown passed through the hands of the treasury. Angelillo de Martino, we have seen, paid some of the tax he collected in 1449 to various banks and part of the proceeds from the sale of the Archbishop of Otranto's property was deposited in the bank of Pere Cimart. The treasury regularly used banks in this manner for the receipt and deposit of revenue, the deposit usually being in the nature of the sprat that attracted the loan or credit mackerel. Both Neapolitan and Catalan merchant bankers shared in this form of royal patronage until in 1448 the king attempted to channel all his monetary transactions through a single bank. A similar arrangement had been introduced in 1446 for the kingdom of Valencia where the bank of Thomas Pujades, a nephew of the treasurer general, became the sole agent for receiving and disbursing moneys of the *curia* and the *generalidad* of the kingdom.[73] In Naples the bank chosen was that of Giovanni di Miroballo, the only native bank of

---

[70] ACA Reg. 2697. 141ʳ, 31 Aug. 1452, Instructions for de Niubo. Two of the ships already had treasury officials aboard: Johan Perez Terre in the ship captained by Luis Solsona, and Antoni Berga in a Venetian ship captained by Lorenzo Russo. Two officials of the *escriva de racio*, Johan Quintana and Nicolau Brusca, were attached to the squadron.

[71] Ibid. 42ᵛ, 2 Dec. 1449.   [72] ACA Reg. 2800. 59ʳ, 18 Apr. 1458.

[73] ACA Reg. 2698. 156ʳ, 27 Feb. 1446, Instructions for the King of Navarre, as *locumtenens* in Valencia, to put the new system into operation. Cf. the arrangement whereby the manager of the Roman branch of the Medici bank had in 1421 been appointed 'depository of the papal chamber' (G. Holmes, *The Florentine Enlightenment 1400–50* (London, 1969), pp. 77–8). Cf. P. Partner, *The Papal State under Martin V* (London, 1958), p. 137.

any importance, and one which had often helped the king out of difficulties.[74] By 1445, at the latest, his bank had begun to receive money on behalf of the treasury; in November of that year the syndics of Sorrento paid their coronation tax to it 'pro parte regie curie'.[75] And in 1448 he bought his way into the ranks of the feudal nobility for the sum of 2,500 ducats which he paid for a fief comprising Lettere, Gragnano, Pimonte, Positano, and Torre Galli, and straddling the neck of the Sorrentine peninsula.[76] That same year was indeed something of an *annus mirabilis* for Giovanni because it also saw him appointed a president of the Sommaria,[77] going as the king's envoy to Rome, and even joining in the assault on Piombino, for which exploit the king himself dubbed him a knight.[78] The financial assistance the crown received from the Miroballo bank had become especially substantial and needful in the difficult circumstances of 1448 when Alfonso was straining his credit to sustain the war against Florence. Giovanni di Miroballo came to the rescue with various kinds of credit amounting to almost 19,000 ducats.[79] Part of this sum was made up of promissory notes and returned bills of exchange which the treasurer in Spain had been unable to meet and which di Miraballo had discharged on behalf of the crown. His bank also held jewels to the value of 5,600 ducats which the king had bought from Genoese merchants on eight months' credit.[80] In this manner Miroballo had assumed responsibility for payment of various creditors of the crown. In return the king directed to his bank a number of payments due to the treasury so that Miroballo might recoup himself, 'ex quibuscunque peccuniis et juribus nostre curie tam focularium collectarum trium novissime in parlamento celebrato Neapoli in toto

[74] In 1442 Giovanni di Miroballo was captain of the Piazza delli Armieri in Naples and contributed 80 ducats—the highest of all individual assessments—towards the king's triumphal entry (BNN Bibl. Branc. MS. IV B10). One may therefore presume that he was among the richest men in the city.

[75] ASN Fasc. Com. Somm. 91ᵛ.

[76] ACA Reg. 2913. 22ʳ, 27 July 1448, Privilege investing di Miroballo with the fief.

[77] ACA Reg. 2913. 60ᵛ, 30 Sept. 1448, Privilege fixing his salary as president at 500 ducats.

[78] Ibid.

[79] ACA Real Patrimonio 2951. In November 1448 the crown owed him 18,973 ducats 3 *tarini* 15 *grana*.

[80] ACA Reg. 2696. 171ᵛ, 25 Aug. 1448, Promissory note for the Genoese merchants. Among the jewels was a diamond for which Alfonso paid 3,240 ducats.

dicto Regno generaliter impositarum quam aliis etiam quibuscumque que omnes in banco vestro Neapoli deponuntur et iussu et ordinatione nostris deponende sunt.'[81] Sums thus received were to be notified to Gabriel Puig, the administrator of the Neapolitan treasury, and entered in Miroballo's ledgers as payments in discharge of the crown's debt.[82]

A month later Alfonso decreed that all payments to and from the crown in the kingdom of Naples should be made through this one bank:

De continent sia manat e scrit a tots tresorers eraris e comissaris e reebedors o collidors sots qualsevol titol o nom nomenats en qualsevol provincies del Reyalme que daquiavant de totes les peccunies que colliran deles entrades dela cort axi de foculers coltes dohana de pecores secrecies e portulanies fondechs de sal ferro e pega cabella dela graxa del flagello e dels sis grans per onza e encara dels quatre per cent dret de tapit e altres qualsevol drets e emoluments diputats en temps passat a pagar salaris del gran Camarlench e Loctinent de presidents racionals e altres officials dela summaria e encara dela vicaria residuums o restes de tresorers eraris e altres qualsevol administradors de peccunia e encara peccunies procehidores de qualsevol contractes faedors per lo dit Senyor Rey, o altres qualsevol persones en nom de aquell, residuums de comptes finats en summaria, o no finats, e finalment totes altres peccunies procehints de qualsevol drets per qualsevol via pertanyents ala Regia Cort deien e sien tenguts respondre e aquelles trametre o portar al banch del dit misser Johan de miraball en Napols de continent que les dites peccunies reebudes hauran sots incorriment de grans penes pecuniaries e altres a arbitre del dit Illustrissimo Senyor Duch imposadores, com la intencio del dit Senyor sia que en lo dit banch vinguen totes les sues peccunies e per aquell sien pagats tots provisionats e salariats e deutes deguts per la sua cort a qualsevol persones.[83]

Even those with a pension assigned upon the taxes of their own vassals had to forego the facility of collecting the money directly: 'each of them can or ought to be satisfied since payment will be made to him in full by the said bank to the very great benefit of the said king, for it behoves him to know clearly the amount of his

---

[81] ACA Reg. 2913. 39ᵛ, 29 Aug. 1448.

[82] '. . . introitum sibi [sc. Puig] faciat et vobis exitum in solutionem debiti huius' (ibid.).

[83] ACA Reg. 2699. 141ᵛ, 3 Oct. 1448. This order formed part of the general instruction sent to the king's council in Naples for a reform of justice and administration. Cf. above, p. 100.

income throughout the kingdom, and in no other way can he see or know this.'[84] Certain categories of persons were nevertheless exempted from the general rule: castellans and castle garrisons were to collect their pay directly from the assigned fund as in the past; also exempted were those serving the king either at court or in the army. It followed that these would have first call upon the revenue, and that other salaried officials, pensioners, and creditors of the crown would have to depend upon the residue that collectors and treasurers deposited with the bank. And since the cash available in the treasury never sufficed to satisfy all the demands upon it, there was little likelihood that the king's account with Miroballo would ever be buoyant enough to pay all those in the unprivileged categories. Miroballo would, therefore, either have to advance sufficient funds from his own resources, or put off the less importunate. A link between the bank and the treasury was provided by Johan Ferrer who had succeeded Gabriel Puig as administrator of the treasury in the absence of Capdevila. Alfonso charged him with the duty of ensuring that the revenues of the crown were duly paid into the bank, keeping watch on all receipts and payments, and issuing the appropriate receipts and quittances which would have been given had the cash passed through the treasury. For these purposes the bank was to furnish him at any time on demand with details of the king's account, 'as is the customary usage and practice between one merchant and another and in no other manner' ('com es acostumat e usat fer e usar de un mercader a un altre e no en altra manera'). This last phrase probably reflects Miroballo's anxiety to keep the royal account on a commercial footing, and in particular to keep his bank free of bureaucratic control. Hence too the provision that the bank should not present accounts in the Sommaria or to any treasury official other than Ferrer. It was, however, obliged to make a daily return of all transactions on behalf of the crown to Johan Dasin, *locumtenens* of the *escriva de racio*, whom Alfonso dispatched to Naples expressly for that purpose. 'The said Johan Dasin shall keep a book both of the receipts and of the payments which may be made, in the same manner as a credencerius keeps a book, and it shall

[84] Ibid.: '... cascun dells pot o deu esser content puix lo pagament li sia fet en lo banch planament per tant gran benefici com al dit Senyor sen sguarda de saber clarament quant munte los introhits de fi en fi de tot lo Reyalme e altrament be no puxa veure ne saber de aço.'

correspond with the book of the bank, the one being collated with the other at least once every week.'[85]

One cannot but wonder whether the king took away from the treasury so significant a part of its functions entirely of his own free will, whether he was content with a situation in which the chief official of his treasury treated with Miroballo 'as between one merchant and another'. Doubt is reinforced by a later paragraph in the same set of instructions which orders that gold, silver, and jewels from the wardrobe in Castelnuovo be given to a number of bankers, first among whom is Giovanni di Miroballo, as security 'for the amounts which they have recently contracted with the Lord King' ('per les quantitats que han novament contractat ab lo dit Senyor Rey'). As a result Alfonso's entire collection of jewels and precious objects went into pawn. None the less the arrangement conferred advantages which must have been appreciated, for when solvency returned he did not bring it to an end. One may also argue that it never came properly into operation because numerous special exemptions were swiftly added to the general categories specified in the instruction. Influential men lost no time in asking for such exemptions. The banker's own relative, Geronimo di Miroballo, was permitted to collect his salary as a counsellor without going through the bank: 'non obstantibus quibusvis ordinationibus de non solvendis annuis provisionibus nisi per manus nostri Thesaurarii et etiam quod omnes pecuniae dictae taxae generalis in banco egregii militis Johannis de Miroballis Neap. deponi debeant'.[86]

For some years Miroballo waxed in dignity and prosperity. He extended his feudal estates by purchasing the barony of Castel San Giorgio and Bracigliano from the Countess of San Severino for 3,500 ducats,[87] and the town of Vieste in Capitanata for 9,100

---

[85] For the *credencerius* see below, p. 347: '... lo qual Johan Dasin tinga libre tant deles dites entrades com deles exides ques hauran a fer en axi que com libre de credencer sia e corresponga ab lo libre del banch faent collacio lo hu ab laltre totes setmanes almenys una volta.'

[86] Toppi, *De origine tribunalium*, ii. 476, Privilege dated 20 Nov. 1449. This clause also refers to an edict issued on 12 Oct. 1449 which ordered that all pensions charged on the revenues from baronial lands were to be paid through the treasurer general and not collected directly. See Gentile, 'Lo stato napoletano' (1937), p. 28. Cf. the privilege permitting Mariano d'Alagno, brother of the king's favourite Lucrezia, to collect an annual provision of 100 *oncie* directly from the vassals of Roberto Sanseverino (ASN Priv. I. 51ᵛ, 5 Dec. 1452).

[87] ACA Reg. 2914. 105ᵛ, 14 Aug. 1450, Privilege by which the king approves the sale.

ducats from the crown.[88] In October 1453 Alfonso asked the pope that the crusading subsidy due from his clerical subjects should be paid to Miroballo's bank in Naples by those resident in the kingdom, and to the branch in Rome by those resident there, 'li quali sono banchi securissimi'.[89] A cloud descended when in 1456 or 1457 the Consilium Pecuniae fined him 30,000 ducats,[90] and it was probably at this juncture that he ceased to act as the king's banker. But since his place was taken by the bank of his sons, Alberico and Durso di Miroballo, the family had obviously not fallen into disgrace.[91]

Ample evidence has survived to illustrate the manner in which the Miroballo bank served the king. Large sums collected as tax were paid to it; for example, 35,040 ducats—virtually all the receipts for the grazing tax in Puglia during the 12th Indiction (1448–9)—were deposited there.[92] The Neapolitan mint sent there 2,210 ducats coined from gold furnished by the *sub camerarius* Pere de Mondrago.[93] Receipts from outside the kingdom also occasionally found their way to the bank, as happened when the king instructed the representative of the College of Merchants of Mallorca to pay to Miroballo the 500 ducats it had offered for a privilege.[94] Payments from the king's account could be made only on the authority of a letter bearing the royal signature— Alfonso issued orders to this effect on 26 November 1448;[95] most of these payments were of a local nature and for relatively small sums. Much larger amounts were involved in the international transactions in which Miroballo served the crown. On 22 January 1451, for example, he advanced a total of 14,000 ducats against three bills of exchange drawn on Perot Mercader and payable to three correspondents in Barcelona.[96] In April of the same year he

[88] ACA Reg. 2917. 34ʳ, 30 May 1452, Instrument of sale; ASN Priv. I. 30ᵛ, 22 Oct. 1452, an order for Miroballo to be placed in possession of the fief. Cf. Gentile, 'Finanze e parlamenti', p. 198, n. 3.

[89] ACA Reg. 2660, 109ᵛ.   [90] Cf. above, p. 120.

[91] A reference to the bank of Alberico di Miroballo and brothers occurs in a bill of exchange for 5,000 ducats dated 12 Aug. 1451 (ACA Reg. 2721. 6ᵛ). Another branch of the same family, Carlo di Miroballo and his brothers, also owned a bank (ibid. 26ʳ, 14 May 1452; 48ᵛ, 12 Oct. 1452).

[92] ACA Reg. 2914. 67ᵛ, 15 June 1450.

[93] ACA Real Patrimonio 2011, Entry for 7 July 1453.

[94] ACA Reg. 2720. 85ᵛ, 11 Jan. 1449; Receipt for the College.

[95] ACA Reg. 2719. 83ᵛ.

[96] ACA Reg. 2720. 169ʳ. The correspondents were Jacobo and Nicolo degli Strozzi, Matheu Capell, and Filippo Pirozzi.

gave another 14,000 ducats on a bill payable in June from a clerical subsidy being collected in Spain.[97] Also it was Miroballo who supplied the letter of credit which Alfonso sent to his *comprador maior*, Andreu Pol, in Flanders so that he might buy a very fine tapestry depicting the story of Nebuchadnezzar.[98]

The agreement of October 1448 with Miroballo did not prevent the king from keeping accounts with other banks. Even moneys which ought, by the terms of the decree, to have been paid to Miroballo were sometimes deposited elsewhere.[99] One of these other banks belonged to the Catalan Pere Cimart (or Simart). The crown kept an account with him in 1447 when a loan of 1,000 ducats was paid into it.[100] In the 13th Indiction (1449–50) no less than 8,400 ducats received from the grazing tax of Puglia[101] were deposited there, so also were 1,200 ducats realized from the sale of the Archbishop of Otranto's effects.[102] During 1449 the balance of the account seems not to have favoured the king, for the 500 ducats owed to Cimart in January of that year had risen to 11,000 ducats by July.[103] Subsequently it swung the other way until the bankruptcy of Cimart in the spring of 1453 found him owing the crown 6,388 ducats.[104] But the failure of his bank appears not to have led to Cimart's ruin, for in 1455 he still held the office of *locumtenens* to the *escriva de racio*. Probably the most important of the Spanish bankers who had dealings with the crown was Marti de la Cavalleria, a member of a Jewish family which had been baptized in 1414 following the Congress of Tortosa.[105] In partner-

---

[97] ACA Reg. 2720. 177ʳ, 27 Apr. 1451. In his confirmatory letter Alfonso urges his officials to see that the bill is paid as quickly as possible: 'com pus prest seran complits los dits cambis, tant pus prest nos porem altra volta servir deles dites quantitats.'

[98] ACA Reg. 2661. 5ʳ, 23 May 1453, Letter to Pol: '... nos vos trametrem credit a misser Johan de mirabal per babtista allata.'

[99] (e.g. the tax receipts which Angelillo de Martino paid into three other banks in 1449 (above, p. 178, n. 50).

[100] ACA Reg. 2940. 34ʳ, 1 July 1447. At that time the bank was a partnership between Cimart and Nicolau Calcer.

[101] ACA Reg. 2914. 80ᵛ, Quittance for the grazing-tax commissioner. For details of the grazing organization in Puglia see below, pp. 359 ff.

[102] Cf. above, p. 180.   [103] ACA Real Patrimonio 2951.

[104] The failure must have occurred before May 1453 when Jacme Marti sent a messenger to Naples to make alternative arrangements for the payment of 126 *oncie* which he was to have received from Cimart for rebuilding the castle of Gaeta (ASN Dip. Somm. 189 (2)).

[105] F. Baer, *A History of the Jews in Christian Spain* (Philadelphia, 1966), p. 276.

ship with his brother Felip, Marti played a major part in the financial operations of the state, and especially in providing the bills of exchange which financed enterprises in Italy by drawing on revenues in Spain, Sicily, and Sardinia.[106] A whiff of suspicion touched him in 1452 when investigations were made into the activities of merchants suspected of illegal trading with Florentines,[107] but he seems to have emerged unscathed, for in the following year he was still transacting business with the crown.[108]

A survey of the means whereby the treasury contrived to keep the state financially afloat would be incomplete without reference to the part played by individuals—mostly merchants and courtiers—who time and again provided the king with ready cash to satisfy pressing creditors. The registers record hundreds of such loans and demonstrate that they were the vital lubricant of the whole financial machine.[109] In 1440 a whip-round among those at court to raise money for the *condotta* of Antonio Caldora produced this result: Berenguer Mercader 200 ducats in cash and 400 in a bill of exchange, the Count of Lauria 300 ducats, the Archbishop of Palermo 200 ducats, Guiso de Licho 150 ducats, Andrea Bonromei 50 ducats, Falduxo Massi 50 ducats, Petro de Gallano 50 ducats, Antoni Guardia 150 ducats, Arnau Fonolleda 100 ducats, Lope Ximenez de Urrea 200 ducats, Francisco de Bartolomio 50 ducats, Ser Rustico de Roma 802 ducats, the Countess of Caserta 160 ducats, and Arnol de Eulalia and Pere Caller (syndics of Teruel) 800 ducats.[110] In May 1450 a merchant of Perpignan, Pere Tallent, paid Bernat Vaquer of the treasury 649 ducats which had been owing to him since 1439 for corn supplied to the court.[111] Joan Traganer, a Catalan merchant, paid Carafello Carafa the 218 ducats owed him on his salary as castellan of Castel Capuano.[112]

[106] One of his largest bills was for 20,000 ducats payable from the clerical subsidy in Spain (ACA Reg. 2720. 184^r, 15 Oct. 1451).

[107] Miquel Bru, the receiver general in Spain, was ordered to examine the books of Bernat de Barqueres who was suspected of dealings with Cosimo dei Medici. Among other things, Bru was to look for transactions involving Marti and Felip de la Cavalleria (ACA Reg. 2660. 35^v, 22 May 1452).

[108] He took a bill for 4,000 ducats on the clerical subsidy on 10 May 1453 (ACA Reg. 2721. 55^v) and on 5 Sept. 1453 he sent 175 pounds of silver to the Neapolitan mint for coining on behalf of the treasury (ACA Real Patrimonio 2011).

[109] Cf. the fragment of treasury receipts for 1440–1 published in Mazzoleni, *Fonti aragonesi*, i. 91–8.

[110] Faraglia, *Storia della lotta*, p. 216, n. 1.

[111] ACA Reg. 2940. 88^v, 25 May 1450.   [112] ACA Real Patrimonio 2951.

Another Catalan merchant resident in Naples, Johan Canals, gave 960 ducats to the master of the choirboys in the royal chapel to cover expenses he had incurred in recruiting choirboys in Spain.[113] No merchant who hoped for favour and business from the crown could avoid rendering this kind of service; neither could the courtier or official looking for favour and advancement. Johan Peyro, a clerk, made a loan of 2,000 ducats,[114] Steve Curto of the *escriva de racio*'s office lent 1,100 ducats free of interest,[115] Giuliano Riccio, *doganerius* of Naples, Gaeta, and Castellammare, advanced 5,000 ducats as a loan and 700 as a gift.[116] Among the nobility one finds the Count of Fondi lending 5,000 ducats,[117] the Prince of Taranto 7,955 ducats,[118] Guillem Ramon de Moncada 4,000 ducats free of interest,[119] and Bernat de Requesens 8,910 ducats.[120] The Bishop of Lerida lent 200 ducats for the care of the sick and wounded during the siege of Piombino.[121]

Sometimes the loan was repaid by the treasury—often the treasury in Spain, thus meeting Italian debts from Spanish revenues. This happened with the Bishop of Lerida, who was told to recover his 200 ducats from Andreu Capdevila, regent of the Spanish treasury. A debt of 2,157 ducats owed to the royal confectioner Bernat Figueras for a mixture of sweetmeats and loans was paid by means of a bill of exchange directed to Perot Mercader.[122] Sometimes repayment was assigned upon a specific item of revenue. Giuliano Riccio, for example, was permitted to recover his loan from the customs revenues under his control, and Gabriel Cardona, treasurer of Calabria, was repaid a loan of 1,000 ducats from the *balia* of Morella in Valencia and, should that not suffice, from his Calabrian revenues.[123] Creditors obviously preferred to have a claim, even if not a first claim, upon a particular source of revenue rather than take their chance with the general fund in the Miroballo bank. The register of 'Creditos contra la curia real de Sicilia 1448–1450'[124] contains sixteen entries for January 1449; of

[113] ACA Reg. 2940. 94ʳ, 2 May 1450.

[114] Ibid. 162ʳ, 10 July 1452.

[115] Ibid. 156ʳ, 4 June 1452.

[116] Ibid. 143ʳ, 1 Jan. 1452.

[117] ACA Reg. 2940. 126ᵛ, 28 May 1451.

[118] Gentile, 'Finanze e parlamenti', p. 198, n. 3, a list of several loans made by nobles in 1452.

[119] ACA Reg. 2940. 97ʳ, 20 Sept. 1450.

[120] Ibid. 76ʳ, 2 Dec. 1449. This amount included 1,500 ducats as the price of thirty slaves bought from Requesens.

[121] ACA Reg. 2720. 98ʳ, 20 Jan. 1449.

[122] Ibid. 119ᵛ, 14 June 1449.

[123] Ibid. 77ᵛ, 25 Nov. 1448.

[124] ACA Real Patrimonio 2951/2.

these, eight show repayment assigned upon the Spanish revenues, five upon specified Neapolitan funds, and only three upon no special fund—and this only a few months after the decree requiring all payments to be made through the bank of Miroballo. The concept of a general revenue fund which lurked behind the reorganization of 1448 still struggled unequally with the fact that much of the crown's income was made up of a multitude of funds disbursed separately by a host of relatively minor officials.

Reference has already been made to the strain which Alfonso's Italian enterprises placed upon the system of accounting and auditing that had previously served the Crown of Aragon. James II had introduced the office of *maestre racional* into Aragon from Sicily; in the Household Ordinance of Peter the Ceremonious it ranked fourth among the officers of state. But the federal nature of the Crown of Aragon made central auditing a cumbersome business, so in 1419 Alfonso began to decentralize by appointing an additional *maestre racional* for the kingdom of Valencia.[125] Similar autonomy was later given to the audit offices of Aragon and Catalonia; the *maestre racional* of Catalonia controlled the accounts of Mallorca and Sardinia.[126] Sicily had throughout its Aragonese period maintained its own court of *maestri razionali*. The kingdom of Naples too had its *magna curia dei maestri razionali*, but there effective control over the accounts of officials had since the reign of Ladislas passed almost entirely into the hands of the *regia camera della Summaria*, commonly known as the Sommaria, which was presided over by a *locumtenens* of the chamberlain.[127] The court of the *maestri razionali* continued none the less to perform its largely empty functions in the building that housed the archives, and Alfonso's chancery continued as a matter of form to notify such matters as tax exemptions to the *maestri razionali* 'resident in

---

[125] Pere Feliu, the *maestre racional* of Valencia, died in 1441 (ACA Reg. 2901. 37ʳ, 21 Oct. 1441). He was succeeded by Guillem de Vich (ibid. 24ᵛ, 28 Oct. 1441) in whose absence Bernat Stellers acted as regent in the office.

[126] Pere de San Climent was *maestre racional* of Catalonia from 1435 until his death in 1455; the office was then given to Francesch dez Valls.

[127] 'Deinde vero eiusdem Regis Ladislai tempore introduci coepit ut rationes ipsae in Camera per presidentes et rationales eiusdem non modo summarie viderentur, sed discuterentur assumerenturque inde dubia et finaliter terminarentur, et per Magnum Camerarium cum eisdem presidentibus et rationalibus quietantiae et omnia que super iis ad Magistrorum Rationalium officium spectabant expedirentur et fierent; sicque exinde hucusque servatum extitit atque servatur magistris rationalibus de iis se nullatenus intromittentibus' (Toppi, *De origine tribunalium*, i. 260; Decree of Alfonso reforming the Sommaria).

the archives of the city' even when Naples, and hence the court, were still firmly held by René of Anjou.[128]

The tribunal of the *maestri razionali* being obsolescent, Alfonso could afford to treat it in this purely formal manner; on the other hand he found it necessary to establish his own Sommaria to control the finances of the kingdom, or such of them as were under his sway. For some years it functioned in Gaeta in a house in 'la plaça de la fruyta' rented from a merchant.[129] Then from June 1441 until the fall of Naples a year later it appears to have been transferred to Aversa.[130] While the king remained in the capital the Sommaria was housed in Castelnuovo, and in Castel Capuano, the residence of the Duke of Calabria, while Alfonso campaigned in Tuscany.[131] Subsequently it followed the king[132] until in May 1451 it became permanently lodged in the house of the chamberlain, Iñigo de Avalos.[133]

The work of the Sommaria fell into two broad divisions: the auditing of accounts and the judicial business arising from the administration of the crown's finances. Officials known as *rationales* (*razionali*) dealt with the audits, and others called *presidentes* with legal matters. These latter had inherited the juridical functions of the *magna curia* in respect of the misdeeds of royal officials employed in any financial office, administrative disputes, and actions between the crown and private citizens involving the revenues of the state. They might also intervene in disputes between private parties if some interest of the crown were involved. For example, the president Jacobo de Cilinis investigated a complaint that some vassals of Orso Orsini, the chancellor, were

---

[128] e.g. notification of tax exemptions granted to the citizens of Chieti to 'magistris racionalibus magne nostre curie residentibus in archivo civitatis' (ACA Reg. 2914. 141ʳ, 19 Aug. 1437).

[129] Faraglia, *Storia della lotta*, p. 124, n. 3. The rent paid was 12 ducats a year.

[130] Many orders issued by the Sommaria from Aversa in this period are to be found in Mazzoleni, *Fonti aragonesi*, I, e.g. a summons to the treasurer in Principato cit. to present his accounts, 21 Sept. 1441 (ibid., p. 27).

[131] In August 1447 it was in Castel Capuano (ibid., p. 61); late in 1448 it had returned to Castelnuovo (ibid., p. 72).

[132] In July and August 1449 it was in Sarno; from November 1449 until March 1450 in Torre del Greco (ibid. *passim*).

Among the expenses which de Avalos as chamberlain authorized in July 1450 were those for repairs to 'quaedam domus in turri Octavi in qua camera eadem Camera [sc. Summariae] regi debebat' (Toppi, *De origine tribunalium*, i. 274).

[133] Gentile, 'Lo stato napoletano' (1937), p. 26, n. 6.

wrongfully withholding the property and rights of their lord.[134] Sometimes they were sent into the provinces with wide-ranging commissions to uncover abuses affecting the revenue. Using the procedure of the sworn inquest, they might summon officials and private citizens alike to testify before them on a great variety of matters. One such inquiry was undertaken by the president Francesco Pagano in the Abruzzi provinces in 1443.[135] His primary objective was to ascertain what taxes had been paid since the death of Giovanna II and to collect any amounts still outstanding. At the same time he looked into irregularities in the conduct of the first census,[136] made inquiries about the customs administration and the activities of several provincial officials, including Antoni Gaçull the treasurer of the Abruzzi, conducted a census of royal churches and chapels, and rounded things off with a feudal inquest. Occasionally *rationales* too would be given commissions of this kind; Nicola Anello Sperandeo, for example, investigated hearth-tax arrears in Principato citra in 1445.[137] Both *rationales* and presidents undertook the assessment of feudal reliefs.[138] Missions of this nature often took the officials of the Sommaria away from their primary task, the inspection of accounts.

The procedure of inspection began with a summons issued in the name of the *locumtenens* of the chamberlain, the presidents and the *rationales* requiring an official to appear on a given day in the Sommaria with his account books. A constable of the Sommaria delivered the summons.[139] If the person concerned did not appear,

---

[134] ASN Priv. I. 160ʳ, 4 Aug. 1454. He was to summon as many witnesses as necessary and compel them to produce their titles.

[135] ASN Div. Som. I. 166: 'Inquisitio collectarum et aliarum funcionum a tempore obitus condam domine regine Johanne secunde et per totum annum quinte indictionis nuper elapsum.' This is the record of the inquest written by Pagano's secretary for submission to the Sommaria. It is followed by 'Inquisitio facta contra Angelum Seripandum de Neapoli et Michaelum Tobiam catalanum regios commissarios in aprucce ultra super numeracione et annotacione focularium de peccunia per eos percepto ab infrascriptis terris et de modo per eos retento'.

[136] Cf. below, pp. 212–13.

[137] ASN Fasc. Com. Somm. 52ʳ, October 1445, Instruction to Sperandeo concerning his commission.

[138] e.g. the assessment made by the president Nicola d'Oferio of the relief payable by Fabrizio de Lagonissa for the town of Telese which he held *in capite* (ASN Rel. Orig. I, Terra di Lavoro e cont. di Molise 25, 20 Nov. 1457). The *rationalis* Jacobo Andrea Cocco assessed the relief payable by the Duke of Sessa at 426 *oncie* (Gentile, 'Lo stato napoletano' (1937), p. 13, n. 5).

[139] e.g. on 10 Jan. 1444 the constable was told to summon Antonio Beccadelli

the aid of a superior was invoked,[140] and if that too proved ineffec-
tive an order went out for the arrest of the defaulter.[141] Usually
the official heeded the order, as did Francesc Monlober, commissioner for the grazing tax in Puglia, who presented himself in
the Sommaria on the appointed day (9 June 1449) with his book of
accounts ('quendam quaternum sue rationis spectantem') for
the preceding financial year.[142] He took an oath 'de ratione ipsa
ponenda fideliter et legaliter ut est moris' and then began the detailed inspection of the accounts ('ipsoque quaterno diligenter et
debite viso discusso ac calculato per presidentes et racionales').
Besides looking for internal errors and inconsistencies, the *rationales*
compared Monlober's book with that kept by his *notarius credencerius*, the deceased Jacobo de Bisignano. This stage of the
audit often took months, even years, so the official normally returned to his post until it had been completed. He was then called
back and given in writing the queries raised by presidents and
rationales. Monlober's replies having been considered and found
satisfactory, his account was closed and a quittance issued by the
locumtenens and presidents on 15 June 1450—almost exactly one
year from the day on which he had submitted his accounts.[143]

to present his accounts as administrator of the Neapolitan customs (Laurenza,
Il Panormita, p. 70).

[140] e.g. the Sommaria ordered the viceroy of Calabria to compel Virgilio de
Giordano to present his accounts for the *secrezie* of Seminara, Reggio, and
Gerace for the 10th, 11th, 12th, and 13th indictions when he failed to appear
before it (Pontieri, *Fonti aragonesi*, ii. 70. The order was issued on 3 Feb. 1451).

[141] e.g. the order for the arrest of Silvestro Sarrocco. Officials in the Abruzzi
are to send him under guard to Naples (Salvati, *Fonti aragonesi*, iv. 39. The
order is dated 18 Oct. 1445).

[142] ACA Reg. 2914. 67ᵛ, 15 June 1450. The final quittance issued to Monlober.

[143] Cf. the quittance given to Monlober for the 8th Indiction: 'Idcircor ationem
ipsam per eundem Franciscum commissarium nostrum sit summarie et finaliter
positam in dicta Camera nostra Summarie ut est dictum coram eisdem officialibus nostris ipsius Camere sufficientem legalem et ydoneam reputantes omnesque
predictas recollectiones et percepciones per eum factas de supradictis peccuniarum quantitatibus ac soluciones liberaciones et retenciones per eum similiter
factas de pecunia supradicta pro premissis causis in suo quaterno particulariter
annotatis tam vigore suarum commissionum quam ad mandata nostra sibi
propterea directa et facta et prout in suo quaterno particulariter continetur'
(Rogadeo, *Codice diplomatico*, pp. 182–8, 13 Apr. 1446). An example of an audited
account, with marginal annotations by officials of the Sommaria, is provided by
the 'Quaternus Rationis Petri Dorta R. Magistri Secreti, Mag. Portulani et
Mag. Salis in provincia ducatus Calabrie citra et ultra . . . a. XIIII et XV Ind.',
published in *Fonti aragonesi*, V. The quittance given Antoni Gaçull in respect
of his accounts as commissioner for the peace aid and other taxes in the Abruzzi

Where the audit revealed deficiencies and no satisfactory explanation was forthcoming, the treasurer received orders to collect the
sums in question from the appropriate official. Thus on 17 January
1456 Perot Mercader was told to take 152 ducats 9 *grana* from
Giuliano Riccio, *doganerius* of Naples, Gaeta, and Castellammare,
for a large number of minor discrepancies in his accounts.[144]
Similar orders might be given for the recovery of tax arrears from
individuals and towns. These demands reached an apogee in
September 1455 when ninety-eight towns and villages in all parts
of the kingdom were ordered to make good deficiencies in aids
from as far back as 1442.[145] Queries raised by the auditors might
also lead to a demand for the production of further documentary
evidence. This happened in the course of the audit of the accounts
of Jacobo de Villaspinosa as commissioner for the collection of
scutage in Principato citra. In order to resolve some doubts, the
Countess of Marsico and San Severino was ordered to send to the
Sommaria all the receipts for scutage issued by the commissioner
in respect of the lands of her son and late husband since the third
indiction.[146]

With such a heavy and constant flow of business passing through
it the Sommaria had need of a comparatively large staff. How many
there were during the years when the tribunal was located in Gaeta
and Aversa is difficult to ascertain. The names of a number of
presidents are known—Pietro Gerunda di Squillace,[147] Carlo
Pagano, Antonio Beccadelli, Marino de Brancadoris,[148] Menelao de
Januario,[149] Pietro de Castiglione,[150] Lancellotto Scrinario,[151]
Jacobo Andrea Ferrillo[152]—but only one *rationalis*, Francisco

is signed by the chamberlain, the Count of Loreto and four *rationales* (ASN
Framm. Somm. 21ᵛ, 15 Sept. 1444).

[144] ASN *Significatorie*, vol. I. 1ʳ. This volume contains many similar orders,
e.g. to collect 240 ducats 6 *tarini* 12 *grana* 4 *denarii* from Carafello Carafa,
magister passuum in Terra di Lavoro (10ʳ, 27 Apr. 1456) and 451 ducats from
Giacomo Sarrocho, commissioner for the salt tax in Terra di Lavoro (17ʳ
13 May 1456).

[145] Ibid. 39ᵛ, 9 Sept. 1456. Tropea alone was called upon to pay 12,018 ducats.

[146] Salvati, *Fonti aragonesi*, iv. 19, 20 Aug. 1444 (i.e. 8th Indiction).

[147] Mazzoleni, *Fonti aragonesi*, i. 30. He was a president in May 1436.

[148] These three are named as presidents in Gaeta in 1437 and 1438 by Toppi,
De origine tribunalium, i. 192.

[149] Laurenza, *Il Panormita*, p. 65. He was a president in August 1438.

[150] Ibid., p. 66: president in September 1438.

[151] Rogadeo, *Codice diplomatico*, p. 77: president in February 1440.

[152] A president in 1440 (Toppi, *De origine tribunalium*, i. 193).

Imperato.[153] From the treasury accounts for August 1444, however, Gentile has been able to extract a list of nineteen presidents and twelve *rationales* employed at that time in the Sommaria.[154] What immediately strikes one about this and later lists of the Sommaria officials is that almost all were Italians, whereas the senior officials of the treasury, as we have noted, were Spaniards. In the second place one might think that this was a rather large establishment, even allowing for the volume of work in the Sommaria. It had resulted from the amalgamation of Alfonso's Sommaria with that which had been serving René of Anjou in the capital, and Alfonso must have had an eventual reduction of numbers in mind when in September 1442 he added yet another president, Angelo Morosini, to the total, for he assured him that he should retain the office for life in the event of the number of presidents being reduced.[155] A further impetus to reform was offered by the corruption and inefficiency that were rife in the Sommaria in the earlier 1440s. A number of scandals were uncovered, among them that of Andrea de Sanctis, treasurer and general commissioner in the Abruzzi, who presented falsified accounts and managed, by bribing officials of the Sommaria, to obtain a quittance. When the fraud was discovered an investigation by the procurator fiscal, Marino Boffa, revealed a total deficiency of 7,300 ducats in de Sanctis's accounts.[156] A still more serious shortcoming from the administrative point of view was the slow pace at which the Sommaria cleared accounts, leaving fraud and inefficiency concealed for years, and depriving the treasury of badly needed revenue.

Alfonso first attempted to improve the performance of the Sommaria by installing a watchdog there. Giliforte de Ursa, who had a high reputation for his skill in examining accounts, was put into the office as 'auditor examinator et revisor' and given the status of a *promotor*.[157] He had authority to participate fully with the presidents and *rationales* in all the work of the Sommaria, but was answerable directly to the king on whose verbal instruction

[153] Mazzoleni, *Fonti aragonesi*, i. 27, an order dated 21 Sept. 1441 mentions him.

[154] Gentile, 'Lo stato napoletano' (1937), p. 24.

[155] ACA Reg. 2902. 98ᵛ, 28 Sept. 1442: '... quam si pro tempore contigerit officia regni huius presentis dicte camere Summarie et numerum presidentium eiusdem modificari et ad certum numerum et terminum reduci.'

[156] ACA Reg. 2909. 47ᵛ, 2 Mar. 1444, Pardon for de Sanctis who had repaid most of the money.

[157] Cf. above, p. 156.

he was to act. Giliforte took up his position in May 1445 and in December of that year was given a salary of 80 *oncie*, a sum considerably above that paid to the regular staff.[158] But his presence in the Sommaria was soon counteracted by the absence of the king in Tuscany; that tribunal, like the other organs of state, slipped back into the lethargy that had been tolerated in the Angevin twilight. Complaints that reached the king are echoed in his letter to the regents in Naples in which he ordered the general administrative shake-up of October 1448. Among other things that reorganization was to remove 'la confusio de molts presidents o altres officials en la summaria dels quals tot jorn lo dit Senyor ha clamors e que dels comptes e fets dela cort dels quals per la dita confusio e multitut a tart si pot haver raho ne fi'.[159] The remedy that had been contemplated in 1442 was now drastically applied with a swingeing reduction in the establishment: the number of presidents was fixed at two (Marino Boffa and Michele Riccio) and the *rationales* at four (Antonio Carusio, Giliforte de Ursa, Bernardo de Raymo, and Nardello Ballester). Both categories of officials were to receive a salary of 300 ducats a year and a quantity of salt which they could dispose of freely. They were to clear all outstanding business with a minimum of delay and afterwards keep all accounts strictly up to date, but they were forbidden to decide 'any matter of importance' without first consulting the king or, in his absence, the Duke of Calabria.

These decisions, taken in a moment of financial crisis and in the hustle of the withdrawal from Piombino, had to be modified once Alfonso had returned to Naples and come to grips with the problems of administration. For one thing, the definition of the points requiring reference to the king was vague in the extreme and hardly encouraged boldness in the dispatch of business in the Sommaria. Also the cut in the establishment had gone too far if the routine business of the tribunal was to be dispatched without delay. The two presidents, Boffa and Riccio, were both members of the royal council required to attend regular meetings of that body and undertake judicial investigations on its behalf. Another problem arose over those made redundant by the reform; some might

---

[158] ACA Reg. 2909. 168ᵛ, 18 Dec. 1445. This privilege fixes the salary at 50 *oncie*. Another (ibid. 170ʳ) of the same date adds another 30 *oncie* considering that 50 was insufficient.

[159] ACA Reg. 2699. 141ᵛ, 3 Oct. 1448.

perhaps be struck off the pay roll,[160] but there were others, such as Angelo Morosini, whose letters of appointment guaranteed them against such treatment. There were also those whom it was impolitic to offend by dismissal: the banker Giovanni di Miroballo, for example, whom Alfonso had appointed a president with a salary of 500 ducats only a few days before ordering the reduction of staff.[161] All the evidence shows that the reduction did not in fact take effect. The chancery was still addressing di Miroballo as a president on 26 November 1448,[162] and he continued to enjoy the privileges until at least October 1452[163] although he seems never to have performed any of the routine duties of a president. Matteo de Campulo, who had become a *rationalis* by September 1444,[164] did not figure among the four nominated in October 1448, yet, together with Boffa, he signed a quittance dated 21 January 1449 as a *rationalis*.[165] The list of those to whom the salt allowance was paid in 1449 gives the names of fourteen presidents in addition to Boffa and Riccio, and seven additional *rationales*.[166] As for those who were nominated, neither Boffa nor Riccio played much part in the Sommaria, Carusio and de Ursa became presidents in 1449, de Raymo was appointed resident commissioner in the Abruzzi, and only Ballester soldiered on as a *rationalis* to the end of the reign. Far from the number of officials in the Sommaria being reduced, it continued to rise fairly steadily until in 1456 there were no fewer than thirty-six presidents and twenty *rationales*.[167] For some like Giannozzo Manetti, who was appointed a president on 30 October 1455,[168] the office was a sinecure. Others had duties which took priority over their function in the Sommaria. Francisco de Pelatis, for example, was already an ordinary counsellor and a lecturer in law when he was appointed a president of the Som-

---

[160] The letter of 3 Oct. had ordered 'que sien pagats tant solament dos presidents e quátre racionals', which might be interpreted to mean that others might retain their title but not their salary.

[161] ACA Reg. 2913. 60ᵛ, 30 Sept. 1448, Privilege fixing di Miroballo's salary.

[162] ACA Reg. 2719. 83ᵛ.

[163] ASN Priv. I. 30ᵛ, 22 Oct. 1452. He paid nothing for this *carta assecurationis*, 'quia presidens Regie Camere Sumarie'.

[164] ASN Fram. Com. Somm. 22ʳ.

[165] ACA Reg. 2913. 88ʳ.

[166] Toppi, *De origine tribunalium*, i. 175.

[167] These are the figures given by Gentile, 'Lo stato napoletano' (1937), p. 24. Toppi (*De origine tribunalium*, i. 181–94) gives detailed information about the presidents appointed after 1449. For the *rationales* see Toppi, iii. 75–8.

[168] Ibid. iii. 261–3.

maria.[169] Pietro Marco de Gipsiis held the additional offices of advocate fiscal and ordinary counsellor.[170] One may therefore conclude on the one hand that the reform of October 1448 utterly failed in its objective of reducing the number of senior officials in the Sommaria, and on the other that the number actually working there was never so great as the nominal strength would suggest.

In addition to the clerk attached to each president and *rationalis*, the staff of the Sommaria included a chief secretary known as the *actorum notarius*, a clerk who kept the registers and a rubricator. The office of *actorum notarius* became a sinecure for one or other of the principal secretaries who appointed a deputy assisted by a clerk to perform the duties.[171] Those responsibilities included the custody of the records of the Sommaria which were stored in a chest with two locks; the *actorum notarius* kept one key and a president the other.[172] The office of clerk of the registers was likewise exercised by deputy. Until 1445 it was in the possession of another secretary, Jacobo Scorza; when he died in that year, Alfonso gave it to his surgeon, Salvador de Santa Fe.[173] The chancery clerk Juan Espanit acquired the post of rubricator of all documents sealed with the great and small seals emanating from the Sommaria.[174] Three constables served the summonses and writs of the Sommaria and kept order on its premises.[175]

The Sommaria functioned as a tribunal as well as an office of audit; its head, the *locumtenens* of the chamberlain, and its presidents were doctors of law. All its officials and their *familiares* were entitled to trial before it. The advocates, procurators, and *promotor* of the crown could appear before it, and it delivered judgement in due judicial form. Many of the cases it heard arose from the misdeeds of revenue officers, such as the frauds committed by Andrea de Sanctis and Enrico de Genaro.[176] The tribunal of the Sommaria

---

[169] He was appointed a president on 22 Mar. 1456 (Toppi, *De origine tribunalium*, i. 193).

[170] Ibid. i. 178.

[171] Beccadelli appointed Jacobo Andrea de Cocco as his deputy. Until 1447 the *actorum notarius* had been paid 36 *oncie* and his clerk 12 *oncie*; in that year the figure was raised to a consolidated 50 *oncie* (300 ducats) on the appointment of Olzina.

[172] ACA Reg. 2906. 49[r], 3 Jan. 1444.

[173] ACA Reg. 2909. 166[r], 20 Dec. 1445.

[174] He was appointed on 25 July 1444 (ACA Reg. 2902. 224[r]).

[175] Salvati, *Fonti aragonesi*. iv. 30.   [176] Cf. above, p. 196.

comprising on this occasion two *rationales* and twelve presidents, met in the house of the chamberlain on 1 January 1444 to deliver its judgement, each member giving his vote in ascending order of seniority.[177] Some cases involved disputes between officials. One between Bernat Lober, *perceptor* of the Vicaria, and Felice Liato, the treasurer of that court, went before Claver as regent of the chancery, but the chamberlain intervened to evoke the case to the Sommaria on the grounds that Lober's accounts, which had given rise to the suit, were then under examination in the Sommaria.[178] Suits involving fiefs held *in capite* could also be heard in the Sommaria. That between the Count of Campobasso and the heirs of Jacobo de Zuzulo began there and was only evoked to the Sacrum Consilium on appeal.[179] The development of conciliar jurisdiction certainly diverted many such private suits from the Sommaria, and the Consilium Pecuniae became for a brief period a formidable rival as a judicial organ for enforcing the fiscal claims of the crown. Nevertheless the Sommaria retained considerable importance as the general dispenser of administrative justice and the source of a substantial body of administrative law.[180]

The Sommaria emerged from Alfonso's reign with enhanced prestige[181] not because he succeeded in effecting any great improvement in its workings, but because he invested it with the powers that had remained in theory with the court of the *maestri razionali*,[182] and so made the Sommaria the sole and supreme organ of financial control for the kingdom. When the nobles of the city of Naples swore fealty to Alfonso on 21 May 1443 they had

---

[177] They were the *rationales* Bernardo de Raymo and Giovanni de Onofrio; the presidents were Giovanni Antonio d'Aquino, Angelillo Scannasorice, Jacobo de Cilinis, Lancellotto Scrinario, Marino Minutolo, Lope de Speyo, Giovanni di San Severino, Michael Rayner, Antonio Beccadelli, Goffredo di Gaeta, Pietro Gerunda, and the senior president, Marino Boffa (Toppi, *De origine tribunalium*, i. 148). Cf. Laurenza, *Il Panormita*, p. 70. Beccadelli voted for a fine nine times the sum involved in the fraud.

[178] Toppi, *De origine tribunalium*, iii. 253–4. The writ to Claver is dated 21 Mar. 1446.

[179] Cf. above, p. 106.

[180] Goffredo di Gaeta, a president of the Sommaria for much of Alfonso's reign and until his own death in 1463, wrote a commentary on the *Riti* of the tribunal compiled by Andrea d'Isernia a century earlier. In his commentary Goffredo expounded the current interpretation of fiscal legislation whose enforcement fell to the Sommaria. Cf. Giannone, *Istoria civile*, iii. 193–4.

[181] Ibid. xxvi, cap. 5.   [182] Cf. above, p. 191.

asked that the privileges of the court of the *maestri razionali* be restored because 'praeter solum nomen quodammodo nihil ultra ut prediximus relictum'.[183] Nothing appears to have been done in answer to this petition until October 1444 when the king confirmed the privileges granted to the *maestri razionali* by earlier rulers.[184] They regained, among other rights, their share in goods confiscated for evasion of customs and tolls—a share which they had lost in 1442 to the chamberlain and officials of the Sommaria[185]—and their control over weights and measures in the kingdom (*ius ponderum et mensurarum*).[186] But these concessions were balanced by another article which reserved to the crown half of all the dues and emoluments accruing to the tribunal. Attempts to defraud the crown of its share led to tighter financial supervision; Jacme Gil of the treasury took control of the receipt and disbursement of fees and salaries from September 1447,[187] and in January 1448 a *magister actorum* was installed specifically to watch over the interest of the crown.[188] Also Alfonso began to make his own appointments of *maestri razionali*. For example, on 18 August 1447

---

[183] Gentile, 'Lo stato napoletano' (1937), p. 35, n. 2, and p. 36, n. 3, where he lists the privileges that the tribunal had been granted by earlier sovereigns.

[184] ACA Reg. 2907. 2ʳ. In registering this privilege the clerk has left a blank space after the preamble, presumably for the insertion of the privileges in question. No date is given, but all the adjoining privileges belong to October 1444. In 1444 the *maestri razionali* numbered 36 (Toppi, *De origine tribunalium*, i. 152) and the judge assessor in that year was Nicola de Fiore (Fuuoard, 'Descrizione della citta di Napoli', p. 751).

[185] On 15 Sept. 1444 the chamberlain ordered Michael Rayner, a president of the Sommaria, to hand to Coluccio d'Afflicto, the *dohanerius* of Naples, a piece of gold brocade and other goods confiscated from a Venetian merchant 'propter fraudem in juribus maioris fundici et dohane neapolis per eum commissam', because it was the duty of the chief customs official to see to the allocation of such goods 'prout sue prudentie melius visum erit' (ASN Framm. Com. Somm. 18ᵛ). Such flouting of their rights must have been behind the petition that the *maestri razionali* presented to the king: 'Item similiter compete alloro la raysone de tucte intercepte et cose fraudate a dohani et cabelle cio che de ipsi la quarta parte abbia lo accosatore et lo restante se sparta infra dohaneri cabelloti et ipsi Magistri Raysonali per equali porcioni delle dicte raysone de turpiti et intercepte al presente non sonno in possessione che laveno applicati ad se lo conte camberlingo et la Summaria dapo la victoria de Napoli havuta per la prefata Maiesta' (ACA Reg. 2912. 123ʳ, 28 Sept. 1447). This privilege for the *maestri razionali* repeats and confirms the favourable answer which Alfonso had given to this petition, presumably in 1444.

[186] Salvati, *Fonti aragonesi*, iv. 45.

[187] ACA Reg. 2912. 116ʳ, 17 Sept. 1447.

[188] Ibid. 167ᵛ, 30 Jan. 1448, Appointment of the notary Agostino de Funce to this office.

he named Gabriele de Mastrillis, a judge of the Vicaria, a *magister rationalis*,[189] and that same day made him a citizen of Naples in order that he should be eligible for the office.[190]

It even seemed for a time as though the king had decided to reverse the trend to desuetude which the tribunal had been following since the reign of Ladislas. A decree issued from the royal camp at Castiglione della Pescaia on 8 February certainly looks like an attempt to bring it back to life. Seeking to put an end to the 'negligentias, tarditates et desidias magistrorum rationalium eorumque locumtenentorum scribarum seu coadiutorum', the edict ordered them without further delay to examine and determine all matters relating to official accounts then pending before their tribunal.[191] Writs were to be issued forthwith for any sums found due to the crown, and should there be doubt as to the ability of a debtor to meet his obligations, they were to take from him in the meantime an adequate surety, or else hold him in detention. Six months were allowed to clear up all outstanding accounts; thereafter all were to be settled within three months of presentation, the penalty for failure to do so being loss of office. To keep them up to the mark, the king ordered them to furnish to the conservator general of the patrimony[192] a list of all accounts then with them, showing when each had been received and what progress had been made with it; similar returns were to be made of all accounts received in the future. Another decree, issued three days previously, had required all receivers of revenues to present six-monthly accounts to the Sommaria and *maestri razionali* within one month of the close of each semester.[193]

These 'perpetual' edicts seem to have been designed to make the existing machine work as efficiently as possible in the king's absence. Once Alfonso had returned to Naples and begun his general overhaul of the administration, his attention fastened on the unsatisfactory situation in which the Sommaria dealt in practice with matters that in law belonged to a non-professional body over which he had little control. The result was a decree issued on 23 November 1450 which transferred all the functions and powers

---

[189] Ibid. 102ᵛ, de Mastrillis was still a member of the court in 1451 (ACA Reg. 2940. 130ʳ, 30 July 1451). Another 'official' member was Nicola Villano, a president of the Sommaria (Toppi, *De origine tribunalium*, i. 195).

[190] ACA Reg. 2912. 101ʳ.   [191] ACA Reg. 2656. 103ᵛ.

[192] For this official cf. below, p. 205.

[193] ACA Reg. 2656. 110ᵛ, 5 Feb. 1448.

of the *maestri razionali* with respect to revenue accounts to the officials of the Sommaria:

Id circho tenore presentium de certa nostra scientia constituimus volumus et ordinamus omnia et singula curiae et officio magistrorum rationalium et personis ipsorum magistrorum rationalium et officialium et personarum eiusdem Curiae hactenus attributa sive concessa et quovismodo ex privilegiis capitulis usu consuetudine vel aliter spectantia et pertinentia eidem Camerae eiusque officio et officialibus et personis eiusdem Camerae omni futuro tempore competere et eisdem attributa atque concessa censeri.[194]

Though shorn of its powers, the *magna curia* of the *maestri razionali* was not abolished. The *seggi* of Naples continued to elect its noble members, and the crown still appointed a receiver to look after its revenues.[195] These derived mainly from its control of measures used in selling dry and liquid commodities; the *maestri razionali* supervised the stamping of them with their mark and organized the distribution of the measures through agents whom they appointed.[196]

One important result of the transfer of the functions of the *maestri razionali* to the Sommaria was that the main administrative archives came under the control of the latter body. They included, besides the closed accounts of the Sommaria, the feudal registers known as *quaterniones* in which were recorded all matters pertaining to fiefs: investitures, confirmations, donations, and subinfeudations. Any change in the ownership of a fief, or in the terms on which it was held, had to be registered within a specified time (usually four months)[197] of the royal grant or assent becoming

---

[194] ACA Reg. 2915. 88ʳ. The decree is printed in Toppi, *De origine tribunalium,* i. 260–1.

[195] Antoni Dodena succeeded Jacme Gil as receiver in 1452 (Mazzoleni, *Fonti aragonesi,* iii. 4).

[196] Cf. the commission given by the 'viri magnifici Magistri Rationales Magne nostre Curie Neapoli residentes in Archivio' to Severo Mercante of Naples to sell stamped measures in Lanciano, Benevento, Salerno and Gaeta (Mazzoleni, *Il Codice Chigi,* pp. 84–5, 14 Aug. 1451).

[197] The privilege conferring the county of Troia upon Garcia de Cabanyells had this provision: 'volumus quod prefatus Garcias eiusque heredes predicti procurent cum solertia debita infra menses quatuor a die adepte corporalis possessionis seu quasi Civitatis . . . inantea numerandos presens nostrum privilegium in libris et quaternionibus nostre camere sumarie penes thesaurarios et officiales nostros apud quos fuerun ɪtranscribi facere et notari' (ACA Reg. 2902. 106ʳ, 12 June 1442). Royal assent to a sale of feudal property given in February 1449 was to be registered within three months (Rogadeo, *Codice diplomatico,*

effective; titles not so registered became null and void. Many tenants-in-chief had taken advantage of the confusion in the kingdom not to register changes in their feudal holdings, and it was only as a systematic series of inquests began to bite that the *quaterniones* became reasonably complete and up to date. A petition in the parliament of March 1450 asking for a full indulgence for those who had failed to register their fiefs 'neli quaterni dela Camera vestra de la Sumaria' shows that administrative pressure on these backsliders was at last making itself felt.[198] The *quaterniones* were considered sufficiently important to have a clerk appointed specifically to keep them. Antonio de Barbastro, a notary of the treasury, was made 'registrator et conservator quaternionum camere nostre in quibus annotantur pheuda et bona pheudalia predicta cum distinctione valoris eorum annui et serviciorum pro illis nostre curie debiturum'.[199] This appointment was made on 15 June 1442, shortly after the registers had come into Alfonso's possession, and it would seem that they remained for some years with the treasury.[200] By the end of the reign Jacobo Andrea de Cocco had succeeded Barbastro as keeper of the *quaterniones*.[201]

The archives of the Sommaria contained in addition several

p. 211). Six months was allowed for the registration of a privilege confirming possession of a fief issued in November 1452 (ibid., p. 292).

[198] Ametller y Vinyas, *Alfonso V de Aragón*, iii. 687. Fillach took action against those who had not registered their fiefs. Commission dated 13 May 1443 (Gentile (1937), p. 42, n. 5).

[199] ACA Reg. 2909. 46ʳ. His salary was 18 *oncie* a year. Barbastro still held the post in 1449 (Toppi, *De origine tribunalium*, i. 45).

[200] Before the fall of Naples the Aragonese administration had endeavoured to compile its own registers. A fief granted to Jacobo della Marra on 18 Sept. 1436 was to be registered in the *quinterniones* 'nostre camere penes nostros thesaurarios' (Rogadeo, *Codice diplomatico*, p. 11). A fief granted in 1443 was entered in the registers 'penes Thesaurariam' (ibid., p. 114). But by 1449 registration was done 'in quaternionibus camere nostre Summariae penes magistros racionales Neapolim in Archivo residentibus' (ibid., p. 211). Evidently the *maestri razionali* had managed to regain custody of them. In November 1452 they seem to have been back with the treasury: 'quaternionibus Camere nostre Summarie penes nostros Thesaurarios' (ibid., p. 292). By August 1457, however, they were 'penes magnum camerarium et presidentes ibidem [sc. Summarie] residentes' (ACA Reg. 2916. 84ʳ, 25 Aug. 1457).

[201] ASN Rel. Orig., vol. 33, fol. 61ʳ: 'Die xxv mensis martii vi Ind. anno domini Millo. CCCCLviii presens privilegium presentatum fuit mihi Jacobo andree coco de neap. Regiorum, quaternionum annotatori et conservatori quod de mandato Regio facto per Magnum Camerarium asserentem dominum regem mandasse eum annotari non obstante lassu temporis annotari feci in quaternionibus ipsis de verbo ad verbum.'

series of registers and other documents directly related to its own judicial and administrative functions. These included registers of executory writs (needed to give effect to any royal provision touching revenues or property of the crown), feudal reliefs, letters to treasurers and other revenue officials, letters of the king addressed to the Sommaria, registers of commissions, and the treasury *cedole* recording details of payments and receipts.[202] Among the loose documents were copies of the *cartae assecurationis* which certified that the king's commissioners had duly installed a tenant-in-chief in possession of a new fief.[203] In 1451 Basilio de Miro, a *rationalis*, became the archivist responsible for these records.[204]

Although ultimate responsibility for the conservation of crown rights and property against infringement lay in the kingdom of Naples with the chamberlain, it had in practice devolved upon the Sommaria. Finding the royal patrimony sadly diminished by wholesale alienations and usurpations, Alfonso decided that some form of control more effective than that of the overburdened Sommaria was needed to screen all acts of the administration that touched upon his demesne, rights, and revenues. He therefore determined to introduce into Naples the office of conservator of the royal patrimony which already existed in Aragon and Sicily. But instead of appointing another conservator specifically for the kingdom, he created a conservator general (just as he had created a treasurer general) 'per omnia regna terras et diciones nostras',[205] and this official he attached to his court. The man chosen was Pere de Besalu who had previously served as a secretary,[206] and he

---

[202] Toppi (*De origine tribunalium*, i. 2, cap. 6) lists the Aragonese records still surviving in the archives of the Sommaria in his day as: Executorialibus Regiae Camerae, Releviorum (from 1440), Vectigaliorum, Erariorum, Literarum regiarum, Commissionum, Consultationum, and the record of the census of 1447. B. Capasso, *Le fonti della storia delle Provincie Napoletane dal 568 al 1500* (Naples, 1902), pp. 214–15, has a fuller list of the Sommaria archives, but many of the series of registers listed by him began later than the reign of Alfonso.

[203] e.g. the order to the commissioner Gregorio Campitello to secure Pirro del Balzo and his wife in possession of Venosa, and to deposit a copy of the instrument recording this act 'in Summaria conservandum in Archivo civitatis nostre Neapolis' (ACA Reg. 2916. 87ᵛ, 31 Dec. 1457).

[204] Toppi, *De origine tribunalium*, i. 45. A special messenger carried records between the Sommaria and other government offices.

[205] ACA Reg. 2912. 137ᵛ, 28 Oct. 1447. This privilege fixes de Besalu's salary at 1,000 ducats a year on the grazing tax.

[206] He was a secretary in August 1439 when Alfonso sent him on a mission to Aragon (ACA Reg. 2651. 125ʳ).

was given the office sometime in the latter part of 1445.[207] In 1446 he paid a visit to Spain, presumably in order to go through the procedures necessary to establish his authority there.[208] He returned to Italy in the summer of 1447, joined the king in his camp at Tivoli, and then initiated a series of measures designed to make his office an effective guardian of the royal patrimony.

He began with a decree made on 14 August 1447 which forbade officials to issue any document involving the financial interest of the crown without first submitting it to the office of the conservator general for approval, registration, and counter-signature.[209] A privilege issued that same day at Tivoli for Roberto di Sanseverino granting him the investiture of the feudal possessions of his deceased brother, the Count of Marsico and San Severino, bears the counter-signature of Besalu.[210] From that date the formula, 'vidit Petrus de Bisulduno regii patrimonii Generalis Conservator', appears on hundreds of documents, for a large proportion of the letters, privileges, writs, etc., emanating from government offices concerned those royal interests which it was Besalu's duty to protect. His attention to his office seems to have been assiduous in the extreme, for, apart from a few absences on the king's business,[211] he attended in person to most of the papers that called for his scrutiny. On those occasions when he was absent, one or other of the senior legal officers of the crown would act for him: Nicolo Antonio dei Monti, Rodrigo Falco, Ramon de Palomar, Cicco Antonio Guindazzo, Valenti Claver, Jacme de Pilaya, Michele Riccio, Nicolau Fillach, Giacomo de Cilinis, and Battista Platamone all countersigned 'pro Conservatore Generali' between 1448 and 1458. The examination and registration of so many documents must have required the services of a fairly large secretariat, but we have no information about the number of clerks assigned to Besalu. Only one appears by name in the registers: Giovanni

---

[207] The exact date is not known, but it must have been later than 31 July 1445 when he was still a secretary (ACA Reg. 2720. 53ʳ).

[208] On 10 Jan. 1447 he wrote from Valencia to Jaime Garcia, the archivist of Aragon, asking for transcripts of certain documents which the king had instructed him to take to Italy (ACA Legajos Fernando I y Alfonso IV, no. 263).

[209] ACA Reg. 2656. 136ʳ.

[210] ACA Reg. 2912. 129ᵛ.

[211] In October 1450 he was sent to Rome to discuss crusading tactics and preparations with the pope (ACA Reg. 2697. 76ʳ). Alfonso refused a request of the Cort of Catalonia that Besalu be sent back to Spain (ACA Reg. 2657. 29ʳ, 4 Jan. 1448).

Perrono de Rivello, who is described as 'egregius', 'nobilis', and 'scriba in officio generalis nostri patrimonii conservatoris'.[212]

The general function of the conservator general having been established, there followed in 1448 a series of decrees defining more precisely the classes of documents that were to be submitted to him, and in effect extending that function to a supervisory role over the operations of the treasury and *maestri razionali*. Among the provisions in the decree of 8 February 1448 concerning the latter body, was an instruction requiring the *maestri razionali* to furnish the conservator general with regular summaries of the accounts before them; 'que omnia pro nostre curie cautela in officio dicti conservatoris conmemorari et annotari iubemus, ut inde cum expediens fuerit informatione habita prout res exigerit a nobis valeat debite provideri.'[213] In the following month another decree ordered the treasurer general or his deputy to submit all records of receipt and expenditure for registration.[214] All receipts, whether of money, bullion, or goods, were to be notified to the office of the conservator general before being accepted by the treasury;[215] payments, on the other hand, were to be notified in a detailed schedule on the day, or the day after, they were made.[216] The decree applied not only to the operations of the treasury in the king's court, but also to those effected in the courts of his *locumtenentes generales*. Therefore, if strictly applied, these procedures would have been enforced in the courts of Queen Maria, Juan of Navarre, and the Duke of Calabria, and would have

---

[212] ACA Reg. 2913. 156ʳ, 30 May 1449. He is instructed to secure Luca di Sanseverino in the counties of Tricárico and Claramonte.

[213] ACA Reg. 2656. 103ᵛ. Cf. above, p. 202.

[214] Ibid. 114ʳ, 20 Mar. 1448. Cf. the decree promulgated in Sicily in 1416 which required that all orders to the treasurer for receipt or payment should be registered by the conservator of the royal patrimony (F. Lionti, *Codice diplomatico di Alfonso il Magnanimo* (Palermo, 1891), p. 17).

[215] 'Quod tesaurarius generalis, eius locumtenens et quicumque alii in officio nostre Thesaurarie receptores et administratores tam in curia nostra quam in curiis nostrorum locumtenentium generalium residentes presentes et futuri nullatenus ammodo per se vel interpositas personas palam quomodolibet vel occulte audeant vel presumant recipere aut recipi facere aliquas peccuniarum summas aurum argentum res merces vel alia quevis bona que in eorum officiis intrare opportuerit nisi prius in officio conservatoris nostri patrimonii generalis notam fuerit.'

[216] 'Ea die qua eas fecerint aut saltem die immediate subsequenti designatis personis in quos distribuerint peccuniarum quantitatibus rebus et bonis distributis per eorum scedulam omnia huiusmodi apperte et . . . distincte continentem officio dicti conservatoris generalis per vos remittendum.'

required deputies of the conservator general to be assigned to each *locumtenens generalis*. In practice Alfonso was chiefly concerned with the treasury in Naples where his son was at that moment *locumtenens*.

A third decree followed hard upon the king's return from Tuscany and reflected, according to the preamble, his determination to turn his attention to the affairs of the kingdom now that he had brought the wars to an end.[217] Firstly he confirmed the constitutions of Roger and Frederick forbidding the diminution of rights and property held by feudal tenure; he then ordered all who had made such 'alienaciones ypothecaciones seu alias quascumque contractas' without obtaining royal assent to make good this omission within six months through the office of the conservator general whom he had specially commissioned for the purpose. They had to present to Besalu the relevant documents, obtain from him the crown's assent, take a new oath of fealty in respect of the diminished fief, and finally enter into the requisite recognizance. All future transactions of this nature were to be subject to notification and registration within the prescribed limit of six months, failing which the offender became liable to the penalties laid down in the original constitutions. A concern for fees doubtless loomed large among the considerations which prompted the revival of these ancient statutes, but it is probably fair to assume that it was also intended to check the erosion of crown rights and revenues, and to make available to the conservator general some of the information needed for the work of his office.

In this manner the conservator general in the space of one year gained an interest in an extraordinary variety of public and private affairs, and a formidable body of paper was directed towards the organization he controlled.[218] Not surprisingly the addition of this new dimension to bureaucratic processes aroused little enthusiasm either among those officials who found themselves subjected to unaccustomed forms of control, or with those private citizens who encountered one more obstacle in the already lengthy and often costly business of extracting a valid document from the state. Some clerks got round the delays, and the checks, simply by

---

[217] ACA Reg. 2656. 135^r, 16 Dec. 1448.

[218] When Marino Curiale was appointed castellan of Bitonto he was required to make three copies of the castle inventory: one for himself, one for the Sommaria, and one for the conservator general (Rogadeo, *Codice diplomatico*, p. 285, 6 Dec. 1452).

forging the required subscription of the conservator general: 'aliqui ex nostris secretariis vel scribis de mandato . . . ipsa conservatoria visione et annotacione completa et integra mandata manibus propriis scribere et apponere ausi sunt.'[219] After Besalu had reported and investigated this malpractice, the king gave him authority to seize and sell property of the offenders to a value of 10,000 Aragonese florins. The chancellor and his subordinates were expressly forbidden to interfere, even though such clerks would normally come under their jurisdiction.[220] On at least one occasion the penalty was exacted. The secretary Martorell was found guilty of having written the *mandatum* on a quittance for Antonio Carusio 'absque visione conservatoris generalis'; Claver the vice-chancellor was instructed to impose the penalty of 10,000 florins.[221]

The last major enactment affecting the conservator general was a decree published in December 1454 to become effective from 1 January 1455.[222] It first provided that all privileges, letters, etc. from the curia which affected 'bonis, preeminenciis vel aliis juribus' of the crown should be registered word for word in Besalu's office. Since documents of this kind had been the subject of the first decree of 14 August 1447,[223] it must be presumed that registration had hitherto been a matter of summary and not verbatim transcription. On the other hand it is possible that the decree was merely rehearsing existing practice in this particular, and emphasizing that no fees would be charged for this registration. It undoubtedly broke new ground by ordering the registration of all documents relating to treasury loans and debts (*albarana, debitoria,* and *cedule maritate*), and above all in requiring that a register be compiled of the ordinary revenue in all provinces of the kingdom. This register was to be drawn up in the manner of a double-entry ledger: 'prout regulantur negociaciones mercatorum, verbi gratia introitus portulanie partium Apulie debent hoc anno Regie curie

---

[219] ACA Reg. 2656. 136ʳ, 1 Jan. 1449.

[220] Ibid. Besalu took this action by virtue of a commission given him on 8 Dec. 1448. The text has not come to light, but it appears to have conferred on him certain judicial power to act in misdemeanours uncovered by his office. One would certainly expect his executive powers to have been accompanied by an appropriate measure of jurisdiction. Cf. above, p. 136.

[221] ACA Reg. 2659. 105ʳ, 24 Aug. 1452. Alfonso wrote on the order: 'Yo la he leyda executalela.'

[222] ACA Reg. 2661. 82ʳ, 22 Dec. 1454.

[223] Cf. above, p. 206.

viginti milia ducatorum, debetur eis quos Regia Maiestas consignavit Ticio vel Gaio cum eius littera tali causa centum.'[224]

Successive decrees had thus endeavoured to bring together in the office of the conservator general the documentation available both for a general and detailed survey of the financial state of the kingdom: feudal records, daily statements of receipt and expenditure in the treasury, a detailed analysis of provincial revenues, a record of all loans and debts contracted by the crown, and a complete register of every grant and privilege that affected the revenue and property of the crown. This was not to duplicate the function of the Sommaria which had to do with completed action and closed accounts. The office of the conservator general was intended to control action at its initial stage, and thus to be an instrument of financial direction and control. The concept of the royal patrimony had merged with the concept of the state, and its conservator had become an embryo finance minister endeavouring, on the basis of a full knowledge of the resources of the state, to guard them against loss and abuse, and to provide the ruler with accurate assessments of his financial prospects. It was not a concept destined to take root in the kingdom of Naples, for on Alfonso's death the office of conservator general disappeared as an alien institution.

In 1444 Borso d'Este reckoned Alfonso's regular income from all sources in the kingdom of Naples to be 830,000 ducats a year. It is a reasonably accurate estimate. The principal constituent of the revenue was an annual direct tax, the imposition and amount of which, in one form or another, were dependent in the first instance on a parliamentary grant. Until he assembled his first parliament in 1443 Alfonso continued to collect the eight aids (*colte*) which had been paid each year to Giovanna II. That parliament replaced the aids with a hearth tax of ten *carlini*—the equivalent of 1 ducat —payable to the crown by all subjects other than tenants-in-chief. Alfonso, who had asked the parliament for a regular income with which to maintain an army, thought he had good cause for satisfaction with the change. A hearth tax offered the advantage of a basic income founded upon an entirely new assessment of the human resources of the kingdom,[225] which the king and his advisers firmly believed would yield substantially more than the aids.

[224] ACA Reg. 2661. 82^r, 22 Dec. 1454.
[225] Any person having his own patrimony or usufruct constituted a 'hearth' irrespective of whether he lived alone or in a family.

The envoy from Barcelona wrote in March 1443: 'The barons of this land in parliament assembled have offered the king 1 ducat for each hearth annually and there are about 400,000 hearths including Naples.'[226] Borso d'Este gave exactly the same estimate of the number of hearths in 1444, so it may reasonably be accepted as the official expectation. Allowing for the *tomolo* of salt which the crown was obliged to distribute free of charge to every household paying the tax,[227] and which Vinyes estimated would cost 25,000 ducats,[228] the anticipated net yield of the hearth tax was 375,000 ducats. In the years between 1290 and 1348, the most prosperous and effective years of Angevin rule, revenue from the aids had amounted to approximately 44,500 *oncie* (267,000 ducats) annually.[229] Nothing in the subsequent century served to increase either the wealth or the population of the kingdom; on the contrary, the general decay of order and administration under the later Angevins makes it unlikely that their income from the aids could have exceeded, or even approached, the earlier figures. There is indeed reason to believe that an aid at the end of Giovanna II's reign was reckoned at 30,000 ducats, so that the eight aids collected by Alfonso in his first years as King of Naples should have given him 240,000 ducats a year.[230] Thus the hearth tax may have been expected to yield 135,000 ducats more than the aids. Had that expectation been realized, the burden of direct taxation on the unprivileged would have increased by some 56 per cent, enough 'da farli di disperare', as Borso d'Este wrote to his brother. In the event it is doubtful whether the hearth tax produced any more than the aids.

Although we do not know the total yield of either the hearth tax or the aids for Alfonso's reign, a comparison can be made of the two in certain towns. Capua, for example, was assessed to pay 50 *oncie* for an aid, so that for the eight annual aids it would have paid 2,400 ducats. For the hearth tax the city and its surroundings

[226] ACB Cart. Com., vol. 13, fol. 24, Antoni Vinyes to Barcelona, Naples, 15 Mar. 1443: '. . . los barons de aquesta terra congregats per lo parlament han offert al Senyor Rey un ducat per foch lany que son entorn CCCCm. fochs comprenent hi Napols.'

[227] Cf. below.   [228] ACB Cart. Com., vol. 13, fol. 24.

[229] Caggese, *Roberto d'Angiò*, i. 613; G. M. Monti, 'Da Carlo I a Roberto di Angiò, Ricerche e documenti', *ASPN* (1933).

[230] Among the king's revenues in 1444 Borso d'Este included a single aid from the clergy reckoned at 30,000 ducats. The two aids imposed by Alfonso for his coronation produced a little over 60,000 ducats.

were reckoned at approximately 2,500 households, furnishing a revenue of 2,500 ducats a year less the cost of salt.[231] The corresponding figures for the demesne town of Aversa give 1,600 ducats for the aids and 1,939 ducats for the hearth tax.[232] In some places the difference was more substantial. In the baronial town of Sessa the aids were assessed at 1,728 ducats and the hearth tax at 2,142 ducats. The Prince of Salerno's town Nola paid 576 ducats for the aids and 932 ducats for the hearth tax. Pozzuoli by contrast paid only 371 ducats for the hearth tax whereas its aid assessment was 1,004 ducats a year. This latter discrepancy probably arises from the prosperity of the town which the hearth tax numeration did not take fully into account. In the province of Calabria similar variations may be noted between the yield of the two taxes, from the reduction in Policastro which paid 500 ducats in aids and 407 ducats for the hearth tax, to the increase in Crotone where the burden rose sharply from 144 to 454 ducats.[233] Making due allowance for remissions of aid granted by Alfonso and his predecessors, the total of tax paid under the older system generally amounted to less than the new hearth-tax assessment. The original aid assessment for Catanzaro, for example, stood at 90 ducats; René of Anjou remitted 30 ducats of this, reducing the annual payment from 720 to 480 ducats; for the hearth tax the town was assessed to pay 1,196 ducats.[234] A more general comparison may be obtained from seven Calabrian towns held by Antonio Centelles before his rebellion in 1444 and afterwards incorporated in the royal demesne. Without making any allowance for remissions of aid, these places were assessed at 3,773 ducats a year for the aids and at 4,113 ducats for the hearth tax.

The few statistics available suggest that the figures for this group of Calabrian towns are reasonably representative of the whole kingdom. They show an increase in tax yield of only some 9 per cent against the 56 per cent anticipated by the government, or a mere 21,600 ducats instead of the expected 135,000 ducats. Moreover, from the former figure must be deducted the cost of the salt which the state had now to supply free of charge to each household; taking that into account the hearth tax could not be expected to yield any extra revenue. What had happened was that those responsible for introducing the new tax had seriously over-

[231] ASN Div. Somm. I. 133, 2ʳ, 5ʳ.   [232] Ibid.
[233] ASN Div. Somm. I. 10, 4ᵛ and 22ᵛ.   [234] Ibid.

estimated the number of 'hearths' in the kingdom. The definition of a 'hearth' left some room for doubt and dispute when the first hearth census was taken in 1443–4.[235] Deliberate frauds also helped to make that census unreliable. Further commissions to uncover those frauds and a second census in 1447[236] improved matters but could not remedy a fundamental miscalculation. The true picture had emerged by February 1449 when a parliament offered the king a general tax (*taxa generale*) of 230,000 ducats a year in place of the *ius focularium*. That figure was based on an estimation that the taxable hearths of the kingdom numbered 230,000 and the king found it wise to accept the proffer rather than rely any longer on the uncertain hearth tax. We may therefore assert with some confidence that the introduction of the hearth tax had not led to any over-all increase in the tax burden on the population of the kingdom.

What Alfonso failed to obtain from the hearth tax he might appear to have gained from a new salt tax which exacted half a ducat from every household in return for one *tomolo* of salt which it was obliged to purchase each year from the state monopoly. That this imposition appeared early in the reign is shown by its inclusion among the heads of the Neapolitan revenue recorded by Borso d'Este:[237]

Item ha da quilli fogi, quatrocentomilia preditti, ogni anno de intrada doxento milia ducati per quatrocento milia tumuli de sale, e metelli mezo ducato el tumulo a chadauno fogo, che e obligato a tuore ogni uno tumulo de sale, e per quello tal tumulo de sale paga mezo ducato al anno.

[235] The instruction given to the census commissioners ran as follows: 'Item siano avisati li supradicti commissarii de scrivere particularamente in ciaschuno foco li capi de casa e in caso che alcuni deli fili o nepoti avessero proprio patrimonio quo ad usufructum e proprietatem simul habitent se debia computare pro uno altro focoleri, ma non avendo proprio secondo di sopra e dicto se debia computare pro uno focolieri. E si non lo figlio habitasse seperato dalo patre e non avesse proprio patrimonio e non viveret ad sua industria sed viveret de substantia patris intelligatur scilicet unum paternum foculare e non duo. Item si morendo lo patre li figli non dividendo la hereditate paterna e simul habitent debiano pagare pro uno focolario tantum nisi acquirerentur alia bona post mortem patris que inter eos non essent communia' (ASN Fasc. Com. Somm. I. 47ʳ).
[236] The parliament of 1443 had stipulated that a census should be taken every three years to ascertain the number of hearths in the kingdom. On 30 Sept. 1445 Francesco Pagano, a president of the Sommaria, received a commission to investigate hearth-tax arrears and frauds in Calabria (ASN Fasc. Com. Somm. 48ᵛ). Officials with similar commissions visited the other provinces.
[237] Foucard, 'Descrizione della citta di Napoli', p. 753.

In September 1445 the Sommaria ordered an inquest into arrears of the 'colte delo mezo ducato delo sale',[238] and a promissory note given to Fonolleda in March 1446 assigned the repayment of a loan on the 'collecte salis per nos noviter imposite'.[239] The true yield of this tax was not, of course, the 200,000 ducats estimated by Borso d'Este, but something around 165,000 ducats less the cost of the salt. One must also take into consideration the fact that in the past subjects had been compelled to buy their salt from the state even though no minimum amount had been stipulated. It is in fact very likely that the compulsory purchase of one *tomolo* was instituted in 1443 following the agreement with parliament that each hearth should receive one free *tomolo* on payment of the hearth tax. Without such a provision the state's income from the salt monopoly would have been drastically reduced because most households might have found it unnecessary to buy additional salt. What appears, therefore, as a substantial new tax proves on closer examination to be little more than the adjustment of an existing imposition.

The only indisputable increase in direct taxation during the reign was that granted by the parliament of October 1456. From it Alfonso obtained a permanent revenue of 2 ducats from each hearth on the basis of the 1449 estimation that there were 230,000 hearths in the kingdom. In return the crown undertook to supply each hearth with one *tomolo* of salt free, as had been done with the hearth tax of 1443. This new tax of 1456 incorporated the existing direct tax—the *taxa generale*—and the extraordinary aids so that henceforth each hearth paid $2\frac{1}{2}$ ducats a year in direct taxes and received two *tomoli* of salt. At first glance it seems a very substantial addition to the tax burden; in practice it amounted to only a modest increase if one bears in mind that it replaced the extraordinary aids which had become a regular feature of Alfonso's fiscal exactions.

Alfonso had promised the 1443 parliament that he would levy no more aids. However, the unexpectedly low yield of the hearth tax and the expense of his wars with Florence and Venice forced him to ask his next parliament in March 1448 for further assistance in that form. He was granted three aids.[240] The parliament of

---

[238] ASN Fasc. Com. Somm. I. 47ʳ.   [239] ACA Reg. 2719, 24ᵛ, 28 Mar. 1446.
[240] Cf. the promise to pay the Count of Cocentayna 5,000 ducats from the proceeds of these aids (ACA Reg. 2940. 50ᵛ, 31 Mar. 1448).

February 1449 gave him a further two aids.[241] Thus, despite the undertaking of 1443, the aid quickly reappeared as the standard form of supplementary direct taxation which Neapolitan parliaments were called upon to vote for the never-ending extraordinary expenditure of the king's wars. From the next parliament—that of March 1450—he demanded three aids:

. . . exposito per nos eidem ut pro defensione nostri status et Regni sucurrendo necessitatibus nobis occurrentibus, et presertim pro stipendis nostrarum armigerarum gentium pro deffensione et conservacione nostri status dictorumque magnatum et baronum aliorumque incolarum et totius rei publice Regni istius nobis de tribus collectis ordinariis ac de aliquibus peditibus subvenire vellent.[242]

When another parliament met in December 1453 it voted not aids but a forced loan of 220,000 ducats. Aids reappeared as a regular feature of taxation when the 1456 parliament granted to Alfonso and his heirs two aids annually as part of the general overhaul of the direct taxes which raised them to a level of 2 ducats a year for each hearth. This last parliament was recognizing that what in theory were extraordinary taxes had become a regular and necessary part of the king's revenue, and it obviously hoped that the new concession would obviate the need for any further supplementary aids. Since Alfonso summoned no more parliaments that expectation was not put to the test.

In addition to the aids granted him by parliaments, Alfonso imposed a number of others in the form of special and feudal aids. After taking the city of Naples he exacted a victory aid at the rate of three ordinary aids.[243] He thoroughly exploited the feudal aids, taking a coronation aid at the rate of two ordinary aids in 1443[244] and aids for the marriages of his three children. In Spain the cities objected strongly to the latter exaction on the grounds that the

---

[241] ASN Div. Somm. I. 133, the accounts presented to the Sommaria by Angelo de Martino who collected the two aids in Terra di Lavoro south of the Garigliano. He received his commission on 16 Feb. 1449 and presented his accounts on 11 Sept. 1450.

[242] Ametller y Vinyas, *Alfonso V de Aragón*, iii. 685.

[243] ASN Fasc. Com. Somm. I. 88ᵛ.

[244] Ibid. 47ʳ. Towns and persons holding privileges exempting them from aids in perpetuity were none the less required to contribute one aid for the coronation tax, 'per che in questa colte non se intendino franchire de speciale persune'. It yielded altogether 61,175 ducats (Tutini, *Discorsi*, p. 80). The coronation never took place. Cf. above, pp. 37–8.

children were illegitimate and there the king had to content himself with an aid at one-third of the customary rate. In the kingdom of Naples he was able to collect two aids each for the marriages of Ferdinand and Eleonor and one for that of Maria.[245] Between September 1441 and the meeting of the parliament in 1456 Alfonso had imposed altogether 37⅓ aids, representing a total of at least 1,120,000 ducats—an average of 75,000 ducats a year over this period, although more than half were taken during the first five years. Arrears amounting to some 66,000 ducats from all these aids were forgiven at the request of the 1456 parliament.[246]

In order to obtain an accurate assessment of the tax burden one must add to these direct taxes the weight of the indirect taxes which fell in one manner or another on most articles of consumption, but to which Alfonso made no significant additions.[247] Feudal dues in cash and kind probably drew at least another 2 ducats a year from each hearth.[248] The Neapolitan taxpayer had also to meet his financial obligations towards the church. In addition to the tithe these involved extraordinary contributions sanctioned by the pope and king such as the Jubilee indulgences of 1450. By a necessarily impressionistic calculation we may estimate the average tax burden on each hearth at 7 or 8 ducats a year. Since the direct tax for each locality was calculated on the total number of households and then apportioned according to an estimation of individual wealth made by local assessors, the sum paid by each household varied very considerably. Assessments tended to discriminate against the poorer members of the community. As for income, a common foot soldier was paid 2 ducats a month,[249] a farm labourer 18 ducats a year,

---

[245] Salvati, *Fonti aragonesi*, iv. 51.

[246] Shortly before the parliament met the Sommaria had issued orders for the collection of these arrears (ASN Signif. I. 39ᵛ, 9 Sept. 1456).

[247] For the indirect taxes see Chapter 10 below.

[248] This calculation is based on a number of reliefs paid by tenants-in-chief. Acerra in the Terra di Lavoro numbered approximately 210 hearths and was held *in capite* by Gabriele del Balzo Orsini, Duke of Venosa. Between 1449 and 1451 it yielded him an average annual revenue of 450 ducats besides a considerable return in kind of fowls, wheat, millet, beans, barley, and wine, worth altogether another 100 ducats (ASN Rel. Orig. i (Lav.), 264). The chief items in the cash revenue were an annual aid given to the lord in August (in some places another aid was given at Christmas), the profits of justice, pasture, mill, and press dues. An assessment of relief for fifteen towns and villages held by Francesco Pandone, Count of Venafro, put the annual value at 1,723 ducats and the number of hearths at 675 (ASN Signif. I. 47ʳ).

[249] Cf. below, p. 277.

and a head cowman 24 ducats a year.[250] Labourers employed in the rebuilding of the castle of Gaeta earned 2 *tarini* 4 *grana* a week, but the work was seasonal.[251] The average household numbered five[252] and if it had two wage-earners among its members it might not find the pressure of taxation too great; but it has to be borne in mind that in many regions paid employment was not easily found and that the system of tax assessment in towns and villages worked against the interests of the poorer inhabitants who often found themselves paying proportionately more than their more prosperous fellow-citizens. Failure to pay on time led to harassment, distraint, and financial penalties which could ruin a man and drive him into outlawry.

[250] Cf. below, p. 363.   [251] ASN Dip. Somm. 189.
[252] This is the estimate of C. J. Beloch, *Bevölkerungsgeschichte Italiens*, i (ed. G. de Sanctis, Leipzig, 1937).

VII

SECRETARIES AND SEALS

THE institutions we have considered in earlier chapters—the treasury, Vicaria, Sommaria, office of the conservator general, office of the *escriva de racio*—each had its own secretarial staff. Here we are concerned with those responsible for writing for the king and his council. The drafting of the king's correspondence, the drawing up of privileges and administrative acts, and the compilation of laws belonged by Neapolitan practice to the protonotary of the kingdom assisted by two secretaries.[1] In Aragon these functions came under the over-all supervision of the chancellor. Beneath him the Household Ordinance of Peter the Ceremonious provided for a protonotary 'learned in grammatical science' to ensure that royal letters were written in a good Latin style; it was also the duty of the protonotary to see to the registration and dispatch of such letters. In addition to the protonotary, the Aragonese chancery had twelve ordinary clerks (*scrivans de manament*) who wrote as directed by the chancellor, vice-chancellor, *oydors*, and royal secretaries, and eight clerks of the register (*scrivans de registre*) who, besides keeping the registers, assisted the other clerks. The royal secretaries, two in number, belonged to the chamber, their duties being to write anything sealed with the secret seal, to record council proceedings, and to write letters on the instruction of the council.

Cristoforo Gaetano, Count of Fondi, on whom Alfonso bestowed the Neapolitan office of protonotary at the beginning of his reign, appears to have exercised some oversight in the dispatch of documents bearing the great seal. As negative evidence one may cite the privilege confirming Guidice Madio as *credencerius* of Trani, Giovinazzo, and Molfetta; it bore the secret seal and was to be regarded as valid even though 'sigillatis non sunt magno nostro

---

[1] Trifone, *La legislazione angioina*, pp. 19–26. Cf. the privilege for the secretary Antonio Beccadelli, 22 Oct. 1455: 'licet de more ac consuetudine huius Regni ac nostro sit ut duobus tantum secretariis nostris ordinariis satisfiat de introitibus dicti sigilli . . .' (Toppi, *De origine tribunalium*, iii. 267).

pendente sigillo nec datum prothonotarii continetur in eis'.[2] The more usual procedure, as in the other Great Offices of state, was for a *locumtenens* to discharge the essential formal functions. Antonio Beccadelli acted in that capacity for the protonotary in 1437 and 1438.[3] Cristoforo's son Onorato, who followed him in the office, managed it in a similar fashion. As chief notary of the kingdom he frequently made appointments to notarial and minor judicial offices 'ex sui officii potestate' and authorized the writing and dispatch of the appropriate diploma 'de mandato prothonotarii'. In October 1442 he appointed Pietro Marco judge and assessor to the captain of L'Aquila;[4] Giovanni Nicola Cicco Simone, after undergoing an examination, was made a public notary with a diploma given 'per manus spectabilis et magnifici viri Honorati Gayetani militis logotete et prothonotarii'.[5] By a commission given 'in civitate Neapolis in hospicio nostre residencie' on 30 March 1450, Onorato Gaetano appointed Monserrat Poch his agent in Calabria for collecting fees due to the protonotary from the judicial officials of the communes,[6] and gave him authority to issue the necessary letters of appointment and confirmation to these officials.[7] The protonotary's authority to license persons to practise medicine and surgery was severely curtailed by the order that any such licence must bear the countersignature of the *protomedicus*,[8] and some appear to have been granted without any reference to the protonotary.[9] Like his father, Onorato left much of this routine work to a *locumtenens*. A fragment of a register of privileges issued by the protonotary *ex officio* between October 1448 and March 1452[10] contains a number authorized by him in person when he was in Naples towards the end of 1448; most are authorized, however, by various *locumtenentes* such as the *rationales* Nicola

---

[2] Rogadeo, *Codice diplomatico*, p. 9. The privilege is dated 27 Aug. 1436.

[3] Laurenza, *Il Panormita*, p. 66. On 27 Dec. 1438 Beccadelli issued a privilege as 'locumtenens magnifici viri Cristofori Gayetani'.

[4] ACA Reg. 2902. 101ᵛ, given in the king's camp 'prope Scaffila'.

[5] Ibid. 18ᵛ, 4 May 1442, given in the camp 'apud Silvam Longam'.

[6] Cf. below, p. 339.

[7] Pontieri, *Fonti aragonesi*, ii. 108–9.

[8] ACA Reg. 2904. 148ᵛ, 23 May 1444; cf. above, p. 79.

[9] e.g. the licence to practise surgery given to Marco Sibilia 'mandato regio facto per Jacobum Quintana regium fiscum prothomedicum' (ACA Reg. 2945. 13ʳ, 20 Dec. 1443). Possibly the protonotary objected to this infringement of his prerogative and obtained, as a compromise, the provision for counter-signature by the protomedicus.

[10] ACA Reg. 2916. 115ʳ ff.

de Statis and Giovanni de Forma.[11] In 1455 we find Antonello Petrucci and Marino de Forma acting in that capacity for letters of legitimization which could also be given *ex officio* by the protonotary.[12] It is none the less evident that in his notarial duties, as in his conciliar functions, the protonotary of Naples had been pushed into a corner where he maintained a certain degree of authority over a very circumscribed range of minor and routine business. Only after Alfonso's death did the Count of Fondi regain a general control of the chancery.[13]

For almost half the reign the protonotary of Aragon ('prothonotarius in regnis nostris occiduis')[14] too performed few secretarial duties in Italy. Pere Ram, the incumbent of that office, appears not to have accompanied the king to Naples; and when he died in 1442, his son and successor, Ferrer Ram, was kept busy travelling back and forth between Italy and Spain until he too died in October 1448.[15] Occasionally Ferrer Ram did write letters to the king's order. For example, in January and February 1444 when he was in Naples he wrote several *debitoria* and bills of exchange which bear the subscription 'Dominus Rex mandavit michi Ferario Ram prothonotario'.[15] Again in March 1446, shortly before leaving for Spain, he drafted a number of letters.[17] When he departed from the court on a lengthy mission, Ram would hand over his office and the seals in his keeping to a deputy. Annotations in the registers record those days on which he relinquished and resumed his functions. One such note reads as follows: 'Anno domini MCCCCxxxxiiii die viii Novembris apud Liciam de territorio Ypsigri ducatus Calabrie fuerunt assignata sigilla regia unacum officio prothonotarii Andree Gaculli Regio scribe ac dictum officium prothonotarii regenti per absenciam prothonotarii.'[18]

---

[11] ACA Reg. 2916. 115ʳ, 1 Oct. 1448: 'Datis in nostris felicibus castris in absentia Spectabilis et Magnifici viri Honorati Gayetani Fundorum Comitis etc., Regni Sicilie citra farum Logothete prothonotarii per nobilem virum Nicholaum de Statis de Monteopulo fidelem familiarem nostrum dilectum in nostris felicibus castris prope Lacedoniam.' Ibid. 124ʳ, for a licence to practise surgery issued by de Forma in Castelnuovo, 13 Dec. 1448.

[12] ASN Priv. I. 172ʳ, Castelnuovo, 28 Dec. 1455 (Marino de Forma); ibid. 179ʳ, 3 May 1455 (Antonello Petrucci).

[13] Documents emanating from the chancery between 1458 and his death in 1494 regularly bear the subscription of his *locumtenens*. Cf. Mazzoleni, *Regesto della Cancelleria Aragonese di Napoli* (Naples, 1951), pp. 216 ff.

[14] ACA Reg. 2690. 106ᵛ, 1 Sept. 1444, referring to Ferrer Ram.

[15] Cf. above, p. 140.

[16] ACA Reg. 2720. 1ᵛ–7ᵛ.

[17] ACA Reg. 2656. 13ʳ, 19 Mar. 1446.

[18] ACA Reg. 2720. 43ʳ.

Gaçull, who acted as regent until Ram returned on 9 August 1445, was probably the senior clerk of the chancery where he had served since at least 1432[19] as well as undertaking a number of diplomatic missions in Italy.[20]

After Ram's death Alfonso gave the office of protonotary for Aragon to his most trusted secretary, Arnau Fonolleda, in whose hands it became once more effectively the post of principal secretary and notary to the crown.[21]

It will be convenient to consider the secretaries in three groups: those appointed according to Neapolitan or Aragonese usage, and those given the title as a mark of honour. Many of the latter were subjects of other rulers. Guiniforte Barzizza, a secretary to Filippo Maria Visconti, was one such. His relationship with the Aragonese court had begun in 1432 with a visit to Barcelona during which he had struck up a friendship with Alfonso's secretary Joan Olzina and was made a *familiaris*. As a member of the Duke of Milan's council he had subsequently advocated a policy of co-operation with Aragon, and after the Duke's death had endeavoured to forge an alliance between Alfonso and the short-lived Ambrosian republic.[22] On 7 December 1447 the king appointed Domenico Ferusino, another ex-secretary of Filippo Maria, his own secretary and counsellor, 'in omnibus et singulis negociis et agendis nostris que e cetero ad Mediolani aut aliis partibus longobardie agi duci tractarive continget per nuncios ambasciatores et comissarios nostros predictos unacum ipsis pro nobis eciam debeat et habeat interesse.'[23] While Ferusino might have played some part in the discussion of northern Italian affairs in the council, his secretaryship was purely honorary. Another secretary in this category was Baltassare de Canova, secretary to the Doge of Genoa Raffaele Adorno, who received the title in September 1444 when relations

---

[19] In 1432 he was attached to the Aragonese garrisons on the Genoese coast, and with Juan Perez of the treasury was responsible for selling some of the king's corn there (Ametller y Vinyas, *Alfonso V de Aragón*, i. 382).

[20] In February 1436 he was sent to the Bishop of Lerida and the Cardinal San Sisto in Florence (ibid. iii. 557), in August 1438 to Milan (ibid. ii. 188), and in the spring of 1443 to Rome and Florence (ibid. ii. 495).

[21] See below, pp. 230 ff.

[22] Barzizza, *Orationes et epistolae*, Letters to Olzina (pp. 87 and 106); to clerk Jorge Catala (p. 121) from Milan, March 1439. In May 1448 Alfonso referred to Barzizza as 'nostro embassatore' to the Milanese republic (ACA Reg. 2719. 52ᵛ, 18 May 1448).

[23] ACA Reg. 2912. 148ᵛ.

between the king and the republic were passing through a cordial phase. The privilege appointing him conferred the usual privileges and salary of 50 *oncie* given to a Neapolitan secretary,[24] but he never performed any secretarial duties in Naples. Pietro de Noxeto, a papal secretary, was similarly honoured in August 1447.[25]

Secretaryships bestowed on a few prominent literary figures were also honorary appointments, intended more to give the recipient a salary and standing in the court than to bind him to routine duties. Among the humanists who adorned these departmental niches, the brightest figure was that of Lorenzo Valla whose scepticism about the temporal power of the papacy accorded very well with Alfonso's own practical doubts on that same subject. Valla first joined the court in 1435 with the title of secretary and a salary of 50 *oncie*.[26] He remained there for thirteen years as its mentor in all things classical, and in particular as the king's Latin tutor, for although Alfonso had an adequate command of low Latin,[27] he needed help with the classical literature that caught his imagination in Italy.[28] The combination of political secularism and Spanish religious fervour which he found in Alfonso's court stimulated Valla to produce his greatest work. Besides his attack on the Donation of Constantine—written in 1441 or 1442, at the height of the quarrel between Alfonso and Eugenius IV—he completed *De libero arbitrio* and *Dialecticae disputationes*, and began *In Novum Testamentum adnotationes* while enjoying his sinecure secretaryship.

A statement on the patronage of scholars, conventional in tone but presumably in harmony with the king's thinking, occurs in the preamble to the privilege appointing Geronimo Guarino, son of the renowned educationist Guarino Veronese, a secretary and counsellor:

Cum animo recensemus decursorum temporum spatia illa nobis quodammodo beata fuisse videri solent in quibus virtutes atque optime artes a principibus culte illarumque professores in precium habiti gratis favoribus ad honores ac dignitates provecti floruerunt ubi cum ipsi premium honostissimi studii sui consequentes ulterior ardentiores

---

[24] ACA Reg. 2909. 196ʳ, 15 Sept. 1444.

[25] ACA Reg. 2917. 54ᵛ, 5 Aug. 1452.

[26] Minieri Riccio, 'Alcuni fatti di Alfonso I', p. 252.

[27] He was able to act as an interpreter for the Emperor Sigismund at the Perpignan Conference in 1415 (Macdonald, *Fernando de Antequera*, p. 223).

[28] His favourite classical authors were Livy, Caesar, Virgil, and Seneca.

ad eas redderentur ceterq. illo quasi stimulo ad eiusdem studii incita-
cionem incitarentur quod coli et in honorem haberi cernerent tempora
sua sic certaturi unusquique plurima laude et gloria illustrarent et
propemodum beata effecerent.[29]

Unlike Valla, however, Guarino did perform the normal duties
of a secretary for approximately two years, as may be seen from the
mandatum on a number of documents,[30] and there is no evidence
that he engaged in any scholarly activity in Naples. Bartolommeo
Facio on the other hand, referred to in 1457 as 'spectati historio-
graphi ac secretarii nostri',[31] devoted himself exclusively to literary
labours, chief among them being his history of Alfonso's conquest
of Naples and the Italian wars.

Among the secretaries appointed according to Neapolitan usage
is one who had much in common with the humanists. Antonio
Beccadelli, or Panormita, to give him his literary name, joined the
Aragonese court about the same time as his great rival Valla. For
many years his legal talents were actively employed in the Sommaria and council, while he vied with Valla as the king's Latin
instructor and promoter of letters at court. Occasionally Alfonso
called upon him to draft letters which required an especially
elegant Latinity. A reference to one of these appears in a letter
he wrote to the king in 1450:

Epistolam ad collegium Cardinalium, quam a me per Matthacum
Joannem secretarium petiisti, per eundem ad te misi recorrigendam, et
emendandam per acri iudicio, ac prudentia tua. Ego quidem, uti ille
tuo nomine mandavit, informavitque ita mentem tuam verbis protinus
explicare conatus sum.[32]

But it was not until September 1455 that Beccadelli, now sixty
years old, was appointed a secretary[33] with particular responsibility

---

[29] ACA Reg. 2912. 143^r, 10 Nov. 1447. The privilege, and hence this passage
was written by Fonolleda. Aurispa had recommended Guarino to Beccadelli in
October 1443 (Laurenza, *Il Panormita*, p. 10). Valla too took an interest in him
and wrote a letter to his father about his prospects (Barozzi and Sabbadini,
Studi sul Panormita, p. 93).

[30] e.g. ACA Reg. 2912. 81^v, Tivoli, 7 June 1447; Reg. 2913. 89^v, Castelnuovo,
21 Jan. 1449.   [31] ACA Reg. 2917. 166^r, 7 June 1457.

[32] Beccadelli, *Epistolae*, fol. 111^r.

[33] Antonello Petrucci received orders to pay him a salary of 40 *oncie* 24 *tareni*
as secretary from the profits of the great seal of the kingdom: 'attamen quia
eundem Antonium inter primos et maiores ac ordinarios nostros secretarios
habemus et prae ceteris pro sua singulari doctrina ac eloquentia carissimum'
(Toppi, *De origine tribunalium*, iii. 266–9).

for diplomatic correspondence with the papacy and other powers of Italy. In that capacity he rendered great service to Alfonso and later to his son Ferdinand.[34]

Giannone has described the early career of another notable Neapolitan secretary, Antonello Petrucci:

Nato in Teano, città presso Capua, di poveri parenti, ed allevato in Aversa da un Notaio, mostrando molto spirito, e grande applicazione alle lettere, fù da costui portato in Napoli, dove lo pose a' servigi di Giovanni Olzina Segretario del Rè Alfonso. L'Olzina, conosciuti i talenti del giovane, dimorando in casa sua il famoso Lorenzo Valla, lo diede a lui perchè lo ammaestrasse; ed avendo Antonello sotto sì eccellente Maestro in poco tempo fatti miracolosi progressi, fù dall'Olzina posto nella Cancelleria Regia, il quale quando gravato d'affari non avea tempo d'andare egli dal Rè, soleva mandarvi Antonello.[35]

In fact Antonello began work as a clerk in the Sommaria. A fragment of a Sommaria register for the months of August and September 1444 contains several pieces written by him: a list of hearths on the lands of the Prince of Salerno, a letter to the viceroy of Calabria, a commission for Joan Gener.[36] Only at the end of the reign did he obtain the position of secretary, or notary in the chamber 'ad conficiendum dictandum et scribendum letteras nostras ex nostra curia sub magno nostro pendente sigillo emanantes et alias tam gratiam quam iustitiam commictas per prothonotarium et camerarium regni nostri sicilie.'[37] Under Ferdinand his fortunes continued to prosper until after the death of Olzina he became principal royal secretary, a post which he held for twenty years. Then, in his old age, he became implicated in the barons' revolt, and was executed on 11 May 1487.[38]

---

[34] e.g. his letters to the governments of Venice, Florence, Ferrara, and Milan on the negotiations for peace between Siena and Jacobo Piccinino (ACA Reg. 2661. 120ᵛ, 6 June 1456) and those to the pope, Milan, Venice, Mantua, Ferrara, Urbino, and Florence, justifying Alfonso's stand in his quarrel with Genoa (ibid. 136ʳ, 10 Aug. 1456).   [35] Giannone, Istoria civile, iii. 457.

[36] ASN Framm. Somm. 11ʳ ff. He signed these documents 'Antonellus de Aversa pro Bernardo' (i.e. the actorum notarius). He was still a clerk in the Sommaria in October 1445, writing now in the name of the new actorum notarius, Luis Cescases (ASN Fasc. Somm. 64ʳ, 29 Oct. 1445, 'Antonellus de Aversa pro Ludovico Cescases'); cf. above, p. 199.

[37] ASN Div. Somm. I. 52 (bis), 76ᵛ. This appointment bears no date. On 16 Jan. 1456 Petrucci was still addressed as sigillator of the great seal (Toppi, De origine tribunalium, iii. 266). In a littera executorialis dated 2 Jan. 1458 he appears as 'regio secretario collaterali' (ASN Fasc. Com. Somm. 13).

[38] E. Pontieri, 'Camillo Porzio storico' ASPN (1958), 126.

Turning back to the earlier years of the reign, we find Luca di Bucchinelli of Caramanico in the office of secretary from at least September 1436.[39] For the 6th indiction (1442–3) he held the captaincy of Isernia, after which he disappears from view.[40] Another Neapolitan secretary, Angelillo di Capua, can be traced only as far as June 1444.[41] Giovanni di Loffredo entered royal service thanks to his fellow-citizens of Manfredonia who, when submitting to the king in November 1442, included this item among their petitions: 'Item supplicano la prefata Maesta per honore et contentecza de questa Universita acceptare per vestro servitore et agregare allo numero delli secretarii della Maesta vostra notaro Janne de loffredo nostro citadino per che e liali practico et bona persona.'[42] That same day he was given a privilege which made him 'secretarium negociorum huius regni Sicilie citra farum ac familiarem nostrum domesticum'.[43] However, he appears to have played no important part in government as a secretary. Apart from one appearance in the council in May 1443,[44] no record survives of his activity at court. In January 1444 he returned to his native Puglia as captain of Foggia.[45]

In contrast to these shadowy figures stand the more substantial personages of Giovanni de Belloflore and Matteo di Girifalco, both of whom were very active as secretaries. Giovanni de Belloflore first appears, whether as a secretary or a clerk we cannot tell, as writer of a privilege given on the instruction of Platamone in Castel Capuano on 8 July 1443.[46] By October 1448 he had certainly become a secretary,[47] and his signature continues to appear in the

[39] Faraglia, *Storia della lotta*, p. 377; Rogadeo, *Codice diplomatico*, p. 12.

[40] ACA Reg. 2902. 174^r, 1 Aug. 1443.

[41] He received confirmation of the annual provision of 36 *oncie* which he had been given by Giovanna II, 2 July 1442 (Faraglia, *Storia della lotta*, p. 301, n. 2). On 26 July 1442 he wrote the commission that empowered Iñigo de Guevara to negotiate a *condotta* with Sforza; on this occasion he signed himself *locumtenens* and *vice* Olzina (ibid. p. 381). This presumably means that he was acting for one of the Aragonese secretaries of the chamber. His latest act is a privilege which he wrote on 10 June 1444 (ACA Reg. 2906. 88^r).

[42] ACA Reg. 2902. 124^r, 6 Nov. 1442.   [43] Ibid. 148^r.

[44] ACA Reg. 2906. 29^r, 20 May 1443. In this document he is described as belonging to the chancery.

[45] ACA Reg. 2903. 113^v, 12 Jan. 1444.

[46] ACA Reg. 2904. 87^v, 'Johannes Bellos Flos mandato regio facto per B. Platamone'.

[47] ACA Reg. 2913. 59^v, 1 Oct. 1448. The appointment of 'Joh. de Bello Flore secretarius' as captain of Atri for the 12th indiction is revoked because it had already been promised to someone else.

registers until 1457.[48] Although Toppi lists him among the presidents of the Sommaria from 1449 onwards,[49] it is quite possible that his post there was of a supernumerary character. Some uncertainty also exists as to the status of Matteo di Girifalco on 21 August 1442 when in Castel Capuano he wrote, on the direction of the council, an order to give effect to its judgement.[50] However, a document referring to his death in 1451 speaks of him as a secretary[51] and it seems probable that he was attached to the Duke of Calabria in his capacity as *locumtenens generalis* in the kingdom.[52] A Tommaso di Girifalco, who was serving as a clerk in the Sommaria in 1445,[53] and who may have been a relative of Matteo, had become secretary to the duke by December 1457.[54]

But the most important of the Neapolitan secretaries was not an Italian at all. Francesc Martorell, who belonged to a prominent Valencian family, came to Italy as a chancery clerk[55] and, thanks to the favour of Valencian influence at court, soon came to the fore. On 20 June 1444 Alfonso appointed him a notarial secretary:

> Quia predecessores nostri bone memorie reges Sicilie citra farum consueverunt habere secretarios ad exercendum officium notariatus in camera regia de dictandis subscribendis et annotandis litteris dictantibus et concernentibus peccunias et res alias fiscales nec alii quidem secretarii in conficiendis litteris ipsis se aliqualiter intromittebant, hunc quidem morem approbantes quia per manus unius ipse littere expediebantur et fiscalia iura in ipsis litteris contenta per varias manus nequaquam ambulabant . . .[56]

Although Martorell did write many letters dealing with the financial

---

[48] ACA Reg. 2946 *passim*.   [49] *De origine tribunalium*, i. 175, 189.
[50] ACA Reg. 2902. 77ʳ.
[51] ACA Reg. 2915. 63ʳ, 22 June 1451. His death had left vacant the office of *credencerius* in the Neapolitan customs.
[52] e.g. the privilege he wrote in Castel Capuano, the residence of the Duke of Calabria (cf. above, p. 54) on 13 Jan. 1448: 'Ferdinandus dominus dux primogenitus et locumtenens mandavit mihi Mattheo de Girifalcho' (ASN Priv. I. 69ʳ).
[53] e.g. ASN Fasc. Com. Somm. 115ʳ, 20 Aug. 1445.
[54] On 26 Dec. 1457, in his capacity as the duke's secretary, Tommaso di Girifalco wrote an instrument testifying that the Count of Gravina had performed homage by proxy (ACA Reg. 2916. 85ʳ).
[55] From Castellammare on 24 Jan. 1437 he wrote a letter to Giovanni di Sanseverino, 'mandato regio per Olzina secretarium' (ACA Reg. 2651. 50ᵛ).
[56] ACA Reg. 2909. 88ᵛ. Martorell is appointed 'notariatus camere nostre ad scribendum seu dictandum notandum et subscribendum litteras nostre maiestatis tam ad sigillum pendentem quam ad sigillum parvum in cartis pergameneis et papireis de solucionibus et exibicionibus peccuniare et aliarum rerum nostrarum fiscalium quibuscumque fiscalis . . .'

affairs of the crown,[57] he was of necessity not the only secretary who dealt with a category of business that loomed so large in royal correspondence.[58] Therefore the appointment gave him status rather than an exclusive function. The Neapolitan secretary's customary salary of 36 *oncie* was also no measure of his wealth. He owned a galley which in 1448 he armed and placed at the king's service;[59] in February 1449 he stood as a creditor of the crown to the tune of 2,500 ducats.[60] To the foundation of this fortune, his property in Valencia, he managed to add some land in Naples which had devolved to the crown on the death of a minor without heirs.[61] The dignity of secretary he amplified in the 1450s with other prestigious offices: that of *magister portulanus* in Sicily,[62] and that of bailiff general and judge ordinary of the Jews in the kingdom of Naples[63]—both very lucrative appointments. With wealth and power he combined some culture which put him on good terms with the humanists of the Neapolitan court, and particularly with Beccadelli who wrote him several letters.[64] The commercial and political rivalry between Valencia and Barcelona may account for his patronage of the 'Busca' party when its envoy Pere Boquet arrived in Naples to negotiate with Alfonso, but like the other patron, the Bishop of Urgell, he expected some reward for his services.[65] His letter to the council of Barcelona chiding it for

[57] e.g. many may be found in the register 'Pecuniae', ACA Reg. 2719. As notary of the chamber he drew up the instrument by which the king sold the town of Caivano to the Count of Fondi (ASN Relevi Originali, Terra di Lavoro e Contado di Molise, vol. 33, fol. 57ʳ, Castelnuovo, 26 July 1456).

[58] On 28 Mar. 1456 Arnau Fonolleda had drawn up a similar instrument for the sale of Caivano to Arnau Sans (ibid.). The Register 2719 'Pecuniae' contains many documents written by other secretaries in no way different from those for which Martorell was responsible.

[59] In June it formed part of a squadron which Alfonso had placed at the disposal of the Doge of Genoa. Martorell himself wrote the instructions for the envoy sent to request the release of the galley for service in the siege of Piombino (ACA Reg. 2696. 157ᵛ, 25 June 1448).

[60] ACA Real Patrimonio 2951.   [61] ACA Reg. 2909. 66ʳ, 23 May 1444.

[62] He held the office by February 1455 (ACA Reg. 2916. 17ᵛ) and exercised it through a deputy, Matteu Pujades, son of the former treasurer. As *magister portulanus* he received a salary of 300 *oncie*.

[63] Gentile, 'Lo stato napoletano' (1938), 29. He was given this office on 29 May 1456 with a salary of 1,000 ducats a year.

[64] Resta, *L'epistolario del Panormita*, pp. 210–11.

[65] Pere Boquet wrote to Barcelona on 16 Aug. 1456: '. . . lo patriarcha e mossen Martorell stan fort mal contents com a lurs treballs e aiudes en aquesta affers dela ciutat nos ha degut sguart' (ACB Cart. Com., vol. 26, fol. 136); cf. above, p. 165.

failing to appreciate Boquet's work in Naples reveals considerable cynicism about the workings of the bureaucracy of which he formed part: 'a man has done a great deal', he wrote, 'who here in eight months does what elsewhere would be done in one'.[66] After Alfonso's death, Martorell left Naples for Sicily to end his career in the service of the new king of Aragon. Besides retaining the post of *magister portulanus* of the island until his death in 1466, he succeeded de Guevara as *alcaide* of Malta in March 1463,[67] and was nominated acting viceroy of Sicily in 1465, but he never assumed this last prestigious office.[68]

Although the number of secretaries appointed according to Aragonese usage substantially exceeded the two *escrivans secretaris* provided for in the Ordinance of 1344,[69] two among them enjoyed a peculiar pre-eminence which placed them among the king's most intimate counsellors: they were Joan Olzina and Arnau Fonolleda.

Joan Olzina came of a Valencian family which had long served the Aragonese crown; a Pere Olzina had been secretary to Juan I in 1392.[70] By 1425, and possibly earlier, Joan had become a secretary, and on the death of Francesc Darinyo in 1428 or 1429 he seems to have risen to the position of one of the two secretaries of the secret seal provided for in the Household Ordinance.[71] Thereafter he remained very close to the centre of state affairs, not only as author of many of the most confidential and important documents of state and of a large proportion of the more routine papers,[72] but also as a trusted emissary and an executant of the royal will. Examples abound of Olzina's activity in this latter role. Having sent him to Sicily in 1432, Alfonso wrote him a letter giving full details of the negotiations then in progress with Naples, the Holy Roman Emperor, Genoa, and other states, as well as a series of instructions dealing with the important assignments for which he had been sent to the island.[73] When the king led his army to Capua in November 1436, Olzina appears to have been left in charge of the administration in the provisional capital at Gaeta

[66] Madurell Marimon, *Mensajeros barceloneses*, p. 567. The letter is dated 21 Feb. 1457.

[67] Vicens Vives, *Fernando el Católico*, p. 145.

[68] Ibid., pp. 159–60.   [69] Cf. above, p. 81.

[70] ACA Reg. 1904. 72.   [71] See ACA Reg. 2692. 34.

[72] The instructions for diplomatic envoys were often drafted by Olzina—e.g. for envoys to Milan, 29 Mar. 1432 (Ametller y Vinyas, *Alfonso V de Aragón*, i. 334); for envoys to Rome, 6 Oct. 1432 (ACA Reg. 2693. 50).

[73] Ametller y Vinyas, *Alfonso V de Aragón*, i. 385.

where he had to deal with such matters as the payment of *condottieri*.[74] Again during the king's prolonged absence from Naples in 1447 and 1448 he served on the triumvirate which advised the Duke of Calabria on the government of the kingdom.[75] In December 1438 he received a general commission to visit all the Aragonese territories, apart from Sicily, to collect moneys owing to the crown.[76] This business kept him away from Italy for almost two years—he returned there in October 1440[77]—during which time he also had dealings on the king's behalf with the Cortes of Catalonia.[78] He did not return to Spain until 1454 when Alfonso sent him to Valencia.

It is rather surprising that a man so well placed to win favours should have obtained for himself no office other than that of secretary. An order given in July 1452 as *locumtenens* of the chancellor[79] is a rare example of his acting in another capacity. Nor did he push the interests of his family to the degree one might have expected. The only relative to benefit greatly from his influence was his nephew Antoni Olzina: in December 1436 Alfonso, at his secretary's instigation, asked his wife to appoint Antoni to the post of secretary to her chamber in the kingdom of Sicily.[80] He did, however, use his position to foster the interest in Italian humanism which had been apparent as early as 1432 in Barcelona when he struck up a friendship with Barzizza.[81] He became a patron of scholars, among them Valla, who described him as 'quasi alter hoc seculo Maecenas',[82] and Beccadelli.[83] On the recommendation of Beccadelli he gave the young Giovanni Pontano a post in the writing office or *scribania*.[84]

[74] e.g. in a letter dated 26 Nov. 1436 the king informed Olzina that he was sending the chancellors of certain *condottieri* to him to collect their stipends. The secretary was to raise the money by loans from courtiers and officials (ACA Reg. 2900. 10ʳ).   [75] Cf. above, p. 100.

[76] ACA Reg. 2651. 115ᵛ, 3 Dec. 1438; ibid. 166ʳ, 7 Oct. 1440.

[77] ACA Reg. 2651. 115ᵛ.

[78] Ametller y Vinyas, *Alfonso V de Aragón*, iii. 648.

[79] Mazzoleni, *Fonti aragonesi*, iii. 10.

[80] ACA Reg. 2651. 46ʳ, 13 Dec. 1436. Antoni Olzina, a knight and preceptor of the order of S. Jaime de Spata, subsequently became *escriva de racio*. Cf. above, p. 88.   [81] Cf. above, p. 221.

[82] A letter of Valla describing the triumphal entry of Alfonso into Sulmona is addressed to Olzina and opens with the salutation, 'Laurentius Valla Olcine Mecenati salutem' (BNN MS. V F19, fol. 166).

[83] Beccadelli apostrophized him thus: 'I nunc, et Maecenas esto, spes musarum, praesidium decusque poetarum' (*Epistolae campanae*, fol. 94ᵛ.)

[84] Ametller y Vinyas, *Alfonso V de Aragón*, iii. 281.

Olzina's reticence in the scramble for offices reflects a rather modest fortune. Like all other officials he was constrained to lend the king money, but his financial succour to the crown consisted almost entirely of minor, short-term transactions, such as a loan of 150 ducats in February 1441[85] or underwriting a bill of exchange to the tune of 700 ducats in October 1436.[86] One important exception to these small-scale dealings was his acquisition of the barony of Huesca and Segura in Aragon. He acquired the barony from the crown in 1438 for 34,000 aragonese florins and administered it until 1455 when Alfonso redeemed it from him in order to resell it to Pedro de Urrea, Archbishop of Tarragona.[87] The transfer of the fief must have uncovered irregularities, for the procurator fiscal demanded that Olzina be prosecuted on a number of charges including the use of bribery and threats to thwart the redemption, ill-treatment of the inhabitants, and general neglect which had diminished the value of the barony. Another charge accused him of the malversation of public funds during his mission to Spain. These accusations against an old and trusted servant distressed the king who, instead of consenting to immediate action against the secretary, instructed his *locumtenens* in Spain, the King of Navarre, to conduct a full inquiry into the allegations, and emphasized that he was anxious to deal leniently with one who had served him long and faithfully.[88] Alfonso died before the investigation had been completed and Olzina ended his career overshadowed by suspicion.

No such eclipse befell Arnau Fonolleda, the younger of the king's principal secretaries. Like Olzina he came of a family established in royal service, for his father, Francesc Fonolleda, had held office in the Aragonese chancery.[89] Socially the family belonged to the urban patriciate—the 'Biga' class—of Barcelona.[90]

---

[85] ACA Reg. 2901. 5ᵛ. The loan was repaid in April 1441.

[86] ACA Reg. 2900. 2ʳ.

[87] ACA Reg. 2943. 49ᵛ, 10 Sept. 1455. The archbishop was to repay Olzina his 34,000 florins and give the king an additional 4,000 florins for the barony.

[88] ACA Reg. 2662. 83ʳ, 29 Oct. 1457, Alfonso to the King of Navarre. The moving spirit behind the attack on Olzina was Jacme de Pelaya of the Consilium Pecuniae (cf. above, p. 119). It was he who countersigned this letter 'ex speciali commissione'.

[89] A receipt drawn up by the notary Antoni Vinyes (19 May 1453) describes Fonolleda as sole heir of his mother Nicola, wife of Francesc Fonolleda (Barcelona, Notarial Archives; Vinyas, *Quintum manuale comune*).

[90] In a letter the council of Barcelona addressed Fonolleda as 'Fill legitim e natural de aquesta ciutat' (ACB Lletres Closes, 322. vi. 9. 1442. 98ᵛ).

Through the usual avenue of a notarial training and working as a writer in the chancery, Fonolleda had by 1436 achieved the rank of secretary.[91] Some of the earliest letters written by him from Gaeta were those under the secret seal which Aragonese procedure required to be written by one of the secretaries of the chamber,[92] but the title of secretary was apparently at this time reserved to Olzina under whose direction Fonolleda, as the junior notary of the chamber, performed his duties.[93] However, this situation lasted for only a few months. When Alfonso left Gaeta for Capua in November 1436, he took Fonolleda with him and Olzina remained behind. Henceforth the younger secretary took his instructions directly from the king. Moreover he it was who constantly followed Alfonso in his peregrinations about southern and central Italy while Olzina performed the duties of chief secretary to the governing councils left behind in the capital. As a result Fonolleda grew closer to the king and acquired a more intimate knowledge of affairs than Olzina. He undertook no missions abroad and left the court only for the briefest spells.[94] Thousands of documents in the extant registers of Alfonso's reign bear witness to his indefatigable application to his duties.

Unlike Olzina, Fonolleda did not rest content with the post of secretary. He held in addition the office of *conservator* of the royal patrimony in the kingdom of Sicily, and only relinquished it in 1446 for the greater dignity of *baile general* of Catalonia.[95] Further honour and revenue came his way in October 1448 when on the

---

[91] In 1435 (March) he was still a writer in the chancery and was then in Messina (Madurell Marimon, *Mensajeros barceloneses*, p. 77). Unlike Olzina, he escaped captivity in the Ponza disaster.

[92] e.g. ACA Reg. 2900, 2^r, 22 Apr. 1436, a letter for Johan de Gallach, regent of the treasury, certifying that he had sold grain belonging to the crown on the verbal instruction of the king. An annotation in the register shows that this letter was given under the secret seal.

[93] In the registers a number of letters bear the annotation, 'Arnaldus fonolleda mandato regio facto per secretarium' (e.g. ACA Reg. 2900. 5^r, 17 Oct. 1436) and 'Fonolleda mandato regio facto per Johannem Olzina secretarium' (e.g. ibid. 6^v, 25 Oct. 1436).

[94] From Castiglione in May 1448, Galceran Dusay wrote to the city council of Barcelona that the king had told him to hand the city's letters to a secretary named Valls, 'qui vuy es secretari e fa los fets de mossen Fonolleda' (Madurell Marimon, *Mensajeros barceloneses*, p. 284). But such absences occurred very rarely.

[95] ACA Reg. 2654, 52^v. The office of *conservator* passed to Guillem Pujades; cf. above, p. 172. After Alfonso's death Fonolleda returned to Spain to serve Juan II as *baile general* of Catalonia.

death of Ferrer Ram Alfonso appointed him protonotary for the Crown of Aragon ('in regnis nostris occiduis') and thus confirmed his status as principal secretary. His duties as *baile general* of Catalonia he had perforce to delegate to a regent. Another member of the family, Berenguer Arnau Fonolleda, became castellan of Crotone,[96] and in July 1443 the king requested a papal dispensation to permit Arnau Marquet Çatrilla, the secretary's nephew, to hold a curacy when only seventeen years old.[97] Fonolleda seems to have acquired no important properties, feudal or otherwise, but he did lend the king substantial sums of money; in June 1449 the crown owed him a total of 5,244 ducats.[98]

By virtue of the enormous number of letters and other documents which he drafted, Fonolleda must rank as one of the most considerable writers of his day. Many of his letters reflect that keen interest in humanistic studies which led Valla, when sending him a copy of Aesop's fables, to call him, 'tu vir litterarum amantissimus'.[99] It was at his request that Jacopo Curlo edited Facio's translation of the life of Alexander by Arrian.[100]

Although the Aragonese Household Ordinance provided for only two secretaries, the number so designated by Alfonso was much larger. A growth in the volume of government business over the course of a century in which the Aragonese empire had also greatly expanded perhaps accounts for this increase. In addition to Olzina and Fonolleda the following secretaries, appointed according to Aragonese usage, served Alfonso in the course of his reign in the kingdom of Naples: Antonio Nogueres, Pere Baucells, Joan Çaborgada, Jorge Catala, Luis Cescases, Jacme Escorta, Andreu Gaçull, Matteu Joan, Bernat Lopez, Pericone de Nasello, Bartolomeu de Reus, Blasco Steve, Gaspar Talamanca, Pere Salvator Valls, and Pere Vicens Vilardo. Not all, of course, were secretaries at the same time. Nothing more is known of Joan Çaborgada after he left for Milan in January 1443 to take part in

---

[96] ASN Div. Somm. I. 10. 26^v.

[97] ACA Reg. 2690, 33^r, 12 July 1443. Two years later he asked for a vacant canonry and priory in Tortosa for the same young man who had meanwhile graduated *bacheler en decrets* (ibid. 144^v. 4 Apr. 1445).

[98] ACA Real Patrimonio 2951. In December 1449 he advanced a further 1,000 ducats on a bill of exchange directed for payment to Pedro Gener, regent in the office of *baile general* of Catalonia (ACA Reg. 2720, 133^v, 13 Dec. 1449).

[99] Barozzi and Sabbadini, *Studi sul Panormita e sul Valla*, p. 80.

[100] Kristeller, *From Renaissance to Counter-Reformation*, p. 66. The manuscript of this work is now in the Vatican library.

negotiations between Alfonso and the pope.[101] Jorge Catala probably died late in 1443[102] and Escorta in 1445.[103] Others earned promotion from the rank of clerk or writer (*scriptor*) during the reign. Luis Cescases, a *scriva de manament*, had become a secretary by March 1443,[104] probably as a reward for his services at the Council of Basle and in negotiations with the anti-pope Felix V.[105] Andreu Gaçull, whose service as a writer extended back at least to 1432,[106] was not promoted until 1445 or 1446.[107] Pericone de Nasello was still a writer in October 1448.[108] Another latecomer was Pere Salvator Valls; in August 1446, when still a writer, he obtained the vacant lieutenancy in the office of *baile general* of Catalonia—perhaps through the good offices of Fonolleda;[109] rather less than three years later, as a secretary, he took to Siena 30,000 ducats to pay the *condottiere* Francesco Piccinino.[110] The status of Gaspar Talamanca is uncertain. After becoming a notary in the office of the Neapolitan chancellor,[111] he was designated secretary to the Duke of Calabria during the Tuscan campaign of 1452–3;[112] in 1454 he was serving in the office of the conservator general,[113] and in subsequent years his signature appears in a number of registers.[114] That not every writer sought promotion is

[101] Ametller y Vinyas, *Alfonso V de Aragón*, ii. 444. An order that he be given 50 ducats for the expenses of this mission is dated 22 Jan. 1443 (ACA Reg. 2901. 107ᵛ). He had undertaken another mission to Milan in August 1441 (Faraglia, *Storia della lotta*, p. 231).

[102] The latest document in the registers bearing his signature is dated 13 Aug. 1443 (ACA Reg. 2905. 200ᵛ).

[103] The post of 'scriba registri apud cameram Summarie' left vacant by his death was given to the surgeon Salvador de Santa Fe on 20 Dec. 1445 (ACA Reg. 2909. 166ʳ). He evidently died in debt to the crown for a commission dated 1 Mar. 1446 authorized the sale of certain property confiscated from his estate (ACA Reg. 2912. 44ʳ).

[104] He was a writer in 1437 (Minieri Riccio, 'Alcuni fatti di Alfonso I', p. 7). Cf. ACA Reg. 2690, 21ᵛ, 27 Mar. 1443.

[105] Giannone, *Istoria civile*, iii. 364.

[106] Ametller y Vinyas, *Alfonso V de Aragón*, i. 382.

[107] When Ram handed the seals to him on 8 Nov. 1444, Gaçull was still a writer (ACA Reg. 2720, 43ʳ). By March 1447, when Alfonso sent him to Rome, he had become a secretary (ACA Reg. 2698. 180ʳ, 19 Mar. 1447).

[108] Minieri Riccio, 'Alcuni fatti di Alfonso I', p. 246.

[109] ACA Reg. 2654, 80ʳ, 3 Aug. 1446. Valls nominated his father as his deputy in the office.   [110] ACA Reg. 2697. 18ᵛ, 10 Apr. 1449.

[111] ASN Priv. I. 27ᵛ.   [112] ACA Reg. 2550. 69ʳ, 29 Aug. 1452.

[113] Rogadeo, *Codice diplomatico*, p. 312.

[114] e.g. ACA Reg. 2946. Classified as 'Speciale Sicilie', this register covers the years 1456–7; ACA Reg. 2916. 28ʳ, 24 Oct. 1455. This letter is addressed to the 'Magister Justiciarius' of Sicily.

shown by the curious case of Francesch Montull, a *scriva de manament*, who was made a secretary against his will at the instance of certain persons who wanted his writer's office. When the intrigue came to light, the king revoked the appointment and restored Montull to his original office.[115]

Montull's experience reveals to what extent Alfonso had relaxed controls over the appointment of secretaries. As a result an unprecedented number of officials bearing that title acquired the power to write letters touching on offices, revenues, and regalian rights, and often it was discovered that a letter written by one secretary conflicted with that written by another.[116] To remedy this state of affairs, Alfonso was obliged in August 1452 to issue an edict forbidding the sealing of any letter of grace or favour ('carta gracia vel preces') not executed by one of four secretaries, namely Fonolleda, Olzina, Valls, and Matteu Joan. He had in effect divided his secretaries into two categories, the larger of which comprised only dignified clerks.

In addition to their routine duties most secretaries found themselves from time to time dispatched on missions to other Aragonese territories and to foreign states. Some indeed were more regularly employed on such business than in their secretarial office. Andreu Gaçull, for example, frequently transacted the king's business with Rome.[117] Pericone de Nasello had more varied assignments: he was sent to Leonello d'Este, Marquis of Ferrara, in 1445,[118] to the Cardinal of Aquileia, the papal chamberlain, in 1449,[119] to Florence and Rome in 1451,[120] and to France and Rome in 1452;[121] in 1456 he carried instructions for the Aragonese fleet operating against Genoa.[122] We have already noted the part played by Luis Cescases as Alfonso's envoy at the Council of Basle; he subsequently undertook missions to Spain,[123] Savoy, and

[115] ACA Reg. 2656. 128ᵛ, 15 June 1448.

[116] ACA Reg. 2917. 49ᵛ, 18 Aug. 1452: 'Cum a curia nostra de una eademque re pro diversis impetrantibus rescripta lettere . . . emanaverint, quod non aliter quam ex secretariorum multitudine contingit . . .'

[117] He was first sent to Eugenius IV in 1436 when that pontiff lived in exile in Florence (Ametller y Vinyas, *Alfonso V de Aragón*, iii. 557). He went to Rome in 1443 (ACA Reg. 2720. 46ʳ), 1447 (ACA Reg. 2699, 70ᵛ), 1451 (ACA Reg. 2697. 91ᵛ), and 1452 (ibid. 119ᵛ).

[118] ACA Reg. 2699. 2ʳ.   [119] ACA Reg. 2697. 38ʳ.

[120] Mazzoleni, *Il Codice Chigi*, pp. 77–8; ACA Reg. 2697. 109ᵛ.

[121] ACA Reg. 2697. 120ᵛ and 146ᵛ; ACA Reg. 2659. 73ʳ.

[122] ACA Reg. 2800. 1ʳ.

[123] He went to Spain in 1442 and again in 1443–4 (ACA Reg. 2690. 21ᵛ).

Burgundy.[124] De Reus went to Rome in September 1453[125] and in the following year to Catalonia.[126] If these diplomatic assignments are taken into account, it will be seen that the number of secretaries available for duty in the court was often well below the nominal strength.

Each secretary had one or more clerks assigned to him.[127] In addition the chancery disposed of a staff of writers (*scrivans* or *scriptores*) which had grown well beyond the number laid down by Peter the Ceremonious.[128] In such matters Alfonso adopted the pragmatic approach evident in the edict by which he permitted Queen Maria, his regent in Catalonia, to increase her staff of writers from seven to ten, and more if needed.[129] Nevertheless there was an establishment in this as in all other offices of the administration, and it could only be increased or exceeded by virtue of a royal edict.[130]

The Aragonese administration in Naples maintained the distinction between the writers of letters and other documents issued in the king's name (*scrivans de manament*) and the somewhat junior writers who kept the registers (*scrivans de registre*),[131] but very often references to these men do not specify to which category they belong. Most commonly they are described simply as belonging to the royal writing office or *regia scribania*. Thus Juan Peiro, who in one document appears as 'Johannes Peyro regius scriba',[132] is elsewhere identified as a 'scriva de munament del Senyor Rey';[133] similarly Rodrigo Vidal is sometimes a 'scriba'[134] and more precisely a 'scriba mandati nostri'.[135] As a general rule it can be assumed that those writers whose names figure in the registers as authors of letters were *scrivans de manament*, but it has

---

[124] ACA Reg. 2656. 175ᵛ, 9 July 1449, Alfonso to the Duke of Savoy; ibid. 176ʳ, Alfonso to the Duke of Burgundy.

[125] Minieri Riccio, 'Alcuni fatti di Alfonso I', p. 424.

[126] Madurell Marimon, *Mensajeros barceloneses*, p. 492.

[127] Pere Boquet in a letter to the council of Barcelona mentioned the clerks of Martorell and Matteu Joan (Madurell Marimon, *Mensajeros barceloneses*, p. 535).

[128] Cf. above, p. 218.   [129] ACA Reg. 2657, 50ʳ, 8 Apr. 1448.

[130] In April 1435 Jacobo de Caxino, a *scriva de manament*, resigned his office so that it might be given to Pere Morell (Madurell Marimon, *Mensajeros barceloneses*, p. 89).

[131] Cf. above, p. 218.

[132] Mazzoleni, *Il Codice Chigi*, p. 56, 18 July 1451.

[133] ACA Real Patrimonio 2011, 4 Sept. 1453.

[134] e.g. ACA Reg. 2907. 129ʳ, 28 July 1445.

[135] ACA Reg. 2914. 90ʳ, 15 Aug. 1450.

to be remembered that *scrivans de registre* sometimes undertook
that duty. The Neapolitan chancery seems not to have made any
such distinction between its clerks. A Francesco della Torina 'de
nostra cancellaria' was appointed in August 1447 to the office of
'regestratorem scriptorem et annotatorem omnium et quorum-
cumque privilegiorum litterarum provisionum et rescriptorum
impetrandorum per quoscunque homines et personas ad nos
et nostram curiam confluentes seu de nostro mandato a nostra
curia emanantium tam graciam quam iusticiam continentium et
tam parvo quam magno sigillis munitarum'.[136] He received as
salary the 12 *oncie* a year which had been assigned to the office in
the reigns of Ladislas and Giovanna II. What is not clear is
whether Alfonso maintained a separate chancery secretariat for
the affairs of his Neapolitan kingdom staffed by clerks such as della
Torina, or whether Aragonese *scrivans* and Italian clerks served
in a common writing office. Since none of the secretaries dealt
exclusively with Neapolitan affairs, the latter alternative seems
the most likely.

Several writers won promotion to the rank of secretary.[137] Others
increased their income and influence by acquiring additional
offices which they could exercise by deputy. Bernat Lober held
the post of treasurer to the court of the Vicaria,[138] Juan Espanit
that of *rubricator* in the *Sommaria*;[139] Juan Steve was *credencerius
ordinarius* in the customs office of the city of Naples.[140] Others
found their supplementary offices further afield; Sergio de Marinis
as *magister actorum* to the justiciar of Abruzzo Ulteriore,[141]
Francisco Maynes as *notarius credencerius* in the salt pans of
Salerno.[142] Several writers found themselves employed as royal
agents and messengers in matters of some gravity. When Alfonso
received a report that the kings of England and France intended
to join forces to deprive the Duke of Burgundy of Flanders,

---

[136] ACA Reg. 2912. 114^r, 4 Aug. 1447.

[137] Cf. above, p. 233. To the examples cited there may be added Bernat Lopez,
a 'scriva de registre de nostra cort' (ACA Reg. 2901. 72^r, 15 Sept. 1442), who
became a secretary.   [138] Cf. above, p. 151.

[139] ACA Reg. 2902. 224^r, Appointment dated 25 July 1444. The *rubricator*
summarized privileges, letters, etc. issued by the Sommaria and entered these
summaries in a register for reference purposes.

[140] ACA Reg. 2902. 25^r, Appointment dated 7 June 1442.

[141] ACA Reg. 2914. 90^r. In August 1450 this post was taken from him and
given to another writer, Rodrigo Vidal.

[142] ACA Reg. 2906. 44^v, Appointment dated 22 Dec. 1443.

Holland, and Brabant so that these might be given to England as compensation for Normandy and Guienne, he sent the writer Pere Pugeriol to the duke with a warning that he should be on his guard.[143] Another writer Michel Garcia went to Genoa in September 1444 to assist Bernat de Requesens in his negotiations with the republic.[144] One of the Italian writers, Domenico de Caiaccia, cut more of a military than a clerkly figure. After fighting for the Aragonese cause against the Angevins, he continued serving Alfonso in his Italian campaigns and not until 1449 did he finally exchange sword for pen.[145]

Documents emanating from the curia were written in the king's name. Alfonso himself wrote a few letters of a peculiarly personal or confidential nature and a number of promissory notes which can be identified by the phrase 'escrita de mi mano' before the date and signature.[146] All other documents were drafted by a secretary or writer on the instruction of the king or of some body or person authorized to act on his behalf. The identity of that authority and of the secretary or writer appears in the formula of the 'mandavit' at the foot of every document; there is stated who authorized the writing and who was responsible for the drafting. For the majority of documents drafted, written and registered by the secretaries and writing office that authority was the king himself, as indicated by the formula, 'Dominus Rex mandavit . . .'. Very occasionally in the earlier years of the reign a direct verbal instruction from the king sufficed; letters thus authorized bore the annotation, 'de mandato regio oretenus facto'.[147] Much correspondence of a political and diplomatic nature must always have originated in this manner, but it fell out of use for documents bearing upon the rights, revenues, and property of the crown; these came to require a written and sealed instruction.[148] Very often, of course, the

---

[143] ACA Reg. 2697. 125ʳ, 12 Mar. 1452, Instructions for Pugeriol.

[144] Minieri Riccio, 'Alcuni fatti di Alfonso I', p. 244.

[145] In January 1449 he assumed the office of *scriptor fiscalis* in the Vicaria which had been granted him when he was still busy in the army (ACA Reg. 2913. 85ᵛ, 12 Jan. 1449). He had also acquired the post of porter in the chancery (ibid. 64ᵛ, 23 Sept. 1448).

[146] Many of Alfonso's autograph letters are registered in ACA Reg. 2940. All are written in Castilian.

[147] e.g. ACA Reg. 2902. 73ʳ, 16 Mar. 1441: 'De mandato regio oretenus facto Lucas de Caramanico'; Faraglia, *Storia della lotta*, p. 377, Document dated 6 Mar. 1437; Rogadeo, *Codice diplomatico*, p. 12, Document dated 18 Sept. 1436.

[148] Cf. below, pp. 244 ff.

authorization came only nominally from the king who was in fact giving effect to a decision reached on his behalf by a competent official. Hence we find employed such formulae as 'Dominus Rex deliberatione consilii mandavit...',[149] 'Dominus Rex mandavit michi Andreu Gacull ad relacionem Arnaldi Fonolleda secretarii',[150] and 'Dominus Rex facta sibi relatione per prenominatos (scil. Claver, Falco, Besalu) mandavit...'.[151]

The royal council too through its president could command the secretaries. A letter ordering the viceroy of Benevento to give effect to a judgement of the council bears the following subscription: 'Matheus de Girifalco ex sententia lata in dicto sacro regio consilio et vidit hanc Episcopus Valentinus presidens in eodem.'[152] A later formula, belonging to the time when the Bishop of Urgell was president of the council, reveals more clearly the *ex officio* authority of the president in relation to the secretaries: 'Johannes Peyro mandato regio facto per Episcopum Urgellensem, Sacri Consilii Presidentem qui has vidit.'[153] Letters based on this form of authority occur frequently in the registers. Much less common are those ordered by other counsellors by virtue of a commission received from the council, for normally that body took collective responsibility for sentences. One such exception was the privilege conferring the powers of guardian and administrator on Francesco de Balzo, son of the Duke of Andria whom Platamone and Beccadelli had certified insane; it was written by Fonolleda, 'mandato regio facto per babtistam de plathamone vicecancellarium et Anthonium de bononia l.d. consiliarios quibus fuit commissum et has viderunt'.[154]

The vice-chancellor, who in the latter instance acted on behalf of the council, can more frequently be found instructing the secretaries *ex officio* as head of the chancery. Following an investigation into titles to the silk toll in Calabria conducted by Platamone, Pietro Guillermo Rocca, and the procurator fiscal, one of the claimants received a privilege issued on the authority of the vice-chancellor:

[149] Rogadeo, *Codice diplomatico*, p. 50, Document dated 5 Dec. 1436.
[150] ACA Reg. 2651. 2^r. 17 Dec. 1437.
[151] ACA Reg. 2917. 13^v, 18 June 1452, Document drafted by Fonolleda.
[152] ACA Reg. 2902. 77^r, 21 Aug. 1442.
[153] Mazzoleni, *Il Codice Chigi*, p. 161, 19 Nov. 1451. Cf. 'Antonellus de Ipolito mandato regio facto per Episcopum Urgellensem Presidentem in consilio qui has vidit' (Rogadeo, *Codice diplomatico*, p. 300, 27 Dec. 1453). I have corrected Rogadeo's transcription of this clause.
[154] ACA Reg. 2904. 115^v, 30 Dec. 1443.

'Johannes Bellas Flos mandato regio facto per B. Plathamone qui has vidit.'[155] An order to the stratigot of Salerno dealing with the guardianship and marriage of a young girl was likewise written at the behest of the vice-chancellor: 'Arnaldus Castello mandato regio facto per Babtistam de Plathamone Vicecancellarium qui has vidit tractatas sub hac forma iam signatas.'[156] Platamone's successor Valenti Claver exercised the same authority,[157] and had indeed used it earlier on those occasions when, in Platamone's absence, he assumed control of the chancery as regent.[158] In other words, a large number of letters initiating judicial action by royal officials were drawn up by the writing office on the instruction of the vice-chancellor or whoever happened to be acting for him. This was in accordance with Aragonese procedure. The chancellor of Naples initiated action in the writing office only as rector of the university of Naples in which capacity he had the power to make certain appointments. Even that function he usually delegated to a deputy. Thus we find Cicco Antonio Guindazzo acting for him in appointing Nicola de Statis as notary to the College of Doctors. To the letter of appointment the secretary Petrucci appended the following authority: 'Antonellus Petrocia mandato regio facto per locumtenentem cancellarium ex officii potestate.'[159] Reference has already been made to the powers exercised by the protonotary, chief physician, and chief chaplain in the drawing up of certain diplomas conferring professional status.[160]

From whatever source the mandate for the drafting of a document might come, a fair amount of latitude in the interpretation of that mandate was left to the writer, unless the document happened to be in common form, in which case standard formulae were employed. Fonolleda managed to slip in an additional privilege for his native city in a memorial which he had prepared for the king,[161]

[155] Ibid. 88ᵛ, 8 July 1443.

[156] Mazzoleni, *Il Codice Chigi*, pp. 47–9, dated 18 July 1451.

[157] e.g. an order to the captain of Atri to investigate a case of alleged unlawful occupation of a house. 'Johannes Oliver mandato regio facto per Valentinum Claver Vicecancellarium qui has vidit traditas iam signatas' (ibid., pp. 300–1, dated 25 Apr. 1452).

[158] e.g. an order to officials in the Abruzzi to dispense summary justice in a claim for debt brought by merchants of Teramo. 'Petrus de Monterubeo mandato regio facto per Valentinum Claver Regentem Cancellarium qui has vidit' (ibid., pp. 65–6, dated 17 Apr. 1451); cf. above, p. 143.

[159] ASN Priv. I. 181ᵛ, 26 Oct. 1454.   [160] Cf. above, p. 219.

[161] ACB Cart. Com., vol. 14, fol. 71, Naples, 11 May 1444.

and Olzina discussed with the envoys of Barcelona the drafting of instructions for an embassy to England.[162] Vespasiano da Bisticci records another incident which illustrates the discretion left to a secretary.[163] Gerardo Gambacorte had obtained from the king letters of reprisal against Florentines for property which he had lost in Tuscany. He proceeded to seize goods from several Florentine merchants in Naples who then asked the ambassador of Florence, Manetti, to intercede with the king. Manetti went to Foggia, where Alfonso was hunting, and early one morning, before the king left for the chase, managed to get him to give instructions that the matter should be dealt with as Manetti desired. The secretary Martorell, who was to write the necessary letters, showed great reluctance to take any action. At first he argued that he could do nothing until he had consulted the king on his return from hunting. When Martorell and Manetti had together seen the king and received confirmation of the earlier instruction, the secretary raised new objections saying that Manetti had not properly understood what had been said because Alfonso had spoken in Castilian. To this the Florentine replied that he had understood perfectly well and was ready to go back to the king yet again if Martorell insisted. Only then did Martorell consent to write the letters in the desired form.

To a certain extent the king was able to control the action of his secretaries by reading and signing the documents they produced. This he did with great care where important state papers were concerned, but a mass of routine and minor papers received only cursory attention or none at all. Indeed it is not certain that the signature 'Rex Alfonsus', which appears on every document issued by his chancery, was always written by the king himself. The earlier Angevin rulers of Naples had signed documents only in special circumstances,[164] and even though the royal signature had become commoner in the time of Ladislas and Giovanna II, it was still regarded at the beginning of Alfonso's reign as an exception. In a privilege given to Barletta on 18 September 1436 we find these words: 'pro ipsarum validiori robore subscripsimus et dedimus propria manu nostra ritu vel observancia nostre Curie quacumque

---

[162] ACB Cart. Com., vol. 14, fol. 119, Naples, 2 Aug. 1444.
[163] 'Vita del Re Alfonso', pp. 395–6.
[164] B. Capasso, *Inventario cronologico-sistematico dei registri angioini* (Naples, 1894), p. LV.

contraria non obstante'.[165] A similar formula had been used in documents of Giovanna II which bore that queen's signature,[166] and it continues to appear fairly regularly in the Aragonese chancery up to 1439. Its subsequent disappearance might either mean that the king signed nothing—an unlikely development—or that his signature had become routine and therefore required no explanation. Even though the latter explanation seems the more plausible, it would have meant that on most documents the king's signature was a mere formality. Hence the value attached to promissory notes written entirely in his own hand, and his habit of writing postscripts to letters when he wished to emphasize the importance of the contents. On a letter to Queen Maria about the arrest of the *justicia* of Aragon Alfonso added these words: 'Avet aquesta letra como si fuesse de mi mano car yo la uviera scrita sino porque es mucha scritura, mas porque conoscays que lo quiero asi por esto e querido fazer estos renglones de mi mano porque conoscays que esta es mi intencio.'[167]

While the king was able, albeit with some difficulty, to control documents dealing with political and diplomatic affairs, he could not cope with the much greater mass of papers that concerned the details of offices, revenues, and properties. In the first years of his reign all letters touching upon the finances of the crown had to be presented in the Sommaria for scrutiny and registration.[168] An order of 21 January 1444 tightened up this procedure by directing that no warrant for the payment of money should be sealed unless it bore the signature of the head of the Sommaria—the chamberlain or his *locumtenens*.[169] Another decree of July 1444 required the countersignature of the chamberlain on all letters of grace, privileges, and letters authorizing disbursement of moneys.[170] This procedure evidently met with some resistance and evasion for it was reiterated in another edict published in April 1445.[171] On a few occasions the chamberlain himself, the Count of Loreto,

---

[165] Rogadeo, *Codice diplomatico*, p. 22.
[166] Minieri Riccio, *Saggio di codice diplomatico*, ii. 72.
[167] ACA Reg. 2651. 136ʳ, 7 Nov. 1439.
[168] e.g. on a letter granting a reduction in the *collectae* to Trani there appears this note: 'presentatum in Regia Camera Summarie coram Domino Magno Camerario die 26 februarii vi indictione et annotatum per me Bernardum de Raymo' (Rogadeo, *Codice diplomatico*, p. 42).
[169] Gentile, 'Lo stato napoletano' (1937), p. 23, n. 2.
[170] ACA Reg. 2904, 165ᵛ, 30 July 1444.
[171] Gentile, 'Lo stato napoletano' (1937), p. 32.

appeared at court and affixed his countersignature to documents,[172] but the task usually fell to his *locumtenens*, Iñigo de Avalos. If the frequency of his signature is any guide, this Castilian favourite of the king discharged his duty most conscientiously both as *locumtenens* and, after 1449, as chamberlain.[173] In the absence of de Avalos—as, for example, in October 1445 when he had gone on the king's business to Milan—Valenti Claver often assumed the function of *locumtenens* to the chamberlain;[174] after de Avalos became chamberlain his regular *locumtenens* was Nicola Antonio de Monti. Since neither de Avalos nor any of the other *locumtenentes* regularly worked in the Sommaria, it is to be presumed that they affixed their signatures only after the document in question had been cleared by that office.

From August 1447 the same classes of documents that required clearance from the Sommaria needed also the countersignature of the conservator general.[175] From August 1452 many of them could be written by only four of the secretaries.[176] Even then experience must have shown that the controls were inadequate for from 1 January 1455 a further annotation, this time by the king himself, was required for all 'cartas regias gratias vel remissiones vel alias largitiones contenentes, aut super aliquo dubio in provinciis quorumvis regnorum nostrorum inter fiscum et privatum occurrente aliquid disponentes'.[177] The words 'Yo he leydo la presente e placeme que assin se faza', written in the king's own hand, henceforth validated all such documents.[178] A further edict issued on 1 June 1455 extended the control to letters patent which, it was stated, had been omitted from the scope of the first edict by a clerical error.[179] Bills of exchange had always borne the king's

---

[172] e.g. a privilege pardoning Andrea de Sanctis a debt of 5,000 ducats bears the subscription, 'vidit francisco de aquino comes laurenti mag. cam.' It is dated Castelnuovo, 11 Sept. 1444 (ACA Reg. 2902. 227ᵛ). A similar 'vidit' appears on the royal assent to a dowry settlement issued from Foggia on 10 Apr. 1445 (ACA Reg. 2907. 129ʳ). In the instructions given to the chamberlain it was required that he should take 'notitiam et conscientiam conditionis et status iurium fisci ac redditionum et proventuum regalium' (ASN Div. Somm. i. 52 (bis), 120ʳ).

[173] De Avalos countersigned a document as *locumtenens* of the chamberlain as early as 5 June 1444 (Rogadeo, *Codice diplomatico*, p. 159).

[174] On 15 Dec. 1447 he signed 'pro locumtenente magni camerarii' (ACA Reg. 2908, 195ʳ).   [175] Cf. above, p. 206.

[176] Cf. above, p. 234.   [177] ACA Reg. 2661. 82ʳ, 22 Dec. 1454.

[178] One may find variations of the spelling such as 'Yo e leydo la presente e plazeme que asi se facza'.

[179] ACA Reg. 2916. 19ᵛ.

personal subscription in a more extended form: 'Yo juro e prometo en la mi buena fe real que assi sera complido como de suso es scripto e por mayor seguredat he querido screvir esto de mi mano.'[180] As a result of these edicts Alfonso had to carry a great burden of reading and signing during the last three years of his life for there were now few documents which could issue from the chancery without his scrutiny. Vespasiano da Bisticci tells a story, gathered probably from Manetti, of a pile of letters being taken to the king for reading and signature just as he was preparing to go to bed.[181] While the procedure may have eliminated some abuses, it smacks of that chronic mistrust of the king's own servants which was concurrently manifest in the operations of the Councils of Money and Subornation.[182] It also created a bottle-neck which effectively slowed down the whole machinery of state.[183]

Having passed through the stages of drafting, correction, approval, and signature, a document received the final stamp of authentication—the seal; without that it had no force or value. The most important of these seals was the bull. Charles I of Anjou had introduced a golden bull.[184] The Aragonese Household Ordinance describes two seals of this type—a golden bull and a lead bull: the former was affixed on grants of great distinction, and the latter to laws, constitutions, grants of baronies, and major grants to towns. Alfonso evidently intended to have a golden bull made for his Neapolitan kingdom, for when making use of the Aragonese bull to seal the privilege investing Alfonso de Cardona with the county of Reggio he explained that this had been done 'cum cugni bullae aureae huius Regni non dum sculpti sint'.[185] In fact such a bull was never made, and the Neapolitan great seal served where in Aragon the bull would have been employed. So when in 1452 Alfonso de Cardona's son and heir was confirmed

---

[180] e.g. ACA Reg. 2651. 41ʳ, Bill dated 11 Dec. 1436.
[181] 'Vita del Re Alfonso', p. 403.   [182] Cf. above, pp. 119–23.
[183] Cf. the complaint of Pere Boquet that 'aquest senyor [scil. Alfonso] se atura mayorment que aci ni vicicanceller ni secretari una tela no metrien que lo Senyor Rey no'n man', Letter to Barcelona, 23 June 1457 (Madurell Marimon, *Mensajeros barceloneses*, p. 589).
[184] Durrieu, *Les Archives angevines*, i. 182. It had been used on the privilege creating the son of Charles II Prince of Taranto (Minieri Riccio, *Saggio* (*Supplemento*), p. 72).
[185] ACA Reg. 2917. 27ᵛ, 17 Nov. 1439. The golden bull of Aragon was again used when Alfonso confirmed de Cardona in possession of the county on 1 Mar. 1443.

in possession of the county of Reggio, the seal used was the great seal of Naples.[186] The Aragonese lead bull appears never to have been affixed to documents of a purely Neapolitan content, though it was used in April 1455 for the instrument appointing the envoys who swore obedience to Calixtus III in the king's name.[187]

A great seal for the kingdom of Naples was ready for use by April 1436. Previously Alfonso had employed a variety of seals. A grant of 8 *oncie* a year to Caterina de Fusco and her brother Pietro made in Gaeta on 10 Feburary 1436 had been sealed 'nostro comuni sigillo negociorum Sicile ultra farum cum alia pro nunc sigilla non habeamus'.[188] To confirm a grant of privileges to Trani on 20 March 1436 he used the secret seal 'cum alia impromptu non habeamus'.[189] A privilege issued on 13 April 1436, however, bore the new Neapolitan seal.[190] Thereafter it was affixed to all privileges, graces, letters of justice, constitutions, and edicts concerning that kingdom and its subjects. A proclamation of 13 March 1456 emphasized its status by requiring that all letters patent not bearing the great seal should be submitted to the chancellor within three months for reissue with that seal.[191] Like the great seal of the Angevins, the great seal of Aragon and papal bulls, Alfonso's great seal was attached to documents by threads of red and yellow silk, hence its name, 'magnum sigillum pendens'.

Much administrative and diplomatic correspondence was sealed with the secret seal[192] which in Aragon, and probably also in Naples, could only be applied to letters that bore the signet seal or some other mark approved by the king. The chamberlain kept the secret seal. Besides serving as a warrant for the secret seal, the signet, the king's personal seal, was also frequently used as a single seal on a variety of promissory notes of a confidential nature. For example, it was used on a letter in which Alfonso promised the writer Arnau Castello that, in the event of his armies taking Florence, Castello should be appointed 'de officio scribanie

---

[186] ACA Reg. 2917. 27ᵛ, 17 Nov. 1439. The date of the confirmation was 24 July 1452.   [187] ACA Reg. 2660. 141ʳ, 28 Apr. 1455.

[188] Faraglia, *Storia della lotta*, p. 55, n. 2.

[189] Rogadeo, *Codice diplomatico*, p. 7.   [190] Ibid., p. 8.

[191] ACA Reg. 2917. 171ʳ.

[192] The secret seal was sometimes placed on warrants for payment—e.g. ACA Reg. 2901. 66ʳ, 12 July 1442, the regent of the treasury is ordered to repay a loan on presentation of letters under the secret seal.

viceregiatus aut gubernacionis totius communitatis Florencie'.[193]
At the end of his life the signet sealed Alfonso's will.[194]

Two other seals remain to be considered: the small or round seal
(*parvus* or *rotundus*) and the square seal (*quadratus*). The small seal
served to authenticate a great variety of documents: minor letters
of justice,[195] instructions to royal commissioners,[196] grants of
limited duration such as annual offices and exemption from customs
duties,[197] provisions concerning the salaries of officials,[198] promissory notes,[199] and in fact for most documents carrying the
status of royal warrants, commanding officials both high and low,
but not having the permanent character which called for the great
seal.[200] There are even documents bearing the small seal which
are expressly stated to be held of no less status than if they bore
the great seal. In a privilege for Molfetta promising that no
Neapolitan should be appointed to any office in that city appears
this clause: 'quas impressione nostri parvi sigilli valituras ac si
essent magno pendente maiestatis nostre sigillo debite roborate
iussimus communiri'.[201] The reason for using the small instead of

---

[193] ACA Reg. 2656. 81ᵛ, 13 Oct. 1447. Cf. promise of office in Puglia for
Jacobo Antonio Silvio (Rogadeo, *Codice diplomatico*, p. 369, 11 Nov. 1456); an
agreement to buy salt from Francesco Antonio de Bertolini against payment in
Barcelona (ACA Reg. 2900, 21ʳ, 22 Jan. 1437).

[194] ASN Priv. I. 186ʳ, 26 June 1458. In the will the signet is described as
'sigillo annli Domini Rogio in quo sculpta erat ethgies maiestatis sue in solio
suo sedentis'.

[195] e.g. ACA Reg. 2913, 112ᵛ, 15 Apr. 1449, Letter for the inhabitants of the
barony of Carapella withdrawing a case from a judge declared partial.

[196] e.g. the instructions given to Simone Cazzetta to collect the 1 per cent
shipping toll in Terra di Bari and Capitanata (ASN Fasc. Com. 58ᵛ, 11 Sept.
1445).

[197] e.g. the customs exemption granted to Jean Morant, ambassador of the
Duke of Burgundy: 'presentes licteras parvo nostro sigillo in pede munitas
vobis propterea dirigentes penes ultimum passuum custodem in confinibus
Regni remansuras' (Mazzoleni, *Il Codice Chigi*, pp. 6–7, 27 June 1451).

[198] e.g. a letter authorizing Luis Amigo to receive his salary as captain of
Montagna di Abruzzo and Cittaducale in Venetian ducats (ibid., pp. 4–5,
13 June 1451).

[199] e.g. for Marino de Andrillo and Nicola Amerosio promising them the toll
on iron etc. in Molfetta and undertaking to issue a privilege under the great seal
at their request (Rogadeo, *Codice diplomatico*, p. 79, 4 June 1440).

[200] Most of the documents registered in the Chigi codex bore the small seal.

[201] Cf. 'Has autem litteras parvo nostro sigillo munitas prefate universitati in
testimonium premissorum concedentes, quas tamen roboris vindicare decerni-
mus ac si essent in carta pergamena scripte et magno maiestatis nostre pendenti
sigillo munite', Document dated 31 May 1445, 'reservato beneplacito' (Rogadeo,
Codice diplomatico, p. 162).

the great seal in such cases seems to be that the favours granted were subject to revocation at the king's pleasure, whereas grants under the great seal were normally of a permanent character. This difference between the two seals was reflected in the physical appearance of the documents to which they were affixed, for while all letters under the great seal were written on parchment, most of those under the small seal were written on paper. One further important use made of the small seal was to authenticate documents under the great seal which could not be affixed to any letter that did not bear the *parvus*. It was, in short, the common administrative seal.

The function of the square seal (*quadratus*) is less clear. It seems to have been employed exclusively by the Sommaria as a measure of control over documents that authorized the disbursement or alienation of crown funds and revenues. Normally, therefore, such documents required both the small and the square seal. A letter to the Sommaria notifying it of a remission of tax and a consequent adjustment in the accounts of the treasurer in Terra di Bari bore both seals;[202] so too did an order to the chamberlain to observe a grant made to Francesco Orsini.[203] In September 1444 the chamberlain ordered those who managed the seals not to affix the great seal to any letters 'fiscalem pecuniam aut alias quascumque res fiscales tangentes nisi prius videritis illas sigillatas parvo et quadrato sigillis'.[204] In his instructions the treasurer general was told to accept the small and square seals as adequate warrant for disbursing money.[205] For some years many letters required all three seals—great, small, and square seals—to the considerable inconvenience and expense of the recipients,[206] until the parliament of 1456 petitioned that the use of the *quadratus* be restricted

---

[202] Rogadeo, *Codice diplomatico*, p. 104, 31 Dec. 1442.

[203] Ibid., p. 110, 3 Jan. 1443: 'Presentes autem literas parvo et quadrato ad usum fiscalis pecunie deputato sigillis nostris munitas.'

[204] ASN Framm. Com. Somm. 16ʳ, 12 Sept. 1444.

[205] ASN Div. Somm. I. 52 (bis), 38ᵛ, probably the instructions for Capdevila.

[206] A privilege dated 4 June 1447 granting the royal page Francesco de Bandino an annual provision of 200 ducats was sealed with the three seals. A notary who later copied the document noted: 'Presens copia fuit abstracta ab originali privilegio in carta membrana scripto manu domini Regis subsignato sigillo eiusdem Maiestatis inpendenti ac aliis sigillis quadrato et rotundo in pede munito' (Rogadeo, *Codice diplomatico*, p. 193). Cf. privilege for Antonello de Fiore of the writing office, 23 May 1445 (ASN Fasc. Com. 119ʳ) and another for Beccadelli dated 22 Oct. 1455 (Toppi, *De origine tribunalium*, iii. 266).

to those documents that had required it in earlier reigns.[207] In reply Alfonso abolished the seal altogether.[208] The development of countersignatures had greatly diminished the regulatory importance of the seals, as the same reply to the parliamentary petition emphasized when it went on to stipulate that for the future all privileges, letters of grace and justice should bear only one seal,[209] which meant in effect either the great or small seal. As a result of this measure it became possible to affix the great seal to most documents without a prior sealing with the small seal.

In addition to the seals of the kingdom of Naples, the chancery also controlled those of the Crown of Aragon and the kingdom of Sicily. For the Crown of Aragon there were, besides the gold and lead bulls, the great seal and the minor or common seal, the latter being employed in much the same manner as the small seal of Naples. A *debitorium* for 6,806 ducats payable by bills of exchange on a clerical subsidy in Catalonia was sealed with it,[210] so too was a letter authorizing Matteu Pujades to raise money by the sale of annuities in the Spanish kingdoms.[211] A privilege regulating Beccadelli's salary charged on the Sicilian revenues was sealed with the great or common seal of that kingdom.[212]

Custody of the Aragonese seals, with the exception of the secret seal, belonged to the protonotary, so we find them controlled successively by Pere Ram, Ferrer Ram, and Arnau Fonolleda. Some of the registers contain notes recording the transfer of the seals to and from Ram on the occasion of his return to or departure from the court.[213] Ultimate responsibility for the great and small seals of Naples lay with the chancellor; in practice each was managed separately by subordinate officials. For the small seal

---

[207] '... dello quatro [sic] se debia ponere ad quelle scripture che se accostumava in tempo deli Rey soy predecessori . . .' (ASN Div. Somm. I. 52 (bis), 171ʳ).

[208] '... Regia Maiestas providet pro beneficio rey puplice regni huius quod sigillum quatrum deletur et annichiletur . . .' (ibid.).

[209] '... proviso quod in quolibet privilegio vel lettera gracie aut justicie non apponatur nisi unum sigillum . . .' (ibid.).

[210] ACA Reg. 2720. 5ᵛ, 4 Mar. 1444. The seal is described as 'sigillo nostro minori Aragonum'. [211] Ibid. 15ʳ, 21 Apr. 1444.

[212] M. C. Tirrito, *Nuovi documenti sul Panormita* (Catania, 1900), p. 196. In the privilege dated February 1450 the seal is referred to as 'lu so sigillu grandi comuni di Sicilia pendenti'.

[213] e.g. 'Anno domini MCCCCxxxxiiii die viii Novemb. apud liciam territorio ypsigri ducat. calabrie fuerunt assignata sigilla Regia unacum officio prothonot. Andree gaculli Regio scribe ac dictam prothonotarii officium regenti per absenciam prothonotarii' (ACA Reg. 2720. 43ʳ).

a single custodian seems to have sufficed; in 1447 that function belonged to one of the clerks, Juan Espanit.[214] The more august character of the great seal and the fees attached to it called for a more elaborate organization and no less than five officials shared in its management: a *conservator*, a *sigillator*, a *credencerius*, a *taxator*, and a *receptor*. The first was general custodian of the seal; the second saw to the use of the seal; the third kept accounts; the fourth assessed fees; and the fifth received the fees. When the great seal was first made Giovanni de Uliante became its custodian,[215] but for most of the reign it was in the care of the *rationalis* Nicola de Statis,[216] who in October 1457 acquired too the office of *credencerius* on the resignation of Tommaso de Vaia de Cilento.[217] The offices of *sigillator* and *receptor* were likewise given to one and the same person during the last decade of the reign; firstly to Jacobo de Villaspinosa[218] and then to the clerk Antonello Petrucci.[219] Bernat Lopez was *taxator* of the great seal through most of the reign.[220] For the Aragonese seals the clerk Joan Peyro acted as *receptor* during the time that Fonolleda was protonotary.[221]

The fees collected from the recipients of documents bearing seals constituted an important source of revenue. In the kingdom of Naples it provided funds from which the king's secretaries were paid;[222] in Aragon the money contributed towards the salaries of

---

[214] A privilege dated 12 June 1447 conferring citizenship of Naples on Espanit, his family, and descendants describes him as 'familiaris scribe parvique sigilli nostri Regni Sicilie citra farum custodis' (ACA Reg. 2912. 68ᵛ). He had earlier been appointed rubricator of all letters under the great and small seals.

[215] On 25 Oct. 1436 de Uliante was instructed to make a payment from the receipts of the great seal 'quod tenetis' (ACA Reg. 2900. 6ᵛ).

[216] A privilege dated 23 Sept. 1448 describes de Statis as 'magni sigilli regni nostri Sicilie citra farum conservatorem' (ACA Reg. 2913. 64ᵛ). Cf. ASN Priv. I. 131ʳ, 6 Apr. 1454; Rogadeo, *Codice diplomatico*, p. 312.

[217] ACA Reg. 2917. 165ʳ, 15 Oct. 1457, Letter of appointment.

[218] On 20 June 1452 he was 'sigillator et conservator regestrorum et receptor sigilli' (Mazzoleni, *Fonti aragonesi*, iii. 1). In September 1444 Jacobo de Civita had been 'sigillatore regiarum litterarum magno regio pendenti sigillo' (ASN Framm. Com. Somm. 16ʳ, 12 Sept. 1444).

[219] Petrucci was appointed *receptor* in July or August 1452 (Rogadeo, *Codice diplomatico*, p. 454). Cf. Toppi, *De origine tribunalium*, i. 201.

[220] He was appointed on 16 Mar. 1442 (ACA Reg. 2904. 48ᵛ). Rogadeo (*Codice diplomatico*, p. 454) prints extracts from a register of fees of the great seal presented in the Sommaria by Lopez on 31 Aug. 1456.

[221] '... receptor iurium sigilli pro magnifico viro domino Arnaldo Fonolleda prothonotario' (Madurell Marimon, *Mensajeros barceloneses*, p. 360, 26 Nov. 1450).

[222] Beccadelli's salary as a secretary was paid from the revenues of the great seal; cf. above, p. 223, n. 33.

writers and chaplains. Because of the absence of the king and his protonotary from the Spanish kingdoms and the employment there of the seals of his *locumtenentes*, Queen Maria and the King of Navarre, the revenue of the seals from that source declined drastically until in 1446 Alfonso ordered half the proceeds from the seals of the *locumtenentes* to be remitted to Naples through the prothonotary.[223] Ferrer Ram managed to collect altogether 7,000 *solidi* to carry back to Naples,[224] a very small sum indeed considering that Fonolleda alone was supposed to receive 6,000 *solidi* annually from that source.[225] In addition to these remittances from Spain, the protonotary of Aragon collected directly the sealing fees for the Aragonese seals administered by the court in Italy. Thus we find Fonolleda, as his deputy, collecting 169s. as 'dret de sagell' on a safe-conduct for Barbary merchants visiting Aragonese territories, 226s. 6d. for twenty-nine provisions concerning the office of *baile general* in Valencia, and 31s. for an edict on the salaries of royal officials.[226]

In both Aragon and Naples elaborate tables of fees prescribed the charges for sealing various kinds of letters.[227] The charges varied depending on whether the letter was in common form, the number and condition of the persons benefiting, and the value of the benefit conferred. It was this last criterion that led to most disputes between those responsible for the seals and the beneficiaries, for the former, having a personal interest in the revenue, tried to drive the best bargain possible. Hence the tussle that ensued between the delegation from Barcelona and the keepers of the Aragonese seals over the sum demanded for sealing some privileges granted

[223] ACA Reg. 2656. 52ʳ, 6 Dec. 1446, Alfonso to the King of Navarre. It is explained that the money is needed 'per obs de quitar nostres capellans e scrivans'. On 4 Dec. 1446 Alfonso had issued a general proclamation warning all officials not to usurp the functions of the protonotary, and especially those that related to the assessment of sealing fees (ibid. 51ʳ). Ferrer Ram had evidently protested that his rights were being ignored in Spain.

[224] Ram died before the money could be distributed and it was not until January 1450 that his heirs handed it to the treasury. See ACA Reg. 2720. 139ʳ, 19 Jan. 1450.

[225] This was his regular salary as a secretary—'gracia ordinaria vestri officii'. It must have been much in arrears, for on 31 July 1445 a provision was made to pay him the amount due for 1441 (ACA Reg. 2720. 53ʳ).

[226] ACA Reg. 2901. 72ʳ, 15 Sept. 1442. Alfonso to the *magister rationalis* of Valencia.

[227] A table of fees for the reign of Charles I is published by Durrieu, *Les Archives angevines*, i. 221–3. B. Mazzoleni has edited a fragment of the 'Quaternus Sigilli Pendentis' for the years 1452–3 in *Fonti aragonesi*, iii.

to the city. From an initial figure of 500 florins, represented to the envoys as 'a special favour', it was brought down, through the intercession of Guillen Pujades, to 300 florins.[228] Similar bargaining must have taken place over the Neapolitan seals, with a general trend towards heavier fees, for the parliament of 1450 petitioned that they should be levied as in the time of Giovanna II and Ladislas. Alfonso granted the petition in respect of the great seal, but for the others he appointed a committee to establish a scale of fees since none had been compiled in the reigns of his predecessors.[229] Whatever improvements may have resulted from these measures, dissatisfaction with the administration of the seals continued to rumble and was heard again in the 1456 parliament. The petition presented on that occasion asked that all letters not normally sealed with the great seal should be written on paper, sealed with the small seal and pay fees 'secondo e solito in questo reame'. In reply Alfonso admitted abuses in the management of the seals[230] and took a number of steps to redress the grievances expressed in the parliament. One of these was the abolition of the *quadratus*; another fixed the fee for the small seal at 5 *grana*; another was the provision that no privilege, letter of grace or justice should bear more than one seal. For the great seal he maintained the existing fees (that is to say, those charged in the reign of Giovanna II) except for letters 'simplicis justitie' which he fixed at 2 *tarini*. The choice of having a letter of justice written on paper or parchment was left to the recipient who paid accordingly; if he chose paper the seal was placed on the dorse, whereas on a parchment it was attached by a silk ribbon.[231]

A note of the fee paid for the seal was made on the original document and sometimes in the registers.[232] Likewise noted was

[228] ACB Cart. Com., vol. 14, fol. 71, Naples, 11 May 1444.

[229] '. . . in aliis vero quorum expressa taxacio non reperitur Regia Maiestas commisit eorum taxacionem arbitrio infrascriptorum videlicet Comitis Concentayne, Valentini Claver, Johannis de Coponibus, Nicolai Fillach et Michaelis Ritzo' (Ametller y Vinyas, *Alfonso V de Aragón*, iii. 689).

[230] '. . . abusiones que sunt in dictis sigillis' (ASN Div. Somm. I. 52 (bis), 171ʳ).

[231] Ibid. This refers to the great seal: cf. above, p. 244.

[232] The sole surviving register of privileges in the Neapolitan archives (ASN Priv. I) has this information, but it is not to be found in the seventeen registers of privileges in the Aragonese archives (ACA Reg. 2902–18). Remembering that a letter might be registered in as many as three offices—the chancery, the Sommaria, and the office of the conservator general—we may conclude that the Aragonese and Neapolitan registers are of different provenance. The latter may well have belonged to the Sommaria and the former to the chancery.

the exemption from the fee enjoyed by certain officials among them the seven great officers of state. A privilege for Iñigo de Guevara bears the note: 'Quia Magnus Senescallus nichil solvit pro jure sigilli',[233] and on another for Giovanni di Miroballo is written 'Nihil solvit pro iure sigilli quia presidens Regie Camere Sumarie'.[234] Other courtiers and officials often obtained exemption as a matter of grace,[235] as did those who were too poor to pay. For those who did pay, the fees exacted covered a wide range as the following examples will show: for the privilege making him a count Guglielmo della Marra paid 8 *oncie*,[236] for a captaincy Angelo Russo paid 1 *oncia*;[237] a privilege conferring a royal chaplaincy cost Nicola di Raynaldo de Carisio 12 *tarini*;[238] the town of Leonessa paid 1 *oncia* for the custody of its castle;[239] a privilege permitting men from within or without the kingdom to settle in certain un-inhabited lands of Raimondo del Balzo cost that noble 4 *tarini*;[240] a very substantial fee of 10 *oncie* was exacted from a group of Genoese merchants for a safe-conduct guaranteeing their safety in trading voyages to the kingdom of Tunis and other parts of the Maghreb;[241] on a licence to practise as a physician Jacobo Constantis paid 1 *oncia*;[242] on his appointment as a president of the Sommaria Buffalo de Diano paid 4 *oncie*;[243] on a confirmation of the *merum et mixtum imperium* the Duke of Andria paid 4 *oncie*;[244] Joan de Torrellas had to pay a fee of 20 *oncie* 20 *tarini* for the privilege that granted him the town of Caiazzo as a fief *in perpetuum*.[245] This last fee was doubtless based on the Sommaria's evaluation of the fief, Caiazzo having been assessed at the rate of 2 *oncie* per *collecta* for tax purposes,[246] but many others must have been arrived at by rule-of-thumb methods. At one time the king even contemplated farming the great seal to the conservator general; a contract was drawn up and then cancelled because, as

<hr/>

[233] ASN Priv. I. 4ᵛ, 2 Sept. 1452.   [234] Ibid. 30ᵛ. 22 Oct. 1452.
[235] A long list of such favours was notified to the conservator general on 12 Nov. 1452: 'Notum facimus et testamur quod subscriptis personis nostro mandato et ordinatione expedite fuerunt gratis et sine aliqua juris sigilli solutione provisiones et lettere infrascripte' (ASN Priv. I. 27ᵛ).
[236] Rogadeo, *Codice diplomatico*, p. 276, 3 Nov. 1452.
[237] Ibid., p. 282, 10 Nov. 1452. Michele Riccio paid the same for the privilege granting him the captaincy of Bitonto (Mazzoleni, *Fonti aragonesi*, iii. 22).
[238] ASN Priv. I. 1ᵛ, 22 Sept. 1452.   [239] Ibid. 2ʳ, 20 Sept. 1452.
[240] Ibid. 16ʳ, 10 Oct. 1452.   [241] Ibid. 61ʳ, 30 Dec. 1452.
[242] Mazzoleni, *Fonti aragonesi*, iii. 21.   [243] Ibid., p. 23.
[244] Ibid., p. 33.   [245] ASN Priv. I. 92ʳ, 13 July 1453.
[246] ASN Div. Somm. I. 133. 2ʳ.

Alfonso wrote in his own hand on the instrument of cancellation, 'Verdad es que lo e leydo e fue por no fazer gratia del sillo por que me ayudasse en mis deudos.'[247]

Besides paying for the seal, the beneficiary of a royal letter was required to pay a fee to cover the costs of material and labour. The sum demanded therefore varied roughly according to the amount of work involved. Bernat Lopez, a writer of the register, received 136s. 6d. for 'putting in form and registering 29 *cauteles*';[248] Pere Baucells, a chancery clerk, got 8 ducats for work on an edict concerning the office of *magister rationalis* in the kingdom of Valencia because the first version had been scrapped and he had had to rewrite it.[249] Sometimes the fees were waived, as when Alfonso gave his assent to a request from Ypsigro that for privileges granted to the town under the great seal 'non siano tenuti pagare cosa alcuna ne per scriptura ne per sigillo'.[250] On a privilege for the married clergy of Terra di Bari appears this note: Jacobo pregate Marino per parte mia che de questa lettera non exigatur pecunias si fieri potest atteso quod sit littera iusta et tassatela Benedictus Lopiz.'[251] The recipients paid 12 *tarini* for the seal, but the document does not reveal whether this plea was successful in exempting them from the secretarial charges. Complaints that the chancery overcharged for these services were often raised in parliaments. In 1450 the barons petitioned as follows:

Supplicano . . . limitare et moderare le spese de qualuncha scriptura che haverano ad usis dela vestra Regale Corte et vestro Sacro Consiglio per forma et modo che li secretarii regestraturi et altri scripturi ali quali apertene siano debitamente pagati de la loro decente faticha et li vestri subditi et vasalli non siano oppressi. Et che la forma de ipso pagamento se facia con deliberacione de ipsi secretarii et regestraturi et ipsi Magnati la quale forma data se debia sempre observare in futurum.

Alfonso returned the answer, 'Placet R. M. de taxacione salarii scripturarum',[252] but the complaint cropped up again in 1456 when in its petition on the seals the parliament included a request that

---

[247] ACA Reg. 2550. 34ᵛ, 8 July 1452.
[248] ACA Reg. 2901. 72ʳ, 15 Sept. 1442, Alfonso to the *magister rationalis* of Valencia notifying him of this and several similar payments.
[249] Ibid.
[250] Mazzoleni, *Fonti aragonesi*, i. 42, 27 Dec. 1444.
[251] Rogadeo, *Codice diplomatico*, p. 391. The 'Benedictus Lopiz' must be Bernat Lopez, the *taxator* of the great seal. This privilege is dated 7 June 1457.
[252] Ametller y Vinyas, *Alfonso V de Aragón*, iii. 689.

the king take measures to moderate charges for writing documents: 'et anche providerene che li scrivani se pagheno moderatamente.'[253] On this occasion the king again made a rather vague promise to look into the matter: 'De scribis autem et eorum solucione Placet Regia Maiestati quod habita de premissis informatione moderentur et taxentur eorum salaria, et idem de secretariis.'[254] The letters of Pere Boquet, the envoy of Barcelona in Naples, suggest that the writers of the chancery looked for more than the proper payments from those seeking to extract letters from them. He complained in May 1455 that 'the writers turn their backs on me and do not listen to me because I do not give them anything', and that 'the notaries and writers will do nothing without payment'.[255] Two years later he was complaining about the sums demanded by Fonolleda for sealing, writing, and registering documents;[256] when these were not paid, Fonolleda threatened to draw bills of exchange on Barcelona.[257] An effective table of fees had evidently not materialized.

Written, signed, and sealed, a letter was ready for dispatch once it had been registered in the chancery. Comparatively few of the vast number of documents written and dispatched by the *curia* during the reign of Alfonso have survived in the original, so our knowledge of the period depends largely upon the registers in which they were transcribed. From the description of administrative practice in this and earlier chapters it will be seen that much emphasis was placed upon registration as a device that enabled different offices, and especially those concerned with finance and regalian rights, to keep watch on those matters that interested them. Thus it could happen that a single letter might be registered in several offices.[258] All, whatever their nature, were registered in the chancery by the clerks of the register who duly noted the fact upon the document. Sometimes they merely wrote, 'Registrata in cancellariam penes cancellarium;' sometimes they were more specific—'Registrata in cancellaria penes cancellarium in registro

---

[253] ASN Div. Somm. I. 52 (bis), 171ʳ.   [254] Ibid.

[255] Madurell Marimon, *Mensajeros barceloneses*, p. 499, Letter dated 28 May 1455.

[256] Ibid., p. 578, Letter dated 13 May 1457: 'Aximateix he fet dita dels trebals e manaments, scriure, cera, veta e pergamena e registres.'

[257] Ibid., p. 599, Letter dated 10 Sept. 1457.

[258] In the reign of Charles I letters had been registered in two series of registers, one for the chancery and the other for the *camera regis*. Charles II added a third series for the protonotary (Durrieu, *Les Archives angevines*, i. 36).

privilegiorum quarto.'[259] Documents were registered in the order in which they reached the clerks, which was not strictly chronological. Taking at random a few leaves of the register known as the Codice Chigi, we find documents registered successively in the following order of date: 5 July 1451, 5 July, 8 July, 6 July, 2 July, 10 July, 10 July, 2 July, 29 June, 9 July.[260] Occasionally registration was deliberately delayed in order to keep a letter secret. In November 1451 Antoni Vinyes wrote to the city council of Barcelona that he had been unable to gain any knowledge of the contents of letters sent to prohibit the election of consuls in the city, 'because they have not yet been registered, so that no one may know what is in them'.[261] The large number of writers who had access to the registers made it difficult to keep the contents of any document confidential, as Vinyes himself demonstrated on another occasion when he was able to send his masters copies of letters close addressed to Queen Maria and the *magister rationalis* of Catalonia.[262] In the registers of the secret seal one finds traces of glue where paper had evidently been placed to cover some of the letters from prying eyes.

In form the Aragonese registers were large octavo volumes consisting of between 150 and 250 leaves of watermarked paper,[263] and were written in a number of hands that show a wide range of style from late Gothic to a fine humanistic script.[264] How they were classified can no longer be determined with complete certainty because the archives were divided after Alfonso's death between his two heirs—Ferdinand in Naples and Juan in Aragon. Moreover those retained in Naples suffered a number of subsequent disasters; our knowledge of them now depends very much upon an onomastic index of 106 registers which was probably compiled soon after the division and is still extant in the Biblioteca Nazionale of Naples.[265] This index gives the following classification of the registers: Justiciae (5 vols.), Comune (27 vols.), Diversorum

---

[259] On a privilege for Crotone, 3 June 1445 (Mazzoleni, *Fonti aragonesi*, i. 46).

[260] Mazzoleni, *Il Codice Chigi*, pp. 20–9.

[261] Madurell Marimon, *Mensajeros barceloneses*, p. 404, 26 Nov. 1451.

[262] He enclosed them in a letter written from Naples on 14 Dec. 1451 (ibid., p. 409).

[263] This was a departure from the Angevin practice of writing the registers on parchment; cf. Capasso, *Inventario cronologico*, p. xlix.

[264] For further details see Mazzoleni, *Il Codice Chigi*, introduction.

[265] It is classified as MS. XIV. A 24; cf. Rogadeo, *Codice diplomatico*, pp. viii, xiv–xv.

Italiae (1 vol.), Regestrum Neap. (35 vols.),[266] Sicilie (1 vol.), Comune Neap. (33 vols.), Judicum (1 vol.), Privilegiorum (3 vols.),[267] Regestrum penes prothonotarium (1 vol.). The registers of Alfonso allocated to Juan II now form part of the archives of the Corona de Aragón under these classifications: Castellae, Commune, Commune sigilli secreti, Corsicae, Curiae, Diversorum Regii Patrimonii, Exercitum, Instructionum, Itinerum, Itinerum sigilli secreti, Litterarum et albaranorum, Majoricarum, Marcarum, Notariorum, Officialium, Officialium Cataloniae, Pecuniae, Privilegiorum Protonotarii Aragonum, Sardiniae, Secretorum, Sententiarum, Gratiarum, Privilegiorum Neap., Venditionum, and 102 registers for Sicily.

Some of the registers in the Aragonese archives have been reclassified, and even misclassified;[268] none the less a comparison of the Neapolitan and Aragonese lists suggests that they do correspond to a reasonable extent, and that they reflect the system of classification used by the Aragonese chancery in Naples. Under Ladislas and Giovanna II the system evolved by earlier Angevin rulers had broken down because of turmoil in the kingdom and the rulers' absence from the capital.[269] Letters were often not registered at all, and when they were it was without regard to subject matter. Alfonso brought order into this chaos by introducing the archival practice of the Aragonese chancery whereby documents were classified and registered primarily according to the nature of their content.[270] Major territorial groups of registers—for Aragon, Naples, Sicily, Sardinia, etc.—were subdivided into subject categories (Comune, Curiae, Privilegiorum, etc.). In addition there were some general registers, such as those for letters under the secret seal which dealt mainly with diplomatic affairs. Doubts sometimes arose as to the most appropriate classification for a

[266] Probably these ought to be described as registers Curie, for this essential classification is otherwise missing from the list.

[267] The surviving register of privileges (ASN Priv. I) is not one of these, which strengthens the likelihood that it belongs to the archives of the Sommaria, not the chancery. Cf. above, p. 250, n. 232.

[268] e.g. ACA Reg. 2910 listed as Privilegiorum Neap. is in fact a register of Comune for Sicily.

[269] Capasso, Inventario cronologico, p. xlviii.

[270] Cf. Capasso, Le fonti, p. 207: 'In questo nuovo archivio nel regno di Alfonso I fu introdotta una nuova classificazione di scritture, ordinata secondo le materie cui ciascun atto apparteneva, ed una nuova distribuzione e denominazione di registri che fu adottata anche posteriormente dalla cancelleria viceregnale.'

letter. A safe-conduct for Giovanni Lombardo, master of a Neapolitan galley, appears in a register of Itinerum sigilli secreti with
the marginal note, 'non bene hic sed in comuni Neapolis'.[271]
Another note is still more specific: 'non bene hic sed in comuni
Neapolis xxviº'.[272] A letter to an unnamed noble ordering him to
meet the king in Apice for urgent discussions was first registered
in Curiae sigilli secreti and then transferred to Curiae Neapolis.[273]
Decisions in such matters seems to have rested with the keepers of
the registers.

Several languages appear side by side in the registers. Most documents under the great seal and communications to other states are
written in Latin. For more ephemeral or personal letters to other
princes and private persons the language of the recipient is used
where Italian, Castilian, or Catalan was appropriate. Thus beneath
a letter to the conservator general written in Catalan appears
the note, 'Sub simili forma in lingua italiana mutatis mutandis
fuit scriptum Nicholao Antonio de Montibus advocato fisci.'[274]
Within the king's own territories the same rule applied: correspondence with Aragon is in Castilian or Latin, with the Catalan
territories in Catalan or Latin; within the kingdom of Naples
the *volgare* was often used, and for Sicily some letters of a private
character are written in the local *volgare*.[275] After Latin the
language most commonly used was Catalan, reflecting the predominance of that nationality in the most important offices of the
central government. Ciphers were frequently employed for secret
correspondence.[276]

[271] ACA Reg. 2795. 117ᵛ, 20 Mar. 1446.

[272] Ibid. 124ᵛ, 26 Mar. 1446. The letter is addressed to some Venetian merchants informing them that the king is sending them a safe-conduct so that they
may bring him a great ruby which he hears they wish to sell.

[273] ACA 2690, 153ʳ, 1 May 1445; cf. ACA Reg. 2660. 120ʳ: 'Non bene hic sed
in pecunie Aragonum.'   [274] ACA Reg. 2658, 168ʳ, 30 Oct. 1451.

[275] e.g. the instructions for an embassy to Rome given to the Sicilian Fr.
Giuliano da Mayali. '. . . dirra per parti dilu dictu Signure: Comu lu predictu
Signuri extimanda lu honuri di la Sua Santita non altramenti ki lu propriu so,
supplica ala Sua Sanctita ki si voglia disponiri ad mandari prestissimamente lu
succursu ki ha deliberatu mandari alu Imperaturi di Custantinopuli atalki sia
a tempu atrovari si illa ala defensioni dilu dictu Imperaturi et contra la potentia
dilu grandi Turchu . . .' (ACA Reg. 2700. 27ᵛ, 6 June 1453).

[276] e.g. a letter to Queen Maria recounting the state of affairs in the kingdom
of Naples written from Gaeta, 9 Feb. 1438. A note in the register indicates, 'fuit
expedita in parva forma et in cifra' (ACA Reg. 2651, 23ᵛ). In May 1452 Alfonso
sent the Emperor Frederick III a cipher to be used for confidential correspondence: 'Serenissime princeps, mitto vobis cifram sicut inter vos et me

Under the early Angevins responsibility for keeping the registers had lain with the chamberlain, and more immediately with the *magistri rationales*.[277] From the time of Giovanna I it devolved upon two archivists, and from 1333 the registers were housed, together with the mint and the tribunal of the *magistri rationales*, in a building near the church of the Augustinians.[278] Bernardo de Raymo, a *rationalis* whose family had held the office of archivist since 1360,[279] was confirmed in that post by Alfonso. In August 1447, however, on the grounds that de Raymo's duties in the Sommaria left him no time to supervise the archives, the king appointed Joan de Boxia 'unum ex archivariis et ordinarium' for life.[280] The instruction that de Boxia is to collect the keys of the archives from de Raymo, or any other person who might hold them, makes it clear that he is henceforth to be the effective keeper and yet his duties as crown *promotor* must have kept him as busy as de Raymo's in the Sommaria.[281] It is unlikely that registers were transferred from the chancery to the archives immediately they had been filled; certainly this could not have happened on the many occasions when the king accompanied by his secretarial staff spent months, even years, away from the capital. At such times a large number of registers would travel in the baggage train. They might even come to grief, as happened at the battle of Ponza when many registers were lost with the royal galley.[282]

To carry its letters the chancery disposed of a considerable number of couriers under the control of the master of the couriers ('hospes seu magister cursorum').[283] In February 1445 the holder of that office, Gregorio Ungaro, had his authority extended from royal couriers to all couriers arriving in the city of Naples.[284] The

deliberatum fuit per quam poteritis michi scribere secreta. Tarditatis causa fuit quia mea propria manu eam scripsi, veniam date' (ACA Reg. 2940. 155ʳ, Pozzuoli, 2 May 1452).

[277] Durrieu *Les Archives angevines*, i. 9–10.
[278] Capasso, *Inventario cronologico*, p. lvii; cf. above, p. 191.
[279] Toppi, *De origine tribunalium*, i. 40–1.
[280] ACA Reg. 2912. 95ʳ, 17 Aug. 1447.
[281] Cf. above, p. 156.
[282] Joan de Boxia lost the original of a privilege during fighting at Pozzuoli, and the register in which it was recorded went down at Ponza (ACA Reg. 2912. 96ᵛ).
[283] The Aragonese Household Ordinance made provision for twenty couriers in the chancellor's office.
[284] ACA Reg. 2906. 144ᵛ, 9 Feb. 1445, Letter appointing Ungaro *magister cursorum* to the city. Nicola de Giovinazzo was master of the couriers in 1454 (Mazzoleni, *Fonti aragonesi*, i. 147), Johan de Valencia in October 1456 (Madurell

effect was to make his house a central mail office to which couriers on arrival delivered all the letters they carried, and from which all letters, both official and private, were dispatched. Towards the end of the reign, if not earlier, the treasurer controlled the dispatch of couriers with the result that private letters were often delayed to suit the needs of government. Pere Boquet of Barcelona complained that 'the treasurer has not allowed the courier who was to have left here on the 14th to depart; it is the greatest difficulty in the world that no courier may be dispatched without leave of the treasurer.'[285] Letters carried from Naples to Barcelona by land usually took at least three weeks.[286] Those sent by sea tended to take longer because they were subject to the delays and diversions of the merchant ships which carried them. When special need arose, relays of couriers were organized to keep the king in constant touch with his fleets, armies, or diplomatic representatives. In September 1444, at the time of Centelles's rebellion, such a relay was established between the capital and Calabria: twelve couriers carried messages from Naples to Cosenza, twelve went between Cosenza and Naples, and ten between Atri and Naples.[287] In June 1452 squires of the household were posted to carry letters daily between Naples and the Duke of Calabria's army in Tuscany,[288] and in 1457 a similar relay of twenty squires posted between Pisa and Naples kept the king in close communication with his fleet operating against Genoa.[289]

Marimon, *Mensajeros barceloneses*, p. 533), and a certain Aligsen in November 1457 (ibid., p. 609).

[285] ACB Cart. Com., vol. 26, fol. 71, Naples, 17 Apr. 1456.

[286] ACB Cart. Com., vol. 14, fol. 93, Envoys of Barcelona to the city from Naples, 11 June 1444. 'Lo present correu senyors parteix daci vuy dada dela present que es dijous e festa del cors precios de Jesu Crist a les quatre hores de mati ans de dinar e deu esser aqui en vint e quatre jorns, per que si compeix placieus fer li donar vint florins, pero per que ell sol esser un aventetios caminador e per fer lo be estirar, li havem offert e promes que per cascun jorn que entrera menys dels xxiiii jorns haie sinch florins per jorn. E apres senyors vos placia que si havets atrametre altre correu per aquests affers o per altre que fessats que aquest vingue, car ultra que es un aventatios caminador nos semble sie aventetiat per que te muller e infants en aquexa ciutat.' This courier delivered his letters in Barcelona on the morning of 3 July, so earning a bonus of 15 florins.

[287] Minieri Riccio, 'Alcuni fatti di Alfonso I', p. 243.

[288] ACA Reg. 2798. 11ᵛ, Alfonso to the Duke of Calabria, 1 July 1452.

[289] ACA Reg. 2800, 14ʳ. One of these couriers was killed and others robbed and beaten by foragers from the camp of Napoleone degli Orsini.

VIII

MILITARY POWER

I t took Alfonso twenty years of intermittent battle by land and sea to win the kingdom of Naples against the opposition of a powerful internal faction and the hostility of virtually all the states of Italy. That opposition and hostility did not vanish with the discomfiture of René of Anjou; it smouldered on to burst into life again soon after Alfonso's death, and it may be argued that he added fuel to it by the 'forward' policy pursued after the conquest of Naples. Whether his military adventures in Italy between 1442 and 1458 were mainly designed to consolidate the Aragonese hold on Naples or as steps towards further conquests is a matter for debate;[1] what is certain is that they kept the kingdom on a war footing for much of the reign, and that the maintenance of his armed forces was consequently Alfonso's major concern.[2]

As far as the land forces were concerned the problem was mainly one of finance. Fiefs held *in capite* of the crown owed one knight's service for every 20 *oncie* of assessed value,[3] or in lieu a scutage calculated at 5¼ *oncie* on every 20 *oncie*.[4] During the years of civil war Alfonso summoned his adherents to perform their service or pay scutage,[5] but after the city of Naples had fallen in June 1442 he never again called on the barons for feudal service. In fact he virtually renounced his claim to it by assenting to a petition of the 1443 parliament for the abolition of scutage and by forbidding the

[1] Cf. Dupré Theseider, *La politica italiana.*

[2] Cf. the judgement of Filippo Maria Visconti, Duke of Milan: 'Lo stato del reame non e simile de li altri et lo bisogna tenere cum la spatta in mano, et per questo ad essa Maiesta convene pensare che la non possa stare de patta, anzi gli e de bisogno o vincere in tutto o perdere in tutto' (ibid., p. 142).

[3] Military service at this rate was stipulated in the privilege confirming Josia d'Aquaviva in possession of fiefs confiscated from his nephew Andrea Matteo d'Aquaviva (ACA Reg. 2908. 140ᵛ, 22 July 1446).

[4] This is the rate given in a privilege concerning the toll on steel and iron in Trani which was held by Simone Cazzetta as a fief 'sub feudale servicio sive adoha unciarum quinque et quarta pro singulis viginti unciis introituum . . .' (ACA Reg. 2915. 196ᵛ, 15 Apr. 1452).

[5] e.g. the order to the royal commissioner in Principato citeriore and Basilicata to collect scutage (Mazzoleni, *Fonti aragonesi*, i. 28, 21 Sept. 1441).

Neapolitan nobles to keep armed retainers.[6] He was relinquishing little of substance. An attempt to collect arrears of scutage for the period from the death of Giovanna II to the end of the fifth indiction (31 August 1442) revealed large numbers of claims, valid and otherwise, to exemption, and a fund wholly inadequate to the military purpose it was meant to serve.[7] In its place the 1443 parliament granted him a hearth tax with which he undertook to maintain a permanent force of 1,000 men-at-arms and ten galleys for the defence of the kingdom.[8] Although military service continued to feature in all grants of fiefs *in capite*, Alfonso had effectively put an end to it.

Where then did he find his troops? One potential source was brought into existence by the parliament of March 1450 which, at the king's request, sanctioned the raising of a militia of 2,300 foot on the basis of one man for every hundred hearths.[9] Its effectiveness was never put to the test, for it could be called upon only to defend the kingdom against invasion and no such emergency arose during the remainder of the reign. Another source of troops mentioned by Borso d'Este in his *Relazione* of 1444 was the royal demesne, where he reckoned that the king might raise 3,000 horse from those

---

[6] Cf. Faraglia, *Diurnali*: 'Rè de Rahona à tolte le gente d'arme a ciascuno signore reservato alo Prencipe di Taranto gran condestabole.'

[7] Francesco Pagano, the commissioner sent by the Sommaria to the Abruzzi, heard claims of exemption by the Count and Countess of Celano, but was not satisfied and assessed them to pay 882 ducats. The Count of Marerio could only produce a privilege which bore no seal in support of his claim to exemption and this the commissioner rejected. On the other hand he did allow the claim of the Count of Tagliacozzo (ASN Div. Somm. I. 166). Efforts to collect the arrears of scutage were continuing as late as 1445 when some horses belonging to Antonio Spinelli were seized for non-payment (ASN Fasc. Com. 83ʳ, November 1445).

[8] Ametller y Vinyas, *Alfonso V de Aragón*, ii. 460; Bianchini, *Della storia delle finanze*, p. 211; cf. above, p. 210.

[9] Ametller y Vinyas, *Alfonso V de Aragón*, iii. 686: 'In primo che li fanti li quali ad requesta de la V. M. li prefati magnati et baroni hanno ordenato che hayate quandocumque questo vestro Regno fosse invaduto da fore chini piaca non li volere operare extra Regnum ne anche supre fuste maritime set solum per defensione terresta et che non li vogliate operare non essendo invaduto lo prefato vestro Regno li quali fanti ascenderanno ad numero de duymilia e trecento ad razone de uno fante per centenaro de fochi. Et che li ditti baruni degiano essere advisati per duy misi inanti aiocheli potzano mandare in debita forma e che lo xercitare deli dicti fanti non se debea compunere in denari. Et durante la operacione delli dicti fanti la Maesta V. non impugna altra nova graveza de fanti comandati.—Placet Regie Magestati salvo quod de vastatoribus et de tempore intimacionis et requisicionis in locis magis propinquis invassioni sit liberum arbitrium Regie Maiestate.'

holding by military tenure.[10] This was almost certainly a figure which he had obtained from official sources, for it corresponds exactly with the estimate of 'lances of the demesne' given by Alfonso in the instructions for ambassadors sent to the pope in March 1443.[11] From Borso's description one might gather that these men served at their own expense; the instructions, on the other hand, make it clear that they had to be paid by the king. Nevertheless it is probable that the royal demesne was a major recruiting ground for Alfonso's armies.

Despite the promise of 1443 to maintain a standing army for the defence of the kingdom, the king had no permanent military force apart from the men employed in garrisoning castles and in his personal guard. The latter, commanded for some years by Rodrigo de Mur,[12] consisted of footmen and archers organized into companies under the command of constables. As one might expect, most of them were Spaniards.[13] Each company numbered twenty or thirty men, and there appear to have been five or six companies.[14] Apart from these guards, a considerable proportion of the household had received the military training customary for nobles and could take up arms when need arose. When the king commanded his armies in person, as he did until the end of 1448, he was accompanied on his campaigns by many great nobles holding offices of state, and by many gentlemen of the household who commanded bodies of troops. Large numbers of Alfonso's household were taken prisoner with him at the battle of Ponza;[15] Pedro de Cardona the chamberlain led the 400 infantry who first broke

[10] Foucard, 'Descrizione', p. 755: 'Item cavalli 3000 pagati per li homeni d'arme dele terre del demanio, zioé che li homeni dele terre del demanio, alquni sono homeni d'arme, i quale ha do, qual tri, qual quatro lance; per modo che seria difficile a saper la nome de tutti quilli homeni d'arme, i quale in tutto hanno cavalli 3000 a soldo delo Re.'

[11] ACA Reg. 2698. 43ᵛ, 26 Mar. 1444. In this memorial for Berenguer d'Erill and Battista Platamone, Alfonso rehearses his military preparations in support of the pope. Among them is the half pay already given to 3,000 lances 'del seu domanio'.

[12] Minieri Riccio, 'Alcuni fatti di Alfonso I', p. 14, and Mazzoleni, *Fonti aragonesi*, i. 91. Both these references are to 1437. The latest mention of de Mur is in October 1446 when he was sent with some infantry to aid the Milanese (Ametller y Vinyas, *Alfonso V de Aragón*, ii. 572).

[13] Minieri Riccio ('Alcuni fatti di Alfonso I', p. 8) lists the constables who received pay in October 1437 as Bartolomeu de Deval, Antoni Soler, Johan Abril, Pasqual de Mora, Bernat Avella, and Bernat Texidor.

[14] Cf. Mazzoleni, *Fonti aragonesi*, i. 89.

[15] Ametller y Vinyas, *Alfonso V de Aragón*, i. 485, a list of the prisoners.

into the city of Naples through the gate of San Genaro;[16] the same
Pedro, his son Alfonso de Cardona, Guillem Ramon de Moncada,
Lope Ximenez de Urrea, and Ramon Boyl commanded the battles
of the king's army at Carpenone;[17] and it was again Pedro de
Cardona with Iñigo de Guevara, Galceran de Requesens, and
Berenguer d'Erill, who led the attack on Piombino. Lesser figures
in the household served with perhaps two, three, or four lances; and
though they received pay for their service,[18] it is clear that they were
expected to offer it when the household was put on a war footing.

Numerous as these knights of the household and their followers
were, they constituted only the nucleus of an army the bulk of
which had to be recruited from the professional captains and
soldiers found all over Italy. According to his needs and the money
available, the king granted *condotte* or commissions whereby a
captain raised so many men at an agreed rate of pay and for a
stipulated time. A few of the greater *condottieri* with established
reputations and followings could raise whole armies. Nicolo Piccinino, perhaps the most famous of Alfonso's *condottieri*, signed
agreements in September 1442 and January 1444 by which he
undertook to serve the king with 4,000 horse and 1,000 foot for
a sum of 168,013 ducats a year.[19] Nicolo's son, Francesco Piccinino,
contracted in the spring of 1449 to provide an army of similar size
and composition.[20] The lord of Rimini, Sigismondo Malatesta,
accepted a *condotta* of 600 lances and 600 foot for one year with
the option of a second year, but he later refused either to serve
or to return the 32,400 ducats paid in advance.[21] Frederico di
Montefeltro of Urbino took the king's pay and served him faithfully. Among the major *condottieri* should also be numbered
Giovanni Antonio del Balzo Orsini, Prince of Taranto. As early
as 1434 he negotiated a *condotta* of 2,000 horse and 1,000 foot[22]

[16] Ametller y Vinyas, *Alfonso V de Aragón*, ii. 410.   [17] Ibid. ii. 417.
[18] A treasury schedule for 1440 contains a long list of payments to members of
the household in respect of the lances they were maintaining in the king's service
(Mazzoleni, *Fonti aragonesi*, i. 100–8).
[19] ACA Reg. 2903. 118ᵛ, 25 Feb. 1444.
[20] ACA Reg. 2697. 18ᵛ, 10 Apr. 1449. Francesco Piccinino first received a
condotta from Alfonso in 1436 (Faraglia, *Storia della lotta*, p. 56).
[21] ACA Reg. 2800. 27ᵛ, 10 Sept. 1457. Alfonso never forgave Malatesta for
this piece of double dealing.
[22] Ametller y Vinyas, *Alfonso V de Aragón*, i. 433. The agreement, signed in
Palermo on 20 Aug. 1434, also provided that the prince should be given the
office of constable.

which was later confirmed as a permanent *condotta* of 500 lances.[23] Until 1442 the prince led his troops in person, but thereafter he delegated the command to his brother the Duke of Andria.[24]

Most lesser *condotte* were stipulated in units of 100 horse or foot, though for mounted troops (men-at-arms) this was often expressed in terms of the 'lance', that is a unit of three horse. Pietro Palagano was given a *condotta* of 100 lances and 100 foot in March 1436;[25] Marino Caracciolo, Count of Sant Angelo, was given thirteen and two-thirds lances in 1441.[26] In March 1452 Carlo di Campobasso, Count of Trémoli, accepted a *condotta* of thirty-three and one-third lances (i.e. 100 horse) with which he was to serve wherever the king pleased from 1 April.[27] The seemingly complete list of *condotte* given by Borso d'Este in his *Relazione* is all expressed in terms of the lance, and ranges from the 500 lances of the Prince of Taranto to the ten lances given to 'messer Aloyse de Aversa'. A schedule of the treasury for 1437 and a Sommaria schedule for 1438 similarly express the *condotte* of mounted men in lances.[28] Only in the 1450s did the 'horse' become more common than the 'lance' in the *condotte* negotiated by Alfonso. In July 1453 Gisperto and Manfredi di Correggio were given 900 horse,[29] and Roberto Orsini 200 horse.[30] Even then the lance is still discernible for the Duke of Calabria, with whose army Roberto was to serve, was told that the *condotta* was conditional upon Ferdinand placing 100 of his own horse under the *condottiere* who would thus have command of 100 lances. Moreover Roberto was promised that the number would be raised to a full 300 in the following year.

[23] Gentile, 'Lo stato napoletano' (1937), 12. For these lances he received an annual stipend of 100,000 ducats.

[24] On 22 July 1444 Alfonso wrote to the prince saying that he wished to send his lances to the March of Ancona as part of a force which he had promised to the papal commander, the Cardinal of Aquileia. He asked the prince to agree to his brother having the command, and also requested him to write to the cardinal with an assurance that his troops would join those of the king (ACA Reg. 2698. 63ʳ).

[25] Faraglia, *Storia della lotta*, p. 57, n. 1.

[26] Ibid., p. 231, n. 2.

[27] ACA Reg. 2914. 188ᵛ.

[28] Minieri Riccio ('Alcuni fatti di Alfonso I', pp. 2 ff.) cites several entries from 'Cedola 1.ᵃ' of the treasury, fols. 199–202 relating to payments for *condotte*. Faraglia (*Storia della lotta*, p. 127, n. 5) gives similar extracts from 'Cedola 2a' of the Sommaria.

[29] ACA Reg. 2799. 7ᵛ, 9 July 1453. It could have been expressed as 300 lances.

[30] Ibid. 7ʳ, 1 July 1453.

Long-term contracts such as this were the exception; usually a *condotta* ran for three months only.[31]

Negotiations for hiring *condottieri* had become part of Italian political and military strategy. Not only was it necessary to muster an army of adequate strength at the right time and place, much also depended upon denying an enemy the services of experienced or strategically placed captains by judicious bargaining. In November 1447 Alfonso empowered dez Puig, his roving ambassador, to hire the services of any duke, marquis, count, or captain willing to accept the king's pay.[32] In the following spring there developed a contest between the king and the Florentines for the services of Frederico di Montefeltro and Sigismondo Malatesta. Again, in the summer of 1453, when preparing to lead an army against Florence, Alfonso informed dez Puig, now his ambassador in Venice, that he intended to leave the kingdom with only a small force and to carry with him the money to pay 1,000 lances 'which we should be able to get from the forces of the enemy'.[33] At the same time he instructed his son to continue negotiations for *condotte* with Alessandro Sforza and Simonetta, even though he believed they were only using them to get better terms from Florence, because in this way they might be kept from joining forces with the Florentines.[34] That he was more concerned to lure Alessandro Sforza away from Florence than to incorporate him in his own army is shown by further letters to the Duke of Calabria in which Alfonso warns that the troops of the *condottiere* must on no account be allowed to mix with those of the duke,[35] and that Ferdinand must 'remember to be careful whom you trust and beware lest some disastrous trick be played upon you'.[36] The earlier Tuscan campaign had witnessed similar overtures to the Duke of Urbino,

[31] Venice commonly offered long-term *condotte* (M. Mallett, *Mercenaries and their Masters* (Bodley Head, 1974), p. 82).

[32] ACA Reg. 2699. 128ᵛ, 18 Nov. 1447.

[33] ACA Reg. 2799. 13ᵛ. 29 July 1453.

[34] Ibid. 18ᵛ, 30 July 1453. Cf. Alfonso's letter to Andrea de Santa Croce, 23 Jan. 1452 (ACA Reg. 2659. 60ᵛ): 'Cum intelleximus spectabilem et magnificum armorum capitaneum Simonectum comitem Castriperii in servitiis florentinorum haud libenter permanere, nec de eis modo aliquo contentari significamus vobis quod si Simonectus ipse nobis servire vellet, illum ad nostra stipendia conducere cuperemus . . .'

[35] ACA Reg. 2799. 36ʳ, 19 Aug. 1453. The king evidently feared treachery and told Ferdinand to use all possible means to persuade Sforza to lead his men against Malatesta who persisted in serving Florence.

[36] Ibid. 37ʳ, 23 Aug. 1453.

who at that time held a *condotta* from Florence. Alfonso let the duke know that he would hire him on the same terms as he had received from the republic and would not require him to fight against it, but only to withdraw from its service. If he remained within his own territory, doing nothing, he was to receive half-pay; if he left it to fight Malatesta, he would have full pay.[37] When Montefeltro's *condotta* expired in October 1454 and he had no further military employment for him, Alfonso none the less took the precaution of granting him an annual pension of 6,000 ducats *ad beneplacitum* in order to retain his goodwill.[38] Because many of the more important *condottieri*, such as Malatesta and Monte-feltro, were also the rulers of minor states, it is sometimes hard to distinguish bargaining over *condotte* from a negotiation for an alliance between states.

Since *condotte* were normally contracted only for short periods and all parties to a conflict endeavoured to entice the others' cap-tains, it was often difficult to ensure faithful performance of an engagement by a *condottiere* who was not a subject of his em-ployer. Comparatively few reneged completely on their under-takings in the manner of Malatesta or Astorre dei Manfredi,[39] but many provided fewer men than the number fixed by the *condotta*. Gisperto and Manfredo di Correggio, for example, were suspected of having served with only 600 instead of 900 horse. Their chan-cellor denied the accusation, but Alfonso ordered his envoy in Tuscany, Antonio di Pesaro, to investigate the matter.[40] The stan-dard safeguard against this malpractice was the muster. Officials of the *escriva de racio* accompanied the armies for that purpose,[41] and the obligation to submit their troops to such verification usually appeared as one of the terms of the agreements made with

---

[37] ACA Reg. 2696. 143ʳ. These terms were set out in a memorial dated 21 Apr. 1448 which Alfonso sent to Ramon d'Ortaffa who was negotiating with Montefeltro.

[38] ACA Reg. 2917. 123ᵛ, 15 May 1455. This privilege grants the pension with retrospective effect.

[39] Astorre, the lord of Faenza, accepted the king's pay for 400 lances and 200 foot for one year with the option of renewal for a further year. After receiving 15,000 ducats of the 36,000 ducats due for the first year, he had broken the contract and kept the money (ACA Reg. 2800. 27ᵛ).

[40] ACA Reg. 2799. 7ᵛ, 9 July 1453.

[41] Cf. Letter from Alfonso to the Duke of Calabria, 13 June 1452: 'Vuy havem desempachats dos de offici de scriva de racio de nostra casa, los quals vos trametem perque continuament seguesquen lo camp e prenguen les mostres, e façen totes altres coses pertenyents allur offici . . .' (ACA Reg. 2798, 5ᵛ).

condottieri.[42] However, a few favoured individuals secured exemption; the abortive agreement with Sforza drawn up in July 1442 stipulated that 'non sia tenuto scrivere, bollare ne fare mostra'.[43] The routine musters too were often carried out in slipshod fashion, so that the king had in August 1453 to warn his son to take a careful muster of the *condottieri* companies to ascertain the exact number of troops in them before renewing any *condotta*.[44]

As a precaution against desertion by the *condottieri*, Alfonso usually demanded some security in the form of money, lands, or hostages. An offer of a *condotta* of 1,200 horse made to Francesco Piccinino in June 1448 carried the condition that he should deposit security in a Neapolitan bank to serve the full term, and in addition hand over to the king castles and lands sufficient to guarantee that he would not for four years after its expiration serve any of the king's enemies.[45] Nanno de Sulmona was asked to hand over his son as security before receiving the first instalment of his *condotta* in March 1440,[46] but it was found that human gages too easily slipped from the king's grasp and he was later inclined to insist upon land or other property. That preference comes out very clearly in a letter to Frederico of Urbino in connection with the *condotta* of Astorre dei Manfredi:

> Quanto al facto de messere Astorre de Favenza . . . vero vedendo li sermini che da lui e altri havemo receputi in caso venissemo ad accordarelo secondo vostro recordo, no haveriamo accepta la securita delo figlolo ne de carne ma de terre o castelle quale mettesse in nostra mano o pleyaria de bancho in quisto Reame nostro e altramente con ipso non accordariamo cosa alcuna.[47]

Despite all the precautions, Astorre still managed to betray Alfonso and defraud him of a large sum. Honours and rewards offered an

---

[42] e.g. the clause in the agreement with Sigismondo Malatesta signed 21 Apr. 1447. The Spanish translation given by Ametller y Vinyas (*Alfonso V de Aragón*, ii. 601) of the original in the Milanese archives reads as follows: 'Item quería S. M. que, luego de haber recibido Segismundo íntegramente el susodicho préstamo por las referidas 600 lanzas y 600 infantes, al cabo de un mes estuviese obligado y debiese pasar revista y alistar y señalar (bollare) las dichas lanzas é infantes, como era costumbre y se hacía por parte de los demás capitanes y caudillos de S. M.'   [43] Faraglia, *Storia della lotta*, p. 382.

[44] ACA Reg. 2799. 36^r, 19 Aug. 1453.

[45] ACA Reg. 2696. 150^r, 17 June 1448.

[46] ACA Reg. 2646. 84^v, 26 Mar. 1440.

[47] ACA Reg. 2659. 67^r, 25 Feb. 1452. Cf. his advice to the Duke of Calabria when treating with the lord of Faenza: 'e sobre la seguretat feu que no sia de persones mas de castells e terres' (ACA Reg. 2799. 5^v, 16 Feb. 1453).

alternative means for securing the loyalty of mercenary captains. An outstanding recipient of both was Nicolo Piccinino to whom Alfonso gave the county of Albe[48] and the right to bear the name and arms of the royal house of Aragon.[49] Though he depended so heavily upon them, Alfonso had a poor opinion of the quality of mercenary soldiers. When urging on Pope Nicholas V the measures needed to support the Albanian leader Scanderbeg against the Turks, he advocated the dispatch of 1,000 infantry and 200 horse, but stressed that they must be 'utili et non de conducta'.[50]

Borso d'Este lists some 3,555 lances in the king's pay in 1444 in addition to the army of Piccinino. Together with the 3,000 horse available from the demesne, this gave the king an army of more than 20,000 horse. But the whole force could be put into the field only if money could be found to pay the initial three months' salary or *prestanza* which, at the usual rate of 60 ducats a lance, would have required an expenditure of little less than half a million ducats for an army of this size.[51] Therefore it is not surprising to find that only a small part of these potential forces were ever brought into action. Borso's estimation that that part did not exceed one-quarter[52] is borne out by what we know of the strength of Alfonso's armies in a number of campaigns. In March 1444 he sent his envoys in Rome a memorial detailing preparations against a possible outbreak of fighting in the March of Ancona.[53] On the day of writing, 26 March, he had dispatched the Duke of Melfi, Cesare di Martinengo, Magno Barrile, and Sancho Carillo, with 800 lances to join Piccinino in the March. Half pay had been given to 3,000 lances from the demesne, and half was being distributed to other captains; the outstanding half he hoped to give shortly, so that by St. George's day (23 April) 10,000 horse

---

[48] Ametller y Vinyas, *Alfonso V de Aragón*, ii. 330. This gift was made in June 1440 when Alfonso wished to secure the services of Piccinino's son, Francesco.

[49] A privilege dated 25 Feb. 1444 styles him 'Nicolao Piccinino de Aragonia' (ACA Reg. 2903. 118ᵛ).

[50] ACA Reg. 2697. 162ʳ, 9 Dec. 1453.

[51] Alfonso claimed that a campaign in the March of Ancona, which lasted for six months in 1443, had cost him 800,000 ducats.

[52] Foucard, 'Proposta', p. 717. Borso also had a poor opinion of the troops that actually took the field: 'E quelle che cavalchano, la Maysta V. sa como le cavalchano, che li non hano ne famigli ne arme ni cavalli . . . Questo tenire de queste grande conducte, e non le pagare, è uno fare perdere lo credito ala V maysta.'

[53] ACA Reg. 2698. 43ᵛ, 26 Mar. 1444.

would be ready for action.[54] Whether Alfonso could have kept
to this timetable we do not know, because on the very day the
memorial was dispatched he fell gravely ill and three months passed
before he was able to join his army.[55] By July the force he proposed
to send in support of the papal army had fallen to 5,000 horse,[56]
and even that number was probably not forthcoming because of
the outbreak of rebellion in Calabria in August which forced him
to divert troops to that quarter. Matters went little better in the
following year when he endeavoured to gather together another
army which he would lead in person against Sforza. Having left
Naples late in July, he found himself on 2 August becalmed in
Teano and sorely embarrassed by the non-appearance of his army.
Pay had been given to Agostino di Sanseverino and Bartolomeo de
Frapiero (according to Borso d'Este each of these had a *condotta*
of twenty-five lances) and 'some lances'; others, who had earlier
received pay, had failed to join his standard. Alfonso urged his
council in Naples to spur on the laggards and to dispatch others as
quickly as possible, for he was being forced to delay his progress
and found it difficult to keep up appearances when passing through
baronial lands with such a poor train.[57] That same day he had had
to leave Capua accompanied only by Luigi di Capua and his
company of twenty-five lances; later in the day Johan de Corella
had joined him, 'and with these alone we are obliged to proceed;
we do not see the others stir'.[58] To give some colour to his slow
progress, he later ordered his huntsmen to attend him and thus
transformed the march into a leisurely chase. Things had not much
improved a month later when, camped on the river Pescara, he had
to warn his commander in the March that, 'considerate le condi-
cione daquisso campo et li modi et animi con che comprehendemo
stanno le gente nostre, ve declaramo che la nostra intencione e che
per non metere lo stato nostro in pericolo debeate tornare piu
tosto in derreto e meterve in alcuna parte forte.'[59] So dire was his

---

[54] In addition to the troops, he promised to send Piccinino 20,000 ducats
within eight or ten days.

[55] A. F. C. Ryder, 'La politica italiana di Alfonso d'Aragona', *ASPN* (1959),
67–8.

[56] Cf. above, p. 263, n. 24.

[57] ACA Reg. 2698. 98ʳ: '... car attes que som exits desacompanyats nos cove
detenir e fer petites jornades e no tirar de trata segons haviem deliberat, e quasi
no sabem com regir nos attes que anam per terres de barons.'

[58] Ibid. '... e ab aquests sols nos cove anar, ne veem los altres moures.'

[59] Ibid. 103ʳ, Alfonso to the Marquis of Gerace, 27 Aug. 1445.

need of troops that he ordered the suspension of proceedings in a lawsuit involving Aimerico di Sanseverino, Count of Capaccio, because the count had announced his intention of joining the royal army with 100 horse at his own expense.[60]

For the spring of 1446 Alfonso hoped, so he informed the Cardinal of Aquileia, to muster an army of 3,000 horse and 1,000 infantry which would eventually be increased to 9,000 horse.[61] Though the grand total was not achieved, he did make a slightly better showing than in 1445. By mid-March the royal forces which had wintered in the March of Ancona (some 2,000 horse and 500 infantry) had received their pay, those in the Abruzzi were about to be given theirs, and it was intended to begin paying 2,000 lances of the main army which the king would lead.[62] Thereafter the tempo slackened. At the beginning of May final dispatch had still not been given to the first 1,000 horse and foot of the main army,[63] and August arrived before 150 of these horse and 800 infantry finally left Naples to join the cardinal's army.[64]

Some indication of the size of the army with which Alfonso invaded Tuscany in 1448 may be obtained from the fact that, on the conclusion of that unsuccessful campaign, he asked the pope to provide winter quarters for the surviving 3,000 horse and 2,000 foot.[65] Even allowing for those lost in the siege of Piombino and those detached to garrison Castiglione della Pescáia, the total strength of the army had probably never been much greater than this. The Duke of Calabria commanded 6,000 horse and 2,000 foot in the Florentine war of 1452–3,[66] a campaign which again

---

[60] ACA Reg. 2698. 103ʳ, 5 Sept. 1445. The council in Naples was told to stop the proceedings 'ab aquelles pus honests colors queus sia possible'.

[61] ACA Reg. 2699. 33ᵛ, 3 Feb. 1446.

[62] ACA Reg. 2698. 165ᵛ, 17 Mar. 1446; Reg. 2940. 7ʳ, 2 May 1446.

[63] Ibid. In this autograph letter to the Cardinal of Aquileia Alfonso wrote: '. . . e mas presto que pensays esta semana en que esto, plaziendo a dios, desempachare j m. cavallos e mil infantes . . .'

[64] Ibid. 15ʳ, Alfonso to the Cardinal of Aquileia, 20 Aug. 1446: 'Señor no vos maravileys si tanto e tardado en desempachar a Babtista de cinguli vestro criado car lo e fecho porque vos levase certidumbre de lo que queria fazer e assi mesino vos levasse algunos cavallos.' The 200 infantry needed to make up the 1,000 promised to the cardinal 'no son aun allegados'.

[65] Ametller y Vinyas, Alfonso V de Aragón, ii. 646.

[66] These are the figures given by Facio (De rebus gestis, X, col. 160) and probably include the 1,000 infantry which Alfonso promised Frederico di Montefeltro in March 1452 (ACA Reg. 2697. 123ᵛ, 3 Mar. 1452). They left Naples on 3 Apr. (Reg. 2659. 81ᵛ) and later, under the command of Frederico, joined the army of the Duke of Calabria.

went so badly that the king had to promise his allies, the Venetians, that he would intervene in person with another army of 3,000 lances.[67] By the end of July 1453 he claimed to have mustered 4,000 horse, but the relief army, whatever its final strength, had not crossed the frontier by the end of October when the king fell ill, and only 1,000 horse[68] were eventually sent under the command of Iñigo de Guevara to succour Ferdinand. It would seem, therefore, that Alfonso could gather together, at the most, 5,000 or 6,000 horse and 2,000 foot soldiers. Though well below those given out to overawe enemies and encourage allies, these numbers compare reasonably well with other Italian armies of the day. Florence is reputed, by Machiavelli, to have had 8,000 men at its disposal to face Alfonso in 1452, but he has in all probability exaggerated the figure because he reckons the king's army to have numbered 12,000.[69] The French army formed by Charles VII in 1445 'numbered little more than 8,000 men'.[70]

The great majority of mounted and foot soldiers in Alfonso's armies were Italian; so too were most of his captains. Of the fifty-four captains holding *condotte* for ten or more lances listed by Borso d'Este in 1444 forty were Italians. When in 1452 he gave his son Ferdinand his first command of an army, Alfonso appointed to advise him a council composed of the most experienced and trusted captains in that army. Only one Spaniard, Garcia de Cabanyells, served on it, and an inner council of three was composed solely of Italians: Orso Orsini, Paolo di Sangro, and Theseo de Savellis.[71] Members of the great noble families of the kingdom

[67] ACA Reg. 2697. 154ʳ, 29 June 1453.

[68] ACA Reg. 2799, 13ʳ, 24 July 1453, Alfonso to Matteu Malferit: '. . . fins ala present jornada havem spachats iiij m. cavalls e continuam desempachar lo restant.' The figure of 1,000 horse is that given by Facio (*De rebus gestis*, X, cols. 176–7); Summonte (*Historia*, IV. 6, p. 179) puts the number at 500.

[69] Corresponding reductions ought probably to be made in Machiavelli's estimates for other armies—e.g. he puts the strength of the Venetian army at Caraveggio at 12,000 horse, and reckons that in May 1452 it amounted to 16,000 horse and 6,000 foot; for Sforza's army in May 1452 he gives figures of 18,000 horse and 3,000 foot.

[70] J. H. Shennan, *Government and Society in France 1461–1661* (London, 1969), p. 36. Charles the Bold of Burgundy could muster an army of no more than 15,000, which figure included the feudal ban and arrière ban (J. Calmette, *The Golden Age of Burgundy* (London, 1962), p. 249). The discussion of the size of armies by Mallett (*Mercenaries and their Masters*, pp. 116–18), which came to my notice after this chapter was written, reaches conclusions in line with my own.

[71] ACA Reg. 2798. 17ᵛ, 15 July 1452. The other members of the council were

at all times figure prominently in the king's armies. In 1437 Giovanni della Ratta, Count of Caserta, was serving with thirty lances,[72] Raimondo Orsini, Count of Nola, with 200,[73] Bertoldo degli Orsini commanded forty lances,[74] Onorato Gaetano, Count of Morcone, commanded eighty.[75] In that same year we also find among the king's captains Giacomo Gaetano, son of the Count of Fondi, Giovanni Battista Carafa, Carafello Carafa,[76] and Orso Orsini.[77] The captains of 1444 included Troiano Caracciolo, Duke of Melfi,[78] Carlo di Campobasso, Agostino di Sanseverino, Antonello della Ratta, Giacomo Zurlo.[79] Many of the infantry commanders too were Italians: Nanne de Alba,[80] Sancho di Maddaloni,[81] Giovanni di Benevento,[82] Antonuccio di Paganico,[83] Leone di Salerno alias Caceta, Russo di Aversa, and Cosimo del Garreto[84] are among those who held the office of 'peditum comestabulus'. Italians also appear among the marshals who were responsible for organizing the lodgings of the army, controlling its supplies of foodstuffs, and administering justice.[85] Rinaldo Bonito was marshal of Ferdinand's army in 1452.[86]

As for the commanders of armies, one often finds Italians leading the king's forces. The greater *condottieri*, such as Nicolo and

---

Carlo di Campobasso, Antonio Caldora, Leonello Aclocciamura, Cola Scarano, Agostino di Sanseverino, Raimondo d'Anechino, and Jacobo di Montagano.

[72] Minieri Riccio, 'Alcuni fatti di Alfonso I', p. 4.   [73] Ibid., p. 5.
[74] Ibid.   [75] Ibid., p. 7.   [76] Ibid., p. 8.
[77] Faraglia, *Storia della lotta*, p. 91, n. 3.
[78] He led a body of troops to the aid of Piccinino in the March of Ancona in March 1444 (ACA Reg. 2698. 43ᵛ).
[79] These names appear in Borso d'Este's list of captains.
[80] ACA Reg. 2904. 78ʳ, 8 Mar. 1443, a pardon for any offences this 'peditum comestabulus' might have committed while serving the king.
[81] ACA Reg. 2907. 119ʳ, 27 June 1445. Sancho and Nanne de Alba are jointly granted the hearth tax in Corbari.
[82] ACA Reg. 2902. 5ʳ, 2 Apr. 1440, Privilege appointing him captain of Montefuscolo.   [83] ACA Reg. 2908. 72ʳ, 6 Oct. 1445.
[84] These three are among the officers of the army in April 1437 listed by Faraglia, *Storia della lotta*, p. 91, n. 3.
[85] The privilege appointing Pietro Palagano a marshal, 'more huius Regni nostri Sicilie citra farum', charges him with 'providendi, ordinandi et collocandi felicem nostrum exercitum mansiones et loca congrua, dandi schyeras et squatras ipsius nostri exercitus collocandi, et eis providendi, iustitiam ministrandi, assisias, statuta et ordinationes condecentes et concedentia super pane, vino, grano, ordeo, carnibus et aliis victualibus quibuscumque ponendi, mittendi et assignandi' (Rogadeo, *Codice diplomatico*, pp. 36–7).
[86] ASN Priv. I. 12ᵛ, 8 Oct. 1452: '. . . nostri consiliarii et marescialli . . . et precipue in bello presentis temporibus in quibus munus marescialli gessit . . .'

Francesco Piccinino and Frederico di Montefeltro, exercised virtually independent command over their troops, so too did the Prince of Taranto.[87] Menicuccio de Amicis dela Aquila held the title of captain general of the king's men-at-arms in 1436;[88] it probably indicates an independent command for it is the title given in that same year to Francesco Piccinino.[89] Another notable captain general was the Sicilian noble, Giovanni di Vintimiglia, Marquis of Gerace. His military career began in 1420 when he served with Alfonso in the siege of Acerra.[90] Muzio Attendolo Sforza took him prisoner in a battle outside Naples in 1423.[91] In 1432 he accompanied the king on his expedition to the island of Djerba and commanded a section of the army in the engagement fought against its ruler.[92] When Alfonso returned to his Neapolitan enterprise he sent the marquis with a body of troops to support the Prince of Taranto.[93] He was taken prisoner at Ponza, defended Capua against Caldora in 1436,[94] and in 1438 took part in an unsuccessful siege of Naples.[95] He received his first independent command in 1443 when he led the advance forces of the king in the March of Ancona. During the following year we find him in the Balkans exercising the office of viceroy in Athens and Neopatria and assisting his brother-in-law Charles Tocco II. Alfonso recalled him in 1445, again to assume command of an army in the March.[96]

In the light of this regular employment of Italian troops, captains, and commanders, how does one explain the charge made by Borso d'Este that Alfonso relied too much upon 'Catalan' troops and captains? The term 'Catalan' must not be taken literally, for as used by Borso it applied to any person of Spanish extraction, including Spanish families long settled in Sicily. Thus men such as Pedro de Cardona,[97] Guillem Ramon de Moncada, and Lope

---

[87] Cf. above, p. 262.

[88] 'Capita general dela gent darmes del Senyor Rey' (Faraglia, *Storia della lotta*, p. 73, n. 2). This reference is to November.

[89] Ibid., p. 56.   [90] Facio, *De rebus gestis*, ii.

[91] Ametller y Vinyas, *Alfonso V de Aragón*, i. 167.

[92] Ibid. 350.

[93] Ibid. i. 442 and 454. In September 1437 he was commissioned to raise 231 lances as a captain of men-at-arms (Minieri Riccio, 'Alcuni fatti di Alfonso I', p. 6).

[94] Ametller y Vinyas, *Alfonso V de Aragón*, ii. 39.

[95] Ibid. 190.

[96] ACA Reg. 2698. 109^r, 27 Sept. 1445, a memorial for the marquis as captain general of the royal army.

[97] Cf. above, p. 61.

Ximenez de Urrea were to him 'Catalans' not Sicilians, and certainly not Italians. More than anything else the overwhelmingly Spanish character of the royal household must have created the impression that the king's most trusted companions-in-arms were non-Italian. Iñigo de Guevara, the *mayordomen*, fought alongside the king at Ponza and Carpenone, in the March of Ancona, and at the siege of Piombino; he again joined the army the king was raising in September 1453 as captain general.[98] His half-brother Iñigo de Avalos likewise engaged in battle only on those occasions when the king in person led his army. The same holds true for the brothers Alfonso and Pedro de Cardona, and for Eximen Perez de Corella. Since the king did command his main armies until the end of 1448, Spaniards and Spanish-Sicilians holding major household offices figured prominently in his military entourage during that period. However, very few of them held regular commissions or *condotte*. If we turn to Borso's own list of *condotte* for 1444, we find among them only a handful of Spaniards of the household: Iñigo de Guevara has 300 lances; Ramon Boyl, a *camerlengus*, has 200; 'lo signor dom Lupo'—probably the chamberlain Lope Ximenez de Urrea—has 150; Jacme Ferrer, a gentleman of the chamber, commands twenty-five lances; Antonio de Luna, Count of Caltabellotta and chamberlain of Sicily, has twenty-five.[99] In subsequent years, and especially after 1448, the part played by Spaniards, whether courtiers or professional soldiers, in Alfonso's armies was greatly diminished. Only a few nobles held military commands of any significance. Fernando de Guevara and Luis dez Puig assumed command of the few Aragonese troops in Milanese territory in July 1449 but did nothing with them.[100] On the other hand, Garcia de Cabanyells, Count of Troia, pursued an active military career and was killed in action in Tuscany while serving as an adviser to the Duke of Calabria.[101] Ramon d'Ortaffa was another Spanish noble who might be described as a professional soldier. He spent some years in Genoa as captain of a thousand men sent by Alfonso to bolster the position

---

[98] Ametller y Vinyas, *Alfonso V de Aragón*, i. 487; ii. 420, 641; ACA Reg. 2799. 42ᵛ, 12 Sept. 1453.

[99] To these it may be necessary to add the *mayordomen* Juan Fernandez de Hijar with twenty-five lances if that is the identity of 'Messer Zuam Dilia catelano'.

[100] ACA Reg. 2697. 33ᵛ, 6 July 1449.

[101] He died 'cum multa sanguinis effusione' (ACA Reg. 2917. 118ʳ).

of the Adorni faction.[102] From 1452 until the end of the reign he served as the king's viceroy in Albania and commanded the small force of Aragonese troops supporting Scanderbeg.[103] Ramon Boyl, a Valencian noble, had a long and continuous military career which entitles him also to be considered a professional soldier. During the civil war he commanded the garrisons of the castles held by the Aragonese in Naples, late in 1439 he besieged and took the castle of Aversa, and at the battle of Carpenone he commanded a reserve division of the king's army.[104] Alfonso left him with 500 lances and 500 foot to guard the Abruzzi frontier during the winter of 1442;[105] in that same region in the following year he successfully besieged the castle of Teramo, and in September again assumed command of the troops there as royal commissioner in the March of Ancona.[106] He it was who took Sforza's last stronghold in the kingdom, the castle of Civitella, in October 1445.[107] October 1446 saw him dispatched to the aid of the Milanese, but though he was able for a brief period after the death of Filippo Maria Visconti to take possession of the castle of Milan, his position there soon became militarily and politically hopeless. Circumstances forced him to hand over the fortress to the newly established republican government, which then arrested him and his men and confiscated their arms and horses. After Alfonso had negotiated his release, Boyl was sent in the autumn of 1448 to take command of a body of troops mustered at Ferrara in order to attack Sforza's position in the Parmigiano in the following spring.[108] By June 1449 money to pay his men had still not arrived, and perhaps it never came, for in February 1451 Alfonso had to ask the Marquis of Ferrara to intercede with Boyl's creditors who had placed a distraint on his arms and horses.[109] This second fiasco seems to have marked the

---

[102] ACA Reg. 2690. 90ᵛ, 3 July 1444, Instructions for him. He was still in Genoa in October 1446 when Alfonso informed him that it was impossible to send money to pay his men (ACA Reg. 2699. 48ʳ, 11 Oct. 1446). At the same time the king expressed satisfaction with his conduct.

[103] C. Marinescu, 'Alphonse V roi d'Aragon et de Naples, et l'Albanie de Scanderbeg', *Mélanges de l'École roumaine en France*, 1 (Paris, 1923), 59. On 15 June 1454 his vice-royalty was extended to cover Greece and Slavonia (ACA Reg. 2661. 70ᵛ).

[104] Ametller y Vinyas, *Alfonso V de Aragón*, i. 441; ii. 274, 282, 397, 418.

[105] Ibid., p. 423.

[106] ACA Reg. 2690. 44ʳ, 26 Sept. 1443, Commission for Boyl.

[107] Ametller y Vinyas, *Alfonso V de Aragón*, ii. 546.

[108] ACA Reg. 2696. 173ʳ, 25 Sept. 1448; Reg. 2697. 16ʳ, 8 Apr. 1449.

[109] Ibid. 21ᵛ, 7 June 1449; ibid. 85ᵛ, 21 Feb. 1451.

end of an otherwise successful military career; in January 1453 Boyl retired with a pension of 1,000 ducats a year.[110]

A few Spanish notables travelled from their home country to make brief appearances with Alfonso's armies in Italy. Hugo Roger de Pallars, the constable of Aragon, was with them in 1444 and 1445.[111] Diego Gomez de Sandoval, *adelantado* of Castile, and his sons, Hernando and Diego, fought at Ponza. The younger son, Diego, may have remained in Italy; if not he returned to serve Alfonso, for on 20 January 1449 the king ordered Perot Mercader to arrange the transport of all the Castilian's horses and men to Naples.[112] Galeotto Bardaxi, an Aragonese knight who had won renown in many states for his prowess in duels and tournaments, was specially summoned to Italy to fight for the king. When he arrived in 1448 he was given an annual provision of 120 *oncie*[113] and soon found an opportunity to distinguish himself in the attack on Piombino.[114] One may suppose that a number of Spanish commoners also found their way to Italy to serve in the king's wars, but no very large bodies of troops were dispatched other than those which accompanied him on his two departures from Spain. Nor were many requested because Alfonso preferred that his western states should support him with money rather than men; the Spanish soldier had not yet attained that reputation which was to make him master of Italy half a century later. On those occasions when Alfonso did ask for troops from Spain, he wanted not mounted men—Italy abounded in these—but crossbowmen. In November 1439 he asked Queen Maria to arrange for 500 to be sent; they were to be in Italy by April 1440 with pay for at least six months.[115] Three hundred sailed from Barcelona in June 1440,[116]

[110] ACA Reg. 2917. 94^r, 6 Jan. 1453.

[111] He appears to have travelled to Naples overland by way of Lombardy and to have been detained there for some time (ACA Reg. 2690. 102^v, 17 Aug. 1444). By October 1445 he was campaigning in the March of Ancona (ACA Reg. 2939. 86^r, 18 Oct. 1445).   [112] ACA Reg. 2720. 106.

[113] ACA Reg. 2913. 1^r, 12 Apr. 1448. The privilege describes him as 'nobilis strenuus qui duelli certamina compluresque alios bellicosos actus tam in Hispania Italia Alamannia Gallia quam aliis mundi partibus strenue agens ita viriliter in illis sese gessit quod victor undique evasit'. Alfonso had sent his herald Calabria to Flanders to assist Bardaxi in one of his duels (ACA Reg. 2939. 125^r, 29 Mar. 1446).

[114] Ametller y Vinyas, *Alfonso V de Aragón*, ii. 643–4.

[115] ACA Reg. 2651. 139^r, 23 Nov. 1439: 200 were to be paid by Catalonia and Majorca, 200 by Aragon and Valencia, and 100 by the crown.

[116] Madurell Marimon, *Mensajeros barceloneses*, p. 209.

and Alfonso was encouraged to make similar requests of Sicily and Sardinia.[117] The struggle with Florence led him in 1448 to demand 1,000 bowmen from the Cortes of Catalonia and an unspecified number from Valencia.[118] Though it is unlikely that either state met his request in full, both had sent contingents which joined his army at Piombino by August 1448.[119] The largest request of all came in July 1454 when the King of Navarre was told to ask the Cortes of Catalonia for 2,000 crossbowmen,[120] later amended to 1,600 bowmen and 400 sailors.[121] None of these was sent, whether from a refusal of the Cortes or from a disappearance of the need after the Peace of Lodi, we cannot be sure. In general we may conclude that in Alfonso's armies the proportion of Spaniards among the foot soldiers was much higher than among the mounted men-at-arms.

Armies commanded by *condottieri* usually had attached to them one or more commissioners whose duty it was to ensure that the general obeyed his instructions and to exercise those political functions that the king did not see fit to entrust to his captains; in short they performed functions similar to those of the Venetian *provedittori*. A commission of this kind was given to the secretary Bernat Lopez in October 1457. It empowered him, as general commissioner with the king's forces under Francesco Piccinino and Frederico di Montefeltro in central Italy, to supervise the execution of the king's orders and to grant *condotte*, truces, safe-conducts, etc., as he saw fit.[122] In June 1452, while the Duke of Calabria moved slowly towards Tuscany to join the Duke of Urbino, the hospitaller Andrea di Candida, prior of Barletta, attended the latter as the king's commissioner.[123]

---

[117] ACA Reg. 2651. 149^v, Alfonso to the viceroy of Sardinia, 22 Apr. 1440. If skilled bowmen are not available in Sardinia the king suggests that the kingdom should provide money to pay the Spanish troops beyond their initial six months.

[118] ACA Reg. 2657. 43^v, 22 Feb. 1448.

[119] ACA Reg. 2696. 170^r, Alfonso to Luis dez Puig, 11 Aug. 1448.

[120] ACA Reg. 2700. 69^v, 27 July 1454.

[121] ACA Reg. 2661. 77^v, 2 Nov. 1454.

[122] ACA Reg. 2800. 41^v, 19 Oct. 1457, the commission for Lopez; ibid. 43^v, 20 Oct. 1457; his instructions, which provide, *inter alia*, that should the Duke of Modena die and his brother Ercole ask for aid in obtaining the dukedom, Lopez is to divert Piccinino from the attack upon Rimini and send his forces in support of Ercole.

[123] ACA Reg. 2798. 2^r, 6 June 1452. In this letter the king instructs the Duke of Calabria to advise di Candida of all correspondence between himself and Montefeltro.

Because mercenaries were plentiful and money was not, men were seldom hired for more than a few months. Although a certain amount of bargaining might take place, it moved within narrow limits, there being in Italy a recognized rate for the hire of mounted and foot soldiers.[124] When giving a *condotta* on a monthly basis, Alfonso usually paid at the rate of 8 ducats for a lance. Thus Carlo Ruffo, on behalf of the king, paid fifty lances a total of 4,800 ducats for twelve months;[125] Sigismondo Malatesta and Luigi Pessa were offered it;[126] the half-pay suggested for the Duke of Urbino in 1448 was to be 4 ducats a month for each lance.[127] Payment at a higher rate seems to have been given only for small bodies of men, and presumably as a special favour. Some defectors from Caldora's army were taken over by the king at $12\frac{1}{2}$ ducats a month in November 1437.[128] Juan de Hijar, Alfonso's viceroy in Calabria, contracted with Filippo, Jacobo, and Troilo Baramonte to serve with twenty horse at the rate of 10 ducats a lance in September 1422 when he was endeavouring to preserve the Aragonese foothold in that province.[129] *Condotte* contracted for a year normally involved an expenditure of 50 ducats a lance, a figure which took into consideration the limited duration of the campaigning season and the difficulty which a mercenary soldier would have in finding employment outside it. In 1449 dez Puig had instructions to negotiate a *condotta* with the Marquis of Mantua at 40 ducats, or at most 50 ducats, a lance.[130] Paolo di Sangro and Carlo di Campobasso were hired at this rate in 1437.[131] A higher figure of 9 or 10 *oncie* (i.e. 54 or 60 ducats) was sometimes paid to those with only one or two lances,[132] but Borso d'Este was incorrect in his statement that 60 ducats was the regular annual stipend for a lance. For a foot soldier the usual rate of pay was 2 ducats a month. Carlo Ruffo paid

---

[124] Cf. M. Mallett, *Mercenaries*, p. 137. The rates paid by Alfonso corresponded closely to those paid by Venice and Milan; at the beginning of the century they had been almost twice as high.

[125] Mazzoleni, *Fonti aragonese*, i. 21. This was in March 1438.

[126] The offer to Malatesta was made in 1447 (Ametller y Vinyas, *Alfonso V de Aragón*, ii. 600). Pessa's *condotta* was for payment purposes expressed at the monthly rate even though it was to be of unlimited duration (ACA Reg. 2700. 107^r, 11 Jan. 1456).

[127] ACA Reg. 2696. 143^r, 21 Apr. 1448; cf. above, p. 265.

[128] Mazzoleni, *Fonti aragonesi*, i. 83.

[129] Pontieri, *Fonti aragonesi*, ii. 33.

[130] ACA Reg. 2697. 21^r, 3 June 1449.   [131] ACA Reg. 2695. 39^r.

[132] Carlo Ruffo made some payments at these rates (Mazzoleni, *Fonti aragonesi*, i. 22).

captains of infantry at that rate in 1438,[133] Nanno di Sulmona
received it for his 300 men in 1440,[134] and it still applied in 1456
when 1,800 ducats was sent to Francesco Piccinino as pay for 300
infantry for three months.[135] When paying the stipend of troops
the treasury normally deducted a commission or *elagio* of 4 per cent,
though the king often waived it.[136]

To give effect to a condotta, Italian custom (*la usanza italiana*)
required an advance payment known as the *imprestanza* to be given
to the captains. Only when that had been completed would they
take the field. The amount to be paid was a matter for negotiation
and seems usually to have been three months' pay, though larger
sums were given when a long period of service was envisaged. The
agreement between the viceroy of Calabria and the Baramontes
in 1422 provided for an *imprestanza* of 40 ducats a lance;[137] in
August 1453 Alfonso was intending to pay 50 ducats a lance to the
army being mustered for a campaign in Tuscany.[138] On this latter
occasion, as on many others, he found it impossible to pay the
whole *imprestanza* in a lump sum, and so had to give it in instalments as money became available; hence the inordinate delays
which often occurred before his armies could be set in motion.
Italian custom further demanded that two-thirds of the *imprestanza*
be paid in cash and one-third in cloth. Putting an army in the field
thus entailed not only finding large sums of ready money, but also
organizing the purchase of considerable quantities of cloth. Since
the kingdom of Naples had no cloth industry, Alfonso arranged
for most of the cloth he needed to be imported from his Spanish
territories. The Aragonese registers record many purchases of this
nature: 1,500 'cloths of those sorts and colours which the said
Lord King is used to have brought from there to give for the

---

[133] Mazzoleni, *Fonti aragonesi*, i. 22.

[134] ACA Reg. 2646. 84ʳ, 26 Mar. 1440, Alfonso to the Count of Campobasso
who was acting as an intermediary with Nanno.

[135] ACA Reg. 2800. 4ᵛ, 17 Nov. 1456.

[136] Mazzoleni, *Fonti aragonesi*, i. 98–9. Faraglia (*Storia della lotta*, p. 299, n. 1)
quotes the instance of Paolo di Sangro who in June 1442 received 8,000 ducats
for 200 lances. From this sum the treasury deducted an *elagio* of 420 ducats
according to Faraglia; this should probably read 320 ducats. In the agreement
reached with Sigismondo Malatesta in April 1447, Alfonso promised not to
exact an *elagio* on his *condotta* (Ametller y Vinyas, *Alfonso V de Aragón*, ii. 600).

[137] Pontieri, *Fonti aragonesi*, ii. 33.

[138] ACA Reg. 2799. 35ʳ, 19 Aug. 1453, Alfonso to Matteu Malferit: '. . . havem
fet donar los deu ducats per lança quels restaven dels cinquanta ducats per
lança quels donam de prestança . . .' Cf. Mallett, *Mercenaries*, pp. 83–4.

imprestanza' were to be bought with part of the proceeds of a clerical subsidy;[139] 5,375 cloths bought in January 1452 from Francesch Giginta of Perpignan at a price of 86,000 ducats;[140] 2,500 'common Perpignan cloths' from Bertran Crexells for 50,000 ducats.[141] They also contain many accounts of the distribution of cloth to the king's captains and *condottieri*. On 25 November 1436 he was urging the secretary Olzina to see that the Prince of Taranto received cloth to the value of 1,000 ducats without delay.[142] Two days later he ordered that Antonuccio Orsini be given cloth to the value of 200 ducats—half in Florentine cloth and half in Majorcan cloth.[143] A warrant addressed to the treasurer on 6 December 1448 authorized the issue of cloth due for 'la emprestanza passada' to Joan Catala and Bernat Vidal, constables of the king's guard.[144] Retrospective payment of the *imprestanza* in this manner would not have been possible had the men concerned been mercenary troops. Red, blue, green, white, and purple were the colours preferred for the cloths.[145] Payment for them was usually charged upon a Spanish source of revenue, and so they represented a substantial subsidy from those territories for the king's military operations in Italy.

Spain also contributed to the king's artillery with pieces ranging from the huge bombard belonging to the *generalidad* of Catalonia to the smaller bombards in whose manufacture the Catalans had become particularly skilled. The great siege piece known as the 'General' is said to have been used by Alfonso in his attack on Marseille in 1423;[146] in 1440 he told Queen Maria to buy it from the *generalidad*,[147] and this she must have done for in February

---

[139] ACA Reg. 2939. 71ᵛ, 17 July 1443: 'draps de aquelles sorts e colors que lo dit Senyor acostuma fer venir e haver deça per dar ala emprestança.'

[140] ACA Reg. 2940. 143ᵛ, 24 Jan. 1452.

[141] Ibid. 138ʳ, 10 Aug. 1451. The Register 2651, 69 ff. records many purchases of cloth made from various merchants in April 1437 for the *imprestanza*.

[142] ACA Reg. 2900. 9ᵛ: '. . . fazet que aya presto los mil ducados en draps de lana, car soy obligado al principe, e dios sabe si soy tenido acerca.'

[143] Ibid. 10ᵛ. Antonuccio was the son of Francesco Orsini, the prefect of Rome. Cloth valued at 400 ducats was given to the Count of Fondi on 4 Nov. 1437 (Minieri Riccio, 'Alcuni fatti di Alfonso I', p. 9).

[144] ACA Reg. 2719. 84ʳ.

[145] A contract signed on 8 Dec. 1451 with Marti dela Cavalleria for 1,100 cloths to be made in Barcelona specified the following colours: 350 red, 250 blue, 250 green, 200 white, and 50 purple (Mazzoleni, *Il Codice Chigi*, pp. 214–17).

[146] Ametller y Vinyas, *Alfonso V de Aragón*, i. 191, n. 3.

[147] ACA Reg. 2651. 170ʳ, 27 Oct. 1440. She was to pay up to 2,000 florins.

1442 he instructed her to send it to Italy.[148] It was brought into
Castelnuovo in March 1443, and in December 1444 transported
by sea to Calabria, together with another siege piece known as the
'San Jorge', for use against Centelles's strongholds.[149] Advances
in the art of smelting in Catalonia and the discovery of a means
whereby bombards could be constructed in sections, thus making
their transportation easier, had given the artillery of that province
a great reputation in Europe.[150] Large numbers of pieces of all
sizes were made there on the king's orders for use in Italy. Carles
d'Olms, procurator royal in Roussillon and Cerdagne, the centre
of the Catalan metallurgical industry, sent two bombards to Naples
in December 1453 and at once received instructions to have
another thirty-five made with longer 'male' (*mascles*) sections.[151]
(The bombard consisted of two sections, the 'male' or muzzle
section fitting into the breech or 'female' section; by lengthening
the 'male', the range of the weapon was increased.) D'Olms delivered these pieces in February 1455.[152] Still not content with his
artillery, Alfonso ordered a further forty bombards with 156
'males'[153] from Spain, but of these only 24 bombards and 96
'males' reached Naples in May 1457; the rest were taken by a
Genoese ship.[154] Besides bringing artillery from Spain, Alfonso
developed the casting of cannon in the arsenal of Naples. One
of his first masters of this art was Bartolommeo di Milano who
was at work in the arsenal in October 1447.[155] Later a Frenchman
known as Guglielmo lo Monaco, a particularly skilled caster,
made some huge bombards for him. One cast in 1454 consumed
65 quintals 87 rotols of bronze.[156] In the following year lo Monaco
made 'La Napoletana', a bombard in three sections which weighed
102 quintals 22 rotols and fired projectiles weighing 2 quintals.[157]

Alfonso used this artillery in sieges and for the defence of fortified positions. Contemporary records give little indication of its

[148] ACA Reg. 2650. 137ᵛ.
[149] Minieri Riccio, 'Alcuni fatti di Alfonso I', pp. 234, 247.
[150] Macdonald, *Fernando de Antequera*, p. 180.
[151] ACA Reg. 2661. 50ʳ, 26 Dec. 1453.
[152] ACA Reg. 2721. 70ʳ. 13 Feb. 1455. Each had cost 100 Perpignan shillings.
[153] The 'male' section tended to wear out quickly. The consignment of bombards delivered in 1455 had a spare 'male' for each piece.
[154] ACA Reg. 2721. 51ᵛ, 11 July 1457.
[155] Minieri Riccio, 'Alcuni fatti di Alfonso I', p. 255.
[156] The metal was delivered to lo Monaco in February 1454 (ibid., p. 429).
[157] Ibid., p. 444. 'La Napoletana' was used against Genoa in 1478 (Bianchini,
Della storia delle finanze, p. 214).

effectiveness. The pains the king took to equip himself with the new weapons may merely reflect his determination not to be outdone in novelties by any other prince. On the other hand, he does appear to have placed much reliance upon them. Costanzo attributes the failure of the Duke of Calabria's attack on Florence in 1452 to the bursting of his bombard on its first shot; without it the duke found it impossible to take fortified towns and was delayed outside the small castle of Castellina for forty-four days.[158] It may have been the setbacks of this campaign that prompted the rapid growth in the royal artillery of subsequent years. By 1452 four large pieces known as 'passavolanti' had already been mounted on a tower to guard the port of Naples;[159] many more bombards were positioned on the shore in June 1453 to defend the city against a threatened Genoese attack.[160] To take charge of his growing arsenal of large firearms Alfonso created the office of master of artillery. Pere de Lartiga was the first incumbent;[161] after his death the office passed briefly to Alessandro Moragues,[162] and then to Guillem Pujades. It was in his possession by 1 July 1444 when the king sent an official of the *escriva de racio* to collect artillery and powder from him,[163] and he appears to have retained it for the rest of the reign.[164]

The paucity of references to handguns in the Aragonese documents leads one to suspect that Alfonso's armies made little use of smaller firearms even though he employed them as early as 1421 in the siege of Acerra.[165] Four spingards were purchased in

[158] Costanzo, *Historia*, iv. 6, p. 160.
[159] 'Come lo Imperatore Federico entrò in Napoli' (1908), 489. Other pieces of artillery were known as 'dragoni' (Minieri Riccio, 'Alcuni fatti di Alfonso I', p. 17: reference to October 1438) and 'serpentini' (ibid., p. 425).
[160] Ibid., p. 418.
[161] Ibid., p. 14: reference to 1438; Faraglia, *Storia della lotta*, p. 165, n. 2: reference to de Lartiga in 1439.
[162] He held it in June 1443 (Minieri Riccio, 'Alcuni fatti di Alfonso I', p. 241).
[163] ACA Reg. 2690. 88ʳ.
[164] As 'tenens custodiam artillerarium' he received the thirty-five bombards from Spain in February 1455 (ACA Reg. 2721. 70ʳ).
[165] Faraglia, *Storia della lotta*, p. 183. Faraglia disputes the assertion of Zurita that René of Anjou was the first to use spingards in the kingdom of Naples: 'Fué este príncipe el primero, que llevó al Reino las espingardas: pero pocos sabían hacer la pólvora: y el Rey mandó hacer gran número dellas: y comenzaron á usarse mucho de allí en adelante como arma ofensiva y terrible' (apud Ametller y Vinyas, *Alfonso V de Aragón*, ii. 273). Since bombards were fairly freely employed, a scarcity of powder is unlikely to have been an important limiting factor in the use of handguns.

November 1441 at 3 ducats apiece,[166] and another twenty in May 1442 for the same price.[167] A purchase of lead to make balls for them figures in the treasury accounts for April 1442.[168] What discouraged the king from adopting them on a large scale was probably a lack of men skilled in their use and the fact that they still possessed no decisive superiority over the crossbow. So long as he could obtain seasoned archers from Spain, he had no reason to abandon the crossbow as the favoured offensive weapon of his infantry. Spain also supplied heavy bolts for the bows[169] and a large quantity of lighter missiles known as *passadors*.[170]

Like most other armies of the time, those of Alfonso were composed largely of mounted men-at-arms; foot soldiers numbered no more than a quarter of their total strength. Yet, despite this emphasis upon cavalry, pitched battles which allowed that arm to be used to full advantage were rarely ventured. In the whole course of his Italian wars Alfonso engaged in very few full-scale land battles, and some of those were the result of accident not design. His campaigns were otherwise a series of skirmishes, sieges, and manœuvrings. Many other Italian princes and *condottieri* employed similar tactics which contemporaries identified with the tradition established by Muzio Attendolo Sforza in contrast to that of Braccio da Montone and his follower Nicolo Piccinino who believed in forcing the enemy to a decisive encounter. Instructions given to royal commanders almost always stressed the need for caution and the avoidance of risk. A letter to the Duke of Calabria in July 1453 is a typical example:[171]

[166] Faraglia, *Storia della lotta*, p. 258, n. 2.

[167] Minieri Riccio, 'Alcuni fatti di Alfonso I', p. 34.   [168] Ibid., p. 32.

[169] ACA Reg. 2901. 17ʳ. 20 June 1441. An instruction to the *magister rationalis* of Valencia to allow in the accounts of Berenguer Mercader expenses for the manufacture of bolts ('viratons') sent to Italy.

[170] Perot Mercader shipped twenty-six cases of *passadors* to Naples (ibid. 151ᵛ, 23 Feb. 1445). In 1455 the *receptor general* Miquel Bru sent fifty cases (ACA Reg. 2661. 103ʳ).

[171] ACA Reg. 2799. 8ᵛ, 11 July 1453: '... havem sentit per diverses parts que los florentins entenen secretament aiustar la llur gent darmes e fer de dos cosas la una, o de venir a trobar vos, o de metrese ales spatles vestres per poder vos tenir clos, per fer vos algun carrech e vergonya o dan ans que nos ab nostre exercit siam en aquexes parts. Perço es mester que haiau consell ab ursino lo qual deura esser ja aqui e ab consell de aquell vos conselleu ab los altres capitans e altres queus aparra que de aquesta materia aconsellar vos deiau e ab aquells delibereu aon deiau star fins atant que siau pus poderos dels enemichs, e si en aquexes parts e altres dels enemichs podeu star sens perill deles coses dessus dites per no perdre la reputacio e conservar la opinio bona deles gents la qual huy ha

We have heard from various sources that the Florentines intend secretly to gather together their men-at-arms and do one of two things: either to come face to face with you, or else to place themselves in your rear in order to hem you in. Their purpose is to harm or discredit you before we with our army reach those parts. Therefore it is necessary that you take counsel with Orsino, who ought already to be there; and with his advice consult the other captains, and anyone else you think should advise you on this matter; decide with them where you should place yourself until you are stronger than the enemy. If you can remain where you are, or elsewhere in enemy territory, without any of the dangers mentioned above, so as not to lose your reputation and keep the good opinion of people—which is today of great weight in most matters —then you should stay there. If you cannot do so without danger, you should go where your reputation will suffer least, and where you and your army are safe from danger and harm.

In giving such orders or advice, Alfonso was often blending an innate caution with a calculation that the enemy might be overcome by financial exhaustion so that his armies would melt away without a trial of armed strength. In June 1452 he advised the Venetians to avoid the pitched battle which Sforza was seeking:

For, as we have written to you on many occasions, to avoid giving battle to him is to destroy him utterly, because the count has to give money, and having no means of getting it, he is of necessity going to lose his following and his state without putting the state of the Signoria in any danger whatsoever.[172]

On the other hand, he was not incapable of urging action when he judged the situation to be favourable or believed that time was running against him and not his adversary. Such a situation existed in the summer of 1452 when, while pressing caution upon the Venetians, he was exhorting his own captains to come to grips with the Florentines because 'to remain undisturbed would redound greatly to the interest of the Florentines now that we have challenged them'.[173]

una gran efficacia en los mes fets ho façau. E on no se pogues fer sens perill anau en aquella part aon menys dela reputacio se perda, e a vos e a vestre exercit sia segur de no haver perill e dan.'

[172] ACA Reg. 2798. 9ʳ, 21 June 1452: '... car segons moltes vos havem scrit, lo deviar de venir ab ell a batalla es destruirlo totalment per que havent lo dit comte a donar diners nous no haura manera de haver los, e axi ve a perdre de necessitat la companyia e son stat sens metre lo stat dela dita S. en perill algu.'

[173] ACA Reg. 2798. 8ᵛ, 21 June 1452. '... redundaria in grande utile deli fflorentini li quali nuy havendo diffidati stariano in reposo.'

As a strategist Alfonso possessed the virtues of indomitable patience and skill in marshalling his considerable but scattered financial and material resources. His greatest weakness was that, having attained his major goal—the conquest of Naples—he had no other clear objective in view and so frittered away his resources in a series of open-ended enterprises. As a tactician his movements were cautious and methodical; there was no brilliance in his generalship.[174] But he was always with his armies, sharing the dangers of battle and the discomforts of camp life to an extent considered unbecoming to his dignity by some contemporaries. Borso d'Este was particularly scornful:

Non pare a nui che la V. Maystà sia quella che, per ogni minimo respecto, debia andare in campo contro uno vostro subdicto, nè etiando, per ogni piccola cossa, meterse a simele sbaraglio e mettersi a pericolo como facia el plu tristo saccomano che habiati, perchè lè ala V, Maystà, a farve, de Re conductero gentedarme, è puocho honore.[175]

Another noteworthy characteristic of Alfonso as a general was the high standard of discipline he sought to maintain among his troops. Panormita and Facio make much of this quality, the former citing the clemency shown to the city of Naples after its capture, and the king's action, in the storming of Biccari, of placing all women under guard until it was safe for them to return to their homes.[176] More impartial testimony is provided by the anonymous diarist who observed, with reference to the storming of Naples: '. . . lo bon Rè de Rahona rende per male bene à Napolitani incontinente intrato dentro con universo banno comando à pena dela forca non fosse persona nulla devesse ponere piu à saccho . . .'[177] Many soldiers who disobeyed the order were hung.[178] Indiscipline in his son's army called forth a severe reprimand from the king, and the following advice in a letter written in his own hand:[179]

---

[174] Cf. Faraglia, *Storia della lotta*, p. 249: 'Non era Alfonso eccellente nell'arte della guerra, ma i baroni catalani e aragonesi ed i capitani italiani colla loro virtú compensavano il difetto di lui.'

[175] Foucard, 'Proposta', p. 718.

[176] Beccadelli, *De dictis et factis*, ii. 20 and 23.

[177] Faraglia, *Diurnali*, p. 124.   [178] Faraglia, *Storia della lotta*, p. 289.

[179] ACA Reg. 2940. 176ʳ, 14 July 1452. Cf. the letter to the duke's council in which Alfonso orders them to put an end to the 'molte cose enorme et disordinate che fanno le gente de quisso nostro campo in le terre extranee et de nostri amici' (ACA Reg. 2798. 17ᵛ, 15 July 1452.)

... dizen me que tu gente faze mucho mal, nole des rienda que quando querras; no los poderas mandar o del mal o el bien el principio es fundador; o te amen o te teman, mas faze que en todas maneras seas obedescido que en otra manera no averas onor.

How strictly Alfonso punished soldiers who molested the civilian population may be illustrated by his action against Ferrando Guzman, a man-at-arms who forcibly abducted a girl from Teano. On the king's instructions, the regent of the Vicaria and the captain of Naples seized them both and put Guzman in the dungeons of Castelnuovo while the girl was placed in a convent.[180] A few days later the regent was told to have Guzman taken to Teano and beheaded in the town square.[181] The intercession of several nobles and the girl's father saved the abductor from death, but he was obliged to marry her and remained for some time in prison.[182] Another incident involving the molestation of a woman occurred when the king was passing through Atri and it too received his immediate attention. The captain of Atri had seized a townsman who had refused to undertake a mission to Penne on the grounds that he could not leave his wife because some troops were quartered in his house. After his arrest one of the soldiers had taken the opportunity to seduce the wife. Alfonso ordered the viceroy of the Abruzzi to conduct an immediate investigation, and to send his report to Fonolleda as quickly as possible.[183] Normally the marshals of the army administered justice in cases involving soldiers.

A review of the military organization would be incomplete without reference to the large number of castles which guaranteed the king's control of strategic points and the major towns and cities. Many had suffered serious damage in the sieges that characterized the struggle between Aragonese and Angevins. The most important were repaired, strengthened and, in some cases, virtually rebuilt.[184]

In contrast to his reliance upon Italians in his field armies, Alfonso showed a marked preference for Spaniards as castellans. The diarist quoted earlier for his praise of the king's clemency,

---

[180] ACA Reg. 2698. 64ʳ, 29 July 1444.   [181] Ibid. 64ᵛ, 3 Aug. 1444.
[182] Ibid. 65ʳ, 5 Aug. 1444.
[183] ACA Reg. 2698. 21ʳ, 7 Nov. 1443.
[184] For the rebuilding of Castelnuovo cf. above, p. 55. For work on the castle of Castellammare and Gaeta cf. above, pp. 179–80. Some shops were demolished in the town square of Traetto in order to enlarge the castle moat (Mazzoleni, *Il Codice Chigi*, pp. 261–2, Order for payment of 20 *oncie* to the owners).

noted in 1450 that, 'Al presente nen taliano tene per parte de Rè de Rahona forteza nesciuna'.[185] He was not wholly correct, for a handful of castles had Italian castellans. Castel Capuano in Naples was governed by Carafello Carafa with a garrison of twenty men,[186] but it was of small military importance having become the residence of the Duke of Calabria after his marriage. In Gaeta the Torre di Mola remained in the custody of the Gaetano family who had been its castellans since the time of Charles II.[187] The courtier Gabriele Curiale collected numerous castellanies including the fortresses of Pozzuoli,[188] Vico,[189] and Ferolito;[190] he almost certainly appointed Italian deputies in each of these strongholds. The same probably happened with the castellanies of Vandra[191] and Bitonto, held by Marino Curiale.[192] Another Italian, Sansonetto Sersari, was castellan of Aiello from 1452.[193] In September of that same year the king restored control of the castle of Leonessa on the Abruzzi frontier to the commune which had lost it when he took the town.[194] The incident which provoked the Neapolitan diarist to the remark quoted earlier was the dismissal of Landolfo Marramaldo, castellan of Barletta: 'In quisto mese d'Aprile del predetto anno [scil. 1450] Rè de Rahona ha tolto a messer Pandolfo Marramalto lo castello de Barletta havea tenuto circa anni 34.'[195] Marramaldo had originally received the castellany from Giovanna II as security for a loan of 15,000 ducats, and in September 1436 Alfonso had confirmed him in possession of it.[196] Accusations that he and some of the castle garrison had participated in a riot early in 1450 led to his

[185] Faraglia, *Diurnali*, p. 135.
[186] He was appointed castellan in June 1442; see ACA Reg. 2903. 34^r, 3 Dec. 1442.
[187] ASN Priv. I. 84^r, 21 July 1453. This privilege confers the castellany on Nicola Gaetano who had earlier renounced it in favour of his father Cristoforo. On the father's death the office reverted to the crown. Alfonso returned it to Nicola in consideration of the service he had rendered in the taking of Gaeta, and of the large sums which he and his father had spent 'in reficiendo fortellitia et muros dicte turris mole ob bellorum calamitatis dirutos'.
[188] These were the Torre and the Belvedere. He was appointed castellan, with power to appoint a deputy, on 29 Aug. 1448 (ACA Reg. 2913. 48^r).
[189] ACA Reg. 2915. 18^v, 10 Mar. 1451, his appointment as castellan of Vico.
[190] Ibid., 10 Mar. 1451.
[191] ASN Priv. I. 27^r. The appointment was probably made in 1451.
[192] Rogadeo, *Codice diplomatico*, pp. 283–6. Appointment dated 6 Dec. 1452.
[193] ACA Reg. 2917. 4^r, 5 June 1452, Privilege confirming Sersari as castellan.
[194] ASN Priv. I. 2^r, 20 Sept. 1452. Previously Laudadeo Tau had been castellan.
[195] Faraglia, *Diurnali*, p. 135.
[196] Rogadeo, *Codice diplomatico*, p. 23, 18 Sept. 1436.

removal from several offices including that of castellan.[197] The circumstances of Marramaldo's dismissal and the subsequent appointment of Italians to other castellanies make it most improbable that Alfonso was bent on the systematic exclusion of his Italian subjects from such posts. Moreover account must be taken of the numerous castles in baronial fiefs over which the king had no control.

But if our diarist was wrong in asserting that, after Marramaldo had lost Barletta, no royal castle was governed by an Italian, he was correct in implying that Alfonso usually entrusted them to Spaniards. 'Illis custodiam castrorum nostrorum in quibus quasi basis et firmamentum totius Regni versatur comuniter consuevimus quorum de fide et industria opinionem et fiduciam singularem habemus.'[198] In an insurrectionary situation—and most castles served to ensure royal control of the provinces, rather than to defend the kingdom against foreign invasion—a castle manned by a native castellan and garrison might make common cause with the king's enemies, whereas a Spaniard saw his own fortunes and safety totally bound up with those of his master. So we find Alfonso appointing Spanish castellans in almost all strategically important fortresses, and moreover garrisoning them with Spanish soldiers. In 1437, for example, we find that first Joan Tomas and then Juan de Castelbisbal were castellans in Gaeta, Joan Metge of Barcelona in Ischia, Joan Perpenya in Capua, and Arnau Sans in Castelnuovo.[199] In July 1443 the treasury made payments to a number of castellans, all of them Spaniards: Joan Perpenya (still in Capua), Perc Aulesa (for the Torre di Capua, i.e. the fortress of Frederick II), Rodrigo Mur (S. Angelo Teodice), Ramiro de Funes (Caiazzo), Rodrigo Gener (deputy of Arnau Sans in Castelnuovo), Juan de Jerez (Troco), Bernat Sans (Rocca Janula), Joan Metge (who held the castellany of Ischia for life), and Gispert Dezguanes (Capri).[200] Castel dell'Ovo in Naples had a garrison of thirty-three 'companyons cathalans' in November 1441,[201] and after the fall of

[197] On 21 Mar. 1450 Marramaldo, described as formerly castellan of Barletta and viceroy of Puglia, received a pardon for his part 'in ipsa novissima rebellione per dictos socios facta' (ACA Reg. 2914. 43ʳ).
[198] These words appear in the privilege appointing Marino Curiale castellan of Bitonto (Rogadeo, *Codice diplomatico*, pp. 283–6).
[199] Minieri Riccio, 'Alcuni fatti di Alfonso I', pp. 7–8.
[200] Ibid., p. 241.
[201] Faraglia, *Storia della lotta*, p. 258, n. 2.

the city Castelnuovo was secured with a garrison of fifty Spaniards.[202]
The castle of Gaeta had a garrison of fifteen Catalans in 1437,[203]
and there is good reason to believe that in other places and other
times Spanish castellans commanded Spanish garrisons.

In September 1443 the castellanies of Traetto and Castelforte,
both strategically important for the defence of the Garigliano, were
taken from Marinello de Medici, 'absque alia sui nota infamia',
and given to Alfonso de Cardenas, viceroy of Gaeta.[204] Of the
castles which dominated the capital, all but one—Castel Capuano—
were commanded by Spaniards.[205] In Puglia the principal royal
stronghold, Manfredonia, had as its castellan Garcia de Cabanyells
and, after his death, Juan de Liria.[206] The castle of Cosenza, 'in
quo fideliter et diligenter cuostodiendo maxima pars status nostri
dicti ducatus Calabrie consistit',[207] was controlled by Francesch
Siscar, the viceroy of the province, who resided there and appointed his own castellan for life.[208] When the king took possession
of the Calabrian fortresses of Antonio Centelles, he entrusted
them all to Spaniards.[209]

Like most other offices, castellanies often served as a means of
rewarding courtiers and officials; such nominal castellans appointed deputies to carry out their duties. For example, we find
the secretary Blasco Steve appointed castellan of Melissa,[210] and
the *reboster* Pere de Botifar castellan of San Severino.[211]

Castles of especial strength and importance were held by
'Spanish custom' ('ad usum et consuetudinem Hispanie') which
required a castellan to surrender a castle to his lord whenever

---

[202] On 8 Aug. 1447 annual pensions of 6 *oncie* were granted to Pedro Cortes and
Gonsalvo de Pontevedra who had served in the garrison of Castelnuovo for
twenty-two years (ACA Reg. 2912. 86ᵛ).

[203] Minieri Riccio, 'Alcuni fatti di Alfonso I', p. 3. The Gaeta garrison was still
composed of Catalans in 1442; see ACA Reg. 2904, 76ᵛ, 24 May 1443.

[204] ACA Reg. 2903. 101ʳ, 17 Sept. 1443.

[205] Arnau Sans was castellan of Castelnuovo throughout the reign. In 1443 the
castellans of Castel dell'Ovo, Castel Sant'Erasmo, and Castel Sant'Angelo
respectively were Pedro de Sesse, Pedro de Lartiga, and Rodrigo Mur (ACA
Reg. 2903, 34ʳ).

[206] ASN Priv. I. 72ᵛ, 28 Dec. 1452, Appointment of de Liria.

[207] ACA Reg. 2912. 67ʳ, 4 July 1447.

[208] Ibid. 62ᵛ, 23 Nov. 1441.

[209] e.g. Crotone to Berenguer Arnau Fonolleda (garrison of 40), Belcastro to
Galceran de Barbara (garrison of 25), Catanzaro to Frederico de Cefalu (garrison
of 29), Cropani and Le Castelle to Alfonso de Vargas, Roccabernarda to Marti
Joan Escarrer.

[210] Mazzoleni, *Fonti aragonesi*, i. 61 (garrison of 12).   [211] Ibid.

called upon to do so.[212] Manfredonia, Bitonto, Melissa, Catanzaro, and Benevento were among those that fell into this category. The remainder were held 'ad usum et consuetudinem huius Regni Sicilie citra farum'[213] or 'ad usum ytalie'[214] which probably signified one and the same usage. An instruction sent to the viceroy of Corsica in 1451 throws a little light on a distinction which is nowhere explained in any detail. Jacme de Besora was to entrust castles 'which are strong and impregnable' to castellans appointed 'a us e costum de Spanya'; others might be granted on whatever terms the viceroy thought advisable.[215]

The payment of castellans and garrisons constituted a prime charge upon the revenue. Often a castellan had authority to collect the stipends of himself and his men directly from a local source, such as the hearth tax or customs dues. Joan Metge, for example, took his pay and that of the twenty men garrisoning the castle of Ischia from the hearth tax in Sorrento, Vico, Massa, and Positano.[216] Alternatively they were accorded a high place among the claimants on a revenue fund; in the case of the garrisons in Naples it was a position of absolute priority over every other charge on the treasury. 'Primum et ante omnia satisfiat suppleaturque stipendiis castrorum tam scilicet sociorum seu custodum quam castellanorum dicte civitatis.'[217] Most castellans received a salary of 10 ducats a month,[218] and their men were paid sums ranging from 2 ducats

---

[212] In a letter to the King of Navarre, Alfonso gives orders that the castellan of Rueyta should surrender his office to a new appointee, 'pues es a uso e constumbre de spanya . . . dins pena dela fieldat e otras que incorren los que tienen castillos a costumbre de spanya e no los rienden a su senyor quando son requeridos . . .' (ACA Reg. 2700. 32ᵛ, 29 June 1453). A little further light is shed on the 'Spanish custom' by the appointment of Macciota de Alagona to succeed Garcia de Cabanyells as castellan of Monte S. Angelo which was held according to that usage. Pere del Forcayo is ordered to receive the castle from the vice-castellan of Cabanyells whom '. . . havem per absolts . . . una dos e tres vegades segons lo us e costum despanya del sagrament e homenatge e altre qualsevol obligacio' (ACA Reg. 2917. 76ʳ, 28 Dec. 1452). Del Forcayo was a porter of the chamber.

[213] e.g. the castle of Barletta (ASN Priv. I. 10ʳ, 16 Sept. 1452).

[214] e.g. the fortresses of Pozzuoli.

[215] ACA Reg. 2697. 106ʳ, 17 Aug. 1451.

[216] ASN Fram. Com. Somm. 19ᵛ.

[217] ACA Reg. 2902. 60ᵛ, 4 July 1442.

[218] The four castellans of Naples were paid at this rate (ACA Reg. 2903. 34ʳ, 3 Dec. 1442); so too was Siscar for the castle of Cosenza (ACA Reg. 2912. 62ᵛ, 28 June 1447). But Blasco Steve and Alfonso de Avalos, titular castellans of Melissa, received only 6 ducats (ACA Reg. 2917, 161ʳ, 3 June 1457, Appointment of de Avalos on resignation of Steve).

a month in Melissa[219] to 3 ducats in Cosenza. The 108 men of the four Neapolitan castles received 2½ ducats a month.[220] The difference is probably attributable to the rations issued to some garrisons in addition to their pay. The twelve men in Melissa, for example, were each entitled to 1 *tomolo* of grain and a barrel of wine a month. All salaries were subject to the *elagio* of 4 per cent. A provisioner of castles saw to the furnishing of supplies.[221]

Considerations of economy decreed that many castles should be left ungarrisoned and in a state of disrepair, though they might still be entrusted to a castellan who received a nominal salary for keeping an eye on the building. One such castle was that of Spinei which was in the care of a female castellan, Giovanella Gattola.[222] In November 1450 Alfonso gave his consent for the payment of a garrison of twelve, but it is clear from the salaries assigned—18 ducats a year for the castellan and 2 *carlini* (one-fifth of a ducat) a month for the men—that the military force in Spinei remained still a scratch, part-time body of locals.[223]

---

[219] ACA Reg. 2907. 60ʳ, 8 Nov. 1444, Appointment of Steve. It was raised to 3 ducats in 1457 when de Avalos became castellan.

[220] ACA Reg. 2903. 34ʳ.

[221] Giovanni de Fossano held this office. In 1422, as Duke of Calabria, Alfonso had appointed Rodrigo de San Juan *provisor* of all royal castles in Calabria on the model of the Sicilian *provisor* (Pontieri, *Fonti aragonesi*, ii. 13).

[222] Cf. the castellany of Amantea which was held from September 1442 by Margarita de Pictavia (ACA Reg. 2915. 205ᵛ).

[223] ACA Reg. 2914. 127ʳ, 16 Nov. 1450.

IX

NAVAL FORCES

ANGEVIN sea power never recovered from the blows inflicted in the wars of the Sicilian Vespers. In the time of Giovanna II the shipping resources of Naples, whether for war or commerce, were of little account among the maritime states of the Mediterranean. For those states, and especially for the maritime republics of Italy, Alfonso's victory meant the incorporation of the kingdom into an aggressive maritime empire, Aragonese in name, but Catalan in nature. Hence the hostility that persisted, with but few intermissions, between Genoa, Florence, and Venice on the one hand and the Aragonese power on the other until the day of Alfonso's death. The Catalans, it is true, had never been over-enthusiastic about the Neapolitan enterprise which cost them a lot of money and Barcelona its political predominance in the Aragonese empire; none the less, the success of their ruler's venture made their quarrels with old rivals more bitter, whetted their appetite for further, and commercially more rewarding, victories, and shifted the focus of naval activity to Italian waters. Naples thus became, for a few years, the centre of a major sea power.

Since much of the substance of that power was drawn from other parts of the king's dominions, those offices of the kingdom of Naples which had to do with the sea played only a minor part in the management of fleets and naval affairs. One of the seven officers of state, the admiral, held titular responsibility for all things concerned with the crown's interest in ships and seamen. That dignity had become hereditary in the Marzano family and, like the other great offices, almost completely non-functional. The decadence of Neapolitan naval power to the point of disappearance had made it unnecessary to supplement the admiral's office with any other of a more substantial nature. Giovanni Antonio di Marzano, Duke of Sessa, by declaring opportunely for Alfonso had secured confirmation of the office with which he had earlier been invested by Giovanna II. With the constable he shared the honour of a marriage alliance with the royal family, for his son Marino di Marzano Ruffo married the king's illegitimate daughter Eleonora in May 1444. Marino became admiral on the death of his father in 1454 and held the office until he joined the revolt of the barons against Ferdinand.

The duties that nominally fell on the admiral were as follows: to supervise the building of ships for the crown, to take care of all naval equipment, to organize the royal fleets, to license privateers and prevent unlicensed privateering. He appointed and dismissed the masters of royal ships and arsenals. Through a court with the usual array of judges, constables, jailers, etc., and functioning according to the procedures of the Vicaria, he exercised jurisdiction over all seafarers.[1] In practice the Neapolitan admiral confined himself to his judicial functions, and even those devolved mainly upon subordinates known as *protontini* each of whom had responsibility for a stretch of coast.[2] The letter of appointment given to one of these officials, Leucio de Palaganis of Trani, grants him jurisdiction in cases between seamen and merchants of Trani, as well as those, both civil and criminal, involving strangers; but he was debarred from trying criminal cases that carried a penalty of death or mutilation. Appeal from his court lay directly to that of the admiral: 'Et quod nullum alium in superiorem tuum et iudicem competentem habeas nisi Regni nostri Admiratum unde tuum officium dignoscitur derivare.'[3] Giovanna II had granted the office to Leucio's father on a hereditary basis, and it had passed to Leucio in December 1436 after the death of his father and elder brother. In August 1450 he sought and obtained confirmation in it because royal officials were interfering with his jurisdiction. He must also have been unpopular in Trani for the city made representations to the king which led to the abolition of the office in

---

[1] The instructions given to Alfonso's admirals have not survived but we have those issued for Roberto Sanseverino in February 1460 following the rebellion of Marino di Marzano Ruffo (Tutini, *Discorsi*, pp. 15–26). They are strikingly similar to those given to Angevin admirals a century earlier, so there is good reason to suppose that Alfonso had been equally conservative in his treatment of a redundant office.

[2] e.g. the admiral appointed Ferruccio Protospatario *protontino* of Crotone with responsibility for the coast between Cirò and the river Rocca (Gentile, 'Lo stato napoletano' (1937), p. 16, n. 1; the appointment is dated 1 Jan. 1454). Another *protontino*, Giovanello Perrone, exercised jurisdiction from Cetraro to Amantea (ibid.). On 10 July 1451 the king confirmed another of the admiral's appointments, that of Luigi Guarna as *protontino* in Salerno (Mazzoleni, *Il Codice Chigi*, pp. 31–2).

[3] ACA Reg. 2914. 91ᵛ, 17 Aug. 1450. The privilege is printed by Rogadeo, *Codice diplomatico*, pp. 225–7.

September 1454 and the transfer of its functions directly to the admiral or his *locumtenens*.[4] However, Palagano fought back and succeeded in having his office restored in July 1456; the king justified this volte-face by accusing the city of not keeping the promises it had made when the office was abolished.[5] Another conflict over jurisdictions arose in Giovinazzo, this time between the *protontino* and the Venetian vice-consul, with the latter complaining of usurpations by the former.[6] How much business was transacted in the admiral's court cannot be ascertained because all its records have disappeared and other sources make very few references to it.[7] That it did function seems certain from such scraps of information as the name of the judge assessor given by Borso d'Este[8] and the exemption from citation before the court in first instance granted to citizens of Massa, Vico, and Sorrento.[9] That it had little to do appears probable if one considers that the *protontini* dealt with most of the matters arising among merchants and seafaring folk in the kingdom, while the captains and commanders of royal ships and fleets exercised jurisdiction over the men under their command. How complete their power was is illustrated by the full jurisdiction granted to Pere de Niubo, captain of the king's ship *Sta. Maria e S. Miquel*; his authority over his crew extended to the land as well as to the sea and he appointed his own *alguaciles* to enforce it.[10]

In the management of naval affairs proper the Neapolitan admiral was completely overshadowed by his Aragonese counterpart. Although their powers and privileges, as set out in their instruments of appointment, were very similar,[11] those of the

---

[4] Rogadeo, *Codice diplomatico*, pp. 319–20, 12 Sept. 1454.

[5] Ibid., p. 360, 29 July 1456.

[6] Mazzoleni, *Il Codice Chigi*, pp. 107–8. A royal letter dated 1 Sept. 1451 ordered all officials in Giovinazzo, and especially the *protontino*, to respect the privileges of the vice-consul.

[7] Gentile ('Lo stato napoletano' (1937), p. 14) refers to documents relating to the court issued from the admiral's residence in Sessa, but he gives no details.

[8] It was 'Piedro Zironda' (Foucard, 'Descrizione', p. 750).

[9] ACA Reg. 2917. 130ᵛ, 27 July 1455.

[10] ACA Reg. 2660. 159ʳ, 13 Oct. 1455.

[11] The duties of an admiral of Aragon, Valencia, Sardinia, and Corsica in the fourteenth century are detailed in a document which probably belongs to the reign of Alfonso IV. In Aragon, as in Naples, these formal letters of appointment hardly changed to represent the true state of affairs (M. Usón Sesé, 'Un formulario latino de la cancillería Real Aragonesa (siglo XIV)', *Anuario de historia del derecho español*, 7 (1930), 456–9).

Aragonese referred to a state with substantial naval power, and to
a man—Berenguer d'Erill—with considerable experience of the
sea. The instrument appointing d'Erill one of the procurators to
swear obedience in the king's name to Nicholas V described him
as 'admiral in all our western dominions'.[12] In February 1448 he
signed himself 'admiratus generalis'.[13] If this latter title means that
he had become supreme naval commander for all the king's
dominions, including Naples, it represents a development similar
in nature to the treasureship general and may have been prompted
by the exigencies of the Tuscan war at the close of which d'Erill
commanded the fleet that attempted to storm Piombino. In 1452
he led a combined Aragonese and Venetian fleet in operations
against the Florentines.[14]

Although he did nothing to give new life to the Neapolitan
admiral's office, Alfonso did, soon after he had gained possession
of Naples, set the naval arsenal to work again with the building
of twenty-six galleys. Antoni Vinyes in his letters to Barcelona
related how on the 14 and 15 March 1443 the king gave orders for
the placing of stocks for these galleys,[15] and how on Lady Day
(25 March) after vespers he had gone to the arsenal with a great
following of nobles to place the stocks. With his own hand
Alfonso set up the first timbers for the stocks of the first galley,
the Duke of Calabria fixed those of the second, the nobles in
his company began the rest.[16] Thereafter shipbuilding went on
steadily in the arsenal. A galley and a caravel were under construction there in 1451,[17] and two large ships in the following
year.[18] In March 1456 Boquet reported that twenty-one galleys
were being built.[19] The Emperor Frederick III was taken on a tour

[12] ACA Reg. 2654. 124ᵛ, 22 Mar. 1447.
[13] ACA Reg. 2656. 111ᵛ, 3 Feb. 1448.
[14] ACA Reg. 2798. 2ᵛ, 11 June 1452, Instructions for d'Erill.
[15] ACB Cart. Com., vol. 13, fol. 24, 15 Mar. 1443: '... e son nomenades sots
les invocacions seguents: Sta. Maria, Sent Miquel, Sent Jordi, Sent Anthoni,
Sent Alfonso, Sent Nicolau, Sent Barthomeu, Sent Andreu, Sent Matheu,
Sent Mercuri, Sent Benet, Sent Bernat, Sent Genaro, Sent Elm, Sent Luys, Sent
Enello, Sent Spreu, Sent Johan evangeliste, Sent Johan babtiste, Sent Pere, Sent
Pau, Sent Sever, Sent Jacme, Sent Marti, Sent Lorens, e Sent Vicens. E les
vi fa dela devisa dela gerreta de nostra dona, e v del siti perillos, e v dels libres,
e v dels mils, e v dels grobs ...'   [16] Ibid., fol. 31, 4 Apr. 1443.
[17] ACA Reg. 2940. 118ʳ, 15 Feb. 1451; Mazzoleni, Il Codice Chigi, p. 22,
8 July 1451.
[18] ACB Cart. Com., vol. 22, fol. 9, 21 Jan. 1452.
[19] Madurell Marimon, Mensajeros barceloneses, p. 513.

of the arsenal which had been almost entirely rebuilt by the time of his visit to Naples. He saw it as a long building with two main wings. On one side were the offices of the *escriva de racio* and the admiral—which admiral the description of the Emperor's visit does not reveal; on the other were storerooms 200 yards long and ten wide for anchors, artillery, sails, ropes, and other naval stores, workshops where anchors and cannon were made, and a dry dock with thirty-two bays.[20] No information has survived as to the nationality of the master shipbuilders who constructed these vessels. The officials of the *escriva de racio* who controlled the financial side of the work were all Catalans: Bernat Marti, Bernat Fench, and Andreu de Vesach.[21] To provide similar facilities in the Adriatic, Alfonso gave orders in 1452 for the establishment of a naval arsenal at Trani.[22] Some of the wood used for shipbuilding at Naples was brought from Calabria and Basilicata,[23] but most of it came from the nearest available forests in the province of Terra di Lavoro. Certain places in that province were obliged to make their carts and draught animals available for hauling the timber needed by the crown for building ships. Aversa was one of the towns subjected to that service.[24] Casanova, near Capua, secured exemption in June 1451 from the obligation, 'inferendo lignaminia pro navibus et triremibus'.[25] Sometimes local sources of raw materials did not suffice and quantities of pine planks, rope, and sailcloth were brought from Spain.[26] When relations between the states permitted, anchors were purchased in Venice.[27]

Besides building ships, the arsenal at Naples was kept busy fitting, repairing, and arming the fleets which Alfonso gathered there for action against his numerous enemies. Thus work was provided for a considerable number of men; more than one hundred smiths were at work in the foundry of the arsenal when

[20] 'Come lo Imperatore Federico entrò in Napoli', p. 488.
[21] Marti supervised the building until 1450, Fench for a few months in that year, and de Vesach from August 1450. Cf. I. Schiappoli, 'La marina degli Aragonesi di Napoli', *ASPN* (1940), p. 35.
[22] Gentile, 'Lo stato napoletano' (1937), p. 14, n. 5.
[23] Ibid., n. 4.
[24] Mazzoleni, *Il Codice Chigi*, pp. 97–8, 276.
[25] ACA Reg. 2915, 65ᵛ, 28 June 1451. Casanova was freed from this and other labour services owed to the crown because of poverty.
[26] e.g. the order for planks of pine to Johan de Cordoba, *baile general* of Catalonia (ACA Reg. 2690. 69ᵛ, 18 May 1444): '. . . per obs de una galera que entenem fer fer açi volem haver taulam de meliç, de pi per cloeuda daquella.'
[27] ACA Reg. 2721. 56ᵛ, 15 May 1453.

the Emperor visited it. But men with the requisite skills could not
always be found locally. For work on the timbers of galleys and to
make masts a large number of craftsmen had to be summoned to
the Neapolitan arsenal from all the Sicilian ports in 1454.[28] Nor
was Naples the only place where the king had ships built. Several
large vessels were built for him at San Feliu de Guixols in Catalonia;[29] Siretto de Vultagio of Genoa contracted to build one of
1,500 *botes* at Castellamare in Sicily;[30] and the old royal ship the
Santa Maria (commonly known as the *Negrona*) was sent to
Messina for breaking up so that a new vessel of around 1,000
vegeti might be built there using whatever parts remained serviceable.[31] In 1446 the king gave orders to the *bailes generales* of
Aragon, Valencia, Catalonia, Majorca, and Roussillon that each
should have a galley built from the crown revenues.[32] Joan Alberti
the procurator royal in Majorca, and a consortium of his friends
had already offered to build five galleys in the island for the king's
service if the crown would meet 50 per cent of the cost.[33] Ships
built by the crown represented, however, only a small proportion
of those that could be pressed into naval service when necessity
arose, for there were no essential differences in construction
between warships and merchant ships. The royal ships themselves
served as often as merchant ships as they did for war. They

---

[28] On 13 July 1454 twenty-five 'mastri daxia' from the arsenal of Messina were
ordered to report to the arsenal of Naples with their tools to work on galleys
(ACA Reg. 2916. 10ʳ). On 23 Oct. 1454 Alfonso wrote to the captains of the
principal Sicilian seaports: 'per fare lu piu prestu che si pocza li arbori dele
nostre nave havemo bisogno equa un grande numero de mastri daxia et cala-
fati . . .' They were to present themselves in the Neapolitan arsenal and receive
their instructions from Lope Ximenez de Urrea, viceroy of Sicily and Naples
(ibid. 14ʳ).

[29] One, referred to as 'la nau grossa', was completed there under the direction
of Pere Sirvent at the end of 1447, armed and then taken to Italy for employment
in the Tuscan war (ACA Reg. 2719. 45ʳ, 28 Jan. 1448; Reg. 2720. 91ᵛ, 10 Jan.
1449). Johan del Buch supervised the building of another ship at S. Feliu (ACA
Reg. 2690. 117ᵛ; Reg. 2698. 162ʳ, 27 Feb. 1446).

[30] ACA Reg. 2940. 89ᵛ, 29 May 1450. By August 1457 'la grossa la ques feu
a Castellamar' was ready to join the attack on Genoa (ACA Reg. 2800. 23ᵛ,
22 Aug. 1457).

[31] ACA Reg. 2690. 169ʳ, 20 Aug. 1445. This was perhaps the ship the Venetians burned at Messina while it was still under construction. The king instructed
that the sails which had been ordered for it from Spain should be used instead
for another ship being built in Naples (ACA Reg. 2720. 131ʳ, 30 Nov. 1449).

[32] ACA Reg. 2699. 45ʳ, 4 Aug. 1446. At the same time he ordered inquiries
to be made to discover where a 'galera negra' could best be built.

[33] ACA Reg. 2699. 45ʳ, 4 Aug. 1446.

frequently carried from Ibiza to Naples the salt needed for distribution in respect of the hearth tax,[34] and sometimes undertook longer voyages, as in 1451 when two galeasses transported from Flanders the merchandise bought for the crown by the *comprador* Andreu Pol.[35] Special arming was necessary when they were needed as fighting vessels.[36]

The true measure of Aragonese naval power was thus not the number of galleys and ships belonging to the crown but the total force that could be mustered from the shipping of all its subjects. Private merchant vessels would be hired or commandeered as warships or transports for any large enterprise. During the siege of Piombino, Luis Bertran, master of a ship from Barcelona, found himself detained in the port by the king's command and obliged to make his vessel available to the attacking force. He received a written promise of compensation of up to 2,000 ducats in the event of the ship and its cargo being lost, and for any loss incurred by the interruption of his voyage to Naples.[37] In this manner five merchantmen were armed for the unsuccessful attack on Piombino. To reinforce his fleet operating against the Genoese in 1457 Alfonso hired several ships, including one belonging to Berenguer de Pontos; it had a total complement of 200 men, and its hire for two months cost the treasury 3,000 ducats.[38] He also chartered the ship of the Catalan merchant Prats to carry supplies to Vilamari's fleet.[39] Since this means of strengthening a fleet was very costly, great efforts were made to persuade the maritime cities to furnish vessels at their own expense. Alfonso announced in 1454 that he intended to ask many cities to contribute two or three galleys to a large fleet which he hoped to gather that summer for an attack on the Turks.[40] If the request was made it produced scant effect on that occasion. But when the Catalans felt their vital interests threatened, as in the war with Genoa, they were ready to provide the king with ships. In the summer of 1457

---

[34] Cf. below, p. 354.

[35] ACA Reg. 2655. 137ʳ, 8 June 1451, Instructions for the voyage given to the captain Francesch dez Valls.

[36] e.g. early in 1442 Berenguer d'Erill was ordered to arm the royal ship *Botifarrer* so that it might be used to prevent the Genoese from carrying provisions to the beleaguered garrison of Naples (Faraglia, *Storia della lotta*, p. 267, n. 1).

[37] ACA Reg. 2940. 54ᵛ, 22 Aug. 1448.

[38] ACA Reg. 2800. 24ᵛ, 25 Aug. 1457.   [39] Ibid. 20ᵛ, 22 July 1457.

[40] ACB Cart. Com., vol. 24, fol. 64, 9 May 1454.

Barcelona armed four large ships, two baleners and two galleys,
to reinforce the fleet attacking the Genoese.[41] Valencia supplied
one ship for the same operation.[42] In 1453 the *pagesos* of Majorca,
in the hope of winning royal favour for their cause, made available
the galley they had built two years earlier.[43] Messina offered a
galley in 1440,[44] and in 1457 the Sicilian parliament offered 60,000
florins for the maintenance of triremes against the Turks in return
for certain privileges.[45] None of the Neapolitan cities appears to
have contributed in this manner to the royal fleet, probably
because none possessed any vessels that would have been useful.
A possible exception was Tropea which was expected in 1445 to
furnish a galley. The king appointed Jacobo Romano, a citizen of
Tropea, to command the vessel, 'que ad nostra servicia per
universitate dicte civitatis nostre Tropea ordinabitur';[46] it does
not appear by name in any document dealing with naval operations, but may have been numbered among the royal galleys.

Even more important than the contribution of cities and states
was that made by individual owners of ships and galleys. Many
wealthy men besides merchants looked upon a vessel as a sound
investment. Mostly they would put them to commercial use, but
when need arose they were armed for war. In April 1440 Alfonso
told the captain of his galleys, Francesch Gilabert Centelles, to
sail at once to Gaeta with his own galley and as many others as he
could find belonging to subjects of the king in order to drive away
a Genoese fleet.[47] When Vilamari, commander of the fleet attacking
Genoa, appealed for reinforcements in May 1457, Alfonso promised to send him the galleys of Valenti Claver (the vice-chancellor), Matteu Joan (a secretary), Joan Torrelles (lord of Caiazzo
and castellan of Barletta) and the Count of Campobasso.[48] A week
later he ordered two galleys belonging to the governor of Catalonia
to place themselves immediately at Vilamari's disposal;[49] and
that same day Matteu Joan's galley left Naples carrying similar

    [41] ACA Reg. 2800. 14ᵛ, 6 Sept. 1457.
    [42] Ibid. 23ᵛ, 22 Aug. 1457. It was a vessel that the Valencians had taken from
the Genoese.
    [43] ACA Reg. 2799. 12ʳ, 16 July 1453.
    [44] ACA Reg. 2646. 86ʳ, 29 Mar. 1440.   [45] ACA Reg. 2946. 110ʳ.
    [46] ACA Reg. 2904. 236ʳ, 6 Mar. 1445.
    [47] ACA Reg. 2651. 149ʳ, 25 Apr. 1440.
    [48] ACA Reg. 2800. 7ʳ, 9 May 1457. The galleys of Claver and the Count of
Campobasso were expected back in Naples after carrying troops to Albania.
    [49] ACA Reg. 2800. 9ʳ, 14 May 1457.

instructions to the galleys of the Count of Oliva and Pere de Besalu in Sardinia. The galley of the Archbishop of Tarragona left Naples to join the fleet on 7 June,[50] followed in July by those of the Prince of Rossano, the Prince of Salerno, and the Count of Fondi.[51] By the end of August other galleys belonging to the Count of Aderno, Pere Cases (prior of Messina), the viceroy of Sicily and the Count of Caltabellota had been armed and were ready for dispatch.[52] Thus it often happened in a large fleet that the private vessels outnumbered those of the crown. When Vilamari sailed from Naples to relieve Castiglione della Pescáia in November 1449, his fleet comprised three royal and seven private galleys.[53]

The Neapolitan nobility, it will be noted, had followed Spanish and Sicilian example in becoming proprietors of galleys. The urban patriciate of Naples, however, seldom did so. A certain Erasmo Arella of Gaeta some time before 1442 armed a galley at his own expense allegedly to serve Alfonso, but his actions—illegally seizing men to row it, provisions to equip it, and then preying indiscriminately upon coastal shipping—amounted to scarcely veiled piracy.[54] In an indirect manner, however, the whole kingdom contributed to the upkeep of the king's ships. The hearth tax granted by the parliament of 1443 was supposed to maintain ten galleys for defence of the coasts.[55] The upkeep of galleys had also been the justification for a tax known as the *nuova gabella* first imposed by Charles III on shipping and merchandise on the western coast between Gaeta and Reggio.[56] Heedless rulers had soon alienated most of the tax, and even those amounts which came into the hands of the crown were never put to their avowed purpose. In a session of the council held on 24 June 1445, Alfonso

---

[50] Ibid. 14^v, 7 June 1457.   [51] Ibid. 20^v, 22 July 1457.

[52] Ibid. 23^v, 22 Aug. 1457. A fleet of seven galleys sailed on 28 Aug. under the command of the prior of Messina (ibid. 25^v). In addition to these galleys, Alfonso had at his disposal in Naples that August two royal galeasses, the ship built at Castellamare, one bought from Antoni Albo, one that had belonged to Prexana, another that had belonged to Madrenchs, one furnished by Valencia, and another captured from the Genoese in Barbary waters: in all eight ships, none of which had yet been armed.

[53] ACA Reg. 2697. 42^v.

[54] He subsequently received a pardon for these excesses (ACA Reg. 2904. 83^r, 12 June 1443).

[55] Cf. above, p. 260.

[56] The tax was levied at a rate of 1 per cent *ad valorem* on all exports and imports, while ships paid a sum according to their burthen.

decreed that the *nuova gabella* should be extended from Reggio to the river Tronto so as to cover the whole coastline of the kingdom.[57] The additional proceeds were likewise devoted, in theory, to the maintenance of galleys. On the western shores Alfonso made no serious attempt to redeem earlier alienations; indeed he made new grants. In Gioia, for example, he gave the *nuova gabella* to Giovanni d'Alagno, and, on his death, to an official named Giorgio di Toraldo.[58] In Capri and Anacapri he granted it to Carletto and Geronimo Cursio *in perpetuum* as a reward for their services in the capture of the islands.[59] In Gaeta it was sold to Raimo Ronco in 1439 and again in 1445.[60] However, on the eastern coast, where the duty first came into operation in 1445, he made no general alienations, and special collectors were appointed to gather it.[61] The kingdom of Naples made yet another financial contribution towards its ruler's sea power with a levy on salaries and pensions granted by the parliament of 1455 for the purpose of building twelve galleys.[62] But, unlike the Cortes of the Spanish kingdoms, the Neapolitan parliament had no means of ensuring that the moneys it granted the crown were employed in the manner intended.

The greatest show of naval power ever mustered by Alfonso was the fleet he gathered in the harbour of Naples to impress the visiting emperor. It comprised thirty galleys, ten ships, four 'galeoni grossi di rimi', and several galeasses for transporting troops and horses. Although it is unlikely that all these vessels belonged to the crown, all the crews wore royal livery for the occasion.[63] His claim that he would gather one hundred galleys in 1454 for a crusade assumed that every subject, every city would furnish every galley asked of them, and hence was as unrealistic as the strength sometimes claimed for the armies. More soberly he informed the King of Bohemia in April 1455 that he hoped to attack the Turks with twenty triremes.[64] For most of his major enterprises he was able to assemble around that

[57] ASN Fasc. Com. Somm. 117[r].   [58] ASN Priv. I. 77[v], 23 Jan. 1453.
[59] ACA Reg. 2903. 94[v], 23 Aug. 1443.
[60] ACA Reg. 2908. 60[r], 20 June 1445.
[61] The official who had collected it at Rodi from 1450 to 1451 was appointed collector in Manfredonia, Fortore, and Térmoli for 1453–4 (ASN Sig. I. 22[r]).
[62] Cf. above, p. 133.
[63] 'Come lo Imperatore Federico entrò in Napoli', p. 488.
[64] ACA Reg. 2661. 86[r], 26 Apr. 1455.

number of vessels. At Ponza he had fourteen ships and thirteen galleys. For the attack on Piombino in September 1448 he mustered ten galleys, four galeasses, and five ships. For the campaign against Genoa (1456–8), which was essentially a trial of strength at sea, he disposed initially of fourteen galleys. By the spring of 1457 that number had fallen to ten, and those, the commander warned, were in no fit state to meet the equivalent number which the Genoese had armed during the winter.[65] They failed in fact to prevent the Genoese from harassing the coast and shipping of the Spanish provinces during the summer of 1457, forcing Barcelona to arm two galleys in its own defence.[66] Galvanized into activity by these setbacks and the threat of French intervention,[67] Alfonso scoured his dominions for vessels and by September had brought the strength of his fleet to twenty-eight ships and galleys. After an unsuccessful attack on the city of Genoa itself launched on Christmas Day 1457, Vilamari the Aragonese commander had to lay up his ships for the winter. By the following spring he again found himself with only eleven galleys, mostly in a bad state of repair, and by May 1458 the best endeavours of Naples had not increased this total beyond fourteen. At this point Jean of Anjou entered Genoa with eleven ships, not the twenty which rumour had attributed to him. The war fleets put to sea by Genoa and Venice resembled those of Aragon; that is to say, they numbered between ten and twenty vessels and could not be maintained above that strength for more than very short periods.

Galleys constituted the main striking force of a war fleet. Ships played an auxiliary role, especially as carriers of the land troops who still did much of the fighting in a full-scale battle at sea. The Genoese and Venetians perhaps relied more on their seamen in naval combat than did the Aragonese. At Ponza the seasoned sailors of the Genoese fleet enjoyed an immense advantage over the knights of the king's army many of whom, besides being seasick, found it impossible to keep their feet on a rolling deck. But all fleets employed basically the same tactics. They are illustrated by an eyewitness account of a battle fought off Piombino

---

[65] ACA Reg. 2800. 7ʳ, 9 May 1457.

[66] ACB Cart. Com., vol. 27, fol. 138, 13 June 1457.

[67] In July the king received a report from Barcelona that eighteen or twenty galleys were arming in Marseille for the relief of Genoa (ACB Cartas Reales, Neg. 2059, Alfonso to Barcelona, 2 Aug. 1457).

written by Arnau de Vildemany who happened to be in the
Aragonese camp on a mission from the Cortes of Catalonia.[68]

The Florentines armed four galeasses and two galliots and brought
into Piombino 300 men, bombards and other weapons without any
hindrance because there were no ships with which to oppose them.
That same evening they returned to Leghorn to load provisions for the
camp of their army . . . and these galeasses came to Porto Barato, which
is six miles from here, to victual their camp. I can tell you that if they
had succeeded the King would have been in as great danger as man ever
was, because the Florentine army was growing stronger every day and
our troops could not reach us. Seeing himself in these straits, the king
put 40 men in each of six galleys and one galliot that happened to be
here, and 60 or 70 men into three small ships, one of 150 *botes* burthen
and the other two of less than 100 *botes*. He made the governor Mossen-
yor Requesens captain of these vessels and ordered him to go out and
fight the seven galeasses of the Florentines. On the morning of Monday
the fifteenth of this month he went out to meet them. I had asked
leave of the king to be allowed to go with the captain and he said that he
was pleased to grant it. It is true that he had not put many men aboard
the galleys and ships, the reason being that he anticipated an attack
by the Florentine army at any moment. Between three and four o'clock
in the afternoon we engaged the galeasses and the fighting went on into
the first hour of the night. Many were killed and wounded: the dead
numbered above 150 and the wounded more than 500 to our knowledge. It pleased God to give us the victory . . . we took two galeasses
and two fled into the night that robbed us of them even though we gave
chase for a good four hours; the wind got up and we lost them, which
was no wonder considering the condition of our vessels.

Had he not feared an attack from the Florentines, the king would
have packed still more soldiers into his ships and reduced their
manœuvrability still further.

Reports of huge fleets, like those of great armies, were put about
for propaganda purposes, and the same limiting factor—money—
made it impossible to set either in motion. A light galley did not
cost a great sum to build: one was constructed in the arsenal at
Naples for 1,000 ducats,[69] while a large ship built in Catalonia

[68] ACB Cart. Com., vol. 18, fol. 99, Vildemany to Luc Civaller, Camp outside
Piombino, 19 July 1448.
[69] ACA Reg. 2940. 118[r], 15 Feb. 1451. The king promises to repay Bernat de
Requesens 1,000 ducats, 'los quals de nostra ordinacio bestreu per fer una
galea nova en la teraçana dela nostra ciutat de Napols'. In the *Llibre de inventaris
de galeres de 1438–1450* of the Generalidad de Catalunya (ACA Generalidad,

cost between 6,000 and 7,000 florins.[70] For the ship that he bought from Prexana the king paid 2,000 ducats.[71] But construction costs were relatively insignificant compared with the cost of arming, provisioning, and paying the crew. When Pere Sirvent went to take command of the royal ship that had been built at San Feliu de Guixols, he took with him 6,300 florins to meet the cost of arming and sailing her to Italy.[72] In other words, commissioning a vessel and getting it to sea cost about the same amount as building it. Some idea of victualling expenses may be obtained from the figure of 168 ducats 17 *grana* which the clerk of a royal ship spent in feeding its crew of 200 men during the month of August 1454.[73] Wages for a galley crew amounted to around 250 ducats a month,[74] and a ship's master was paid up to 300 ducats a year.[75] To have maintained a fleet of twenty vessels in constant readiness would thus have cost something more than a quarter of a million ducats a year. Not surprisingly the treasury often found itself unable to pay the king's ships, although it did make efforts to give the crews something every one or two months.[76] When pay fell too badly into arrears, ships voluntarily in the service of the crown might threaten to withdraw. This happened with three galleys guarding Gaeta and Castellammare di Stabia in January 1437. In face of their ultimatum to leave within a week, Alfonso ordered his treasurer to give them 500 ducats immediately and warned that

fol. 131/2) the value assigned to a number of galleys is as follows: 1,950 libres (the Barcelona pound), 500 libres, 370 libres, 450 libres, 180 libres, 400 libres, 600 libres. These valuations made allowance for depreciation. The Barcelona pound was worth rather more than the ducat, the exchange rate varying between 15 and 18 shillings to the ducat.

[70] In 1453 the Cortes of Catalonia proposed the construction of nine ships, including three of 1,500 *botes*, within this price range (ACB Lletres Closes, 330, VI. 17. 193ʳ, 5 Sept. 1453). The florin was worth 12 or 13 Barcelona shillings.

[71] ACB Cart. Com., vol. 22, fol. 9, 21 Jan. 1452.

[72] ACA Reg. 2719. 45ʳ, 28 Jan. 1448, Order to the receiver general in Spain to provide Sirvent with this money.

[73] Mazzoleni, *Fonti aragonesi*, i. 146.

[74] Two galleys sent to Puglia in 1438 were given 1,000 ducats as pay for two months (ACA Reg. 2651. 1ᵛ).

[75] This was the salary of Pere Sirvent, one of the most experienced masters (ACA Reg. 2661. 54ʳ).

[76] In September 1453 Vilamari was sent 400 ducats for distribution to each of the galleys under his command (ACA Reg. 2799. 46ᵛ). In September 1456 he received 1,000 ducats for each galley (ACA Reg. 2800. 1ʳ), and in May 1457 500 ducats for each (ibid. 9ᵛ).

they would have to be given another 500 ducats by mid February at the latest.[77]

Some of the money expended on his fleets Alfonso managed to recover from the clergy and laity of his dominions through taxation sanctioned by the pope; the justification was always that the money would be used for a crusading venture. Half the proceeds from the Jubilee indulgence of 1450 in all his lands was granted to the king so that he might maintain a fleet against the Turks, but the proceeds were disappointing, thanks—so Alfonso complained to the pope—to 'the scant devotion that men have shown, especially in our western states'.[78] To make good the deficit he asked the pontiff for a dispensation permitting him to sell foodstuffs to the infidel, the profit from which would maintain a fleet for their destruction.[79] In June 1453 he asked for the fruits of vacant benefices up to a value of 300,000 ducats to pay for the upkeep of his galleys at a time when the Turkish attack on Constantinople was causing alarm in Europe.[80] A little later, after news of the fall of that city had spread further consternation, he seized the opportunity to demand a concession for three years of the revenues from all vacant benefices in order to keep a fleet in action in the eastern Mediterranean.[81] Nicholas V carefully avoided these requests, but the more naïve Calixtus III granted him a crusading tithe on all ecclesiastical revenues.[82]

The expense of naval operations was also offset to some extent by prize. Privateering was a highly developed business in which both rulers and subjects eagerly participated. When the procurator royal of Majorca proposed that he and his friends should build galleys in partnership with the crown,[83] he had in mind a privateering syndicate, and before clinching with them Alfonso insisted that agreement be reached on the sharing of prize.[84] He regularly dispatched privateering expeditions made up of his own ships and private vessels whose owners contracted to serve the crown for the voyage under a commander appointed by the king. One of

---

[77] ACA Reg. 2651. 49^v, 24 Jan. 1437.
[78] ACA Reg. 2697. 109^v, 21 Oct. 1451.
[79] Ibid.: 'Otherwise, he threatened, the king can no longer maintain them.'
[80] ACA Reg. 2700. 27^v, 6 June 1453.
[81] ACA Reg. 2661. 35^r, 12 Oct. 1453.
[82] ACA Reg. 2662. 32^r, 25 May 1456. The bull granting the tithe was dated 11 Sept. 1455.
[83] Cf. above, p. 296.   [84] ACA Reg. 2699. 45^r, 4 Aug. 1446.

these expeditions was organized in December 1449 under the command of Bernat de Requesens. Alfonso gave him three ships: one of them a royal ship fitted out in Naples; the other two belonged to Pere de Prexana and Joan Madrenchs who had each received 1,000 ducats to fit their ships and a promise of a half share in any prize taken.[85] The instructions given to Requesens ordered him to go to Sicily, where the two private vessels were being fitted out, and to lead them to an agreed rendezvous when he received word that the royal ship had left Naples. Once his squadron had assembled, he was to transfer himself to the royal ship and sail eastwards attacking any vessels he might meet belonging to Venice, Florence, Anjou, and the Moors. He was also authorized to undertake operations on land with the object of seizing castles and territory; if feasible, these were to be held in the king's name, and if that was not possible they were to be sacked and burned. Captives taken by land or sea were to be ransomed whenever possible. Captured vessels might be brought home if in good condition; otherwise they should be burned. The decision whether to sell captured goods or bring them home was left to the commander's discretion. If he decided to sell them, the proceeds of the sale, as well as any bullion taken, were to be handed to the treasury representative aboard the king's ship. Also on board was an official of the *escriva de racio* to keep the accounts. Requesens had authority to requisition the services of any Aragonese corsairs he might meet in the course of his expedition on which the king placed a time limit of three months by requiring him to be back in Naples or Gaeta by the end of March 1450.

A month or so after Requesens sailed from Sicily, another fleet of ten galleys left Naples under the command of Bernat Vilamari to attack similar targets. Only three of these galleys belonged to the crown. Vilamari's instructions[86] told him to go first to Messina and Catania to take on board the biscuit and bread that had been prepared in Sicily. Once fully provisioned, he was to cruise in those parts of the eastern Mediterranean where, in his judgement, most damage might be inflicted on the king's enemies, particularly the

---

[85] ACA Reg. 2697. 41ᵛ, 22 Nov. 1449. As a special concession their share of prize was exempted from the normal deduction of one-fifth for the crown. They were also promised a supplementary payment of 1,000 ducats each in the event of any prize being taken.

[86] ACA Reg. 2697. 51ᵛ, 21 Jan. 1450.

Venetians. He was not, however, to permit any killing of Venetians and other Christians;[87] the same prohibition presumably did not apply to Muslims. Prize was divided into two equal shares—one for the king, the other for the owners of the private galleys—and, because the galleys could not conveniently carry much cargo, the royal share was either to be sold by the treasury representative, or else sent back to Naples or Sicily in a convenient ship. Vilamari was to return to Sicily by the end of March unless he judged it prudent and profitable to continue the cruise. In the event he took advantage of this discretionary instruction to prolong his operations until the middle of July. A triumphal reception to celebrate his 'victory' over the Venetians greeted him on his return to Naples. The envoys from Barcelona have left a brief description of it:[88]

On Sunday morning we went out to receive the captain at the city mole, where were gathered the council appointed by the lord king and many other notable people. The galleys, together with the galley of our embassy and that of mossen. Pachs of Majorca, left the Castel dell'Ovo and with great triumph approached the city mole where the captain was received with great honour. Accompanied by a large number of people on horseback, he and the masters of the galleys were led to the cathedral. They went in this order: the Count of Fondi, head of the Lord King's council, Johan de Marimon and the captain between them; behind them rode the Count of Brienza, Bernat Çapila and mossen. Gonsalvo de Nava, one of the masters; and after them many notable persons and courtiers of the king, each according to his degree.

The nature of the victory remains obscure, for we know only that Vilamari had cruised in the Adriatic and Aegean, and that the Grand Master of Rhodes had prevented him selling goods seized from subjects of the Sultan of Egypt.[89] In another prolonged operation, which lasted altogether from September 1450 until September 1452, Vilamari took the small island of Castelorizo

---

[87] '. . . no permetant empero que sia feta guerra drua ço es do matar als dits venecians ne altres cristians', ACA Reg. 2697. 51ᵛ, 21 Jan. 1450.

[88] ACB Cart. Com., vol. 20, fol. 163, 17 July 1450.

[89] Vilamari must have been in the Adriatic in February when the *magister portulanus* of the Abruzzi received orders to furnish his galleys with biscuit (ACA Reg. 2697. 54ʳ, 26 Feb. 1450). For the dispute with Rhodes see N. Iorga, *Notes et extraits pour servir à l'histoire des croisades au C. 15* (Paris and Bucharest, 1899–1915), ii. 440; and F. Cerone, 'La politica orientale di Alfonso d'Aragona', *ASPN* (1902), 450–4. The Grand Master had a treaty with the sultan.

near Rhodes, built a castle there, and so turned it into a base for Aragonese naval operations in the eastern Mediterranean.[90]

The prize that aroused most interest and controversy was a Genoese ship of 1,800 *botes* belonging to the merchant Squarciafico. Joan Llull, commander of two of the king's ships, took it in June 1453 during a cruise off the coast of Africa.[91] The loss of a ship with a cargo valued at 150,000 florins in a time of peace between Aragon and Genoa caused consternation in the republic, and an embassy was sent to Naples to negotiate its recovery. Eventually Alfonso ordered the release from his galleys of Genoese taken prisoner in the ship and the return of their jewels to the women passengers, but he kept the ship and its cargo.[92] Although this was a uniquely rich haul, one must assume that most of these expeditions proved profitable, otherwise they would not have been mounted so regularly.[93]

The crown also derived profit from privateering enterprises in which it took no part other than to authorize the arming of a vessel and commission its owner to attack the king's enemies, for the king was entitled to one-fifth of any prize taken by a subject.[94] Many, of course, sought to evade that levy; among the crimes for which the Count of Campobasso received a pardon in 1457 was his failure to pay the crown its share in the prize taken by his galley in the eastern Mediterranean.[95] Sometimes the king would renounce his fifth in return for an agreed payment in advance or even make an outright grant of it.[96]

Although it was a relatively cheap way of harassing an enemy, a policy of encouraging privateers had its drawbacks. Once a subject

[90] Vilamari's instructions for this operation are to be found in ACA Reg. 2697. 69ᵛ, 20 Sept. 1450. For the seizure of Castelorizo see Facio, *De rebus gestis*, IX. The Knights Hospitallers, nominal suzerains of the island, protested in vain to Rome against the Aragonese occupation (ACA Reg. 2939. 130ᵛ, 25 July 1451).

[91] Facio, *De rebus gestis*, X; ACB Cart. Com., vol. 23, fol. 57, 30 June 1453. This letter was written the day Llull brought his prize into Naples.

[92] Iorga, *Notes et extraits*, ii. 488–92.

[93] Details of many privateering expeditions are given by C. Marinescu, 'Notes sur les corsaires au service d'Alfonse V d'Aragon, roi de Naples', *Mélanges d'histoire générale de l'Université de Cluj*, I (1927).

[94] e.g. acknowledgement of receipt from the procurator royal in Majorca of 1,296 ducats, being the royal fifth in a Genoese ship *La Serrana* taken by Pere dez Pla (ACA Reg. 2720. 10ᵛ, 20 Apr. 1444).

[95] ASN Div. Somm. I. 52 (bis), 23ʳ, 10 Oct. 1457.

[96] The register ACA Reg. 2945 (Gratiarum) contains fifteen privileges waiving the crown's claim to the fifth. They cover the years 1443–58; twelve are for Catalans and three for Portuguese.

had obtained permission to arm a vessel, it became difficult to control his activities. The Mediterranean swarmed with privateers of all nations, many of whom were not particular to confine their attentions to the shipping of enemy states, but would fall upon any lucrative and easy victim even if it belonged to a fellow citizen. Nicolau Binot of Majorca was found guilty of the piratical seizure off Calabria of a vessel belonging to Zullio di Viterbo of Messina.[97] Gilabert de Lupia, brother of the *baile* of Perpignan, even ventured to take a caravel belonging to Alfonso's sister, the Queen of Portugal.[98] A very uncertain line divided privateering from piracy and no special opprobrium seems to have attached to those who crossed it. Even Galceran de Requesens, governor of Catalonia, was accused of acts of piracy under cover of the royal ensign, and the king himself admitted the lawlessness of his own vessels.[99] While individuals and the state might make occasional profits in these conditions, international relations and commerce suffered grievously.

From time to time governments sought to redress the balance by curbing the wilder excesses of their subjects. Once he had driven the Duke of Anjou from Naples, Alfonso attempted to deal with the shoal of privateers that had proliferated in the confusion of the preceding years. He decreed that all galleys, save those in royal service, were to be disarmed, and that for the future no subject should arm a vessel without his leave on pain of death.[100] To bring under control those galleys retained in the service of the crown, he directed that they should all gather in Palermo, where they would be put under the command of a 'good captain'. Efforts were also made to arrest ships which, though armed under royal licence, had failed to give the required security against harming allies and subjects of the crown. Those that, having failed to give security, had harmed subjects and allies of the king were to be taken and disarmed, and their masters sent under

---

[97] ACA Reg. 2918. 4ʳ, 3 July 1451. Binot was sentenced to pay di Viterbo 4,000 ducats in compensation.

[98] ACA Reg. 2651. 156ʳ, 13 Sept. 1440, Order to the governor of Majorca to see that it is returned immediately.

[99] '... considerant los dans e maltractaments que les galeres e galiotes del dit Senyor stants disperses e separades van fahent a diverses conditions de gents e pus tot als amichs e vassalls del dit Senyor que als enemichs' (ACA Reg. 2939. 59ʳ, 21 Jan. 1443).

[100] ACA Reg. 2939. 59ʳ, 21 Jan. 1443; ibid. 64ᵛ, 16 July 1443, Instructions to Queen Maria to put these regulations into effect in the territories under her control.

secure guard to the king with a statement of their offences. Those that had committed no offence were to be disarmed.[101] Stern action was ordered against notorious pirates such as Loys Garcia whose galliot had wrought indiscriminate havoc among shipping. In December 1443 Alfonso instructed Diego de Graieda, master of a royal galley, to seize him and carry him prisoner to Naples for punishment.[102] But either Garcia evaded capture or he was able to buy his way out of trouble for one year later he was still pursuing his piratical career.[103] In 1447 Catalan pirates infested the coasts of Calabria. Alfonso acknowledged the menace in a letter to his council in Naples:

We have received your letters in which you inform us of the robberies committed on the coasts of Calabria and in other parts of this kingdom by Pons dez Catlar and Ferrando de Valdaya and others with their vessels, both in taking men by force and in seizing any goods and chattels they may come upon, without regard whether they belong to our subjects, confederates and friends; they behave rather as pirates and common robbers, stealing from everyone, paying little heed to the disservice they do us, caring only for their desire to advance their own interests by one means or another. And though we have received so many complaints about them, we have until now chosen to dissemble, in the hope that they would mend their ways and abandon their evil doings.[104]

This extraordinary tolerance was brought to an end by an order to the Count of Cocentayna to send any galleys available in pursuit of the miscreants. Yet in 1452 it was still found necessary to order

---

[101] ACA Reg. 2690. 49ᵛ, 20 Jan. 1444, Instructions for Gilabert de Lupia who, as commander of a royal galley, was to search for the offending vessels.

[102] ACA Reg. 2698. 21ᵛ, 29 Dec. 1443. Despite his misdeeds, Garcia had hitherto enjoyed a safe-conduct which was now revoked.

[103] ACA Reg. 2795. 9ᵛ, 16 Nov. 1444, Order to Queen Maria to effect the release of some Dalmatians whom Garcia had seized, 'more piratorum', and put to the oars of his bireme.

[104] ACA Reg. 2699. 76ʳ, 10 May 1447: 'Vestres letres havem reebudes per les quals nos avisau deles roberies quis fan en les marines de Calabria e altres de nostre Regne de Sicilia deça far per Ponc dez catlar e ferrando de Valdaya e altres ab lurs fustes axi en pendre homens per força com encara robes e bens qui davant los venen no attenent si son de vassalls ne subdits confederats e amichs nostres ans com a cossaris e publichs ladrons van a roba de totes gents poch attenent al deservey que a nos fan no curant sino de lur ambicio per fer lurs fets o per una via o per un altra, e ab tot a tantes clamors quantes dells nos son vengudes fins huy ho haiam volgut dissimular sperant ells se corrigissen es smenassen del mal fet . . .' Valdaya appears to have used Ischia as his base of operations.

the seizure of galleys ignoring the decree of 1443 which required
a royal licence to arm any vessel.[105] Impossible as it may have been
to stamp out entirely the evils of unlawful privateering and
piracy, one suspects that Alfonso hesitated to inflict exemplary
punishment on those who broke his own laws against them from
fear of offending Catalan interests upon which he relied to
provide the backbone of his sea power.

Command of the king's ships and galleys was almost exclusively
in Catalan hands. Two types of command need to be distinguished:
one, the command of individual vessels, was of necessity given to
professional seamen; the other, command of fleets or squadrons,
might be given to a noble or official who was not an experienced
sailor, but who had the authority to ensure that the fleet carried
out its assignment. In the first category Catalans enjoyed a monopoly, as may be seen from the list of masters of vessels belonging
to the crown: Thomas Thomas, Pons dez Catlar, and Pablo
Sureda of Majorca, Diego Graieda, Joan Madrenchs, Pere Sirvent,
Luis Sirvent,[106] Jacme de Mascort, Miquel Romeu, Luis Solsona,
Joan Llull, Bernat Çamaso, Bernat de Pachs, Huguet de Pachs,
Gregori Junquers, Jacme Pipinelli, Gilabert de Lupia, Joan
Salvador, Pere Pujades, Macia Vinyes, Galceran Gener, Gonsalvo
de Nava, Pere de Niubo, Berenguer de Pontos, Guillem Torells,
Pere de Prexana, Salvator Sureda, Rafael Julia, Luis Castellin.
The envoy of Barcelona in Naples wrote in January 1452 that all
the ships in the king's service, both those at sea and two being built
in Naples, then had masters who were natives of the Catalan
capital.[107] He exaggerated a little, but not outrageously.

The second category of commanders exhibits rather more
variety, though Catalans still predominated. Iñigo de Avalos and
Bernat de Requesens commanded privateering expeditions. The
secretary Olzina was captain of six galleys sent to Genoa in March
1446. Command of a privateering expedition fitted out in 1457
was given to the Catalan noble Pere Joan de Sent Climent. There
were those in the Consell de Mar who opposed his appointment

---

[105] ACA Reg. 2659. 110ᵛ, 19 Nov. 1452, Order to de Graieda to seize such
vessels, putting their crews to the oars of his own galley and sending their
officers prisoners to the king.

[106] On 28 Dec. 1453 Alfonso gave a feast aboard the royal ship commanded by
Sirvent when it lay in the harbour of Gaeta (Minieri Riccio, 'Alcuni fatti di
Alfonso I', p. 428).

[107] ACB Cart. Com., vol. 22, fol. 9, 21 Jan. 1452.

on the grounds that he had no experience of the sea, but the king insisted. While his three ships were fitting Pere Joan spent all his time in the arsenal either seeking to give the lie to his detractors, or else to make good his deficiencies.[108] The only Italians given a command of this kind were Francesco de Riccardis, an army captain, who was appointed captain general of five galleys sent to join the fleet off Genoa in 1457,[109] and Carafello Carafa who took command of three galleys sent to seize the castle of Leghorn in March 1452.[110]

General command of the king's warships, which belonged by tradition to his admirals, did not become a matter of practical concern so long as the vessels operated independently or in small squadrons. The title of 'captain of the galleys' did exist before 1440, but the office was apparently not then of great importance. Francesch Gilabert de Centelles, a Catalan who held fiefs in Sardinia and who later became Count of Oliva, was reinstated in it in April 1440. His command consisted only of his own galley and any others belonging to other subjects of the king that he might be able to recruit.[111] Nor did his second spell of office last long, for by September 1440 he was witnessing an act as *marescalcus*[112] and in the course of a long career was never again mentioned as 'captain of the galleys'. Only in the summer of 1443 when Alfonso mustered his galleys in Palermo with the intention of putting them under the command of a 'good captain' did the title begin to assume real importance.[113] It was probably at this juncture that he bestowed it on the Catalan Bernat Vilamari; Vilamari had certainly assumed it by September 1444 when, as 'captain of our galleys', he was recalled from his operations in the Adriatic, where he was supporting the land forces in the Abruzzi, in order to join in the attack on Centelles's possessions in Calabria.[114]

[108] ACB Cart. Com., vol. 27, fol. 132, 5 June 1457; ACA Reg. 2800. 16ᵛ, 4 June 1457.

[109] ACA Reg. 2800. 20ᵛ, 22 July 1457.

[110] ACA Reg. 2697. 126ʳ, 9 Mar. 1452. The castellan had promised to betray the castle, but the scheme misfired.

[111] With these galleys he was told to go at once to defend Gaeta against a Genoese force of three galleys and two galliots (ACA Reg. 2651. 149ʳ, 25 Apr. 1440).

[112] Ibid. 163ᵛ, 18 Sept. 1440. He still used the title of marshal in 1448 (ACA Reg. 2945. 87ʳ, 21 May 1448).

[113] Cf. above, p. 308.

[114] ACA Reg. 2698. 69ʳ, 24 Sept. 1444.

His next major operations were the cruises in the Adriatic,
Aegean, and eastern Mediterranean from 1450 to 1452 discussed
earlier in this chapter. In 1453 he took over from Berenguer d'Erill
command of the naval side of the Tuscan war, and it was probably at this juncture that he acquired the title 'captain general of
the fleet[115] and the governorship of Roussillon and Cerdagne. The
title was not coined especially for him—it had previously been
granted to Benedetto Doria, presaging the service which that
Genoese family was to render to Alfonso's descendants[116]—but
it assumed for the first time a practical significance. Frequent
reference has already been made to Vilamari's greatest enterprise,
the naval campaign against Genoa which he conducted from
September 1456 until Alfonso's death. It came near to success in
that he managed to bottle up Genoese shipping and harry the
coast of the republic virtually at will, but he failed in a direct
attack on Genoa itself and drove the republic to the desperate
expedient of calling in French aid. After the king's death Vilamari
remained in Naples as Ferdinand's naval commander, an office
which passed eventually to his son.[117]

Seamen to man the king's ships were drawn mainly from the
Spanish territories and Sicily. Rowers for the galleys came from
all parts, including certain coastal towns and cities of the royal
demesne in the kingdom of Naples which were required to furnish
a quota of oarsmen for the galleys.[118] Criminal and other 'un-
desirable' elements of society were regularly pressed into service.
On one occasion Queen Maria was instructed to put to the oars
of Pablo Sureda's galley all available 'lenones et desides alii qui
vitam in otio transigunt et etiam ceteri criminosi quorum flagicia
galearum servitium mereantur'.[119] When preparations were made
to arm the galley of the governor of Valencia, Alfonso told the
King of Navarre to take men from the prisons if sufficient oars-

---

[115] A safe-conduct for ships from Piombino was notified to Vilamari as 'generali
nostre classis capitaneo' on 4 June 1453 (ACA Reg. 2917. 112ᵛ).

[116] The title was bestowed in Doria on 23 June 1448 (ACA Reg. 2656. 128ᵛ).
He was at that time a supporter of the pro-Aragonese Campofregosi faction
which held power in Genoa.

[117] The son commanded Ferdinand's naval forces in the war of 1486 (E. Pontieri, 'La "Guerra dei Baroni" ', *ASPN* (1972), 119).

[118] Cf. pardon issued to Maratea for penalties incurred 'ex eo quod non mise-
runt homines remigeros comandatos ad galeateas nostras' (Mazzoleni, *Il Codice
Chigi*, pp. 35–6, 10 July 1451).

[119] ACA Reg. 2690. 110ʳ, 12 Sept. 1444.

men could not otherwise be found.[120] Prisoners taken at sea from enemy ships and those contravening the laws on privateering were also liable to find themselves pulling the oars of a galley. Sometimes masters of galleys pressed to complete a crew were indiscriminate in their methods. When the King of Castile complained that some of his subjects had been wrongly put to the oars of Alfonso's galleys, the King of Aragon replied that this could only have happened to desperate criminals arrested within his domains who had been spared worse punishment. Nevertheless he arranged for the Castilian ambassador then in Naples to inspect his galleys and permitted the release of Castilians found in them; he also promised to have the same done with the other galleys when Vilamari brought them back from a cruise in the Levant.[121]

But the prisons could not always furnish enough galley fodder and a broader appeal to the desperate and criminal became necessary. A curious example of this kind of recruiting is provided by a letter which Alfonso sent to the King of Navarre on behalf of the Count of Caltabellota who had built in the arsenal of Naples a galley for the crusading fleet of which there was so much talk in the summer of 1456. The letter asks the regent in Aragon to grant a pardon for any crime to all who enlisted for service in the count's galley, excepting only traitors, heretics, sodomites, and coiners. Debtors were to be encouraged by a promise of a stay upon all action for debt during the period of their service and for six months after their return home.[122] Many gladly took this way out of their difficulties, but, having secured the pardon and their wages, large numbers of them deserted in Sicily.[123] The law did not permit the impressment of free men, and masters were sometimes warned not to resort to it. Thus when Jacme Pasqual took a royal galley to Spain in August 1446, he was ordered to return to Italy as quickly as possible, 'but without impressing men'.[124] At other times authority chose to close its eyes because it needed the galleys. Erasmo Arella of Gaeta, who had armed a galley to serve the king, received a pardon for a number of crimes including

[120] ACA Reg. 2700. 32ᵛ, 29 June 1453.
[121] ACA Reg. 2660, 121ᵛ, 29 July 1454, Letter to the King of Castile.
[122] ACA Reg. 2946. 4ᵛ, 23 Sept. 1456.
[123] Ibid. 61ʳ, 2 Sept. 1457, Commission empowering Giovanni di Pisano of Messina to apprehend the deserters.
[124] ACA Reg. 2699. 45ʳ, 4 Aug. 1446.

impressment, 'prout comuniter per consimiles galee patronos consuevit fieri'.[125] But the press gang on occasion overstepped the mark. It did so when the master of the galley belonging to the Count of Oliva had Antoni Lopez seized by force from his house in Naples, gagged with a towel, and carried off to the galley. Lopez had come to Naples to work on the rebuilding of Castel-nuovo, so the king angrily ordered that he and all others similarly impressed in the city of Naples should be released from the galley.[126] Others with less claim to royal attention might not have been so lucky.

Such rough and ready methods might serve to furnish the galleys with rowers, but they could not provide an adequate number of experienced seamen. These had to be recruited by the promise of pay and the prospect of a share in prize—prize taken by royal ships was shared half and half between the crown and the crews—from the seafaring population of the Aragonese dominions. As one might expect, a fleet which drew most of its masters from the Spanish territories found most of its seamen there too.

The emergence towards the end of the reign of a council for naval affairs has been mentioned in a previous chapter.[127] A need for such a body, which would keep a closer watch on these matters than was possible in the general council, had made itself felt in 1450 when Alfonso had begun to step up his naval operations in the eastern Mediterranean and had sent his first contingent of soldiers to aid the Albanians against the Turks. These were the initial moves in an ambitious policy designed to take advantage of the break-up of the state structure in the Balkans and Levant in face of Turkish pressure. Its success depended very much upon sea power, and the fact that the Turks could be presented as the main targets of attack made it a respectable enterprise in the west. But the brunt of the naval power organized by the council fell in the end not upon the Turks but upon Genoa.

---

[125] ACA Reg. 2904. 83ʳ, 12 June 1443. Arella had committed the offence 'ut gentes habere posset necessarias vi nonnullos homines tam vassallos nostros quam alios cepit atque pro usu et exercicio galee eiusdem ad remum et alias detinuerit.'

[126] ACA Reg. 2656. 177ʳ, 31 July 1449; ibid. 179ʳ, 1 Aug. 1449: 'no content vos o lo patro o altres de vestra galea de pendre ġent per forsa contra nostra voluntat . . .'

[127] See above, pp. 123–4.

For the kingdom of Naples this renaissance as a naval power did not outlast the king who brought it about. Severed from Sicily, Catalonia, Valencia, and the Balearics, the kingdom ceased to play an important strategic role in the naval affairs of the Mediterranean, its coasts fell prey to the ravages of corsairs, and in the reign of Ferdinand a Turkish fleet was able to seize the city of Otranto.

X

POWER IN THE PROVINCES

THE breakdown of royal authority under Giovanna II was most starkly evident in the central government's loss of control over the provinces. In this sphere Alfonso's chief concern was, therefore, to re-establish that control, partly in order that law and obedience might be restored among his subjects, partly from a need to gather as much tax as possible from them. He pursued those objectives primarily by restoring efficiency in the central organs of finance and justice, and by resuscitating the Angevin machinery of provincial and municipal government. At the highest level—the government of provinces—he introduced greater flexibility than had existed hitherto by employing a variety of officials—viceroys, commissioners, captains general—with degrees of authority that could be adjusted to meet the local situation. In general, however, he refrained from gratuitous assaults on Neapolitan institutions and traditions, preferring to emphasize the element of continuity in his rule and to deal with Neapolitans through Neapolitans. Customary law too proved a powerful defender of the status quo in local government. It was so entrenched that it often successfully resisted efforts to modify the privileges and constitutions of towns and cities. The demesne cities of Abruzzo citeriore, for example, in 1448 petitioned against numerous official infringements of their jurisdictional privileges and obtained from the king's council general satisfaction in accordance with a strict interpretation of customary law.[1] Most, and probably all, such assaults on municipal rights arose from attempts on the part of royal officials to enlarge the size and scope of their perquisites, not from government policy. Where the king did sometimes run deliberately into conflict with the established order was in the alienation of demesne land, but even here well-documented custom could prevail over his wishes and need for money. The town of Francavilla al Mare in the Abruzzi forestalled its sale to

[1] ACA Reg. 2913. 117ʳ, 9 Jan. 1449, Royal letter in favour of the petitioners ordering a strict observance of their privileges and constitutions.

the Count of Loreto by sending to the king a deputation backed by other towns of the royal demesne which were anxious that an unfavourable precedent should not be established. The council considered the case and gave its decision in favour of Francavilla, following the principle enunciated in the privilege which gave effect to its judgement:[2]

Cum reges et principes multipharie famam adquirere soleant ex nulla tam re nomen suum magis immortalitati conferiatur quam civitates terras et castra regnorum suorum in iustitia manutenere ac prothegere et que in legem partionatam sibi per eos concessa sunt inviolabiliter observare et a demanio seu diademate regio eas non separare.

If the king was restricted by law and custom in his dealings with those of his subjects living within the royal demesne, his routine control over the other inhabitants of his kingdom was virtually non-existent. This was a limitation of great moment in a state where out of some 1,500 *universita* only between 100 and 200 belonged to the crown.[3] Although these figures disguise the fact that most of the major cities belonged to the demesne, there were whole provinces—notably Terra d'Otranto, Basilicata, Principato ulteriore, and Molise—in which the crown was virtually landless. The greatest of the Neapolitan barons, the Prince of Taranto, possessed some 300 *universita* and with them complete control of the heel of Italy.[4] Josia d'Aquaviva, Count of San Flaviano, whose son married a daughter of the Prince of Taranto held forty-eight *universita* in the Abruzzi provinces.[5] In Calabria the Duke of San Marco, a member of the powerful Sanseverino family, held forty-seven *universita*, while his son-in-law, the Count of Sanseverino, held another thirty. The church, by contrast, held

---

[2] ACA Reg. 2690. 106ᵛ. 1 Sept. 1444.

[3] Gentile ('Lo stato napoletano' (1937), p. 47) gives the figure as 102 out of 1,550. Bianchini (*Della storia delle finanze*, p. 183) makes it 200 out of 1,550. My own count gives 134 *universita* in the royal desmesne following the confiscation of the estates of Centelles in 1444–5. The discrepancies probably arise from taking different points in time for the counting and different interpretations of the term *universita*. I have taken it to mean an autonomous inhabited place having its own municipal officials.

[4] According to Costanzo the Orsini family held seven metropolitan cities, more than thirty of which were the seats of bishoprics and more than 300 castles. Tristan Caracciolo asserted that the Prince of Taranto could travel from Naples to Taranto spending every night in a house of his own.

[5] Bianchini, *Della storia delle finanze*, p. 183; G. Incarnato, 'Il possesso feudale in Abruzzo ultra dal 1500 al 1670', *ASPN* (1972), 222–3.

only forty-three *universita* throughout the kingdom. Alfonso was not responsible for the dilapidated condition of the royal demesne; his predecessors, and in particular Giovanna II, had alienated large parts of it to the Sforzas and Colonnas.[6] But his own policy of winning over the Neapolitan nobility by generous grants of land and planting trusted Spaniards among them had prevented him from strengthening the demesne with fiefs seized from irreconcilable enemies. For example, the county of Troia, taken from Francesco Sforza, was given to Garcia de Cabanyells,[7] and those of Ariano and Apice to Iñigo de Guevara.[8] Only the forfeiture of Centelles's estates in Calabria brought any permanent and substantial additions to the royal demesne; they numbered in all twenty-nine *universita*.

In all these lands outside the royal demesne tenants-in-chief exercised the rights of *merum et mixtum imperium* granted to them in the parliament of 1443. At first Alfonso would do no more than confirm privileges already granted and he answered the barons' petition for a general concession with the words: 'Placet Regiae Maiestati observari facere privilegia iurisdictionum concessarum.[9] On 9 March he withdrew this reservation and made the concession a general one. In practice he was conceding very little.[10] Just as numerous exemptions from scutage had rendered that imposition of small significance both financially and militarily, so earlier grants of jurisdiction to the barons—especially in the reigns of Ladislas and Giovanna II—had been so widespread as completely to undermine the crown's pretensions to administer justice to all its subjects. In addition to this general delegation of jurisdiction to the barons, many favoured individuals received further privileges which had the effect of excluding royal officials from

---

[6] Pontieri, 'Muzio Attendolo e Francesco Sforza', p. 103.

[7] ACA Reg. 2902. 106[r], 12 June 1442, Privilege conferring the city on Cabanyells with the title of count.

[8] ASN Priv. I. 40[v], 23 Oct. 1452, Privilege confirming the original grants of 1435 and 1440.

[9] de Bottis, *Privilegii*, fol. 6.

[10] The concession of *merum et mixtum imperium* was made *ad beneplacitum*. This was expressly stated in the privilege conferring the county of Troia on Giovanni di Cabanyells. The original grant in 1442 had not included the *merum et mixtum imperium*; it is now granted 'prout comites et barones terrarum et barones et locorum in eadem provincia capitanate in eorum terris et locis utilius melius et favorabilius tenent possident et exercent ac de jure usu vel consuetudine tenere et exercere possunt seu quomodolibet possidere nostro tamen beneplacito perdurante' (ACA Reg. 2917. 113[r], 3 Jan. 1453).

their estates more or less completely. An outstanding example was the Prince of Taranto who exercised virtually complete sovereignty over his vassals. In 1445 an inquest into royal rights in his lands had to be called off in face of his protests.[11] When Carlo Ruffo, Count of Sinopoli, took the captaincy and castellany of Seminara as security for a loan to the crown of 3,500 ducats, those offices were exempted from the jurisdiction of the viceroy and justiciar of Calabria.[12] Similar concessions, prompted by the need to reward services or satisfy creditors, occurred regularly throughout the reign. In these circumstances the greater part of the routine business of local government—justice, police, taxation, and the regulation of economic life—rested in the hands of the feudal nobility who for that purpose maintained their own administrative organizations with chancellors, treasurers, secretaries, judges, and a host of minor officials.[13] For the crown there remained the functions of providing a similar routine administration in the royal demesne and exercising its higher powers of supervision over its vassals. The former function, governed by the constitutions of the kingdom and customary law, admitted of little experiment or innovation; the latter posed urgent political problems to which Alfonso responded primarily by reinforcing the authority of the *curia* and its executive organs. Parallel to the reassertion of royal authority from that direction, the slow but steady subjection of the kingdom by force of arms enabled him to re-establish the agents of the crown in a position of authority in most of the provinces.

With a few modifications the division of the kingdom into provinces still followed the pattern established by Frederick II. In the reign of Alfonso there were twelve of them: Terra di Lavoro, Molise, Principato citeriore, Principato ulteriore, Basilicata, Capitanata, Terra di Bari, Terra d'Otranto, Abruzzo citeriore, Abruzzo ulteriore, Calabria, and the two districts of Valle del Crati and Terra Giordana which were administered as a single province. In terms of population, strategic and economic

[11] ASN Fasc. Com. Somm. 85^r, 12 Nov. 1445. That same day the commissioner collecting marriage aids in Terra di Bari and Terra d'Otranto was ordered not to collect them in the lands of the prince, his mother, and his brothers, the Dukes of Andria and Venosa (ibid. 93^v).

[12] ACA Reg. 2909. 5^r, 4 July 1443.

[13] It was customary for the greater feudataries to appoint deputies who bore titles such as *vice comes*, *vice dux*, etc.—e.g. the royal order addressed *inter alia* to the 'Viceduci Suesse Vicecomiti Fundorum' (Mazzoleni, *Il Codice Chigi*, p. 191, 30 Dec. 1451).

importance, the provinces differed greatly one from another. The most heavily populated were Terra di Lavoro and the two Calabrian provinces, followed by the Principati and Abruzzi. The least populous province was the Terra d'Otranto, a reminder that the power of the Prince of Taranto was not entirely commensurate with his estates. Until Sforza had been driven from the Roman Marches and peace made with the papacy, Abruzzo ulteriore and the district of Terra di Lavoro beyond the Garigliano remained of vital importance to the land defences of the kingdom. Later the threat from external enemies hung mainly over the sea coasts, and in particular over the major ports of Terra di Lavoro, Calabria, Terra di Bari, and Capitanata which had to be fortified against raids by Venetian or Genoese fleets. Capitanata, Terra di Bari, Basilicata, and Calabria were the chief grain-producing regions, and the provinces of Puglia regularly exported a surplus through the Adriatic ports. Large quantities of salt were manufactured around Manfredonia and Barletta and, on a smaller scale, in Calabria. Puglia was of great importance to the crown as the region of winter pasture controlled in its interest by the *dogana della mena delle pecore*.[14] The concentration of population in Terra di Lavoro, and especially in the capital, made that province an important centre of internal and external commerce. These differing degrees of importance, combined with the varying extent of the royal demesne, meant that provinces were susceptible to a range of influence by the central government. Thus, to take extreme examples, the affairs of the Terra di Lavoro were closely regulated, while the Terra d'Otranto was almost entirely neglected.

As Alfonso had conquered the provinces piecemeal and been obliged to hold them against René of Anjou and his supporters, he had found it necessary to subject them initially to the control of officials unbound by the constitutional provisions that regulated the appointment and conduct of the regular governors, the justiciars. He accordingly entrusted the provinces to omnicompetent viceroys. Some precedent existed for the use of such officials in the kingdom: Ladislas had made much use of them in the early troubled years of his reign; Giovanna II had appointed a viceroy for Calabria, Alfonso systematically

[14] See below, pp. 359 ff.
[15] A. Cutolo, *Re Ladislas d'Angiò Durazzo* (Naples, 1969), p. 157.

developed the office, appointing trusted Spaniards, and less often
Italians, as the cornerstones of his military and political mastery
of the kingdom. At first they commanded not whole provinces but
districts or cities obedient to the king from which they endeavoured
by force or persuasion to extend their authority. Garcia Aznares,
Bishop of Lerida, was viceroy of Gaeta in 1436;[16] in 1437 Angelo
Morosini held that office in the duchy of Amalfi;[17] Ramon Boyl
held it in Aversa in 1440.[18] In contrast to these very restricted
areas of authority, Francesco d'Aquino, the chamberlain of the
kingdom, was in 1438 given the titles of viceroy and commissioner
for the whole of the Abruzzi region where Alfonso at that time
held very little territory.[19] As the king effectively extended his
sway over whole provinces, the scope of viceregal authority was
adjusted to conform to the provincial pattern until by 1444, when
Sforza and the last Angevin partisans had been cleared from the
Abruzzi, viceroys had been appointed for all the provinces except
the Terra d'Otranto, the preserve of the Prince of Taranto, and
the relatively unimportant Molise.[20] Other viceroys governed
Terracina and Benevento—papal cities entrusted to Alfonso for
the period of his life—and the district of Cassino. The older
pattern reappeared briefly in Calabria during the revolt of Centelles when no less than three viceroys were commissioned to
restore order in that province. Once that task had been accomplished a single viceroy resumed the government.

As agents of the king invested with the full authority of the
crown and assisted by *alguaciles*,[21] the viceroys wielded greater
power than the former justiciars, but they had no place in the
constitutions of the kingdom and their presence aroused considerable misgiving among the Neapolitan nobility. Therefore
Alfonso did not attempt to retain them in most provinces once

---

[16] ACA Reg. 2900. 16ᵛ, 26 Dec. 1436, Letter from the king to the bishop as
viceroy.

[17] ACA Reg. 2902. 1ʳ, Reference to a privilege issued by Morosini as viceroy
at Cava, 1 Aug. 1437.

[18] ACA Reg. 2646. 93ʳ, 13 June 1440. Late in 1439 Boyl had led the forces
that took the castle of Aversa.

[19] ACA Reg. 2909. 119ʳ, Confirmation of a privilege issued by d'Aquino in
his capacity as viceroy, 12 July 1438.

[20] In his description of the kingdom Borso d'Este named the most important
viceroys in 1444 as Ramon Boyl (Abruzzi), Eximen Perez de Corella (Terra di
Lavoro), Garcia de Cabanyells (Puglia), Antonio Centelles (Calabria), and
Carafello Carafa (the Cassino district).

[21] Cf. above, pp. 162-3.

all danger of armed rebellion had disappeared, but reinstated the justiciars in their former role. By the last years of the reign viceroys ruled only in Calabria and the region of the Terra di Lavoro beyond the Garigliano; in the Abruzzi there governed a commissioner general with powers similar to those of a viceroy.[22] In Calabria Alfonso could claim to be following a practice instituted by the Angevins. As for the frontier regions of the Terra di Lavoro and Abruzzi, considerations of security may have prompted the retention of a viceroy. It is also possible, in the case of the Garigliano district, that the king refused to remove a trusted servant, Alfonso de Cardenas, from a prestigious office. Garcia de Cabanyells, another Spaniard who had served Alfonso well in his wars, kept his title of viceroy in the Puglian provinces until his death in 1452, and in the Abruzzi the title did not disappear until the holder, Ramon Boyl, fell into disfavour as a result of his failure to carry out a projected attack on Sforza.[23] Well before then his exercise of the office had been little more than nominal, if we may believe the complaint of Rodrigo Vidal that he had made nothing from his post as *magister actorum* to Boyl and his deputy because they were rarely in the province.[24] Another type of viceregal appointment that may have persisted was that made in favour of certain nobles in respect of their fiefs; they had the effect of excluding all royal officials from those fiefs.[25]

The privilege dated 16 July 1443[26] that appointed de Cardenas viceroy in Terra di Lavoro beyond the Garigliano made him responsible for garrisoning and provisioning all castles in that region, and for the appointment of their castellans; he had authority

---

[22] Bernardo de Raymo, a *rationalis* of the Sommaria, appears to have been given this office in the 14th indiction (1450–1). In May 1451, after expressing satisfaction with his conduct, the king confirmed him as commissioner general for the remainder of that indiction and the whole of the 15th indiction (ACA Reg. 2915. 19ᵛ, 24 May 1451).

[23] Cf. above, pp. 274–5.

[24] ACA Reg. 2914. 90ʳ. Vidal first obtained the office in August 1442. Alfonso renewed the appointment—but now as *magister actorum* to the justiciar—from September 1451 so that Vidal might derive some benefit from it. Diego de Speio was Boyl's deputy in his last years as viceroy (Mazzoleni, *Il Codice Chigi*, pp. 338–9, 12 June 1452: de Raymo is ordered to conclude a case begun before de Speio).

[25] e.g. appointment of Francesco Orsini, Count of Conversano and Gravina, as viceroy in all his possessions (ACA Reg. 2909. 147ʳ, 28 June 1445).

[26] ACA Reg. 2903. 82ᵛ, Letters patent, *quod pareatur*, enjoining obedience to him as viceroy were issued on 18 July 1443 (ibid. 88ʳ).

to pardon all crimes, whether public or private, committed to that date, and to issue safe-conducts to rebels wishing to make their peace with the king. Three days later he received additional powers to deal with the bandits who infested the roads between Naples and Rome; freed from strict observance of the law, he could proceed against them 'deum et justiciam solum habens pre oculis' and invoke the emergency regulations promulgated by Charles I for the suppression of robbers.[27] Much greater power was delegated to the Aragonese noble Lope Ximenez de Urrea who became viceroy and *locumtenens generalis* in Calabria in November 1443.[28] His jurisdiction covered all criminal cases including treason, and all civil cases, even those involving tenants-in-chief and those pertaining to the Vicaria and Sommaria. His authority over castellans extended to those who held by Spanish usage, and he wielded the power—usually reserved to the crown—of appointing and removing captains of towns. In financial matters he was able to appoint collectors of the hearth tax where none had been appointed by the king, and to oblige these and other revenue collectors to render accounts to him. Finally, he was empowered to use the forces of the crown against rebels in the province. This last provision explains the exceptionally sweeping character of the others, for baronial unrest in Calabria, led by no other than the previous viceroy Antonio Centelles,[29] was gathering to the storm that was to break in the summer of 1444. Francesch Siscar, the Valencian whom Alfonso appointed viceroy of Calabria once the back of the rebellion had been broken,[30] exercised more restricted authority: appeals from lesser tribunals, cases of denial of justice, enforcement of the judgement of the supreme tribunals. The king took back into his own hands the appointment of captains and castellans in that province.[31]

---

[27] Ibid. 88ᵛ, 19 July 1443.   [28] ACA Reg. 2906. 39ᵛ, 16 Nov. 1443.

[29] Since Borso d'Este names Centelles as viceroy still in 1444, it is possible that he had not been deprived of the office but supplanted by a viceroy with greater powers. Such a mark of disfavour might have stimulated his resentment against Alfonso.

[30] The date of his appointment is not known, but he was viceroy by 5 Mar. 1445 (ACA Reg. 2908. 52ʳ).

[31] Siscar's administration of Calabria is exceptionally well documented thanks to the survival of fragments of registers from his chancery among the records of the Sommaria. ASN Fasc. Com. Somm., fols. 1–17 covers the months April and May 1452. Fasc. Com. Somm., fols. 124–51, covers May and June 1453. This latter fragment has been edited by Pontieri in *Fonti aragonesi*, ii.

Although the justiciars suffered partial eclipse as the chief provincial representatives of the crown, their office continued to exist under the shadow of the viceroys, until the disappearance of the latter in most provinces allowed it to regain its former authority. This return to normal brought Neapolitans back into the government of the provinces, for while almost all viceroys were Spaniards, justiciars were chosen with an equal hand from Spanish and Italian subjects. Of the thirteen mentioned in the records, six were Spaniards and seven Italians, all of them natives of the kingdom. Two of the Neapolitans (Giovanni di San Severino and Francesco d'Aquila) became justiciars in Principato citeriore only during temporary renunciations of the office by the Catalan Pere de Botifar, to whom it had been granted for life.[32] On the other hand, in 1451 a Neapolitan, Giovanni di Somma, became justiciar of Molise for life.[33] In practice Neapolitan participation in the office was almost certainly greater than this partial record suggests for many justiciars, Spaniards and Italians alike, performed their duties through deputies who were usually natives of the kingdom. Those serving in the household or in some branch of the central government regularly obtained leave to appoint deputies in their provincial posts. That concession appears in the privilege appointing Fernando de Argiona, the *sobrecoch*, justiciar of Basilicata,[34] in that for Antoni de Cetina of the wardrobe as justiciar in Valle del Crati and Terra Giordana,[35] and in that of Giovanni di San Severino, the regent of the Vicaria, for Principato citeriore.[36]

Justiciars, unlike viceroys, were subject to certain provisions in the laws promulgated by Frederick II: these required that they should not be prelates, barons, or natives of the province to which they were appointed, limited their tenure of office, and attached to them a staff of professional judges, Alfonso adhered to these statutes, enjoining one justiciar to administer justice, 'juxta quod

[32] Botifar received the office on 31 Oct. 1444. He renounced it in favour of San Severino for the 9th and 10th indictions (ACA Reg. 2908. 70ʳ, 2 Oct. 1445). He renounced it again for the 11th indiction in favour of d'Aquila (ACA Reg. 2912. 82ʳ, 1 Aug. 1447). In May 1450 he finally relinquished the office in return for a pension of 100 *oncie* (ACA Reg. 2914. 66ʳ).

[33] ASN Priv. I. 18ʳ, 2 Sept. 1451.

[34] De Argiona renounced the office in favour of Jacobo de Vilaspinosa for the 7th and 8th indictions (ACA Reg. 2903. 106ʳ, 29 Nov. 1443; Reg. 2902. 221ᵛ, 6 Aug. 1444).

[35] ACA Reg. 2906. 157ʳ, 7 Mar. 1445.

[36] ACA Reg. 2908. 70ʳ, 2 Oct. 1445.

tempore quondam federici olim Romanorum imperatoris didicimus observantia . . .',[37] and telling another, 'dictum justiciaratum exerceri debere iuxta modum ritum et ordinem sacrarum regni huius constitutionum et capitulorum volumus'.[38] A petition of the 1450 parliament asking that justiciars should render an annual account of their administration (*sindicare*), 'secundum constituciones et capitula regni', met with royal approval, while a further request that they should be changed annually and not be permitted to exercise the office by deputy was rejected because such concessions would have placed new limitations on the royal prerogative.[39] Whether justiciars did afterwards submit themselves to annual syndication is doubtful, because the parliament of 1456 renewed the demand that they should do so; once again the king replied, 'Placet Regio Maiestati quod constitutiones et capitula regni serventur.'[40] And however much or little the justiciars abided by the constitutions of the kingdom, it was inevitable that they should find their jurisdiction overlapping and conflicting with that of the barons. Fundamentally disputes over the justiciars' jurisdiction reflected a deeper struggle between royal and private jurisdiction, with the crown trying—not always from the best of motives—to countervail the great access of strength that the baronage had gained in the period of Angevin decadence and civil war. One of the most important aspects of the conflict is highlighted by an article of the March 1450 parliament:[41]

Item supplicano li predicti che considerato le intollerabile extorsiuni et nove inventuri trovate per li justicieri dele provincie de questo Regno piatza a la V.M. decernere et ordenare che daquesto nante nullo justiciere daquesto Regno se habea ad intramettere de primis causis tanto civili quanto criminali deli subditi officiali et vasalli de ipsi magnati et baruni li quali hanno lo mero et mixto imperio nisi dum taxat tantum in casu denegato justicie dele quale denegacione de justicia prius et ante omnia debia legitimamente constare, et che li prefati magnati et baruni et loro subditi non siano tenuti a dare expense et pransi ali predicti justicieri secundo per li dicti justicieri erano recercati.

[37] ASN Div. Somm. I. 52 (bis), 152^r, n.d.
[38] ACA Reg. 2908. 194^v, 15 Dec. 1447, Appointment of Domingo Garcez as justiciar of the district of Taverna.
[39] Ametller y Vinyas, *Alfonso V de Aragón*, iii. 688. In his first parliament in 1459 Ferdinand conceded the annual appointment of justiciars (Gentile, 'Lo stato napoletano' (1937), p. 54, n. 1).
[40] ASN Div. Somm. I. 52 (bis), 171^r.
[41] Ametller y Vinyas, *Alfonso V de Aragón*, iii. 688.

To this petition the king returned the answer: 'Placet Regie Magestati nisi in casu prevencionis quam Regia Maiestas sibi et dictis justiciariis specialiter reservat.'[42] He could hardly have done otherwise since the barons had correctly stated the formal line of division between baronial and royal jurisdiction. The conflict arose from differences over a definition of the exceptional circumstances which permitted the intervention of a justiciar. When did a plea cease to be 'de primis causis'? Who was competent to determine when denial of justice had arisen? On one side stood the justiciars anxious to extend their authority and the fees that derived from it; on the other the barons, determined to resist any royal encroachment on their hold over their vassals; and in the middle these same vassals, appreciating royal justice as their ultimate refuge against baronial oppression, yet concerned to avoid the heavy expense of litigation which too unrestrained a competition between justiciar and feudal overlord might involve.[43] The baronial petition of 1450 and the king's response did little more than state the problem, as happened again in the 1456 parliament when the barons renewed their protest against the action of justiciars in calling cases of first instance into their courts.[44]

Towns in the royal demesne had to fight a similar battle to secure for the captain's court cognizance of cases of first instance against the encroachment of the justiciars. In 1444, for example, the *locumtenens* of the justiciar in Captitanata had to be instructed to respect the privilege of Lucera which reserved to the captain's court all cases of first instance other than those involving fiefs, coining, treason, and offences against the poor, widows, and wards, all of which belonged to the Vicaria.[45] In 1449 the de-

[42] Ametller y Vinyas, *Alfonso V de Aragón*, iii. 688. As a special favour the barons were promised that the justiciars would not, for one year, enter their lands 'eciam in casu prevencionis'.

[43] An order to royal officials not to take cognizance of civil and criminal cases 'in primis instantiis et in causis etiam primarum appellationum' arising in lands of the Prince of Rossano is represented as arising from the intercession of the prince 'qui pro parte dictarum suarum omnium civitatum terrarum castrorum atque locorum . . . nobis instantissimas supplicationes efudit' (ASN Priv. i. 177ʳ, 13 Aug. 1454).

[44] The petition reads: 'Item che li vaxali deli dicti baroni non se posano trahere davanti li justicieri delle provincie in le prime cause nisi in causa denegate justicie.' The king replied: 'Placet R.M. preterquam in causam preventionis negligentie et denegate justitie' (ASN Div. Somm. i. 52 (bis), 171ʳ).

[45] ASN 'Pergamene dell'Archivio di Stato: Pergamene di Lucera', Ic, 14 Nov. 1444.

mesne towns of Abruzzo citeriore presented to the king a joint petition against numerous infringements of their jurisdictional liberties perpetrated by the justiciar and his officials.[46] How far such protests were motivated by zeal for the welfare of the whole community and how far by the interests of town oligarchies could only be determined by a close study of the town concerned, and such a detailed examination of the urban life of this period is seldom feasible.

It is also difficult to estimate to what extent the crown was encouraging the justiciars in a more interventionist attitude. The knowledge that behind them stood a ruler with a high regard for his sovereign power must have stiffened the justiciars. Extraordinary powers conferred by the crown sometimes added greatly to their authority. To deal with bandits in Principato citeriore Giovanni di San Severino was granted special jurisdiction similar to that conferred on the viceroy de Cardenas.[47] Still more extraordinary was the suspension of all mesne jurisdiction decreed in Basilicata for the two years (1445-7) during which Bernardo di San Severino was justiciar.[48] No emergency can have inspired the suspension, for it was decided upon almost one year before the justiciar was due to take up his office.[49] Deliberately or incidentally it made the office of justiciar exceptionally lucrative, and yet there is no evidence to show that Bernardo di San Severino was ever an important creditor of the crown. It also enabled the king to do good business by selling exemptions from the suspension.[50] Whatever his motives, Alfonso's action brought home to the nobility in dramatic fashion that his recent grant of the *merum et mixtum imperium* had indeed been made *ad beneplacitum*,

---

[46] ACA Reg. 2913. 117ʳ, 9 Jan. 1449.

[47] ACA Reg. 2908. 161ᵛ, 11 Aug. 1446. Cf. above, p. 323.

[48] '... suspendentes pro tempore videlicet duorum annorum a die date illius privilegii per nos sibi concessi in antea continuo computandorum omnem et quamcumque iurisdicionem civilem et criminalem merumque et mixtum imperium et aliam quamvis gladii potestatem quam et quod quivis principes duces comites seu barones et utiliter domini quarumlibet civitatum terrarum castrorum seu locorum dicte provincie exercerent seu exercere possent ...' (ACA Reg. 2906, 131ʳ).

[49] Bernardo's letter of appointment is dated 14 Oct. 1444 and was to take effect from the 9th indiction (i.e. 1 Sept. 1445) (ACA Reg. 2904. 174ᵛ). He received this appointment because of the king's satisfaction with the manner in which he had performed his duties as justiciar in Principato citeriore.

[50] Antonio Dentice, a Neapolitan noble with fiefs in Captitanata, secured such an exemption (ACA Reg. 2906. 131ʳ, 4 Dec. 1444).

and that subjects exercised justice as a matter of grace and not of right. It is possible, therefore, that later parliamentary protests were not directed mainly against petty poaching by the justiciars in the domain of baronial jurisdiction, but against a royal policy which aimed at minimizing earlier concessions.

A concentration by rulers and ruled alike upon the judicial function of the justiciar reflects the principal activity of an official appointed *ad iusticiam et ad guerram* in times when internal peace was generally assured. Privileges appointing justiciars carry the same emphasis, beginning with this general proposition:[51]

Ad bonorum custodiam malorumque vindiciam portat princeps gladium et exercet imperii potestatem qui dum iuste sevit in reprobos pacificos servat in tranquillitate securos ut igitur executio iustitiae vigeat et nervus discipline publice non lentescat providi constituendi sunt istos qui ab iniuriis innocentes custodiant et patulis hostiis equaliter omnibus iura reddant.

To these ends the justiciar is appointed *ad beneplacitum* with jurisdiction comprised of the *merum et mixtum imperium* and *gladii potestas*, in other words full civil and criminal jurisdiction with the power to inflict all manner of penalties. Having taken the required oaths of fidelity and good conduct, he would present himself at the appointed time—usually the beginning of an indiction—in the principal royal city of the province to assume his office. His duties were defined in general terms as administering justice to all who sought it, and more especially the protection of the church, the clergy, widows, wards, orphans, 'et alias miserabiles personas' by a faithful adherence to the 'jura comuna constituciones et capitula pro regni statu et fidelium reformacione composita'. A judge and a notary, who normally received annual salaries of 22 and 16 *oncie*, assisted him in his judicial duties.[52] The normal salary of the justiciar himself was 100 *oncie* a year; in the small province of Molise it was only 150 ducats,[53] but in many others the office was worth considerably more than the bare salary thanks to numerous perquisities and the profits of justice.

---

[51] e.g. ACA Reg. 2908. 194^v, Appointment of Domingo Garcez.

[52] Often these offices were given to highly placed individuals who appointed deputies to do the work. Fonolleda held the position of *actorum notarius* to the justiciar of Cosenza with the exceptionally high salary of 45 *oncie* a year (ASN Div. Somm. I. 10, 16^v).

[53] Gentile, 'Lo stato napoletano' (1937), p. 52, n. 5.

An attendant knight, ten armed retainers for prison guard and similar duties, and two messengers completed his usual retinue. The demesne towns of Abruzzo citeriore evidently considered this company inadequate, for in their petition of 1449 they asked that it be increased to the twelve mounted men and fifteen footmen sanctioned by *antiquissimus ritus*.[54] In Calabria a special advocate was appointed to watch over the crown's interests in the courts of the viceroy and justiciar.[55] The same may have been done in other provinces where the crown had extensive demesne and fiscal interests, but such appointments have not yet come to light.

The first act of the new justiciar would be to take over from his predecessor all prisoners held in custody together with a statement of the charges against them; he likewise received the records of all other cases pending, whether of the crown or of private persons. A seal bearing his arms in the centre and his name around the circumference authenticated these and all other documents issued by a justiciar. The outgoing official was required to undergo syndication, that is to submit to an inquest upon his acts in office before leaving the seat of government. It was this process which parliaments attempted, apparently in vain, to make an annual one.[56] Usually the inquest would be conducted by a judge and a leading citizen; it covered also the actions of the justiciar's subordinates, and might extend to twenty days for each year of office. Once it had been completed, the justiciar was supposed to make restitution to those whom he had been shown to have wronged. Because it usually proved difficult to collect such damages, the March 1450 parliament asked that justiciars be obliged to deposit an adequate sum as security in the Sommaria before assuming office. The king assented and promulgated a statute to that effect.[57]

---

[54] The king gave his assent to this petition. The towns were probably concerned to avoid the impressment of their citizens into the justiciar's bodyguard and other demands for service.

[55] 'Considerantes quod in provincia calabrie curia nostra diversa patitur incomoda eo quod nullus est qui iura et res fisco nostro pertinentia et pertinentes patrocinetur et tueatur' (ASN Priv. I. 149ʳ, 15 Mar. 1454). Coluccio Gallardi of Cava was appointed to this new office.

[56] Cf. above, p. 325.

[57] The privilege appointing Giovanni di Somma justiciar of Molise refers to this statute: 'Volumus tamen quod ante ingressus exercicii ipsius justiciaratus officii tenearis cave re ydonee in Camera nostra Summarie de stando sindicatui et de solvendo iniuratis vel damna passis siquid eis fuerit restituendum et alia in super faciendo que in pragmaticam per Maiestaem nostram noviter edictam continetur' (ASN Priv. i. 18ʳ, 2 Sept. 1451).

At least one justiciar—Giovanni di Carrenyo, justiciar of Basilicata—was subsequently called to give account of his administration before the Sacrum Consilium, and it may be that the statute,
the text of which has not yet come to light, transferred the inquest in certain circumstances to that august body.[58] Such a move
would have been in keeping with the general mood of Aragonese
government.

The extant records of the central government rarely afford any
glimpse of the day-to-day activities of the justiciars. One of the few
occasions on which they do concerns Bernardo di San Severino,
justiciar in Basilicata. While Alfonso was directing operations
against Centelles in Calabria, a deputation from Saraceno in
Basilicata appeared before him to plead that the town be given
some tax relief because a fire had devastated a large part of it.
The king ordered the justiciar to investigate and Bernardo had
gone to Saraceno in person with some officials of the Vicaria.
As a result of his inquiry a list was compiled of the houses destroyed, and the owners were granted exemption from all taxes for
the space of eight years.[59] Much of a justiciar's time must have
been occupied with the kind of business that is recorded in the
registers of the viceroy of Calabria, for viceroys and justiciars
perfomed essentially similar functions. In May 1453 Siscar dealt,
among other matters, with a complaint from the Marquis of
Gerace that two of his officials had left their posts without submitting to syndication; with a petition from the town of Calanna
against the tyrannies of the Count of Sinopoli; with an appeal by
the Jewish community of Catanzaro against a tax intended for
a specifically Christian project in the city; and with a complaint
from the Archbishop of Messina that the captain of Feroleto was
hearing cases that belonged to the archiepiscopal court.[60]

---

[58] On 25 Mar. 1453 Pavone de Lupis was appointed to administer the office
pending a decision of the Sacrum Consilium whether di Carrenyo should be
dismissed (ACA Reg. 2917. 99ᵛ). Referring to di Carrenyo, the letter explains
that '. . . in jus vocatus stet sindicatui rationem de administratis per eum in
dicto justicieratus officio redditurus huiusmodique eius sindicatus examen
pendeat impresentiarum in nostro sacro consilio . . . quousque causa dicti
Johannis cognita et decisa sit et per merita sindicationis predicte per idem
nostrum sacrum consilium iudicatum et determinandum privari ne debeat
prefatus Johannes officio predicto . . .'

[59] ACA Reg. 2909. 123ʳ, 19 Apr. 1445.

[60] The action taken by Siscar in all these matters is recorded in *Fonti aragonesi*
ii. 180–200.

The perils that could befall an imprudent justiciar or viceroy are illustrated by the riot that caused Ramon Boyl to flee from Atri in January 1445. A pardon subsequently given to the townspeople tells what happened.[61]

Viro magnifico Raymundo Boyl milite utriusque nostre Aprutine provincie vicerege in dicta civitate nostra Adrie assiduam residenciam faciente, operante humani generis inimico et pacis emulo dante causam ac parientibus oneribus multiplicibus angariis gravissimis universitate et hominibus ac specialibus personis civitatis ipsius per dictum viceregem indesinenter et insaniter imponatis, factus est casus quod universus populus dicte civitatis nostre Adrie die scilicet quintadecima proximi preteriti mensis Januarii presentis anni viii Indictionis ad rumorem et tumultum vehementem prorumpens fecerunt impetum et insultum adversus personam dicti Raymundi Boyl viceregis nostri ac personas etiam armigerorum et familiariorum eiusdem armata huic inde in medio plathee maioris manu conserta, propter quod demum nonnullis armigeris et familiaribus obtruncatis ipse vicerex ut ab huiusmodi furore illesus evaderet mox per menia civitatis ipsius se raptim eiciens equis armis cunctisque impedimentis in civitate relictis pedester et paucis eum comitantibus abire compulsus est.

The king obviously considered that Boyl had acted unwisely and was prepared to blame him openly for the rising. One suspects, however, that Atri had to pay something for its pardon.

Whether the ultimate authority in a province lay with a viceroy or a justiciar, the immediate government of cities and towns and the adjacent countryside was in the hands of a class of officials who usually bore the title of captain. Charles II had introduced these officials in place of the Hohenstaufen bailiffs.[62] Alfonso appointed a number of captains general or governors—men who controlled several towns—in districts of special importance to the crown. Joan Llull and Jacme Ferrer served successively as captains general of the Sorrento peninsula,[63] Joan de Liria as captain general of Manfredonia and Monte Sant Angelo,[64] Rainaldo

---

[61] ACA Reg. 2907. 53ᵛ, 10 Feb. 1445.

[62] Capasso, *Inventario cronologico*, p. xxxix.

[63] Llull's appointment as captain general and governor is dated 14 May 1443. It covered the towns of Sorrento, Massa, Vico, and Positano (ACA Reg. 2904. 70ᵛ). Ferrer was appointed 8 May 1444 (ACA Reg. 2902. 202ᵛ) and on 9 Nov. 1448 was confirmed in it for life or *ad beneplacitum* (ACA Reg. 2913. 69ᵛ).

[64] ACA Reg. 2903. 32ʳ, 16 Nov. 1442, Appointment of de Liria as captain general and governor with power to appoint and dismiss captains in the towns under his control.

Loliante in the lands once held by Centelles,[65] and Gispert Dezguanes in Capri and Anacapri.[66] The majority of towns, however, had individual captains, appointed annually by the king if they were in the royal demesne, and elsewhere by the feudal lord. The privilege of L'Aquila which permitted it to nominate its own captain, subject to confirmation by the king, was quite exceptional;[67] and even there pressure was sometimes exerted in favour of a royal nominee.[68] Another peculiarity of the captaincy of this city was that the term of office lasted for only six months. Sometimes a town would ask to have a certain person as its captain—Castrovetere, when captured from Centelles, petitioned that the office be given to Antonio Carafa of Naples, 'considerato la virtu et honesta honorevoli usati et operati . . . circa la reductione de Castrovetere'[69] but such petitions were rarely granted. On the other hand, petitions asking that no native of the town be made captain were sympathetically received, for with these, as with most provincial appointments, the established principle, that a native of a town or province should not hold office there, prevailed.[70]

Captains, like justiciars, were appointed 'ad justiciam et ad guerram'; in fact virtually identical formulae were used in the privileges appointing both kinds of official. Except in L'Aquila, the captain's term of office ran for one year—the indiction not the calendar year—although most appointments allowed for an

[65] He was appointed in July 1448 with full viceregal powers because of the emergency created in the area by the war with Venice (ACA Reg. 2913. 15^r, 8 July 1448).

[66] His appointment is dated 13 June 1447 (ACA Reg. 2908. 220^v).

[67] In a privilege confirming the city's nomination of Corrado d'Aquaviva the captain is described as, 'vos quem universitas et homines civitatis nostre aquile iuxta ipsius capitulam et consuetudinem pro capitano nominaverunt' (ASN Priv. i. 109^v, 3 Feb. 1454).

[68] e.g. the letter written to the city asking it to elect Taddeo de Cataldo of Urbino 'per lo primo semestre per lo quale non vi avimo ia scritto per altro' (Mazzoleni, Il Codice Chigi, pp. 224–5, 26 May 1452).

[69] ACA Reg. 2904. 229^v, 15 Feb. 1445. The king rejected the request.

[70] Cf. the petition from Penne in the Abruzzi: 'Item dignetur maiestas ipsa providendo de officiali in dicta civitate seu provincia eadem pennosi ponere officialem ydoneum et sufficientem qui non sit de provincia nec aliquomodo affeccionatus in ista provincia propter divisiones et parcialitates que hactenus orte fuerunt in provincia ipsa propter discrimina guerrarum et aliarum rerum extranearum que incubuerunt in ipsa provincia et status ipsius maiestatis continue augeatur.' To this petition the king returned a 'Placet' (ACA Reg. 2902. 79^v, 22 Sept. 1442).

extension *ad beneplacitum* following the indiction for which they were initially granted. Towns of the royal demesne held it a matter of particular concern that their captains should not serve for more than one year lest a long tenure of the office undermine their liberties. All therefore took care to include a petition to that effect among the *capitoli* which they presented to the king on submission. For example, Manfredonia, which submitted to Alfonso in November 1442, placed in the first item of its *capitoli* the request that 'annuatim debia mandare lo capitanio in nome dela sua Maiesta . . . el quale capitanio alla fine del suo anno debia stare ad sindicato'.[71] Custom being on their side, Alfonso never rejected such requests from his demesne subjects, and on occasion the chancery included in its documents statements which affirmed the principle of annual appointments for captains. Thus, when Sorrento was asked to accept Angelo Molicelli as its captain for the unexpired portion of a year, it was assured, 'che nostra intencione e che venendo lo primo di de septembre providere et mandareve altro capitaneo et quello motareve de anno in anno si como facemo a le altre nostre terre demaniale'.[72] And in July 1444 Pietro Paolo de Corbis received orders to surrender the captaincy of Capua for the coming indiction in accordance with the 'consuetudines Regni huius et privilegia civitatis ipsius.'[73] None the less captains were sometimes appointed for initial periods exceeding one year; Rescamuccio de Capograsso was given the captaincy of Vittorito, Pentonia, Roccasasale, and Pratola for three years in November 1443.[74] More common still were captaincies bestowed for life: that of Cava on Pedro de Aragonia 'pro sequente proxime anno septime indictionis et ab inde in antea dum vitam duxeritis in humanis';[75] the captaincy and castellany of Castrovetere for Gabriel Davo;[76] Tocco for Iñigo de Avalos;[77] Archi for Antoni Gaçull.[78] Italians as well as Spaniards benefited from the royal infringement of custom: the captaincy of Scafati was granted for

---

[71] ACA Reg. 2902. 124ᵛ, 6 Nov. 1442. All the towns taken from Centelles made the same request.

[72] Mazzoleni, *Il Codice Chigi*, p. 255, 5 Mar. 1452.

[73] ACA Reg. 2903. 134ᵛ, 1 July 1444.

[74] ACA Reg. 2904. 107ᵛ.   [75] ACA Reg. 2902. 87ᵛ, 2 Oct. 1442.

[76] ACA Reg. 2907. 90ʳ, 5 Apr. 1445.

[77] ACA Reg. 2915. 99ʳ, 13 Oct. 1451.

[78] ACA Reg. 2908. 80ᵛ, 15 Sept. 1445. Gaçull and, if necessary, his heirs were to hold the captaincy and castellany until such time as they had been repaid 1,000 ducats lent to the crown.

life to Nicolo Tomacelli,[79] that of San Mauro to Giovanni della
Via,[80] that of Castelnuovo near Cassino to Nicola de Victo,[81]
Feroleto to Pietro Carbone,[82] Rosarno to Pietro di Curropulo.[83]
Not that such a grant guaranteed its recipient a lifelong possession
of the office, for he might, as happened to Pietro di Curropulo,
find himself superseded a month later by another life incumbent.[84]

Two motives appear to have inspired the concession of captaincies beyond the normal term. One was a desire to reward
services rendered to the king, services such as those of Pedro de
Aragonia a military captain, Nicola de Victo a chamberlain who
had served in the household since his youth, or of della Via an
official of the treasury. When Alfonso wanted to give his chamberlain Joan Guallart a wedding present of 2,200 ducats and found
that the treasury could not conveniently pay in cash, he appointed
Guallart captain of Castellammare and Gragnano until such time
as the office should have yielded him that sum.[85] Pietro Carbone
who obtained the captaincy of Feroleto for life was probably
identical with the Pietro Carbone who commanded the castle of
Crotone for Centelles and surrendered it to the king after only
a token resistance; if so, his life office was no doubt part of the
price paid for that opportune surrender. The other motive was
pecuniary: a captaincy was an acceptable gage for creditors of the
crown and men were prepared to pay for the office as an investment. Ten days after Andrea de Sanctis became captain and
castellan of Archi the king promised not to remove either him or
his heirs unless they were first repaid a loan of 1,000 ducats. His
return on this investment was a salary of 210 ducats a year plus
the profits and perquisites which a captain might expect from his
office.[86] Two years later Antoni Gaçull gave the king the 1,000
ducats needed to repay de Sanctis and he in turn received 'permanent' possession of the captaincy on similar terms. Gabriel
Davo, the *emptor* of the household, made a loan of 1,100 ducats
linked to the captaincy of Catanzaro; 100 ducats went to the

[79] ACA Reg. 2907. 176^r, 26 Dec. 1446.
[80] Ibid. 76^r, 8 Jan. 1445. He also held the castellany.
[81] ACA Reg. 2907. 82^v, 3 Apr. 1445. The appointment included the castellany.
[82] Ibid. 62^v, 19 Jan. 1445. This too included the castellany.
[83] Ibid. 63^v, 19 Jan. 1445. This too included the castellany.
[84] Stefano di Gennaro was appointed captain and castellan of Rosarno for
life on 22 Feb. 1445 (ACA Reg. 2904. 192^r).
[85] ACA Reg. 2906. 92^r, 18 May 1444.
[86] ACA Reg. 2905. 200^v, 13 Aug. 1443.

previous captain Alfonso Salazar who could not be removed until he had recovered that sum; Davo in turn was to keep the office until his loan had been repaid.[87] Rainaldo Loliante gave 1,200 ducats to become captain and castellan of Martirano Lombardo in August 1443 with the right to all profits of justice. Alfonso justified the transaction by his need of money to pay his troops.[88] Even a city as important as Capua could find itself subject to an arrangement of this kind, its privileges notwithstanding. In September 1449 the *reboster* Pere de Botifar gave the king 1,000 ducats to obtain the captaincy of Capua for himself and his heirs; it had first to be redeemed from Juan de Luna with a payment of 525 ducats.[89] The captaincies of Trani, Barletta, Molfetta, and Giovenazzo went to Antoni Olzina, a chancery clerk, for 1,000 ducats in February 1448.[90] The Neapolitan nobility shared in these transactions: Carlo Ruffo, Count of Sinopoli, was invested with the captaincy and castellany of Seminara as security for a loan of 3,000 ducats; together they yielded him an annual revenue of 300 ducats.[91]

With captaincies being promised, sold, redeemed, confirmed, and withdrawn according to political or financial exigencies, or in response to pressure exerted at court by interested parties, one is not surprised to find that confusion often reigned and that two or more claimants appeared for a single office. This happened with the captaincy of Atri for the 11th indiction; first it was given to Cristoforo de Firmanis and then to Pere Blesa who took possession. De Firmanis next received a promise of it for the following indiction—an action which involved revoking another promise for that year already given to the secretary Giovanni de Belloflore.[92] To lessen the possibility of conflicting appointments being made, a statute was promulgated either in 1447 or 1448; it provided that the office of captain could be sought and granted only in the year immediately preceding that in which it was to be exercised.[93]

---

[87] ACA Reg. 2914. 128ʳ, 21 Oct. 1450.
[88] ACA Reg. 2903. 96ʳ, 25 Aug. 1443.   [89] ACA Real Patrimonio, 2951.
[90] Ibid.
[91] ACA Reg. 2909. 5ʳ, 4 July 1443. The justiciar and viceroy of Calabria were to exercise no jurisdiction in Seminara during the count's tenure of the office of captain.   [92] ACA Reg. 2913. 59ʳ, 1 Oct. 1448.
[93] A privilege appointing Andrea de Giovanni di Castro captain of San Severo for the 12th indiction was annulled because it contravened this statute: '. . . contra formam statuti et ordinacionis per nos in dicto Regno Sicilie citra farum facti, videlicet quod officia capitaniatis in dicto regno non impetrarentur nec

From the details given above of a number of appointments, it will have become apparent that in many towns the offices of captain and castellan were held by the same person. Usually this happened in those places where neither the town nor the castle was sufficiently important to justify having separate officials. However, an arrangement which concentrated so much influence in the hands of a single man often aroused opposition. Atri petitioned in 1447 that the king should desist from the practice of giving the captaincy to the castellan; but though it received a promise that it should cease after the coming indiction, for which the captaincy had already been granted to the castellan,[94] that promise was not kept and the castellan, Pere Blesa, once more became captain for the 14th and 15th indictions.[95] Nor was Atri any more successful with another petition asking that its captains be not allowed to exercise their office by deputy. Alfonso's *placet* did not prevent him from granting that concession to Cristoforo de Firmanis for the 12th indiction.[96] These actions may not, of course, have been deliberate violations of promises given to Atri, but may have arisen from failure on the part of the king's advisers to consult the records, or from deliberate neglect to remind him of conditions that stood in the way of certain persons. A system of government that permitted so many exceptions to every rule could easily fall into unwitting error. Permission to exercise the office of captain by deputy was generally granted to those fully occupied in more important posts.[97] Pere de Capdevila the treasurer, for example, held a number of captaincies,[98] so too did the *sobrecoch* Fernando de Argiona.[99] On the other hand, a captaincy could sometimes

concederentur nisi anno precedenti pro anno subsequenti immediate . . .' He was later appointed for the 13th indiction (ACA Reg. 2913, 66ʳ, 15 Oct. 1448).

[94] ACA Reg. 2912. 36ᵛ, 18 June 1447.

[95] ACA Reg. 2914. 79ʳ, 10 July 1450; ibid. 152ʳ, 16 June 1451.

[96] ACA Reg. 2913. 59ᵛ, 1 Oct. 1448.

[97] In the appointment of Pedro de Aragonia as captain of Cava it is stated, '. . . ceterum quia vos dictus Petrus de Aragnonia capitaneus in dicta civitate Cave modo ordinatus habetis continue cum vestri armigeriorum comitiva ad alia nostra ardua et magis negocia vaccare servicia propter quod in ipsum capitanie officium non poteritis personaliter interesse...'(ACA Reg. 2902. 87ᵛ, 2 Oct. 1442).

[98] Castelle ad Mare, Barbaro, Cropani, Zagarise, and Castel Alfonsina—all in Calabria (ASN Priv. I. 85ʳ, 28 July 1453; ibid. 86ᵛ, 29 July 1453).

[99] At different times he held the captaincies of Cava, Catanzaro, Taverna, and Cirò. In the latter town his kinsman Gonsalvo de Argiona acted for him, 'non potens in exercendo huiusmodi officium nostris serviciis occupatus personaliter interesse' (Mazzoleni, *Il Codice Chigi*, p. 141, 21 Oct. 1451).

take precedence over another post. Thus Luis Amigo, *emptor maior* of the household, was told to go in person to the Abruzzi to perform his duties as captain of Cittaducale and the region known as Montagna di Abruzzo.[100]

Looked at from the point of view of nationality, the appointments to captaincies do not show that bias towards Spaniards which is evident among the viceroys and, to a lesser extent, among the justiciars. A count of captaincies recorded in the registers reveals a proportion of roughly two to one in favour of natives of the kingdom. Most of the Spaniards were soldiers, household or government officials of the middle rank, and the majority of these appointed deputies who were often Italians. The majority of Italian captains came by contrast from the ranks of the minor urban and provincial nobility. Nor were Italians excluded from office in the most important cities. Only in Naples itself do Spaniards appear to have monopolized the office. In 1444 the captain of the capital was a Spaniard whose name Borso d'Este rendered as 'Bisance'—most probably Pedro Sanchez who was captain again in 1451.[101] During the 10th indiction (1446–7) Gispert Dezguanes held the office through a deputy.[102] Gaeta had Spanish captains in the earlier part of the reign, among them Alfonso de Cardenas[103] and Gispert Dezguanes;[104] from the 11th indiction, however, Blasio Frangipane of Terracina took over the office,[105] which later passed to Pratito Gaetano[106] and Pietro Carbone.[107] A rather similar pattern is discernible in the principal ports of the eastern coast. The privileges of Manfredonia required the captain to be appointed annually, so Alfonso named the *mayordomen* Joan de Liria captain general for Manfredonia and Monte Sant Angelo *ad beneplacitum* and left it to him to nominate subordinate annual captains.[108] At the time of his death Garcia

---

[100] Ibid., pp. 90–2, 14 Aug. 1451.

[101] Mazzoleni, *Il Codice Chigi*, p. 131, 18 Oct. 1451.

[102] ACA Reg. 2907. 156^r, 27 Dec. 1445.

[103] He was captain of Gaeta until June 1443 when he became viceroy of the whole region (ACA Reg. 2902. 177^r, 24 June 1443).

[104] He held the office from June 1443 to September 1444, and again in 1447.

[105] ACA Reg. 2912, 60^r, 27 June 1447. He performed the duties by deputy.

[106] ACA Reg. 2914. 104^v, 23 Oct. 1450. Gaetano, an *armorum uxerius*, was captain for the 15th indiction (1451–2).

[107] ACA Reg. 2917. 139^r, 6 Apr. 1456: captain for the 5th indiction (1456–7).

[108] ACA Reg. 2903. 32^r, 26 Nov. 1442. De Liria was able to appoint a deputy for his own office.

de Cabanyells, the viceroy of Capitanata, held the captaincy of Manfredonia; a Neapolitan, Nicola de Vito of Gaeta, stepped into his place.[109] Barletta, the chief grain port of Puglia, had at least two Neapolitan captains—Bartolomeo Curiale (or Correale) of Sorrento[110] and Pietro Paolo de Corbis of Atri.[111] In Capua the captaincy went impartially to Spaniards and Italians until Botifar obtained control of it in 1449.[112] In Lanciano, a major trading centre with an international market, most of the captains were Italians.[113]

The duties of a captain were to supervise the administration of his town and administer justice. His jurisdiction extended to all crimes except treason, heresy, and coining; he could erect gallows, a whipping post, stocks, and any other necessary instruments of punishment; he had the power to torture suspects and inflict all manner of punishments; and he was granted use of the four 'arbitrary letters'. Like the justiciar, he was assisted by a judge assessor and a notary, both of whom he could appoint himself subject to the approval of the crown. In fact it was the protonotary who *ex officio* issued the necessary letters of appointment to these subordinates,[114] many of whom were relatively well-placed officials enjoying the profits of posts which they entrusted to deputies. The most extraordinary judge assessor was perhaps Francesco d'Antignano, a noble of Capua who obtained the office in that city for life; having no legal training, he had then to obtain a privilege which allowed him to appoint a lawyer to carry out his duties.[115]

Under the captains towns and cities enjoyed varying degrees of self-government according to the privileges which they had been

---

[109] ACA Reg. 2917. 73^v, 16 Jan. 1453.

[110] ACA Reg. 2908. 210^r, 12 Mar. 1447. Bartolomeo was the father of the much favoured page Gabriele.   [111] ACA Reg. 2903. 130^v, 3 July 1444.

[112] The earlier captains were Pietro Paolo de Corbis (ACA Reg. 2903. 134^v, 1 July 1444), Antonuccio di Castro (ibid. 133^v, 1 July 1444), Joan Capellades of Barcelona (ACA Reg. 2908. 53^r, 31 July 1445), and Gispert Dezguanes (ACA Reg. 2912. 53^v, 19 June 1447).

[113] Antonio Guastaferro of Gaeta was captain in 1443 (ACA Reg. 2903. 89^v, 30 July 1443). He was succeeded by Gabriele Matte of Sulmona (ibid.) then came Giovanni di Maio of Naples (ibid. 129^r, 30 Oct. 1443), Ristanuccio Capograsso of Sulmona (ACA Reg. 2908. 56^v, 24 Aug. 1445), Antonuccio di Castro (ibid.), and Michele di Maio of Naples (ACA Reg. 2912. 30^r, 1 June 1447).

[114] e.g. for Antoni Olzina as judge and *actorum notarius* to the captains of Trani, Barletta, Molfetta, and Giovinazzo (ACA Reg. 2909, 26 Nov. 1443). This privilege in effect gave Olzina control of eight posts which he was free to fill with his own nominees.

[115] ACA Reg. 2915. 11^v. This privilege was issued by the protonotary, the Count of Fondi.

able to win from the crown or their feudal overlord. Most were permitted to elect their communal officers annually. In Calabria the viceroy issued instructions on 25 August to all captains of the royal demesne ordering them to summon a general meeting (*parlamento*) in each *universita* for the purpose of making these elections. The meeting took place on 1 September under the presidency of the captain who could nominate to offices in case of disagreement among the electors. The composition of the *parlamento* varied from place to place; everywhere the poorer members of the community (the *popolo minuto*) were excluded,[116] and in some towns nobles and the wealthier commoners (the *borghesi*) each had their own organizations which reached an understanding on the sharing of offices. In feudal towns the nomination of the communal officers was subject to the will of the lord. Although royal assent was needed to validate these feudal nominations, the later Angevin monarchs had neglected to enforce that control with the result that Alfonso's attempts to do so met with strenuous protests. A baronial petition in the 1456 parliament asked for complete freedom in this matter:[117]

Item li predicti baroni possano creare annuatim li jodici annali et camerlengi nele loro terre et altre quale se voglia officiali como hanno accostumati et sonno consueti ad loro arbitrio et voluntate sensa alcuno pagamento o confirmacione de sua Maesta et de soy officiali anche delo diricto che la Regia Corte pretendevu havere per lo passato et per lo advenire deli dicti jodici annali et mastri jurati siano liberi et exempti et habranno de perpetue remissione et gracia et ipsi selli poxano eligere creare removere et cassare ad loro arbitrio et voluntate.

In reply the king gave them the right to appoint 'judices annales ad justitiam reddendam' without licence of the crown or the payment of any fee. Such justices, who usually had no legal training, were not, however, to witness public or private contracts save in places with less than 250 households where they might do so 'auctoritate Regie Maiestatis'. In all larger towns the appointment of officers empowered to witness contracts drawn up by notaries (that is, the *judices ad contractus*) remained subject to confirmation by the crown and payment of the requisite dues.[118] He likewise

---

[116] This is the conclusion reached by Gentile ('Lo stato napoletano', p. 33).

[117] ASN Div. Somm. I. 52 (bis), 171ʳ.

[118] A decree of 4 Feb. 1456 fixed the fee at 12 *tarini* a year (Gentile, 'Lo stato napoletano' (1938), p. 39).

reserved the right of assent to the election of the *magistri jurati* or *camerlengi* as they were called in the baronial petition; they were to take an oath before the justiciars and pay a fee for their commissions issued under the great seal. In effect the king had stood his ground and rejected the substance of the petition. *Magistri jurati* exercised police functions and petty criminal jurisdiction, being responsible for the arrest of criminals caught in the act, for organizing the watch, and enforcing the ban on prohibited weapons; they also regulated the prices of essential foodstuffs and supervised the markets.[119] In the performance of these duties they were assisted by the *baiuli* or bailiffs, the number of whom varied according to the size of the town. Nobles were exempted from serving in this office.[120] The judges elected annually by the *universita* (usually they were four in number) judged in the first instance those petty offences that did not involve corporal punishment or fines exceeding one *oncia*, and which did not involve the nobility or clergy. The fines they inflicted, together with the fines for false weights and measures, and tolls and dues of various kinds,[121] constituted the *gabella baiulacionis* which belonged by right to the crown. In most feudal towns it had long since been granted to the feudatory, and even within the royal demesne it was often given to a town or individual as a favour; most commonly it was farmed annually to the highest bidder.[122] The financial affairs of the *universita* were entrusted to one or more *sindaci* and a treasurer elected annually or, as usually happened in baronial towns, nominated by the lord. These officers apportioned taxes and administered the communal revenues, functions which often led to dissension in the community.[123] The custom which assured nobles and commoners of an equal share in the offices did little to prevent quarrels between the two groups

---

[119] The functions of the *magistri jurati* are discussed by Capasso (*Inventario cronologico*, p. xxiii) and Gentile ('Lo stato napoletano' (1938), p. 37). Minieri Riccio (*Saggio*, Suppl. i, p. 45) prints the capitoli for *magistri jurati* issued in 1280.

[120] Gentile, 'Lo stato napoletano' (1938), pp. 39–40.

[121] The *gabella* included tolls, dues from the forest, market, customs, slaughterhouse, and the profits of petty justice.

[122] Cf. the petition of Taverna that it be granted the *gabella baiulacionis*, including the mill, for 40 *oncie* a year. The king rejected this petition and directed that it should go to the highest bidder, as in the rest of the demesne (ACA Reg. 2904. 240ʳ, 5 Dec. 1444).

[123] Gentile, 'Lo stato napoletano' (1938), pp. 46–7.

over tax assessment; often enough the disagreements led to disorder which the captain had to quell. All elected officers were syndicated.

Despite their association with a judicial and fiscal system that weighed heavily on the communes, captains sometimes enjoyed a measure of popularity with those they governed. When Cirò, one of Centelles's towns, surrendered to the king, it asked that the captain Cola Cagnigroi, 'citadino nostro', be taken into the king's favour and appointed royal captain for the year.[124] Santa Severina likewise recommended its captain Giovanni Calbeto to the king, and asked that he be given a pension.[125] Melissa petitioned for a safe-conduct for the person, family, and property of its former captain Frederico di Rocca in consideration of his good government.[126] Most requested at least a safe-conduct for the captain, and none that he be punished for any misdeeds. The other side of the picture is presented by captains such as Tommaso Carafa who was alleged to have carried away from Sulmona goods belonging to a fugitive and to have extorted money from other citizens.[127] Michele Pampini, a Venetian merchant, complained to the viceroy of Calabria about the arbitrary behaviour of the captain of Crotone, Marti Joan Escarrer, whom he alleged had demanded that he deposit security *de stando iuri* when no one had brought any action or complaint against him. To Pampini's protest—'Come me constringite ad dare quista pregiaria che non est homo che la dimandi da me, e la Signoria Vestra non po essere tucte e parte'—Escarrer had replied by ordering him to be imprisoned in fetters, and had kept him there even when the Venetian promised to furnish the security. Eventually the castellan of Crotone and another Venetian, Giannozzo de Chiarchio, secured his release, while his brother Andrea promised to represent him in any action that might arise in his absence. However, no sooner had Pampini left Crotone than Escarrer seized and imprisoned his brother on the same pretext. Accepting the plea that the captain was not an impartial judge, the viceroy commanded Escarrer to release Andrea and return all goods belonging to the brothers, who were to deposit adequate surety with the viceroy to

---

[124] ACA Reg. 2903, 173ʳ, 8 Nov. 1444. The petition was rejected.

[125] Ibid. 178ᵛ, 20 Nov. 1444. Alfonso assented to this.

[126] ACA Reg. 2904. 187ᵛ, 8 Nov. 1444.

[127] ASN Div. Somm. I. 166. 29ᵛ, Record of the inquest into his conduct by Francesco Pagano in the summer of 1443.

appear in his court if summoned.[128] Some captains found themselves in trouble for neglecting to carry out the orders of the crown. In January 1452 the viceroy of Calabria was ordered to summon before him the captain and castellan of Santa Severina, the castellan of Tacina and the *magister juratus* of Cutro who were to show cause why they had disobeyed letters patent from the king.[129] Some were negligent in the administration of justice,[130] but few aroused the degree of animosity which led to the murder of the captain of Trani in May 1458. This unfortunate or foolhardy official first had his throat cut, was then hung on his own gallows, cut down, and dragged back to his own house which the mob burned with the body. After looting some more houses, the rioters took a ship and fled across the Adriatic.[131]

In the baronial towns the behaviour of captains and other municipal officers tended to reflect the character of the lord who appointed them. Some who enjoyed the confidence of a great magnate could do virtually as they pleased. One such was Jacobo de Monte whose death was recorded by the anonymous Neapolitan diarist:[132] 'Ali 6 de settembre 1449 in la citta de Lezze fo morto messer Jacobo de Monte che per parte del Ill°. Prencipe de Taranto in terra de Bari era un gran maestro, facea et disfacea ad suo commando et voluntà, et tutto l'era accettato.' In Calabria one might cite the attitude of Centelles's towns towards their captains in support of Pontieri's contention that relations between nobles and their vassals were generally good in that province.[133] Against it one would have to take note of nobles such as Carlo Ruffo, Count of Sinopoli, and Tommaso Caracciolo, Marquis of Gerace,[134]

---

[128] ASN Fasc. Com. Somm. 124ᵛ, 5 May 1453.

[129] Mazzoleni, *Il Codice Chigi*, pp. 228–9, 19 Jan. 1452: 'Procehiu contra ells e sos bens segons trobareu per iusticia en manera que conegen quina cosa e no obeyr nostres manaments, e sia a ells castig e a altres exempli.'

[130] Cf. the instruction to Bernardo de Raymo, commissioner general in the Abruzzi, to take action against the many criminals who are left unpunished by captains and nobles holding the *merum et mixtum imperium* (ACA Reg. 2915. 19ᵛ, 24 May 1451).

[131] The incident is described by Pere Boquet in a letter written to Barcelona from Naples between 8 and 15 May 1458 (ACB Cart. Com., vol. 28, fol. 108). Gentile thinks that the captain who lost his life was probably Giovanni Serignaro ('Lo stato napoletano' (1938), p. 56, n. 4).

[132] Faraglia, *Diurnali*.

[133] E. Pontieri, *La Calabria a metà del secolo XV e le rivolte di Antonio Centelles* (Naples, 1963).

[134] Gentile, 'Lo stato napoletano' (1938), p. 43, n. 1.

whose misdeeds, perpetrated personally and through their municipal officers, constantly echoed in the viceroy's court. The town of Borelli, for instance, complained to Siscar that the captain appointed by Ruffo had left without rendering any account at the end of his term of office, and that the count was taking advantage of the situation to make them pay their taxes twice over.[135]

Viceroys, justiciars, and captains discharged the peace-keeping and law-giving functions of the crown in the provinces. Its fiscal interests were looked after by another body of officials whose activities came under the control of the Sommaria. Their efficiency was of vital concern because on it depended the bulk of the crown's revenue and hence the life of the state; it had moreover considerable political significance because they functioned in the feudal domains more effectively and intensively than did the judicial officers of the crown.

For fiscal as for judicial purposes the province constituted the principal administrative unit. Even the Terra d'Otranto did not entirely escape the attention of revenue commissioners. In the autumn of 1445 the Sommaria ventured to dispatch Andrea Barzello to that stronghold of the Prince of Taranto with instructions that he should 'pigliare informatione dele rasune che spectano ala regia corte in dele cita, terre e porte seu maritimi che lo dicto principe tene e quelle notificare ala regia corte'.[136] But when the prince protested that such an inquest infringed his privileges, the commissioner was called off.[137] Elsewhere the attention which the Sommaria devoted to a province depended on its wealth measured in terms of trade, agricultural production, and population; it was far more active, for example, in Terra di Lavoro and Terra di Bari than in Molise and Basilicata.

Direct taxes—the hearth tax and aids—were normally collected by officials dispatched to the provinces for that purpose by the treasury, although in the earlier part of the reign the viceroys had sometimes organized the collection.[138] In November 1448 Alfonso

[135] Pontieri, *Fonti aragonesi*, ii. 151–5, 24 Nov. 1452.
[136] ASN Fasc. Com. Somm. I. 85^r, 12 Nov. 1445.
[137] Ibid.: 'Fin che non averra altro comandamento dela regia corte non debia exercire suo officio in dela dicta provincia, non obstante che abia la commessione e le instruccione de fare lofficio in dela dicta provincia.'
[138] Cf. the final quittance given to de Cardenas for two instalments of the hearth tax for the 11th indiction which he had collected in his viceroyalty. He had also collected the tax arrears for the previous five years (ACA Reg. 2913, 86^v, 21 Jan. 1449).

regularized the procedure by decreeing that, with effect from the Christmas instalment of that year, five special commissioners were to be responsible for the hearth tax. Each was assigned a group of provinces and a headquarters: one commissioner for Terra di Lavoro and Molise was to reside in Naples; another for the two Principato provinces and Basilicata had his seat in Benevento; Cosenza became the centre for Calabria, and Sulmona for both the Abruzzi provinces; Terra d'Otranto, Terra di Bari, and Capitanata were grouped together under a commissioner resident in Trani.[139] Other commissioners were appointed for the aids and salt tax. The communes in each of these areas had to deliver their tax at the designated centres through their syndics, often at great inconvenience and expense.

Collection of the indirect taxes called for a much larger body of relatively petty officials, because these imposts consisted, in the main, of a host of duties on the movement and sale of raw materials, manufactured goods, agricultural produce, and animals. Ports and major market towns were therefore the principal centres for this form of taxation.

The most productive taxes were the customs duties, levied on all species of goods brought into or taken out of the kingdom, and the numerous port dues imposed on shipping. They were administered by the port masters (*magistri portolani*) each of whom controlled a stretch of the coast. The *magister portolanus* of the Abruzzi covered the Adriatic shore from the river Tronto to the river Fortore, so that the province of Molise, which contained no port of any significance, also fell within his jurisdiction. Capitanata and Terra di Bari were jointly administered by the *magister portolanus* of Puglia. Terra d'Otranto and Basilicata constituted another unit, while Calabria, Principato citeriore, and Terra di Lavoro each had its own *magister portolanus*. Such was the pattern which emerged at the end of the reign after a number of experiments and reshufflings. Until 1446 Puglia, Basilicata, and Terra d'Otranto all came under one *magister portolanus*, Landolfo Marramaldo; for some years Terra di Lavoro had two *magistri*

---

[139] ACA Reg. 2913. 75ʳ, 20 Nov. 1448. These cities had been designated as the centres for payment of the hearth tax by the 1443 parliament which had introduced that tax (Gentile, 'Lo stato napoletano' (1937), p. 56). Some further modifications were made: e.g. in 1453 when Bernat Mattes of the treasury became tax commissioner for Basilicata and Terra di Bari (ACA Reg. 2917. 103ᵛ, 24 Mar. 1453).

who appear to have acted jointly;[140] the region of Valle del Crati had its own official in 1449.[141] Naples and Gaeta, it should be noted, formed a separate administrative unit for customs purposes outside the jurisdiction of the *magister portolanus* of the Terra di Lavoro. The *magistri* held their offices usually on a life tenure which was often tied to some financial deal with the crown. Bernabo della Marra, who became *magister portolanus* of Puglia in February 1446, undertook to lend the king 4,000 ducats, including cloth to the value of 1,000 ducats for the hire of troops. He was to recoup this sum from the proceeds of his office which he was to retain for one year after the full amount had been recovered.[142] By June 1449 della Marra had been replaced by Simone Cazzetta who appears in a list of the crown's creditors for the sum of 3,000 ducats which he too was expected to recover from the receipts of his office.[143] Similar arrangements, which enabled the king to anticipate his revenues, were probably made with other *magistri portolani*.

A *magister portolanus* or his deputy—for they all received permission to exercise the office by deputy—appointed subordinate *portolani* to carry out his functions in those ports of the royal demesne where traffic was permitted. The instructions given to della Marra for Puglia divided these ports into three categories: the main ports (Manfredonia, Barletta, and Trani) to be served by four *portolani* in each; lesser ports (Molfetta, Giovinazzo, and Santo Stefano) with two *portolani*; and small harbours (Fortore and Mola) with only one apiece. In all other harbours, including those belonging to feudataries, traffic was strictly forbidden, ships being allowed to enter them only in the event of storm or dire emergency.[144] *Portolani* were expected to enforce the ban by watching the coast for illegal shipping, seizing any vessel found

---

[140] They were Bartolomeo di Gennaro and Ciarletta Gattola (see ACA Reg. 2913. 45ʳ, 21 Aug. 1448). Before July 1451 they had been replaced by a single official (Mazzoleni, *Il Codice Chigi*, pp. 58–9, Order to the *magister portolanus* of Terra di Lavoro, 15 July 1451).

[141] Mazzoleni, *Fonti aragonesi*, i. 72. He was Giovanni Setario.

[142] Rogadeo, *Codice diplomatico*, pp. 169–70. He received a salary of 600 ducats.

[143] ACA Real Patrimonio 2951, Credit entered under October 1449; Reg. 2913. 157ᵛ, 9 June 1449, an order addressed to him as *magister portolanus* of Puglia.

[144] Among della Marra's instructions was a requirement that he should issue a proclamation by crier forbidding the loading of dutiable cargoes in any harbour belonging to a lay or ecclesiastical lord.

infringing it, and taking care that no feudatory established a port.[145]

The dues collected by the port masters included those levied on ships according to their burthen, and a variety of port charges, such as payment for loading, warehousing, and berthing facilities. Assessment and collection of duty on cargoes was the province of the customs officials (*doganieri*) subject to the over-all control of the *magistri portolani*. As soon as his ship entered harbour, the captain was required to submit a list of his cargo, and only under the supervision of the customs officials could it be unloaded into the customs warehouses for detailed inspection and calculation of the duty payable.[146] Customs duties varied between provinces, partly because of differences in local units of measurement, and partly because some products were much more important in some regions than in others. Each *magister portolanus* therefore received from the Sommaria a table of charges appropriate to his area. The tables for Puglia emphasized the duty on grain exports—*ius exiture seu tracte*—which was fixed at a standard rate of 4 ducats a *carro* for wheat, though della Marra had authority to negotiate reductions to $3\frac{1}{2}$ or even 3 ducats with merchants if he considered it advantageous to the crown. In effect he had to consider the rate which best suited his own interest since he was recovering his loan from the income of the office. Grain carried from a port in Puglia to another port within the kingdom paid a duty of 15 *carlini* a *centenario*. In Principato citeriore customs duties on grain were calculated according to Neapolitan measures: 30 *rotoli* made 1 *tomolo*, 8 *tomoli* made 1 *salma*. There the *magister portolanus* was instructed in 1446 to levy the grain duty at a rate of 7 *grana* for every *tomolo* of wheat exported and 7 *grana* for a *centenario* shipped within the kingdom.[147] A decree promulgated in 1455 eliminated many of these differences by imposing a uniform duty of 12 *grana* for a Neapolitan *tomolo* on all wheat exported from the kingdom.[148] Timber cut from the forests of Principato figures prominently in

[145] Cf. the instructions given to Giuliano Riccio as *magister portolanus* of Principato citeriore, 11 Mar. 1446, which are published by Minieri Riccio, *Saggio*, ii, pt. 2, pp. 1–3.

[146] Gentile, 'Lo stato napoletano' (1938), pp. 11–12. Gentile summarizes the customs regulations issued in 1452 and repeated in 1457.

[147] The rate for other cereals and foodstuffs in Principato citeriore was half that levied on wheat.

[148] Gentile, 'Lo stato napoletano' (1938), p. 4.

the customs table for that province.[149] Other items mentioned there are biscuit, pitch, pigs, sheep, goats, mules, and horses. The *magister portolanus* could seize and imprison any ship's master who attempted to sail without paying the customs and other dues; the vessel too would be detained pending determination of the case by the Sommaria. His authority also extended to wreck and jetsam which, if not claimed within one year of being taken into his custody, became the property of the crown.

In each port the *magister portolanus* and his subordinates kept a register showing the details of exports: quantities, date, names of vessels and masters, destination, and, in the case of restricted goods, the details of sureties given.[150] To guard against fraud the crown maintained another agent known as the *notarius credencerius* attached to each *magister portolanus*. It was his business, with the assistance of his subordinates in each port, to keep his own record of the port transactions, and to ensure by regular inspection that the *portolani* kept their books in proper order. He performed the same function with those individuals to whom the port and customs duties were farmed by the *magister portolanus* whenever an adequate offer was forthcoming.[151] At the end of the financial year both *magister portolanus* and *notarius credencerius* submitted their accounts to the Sommaria.[152]

Control of traffic across the land frontiers presented great difficulties because they ran through the most mountainous and uninhabited regions of the peninsula. For many years hostilities

[149] It paid a duty (*ius portulanie*) varying from 3 *tarini* a hundred on planks to 1 *tarin* a hundred on logs. Shipbuilding timber paid one-tenth *ad valorem*.

[150] In the privilege appointing Cristoforo Gentile *portolano* of Manfredonia he is warned to enforce the edicts of the church against the export of food and arms to infidels (ACA Reg. 2915. 196^r, 8 Mar. 1452).

[151] Cf. the instructions for the farming of duties given to della Marra (Rogadeo, *Codice diplomatico*, pp. 169–70).

[152] Cf. the instructions given to Thomas de Aulesia, the royal librarian, who was given the post of *notarius credencerius* to the *magister portolanus* of Puglia with a salary of 42 *oncie* a year (ACA Reg. 2909. 160^r, 25 Nov. 1445); also the appointment of Joan Ferrer to the office in the Abruzzi (ACA Reg. 2908. 164^r, 29 Apr. 1446). Among the deficiencies charged to Laudadeo Tau, *magister portolanus* of the Abruzzi for the 1st, 2nd, and 3rd indictions, was a sum of 3 ducats, being the duty on 1 *carro* of wheat 'quod asserit fuisse delatum ortonam et credencerius nullam facit mencionem' (ASN Signif. I. 35^v, 26 Aug. 1456). In 1457 the *magister portolanus* of Basilicata and Terra d'Otranto, Guerrerio d'Ischia, and his subordinates were convicted in the Sommaria of fraud and extortion. They were dismissed from office and punished (Gentile, 'Lo stato napoletano' (1937), p. 47, n. 4); ASN Dip. Somm. 48; Signif. I. 10^r.

with the neighbouring papal states and with Francesco Sforza added to the problem, so it was not until 1443 that Alfonso managed to establish effective customs control on the frontier of the Terra di Lavoro, and it was 1445 before he achieved it in the Abruzzi. As with the sea coasts, a number of places were designated as customs posts and in these all merchandise and cattle taken into or out of the kingdom had to be submitted to the inspection of the king's officials. On the Terra di Lavoro frontier these posts, or *passi* as they were called, began with San Germano (near Montecassino) and continued in a chain with Isoletta, Sora, Balsorano, 'Insula filiorum petri' (Isola del Liri?), a 'Turris Campi Latri' which I have been unable to identify, Roccavivi, Pontecorvo, Terracina, Sant'Angelo Theodice, and Arce. In the Abruzzi there were three groups of *passi*. One consisting of Tagliacozzo, Avezzano, and Capistrello continued the line of posts in the Terra di Lavoro to the head of the valley of the Liri. The second group had its headquarters in Sulmona; posts in that city, in Chieti, and in Lanciano served to control traffic on the upper and lower reaches as well as the plain of the river Pescara; Castel di Sangro guarded the route along the valley of the Sangro. A third group of posts in L'Aquila, Montereale, and Teramo controlled the river routes of the Aterno and Tordino on the most northerly frontier. Except in the valley of the Liri, these posts stood well behind the frontiers of the kingdom at distances varying from ten to fifteen miles. Most of them were not much used because little commercial traffic went through this wild, difficult country.

The supervision of traffic across the land frontiers was entrusted to commissioners who appointed their own deputies in the designated posts. Carafello Carafa, viceroy of Cassino, became commissioner for the Terra di Lavoro frontier from San Germano northwards sometime between 1443 and 1446.[153] The rest of that frontier from San Germano to the coast at Terracina was for some years the responsibility of the Count of Fondi, whose estates dominated that region; but by 1454 at the latest the whole frontier of the province had become the responsibility of Carafa.[154] In the

---

[153] Instructions issued to Carafa on 30 Apr. 1446 (ASN Dip. Somm. 48) make it clear that he had been performing the duties for some time, perhaps since he became viceroy of Cassino early in 1443. However, that he was not the first commissioner is shown by a reference to 'li statuti . . . declarati per la nostra corte alle toy predecessori'; cf. ACA Reg. 2903. 82ᵛ.

[154] Gentile, 'Lo stato napoletano' (1938), p. 7; ASN Signif. I. 10ʳ, 27 Apr. 1456.

Abruzzi provinces the situation was complicated by the grants made by Giovanna II of the most valuable constituent item of the customs, the duty on exported foodstuffs, the *gabella grassie*.[155] An inquest into the administration of that duty conducted in 1443 led to a judgement of the Sommaria revoking the grants made by Giovanna, but Alfonso then proceeded to give the *gabella* to Iñigo de Avalos for life with permission either to administer it through his own officials or to farm it.[156] In 1444 the Sommaria instituted another inquest into the conduct of other officials responsible for the control of traffic across the Abruzzi frontiers.[157] By September 1451 Francesco de Paganis of Tagliacozzo had become 'magister passuum Aprutii' and he held the office still in 1456.[158]

A detailed picture of the administration of the land customs emerges from the instructions given to Carafa in 1446. Export dues were levied on slaves, war horses, colts, foals and fillies, mares, common riding horses, mules, oxen, sows, sheep, rams, goats, and all foodstuffs. Horses above a certain size required in addition a special export licence—a measure intended to conserve the stock of horses suitable for war.[159] The export of coins and bullion likewise required a licence, smuggling of them being treated as a

[155] Giovanna II had granted it first to Giovanni Dentice and Gualterio Caracciolo, and later to Monaco de Anna and Urbano Crivino (ACA Reg. 2908. 63ʳ). In L'Aquila it was granted to Battista de Camponeschis whose heirs continued to collect the dues after his death. They unsuccessfully petitioned Alfonso to confirm them in possession and were in 1451 ordered to pay to the treasury the money held to have been collected illegally (Toppi, *De origine tribunalium*, i. 277).

[156] The 'inquisitio grassie aprucii et contra ipsius administratores' was conducted by Francesco Pagano. After some questioning of the officials he handed over to Antonello Baroni who had been sent especially for that purpose by the Sommaria (ASN Div. Somm. I. 166. 16ʳ). The letters granting the *gabella* to de Avalos are dated 2 Aug. 1444 (ACA Reg. 2908. 63ʳ).

[157] Gentile, 'Lo stato napoletano' (1938), p. 6.

[158] Mazzoleni, *Il Codice Chigi*, p. 119, 18 Sept. 1451, an order addressed to de Paganis. An order for the recovery of deficiencies discovered in his accounts for the 3rd indiction is dated 28 July 1456 (ASN Signif. I. 28ʳ).

[159] The registers contain numerous letters authorizing the export of horses. A traveller leaving with a horse which he had not brought into the kingdom had normally to provide sureties to guarantee its return within a stated period. A letter patent 'expedita fuit in forma camere pro Johanne Martini et Michaele Falagera catalanis pro duobus equis pili sauri pretii et stature non prohibitis et ducatis xv pro quolibet pro eorum impensis pro quibus caverunt Bartholomeus de Afelatro sellarius et Johannes Januense panicterius habitator in plathea francesche reducere dictos equos et presentare in hac camera infra menses duos' (ASN Lictere Passus I. 6ᵛ, 19 Apr. 1458).

capital offence.[160] Anyone entering or leaving the kingdom had to declare on oath to the customs officials that he carried no letters or writings prejudicial to the king, and should such things be found upon him, he was arrested and sent to Naples for interrogation. In Carafa's instructions a distinction is made between those found with contraband goods away from frequented routes and those attempting to pass with it by the main highways. Against the former a presumption of guilt was permitted, so both they and their goods were placed under arrest. The latter, if they were Neapolitan subjects, lost the contraband articles but were not imprisoned; if they were foreigners, but not merchants, ignorance was presumed and their goods were impounded while they returned to the Sommaria to obtain the necessary licences. Merchants were less fortunate: if caught breaking the customs regulations, they lost their goods and faced the prospect of a year in the prison of the Vicaria. A Neapolitan subject known to have smuggled goods without being caught in the act could be arrested later by the customs officials and sent for trial.[161] To prevent abuse of this power, officials were not permitted to accept composition from any person against whom such a charge had been laid, nor were they able to hold him in custody for more than three days. Public proclamations in Naples, Capua, Gaeta, Aversa, 'et altri lochi famosi de terra de lavoro', endeavoured to ensure that people knew which articles were subject to customs control.

From his accounts it would appear that Carafa kept only one man in each of the *passi* under his control, and since they received an average salary of only two ducats a month, it is hardly likely that they could have paid subordinates. However, the Sommaria must have accepted this staffing as adequate to the posts. In the Abruzzi the numbers were larger. In Sulmona in 1443 Pagano found a deputy commissioner and fifteen minor officials; in both Taglia-cozzo and L'Aquila there were seventeen.[162] That they often

---

[160] Benko Kotruljević (Benedetto Cotrugli) of Ragusa, condemned in his absence to the loss of life and property for the unlicensed export of coins, was pardoned at the instance of the Duke of Bosnia (ACA Reg. 2917. 121ᵛ, 15 Apr. 1455). Kotruljević was the author of *Della mercatura et del mercante perfetto*, published in Venice in 1573.

[161] Such arrests would presumably have arisen from denunciations of the offences. Anyone making a denunciation stood to gain one-quarter of the goods forfeited if the prosecution proved successful.

[162] ASN Div. Somm. I. 166. 16ʳ. A *notarius credencerius* was attached to each customs commissioner in the same manner as to the *magister portolanus*. Bernardo

tyrannized travellers and accepted bribes to allow the passage of contraband goods is suggested by the warnings against such practices in Carafa's instructions. The commissioners assisted by a judge had the power to try and punish their subordinates for official misdemeanours with penalties up to the loss of life and property.

The customs duties levied on goods carried across the frontiers of the Terra di Lavoro in 1446 were as follows: sheep and goats paid 4 ducats a hundred, pigs 10 ducats a hundred, oxen 1 ducat a head, cows 60 ducats a hundred, and all foodstuffs one-tenth of their value. These charges must have represented an increase on those levied in the previous reign because in the parliament of March 1450 the barons petitioned that customs duties be levied at the rates prevailing in the reign of Giovanna II. Alfonso answered, 'Placet Regie Maiestati quod cabella grassie exigatur et recolligatur prout exigi consuevit tempore Regis Ladizlai vel Regine Johanne secunde ad eleccionem et arbitrium Regie Maiestati.'[163] The result, one imagines, was a combination of charges from both reigns most advantageous to the crown. But revenue was not the sole consideration of the crown in its management of the customs; concern for food supplies within the kingdom caused a ceiling to be placed upon the number of animals that might be exported in any year. For the Terra di Lavoro frontier the instructions of 1446 fixed the annual quota at 10,000 sheep and goats, 6,000 pigs, 130 oxen, and 370 cows. Had these numbers been reached, they would have yielded an annual revenue of 1,352 ducats, whereas Carafa's total receipts for foodstuffs as well as animals, over a period of eighteen months in 1448 and 1449 amounted to only 744 ducats. It would seem, therefore, that the number of animals exported fell well below the permitted maximum. Nevertheless in 1449, perhaps because of the outbreak of war with Venice and a bad harvest, the king imposed a total ban on the export of animals and foodstuffs, and he refused to lift it at the request of the parliament which met in March 1450.[164] Representations from the papacy,

de Raymo was given that post in the Abruzzi (ACA Reg. 2915. 97ʳ, 14 Oct. 1451).

[163] Ametller y Vinyas, *Alfonso V de Aragón*, iii. 689.

[164] Ibid. Article XIII of the parliament reads: 'Item supplicano li predicti che considerato che a tutti li vestri subditi et vassalli e necessario de subvenire a la V.M. per diversi paghamenti et per la V.M. e stato facto bando et comandamento che non se debia cazare fore questo vestro Regno victuaglie e bestiamis,

whose subjects were the principal sufferers from the embargo, eventually caused it to be raised, but traffic across the land frontiers remained insignificant compared with that through the ports. It consisted mainly of the baggage of travellers together with a few animals and animal products destined for consumption in the neighbouring lands of the church.[165] The kingdom, it must be remembered, produced no manufactures which were in demand elsewhere in Italy. Moreover travellers by land faced the perils of brigands and the hazards of bad roads. Alfonso attempted to deal with both these handicaps to traffic: with the former the manner described in an earlier chapter;[166] with the latter by appointing commissioners charged with the repair and improvement of roads and bridges. The demands made on the communities by these agents caused so much complaint that, according to a petition of the 1456 parliament, Alfonso revoked the commissions of all but Brunoro Sparella 'qui remaneat pro reparandis viis publicis extra civitates'.[167]

Within the kingdom the crown derived revenue, other than the direct taxes, from its monopoly of the sale of certain commodities —salt, iron, steel, and pitch—and from a host of duties known as the old and new *gabelle*. These revenues were administered by *secreti*. Because the duties were farmed whenever possible, and because most of them yielded very little when collected by the agents of the crown, the office of *secretus* was almost always combined with some other that concerned the revenue. Most commonly it was held together with the charge of *magister portolanus*, as happened in Calabria, Puglia, Basilicata, and Terra d'Otranto.[168]

nen altre mercancie et per questo li dicti vestri subditi et vasalli non potendo vendere loro victuaglie bestianne et altre mercancie extra Regnum non foreja abile fare li dicti paghamenti ne anche vivere loro. Et per questo piaca a la V.M. concedereli de gracia che possano vendere loro victuaglie cio e grano, vino, oglio, carne salata, et omne altra cosa pertinente ad vita de homo, nec non omne generacione de bestiame et altre mercancie fora questo vestro Regno ad che loro piacera.' The petition goes on to ask for the reduction in customs rates mentioned above.

[165] The chief items exported from the Abruzzi 1454–5 were sheep, cheeses, and a small number of oxen (ASN Signif. I. 28ʳ, 28 July 1456).

[166] See above, pp. 161–2.

[167] ASN Div. Somm. I. 52 (bis), 171ʳ; cf. Gentile, 'Lo stato napoletano' (1938), p. 9.

[168] e.g. Marinello de Medici was appointed to both offices in Basilicata and Terra d'Otranto by a single privilege (ACA Reg. 2912. 73ʳ, 5 July 1447). Gabriel Cardona held both in Calabria from 1445 until 1451 when he fled leaving his accounts in disorder (Gentile, 'Lo stato napoletano' (1937), p. 55, n. 3). Pedro de Orta succeeded him from March 1451 (ASN Priv. I. 49ʳ).

In the Abruzzi the official known as the treasurer general or commissioner and treasurer of the region held it.[169] A rare example of a *secretus* simple may be found in Calabria where Frederico Sparella held that office alone until May 1444 when Tristan de Queralt became both *magister portolanus* and *secretus*.[170] In similar fashion, the functions of the *credencerii* in the office of the *secreti* were normally doubled, so that Joan Ferrer became simultaneously *notarius credencerius* to both the *secretus* and the *magister portolanus* of the Abruzzi.[171]

One other office often combined with that of *magister portolanus* and *secretus* was the administration of the crown's salt monopoly. Always by far the most lucrative of the monopolies, salt assumed particular importance in 1443 when it became linked with the new hearth tax. In return for the payment of 1 ducat from each hearth, the crown undertook to supply one *tomolo* of salt free of charge; failure to deliver the salt by November in each year was supposed to entail a reduction of the tax by half. Soon afterwards the crown made compulsory the purchase of an additional *tomolo* each year for every household.[172] Hence the emphasis laid upon efficient administration in the salt monopoly by the *magistri salis*. Although not entirely self-sufficient in salt, the kingdom of Naples produced a great deal, especially in the Barletta–Manfredonia district which accounted for perhaps half its requirements. There were other centres of salt production at Castellaneta, Siponto, Taranto, Altomonte, Rossano, Neto, Amalfi, Santa Severina, and Salerno. Only strict control of the manufacture of salt could guarantee the monopoly of its sale, so the crown systematically took the salt pans from private hands (including those of Barletta in 1441) and thereafter had salt made there by contractors who could only dispose of it to the crown at a fixed price.[173] Armed men on horse

---

[169] Andrea de Sanctis held these offices until 1443 when he was replaced by Antoni Gaçull.

[170] See ACA Reg. 2909. 42ᵛ, 14 Feb. 1444. *Vice-secreti* were appointed in the principal towns of the royal demesne to collect the duties and enforce the monopolies.

[171] ACA Reg. 2908. 164ᵛ, 28 Apr. 1446.   [172] See above, p. 213.

[173] Bianchini, *Della storia delle finanze*, p. 201. Between 1442 and 1445 Pietro Bailardo and Blasio di Marinello of Barletta manufactured 6,530 *carri* at the rate of 2½ *tarini* a *carro* under a contract with Landolfo Marramaldo, the *secretus* of the salt pans at Barletta (Rogadeo, *Codice diplomatico*, p. 164). The conditions laid down by the crown for the manufacture of salt at Barletta are given in Salvati, *Fonti aragonesi*, iv. 59. Those for Manfredonia may be found ibid., p. 60.

and foot guarded the salt pans,[174] and the master of the salt (the *magister salis*) had jurisdiction over all employed there. In these circumstances a licence for the private manufacture of salt became a highly prized privilege granted to only a few favourites. Luisa d'Alagno, for example, was permitted to make 1,000 *carri* a year and to sell them as she pleased.[175]

Since most of the centres of salt manufacture were in Puglia and Calabria, difficulties of transport caused the bulk of what was produced there to be distributed in the eastern and southern provinces and in the Abruzzi. For households in the Terra di Lavoro and Principato the king promised in 1443 to supply the 'red' salt imported from Ibiza.[176] It proved difficult to organize adequate shipments of this salt, with the result that by September 1444 its distribution had fallen one year in arrears in some parts of Principato ulteriore.[177] Even those government stores (*fondachi*) supplied with local salt often found themselves without stocks through a breakdown in production or negligence on the part of the *magister salis*. Domenico d'Afflicto, the *magister salis* of Puglia, was fined for not keeping the store at Lucera supplied with salt; he had instead sold it abroad.[178] On 22 January 1449 when Nicola d'Afflicto, presumably a relative of Domenico, arrived in Bitonto to inspect the salt store, he found it empty; the official in charge, the *doganerius*, protested that the fault was not his since he had frequently but vainly asked for supplies from Paolo de Damiano the commissioner in charge of the main store at Barletta.[179] Not only were the *fondachi* often ill stocked with salt, they

---

[174] At Barletta there were six mounted men and four footmen (Rogadeo, *Codice diplomatico*, p. 176).

[175] Ibid., p. 438.

[176] In instructions sent to Queen Maria on 16 July 1443 there is the following item: 'A lo que diu la dita Senyora haver provehit en fer venir sal deles parts deça respon lo dit Senyor que es molt necessari axi se execute e qui la execucio de aço no se tarda molt massa considerat que es tengut de dar dela sal de Eviça un turno per foch en tres provincies per tot lo mes de agost, e altretanta per tot lo mes de octubre seguents. En altra guisa pert la Cort mig ducat per turno, e troba se vuy la doana de Napols molt buyda de sal segons la quantitat ques deu exit' (ACA Reg. 2939. 64ᵛ).

[177] ASN Framm. Com. Somm. 15ᵛ.

[178] Gentile, 'Finanze e parlamenti', p. 219, n. 3: 'Lo stato napoletano' (1938), p. 19, n. 1.

[179] F. Carabellese, *La Puglia nel sècolo XV da fonti inèdite* (Bari, 1901), pp. 110–11. Cf. the order to Antoni Gaçull, treasurer general of the Abruzzi, to give the convent of St. Francis in L'Aquila its annual assignment of 8 *tomoli* of salt from the *fondaco* of L'Aquila, even though it should have come from the

were also few and far between for a population which had to rely upon them for an essential commodity. For example, in Puglia, the main centre of production, there were stores only in Barletta, Manfredonia, Trémoli, Lucera, and Venosa.[180] The government had no desire to open more, but tried on the contrary to close small ones where the amount of business did not justify the cost of maintaining the store and its staff. The treasurer of Calabria proposed to close the *fondaco* in Monteleoni (Calabria) for these reasons, but the town protested that it had been there 'from time immemorial'.[181] Such a situation encouraged a clandestine trade in salt despite the efforts of the crown to protect its monopoly by forbidding private manufacture and sales. As soon as Alfonso had gained firm control of the kingdom he took action to suppress or bring under the crown all those salt manufacturies which had come into private hands during the preceding chaos. Those dispossessed received compensation when the king thought it politic to placate them,[182] but further trespass on the crown monopoly brought down heavy retribution on the offender. One of the charges brought against Centelles concerned 'le occupacione facte per lo dicto don Antonio dele saline . . . apertenente ala Corte'.[183] There followed in 1445 a campaign, waged by the Sommaria through a body of special commissioners, to gain control of all private stocks of salt.[184] However, the shortcomings of the government salt stores led eventually to some relaxation of the policy of a rigid monopoly of sales; an edict of 20 September 1449 permitted any person to resell salt bought from a *fondaco* or any other authorized source, provided that the price did not undercut that

---

fondaco of Pescara, 'cum non fiat sal in salinis dicte terre Piscarie neque inibi nostre Curie fundicus minime teneatur' (Mazzoleni, *Il Codice Chigi*, p. 81, 24 July 1451).

[180] In Barletta and Manfredonia, the main *fondachi*, salt was sold at 5 *carlini* a *tomolo*; in the three subsidiary *fondachi* the price was increased by 1 *grana* to cover the cost of carriage (Rogadeo, *Codice diplomatico*, p. 176, Instructions for Bernabo della Marra).

[181] ASN Fasc. Com. Somm. 65^r.

[182] e.g. the Duke of Andria, who claimed certain rights in the salt pans of Basilicata, was granted 5 *carri* of salt each year from the salt pans of Torre a Mare, with the right to export it free of duty or else keep it for the use of his household (ACA Reg. 2909. 202^r, 2 Mar. 1446). Cf. Gentile, 'Lo stato napoletano' (1938), p. 15, n. 1.

[183] ACA Reg. 2698. 67^v, 18 Aug. 1444.

[184] ASN Fasc. Somm. I. 70^v, 3 Nov. 1445, Letter informing the captain of Nola of the arrival of the special commissioner, Tristan de Queralt.

charged by the crown.[185] A sharp fall in revenue resulted, so in October 1455 a new modification of the salt regulations restricted private sales to towns which had no royal store.[186]

Iron, steel, and pitch, the ancient royal monopolies known as the *secrezie*, were all controlled by the *secreti* who sold them at fixed prices from the *fondachi* in the major demesne towns. The last turbulent years of Angevin rule had witnessed numerous encroachments on these monopolies, encroachments which the crown now endeavoured to eliminate. On 9 January 1446 the council ordered those nobles claiming a right to a toll on iron, steel, and pitch sold within their fiefs to produce their titles; among them were the Prince of Salerno, the Duke of Melfi, the Duke of Andria, and the Count of Lauria.[187] After scrutiny of their privileges, some lost their rights to the tolls—the Duke of Andria, for example, had to surrender the toll on iron;[188] others, like the de Sardis family of Sulmona, succeeded in maintaining their claims.[189] Most of the small quantity of iron produced within the kingdom was mined in Calabria where the Duke of San Marco's foundry at Malvito accounted for a large proportion of the output. After the procurator fiscal had brought an unsuccessful action claiming for the crown a *ius terciarie* on the iron produced in the foundry,[190] the crown attempted to develop mines within the demesne,[191] but its prospecting achieved little result and most

[185] The *magister portolanus* of Puglia was ordered to permit Nicola di Buccino of Trani to sell a quantity of salt 'emptos olim per eum a quibusdam mercatoribus' in accordance with 'pracmatica sanctio a nobis edita quia voluimus et ordinavimus ut quivis baro, universitates et singulares persone huius Regni nostri Sicilie recepto a nostra Curia quolibet anno uno tumino salis pro quolibet foculari, possint ad sue libitum voluntatis sal emere et vendere' (Mazzoleni, *Il Codice Chigi*, pp. 60–1, 10 July 1451).

[186] Gentile, 'Lo stato napoletano' (1938), p. 19.   [187] Ibid., p. 15.

[188] ACA Reg. 2909. 202ʳ, 2 Mar. 1446.

[189] Matteo and Silvestro de Sardis had obtained the 'cabella ferri aczari picis et vomerum' in the Abruzzi from Giovanna II and were confirmed in possession of it by Alfonso (ACA Reg. 2914. 141ʳ, 19 May 1451). In Barletta these *gabelle* had been granted to Jacobo della Marra as a fief *in perpetuum* by a privilege dated 18 Sept. 1436 (Rogadeo, *Codice diplomatico*, p. 10).

[190] Mazzoleni, *Il Codice Chigi*, pp. 333–4, 30 May 1452, Order to the viceroy of Calabria not to interfere with the Duke's collection of the *ius terciarie* pending determination of the suit. A document entitled 'Introitus ex demaniis Calabrie 1456–8' (ASN Div. Somm. I. 10. 15ʳ) has this note: 'Item vero quod dominus dux Sancti Marci habet certas ferrerias in dicta provincia que faciunt magnam ferri quantitatem propter quas dictus fundicus modicum valet.'

[191] A privilege dated 27 Sept. 1452 gave jurisdiction over the miners and prospectors to Pedro de Orta of the treasury (ASN Priv. I. 48ʳ).

of the metal sold in its stores had to be imported. The greater part was purchased from Venetian merchants who obtained it from Balkan mines; the remainder came from Spain.[192] The price paid by the crown remained steady at 4 ducats a quintal; the *secreti* sold the iron at 6 ducats a quintal, one-third of this sum representing the *cabella* or *ius terciarie*. Steel sold at 7 ducats a quintal with the same profit margin of 50 per cent as iron. The tax on pitch (a *quintaria*) yielded the crown a profit of 25 per cent.

These lesser monopolies created problems for crown and consumer very similar to those which arose from the salt monopoly. In some *fondachi* the quantities sold were so small that the crown attempted to close the stores. The Sommaria disallowed part of the salary paid by the *secretus* of Basilicata and Terra d'Otranto to his deputy in the *fondaco* of Atella for the third indiction (1455–6) 'quia considerata parva utilitate dicti fundici non meruit dictum salarium'.[193] Even in the large cities only relatively small transactions were recorded in these commodities. The iron received into the store at Naples in the year 1451–2 amounted to only 199 quintals;[194] sales in Gaeta in that same year totalled 109 quintals 4 rotols, and fell in the following year to 45 quintals 4 rotols. The *fondaco* in Castellammare di Stabia sold a mere 20 quintals of iron in 1451–2.[195] This small demand reflects the lack of manufacturing activity requiring these raw materials outside the royal arsenals. Alfonso promised to consider a petition from the 1450 parliament asking that subjects be allowed to retail within the kingdom iron bought from the royal stores, but we do not know what he decided.[196]

[192] e.g. the contract with Bertran Crexells, a merchant of Perpignan, whereby he undertook to deliver 4,000 quintals of iron in Naples (ACA Reg. 2721. 56ʳ, 15 May 1452). In the peace negotiations with Piombino Alfonso unsuccessfully sought to have the annual tribute due to him from that state fixed at 1,000 or 2,000 quintals of iron (ACA Reg. 2697. 47ᵛ, 18 Jan. 1450).

[193] ASN Signif. I. 57ʳ, 15 June 1457.   [194] Ibid. 1ʳ.

[195] The accounts of Giuliano Riccio, administrator of customs in Naples, Gaeta, and Castellammare, show that in the second indiction he sold the *gabella ferri* of Gaeta to Antonio Russo for three months for 80 ducats 2 *tarini* 12 *grana*. Joan Ferrer paid 176 ducats 2 *tarini* 3 *grana* to have it for the remainder of the financial year. From the *ius ferri et picis* of Castellammare which Riccio collected himself in the second indiction he realized altogether 21 ducats 5 *tarini* 8 *grana* (ACA Reg. 2917. 151ᵛ, 23 Feb. 1457).

[196] 'Item supplicano li predicti che considerato che in alcuna parte de questo vestro Regno e gran penuria de ferro et non hanno li fundichi vicini dove loro possano comprare che sia licito ali tali regnicoli comprare lo ferro neli fundichi statuti et paghare la debita gabella de esso ferro et dapoy poterelo vendere ad

Most of the other dues and indirect taxes—the *gabelle*—whether 'old' or 'new' were more irksome than profitable to the treasury. A large number had long since been alienated to individuals and corporations who made their own arrangements for the collection. Alfonso introduced no new taxes of this sort and continued to use those that existed as a convenient fund of favours. A general scrutiny of the titles by which they were held began with an inquest in the autumn of 1445.[197] In the city of Naples those claiming a right to any *gabelle* were given three days following a personal summons within which to present their titles before the Sommaria. The Prince of Taranto succeeded as usual in keeping the commissioner out of his domains.[198] Because most of the *gabelle* remaining in the hands of the crown involved the collection of numerous small sums in scattered localities, they were, whenever possible, farmed annually to the highest bidder. Only if no satisfactory offers were forthcoming would the *secreti* collect them directly. Feudal lords adopted the same policy and some were accused by their vassals of forcing the farms upon them at inflated prices. Where the farm affected only a locality, it became the responsibility of the *secretus* to negotiate it. If it affected more than one province, or the whole kingdom, the treasury undertook the negotiations, as it did when the duty on coral (*cabella coralli*) was farmed to a Venetian merchant, Jacobo de Giovanni.[199] Sometimes a number of *gabelle* were lumped together in one transaction; this happened in 1457 when the *gabelle* of the city of Naples known as *vino, marittima, carne, quartatico, buon denaro, piazza maggiore*, and *cavalli* were farmed together for 23,000 ducats.[200]

In those spheres of provincial administration so far considered the crown took a generally conservative line, making few innovations

minuto ad chi lo volesse comprare per che omne uno non po andare al fundico ad comprare ad minuto. Regia maiestas habita informacione providebit' (Ametller y Vinyas, *Alfonso V de Aragón*, iii. 690).

[197] The instructions issued by the Sommaria to the commissioner for Naples informed him: 'Scire te volumus quod regia paterna maiestas et sua curia certis bonis respectibus plenam informationem habere intendit de omnibus et quibuscumque cabellis et aliis iuribus fiscalibus ad dictam regiam curiam spectantibus et pertinentibus ubique in toto predicto regno Sicilie citra farum et presertim in provincia Terra Laboris et in hac civitate Neapolis que per quoscumque tenentur et possidentur ac quo iure et titulo' (ASN Fasc. Com. Somm. I. 83ʳ, 9 Nov. 1445). [198] Ibid. 85ʳ.

[199] ACA Reg. 2720. 62ʳ, 1 Nov. 1446. Pedro Saldundo was appointed *credencerius* for the crown to the farmer of this tax (ACA Reg. 2909. 206ᵛ, 11 Mar. 1446). [200] Bianchini, *Della storia delle finanze*, p. 200.

either in procedures or personnel. In the administration of the
grazing lands of Puglia and of the royal farms, by contrast,
Alfonso introduced radical reforms. Since the days of the Roman
Republic sheep and cattle had been brought from summer
pastures in the uplands of the Abruzzi and the central Apennines
to winter in the lowlands of Terra di Bari and Capitanata. It was a
mass movement of men and animals regulated by tradition in its
timing and in the routes it followed. To the landowners of Puglia,
the crown among them, it represented an important source of
income derived from the sale of pasture rights; in addition the
crown had raised revenue from a grazing tax that dated back at
least to Frederick II and possibly to the Normans.[201] Not content
with this income, Alfonso set up an organization to take full
control of the transhumance by obliging all those bringing animals
to winter pasture to deal directly with a royal commissioner who
assigned grazing to them and collected a fee based on the number
of animals. Landlords were forbidden to deal directly with those
who sought the grazing; instead they had to lease their pastures to
the commissioner who paid for them at a rate fixed by the treasury.
In effect the king had transformed the transhumance or *mena delle
pecore* into a royal monopoly. Some steps in this direction must
have been taken in the previous reign because the parliament of
1443, which protested against the innovation, asked that all landowners be permitted to sell their grazing freely as in the time of
Ladislas,[202] and the commissioner appointed in January 1443 was
given the salary 'prout solitum fuit et erat exigi et haberi tempore
Illustrorum regum Ladislai et Regine Johanne secunde'.[203]
Nevertheless the conditions of the preceding years must have
made any rigorous enforcement of crown control impossible and
it was only from the beginning of 1443 that the monopoly began to
bite. In reply to the baronial petition Alfonso promised that they
should receive for their pasture a price not less than that given in
the reign of Ladislas, but he carefully avoided the issue of their
freedom to sell the grazing as they pleased.[204] A year later Borso

---

[201] For a discussion of the grazing tax in the time of Robert of Anjou see R.
Caggese, *Roberto d'Angiò e i suoi tempi* (Florence, 1921), i. 509.
[202] de Bottis, *Privilegii*.
[203] ACA Reg. 2902. 156ᵛ, Appointment of Matheucio Vacaro.
[204] 'Placet Regiae Maiestati verum quod herbagia vendi habeant non minori
pretio quam solita fuerunt vendi tempore bonae memoriae regis Ladislai'
(de Bottis, *Privilegii*).

d'Este put the organization of the *mena* first among the causes of Alfonso's unpopularity with his Neapolitan subjects because it had deprived them of their revenues.[205]

Croce saw the *mena* as another example of the subjection of Naples to Spanish institutions, for he believed that Alfonso had taken the Castilian *mesta* as his model.[206] While his knowledge of the *mesta* might have convinced the king of the potential monetary value of a carefully controlled transhumance, there were important differences between the Castilian and Neapolitan systems; in particular there was in the Italian kingdom nothing equivalent to the powerful guild which in Castile administered the whole operation. Moreover it is evident that Alfonso was developing a native institution, not imposing a wholly alien custom.

By January 1443, at the latest, the organization of the *mena* had already taken definitive shape. At its head stood a commissioner: 'comissarium et magistrum seu ductorem vel gargarium mene seu dohane vel gargarie ovium seu pecudum aliorumque animalium minutorum et grossorum descendentium tam ab extra quam intra Regnum hoc ad partes Apulie ad pasculandum seu pascua summendum'.[207] He negotiated with the landowners of Puglia the price at which they would make their pastures available[208] and allocated these to the flocks at rates fixed by the king.[209] He exercised full jurisdiction, both civil and criminal, over all those engaged in the transhumance and was empowered to give guarantees for the safety of the drovers, their animals, and their goods. Edicts forbidding the owners of animals to send them to winter pasture elsewhere than in Puglia ensured that the crown had

---

[205] Foucard, 'Proposta', p. 714.

[206] Croce, *La Spagna nella vita italiana*, p. 43. For the *mesta* see J. Klein, *The 'Mesta'* (Cambridge, 1920).

[207] ACA Reg. 2902, 156ᵛ. This privilege promises Vacaro the office of commissioner for a period of five years with effect from 1 Sept. 1447. He never assumed the office.

[208] '. . . pro parte nostre curie dicta herbagia earundem partium Apulie a patronis illorum pro precio quo poteritis meliori et prout convenire melius et concordare potueritis cum eisdem ut animalia ipsa patulentur in hiis omnibus nostre curie comodum quantum poteritis procurandum' (ibid.). The effect of the undertaking given to the 1443 parliament was to ensure that these payments would not be lower than those made for the pastures in the reign of Ladislas.

[209] 'Ius dicte mene tam pro cabella quam passibus et omnibus aliis exinde debitis secundum quod a nobis et nostra curia habueritis in mandatis oretenus vel in scriptis . . .' (ibid.).

full control of the movement.[210] The area devoted to winter grazing lay in the great plain known as the Tavoliere stretching south of the river Fortore. Flocks and herds entered it in November and left in May. An attempt to develop a similar grazing area on the coastal plain of the Abruzzi was made in 1447 but met with little success. The hopes of attracting herds from the Abruzzi mountains and the papal states foundered on immemorial pasture habits.[211]

From September 1443 until the end of the reign Francesc Monlober held the office of commissioner in charge of winter grazing in Puglia.[212] A *notarius credencerius* kept watch on his accounts.[213] Foggia, a demesne city in which Monlober also held the office of captain, was the administrative centre for the *mena*.

A very large number of animals wintered in these pastures and fully justified the crown's expectations of profit. For the 8th indiction (1444–5) the sheep totalled 424,642 and the cattle 9,169; by the 12th indiction the numbers had risen to 925,712 sheep and 16,490 cattle.[214] In the following year the *mena* achieved a record 1,019,821 sheep and 13,503 cattle.[215] One hundred head of sheep from within the kingdom paid 8 ducats, while those from outside paid sums varying from 4 to 7 ducats a hundred. Larger animals paid at the rate of 25 ducats for every hundred head.[216] These payments exempted the flocks and herds from all tolls on the roads and entitled their owners and drovers to buy salt at half the usual price. In addition to the lower rates charged on animals brought into the kingdom, the commissioner could, at his discretion, waive the toll altogether in order to attract more animals,[217]

---

[210] '. . . possitis et libere valeatis precipere et mandare . . . quod nullatenus a predicto Regno presumant extraere seu extrahi facere animalia supradicta tam grossa quam minuta nec aliorum ea transmittere pro usu pascua sumendi nisi in dicta Apulie provincia . . .' (ibid.).

[211] Gentile, 'Lo stato napoletano' (1938), p. 25.

[212] A privilege dated 1 Aug. 1448 confirmed him in the office for life (ACA Reg. 2913. 42ʳ). He had a salary of 700 ducats and free grazing for 1,000 animals.

[213] Jacobo di Bisignano held that post from 1441 until his death in 1449 (see ACA Reg. 2912. 125ʳ). Gabriel dez Puig succeeded him. The *credencerius* to the *mena* received a salary of 200 ducats.

[214] ACA Reg. 2914. 67ᵛ, 15 June 1450, Quittance for Monlober.

[215] Ibid. 80ᵛ, 31 July 1450, Quittance for Monlober. In the 14th indiction the figures were 855,731 sheep and 18,763 cattle.

[216] Details of these charges appear in the quittances issued to Monlober.

[217] In the 14th indiction Monlober admitted approximately 6,000 sheep and 600 cattle without payment, 'ex iustis et rationalibus causis eum moventibus pro

but despite these inducements only between 10 and 20 per cent of the flocks and herds came from across the frontiers. Revenue from the *mena* fluctuated around 50,000 ducats a year at the beginning;[218] for the 12th, 13th, and 14th indictions it amounted to 92,972 ducats, 103,011 ducats, and 85,798 ducats—one of the most substantial items of crown revenue. The principal head of expenditure set against the income was payment to landowners for passage and grazing rights. At a standard rate of 20 ducats for every 1,000 head of sheep[219] these payments amounted in the 12th indiction to 21,277 ducats, and in the 14th indiction to 18,675 ducats. Some expense was also incurred in compensating land-owners for damage caused by the animals, for Monlober had instructions to settle all claims for damage done by them to cultivated and enclosed land.[220] But either little damage was done, or else the commissioner refused to meet many claims, for in the 12th indiction he paid out only 217 ducats on this account.

It has been alleged, by Bianchini and Croce among others, that the grazing toll as managed by Alfonso was ruinous to the economic prosperity of Puglia in general and especially to the development of crop cultivation in that region. This thesis ignores the fact that the Aragonese dynasty did not introduce the practice of transhumance into Puglia: it was an age-old custom closely bound up with the equally ancient *latifundia*. The essence of Alfonso's reorganization was a strict enforcement of crown control over the movement of animals and the allocation of pastures. Admittedly he was motivated by financial considerations, but the pasture

utilitate dicte nostre Curie et augmento dicte dohane ut maior numerus pecudum conduceretur in apuliam' (ACA Reg. 2914. 153^v, Quittance for the 14th indiction).

[218] Figures for revenue in the earlier years are given by Gentile, 'Lo stato napoletano' (1938), p. 22.

[219] This is the figure mentioned as standard in a record of payments to the Prince of Taranto—even he was compelled to submit his pastures in Puglia to the discipline of the *mena*! His treasurer in Ascoli received from Monlober 103 *oncie* 10 *tarini* in April 1451 for the pasture of 31,000 animals on his lands (ASN Dip. Somm. 547). On the other hand, many nobles enjoyed the privilege of free pasture for a stated number of animals—e.g. the Count of Fondi was allowed free pasture for 1,200 sheep (ACA Reg. 2909. 86^r, 30 Sept. 1444).

[220] The instructions given him in 1448 stipulated: 'si pecudes et animalia ipsa per inadvertenciam pastorum pascerent aut dampnum facerent in agris et terri-toriis seminatis et prohibitis quod nullam penam propterea incurrant patroni dictarum pecudum et aliorum animalium, sed illi qui dampna passi fuerint omnino recursum habeant ad vos prefatum commissarium.'

rights would still have been sold by landowners directly had the crown not enforced its claim to act as middleman. To argue that, but for the state's encouragement of transhumance, more land would have been turned to cultivation, presupposes a wholly different outlook in the landowning class to that which had prevailed for centuries and, by implication, a wholly different social and political structure in the kingdom.[221]

That Alfonso had some interest in the improvement of agriculture is shown by the measures taken to develop his own demesne farms in Puglia, Terra di Lavoro, Valle Beneventana, and Calabria. The most extensive and productive were in Puglia where Alfonso established a number of new farms or *massarie*. A privilege appointing Johan Andreu de Vesach manager (*magister massari*) of such a farm explains that 'statuerimus quendam in partibus Apulie massariam tam agrorum quam eciam bovium vacarum aliorum animalium componere et construhi facere'.[222] Another privilege appointing a *credencerius* to a farm manager refers to 'massarie nostre agriculture et armentorum quas de novo fecimus in Apulie partibus'.[223] The Puglian farms were controlled by a commissioner, several fragments of whose accounts have survived covering the years 1452 and 1454.[224] The commissioner Bernat Macthes had succeeded another Catalan, Bartholomeu Soler, who had died in September 1451.[225] He supervised a group of farms in the plain around Lucera and Foggia where many small villages still bear the name 'Massaria'.[226] His labour force numbered 217 in 1452 and 254 in 1454, but some were casual labourers who worked on the farms for only a few weeks or months in the year. For a full year's work a labourer received 18 ducats and his food, a head cowman 24 ducats, and a mill-hand 14 ducats 2 *tarini*.[227] Food and drink were reckoned to cost 4 *tarini* a month for each man. At harvest time the farms recruited additional labour from the

---

[221] Cf. the judgement of Gentile ('Lo stato napoletano' (1938), p. 20): 'Il Re non solo aveva avuto di mira un fine giustissimo, di creare, cioè, una nuova e copiosa fonte di risorse per l'erario dello Stato, ma si rese degno di lode per aver dato incremento ad una cospicua industria, all'allevamento del bestiame.'

[222] ACA Reg. 2914. 58ᵛ, 6 June 1450.

[223] ACA Reg. 2915. 132ʳ, 15 Apr. 1451.

[224] ASN Dip. Somm. 631 (1) and 41 (1).   [225] ASN Signif. I. 23ᵛ.

[226] The farms under Macthes were Vulgano, Celone, Bardamento, Casalnuovo, and Fiorentino.

[227] These wages were considerably higher than those paid in the time of Robert of Anjou. Cf. Caggese, *Roberto d'Angiò*, i. 502 f.

uplands to the west and south. The harvesters worked in bands each under a leader from its own village who received all the wages on behalf of his team. Wages for such casual labour ranged from 15 *grana* to 1 *tarino* 10 *grana* a day exclusive of incentive payments.[228] In 1454 when the harvest amounted to 382 *carri* 52 *tomoli* of wheat and 128 *carri* 56 *tomoli* of barley, the harvest labour cost 571 ducats 9 *grana*. The yield of approximately sixfold in the grain crop of 1454 represents the average yield from average land in that age.[229] It was in the rearing of animals that the royal farms played an innovatory role. Much was done to improve the breed of horses, and merino sheep were introduced from Spain in order to stimulate the local manufacture of woollen cloth. A ban on the use of foreign woollen cloth imposed in 1465 signalled the success of this latter measure.

[228] e.g. the 4 ducats 10 *grana* given to Jacobo and Antonio Anteniri, 'li quali li donai cum loro sollicitudini facendoli metiri nante di et usque ad calata de soli quasi ad hori doy de nocte lo fecero meteri in una jornata ac per beveragio ut moris est.'

[229] *The Cambridge Economic History of Europe*, i. 377.

CONCLUSION

CROCE observed that one reason for the comparative neglect of southern-Italian history by historians was the failure of that region to give birth to a nation state.[1] Even as a regional state the kingdom of Naples in the latter centuries of its existence played only an undistinguished part in Italian and wider European affairs. Those years under Frederick II, Charles I, or Alfonso I, when it took the centre of the stage were, it might be argued, brief alien phases, false dawns of a great destiny which never came to light because their energy and inspiration came not from within. As long as the kingdom of Sicily remained united, the strength of the monarchy in the island, where feudalism on the grand scale had not taken root, more than made good its weakness on the mainland where the feudal nobility held predominant power. Furthermore, the great foreign rulers mentioned above could count on still broader support from their non-Italian possessions. Thus they were able to impose on the mainland territory a centralizing, authoritarian administration strong enough to cow or beat into submission the recalcitrant feudal aristocracy. Those rulers, on the other hand, who found themselves after the Sicilian Vespers confined to the kingdom of Naples were driven, either in consequence or in fear of baronial rebellion, to emasculate the royal administration. Ideas and institutions which might have provided the foundation for a modern state lacked here the room and sustenance for growth. Within fifty years of Alfonso's death the kingdom had been swallowed up as a mere province of his nephew's Spanish empire.

The later metamorphoses of the kingdom of Naples cannot, however, give a true measure of great periods in its history any more than the Florentine republic can be judged by its final off-spring, the Grand Duchy of Tuscany. That ideas know no frontiers is a commonplace; the same may be said of their manifestations as social and political institutions. Inspired solutions to administrative problems, like scientific discoveries or mechanical inventions, have an application wider than their original context and often

[1] B. Croce, *Storia del regno di Napoli* (Bari, 1944), p. 13.

far beyond the dreams of those who originate them. To determine how far and in what manner the apparatus of government which Alfonso created in Naples influenced the evolution of states elsewhere in Europe would require a study beyond the scope of this essay. In one direction at least the line of development is quite clear: the heir to that system was not viceregal Naples but imperial Spain.

What made the Neapolitan state of Alfonso rich in seminal principles was a fruitful interaction of Spanish and Italian genius, of energizing forces sufficiently akin in their common Mediterranean culture to harmonize, sufficiently dissimilar in their historical development to yield a hybrid of tough originality.[2] Like all states of the period, those of Italy and Spain took territorial expansion as the ultimate goal of political action—even Venice had turned in that direction—but whereas the Italian struggle to expand was largely internecine in character, that of the Iberian peoples looked outwards to the conquest of alien territory. The last Moorish foothold in the peninsula preoccupied Castile; Portugal was making rapid progress towards the acquisition of trade and territory in Africa and the islands of the Atlantic; Aragon pursued its aim of Mediterranean empire mainly at the expense of Italian rivals. Centuries of struggle against the vast world of Islam had played a major part in forging the Spanish political mentality; in Spanish religion it had bred a combative, disciplined quality which produced an identification of secular and ecclesiastical authority and virtues, a church obedient to the state. In Italy, on the contrary, the long-established antagonism between the papacy and temporal rulers and the newer impact of humanism had undermined the ideological efficacy of Catholicism and encouraged a secular understanding of political authority. Monarchical forms of government had given the Iberians an administrative and political education very different from that of all Italians save those who lived under the Sicilian crown. In this latter contrast some advantage lay with Spain for the future belonged to the absolute monarchy able to organize great populations and territories, not with those states, however sophisticated

---

[2] The theme of Spanish and Italian elements in the territories of the Corona de Aragón under Alfonso was discussed at a Congress held in Naples in April 1973. M. del Treppo has published a preliminary report, 'The "Crown of Aragon" and the Mediterranean' in *Journal of European Economic History*, 2 (1973), 161–85.

their government, whose interest could not transcend a single city or region.

In the fifteenth century the nature of international conflict had not yet laid bare the inherent weakness of the Italian states. On the contrary they possessed the means to hold their own with assurance against the other powers of Europe and to lead them in statecraft as in other arts. In the diversity of its political systems Italy offered a stimulating challenge to the Aragonese monarchy, forcing it to justify its ideals and practices in the face of rival concepts.[3] Interaction between Spain and Italy gained heightened significance at this time because that phase of cultural innovation known as the Renaissance made Italy the intellectual hub of Europe. Aragonese domination of the south exposed that Spanish kingdom earlier and more intensively than any other non-Italian state to Renaissance ways of thinking and seeing. The kingdom of Naples did not, it is true, make any significant contribution from its own cultural resources; a century of misgovernment had enfeebled artistic and intellectual life there to an extent where Alfonso himself was able to play the part of a great reviver of the arts, calling to that end upon the resources of Spain as well as Italy. He had also, as we have emphasized, to restore a very dilapidated edifice of state, but in this task the kingdom was able to afford a major contribution of materials, for it was endowed with institutions and administrative experience which still retained some of the lustre with which they had once outshone all of Europe.

The combination of Spanish and Italian genius in this challenging environment carried forward the evolution of the modern European state in a degree no whit less important than the advances achieved under Alfonso's great Norman, Hohenstaufen, and Angevin predecessors. Considering the short space of time in which so many innovations and reforms were accomplished, the concentration of change upon the centre of administration, and the apparent determination to alter the balance of power within the state which motivated that change, one might indeed claim that here was a revolution in government. And it was a revolution that succeeded. Alfonso's achievement in reinforcing the power of the crown, so reversing the swing which had for a century favoured

---

[3] e.g. the controversy with the papacy in the polemics of which Valla played a notable part. Cf. above, p. 222, and Holmes, *The Florentine Enlightenment*, p. 136.

baronial pretensions, survived desperate attempts to redress the balance in the reign of his son; an irreversible adjustment had been achieved at the expense of one of the best entrenched feudal aristocracies of Europe.

Undue attention to Alfonso's concessions of jurisdiction to the baronage has obscured his success in reducing them effectively to the status of subjects. This he did by freeing the crown from dependence upon feudal modes of finance and military service. Throughout Italy warfare was becoming increasingly the business of hired professionals whose service was regulated by flexible agreements (*condotte*) drawn up as formal contracts between themselves and governments.[4] Under the later Angevins that method of conducting war, with all the advantages it carried over the rigid formality imposed by reliance upon a feudal host, had penetrated into the kingdom even though the feudal military system was more firmly rooted there than in any other part of Italy. Alfonso took the decisive step of abandoning feudal military service altogether. The Neapolitan nobility remained still a warrior caste, but they were converted into *condottieri*, permitted to bear arms and recruit followers only in the service of the state.

A ruler who thus transformed the nature of his military power had also to revolutionize his finances, for the hired army could only be assembled and put into action by a large and reliable flow of cash. The old convention that the king should 'live of his own', aided in exceptional circumstances by extraordinary grants of taxation, broke down completely in face of these novel military demands. The sadly diminished royal demesne had in practice long since ceased to be the backbone of royal finance. Alfonso made no attempt to restore it to that role or to refurbish the medieval panoply of tax-gathering instruments; instead he developed the concept and administrative competence of the Royal Patrimony so that it became virtually synonymous with the public wealth of the state. Permanent, direct taxes became the most substantial items of the revenue.

The broader fiscal foundation on which Alfonso established his government received its sanction from parliaments only one of which was composed exclusively of tenants-in-chief. In admitting representatives of the demesne to all but the first of these assemblies, Alfonso was consciously harking back to the more universal

---

[4] Cf. Mallett, *Mercenaries and their Masters*.

concept of them which had inspired Frederick II. The feudal nobility found their influence thereby diminished, for the tenants-in-chief could no longer confront the crown as sole spokesman for the whole community. They lost ground in still more telling fashion in the offices of central government to the cohorts of middle-rank professionals—men of law and business to whom Alfonso entrusted the management of affairs. Behind their protests can plainly be heard the march of the authoritarian, bureaucratic state.

The struggle which Alfonso waged against the forces of particularism within the kingdom of Naples was matched by a wider contest with equivalent forces in the many kingdoms and principalities he ruled from Naples. In both endeavours he was motivated primarily by military necessity. Having embarked on a policy of Mediterranean expansion which could only succeed by concentrating the resources of all his territories, he was driven to devise machinery for that purpose. Overarching the federative empire of Aragon he brought into being a number of offices and tribunals with a general competence—a treasurer general, an auditor general, a conservator general, the Sacrum Consilium, and the Consilium Pecuniae are those to which we have drawn particular attention in this study. Considerations of finance played a major part in determining the initial direction of this development, but it had a far more general significance in that it set the course of that imperial administration which Spain was to elaborate in a spectacular manner in the following century.

Most states of Europe were following a similar path towards a greater emphasis on sovereignty, the consolidation of monarchical power against the competing authority of magnates, and the associated concentration of military, bureaucratic, and judicial powers in the apparatus of a centralized state. In the Italian context the Neapolitan baronage may have enjoyed peculiar licence, but their anarchical spirit hardly outdid the strong-arm behaviour of the English nobility[5] or the chronic disaffection of the French;[6] in Castile the authority of the crown over the nobility had suffered a setback in the struggle between Pedro and the Trastamares

[5] Cf. M. Keen, *England in the Later Middle Ages* (London, 1973), pp. 500–1; B. Wilkinson, *Constitutional History of England in the Fifteenth Century, 1399–1485* (London, 1964), p. 335.

[6] P. S. Lewis, *Later Medieval France* (London, 1968), pp. 226–37.

from which it was not to recover until the reign of Ferdinand and
Isabella.[7] The response of rulers to these challenges took forms
which had much in common, partly, one suspects, because they
were ready to adopt measures that had proved their worth elsewhere. Thus Charles VII of France, like Alfonso, seized the
opportunity offered by the ending of civil war to strip his nobles
of their private armies. In England the effective consolidation of
military power and initiative in the hands of the ruler had to await
the victory of Henry VII, but the transformation of the king's
court and council from the appendages of personal monarchy into
the bureaucracy of an 'impersonal crown' made slow progress
throughout the fifteenth century.[8] A great expansion of the
English council's judicial functions and the growing distinction
between the advisory privy council and the continual council for
justice and administration had much in common with developments in Naples, although the greater influence of court and
nobility in the English council left it still uncertain whether its
enhanced authority would in the end reinforce the power of the
crown or that of the magnates. A fair measure of the different
character of English and Aragonese government can be gathered
from the fact that of fifty-nine identified counsellors in the reign of
Edward IV, a king of authoritarian bent, a very large majority
were 'lords of council' and only eight doctors of law. In the
Aragonese council, where the balance of authority had tipped
decisively towards professional servants of the crown, the propor-
tions were almost exactly reversed. The French royal council, like
the English, remained very susceptible to noble influence,[9] and it
lagged behind the latter, and still more that of Alfonso, in the
degree to which its functions had become differentiated.

A common preoccupation with war and armies produced a
common attention to revenues and expenditure, so that in this
sphere of government too some comparison of states is possible.
In sophistication the fiscal system which Alfonso elaborated in
Naples for his Italian kingdom and his wider dominions can
fairly be claimed to have outranked its contemporaries. French
financial administration lacked the unity and definition achieved
by the Neapolitan Sommaria and treasury; and whereas Alfonso

---

[7] Cf. M. Keen, *A History of Medieval Europe* (London, 1967), p. 231.
[8] Wilkinson, *Constitutional History*, p. 214.
[9] Lewis, *Later Medieval France*, p. 129.

imposed an ever tighter central control upon the financial offices of the crown, the kings of France permitted a contrary trend of decentralization which gave a large part of financial supervision to regional *parlements* and *chambres des comptes*. In England the fifteenth century witnessed no great advances in administration;[10] medieval devices, such as seals and tallies, continued to enjoy an anachronistic importance in the management of finance. The 'new' state of Burgundy, by contrast, came much closer to Aragon in the degree and style of administrative innovation exemplified by the Thionville Ordinances of 1473.[11]

Within Italy the comparisons are less easily drawn because of the very different nature of government in Naples and in most other states of the peninsula. Nevertheless many of the bureaucratic procedures adopted by Alfonso were plainly of Italian origin and his preoccupation with administrative reform was itself much influenced by a need to take account of trends in those Italian states with which he found himself in conflict. The Visconti of Milan had begun to counter local particularism with the creation of central councils and a provincial organization staffed by 'new men'.[12] Medicean influence in Florence depended a good deal upon the recruitment to its cause of lawyers who were ready to make the processes of law serve the will of the executive.[13] More importantly the King of Naples was forced to heed those new methods of military organization which his Italian rivals adopted. This competitive exposure of Aragon to the more sophisticated bureaucratic techniques of the Italian communal states and lordships reinforced the influence of that urban patriciate in Catalonia and Valencia which lived in the same world of business and culture as the oligarchies of Italy. It is no accident that Alfonso drew most of the technicians of his regime from that class; the needs of the king in Italy gave them and their master their head in a setting free from the rein which constitutions and custom placed upon them in their homeland.[14] The result was a significant leap forward in the development of the European state.

[10] Wilkinson, *Constitutional History*, p. 271.

[11] Cf. J. Calmette, *The Golden Age of Burgundy* (London, 1962); R. Vaughan, *Philip the Bold* (London, 1962); M. Keen, *Medieval Europe*, pp. 236–8. It is perhaps significant that cordial relations existed between the Aragonese and Burgundian courts during Alfonso's reign and thereafter.

[12] Cf. B. Pullan, *A History of Early Renaissance Italy* (London, 1973), p. 270.

[13] Cf. ibid., pp. 281–2.   [14] Cf. above, p. 18.

SOURCES

A. Manuscript Sources

I. ARCHIVIO DI STATO DI NAPOLI

THE years of Alfonso's government in Naples led to the accumulation there of a great volume of archival material relevant to all parts of the Aragonese empire. The division of that empire at the king's death led to an immediate, and probably hasty, division of these records between his two heirs—Ferdinand, the new ruler of Naples, and Juan II of Aragon.[1] A mass of documents belonging to the Neapolitan administrative offices, and notably the archives of the Sommaria, remained in Naples. So too did 106 chancery registers concerned solely with the kingdom.[2] Of the latter volumes only one has survived the Neapolitan risings of 1647 and 1701.[3] Most of the Sommaria records perished in 1943.

Privilegiorum I

Diversi della Regia Camera della Sommaria

I. 4   Istrumenti etc. per la mensa vescovile di Potenza etc.

I. 10   Introitus ex demaniis Calabrie et inquisitio terrarum Calabrie a. 1456–1458.

I. 52 (bis) Commissionum diversorum regum et variorum annorum.

I. 133   Cedulare Provincie Terre Laboris citra flumen Garigliani duarum collectarum recollectarum per Angelum de Martino commissarium.

I. 149   Privilegi varii di Alfonso I e Ferrante per Reggio ed i Cardona.

I. 166   Inquisitio collectarum et aliarum funcionum a tempore obitus condam domine regine Johanne secunde et per totum annum quinte indictionis nuper elapsum a. 1442.

---

[1] R. Moscati, 'Ricerche su gli atti superstiti della cancelleria napoletana di Alfonso d'Aragona', *Rivista storica italiana* (1953).

[2] See above, p. 254.

[3] This is the volume of privileges described as 'Registrum Secundum' in the onomastic index of these registers (BNN MS. XIV. A24). Cf. J. Mazzoleni, 'Fonti per la storia dell'epoca aragonese esistenti nell'Archivio di Stato di Napoli', *ASPN* 1951, 1952, and 1956.

Dipendenze della Regia Camera della Sommaria

41 (1)   In nel presente libro se contene particularitamente tucto
         lo introyto et exito tanto de dinar quanto de victuaglye
         et altre cose administrate per Bernardo Macthes Mastro
         Maxaro del S. Re in ne la provincia de pulya in presente
         anno tercie Ind. MCCCCLiiii.

48   Quaterno ad rasone de la gabella de la grassia de la pro-
         vincia de terra de labore ordinato et facto per lo Magnifico
         misser Carrafello Carrafa commissario deputato per la Ma:ª
         del S. Re sopra la dicta gabella presentata et assignata per
         ipso inde la regia Camera de la Summaria continente
         intrata et uscita de tucto dinaro che ave perceputo assignato
         et pagato tanto per parte de lo anno de la xij. Ind. quanto de
         lo anno de la xiij. Ind.

178   Cedula prima de la fabrica de Castellammare de Stabia per
         me Joanne Rubio regio commissario a. 1451.

189 (1) Conto della fabrica del castello di Gaeta a. 1449.

    (2)   Registro di conti a. 1453.

314 (1) Quaterno continente lo introytu et exito dele spoglie delo
         quondam archiepiscopo de Idronto che in mano ad paulo
         de brosco de Atella de la Regia Thesauraria et in questo
         regio commissario so pervenute.

547   Quaternus factus et ordinatus per me octavianus de ho-
         stunio officii erariatus civitatis Ascoli ac Baronie vici et
         flumari et terrarum et locorum aliorum infrascriptorum
         continens particullariter introytum eorum et exitum
         quorumcumque iurium et introytuum ipsarum spectantium
         et pertinentium principali curie exactarum per me pre-
         scriptum erarium infra annum presentem xiii. Ind. ac de
         omnibus pecuniis solutis et liberatis nomine principalis
         curie per me prefatum principalem generalem erarium infra
         tempus predictum.

568 (1) Questo e lo quaterno de lo mezo thomolo de lo sale de
         Septembro quinte Ind. liberato per me paris Antello
         erario de la citate de Aversa ali homini de la dicta cita porta
         per porta.

631 (1) En lo present libre se conte particularment tota la entrada
         e exida axi de diners com de forments ordis e altres vitualles
         percebides dela maçaria del Senyor Rey e pervengudes en
         mans de Bernat Mates mastro maçaro dela dita Maçaria
         la qual mana fer lo dit S. en la provincia de pulla en lany
         present dela xv. Ind. MCCCCLii.

(2)   Quaterno denunciacionum anni ii. Ind. MCCCCLiiii curie domini viceregis Calabrie.

Frammento di Comune Summarie (presso il museo degli Archivi di Stato)
A fragment of 12 leaves numbered 11 to 22, August–September 1444.

Fascicoli Comune della Sommaria (presso il museo degli Archivi di Stato)
I. ff. 47–104, September–December 1445.
   ff. 111–24, August–December 1445.
   ff. 1–17,   April–May 1452.
   ff. 124–41, May–June 1453.
   f. 13,   2 January 1458.

Lictere Passus I
Relevi Originali
vol. 1.   Terra di Lavoro e Contado di Molise.
vol. 33. Terra di Lavoro e Contado di Molise.
vol. 252. Principato Citra e Basilicata.
vol. 287. Principato Ultra e Capitanata.

Significatorie vol. I
Pergamene dell'Archivio di Stato
Pergamene di Lucera
Pergamene di Aquila

II. ARCHIVO DE LA CORONA DE ARAGÓN

The registers transferred to Spain after Alfonso's death fared better than those left in Naples for they, in common with the other records in the *Archivo de la Corona de Aragón*, have escaped devastation. Consequently they represent by far the most important source of original material extant for the study of Aragonese rule in Naples from 1435 to 1458.

The main series of chancery registers has been numbered consecutively from the earliest to the latest. Those belonging to the reign of Alfonso V range approximately from number 2,400 to 3,300. Within that range are three main divisions for the registers produced by the chanceries of the king and those of his two *locumtenentes generales*, Queen Maria and Juan of Navarre. Those brought from Naples belong to the first category, the Registros del Rey. They have lost their original numeration, but the classification appears to follow that employed in the Neapolitan chancery. Some confusion was introduced by a reclassification carried out by the archivist Carbonell (1476–1529) and in the process of binding the registers in the eighteenth century. Carbonell went carefully through the registers embellishing blank leaves with his signature and misclassifying some of the volumes. For those volumes concerned with Neapolitan affairs he established a division which he called Cancillería de Napoles. In it he included register 2901, which is devoted almost entirely to the accounts of the treasurers in Spain, and registers 2910 and 2919, which belong in fact to the Sicilian series. On the other hand, there are many registers outside the Cancillería de Napoles which contain documents directly related to the affairs of the kingdom. Those responsible for the binding frequently put together two or three small registers or fragments of registers in order to make one volume of average size. Register 2800, for example, consists of two fragments, one of sixty-three leaves and another of twenty-seven leaves, bound together. When, as in this instance, both fragments belong to the same category, no great difficulty arises. In register 2908 (Privilegiorum), however, one discovers that the first fifty-one leaves are a fragment of a *Comune* register. Register 2916 (classified as Privilegiorum from the Cancillería de Napoles) is still more mixed in character: it contains several fragments, only one of them having privileges for the kingdom; one consists of letters to officials in Sicily, and another of privileges issued *ex officio* by the protonotary of Naples. These are, however, minor defects in an archive which poses for the scholar the more rewarding problems of superabundance.

Registros del Rey

Commune (1416–58)	2455–559
Commune sigilli secreti (1416–41)	2560–84
Officialium (1444–58)	2598–602
Officialium Cataloniae (1416–58)	2603–8
Diversorum Regii Patrimonii (1416–57)	2609–25
Curiae (1416–58)	2641–62
Curiae sigilli secreti (1416–46)	2663–90
Secretorum (1416–58)	2691–700
Pecuniae (1416–58)	2701–22
Sententiarum (1416–56)	2737–46
Itinerum (1416–49)	2747–80
Itinerum sigilli secreti (1420–46)	2781–95
Exercitum et Curiarum (1419–58)	2796–800
Curiae (Cancillería de Napoles) (1436–46)	2900–1
Privilegiorum (Cancillería de Napoles) (1440–58)	2902–19
Marcarum (1416–55)	2924–5

Notariorum (1425–58)	2928–31
Instructionum (1440–53)	2939
Litterarum et Albaranorum (1446–52)	2940
Venditionum (Cancillería de Napoles) (1444–58)	2943
Gratiarum (Cancillería de Napoles) (1443–58)	2945
Speciale (Siciliae) (1456–8)	2946

Real Patrimonio

1411
2011 Seca de Napoles
2910(3) Maestre Racional
2951 Creditos contra la curia real de Sicilia (1448–50)

III. ARCHIVO DE LA CIUDAD DE BARCELONA

Lletres Closes

322, ser. vi. 9, 1442–4.
323, ser. vi. 10, 1444–5.
328, ser. vi. 15, 1450.

Cartas Comunas Originales Recibidas

487, ser. x, vol. 12, 1442.
488, ser. x, vol. 13, 1443.
489, ser. x, vol. 14, 1444.
492, ser. x, vol. 17, 1447.
493, ser. x, vol. 18, 1448.
495, ser. x, vol. 20, 1450.
496, ser. x, vol. 21, 1451.
497, ser. x, vol. 22, 1452.
498, ser. x, vol. 23, 1453.
499, ser. x, vol. 24, 1454.
500, ser. x, vol. 25, 1455.
501, ser. x, vol. 26, 1456.
502, ser. x, vol. 27, 1457.
503, ser. x, vol. 28, 1458.

IV. BIBLIOTECA NAZIONALE DI NAPOLI

MS. X. B 2   Afeltri Antonii. Excerpta autographa ex regiis monar-
chicisque archivis etc.

MS. XIV. A 24 Onomastic index to the chancery registers of Alfonso
which were retained in Naples.

Biblioteca Brancacciana
MS. II. F 6   Notar Giacomo.
MS. III. E 7   Diario di cose occorse in Neapoli dal 1266 al 1478.
MS. IV. B 10   Chronica di Matteo Spinello.

B. Printed Sources

AENEAS SYLVIUS (PICCOLOMINI) *Commentarius in libros Antonii Panor-mitae de dictis et factis Alphonsi regis* (Basle, 1538).

—— *Pii Secundi Pontificis Maximi commentarii* (Frankfurt, 1614).

ALBÉRI, E., *Relazioni degli ambasciatori veneti al Senato*, 15 vols. (Florence, 1839–63).

ALTAMURA, A., *L'Umanesimo nel Mezzogiorno d'Italia* (Florence, 1941).

AMETLLER Y VINYAS, J., *Alfonso V de Aragón en Italia y la crisis religiosa del siglo XV*, 3 vols. (Gerona, 1903–28).

ANON. 'Come lo Imperatore Federico entrò in Napoli e poi lo 4 dì entrò l'Imperatrice in Aversa', *Archivio storico per le province napoletane* (1908).

—— 'Racconti di storia napoletana', *Archivio storico per le province napoletane* (1908).

BAER, F., *A History of the Jews in Christian Spain* (Philadelphia, 1966).

BAROZZI, L., and SABBADINI, R., *Studi sul Panormita e sul Valla* (Florence, 1891).

BARZIZZA, G., *Orationes et epistolae* (Rome, 1723).

BECCADELLI, A., *De dictis et factis Alphonsi regis* (Basle, 1538).

—— *Epistolae campanae* (Venice, 1553).

BELOCH, C. J., *Bevölkerungsgeschichte Italiens*, vol. i, ed. G. de Sanctis (Leipzig, 1937).

BIANCHINI, L., *Della storia delle finanze del Regno di Napoli* (Palermo, 1839), 2nd edn.

DA BISTICCI, V., 'Vita del re Alfonso d'Aragona', *Archivio storico italiano*, IV, pt. 1 (1843).

DE BOFARULL Y MASCARÓ, P., *Coleccion de documentos inéditos del Archivo General de la Corona de Aragón*, cuadernos 22, 23, 24 (Barcelona, 1850).

DE BOTTIS, N., *Privilegii et capitoli con altre gratie concesse alla fidelissima città di Napoli, e Regno per li Sereniss. Rè di Casa de Aragona* (Venice, 1588).

DE BOÜARD, A., *Documents en français des archives angevines de Naples*, 2 vols. (Paris, 1933).

BURCKHARDT, J. C., *The Civilisation of the Renaissance in Italy* (Phaidon Press, London, n.d.).

CADIER, L., *Essai sur l'administration du royaume de Sicile sous Charles I et Charles II d'Anjou*. Bibliothèque des Écoles françaises d'Athènes et de Rome, fasc. 59 (Paris, 1891).

CAGGESE, R., *Roberto d'Angiò e i suoi tempi*, 2 vols. (Florence, 1921).

CALMETTE, J., *The Golden Age of Burgundy* (London, 1962).

CANELLAS, A., *El Reino de Aragón en los años 1410–1458*, IV Congreso de Historia de la Corona de Aragón (Palma de Mallorca, 1955).

CAPASSO, B., *Le fonti della storia delle province napoletane dal 568 al 1500* (Naples, 1902).

—— *Inventario cronòlogico-sistematico dei registri angioini* (Naples, 1894).

CARABELLESE, F., *La Puglia nel secolo XV, da fonti inedite* (Bari, 1901).

CARACCIOLO, T., *De varietate fortunae. Rerum italicarum scriptores*, XXII (ed. Bologna, 1934).

CARUSO, A., 'Circa l'origine del Sacro Regio Consiglio', *Il rievocatore* (Naples, 1956).

DELLA CASA, G., 'Alfonsi regis vita', *Opere*, iv (Venice, 1728).

CASPAR, E., *Roger II (1101–1154) und die Gründung der normannisch-sicilischen Monarchie* (Innsbruck, 1904).

CASSANDRO, G., 'Sulle origini del Sacro Consiglio napoletano', *Studi in onore di Riccardo Filangieri*, ii (Naples, 1959).

CERONE, F., 'La politica orientale di Alfonso d'Aragona', *Archivio storico per le province napoletane* (1902).

CHAYTOR, H. J., *A History of Aragon and Catalonia* (London, 1933).

CHIOCCARELLO, B., *Archivio della reggia giurisdizione del Regno di Napoli* (Venice, 1701).

VAN CLEVE, T. C., *The Emperor Frederick II of Hohenstaufen* (Oxford, 1972).

DI COSTANZO, A., *Historia del regno di Napoli* (Naples, 1710).

CROCE, B., *Storia del regno di Napoli*, 3rd edn. (Bari, 1944).

—— *La Spagna nella vita italiana* (Bari, 1917).

—— *Storie e leggende napoletane*, 3rd edn. (Bari, 1948).

CUTOLO, A., *Re Ladislao d'Angiò Durazzo* (Naples, 1969).

DUFOURCQ, C.-E., *L'Espagne catalane et le Maghrib aux XIIIᵉ. et XIV. siècles* (Paris, 1966).

DU MONT, J., *Corps universel diplomatique du droit des gens* (Amsterdam, 1726).

Dupré Theseider, E., *La politica italiana di Alfonso d'Aragona* (Bologna, n.d.).

Durrieu, P., *Les Archives angevines de Naples. Études sur les registres du roi Charles I (1265–1285)*, 2 vols. (Paris, 1886–7).

Eubel, C., *Hierarchia Catholica medii aevi*, ii (Münster, 1913).

Facio, B., *De rebus gestis ab Alphonso primo Neapolitanorum rege commentariorum libri X*, in J. G. Graevius and P. Burmannus, *Thesaurus antiquitatum et historiarum Italiae* (Leiden, 1723).

Faraglia, N. F., *Storia della lotta tra Alfonso V d'Aragona e Renato d'Angiò* (Lanciano, 1908).

—— *Diurnali detti del Duca di Monteleone*, ed. (Naples, 1895).

—— *Codice diplomatico sulmonese* (Lanciano, 1888).

—— *Il comune nell'Italia meridionale* (Naples, 1883).

Fazello, T., *De rebus siculis decades* (Palermo, 1558).

Filangieri, G., 'Nuovi documenti intorno la famiglia, le case, e le vicende di Lucrezia d'Alagno', *Archivio storico per le province napoletane* (1886).

Filangieri di Candida, R., *Castel Nuovo, reggia angioina ed aragonese di Napoli* (Naples, 1934).

——, 'La peinture flamande à Naples pendant le 15e siècle', *Revue belge d'archéologie et d'histoire de l'art*, 2 (1932).

Foucard, C., 'Descrizione della città di Napoli e statistica del Regno nel 1444', *Archivio storico per le province napoletane* (1877).

—— 'Proposta fatta dalla Corte Estense ad Alfonso I Re di Napoli', *Archivio storico per le province napoletane* (1879).

de Frede, B. C., 'Un medico-filosofo del Rinascimento', *Archivio storico per le province napoletane* (1958).

—— 'Roberto Sanseverino Principe di Salerno', *Rassegna storica salernitana* (1951).

Fueros y observancias del Reyno de Aragón (Zaragoza, 1667).

Gentile, P., 'Finanze e parlamenti nel Regno di Napoli dal 1450 al 1467', *Archivio storico per le province napoletane* (1913).

—— 'Lo stato napoletano sotto Alfonso I d'Aragona', *Archivio storico per le province napoletane* (1937 and 1938).

Giannone, P., *Istoria civile del regno di Napoli*, 5 vols. (Palermo, 1762).

Giesey, R. E., *If not, not* (Princeton, 1968).

Goffredus de Gaeta, *Ritus regiae Camerae Summariae regni Neapolis* (Naples, 1689).

GOTHEIN, E., *Il Rinascimento nell'Italia meridionale* (Florence, 1915).

GREGORIO, R., *Opere scelte* (Palermo, 1845).

HASKINS, C. H., 'England and Sicily in the twelfth century', *English Historical Review* (1911).

HAY, D., *The Italian Renaissance in its historical background* (Cambridge, 1966).

HEER, F., *The Medieval World* (London, 1962).

HIGHFIELD, R., *Spain in the Fifteenth Century, 1369–1516* (Macmillan, London, 1972).

HOLMES, G., *The Florentine Enlightenment, 1400–1450* (London, 1969).

INCARNATO, G., 'Il possesso feudale in Abruzzo ultra dal 1500 al 1670', *Archivio storico per le province napoletane* (1972).

IORGA, N., *Notes et extraits pour servir à l'histoire des croisades au XVᵉ siècle*, 3 vols. (Paris and Bucharest, 1899–1915).

JAMISON, E., 'The Norman administration of Apulia and Capua, more especially under Roger II and William I', *Papers of the British School at Rome*, VI (London, 1913).

KEEN, M. H., *A History of Medieval Europe* (London, 1967).

—— *England in the Later Middle Ages* (London, 1973).

KLEIN, J., *The 'Mesta'* (Cambridge, 1920).

KRISTELLER, P. O., 'The humanist Bartolomeo Facio and his unknown correspondence', *From Renaissance to Counter-Reformation*, ed. C. H. Carter (London, 1966).

LAUER, P., 'Les reliures des manuscrits des rois aragonais de Naples conservées à la Bibliothéque Nationale', *Bulletin philologique et historique*, 1928–9.

LAURENZA, V., 'Il Panormita a Napoli', *Atti della Accademia Pontaniana*, XVII (Naples, 1936).

LÉONARD, E. G., *Les Angevins de Naples* (Paris, 1954).

LEWIS, P. S., *Later Medieval France: the Polity* (London, 1968).

LIONTI, F., *Codice diplomatico di Alfonso il Magnanimo* (Palermo, 1891).

MACDONALD, I., *Fernando de Antequera* (Dolphin Press, Oxford, 1948).

MACK SMITH, D., *A History of Sicily. Medieval Sicily, 800–1713* (London, 1968).

MALLETT, M., *Mercenaries and their Masters: Warfare in Renaissance Italy* (London, 1974).

MADURELL MARIMÓN, J. M., *Mensajeros barceloneses en la corte de Nápoles de Alfonso V de Aragón, 1435–1458* (Barcelona, 1963).

MARINESCU, C., 'Alphonse V roi d'Aragon et de Naples, et l'Albanie de Scanderbeg', *Mélanges de l'École roumaine en France*, I (Paris, 1923).

—— 'Notes sur les corsaires au service d'Alfonse V d'Aragon, roi de Naples', *Mélanges d'histoire générale de l'Université de Cluj*, I (1927).

—— 'Notes sur le faste à la cour d'Alfonse V d'Aragon, roi de Naples', ibid.

MARINIS, T. DE, *La biblioteca napoletana dei re d'Aragona* (Milan, 1948).

MARLETTA, F., 'Un uomo di stato del Quattrocento: Battista Platamone', *Archivio storico per la Sicilia*, I (1937).

MARONGIU, A., 'Il parlamento baronale nel 1443', *Samnium* (1950).

—— *Il parlamento in Italia* (Milan, 1962).

MARTORELL, F., *Alguns aspectes de la vida intima d'Alfons el Magnanim* (Barcelona, 1938).

MASIÁ, A., 'El maestre racional en la Corona de Aragón: una pragmatica de Juan II', *Hispania*, 38 (1950).

MASSON, G., *Frederick II of Hohenstaufen* (London, 1957).

MAZZATINTI, G., *La biblioteca dei Re d'Aragona in Napoli* (Naples, 1897).

MAZZOLENI, B., *Frammento del 'Quaternus Sigilli Pendentis' di Alfonso I (1452–1453). Il Registro 'Sigillorum Summarie Magni Sigilli XLVI' (1469–1470). Fonti aragonesi*, iii (Naples, 1963).

MAZZOLENI, J., *Regesto della cancelleria aragonese di Napoli* (Naples, 1951).

—— 'Fonti per la storia dell'epoca Aragonese esistenti nell'archivio di Stato di Napoli', *Archivio storico per le province napoletane* (1951), (1952), (1956).

—— *Il registro privilegiorum summarie XLIII (1421–1450); Frammenti di Cedole della tesoreria di Alfonso (1437–1454). Fonti aragonesi*, i (Naples, 1957).

—— *Il 'Codice Chigi', un registro della cancelleria di Alfonso I d'Aragona Re di Napoli per gli anni 1451–1453* (Naples, 1965).

MERRIMAN, R. B., *The rise of the Spanish Empire in the Old World and in the New*, 4 vols. (New York, 1934–6).

MINIERI RICCIO, C., 'L'ordine della Giarretta', *Archivio storico per le province napoletane* (1877).

—— 'Alcuni fatti di Alfonso I di Aragona dal 15 apr. 1437 — 31 maggio 1458', *Archivio storico per le province napoletane* (1881).

—— *Saggio di codice diplomatico*, ii (Naples, 1880). Suppl. I (Naples, 1878). Suppl. II (Naples, 1883).

MONTI, G. M., 'Da Carlo I a Roberto di Angiò. Ricerche e documenti', *Archivio storico per le province napoletane* (1933).

—— *Nuovi studi angioini* (Trani, 1937).

382 SOURCES

MOREL-FATIO, A., 'Fernand de Cordoue', *Recueil de travaux à J. Havet* (Paris, 1895).

MOSCATI, R., 'Ricerche su gli atti superstiti della cancelleria napoletana di Alfonso d'Aragona', *Rivista storica italiana* (1953).

MUTA, M., *Capitulorum regni Siciliae constitutionum et pragmaticarum,* iv (Palermo, 1614).

PAGÉS, A., *Ausias March et ses prédécesseurs* (Paris, 1911).

PALUMBO, L., *Andrea d'Isernia* (Naples, 1886).

PARTNER, P., *The Papal State under Martin V* (London, 1958).

PASTOR, L., *The History of the Popes from the close of the Middle Ages,* ii (London, 1891).

PECCHIA, C., *Storia civile e politica del Regno di Napoli* (Naples, 1783).

PONTIERI, E., *L'età dell'equilibrio politico in Italia (1454–1494)* (Naples, n.d.).

—— 'Muzio Attendolo e Francesco Sforza nei conflitti dinastico-civili nel regno di Napoli al tempo di Giovanna II d'Angiò-Durazzo', *Divagazioni storiche e storiografiche* (Naples, n.d.).

—— 'Alfonso V d'Aragona nel quadro della politica italiana del suo tempo', ibid.

—— 'Camillo Porzio storico', *Archivio storico per le province napoletane* (1958).

—— *I registri della cancelleria vicereale di Calabria (1422–1453). Fonti aragonesi,* II (Naples, 1961).

—— *La Calabria a metà del secolo XV e le rivolte di Antonio Centelles* (Naples, 1963).

——, 'La "Guerra dei Baroni" ', *Archivio storico per le province napoletane* (1972).

POSTAN, M. M. (ed.), *The Cambridge Economic History of Europe,* I, 2nd edn. (Cambridge, 1966).

PULLAN, B., *A History of Early Renaissance Italy from the mid-thirteenth to the mid-fifteenth century* (London, 1973).

PYBUS, H. J., 'Frederick II and the Sicilian church', *Cambridge Historical Journal* (1930).

RESTA, G., *L'epistolario del Panormita* (Messina, 1954).

RODRIGUEZ MARÍN, F., *Guia histórica de los archivos de España* (Madrid, 1916).

ROGADEO, E., *Codice diplomatico barese,* vol. ii (Bari, 1931).

ROSSI, G. C., 'Sulmona ai tempi di Alfonso il Magnanimo', *Archivio storico per le province napoletane* (1964).

RUNCIMAN, S., *The Sicilian Vespers* (Harmondsworth, 1960).

RYDER, A. F. C., 'La politica italiana di Alfonso d'Aragona', *Archivio storico per le province napoletane* (1959–60).

——, 'The evolution of imperial government in Naples under Alfonso V of Aragon', in *Europe in the late Middle Ages*, ed. J. Hale, R. Highfield, B. Smalley (London, 1965).

SALVATI, C., *Frammenti dei registri 'Commune Summarie' (1444–1459)*; *Frammenti di cedole della tesoreria di Alfonso I (1446–1448)*. *Fonti aragonesi*, IV (Naples, 1964).

SANCHIS Y SIVERA, J., *Dietari del capellá d'Anfos el Magnànim* (Valencia, 1932).

SCHIAPPOLI, I., 'La marina degli Aragonesi di Napoli', *Archivio storico per le province napoletane* (1940).

SHENNAN, J. H., *Government and Society in France, 1461–1661* (London, 1969).

SOLDEVILA, F., *Historia de Catalunya* (Barcelona, 1938).

SUMMONTE, G. A., *Historia della città e Regno di Napoli*, 6 vols. (Naples, 1748–9).

TIRRITO, M. C., *Nuovi documenti sul Panormita* (Catania, 1900).

TOPPI, N., *De origine tribunalium urbis Neapolis*, 3 vols. (Naples, 1659).

DEL TREPPO, M., 'The "Crown of Aragon" and the Mediterranean', *Journal of European Economic History*, 2 (1973).

TRIFONE, R., 'Il pensiero giuridico e l'opera legislativa di Bartolommeo di Capua', *Scritti per A. Maiorano* (Catania, 1913).

—— *La legislazione angioina* (Naples, 1921).

TUTINI, C., *Discorsi de sette officii overo de sette grandi del regno di Napoli. Parte prima, nella quale si tratta del contestabile, del maestro giustitieri, e dell'ammirante* (Rome, 1666).

ULLMANN, W., *The medieval idea of law as represented by Lucas de Penna* (London, 1946).

—— *Principles of government and politics in the Middle Ages*, 2nd edn. (London, 1966).

——, *The Individual and Society in the Middle Ages* (London, 1967).

USÓN SESÉ, M., 'Un formulario latino de la Cancillería Real Aragonesa (siglo XIV)', *Anuario de historia del derecho español* (1930).

VARIUS, D. A., *Pragmaticae edicta decreta interdicta regiaeque sanctiones regni napoletani*, vol. i (Naples, 1772).

VAUGHAN, R., *Philip the Bold: the formation of the Burgundian state* (London, 1962).

VICENS VIVES, J., *Fernando el Católico* (Madrid, 1952).

VICENS VIVES, J., *Els Trastamares* (Barcelona, 1956).

VITALE, V., *Trani dagli angioini agli spagnuoli* (Bari, 1912).

WALEY, D., *Later Medieval Europe* (London, 1964).

WEISS, R., 'The translators from the Greek of the Angevin court of Naples', *Rinascimento* (1950).

—— 'The Greek culture of south Italy in the later Middle Ages', *Proceedings of the British Academy* (1953).

WILKS, M., *The problem of sovereignty in the later Middle Ages* (Cambridge, 1963).

WRONOWSKI, M. M., *Luca da Penna e l'opera sua* (Pisa, 1925).

ZURITA, G., *Anales de la Corona de Aragón* (Zaragoza, 1610).

THE KINGDOM OF NAPLES

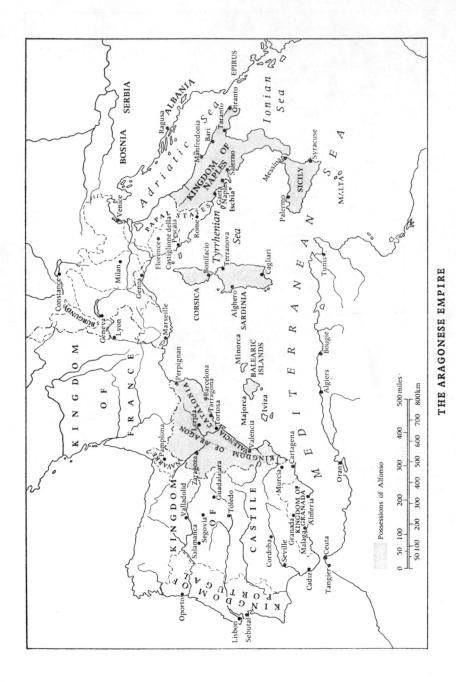

THE ARAGONESE EMPIRE

INDEX